| DATE | | | |
|---|---|---|---|
| | | | |
| | | | |
| | | | |
| | | | |
| | | | |
| | | | |
| | | | |
| | | | |
| | | | |
| | | | |
| | | | |
| | | | |
| | | | |

# TOPICAL CHILD DEVELOPMENT

# TOPICAL CHILD DEVELOPMENT

Roberta M. Berns

Delmar Publishers Inc.™

I T P™

# NOTICE TO THE READER

Cover photo: Reprinted from *Woman's Day* Magazine. Copyright 1993 Hachette Magazines, Inc.

**Delmar staff:**
Acquisitions Editor: Jay Whitney
Developmental Editor: Christopher Anzalone
Project Editor: Theresa M. Bobear
Production Coordinator: Sandra Woods
Art & Design Coordinator: Karen Kunz Kemp

For information, address Delmar Publishers Inc.
3 Columbia Circle, Box 15-015
Albany, NY 12212-9985

Printed in the United States of America
Published simultaneously in Canada
by Nelson Canada,
a division of The Thomson Corporation

1   2   3   4   5   6   7   8   9   10   XXX   00   99   98   97   96   95   94

**Library of Congress Cataloging-in-Publication Data**
Berns, Roberta
    Topical child development/Roberta M. Berns.
        p. cm.
    Includes bibliographical references and index.
    ISBN 0-8273-5727-3
    1. Developmental psychology.   2. Child development.   3. Nature and nurture.   I. Title
BF713.B48   1994                                              93-20927
155.4--dc20                                                   CIP

# Brief Contents

# CONTENTS

# PREFACE

In the fifteen years I have been teaching developmental psychology I always seem to end the course with a feeling that there was still "something" missing in the students' comprehension of the discipline. Until recently, I could not label the "something." An encounter with a 7-year-old, Jessica, clarified what I felt my students were lacking. Jessica was bragging about how she had just learned to spell and she proceeded to rattle off some words form her spelling list. She then requested that we ask her to spell some word of our choosing. My husband said, "Can you spell bicycle?" She said, "No, I can't." "Well, how about bike?" replied my husband. "Oh, I can figure that one out, it's b-i-k-e," she retorted. "How did you figure it out?" we both asked. "When you have two vowels and the first is long, the second is silent," she said. Then it hit me—a first-grader had learned to apply a rule to a new situation, my students had not. My students finish the course able to describe various stages about how and why development occurs. They have no rules or structures to apply outside of their text.

Most development textbooks deal with the question of *how* and *when* children develop and *what* is the result of their development. Yet, throughout all my years teaching, *why* is the most common question students ask—Why are there birth defects? Why are some siblings so different even though they come from the same family? Why do some parents abuse their children? Of course there are no simple answers because the answers must touch a variety of possibilities. I realized the most effective way to delve into the *whys* was to use a topical approach. I believe that by examining developmental topics separately, understanding and study are simplified. My rationale is that scientific analysis and research breaks human behavior into parts even though the parts may operate simultaneously, be interrelated, and even depend on one another.

---

To introduce students to this approach of breaking development into parts, each chapter begins with a vignette related to the area of development being examined. These vignettes are developmental profiles of two children from birth to adolescence, their family, and friends. The profiles are generic in nature to allow students from a wide variety of ethnic and social backgrounds and different geographic areas to relate to them. They provide a picture of how development unfolds in real life, and they provide a continuity for the theories and research discussed in each chapter. This connection is accomplished by raising questions about the developmental profiles at the beginning of the book in order to stimulate the student's curiosity and desire to delve into the answers provided by the scientific research that follows.

As I began to organize this book into aspects of development, thinking of the *whys* of each topic, I developed the following model for each chapter:

- About the Topic
- Biological Influences on the Topic
- Contextual Influences on the Topic
- Interaction of Biological and Contextual Influences on the Topic

This organization enables the student to progress through a hierarchy of levels of learning to reach the highest one—Critical Thinking.

The **About the Topic** section provides *knowledge* and *comprehension*. The **boxes** and **activities** provide *application* of knowledge.

The **Biological Influences** and the **Contextual Influences** sections provide *analysis*.

The **Interaction of Biological and Contextual Influences** section provides *synthesis*.

And the **Critical Thinking and You** provides *evaluation*. By doing these exercises at the end of each chapter, students come to realize the complexity of developmental psychology—unlike the physical sciences, answers are not clear-cut. They also enable students to learn the importance of supporting their opinions with data while affording them the opportunity to form their own hypotheses.

The **Biological/Contextual/Interactional** approach provides an analytical model for the student. Put simplistically, today's zeitgeist is that the child and his environment interact to affect his development. For students whose first exposure to the field of developmental psychology is this course, the interactional explanation is too difficult a concept to comprehend because they do not have the background knowledge. Breaking the interaction into its simpler components of **biology** and **context** and then showing how biological and contextual influences interact to affect development, provides an easier-to-understand picture. Many college students are still thinking at a concrete level, in Jean Piaget's terms, especially in subjects that are new to them. Thus, the approach I have implemented in this book is similar to that used by those who teach a new skill, such as dancing—the dance is broken down into steps; when the steps are mastered, they are put back together.

I have included examples of **atypical development** in each chapter so students can relate the information to the *whats*, *hows*, and *whys* of the topics being examined.

After the topics are discussed, I put "Humpty Dumpty" back together again by examining the **development of the self** in chapter 15.

In each chapter, I have included a feature entitled **Research in Review**, which explores recent, published research addressing topics discussed in the chapter. The purpose is to expose the student to accepted research methodology while at the same time reinforcing the topics discussed in the chapter.

Another feature in each chapter is the **FYIs**. These are anecdotal bits of information that answer questions on anatomy, research findings, and general interest. They round out the learning process.

In sum, my goal in writing this book is not only to teach how development is studied and what developmentalists have learned, but also to stimulate curiosity in those who read it to want to learn more about this fascinating field.

# SUPPLEMENTS

*Instructor's Resource Package*. The binder includes class outlines, chapter summaries, key terms, lecture topics and suggestions, questions, activities, demonstrations, readings, media resources, objectives, handouts, a testbank with more than 1,500 objective questions, color transparencies, and answers to all text and study guide questions.

*Computerized Testbank*. More than 1,500 objective questions found in the instructor's resource package will also be available on computer diskettes for use with IBM PCs and MacIntosh computers.

*Video Package*. A series of ten 30-minute videos from the award-winning television series *Raising America's Children* by Thelma Harms and Debby Cryer in cooperation with the University of North Carolina at Chapel Hill. Each video focuses on one aspect of development, showing children and adults in a wide variety of real-life settings. An illustrated **study guide** and **instructor's guide** accompany the series.

*Student Study Guide*. Reinforces key concepts and objectives with chapter summaries, self-paced student quizzes, essay and research questions, and referenced answers.

# ACKNOWLEDGMENTS

I would like to thank my colleagues across the country who reviewed the manuscript in sections or in its entirety. Their thoughtful comments and suggestions have enabled me to write a better child development textbook. In particular, a few of the reviewers I want to thank by name are: Dr. James Allen, College of Saint Rose, NY; Dr. Marcia Guinn, Rose State College, OK; Judy Hoy, Chesapeake College, MD; Dr. Claire Kopp, University of California-Los Angeles; and Dr. Gary Shaw, Wabash Valley College, IL.

# 1

# What Is Development?

*Growth is the only evidence of life.*
**John Henry, Cardinal Newman**

# DEVELOP-MENTAL PROFILES

## Kenneth Johnson

Kate had met Michael in high school. They were engaged by graduation and married before either finished their business degrees at a community college. Kate's parents approved because this was the way it had been for generations of girls in their Italian family. While Michael was not Italian, he seemed strong enough to head a family and could support his family by working at his father's service station.

Kate and Michael had only one car. It was ten years old, but had a new engine, and servicing it was not a problem. Michael used the service truck owned by his father to drive to work. Michael worked hard. Michael's salary was just enough to pay the mortgage and feed and clothe the family. In addition to Kate, the family consisted of Darla, 3, who had outgrown diapers and had started morning preschool; Jason, 6, and George, 8, who were tornadoes of activity with school and the boys' club. All the children were constantly needing clothes, shoes, pencils for school and other things. Because money was a problem and the family lived on a tight budget, Kate went to work in a local supermarket. The money was not great, but the hours were flexible and health insurance was a benefit. Her mother, who lived down the block, watched the children in the afternoons when they got home from school.

Although Kate wanted only to be a good wife and mother, most of the time she felt stifled.
*(continued on page 31)*

## Jennifer Mason

Jennifer Mason's parents did not choose her precise birthday of January 20, 1970. But they knew this was the time in their lives they wanted a child. Robin and Lloyd had been married for seven years, traveled the world, owned a four-bedroom suburban home where neighbors often had barbeques or pool parties. They were established professionals in their fields and often worked more than ten hours a day. Usually, in the evenings they talked about their careers, except during the past year when they had begun to talk about having a family.

When Robin, 32, finally became pregnant, she immediately began shopping for furniture, baby items, and clothes. Finally, two weeks before the due date, Robin took a leave of absence. Lloyd had read many infant care books. However, he worked 60 miles from their home at an architecture firm and found it very difficult to be at home helping Robin prepare for the birth of their child. When Robin went into labor in the middle of the night, he was there, and so were all four grandparents, who had flown from other cities to see their first grandchild.

The day Lloyd came to take Robin and his newborn daughter home from the hospital, he wore his favorite suit and tie because he wanted to look his best. They wrapped Jennifer in a yellow blanket and knit cap Lloyd's grandmother had made. On the way home, Lloyd pointed out all the sites of interest, but Jennifer had fallen asleep.
*(continued on page 35)*

# ABOUT DEVELOPMENT

You now have an overview of Kenneth's and Jennifer's infancy, toddlerhood, preschool years, school years, and adolescence. Their stories stop at a critical point in their development, a point at which they have to look at themselves—who they are and where they are going. What elements or factors influenced them to get to this point? What role did they personally play in the process? How will the consequences of these influences and their roles affect their future development?

## FINDING CLUES TO DEVELOPMENTAL OUTCOMES

In this book we will explore aspects of development in depth—heredity, prenatal, birth, physical, perceptual, behavioral, cognitive, language, emotional, social and personality, gender role, moral, and then we will tie all aspects together for development of the self. We examine aspects of development separately to simplify understanding and because study, scientific analysis, and research break human behavior into parts although the parts can operate simultaneously, be interrelated, or dependent on each other. For example, while an infant is developing physically, her thought processes are simultaneously developing. A child's thought processes are related to her language development.

In our study of development, we will encounter explanations that apply to children in *general* and explanations that account for individual differences in *specific* children. Knowing how all children progress through the same developmental stages is as significant as knowing how children's developmental outcomes differ. To explain Kenneth's and Jennifer's crises, developmental psychologists probably would consider their ages, gender, temperaments, physical development, family/social interaction patterns, era during which they grew, and so on.

Generalizations can be made about Kenneth's and Jennifer's development based on their similarities:
- They are the same age.
- Both grew up during the 1970s and 1980s.
- Both have intact caring families.

The crises Kenneth and Jennifer both find themselves in at the adolescent stage of development are normal. Although each crisis is different, both center on growing up and taking responsibility for oneself.

A general explanation of Kenneth's and Jennifer's crises is that the crises are part of a process that all children experience when growing. However, this explanation does not provide specific causes of Kenneth's or Jennifer's behavior—Why did their common struggle to become their own person manifest itself the way it did? To arrive at some possible explanations, we must first analyze how Kenneth's and Jennifer's lives differed:
- They have different temperaments—Kenneth is easygoing whereas Jennifer is slow to warm up.
- They are different genders.
- Their families are different sizes and represent different socioeconomic statuses and ethnic groups, so Kenneth and Jennifer have different resources and role models.
- Their families have different cultural and religious educational backgrounds and beliefs.

A topical approach to the study of human development entails the examination of individual aspects of development rather than chronological (by age) or stage (all aspects of development relevant to a specific period such as the toddler stage).

Experiences with adults and peers at home, in the community, and at school have profound influences on development.

**Developmental profiles provide a wealth of clues and indicators as to how and why a particular person became a particular and unique individual.**

- Parenting styles are different.
- Preschool experiences and after-school experiences are different.
- Kenneth matured late compared with his friends, whereas Jennifer matured early.

These individual differences are significant when studying development. They give us clues about specific questions to ask when we want a specific explanation, and they enable us to see if the general explanation holds true despite individual differences.

Kenneth's developmental profile provides clues for the following questions as to why Kenneth impregnated his girlfriend and, thereby, risked his future options:

- Did he have sex with the first willing girl because it was expected of him? (He did not hesitate to tell his friends.)
- Was he too embarrassed to buy condoms at the local store?
- Did he not consider the future consequences of his behavior because adolescents usually ignore this aspect?
- Did his temperament, self-concept, relationships with family or friends, or childhood experiences have any effect or influence on the dilemma Kenneth faces?

Jennifer's developmental profile also provides clues for the following questions explaining why Jennifer became bulimic.

- Was she unconsciously rejecting her parents' expectations of her?
- Was she lonely so she ate to soothe herself and then hated herself for binging, and thus had to purge herself by vomiting?
- Did she unconsciously want attention? Was her behavior a cry for help?
- Did she have a physiological disorder so she never felt "full" when she ate and consequently consumed too much?
- Did her temperament explain developmental outcomes?

You will learn about scientific theories that explain apparent relations or underlying principles of certain observed phenomena. Some theories deal with a particular aspect of development such as language or thinking. Other theories are more global and explain the complex settings that influence many aspects of a child's development. Some theories examine the interaction between a child and his environment, explaining how the individual is constantly modifying and being modified by his environment.

The role theories play in explaining development is to provide a useful method to organize data and make predictions. Human development contains many mysteries, and the existing theories help save time in solving these mysteries.

## DEVELOPMENT DEFINED

Before looking at developmental theories, we need to define *development*. **Development** refers to progressive changes over time. These changes can be *quantitative* , referring to change in amount, as in physical growth or vocabulary. Quantitative changes can be measured objectively. For example, physical growth can be measured in inches; vocabulary words can be counted. Developmental changes can be *qualitative,* referring to change in kind, as in moral understanding or social adaptation. Qualitative changes have to be observed subjectively. For example, infants and toddlers do not know the difference between right and wrong behaviors so they cannot be said to have moral understanding.

Since development refers to progressive changes over time, how do we classify these changes? Developmental changes are *orderly*, *directional*, and *stable*. They are *orderly* in that they occur in a sequence or a series. For example, an infant lifts the head before the chest; an infant learns to sit before standing. Developmental changes are *directional* because they show some kind of accumulation or organization of components; each change in sequence builds on the results of preceding changes. This progressive sequence results in a more advanced or superior form of functioning than what preceded it. For instance, crying precedes babbling, which precedes the first word. Last, developmental changes are *stable* in that their effects do not disappear in a short time. For example, after you have developed the coordination to ride a bike, you can still ride one year later.

Human development is an area in which professionals from many fields of inquiry are interested. They include psychologists, educators, child caregivers, sociologists, anthropologists, health professionals, medical researchers, and many others. Each professional brings a unique expertise to the quest for knowledge.

The science that studies how individuals change over time and the factors that influence or produce the changes is called **developmental psychology**. Developmental psychologists describe human development by delineating sequences and times in which various events occur. For example, most infants say their first word when they are about one year old. Developmentalists explain how and why humans develop as they do. For example, infants must have the ability to mentally picture their mothers and remember her image before they can label her "mama." Developmentalists predict how humans will develop. For example, infants who do not hear language for their first six months stop babbling and can be delayed in developing speech.

Human development is studied to understand who we are, why we are the way we are, how we got this way, and what we can do to improve ourselves. Although development continues throughout life, this book concentrates on children and adolescents. We now will look at some developmental theories to get an understanding of how scientists approach the study of human development.

# THEORIES EXPLAINING INFLUENCES ON DEVELOPMENT

A **theory** is a set of statements that relate different facts or events, explain events, and predict future outcomes. The theories presented here deal with various aspects of development. For example, Erik Erikson's theory deals with personality development; Jean Piaget's theory involves cognitive development; Noam Chomsky's theory is about language development; and Lawrence Kohlberg's theory deals with moral development. Theories are a method of explaining development. They serve to organize research that has been done and to stimulate new research. To simplify our general theoretical overview, we can use three designations to categorize the diverse major theories. The three are based on overall degree of emphasis rather than on specific components. They examine development from the perspective of:
1. forces primarily within the child (biological influences);
2. forces primarily outside the child (contextual influences);

Development can refer to objective items such as the physical growth of the brain and bones or to more subjective concepts such as behavior and intelligence.

3. interaction between forces within the child and outside the child (interactional influences).

Table 1.1 illustrates these three major categories of developmental theories.

As more research is analyzed by sophisticated technology, theories are continually being refined to incorporate new information.

Some theories are useful because they generate much research; some stand the test of time in that newly discovered facts can be explained by the theory; and some do not do either. To evaluate the usefulness of a theory, the following criteria can be applied (Salkind, 1985):

- Inclusiveness—Is the theory broad or narrow in relation to how many phenomena it addresses?
- Consistency—Can it explain new discoveries without changing the assumptions on which it is based?
- Accuracy—What is the degree to which it correctly predicts future events or explains outcomes?
- Relevance—Is there a link between the theory and the data collected?
- Fruitfulness—How productive is the theory in generating new ideas for future research?
- Simplicity—What is the degree of detail? Is the theory easy to understand and test?

## MAJOR THEORIES OF DEVELOPMENT

### TABLE 1.1

| Some Developmental Perspectives | Focus | Sample Theories | Key Theorists |
|---|---|---|---|
| **Forces within the child (biological influences)** | Biology | Maturation<br>Ethology | Gesell<br>Lorenz, Bowlby |
| **Forces outside the child (contextual influences)** | Learning<br><br>Culture | Behaviorism<br>Social Cognitive<br>Sociocultural<br>Historical | Watson, Skinner<br>Bandura<br>Vygotsky<br>Elder |
| **Interaction between forces within and outside the child (interactional influences)** | Psycho-analysis<br>Cognition<br><br><br><br>Systems | Psychosexual<br>Psychosocial<br>Cognitive-Developmental<br>Information-Processing<br>Ecological | Freud<br>Erikson<br>Piaget<br><br>No major theorist<br>Bronfenbrenner |

## FORCES PRIMARILY WITHIN THE CHILD: BIOLOGICAL INFLUENCES

Forces within the child that influence development include genetics (heredity), anatomy (structure of organs), and physiology (function of organs). On a *general* level, these forces are related to evolution of the human species. On a *specific* level, they are also related to maturation and behavior of individual human beings. Theories explaining development in terms of evolution, genetics, or maturation are classified as biological theories.

## Biological Theories

The two major biological perspectives are *maturation* and *ethology*. **Maturation** is the unfolding of genetically determined traits, structures, or functions. **Ethology** is the study of the behavior of different species in their natural habitats.

### Maturation.

Maturational theorists believe development is a result of biological and evolutionary forces. Maturation involves structure and function. The structure of an organ must develop *before* its function can. For example, the muscles in the eyes (structure) must develop before they can be coordinated to read (function). Arnold Gesell believed that development occurs in an orderly sequence that is determined by evolution of the species and the individual biological makeup of each person, namely his genes. Even though the sequence of development is fixed in that it occurs in the same order for everyone, the rate at which an individual progresses through the sequence is different (Gesell 1940, 1954).

Gesell observed and described the ages at which different behaviors emerged, such as walking and talking. Like other maturational theorists, he believed these skills developed following each child's inner timetable, regardless of learning or experience. Learning could occur only *after* the individual was biologically developed. Maturation theory led to the observation of many age-related patterns of behavior to establish **norms**, scientifically established averages or standards of performance. Gesell used these norms to specify the ages at which individuals reach **developmental milestones**, significant events in the life of a person, such as sitting up, standing, and walking. A table of developmental milestones from birth to adolescence is provided at the end of this chapter (table 1.5, page 24).

Biological forces that affect maturation determine when an individual reaches a particular developmental milestone. Rushing a child to perform before he is biologically ready can cause psychological problems. For example, demanding that a preschool child learn to read before he shows an interest can cause that child to not want to read. If adults understand the developmental norms, they are less likely to expect too much from the child (ILG, Ames & Baker, 1981).

With Jennifer's introductory developmental profile, a maturationist probably would explain her resistance to attending school as a reaction to being forced to perform on a specific academic level and to read and write before she was ready to do so. Specifically, Jennifer may not have been able to sit still and follow directions and concentrate; her eyes may not have been mature enough to focus for long periods on printed material or the blackboard.

With Kenny's introductory developmental profile, his mother's attitude to let him suck his thumb as long as he needed is a maturational view.

### Ethology.

Ethology stresses the role of biological processes in the individual and his culture. Ethologists believe development is a result of evolution; specifically those inherited tendencies from earlier generations that foster *adaptation* to the environment. **Adaptation** is a change in structure, function, or form that produces better adjustment in an organism to its environment. The individuals who have survived because they have adapted to changes in their environment are the most fit. These individuals pass their genes with their sets of instructions for characteristics and behaviors on to the next generation. This is termed *natural selection*.

Temper tantrums are common in preschool-age children because of their immature ability to deal with frustration. Knowing this, parents can ignore the tantrums rather than making them worse by demanding self-control.

Ethnologists study children from different cultures and societies to determine profiles relating to motor development or peer relationships. They then compare them with children in similar circumstances in different cultures or societies.

Lorenz, like these children, observed developmental profiles of ducklings, Lorenz concluded that ducklings have certain predisposed patterns of learning that are difficult to alter; he called these patterns imprinting.

Ethologists are concerned not merely with questions about the immediate causation and development of behavior, but also with its function and evolution. Thus, they might ask not only what is the developmental course of smiling in the individual, but also how did smiling evolve (…and what were the advantageous consequences of smiling through which natural selection acted in the course of its evolution? [Hinde, 1989, p. 253]).

To gain a better understanding of evolution, ethologists study individuals from different cultures in their natural settings. Ethologists develop detailed descriptions and classifications of behavior and explain them in terms of adaptiveness. For example, they might observe and record types of body language such as facial expression in communication—In what situations is a smile or a frown used? They might conclude that a smile is more adaptive today in successful communication than is a frown because contemporary society values the person who gets along well with others.

Ethologists address the functional significance of behavior in terms of its success in achieving the biological goals of survival and reproduction. To illustrate, Konrad Lorenz (1952) studied the adaptive behavior in ducks and geese. He observed that newly hatched birds followed the first moving object seen whether it was their mother, a ball, or Lorenz himself. Lorenz concluded that seeing a moving object stimulates the bird's genetic instinct to follow. Apparently, following behavior has survival value; it ensures the young will stay close to their mother until they are old enough to care for themselves.

John Bowlby (1979, 1980, 1982) points to the parallels between animal and human behavior. Bowlby's research with infants suggests humans have an inherited tendency to form affectional bonds. Infants tend to cling and stay in visual contact with the mother. Such behavior has definite survival value in that it stimulates the mother to respond. The mother's response to the infant provides the basis for attachment. Attachment in turn provides the basis for healthy socioemotional development (Ainsworth, 1978).

An ethologist would explain Jennifer's fussiness as an infant as an adaptive response to attract her mother's attention to maintain closeness. Kenny's propensity for fighting, although his mother forbade it, would be explained as an adaptive response to survive among his peers.

## FORCES PRIMARILY OUTSIDE THE CHILD: CONTEXTUAL INFLUENCES

Forces outside a child include behaviors of individuals in various contexts such as family, school, peer group, or community that affect the child's development. Developmental outcomes are attributed to environmental (such as sociocultural or historical) rather than biological factors (such as evolution or genetics). Development is viewed as a function of learning. *Learning* is defined as permanent changes in behavior that result from experience (Gagne, 1968). For example, as you practice what your tennis coach has taught you—forehand, backhand, serve, and volley—you can say that you have *learned* the basics of tennis.

### Learning Theories

Two general theoretical models explain how learning takes place: *behaviorism* and *social cognitive theory*. Behaviorism deals with learning based on doing, whereas social cognitive theory also includes learning based on observing.

**Behaviorism.** Behaviorism is the school of psychology that focuses on observable behavior only and investigates relations between stimuli and responses. Behaviorism emerged from the work of John Watson, who thought only observable behaviors were worthy of serious study. He focused on stimuli in the environment and responses, or consequent behavior, in organisms (Salkind, 1985).

Watson's main assumption was that adult complex behaviors were developed from infants' simple inborn reflexes, which were continually being refined through life experiences. A *reflex* is an unlearned, involuntary *response*, or reaction, of a part of the body to an external stimulus. A *stimulus* is anything to which a person reacts. The stimulus precedes the response. Watson described complex sequential behavior as being composed of chains of stimulus-response (S-R) units that become associated through learning.

Watson had been influenced by the work of Ivan Pavlov, a Russian physiologist. Pavlov was the first scientist to study the direct relation between behavior and events in the environment. He demonstrated how a response could be conditioned. *Conditioning* is the process of learning that occurs through association of stimuli. He trained dogs to salivate to the sound of a bell by repeatedly ringing the bell before presenting food (Pavlov, 1927). This experiment demonstrated *classical*, or *simple, conditioning,* which is when a reflex action (salivation in this case) comes to be associated with a stimulus (the bell in this case) that does not ordinarily elicit it.

Watson's perspective on development can be summed up as follows:

> Give me a dozen healthy infants and my own specified world to bring them up in, and I'll guarantee to take any one of them at random and train him to become any type of specialist I select—doctor, lawyer, artist, merchant, chief, and yes, even beggar man and thief, regardless of his talents, penchants, tendencies, abilities, vocations, and race of his ancestors (Watson, 1925, p. 104).

In other words, Watson felt that even complicated behavior could be conditioned by providing the appropriate stimuli.

On the other hand, B. F. Skinner believed that behavior is a function of its consequences rather than its precedents, or stimuli (Skinner, 1938, 1953). So, if you wrote a letter to your senator and received a reply, you would likely write again. Whereas if you never received an answer, you might stop writing letters to politicians.

Skinner's theory described *operant learning,* or *conditioning.* An *operant* is a response that produces an effect. Operant conditioning refers to a non-reflexive response (not a natural reflex like salivation or blinking) that an individual can make (for example, catching a ball) as the result of the response being rewarded, or *reinforced,* after it is initially made. Toilet training is a good example of operant learning. A child's first defecation in the toilet usually is by accident. The parents' excitement over the accomplishment is the reinforcement that motivates the child to use the toilet again when the urge occurs.

Behaviorism would explain Jennifer's change in behavior from refusing to go to school to agreeing to go because of the reinforcement given to her for

The stimulus here is the presence of a traffic officer with hand raised; the individual driving a car responds to this gesture by stopping his car. More complex sequential behavior is exhibited by how we learn to obey authority.

**F.Y.I.**

In 1948 Skinner wrote a novel, *Walden Two* describing a utopian community governed by his theory of operant learning. It illustrates how behavior is *shaped* by reinforcing desirable behaviors and *extinguishing,* or eliminating, undesirable ones.

This young girl is modeling her parents who are building a deck to their house. She does this because she admires them and has observed that they enjoy what they are doing.

This boy likes to pretend he is a police officer because his favorite television show is about police putting the "bad guys" in jail.

going, such as a new doll. Also, it would explain Jennifer's dislike of her maturing body caused by her father's uneasiness and apparent rejection of her growing up. He did not want her displaying herself around the house. Thus, his negative response made her want to hide her body rather than be proud of it.

Behaviorism has been refined to include more complex interactions between the individual and environmental events. The revised theory is called *behavioral analysis* (Bijou, 1989). One revision is the unit of analysis. This has been expanded from a simple relation between stimulus and response to a functional relation, which includes the meaning of a stimulus to an individual as a consequence of previous contacts with the object or event. Another revision is that which constitutes "behavior." Whereas, Watson and Skinner studied only observable behavior, behavior analysis includes perception, cognition, and emotion. Still another revision is the change in the concept of setting. Behaviorism conceived of a setting as a stimulus-response interaction that affects other stimulus-response relations that follow. Behavior analysis views a setting as a condition affecting the interactional sequence between stimuli and responses by altering the strengths and weaknesses involved in the interaction.

**Social Cognitive Theory.** Behaviorism requires that organisms act in order to learn. Organisms respond to stimuli, and these responses are gradually shaped by their consequences. However, according to Albert Bandura (1977, 1986, 1989), learning also occurs by observing the behavior of others. The behavior change in the form of imitation that results from observing another person perform actions and experience consequences is termed **social learning,** or **cognition.**

Social learning, or social cognitive, theorists maintain that development comes from watching others rather than only through the direct shaping or conditioning of responses (Bandura, 1977, 1986, 1989). Bandura's theory explains how we are socialized, that is, how we learn to cooperate and be helpful, how we learn appropriate gender roles, and so on.

Bandura (1962) noticed that when children learn new songs or role play, for example, play police officer, they reproduce long sequences of new behavior. This behavior, is learned by observation. Thus, in social situations people often learn behaviors rapidly by watching the behavior of others. However, for observational learning or social cognition to occur, certain skills are required. Skills include the ability to pay attention, the capacity to remember what was observed, the ability and motivation to reproduce the behavior, and reinforcement for having reproduced the behavior (Bandura, 1977, 1986, 1989). For example, when learning how to write the letter "o," a child must carefully observe how the teacher makes the letter on the blackboard, remember where to start (top or bottom) and which way to go (left or right), be able to hold a pencil firmly to write the letter and be praised for having written it correctly.

Social cognitive theory explains why Kenny assumed he could cause laughter by calling his teacher Mrs. Simmons "Toots," like his dad called his mom. It also explains Jennifer's play with her Barbie dolls who were dressed up and went to dinner.

## Cultural Theories

**Culture** refers to the concepts, habits, skills, art, instruments, institutions, and so on of a given people in a given period. Thus, we can examine the influence of cultural contexts any time, presently or historically.

Cultural contexts in which children develop provide a natural laboratory for study. Viewing the contrasts in life's arrangements in different cultures has enabled psychologists to examine basic assumptions about developmental goals and specific skills that are learned (Rogoff & Morelli, 1989).

That cultural context influences human behavior can be illustrated by Glick's report of Kpelle subjects' treatment of a classification problem. They sorted 20 objects by functional relations (knife with orange, hoe with potato) rather than likeness (tools, foods). When questioned how they arrived at that classification system, they replied, "That's how a wise man would do it." The desperate experimenter finally asked, "How would a fool do it?" The Kpelle subjects then sorted the objects into piles by similarity (Glick, 1975, p. 636).

According to Super (1981) infant sleep patterns vary as a function of cultural expectations.

In the United States where infants commonly sleep in their own beds, the common developmental milestone of "sleeping through the night" is regarded as a sign of neurological maturity and usually occurs by 4–5 months of age. Parents are encouraged not to attend to their infants at the first whimper after this age so infants will learn to comfort themselves back to sleep. If infants are still waking up at night by one year of age, it is not considered "healthy."

However, in many other cultures an infant sleeps with the mother and is allowed to nurse on demand. There is minimal disturbance of adult sleep and therefore less parental motivation to encourage the infant to sleep through the night in his own bed. Thus, it appears this developmental milestone, in addition to its biological basis, is a function of the cultural context in which it develops.

**Sociocultural.** The theory of Russian psychologist Lev Vygotsky (1978) explains how human development is inseparable from human social and cultural activities. Vygotsky recognized the role of forces within the child. But he suggested that a complete understanding of development, specifically cognition, requires the study of the expectations, tools, skills, models, and interactions provided by a child's culture.

On the social level, Vygotsky focused on how children are aided in the development of higher mental processes, such as reasoning and problem solving, by guidance from people who are already skilled in using these cognitive tools. For example, when many students enter college, they are inundated with numerous exciting activities, and challenging courses in addition to living independently from parents for the first time. It is difficult for many to organize their time, prioritize, and carry out their responsibilities. Once they realize how much time is required for the things they *have* to do, they can see how much time is left for the things they *want* to do. Only then can they begin to prioritize their free or leisure time. Learning to manage time effectively is a long process for some that requires intermittent input from an experienced person.

The sociocultural and historical contexts that influenced the development of the grandfather will in turn impact his granddaughter's development because of their personal ties.

This type of adult support that permits children as well as young people to accomplish, with assistance, skills that they will learn later to accomplish independently is what Vygotsky called the zone of proximal development. He defined the **zone of proximal development** as "the distance between the actual developmental level as determined by independent problem solving and the level of potential development as determined through problem solving under adult guidance or in collaboration with more capable peers" (Vygotsky, 1978, p. 86).

The term *proximal* indicates that the assistance provided is close to but slightly beyond a child's or young person's current competence. Thus,

Young children growing up in financially distressed families generally experience lower grades, aspirations, and self-esteem.

There has been a tremendous amount of research on the effects of television on family relationships. Television viewing, for example, interferes with playtime.

the assistance complements and builds on the individual's existing abilities rather than teaching new skills.

On the cultural level, Vygotsky believes that the tools (e.g., a map) and the institutions (e.g., school) available to a child facilitate learning appropriate solutions to problems. For example, in the United States children are taught how to use maps to travel from one place to another whereas in a society living in the jungle or desert, children would be taught to travel by noting certain landmarks or observing the position of the stars.

The sociocultural approach is one explanation of Kate's marriage after high school: girls in her family were expected to marry and have children. The sociocultural approach also provides a clue as to why Kenny did not consider using birth control when having intercourse with Ellen. Birth control was not allowed according to his religion.

**Historical.** Human development is influenced by significant events and conditions existing in a given historical period and how these evolve over time (Hetherington & Baltes, 1988).

An example of a significant historical event affecting human development was the Great Depression. Glen Elder analyzed the effects of the Great Depression on children and found that it did not affect all families similarly (Elder, 1974). Elder compared the stability and change in the psychological development of children in deprived families (those families whose income was reduced by at least 30 percent) with those in nondeprived families. He found that, in general, adolescents in deprived families participated more in domestic roles and outside jobs compared with those in nondeprived families. Boys who suffered economic loss made firm vocational commitments in late adolescence and had much motivation to achieve and a desire to excel. Girls who suffered economic loss modeled the maternal roles to which they were exposed during the Great Depression. They tended to marry early and stop work at the time of marriage.

Since the 1950s the evolution of television is an example of a condition affecting children who grew up after that time. One effect emerging from the introduction of television into family life was how time was used. Less time was spent reading, doing hobbies, playing games, and interacting (Condry, 1989). Another effect of television viewing is its influence on attitude and belief systems; for many it is a primary source of information. Viewers who watched a lot of television (heavy viewers) were less trusting and more fearful of crime and violence compared with viewers who seldom watched television (light viewers) from the same socioeconomic status and who live in similar neighborhoods. Additionally, heavy viewers are more likely to perceive age, gender, and ethnic stereotypes portrayed on television as real (Comstock, 1991).

The historical approach is one explanation for Jennifer's obsession with her body image; the idealized female body has changed throughout history. In the 1900s the ideal female shape was an hourglass figure. In the 1920s it was fashionable to be flat-chested and have small hips. In the 1940s a shapely figure was ideal, and in the 1960s a boyish, thin figure was in vogue. In the 1980s the ideal female body type was slim, curvy, and muscular. Due to the mass media, especially television and magazines, the idealized female body became a standard for many girls. Jennifer compared herself with this standard, and in wanting to achieve it, perceived she could do so by vomiting.

# INTERACTION BETWEEN FORCES WITHIN AND OUTSIDE THE CHILD: INTERACTIONAL INFLUENCES

The interaction between forces within a child and outside a child includes the conflict between instincts and societal demands as in *psychoanalytic* theories, the relation between maturation of the brain and a child's experiences in the environment as in *cognitive* theories, and the mutual accommodation between the growing human being and the changing properties of the settings in which that person lives as well as the larger contexts in which the settings are embedded as in *systems* theories.

## Psychoanalytic Theories

**Psychoanalytic** theorists analyze the unconscious forces that motivate behavior. Psychoanalysts view development as the redirection of instinctual drives, such as sex or aggression, into socially acceptable behaviors. Two psychoanalytic theories are Sigmund Freud's **psychosexual theory**, so-called because it focuses on the sexual instinct as the factor influencing behavior, and Erik Erikson's **psychosocial theory,** so-called because it focuses on social interactions as factors influencing behavior.

**Sigmund Freud (1856–1939)**

**Psychosexual Theory.** Sigmund Freud was a physician who specialized in the treatment of nervous disorders. His therapeutic techniques of talking out problems revealed to him dynamic forces responsible for creating the abnormal symptoms he was treating. Freud eventually assumed that most of these forces are unconscious (Hall, 1979).

Freud's psychoanalytic theory was influenced by the *zeitgeist*, or trend of thought, of the time—the discovery that energy is conserved. Freud applied this concept to human behavior, and identified it as psychic energy.

Freud assumed that the primary source of psychic energy is *instincts*, or unlearned psychological drives. Instincts originate from biological needs such as the need to survive and the need to procreate; thus, instincts govern behavior. Freud called the personality part that is the seat of the instincts the *id*. The id seeks pleasure and wants immediate gratification.

But human behavior also is governed by reality. Thus, when individuals interact with objects and people, they must accommodate their needs to that that exists and to others' needs. For example, a child learns not to eliminate body wastes in his clothing whenever the urge strikes but rather to find a toilet. Freud called this system an *ego*. The ego deals with reality and makes rational decisions.

Infants are driven exclusively by the id in that they only seek immediate gratification without rational thought (ego) or consideration for the consequences (superego).

Further, human behavior is governed by societal rules. In early childhood through the use of reward and punishment, these rules become internalized and are called the conscience. The conscience stands for morals—what we believe is good or bad. Freud called this system the *superego*. It develops as a product of *socialization*, the process by which children learn the ways of their society. The superego punishes bad behavior with guilt and rewards good behavior with a feeling of well-being.

In summary, Freud believed that in a healthy personality the ego considers the biological needs represented by the id and societal demands represented by the superego and weighs them against reality when behaving or interacting with others. Freud's theory was termed psychosexual because he proposed that development consisted of *stages*, each characterized by the focusing of psychic energy of the sexual instinct on different areas of the body called *erogenous zones*—mouth, the anus, and the genitals.

A **stage** is a period of development that differs significantly in quality from other periods. At each stage an individual could be gratified with the release of tensions from the particular erogenous zone, for example, the mouth by sucking. However, the individual could also be frustrated at any stage if the appropriate stimulation did not occur. Frustration, or the absence of gratification, especially during the first five years of life, was Freud's explanation for emotional or psychological problems occurring later. For example, the adult behavior of chain smoking could possibly be linked to early deprivation of sucking during the oral stage. Thus, Freud believed

**Erik Erikson (born 1902)**

## A COMPARISON OF PSYCHOSEXUAL AND PSYCHOSOCIAL THEORIES

### TABLE 1.2

| Approximate Age | Freud's Psychosexual Theory | Erickson's Psychosocial Theory |
|---|---|---|
| *Infant:* 0–18 months | *Oral:* psychic energy concentrated on need of hunger | *Trust vs. Mistrust:* develop sufficient trust in others to explore the world |
| *Toddler:* 18 months–3 years | *Anal:* psychic energy concentrated on need for elimination | *Autonomy vs. Doubt:* develop control over behavior; carry out intentions |
| *Preschooler:* 3–6 years | *Phallic:* psychic energy concentrated in genital organs | *Initiative vs. Guilt:* develop sense of responsibility for own actions |
| *Schoolage:* 6–12 years | *Latency:* sexual energy channeled into other behavior | *Industry vs. Inferiority:* develop sense of self-esteem through inter-action with peers |
| *Adolescence:* 12–20 years | *Genital:* earlier resolution of conflicts return for reconsideration | *Identity vs. Role Confusion:* develop sense of identity |
| *Young Adult:* 20–40 years | | *Intimacy vs. Isolation:* develop relationship with another person |
| *Middle Adult:* 40–65 years | | *Generativity vs. Stagnation:* develop sense of productivity in work and raising families |
| *Old Adult:* >65 years | | *Integrity vs. Self-Despair:* develop sense of satisfaction with one's life |

that personality developed in a predictable pattern of psychosexual stages from birth to adolescence, as briefly described in table 1.2.

Freud might have explained Kenneth's irresponsible sexual involvement with Ellen as a result of the absence of gratification during the genital stage or his not having developed an adequate superego to control his sexual impulses. He might have linked Jennifer's bulimia to frustration during the oral stage or to repressed sexual urges.

**Psychosocial Theory.** Erikson expanded Freud's theory of development. According to Erikson, healthy psychological development results from the resolution of conflicts between biological needs and the societal demands and social forces daily encountered (Erikson, 1963). Erikson's theory is described as psychosocial because it examines the influence of one's social interactions on one's psychological development. The theoretical basis for Erikson's work is *epigenesis,* meaning "upon emergence," and comes from embryology. It refers to the step-by-step growth of the organs after conception to form an embryo. He explained that every growing thing has a basic plan and out of this plan specific parts grow, each having a particular time to ascend, until all the parts have arisen to form a functioning whole (Erikson, 1963). Thus, he believed that all living things have both a biological and psychological developmental plan, and the parts of this plan have a certain order of emergence.

Erikson assumed the existence of stages of development from birth to death, governed by underlying maturational forces and the presence of a conflict due to social experiences at each one of eight stages: *trust versus mistrust, autonomy versus doubt, initiative versus guilt, industry versus inferiority, identity versus role confusion, intimacy versus isolation, generativity versus stagnation, integrity versus self-despair.* (Refer again to table 1.2 that briefly describes the stages.)

Each stage can be a time of great vulnerability or great potential depending on how the crisis is resolved. Thus, in each stage previous conflicts must be revisited to confront the new conflict. For example, during adolescence in trying to establish a personal identity, all the previous conflicts resurface yet on a different level (Erikson, 1968). To illustrate:

- *Trust versus mistrust* centers on the infant's relationship with parents; in adolescence the crisis centers on friends and other adults.
- *Autonomy versus doubt* centers on toddlers' attempts to control their bodies and do things that they are capable of successfully doing independently; in adolescence the crisis centers on controlling their actions and decisions and taking responsibilities for them.
- *Initiative versus guilt* involves the preschool child making and exhibiting curiosity comfortably within the family or preschool; the adolescent must exhibit this in the school and community as well.
- *Industry versus inferiority* centers around school, in adolescence it focuses on work and sports as well.

**This school-age child's interaction with the computer enables her to be an active participant in learning new concepts. She may learn how to perform division by the games she plays, thus influencing a developmental change.**

Erikson might have explained Jennifer's bulimia as a reaction for failing to resolve the crisis of autonomy versus doubt when she was a toddler, and now during adolescence the crisis has returned so binging and purging are

**Jean Piaget (1896–1980)**

her methods of regaining control. She also may not have resolved the crisis of initiative versus guilt during her preschool years because she felt she had to keep her questions to herself. Becoming bulimic allowed her to show initiative and get rid of guilt by vomiting. Kenneth may have felt inferior in school because he was just an average student or because he was slower to mature physically than peers. Having a girlfriend who was beautiful and willing to have sex with him made him feel superior.

## Cognitive Theories

Cognitive theories explain mental activities and functions such as thought, language, intelligence, dreams, fantasies, and so on. The word comes from the Latin word *cognoscere* meaning "to know."

**Cognitive-Developmental Theory. Cognitive-developmental theory** views the individual as an active participant in the developmental process. The individual interacts with the environment and thinks about it in ways that complement his or her maturity and previous experiences. Development then is the result of the interaction. For example, when Darla was 4 years old, she loved to paint in preschool. She named the colors she was putting on her painting red, blue, green, and yellow. She had the mental maturity to represent the colors in her mind with the appropriate words. By accident, another child bumped her elbow, and Darla put her freshly dipped red-covered brush on the wet blue circle on her paper. As Darla painted over the blue spot with the red paint, she excitedly said, "Look, I made purple!" She had known what purple was; she just did not know it could be made by mixing red and blue. Thus, by acting on her environment, she came to understand the components of the color purple. A new kind of thinking had been reached; she discovered that new colors could be made by mixing certain colors together—developmental change had occurred.

The cognitive-developmental perspective on development is best represented through the work of Jean Piaget. According to Piaget (1963), development occurs in an ordered sequence of qualitatively distinct stages and is characterized by an increase in complexity of thought, such as the progression from intuition to logic. Such a progression can be illustrated by the following statements:

"Do you think it is going to rain tomorrow?"
"Yes."
"Why?"
"I can tell." (intuitive)
"How?"
"Because there are clouds and the barometric pressure is dropping."
 (logical)

Piaget's theory deals with a child's acquisition and use of knowledge. As a result of his work in biology, Piaget believed that animal behaviors were the result of adaptation to the environment via the genes. Piaget applied this concept to human cognitive development. That is, thinking is a behavior that involves adaptation to an environment and results in organization of the mind.

The organized patterns of thoughts are called *schemes*. Infants' schemes are action patterns such as grasping or looking; adults' schemes are concepts such as justice or love. Cognitive development is a continuous process resulting from the successive addition, modification, and reorganization of schemes. The process of adding schemes is termed *assimilation*; for example, when you see a bird never seen before, you add it to your classification of "bird." The process of modifying schemes is called *accommodation*, for instance if you encounter a butterfly for the first time that does not fit your scheme of "bird," you modify your scheme of flying objects to include another classification to accommodate the scheme of butterfly. When new knowledge is encountered, the person is in a state of *disequilibrium* until the new knowledge is assimilated and/or accommodated. After this occurs, a state of *equilibrium* is reached; equilibrium is the resulting reorganization. It represents a state of balance, or organization, between new knowledge taken in and existing knowledge. It is like the final draft written after several attempts to combine library research with knowledge gained in class. Equilibrium signifies developmental change (Piaget, 1970).

Beginning with his own children, Piaget kept detailed diaries of developmental progress. He recorded their behavior in a systematic fashion and used this information as the basis for identifying the different stages of development through which children pass: *sensorimotor, preoperational, concrete operations, formal operations* (Piaget, 1963). Each stage is qualitatively different from the preceding one. For example, the sensorimotor is characterized by actions on objects. The preoperational stage is characterized by the ability to symbolize. The concrete operational stage is characterized by the understanding of cause and effect between real objects. The formal operational stage is characterized by the ability to think logically about abstract problems. A brief outline of Piaget's delineated stages follows in table 1.3.

Piaget might explain Kenny's difficulties in counting and recognizing letters when he entered first grade as a result of not having reached the stage of concrete operations. This is the stage in which children understand that

## PIAGET'S STAGES OF COGNITIVE DEVELOPMENT

### TABLE 1.3

| Approximate Age | Stage | Activity |
| --- | --- | --- |
| 0–2 years | Sensorimotor | Action on environment through motor activity (e.g., touching) and perceptual activity (e.g., seeing) |
| 2–7 years | Preoperational | Development of language (use of symbols to represent actions) |
| 7–11 years | Concrete Operations | Development of reasoning ability on real objects or experiences |
| 11–15 (+) years | Formal Operations | Development of reasoning on abstract and hypothetical problems |

**By understanding how children process information, teachers and coaches can better assist children who are having learning problems.**

symbols stand for real objects. Likewise, Jennifer, who had been drilled in letters and numbers, had difficulty putting the symbols together to read. Piaget would probably describe her in a state of disequilibrium. When Jennifer's disequilibrium is resolved, she would have the ability to assimilate the letters in groups to form words and to accommodate these words to read.

**Information Processing Theory.** *Information processing* refers to how the mind receives sensory information, stores it as memory, and recalls it for later use. Information-processing theorists attempt to explain what happens when a child receives sensory impressions such as seeing or hearing from the environment and responds to them through behavior such as talking—"Look at that caterpillar!" The process is similar to a computer. Simply explained, the *input* comes from the environment via the senses, the memory (short term and long term) and the control of what is remembered are the *throughput*, and the behavior is the *output* (Thomas, 1985) (figure 1.1). Information-processing theorists, however, do not agree on one model to represent cognitive development (Klahr, 1989).

The information-processing theory has refined both learning theory, which states that development results from repeated responses to stimuli, and cognitive-developmental theory, which states that development results when equilibrium is established between assimilation and accommodation. It attempts to explain what occurs mentally between the input and the output; that is, it attempts to explain what mental operations occur for a person to reach a state of equilibrium.

Here is an illustration of how information-processing theories take on where learning and cognitive-developmental theories leave off. You are taking a multiple choice examination. There are five choices for each question. On one question you have narrowed the choice of answers down to two (input). You are having trouble choosing because the wording of the answers is different from the way you studied (coding). You picture your lecture notes and the text (long-term memory), retrieve some information, and finally mark your choice (output).

Theories of how children process information are useful to teachers. They can explain how children take information from the environment, commit it to memory, and retrieve it to solve problems. For instance, children can be taught attentive skills such as taking notes or retrieval skills such as word-picture associations.

**FIGURE 1.1
HOW INFORMATION IS
PROCESSED
(Atkinson & Shiffrin, 1971)**

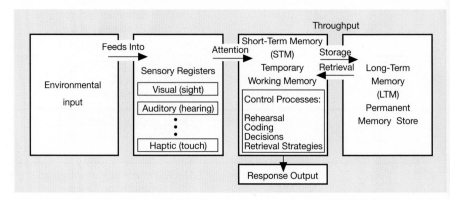

Information processing might explain Jennifer's slow progress in reading in the first grade as perhaps due to an attention deficit or memory problems in coding or information retrieval. Jennifer certainly had a stimulating home environment to which she responded favorably, so it can be assumed her sensory registers were operating normally. It is possible that she felt uncomfortable in school and missed home and, therefore, had trouble paying attention. Also, it is possible that because she was doted on by her parents and caregivers, she did not have to exercise her memory because of the adults' constantly reminding her of things to do.

## Systems Theories

**Systems** are sets or arrangements of elements linked to each other in order to function as a whole; the functioning of the whole is qualitatively different from the sum of its parts. For example, a family system consists of the relationships of its members operating together as a system; it differs from the characteristics of each individual member. Systems theories view development as a joint function of the person and the environment. The environment can include the immediate settings in which a person interacts such as the family, peer group, and community. The environment also can include the contexts in which these immediate settings are imbedded such as culture, or time (period of history).

A main proponent of systems theories is Urie Bronfenbrenner, known for his ecological theory. Systems theories consider the role of the individual in influencing interactions in her environments. For example, a child's stubbornness could influence the parents' childrearing techniques in that the parents might become more restrictive and punitive when the child is defiant (Patterson, 1982). Systems theories also acknowledge the role the individual plays in creating her own environment (Scarr & McCartney, 1983). For example, a child who is muscular and well coordinated may choose to become involved in sports. Her selection of a particular sport could influence subsequent friendships and activities, thereby creating new settings for further interaction. Environments can be changed as people respond to them; in so doing people change, too (Vygotsky, 1978; Luria, 1976; Cole & Scribner, 1974). For example, when the Soviet Union became a federation of states, tremendous political and economic change occurred. As the country moved from socialism to free enterprise, the attitudes and behavior of the Soviet people changed accordingly.

**Ecological Theory.** **Ecological theory** views development in terms of the settings one is in at a particular time and their relations.

Bronfenbrenner defined the ecology of human development as involving "the scientific study of the progressive mutual accommodation throughout the life course between an active growing human being and the changing properties of the immediate settings in which the developing person lives, as this process is affected by the relations between these settings, and by the larger contexts in which the settings are embedded" (Bronfenbrenner, 1989, p. 188).

According to Bronfenbrenner (1979, 1989) the ecological environment, or the environment relevant to human development, is composed of four different systems—*microsystems, mesosystems, exosystems, macrosystems.* Table 1.4 illustrates these systems.

**Developmental profiles at home...**

**At school...**

**In the community and among peers...**

## ECOLOGICAL SYSTEMS AND INFLUENCES ON DEVELOPMENT

### TABLE 1.4

| Ecological Level | Definition | Examples | Issues Affecting Children |
|---|---|---|---|
| Microsystem | Situations in which the child has face-to-face contact with influential others | Family, school, peer group, church | Is the child regarded positively? Is the child accepted? Is the child reinforced for competent behavior? Is the child exposed to enough diversity in roles and relationships? Is the child given an active role in reciprocal relationships? |
| Mesosystem | Relationships between microsystems; the connections between situations | Home-school, home-church, school-neighborhood | Do settings respect each other? Do settings present basic consistency in values? |
| Exosystem | Settings in which the child does not participate but in which significant decisions are made affecting the child or adults who do interact directly with the child | Parents' places of employment, school board, local government, parents' peer group | Are decisions made with the interests of parents and children in mind? How well do supports for families balance stresses for parents? |
| Macrosystem | "Blueprints" for defining and organizing the institutional life of the society | Ideology, social policy, shared assumptions about human nature, the "social contract" | Are some groups valued at the expense of others (e.g., sexism, racism)? Is there an individualistic or a collectivistic orientation? Is violence a norm? |

**(Garbino, 1992)**

The microsystem involves the interaction between a child and others in an immediate setting such as the home or community.

The mesosystem involves the relationships among the various settings in which the child participates, for instance, home and school (parent-teacher conferences).

The exosystem includes the institutions in which the child does not participate but that influence her development indirectly; for example, the parents' work schedule determines the hours available to the child.

The macrosystem consists of basic values, beliefs, or ideologies that influence the ways in which special institutions are organized. For example, the fundamental characteristics of American democracy influence human behavior.

Ecological theorists might explain the Kenneth's dilemma as a result of many related factors such as hormones, relationships with family members, and value systems. The development of Kenny's attitudes were influenced by observing relatives, neighbors, role models on television, and discussing things with friends. Kenny had to choose between his family's and religion's value system and that of his peer culture and the media, while being biologically ready to have sex with a willing partner.

Ecological theorists might explain Jennifer's eating disorder as a result of many related factors such as relations with family, role models, and the value system of her culture. Jennifer was exposed to pressures beyond her maturational ability to deal with them—pressures to be in control, to be thin, to rely on herself and not others, and to make her parents proud.

# WHAT IS THE VALUE OF KNOWING DIFFERENT THEORETICAL PERSPECTIVES?

The advantage of knowing the different theoretical perspectives on development is that we can choose those that apply to a particular problem. If appropriate, we can combine aspects of several theories; this is known as the **eclectic** approach. We can also choose a theory to help us organize factors to study. The eclectic approach is illustrated in the Research in Review section.

## RESEARCH IN REVIEW

### WHAT IS THE RELATIONSHIP BETWEEN MATERNAL FUNCTIONING AND CHILDREN'S BEHAVIOR?

Hammen, C., Burge, D., & Stansbury, K. (1990). Relationship of mother and child variables to child outcomes in a high-risk sample: A causal modeling analysis. *Developmental Psychology, 26*(1), 24–30.

Children of depressed mothers have been shown to be at risk for psychological dysfunctions. Because depression is a common experience for women of childbearing age, large numbers of children may be at risk. This study was designed to examine factors influencing the effect of women's depression on their children.

Some studies have shown one factor to be genetic and claim that depression is inherited. These studies have a biological perspective. Other studies have shown that the parent–child relation-

ship is a factor. These studies have a contextual perspective. Still other studies have pointed to the differential impact of risk factors on children of different developmental stages. These studies have an interactional perspective.

This particular study tries to understand children's outcomes as a complex consequence of multiple related factors thereby taking an eclectic approach.

The study participants included 14 children of depressed mothers, 12 children of manic-depressed mothers, 14 children of chronically medically ill (diabetes, arthritis) women, and 24 children of normal women. All children were 8–16 years of age. There *(continued on following page)*

*(continued from previous page)*

were 32 boys and 32 girls. The women were recruited from various clinics and private practices.

Maternal functioning was evaluated via a self-report assessment scale containing questions of occupational performance, social and leisure activities, relationships with family members, performance in parental role, and so on.

The children were diagnosed as having no disorder, a minor disorder, or a major disorder by clinical interviewers. Behavior and social competence of the children were assessed by the mothers via a checklist. A self-concept scale was administered to the children to assess self-attitudes.

Mother–child interaction behaviors were videotaped in a five-minute discussion of a topic they had reported disagreeing about such as homework or bedtime.

When all the data were analyzed, it was concluded that a child's exhibition of behavior problems was related to how poorly his mother functioned (contextual influence). Maternal functioning that is maladaptive includes the experience of ongoing strain across various role areas, depressive symptoms, and an interactional style with the child marked by negative and critical communications. Whether the child had a disorder depended on the child's characteristics such as age, temperament, and self-concept (biological influence). Finally, the child's characteristics both were caused and were the effect of maternal functioning (interactional influence). Apparently, depressed mothers elicit negative reactions from their children that then intensify their unhappiness and negativity, which in turn elicits more distress from their children. Thus, a cycle of mutual distress and dysfunction results.

Maternal functioning contributes to the development of psychopathology in children. Using a model to show causes and effects of maternal functioning helps identify areas needing intervention.

# DEVELOPMENTAL MILESTONES

Developmental milestones consist of significant events in a person's life such as learning to walk and read. The following table is a chart of the scientifically established averages, or *norms*, at which most children reach specific developmental milestones. Norms are useful because they provide a reference point for the normal course of development. Some children will reach a developmental milestone earlier and some later. However, great deviance indicates a child has a problem (box 1.1).

Box 1.1 **EARLY WARNING SIGNS OF CHILDHOOD PROBLEMS**

Recognizing early warning signs of childhood problems can improve your child's chances for a happy future.

Your child is special to you.

Sometimes even the most concerned and loving parents are unaware of problems their child may be having. Problems a child is born with or that he may acquire could ultimately interfere with his normal growth and development.

This doesn't have to happen. Many conditions can be corrected if parents recognize the early warning signs and seek help.

Here are some very simple things to watch for as your young child develops. These are some of the more common indicators of problems in small children.

If you suspect that your child may have a problem, call for qualified help. Don't delay. Immediate attention can make all the difference in the world for your child and for you.

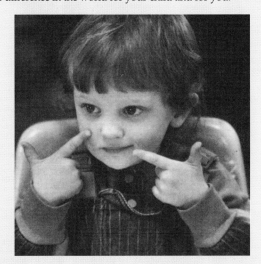

**Seeing**
If your child…
• does not follow objects with his eyes by age 6 months
• is often unable to locate and pick up small objects which have been dropped
• frequently rubs his eyes or complains that eyes hurt; or has reddened, watering or encrusted eyelids
• holds head in a strained or awkward position…(tilts head to either side–thrusts head forward or backward) when trying to focus on someone or something
• sometimes, or always, crosses one or both eyes
• fails to notice objects, people or animals around him when other children do

**Talking**
If your child…
• cannot say "Mama" and "Dadda" by age 1
• cannot say the names of a few objects and people by age 1 ½
• is not attempting nursery rhymes or short TV jingles by age 2½
• is not talking in short sentences by age 3
• is not understood by people outside the family by age 3

**Playing**
If your child…
• does not try to put toys in his mouth by age 7 months
• does not play games such as peek-a-boo, patty cake, and wave good-bye by age 1

• does not imitate parents doing routine household chores by age 2 or 3
• does not play group games such as hide-and-seek or tag with other children by age 4
• does not share and take turns by age 5

**Hearing**
If your child…
• doesn't turn to face the source of strange sounds or voices by six months; or if he sleeps through most noises
• rubs or pulls at his ears repeatedly; has frequent ear aches or runny ears
• talks in a very loud or soft voice
• does not react when you call from another room
• turns the same ear toward a sound he wishes to hear

**Thinking**
If your child…
• doesn't respond to her own name when called by age 1
• is unable to identify hair, eyes, ears, nose and mouth by pointing to them at age 2
• does not understand simple stories told or read by age 3
• doesn't give reasonable answers to such questions as "What do you do when you are sleepy?" or "What do you do when you are hungry?" by age 4
• does not seem to understand the meanings of the words "today," "tomorrow" and "yesterday" by age 5

**Moving**
If your child…
• is unable to sit up without help or support by age 9 months
• uses one hand predominantly before 18 months
• cannot walk by age 2
• does not walk down steps by age 3
• is unable to balance on one foot for a short time by age 4
• cannot throw and catch a large ball bounced to him by age 5

**Living Skills**
If your child…
• doesn't drink from a cup or use a spoon by age 2
• can't help with dressing by age 3
• can't dress without supervision by age 5

**(National Easter Seal Society)**

## TABLE 1.5
## Age Birth—8 months

### Physical Development
**Birth:** *Average size:* 7½ lbs. 20 in. long.
**1 month:** *Average size:* 10 lbs., 1 in. long. *Sleep:* needs 16 hrs. per day. *Hearing:* can perceive differences among various sounds.
**2 months:** *Perception:* preference for fixation on faces and for red and blue colors rather than greens and yellows.
**3 months:** *Sleep:* needs 14 hrs. per day.
**4 months:** *Hearing:* can locate source of a sound.
**6 months:** *Average size:* 16½ lbs., 26 in. long. *Teeth:* lower central incisors appear, total of 2 teeth. *Perception:* depth perception begins to develop.
**7 months:** *Teeth:* lower lateral incisors appear, followed by the central incisors, total of 6 teeth.

### Motor Development
**Birth:** moves around a lot, kicks, lifts and turns head, waves arms, head sags when not supported.
**1 month:** lifts chin when lying on stomach.
**2 months:** holds head erect when held.
**3 months:** steps when held erect, turns from side to back, reaches for objects but misses them, hands mostly open; no grasp.
**4 months:** sits with support, hands open and close, stares at and shakes objects held in hands.
**5 months:** sits on another's lap, rolls from back to side, grasps objects without using thumbs.
**6 months:** sits in high chair, uses hands for support when sitting alone, reaches with one hand, grasps dangling objects, moves objects from one hand to the other.
**7 months:** sits without support, attempts to crawl, rolls from back to stomach.
**8 months:** stands with help, crawls (arms pulling body and legs), uses thumb in grasping, picks up small objects with thumb and fingers.

### Language Development
**1 month:** cries, makes small throaty noises.
**2 months:** crying markedly decreased at 8 weeks, begins producing vowel-like cooing noises; sound, however, not like adults.
**3 months:** cries less, coos, gurgles at the back of the throat, squeals, and occasionally chuckles.
**4 months:** eyes seem to search for speaker, cooing becomes pitch-modulated; vowel-like sounds begin to be interspersed with consonantal sounds, smiles and coos when talked to.
**5 months:** vowel sounds are interspersed with more consonantal sounds (*f, v, th, s, sh, z, sz,* and *n* common) which produces one-syllable babbling. Displays pleasure with squeals, gurgles, and giggles and displeasure with growls and grunts.
**8 months:** displays adult intonation in babbling; often uses two-syllable utterances such as *baba, didi, mama,* imitates sounds. Reduplication or more continuous repetition becomes frequent. Utterances can signal emphasis and emotions.

### Cognitive/Piagetian Development
**Birth–1 month:** *Sensorimotor development—substage 1: Reflexes:* activating reflexes, sucking, grasping, staring, listening are actions that trigger reactions or responses. *Object permanence:* objects have no independent existence. *Space:* no single organized space exists, rather a collection of separate spaces related to specific sensorimotor schemes (e.g., visual space, tactile space). *Causality:* no sense of cause and effect, at most events are related to needs and tensions. *Time:* it is "practical" and linked to feelings of need and effort.
**1–4 months:** *Sensorimotor—substage 2: Primary circular reactions:* first acquired adaptations, assimilation becomes separated from accommodation and there is a coordination of reflexes, sucking a pacifier differently from a nipple or grabbing a bottle to suck it. *Object permanence:* no interest in vanishing objects, they exist only as part of an action.
**4–8 months:** *Sensorimotor—substage 3: Secondary circular reactions:* tries to preserve interesting sights, responds to people and objects, actions are repeated because of their consequences. *Object permanence:* objects just seen are searched for, if thrown there is an anticipation where they may fall, if objects are partially hidden they are reached for, objects are also associated with others' actions. *Space:* initial awareness of spatial relations between objects but still defines all space in terms of actions. *Causality:* perceives own actions as having effect. Magical since of causality, feeling of efficacy, of relating to acts. *Time:* elementary sense of before and after as part of action, recollects the immediate past but own acts remain central to sense of time.

*Ages indicated within this chart are approximations or averages. For example, not all children weigh 7½ pounds at birth. Some weigh 6 pounds and others weigh 9 pounds, and all of these weights are normal. The age ranges should be understood as guidelines for the order, timing and relatedness of changes in these domains.*

## Age Birth—8 months

### Social Development

*Attachment:* 0–3 months; reacts to other people and environmental events indiscriminately; uses sucking, rooting, grasping, smiling, gazing, cuddling, and visual tracking to maintain closeness to primary caretaker; at 6 months seeks out mother and reacts to her especially (Bowlby).

*Period of trust vs. mistrust:* will last until age 2. Mother is main human relationship; successful outcomes of a dilemma at this stage produce hope and trust in the environment and the future knowing that others will care for the basic needs of nourishment, sucking, warmth, cleanliness, and physical contact (Erikson).

*Play:* 1½ months, smiles responsively; 3 months, smiles spontaneously; 7 months, plays peek-a-boo. *Oral stage:* the mouth is the focus of pleasurable sensation and feeding is the most stimulating activity (Freud). *Emotions:* distress to 6 months expressed by cries because of hunger, fatigue, pain, cold, loud noises, or sudden loss of support. Pleasure and contentment occur when securely wrapped or cuddled, rocked, or well fed. Enjoys hearing soothing sounds and looking at interesting sights. Smiles a half smile at pleasant sounds or full stomach at 6 weeks; social smile or grins at another's face at 4 months; laughs and smiles broadly at something particularly exciting at 6 months. *Fear:* at 1 month, often looks scared when placed in a warm bath or held high up; at 6 months, intrigued rather than intimidated; at 7 months, wariness sets in.

### Self-Development

**0–1 month:** shows no awareness of body.
**2 months:** "discovers" hands when catches of sight of them, becomes fascinated by their movement, but "loses" them when they move out of line of vision.
**4 months:** smiles at self in mirror.
**7 months:** pats own mirror image.
**8 months:** still has no concept of where own body ends and someone else's body begins.

## Age 9–17 months

### Physical Development

**9 months:** *Teeth:* upper lateral incisors appear, total of 8 teeth.
**10 months:** *Sleep:* needs 13½ hrs. per day.
**12 months:** *Average size:* 22 lbs., 30 in. long. *Teeth:* lower 1st molars appear, total of 10 teeth. *Body changes:* child has average body temperature of 99.7 F.
**14 months:** *Teeth:* upper 1st molar appears, total of 12 teeth.
**16 months:** *Teeth:* lower cuspids appear, total of 14 teeth.

### Motor Development

**9 months:** stands holding on to furniture.
**10 months:** sits up easily, pulls up to stand, creeps (arms and legs alternate, body free).
**11 months:** creeps on hands and feet, walks when led.
**12 months:** seats self on floor, walks a few steps without help, holds and releases a ball.
**13 months:** crawls up stairs.
**14 months:** stands alone, will take a few steps unaided.
**15 months:** walks alone.

### Language Development

**10 months:** understands some words and associated gestures (e.g., "no" and shakes head); may pronounce *dada* or *mama* and uses holophrases (single words with many different meanings).
**12 months:** employs more holophrases such as *baby, bye-bye,* and *hi;* may imitate sounds of objects, such as *bow-bow;* has greater control over intonation patterns, gives signs of understanding some words and simple commands (e.g., "show me your eye"). Has produced the sounds of many languages and mastered the sounds of his own.

### Cognitive/Piagetian Development

**9 months:** *Sensorimotor—substage 4: Coordination of secondary circular reactions:* adaptation and anticipation occur; becoming more deliberate and purposeful in responding to people and objects; schemes now have goals. *Object permanence:* pursues hidden objects presumed to be at a previous site. *Space:* comprehends relation between object in front of and behind a barrier; interested in displacement of objects seen from different perspectives. *Causality:* understands means-ends relationships; uses others to achieve effects. *Time:* emergence of ability to remember events when own acts are not central; continued confusion of time and space.

## TABLE 1.5 *(continued)*
## Age 9–17 months

### Cognitive/Piagetian Development
**12 months–18 months:** *Sensorimotor—substage 5:* exploration and experimentation by varying behavior to achieve goals. *Object permanence:* monitors all visible displacements. *Space:* understands body as occupying space, moves objects all around and studies relations among them. *Causality:* understands that cause is external to self, takes into account spatial factors in cause-effect relationships. *Time:* can retain more events and an event series for a longer interval: more differentiation of time from own reactions occurs.

### Social Development
*Attachment:* at 9–12 months, maintains attachment link over some distance with eyes, increasingly takes initiative in contacts; begins to fear strangers. Mother is central figure to whom infant seeks physical proximity and contact (Bowlby). *Play:* spends most time in solitary play but will increasingly spend more time in play with mother; at 9 months, plays pat-a-cake; at 13 months, plays ball with another older person; at 16 months, imitates housework. *Social skills:* at 14 months, drinks from a cup. *Anal stage:* at 1 year the anus is the focus of pleasurable sensations (Freud). *Emotions:* at 12 months, cries of frustration when forced to do something against will; cries when can't reach toy on a table; at 13½ months, indicates wants without crying. *Pleasure:* smiles and laughs for same reasons most young children do; great joy is expressed for actions performed and at play with others. *Fear:* from 11–18 months, frightened by height and depth, a strange adult, a jack-in-the-box, a toy dog that moves, a mask, a loud noise.

### Self-Development
**10 months:** responds to own name.
**12 months:** with development of object permanence, begins to realize that other people exist; can name family members (e.g., "dada, mama, baby").
**16 months:** teases and plays with parent.

## Age 18–24 months

### Physical Development
**18 months:** *Average size:* 24 lbs., 32 in. tall. *Teeth:* upper cuspids appear, total of 16 teeth.
**20 months:** *Teeth:* lower 2nd molars appear, total of 20 teeth.
**23 months:** *Sleep:* needs 13 hrs. per day.
**24 months:** *Average size:* 27½ lbs., 34 in. tall. *Body changes:* brain development at 75% its full adult weight.

### Motor Development
**18 months:** runs awkwardly and falls a lot, pulls and pushes toys, throws a ball, fills a spoon but spills it when inserting it into mouth.
**24 months:** walks smoothly, runs well and with legs apart, walks alone up and down stairs, jumps, kicks large ball, builds tower of 6 or 7 blocks, turns book pages singly, holds glass in one hand, places marks on paper, uses scribbles (vertical and circular) to cover all or part of a page.

### Language Development
**18 months:** vocabulary of about 30 words, increasing rapidly. Some words begin to have a general meaning (e.g., *dog* means any dog; *black* or *white*, *live* or *toy*, *big* or *small*). Words that are easily produced (*beep-beep*, *tu-tu*) said one at a time. Sounds heard are easily imitated. Babbling is reflective of adult speech, more intricate intonation patterns used.
**20 months:** begins to use 2- or 3-word sentences.
**24 months:** begins to use 4- or 5-word sentences. Vocabulary has 50–400 or more words. Easily repeats words and simple sentences produced by adults. Speech becoming a mechanism to communicate a request, a wish, an impression. During play, speaks a lot about own actions and speech is more emotionally expressive. All phrases appear to be own creation.

### Cognitive/Piagetian Development
**18–24 months:** *Sensorimotor—substage 6: Beginning of thought:* new schemes or meanings devised through mental combinations before acting, thinking before doing and creating in new ways. *Object permanence:* can now take invisible displacements into account. *Space:* understands that goals may be reached by many different paths. *Causality:* infers causes from effects and effects from causes by mental representation. *Time:* can recall remote events; represents past and future; time exists apart from individual experiences.
**24 months:** *Beginning of preoperational or symbolic stage:* becomes able to represent something with something else; uses representation and mental imagery in speech, play, gestures and with mental pictures.

## Age 18–24 months

### Social Development

*Attachment:* at 20 months, long-term separation from mother will lead to protest, then despair, followed by relative detachment (Bowlby). *Period of autonomy vs. shame and doubt:* will last until age 4. Parents are main human relationship; child learns to be self-sufficient in many activities, and opportunities to try out these skills will lead to a sense of self-control, self-esteem, and autonomy; overprotection or a lack of support will lead to doubt (Erikson). *Play:* by 2 years, involved in parallel play with peers; decrease in time spent playing with mother. *Social skills:* at 18 months, uses a spoon; at 22 months, helps with simple tasks in the house. *Emotions:* has developed empathy, shame, embarrassment, and pride. *Fear:* decline begins to occur again. Aggression: begins to appear at 2 years.

### Self-Development

**18 months:** self-consciousness emerges.
**24 months:** labels self using own name. Able to recognize mirror image.

## Age 3–4 years

### Physical Development

**3 years:** *Average size:* 32 lbs., 38 in. tall. *Sleep:* needs 12 hrs. per day. *Perception:* still slightly farsighted—easier to see distances.
**4 years:** *Average size:* 37 lbs., 40 in. tall.

### Motor Development

**3 years:** rides tricycle, can walk on tiptoe, hops with both feet, runs smoothly, walks up and down stairs one foot on each step, buttons and unbuttons, pours from a pitcher, builds tower of 9 blocks and makes bridge with 3 blocks, tries to make the basic shapes (triangles, circles, and squares), catches ball, arms straight.
**3½ years:** uses basic shapes, scribbles to make designs, uses circles within circles, etc.
**4 years:** balances on 1 foot for 5 seconds, hops on 1 foot, can walk forward heel to toe, throws ball overhand, dresses self, catches small ball, elbows in front of body, does stunts on tricycle, descends short steps, alternating feet, hand preference nearly established.

### Language Development

**3 years:** sentences contain many words with plural endings. Uses the declarative in a raised tone to ask questions. Sometimes uses nouns or other substantives with a negative word to express negation. A greater variety of emotions is now reflected in speech. Vocabulary is about 850 words. Can understand meaning of adult speech about events that have not personally been experienced. Easily repeats songs. Begins to use subordinate sentences. Most pronunciation correct except *r, l,* and the hissing sounds.
**4 years:** vocabulary of about 1500 words; most grammatical endings now known; deviation from adult speech more style than grammar. Begins to use future tense; two or more ideas are regularly expressed in complex sentences. Comprehends feelings (e.g., cold, tired) and prepositions; recognizes color names.

### Cognitive/Piagetian Development

**3 years:** *Symbolic phase of preoperational stage* still in effect. *Imagination:* ability to pretend during play develops; engages in dramatic play. *Conservation:* beginning development of the conservation of amount. *Egocentrism:* reduction in the amount of egocentrism; more able to take other people's perspectives into account. *Classification:* objects are included in a particular class for personal reasons (e.g., "this makes a house"). *Time:* talks almost as much about the past and future as about the present; often pretends to tell time and talks about time a great deal; tells how old he is, what he will do tomorrow or on his birthday.
**4 years:** *Intuitive phase of preoperational stage* begins to operate; the thought processes begin to involve such things as a new understanding of relationships. *Motivation:* rewards continue to need to be fairly immediate and sensual; still very sensitive to praise and attention. *Time:* past and future tenses very accurately used; refinement in the use of time words; broader concepts expressed by use of month, "next winter," "last summer" a much clearer understanding of daily sequence of events emerges.

### Social Development

*Attachment:* by age 4, will accept temporary absence of mother without protest and will accept substitute attachment figures (Bowlby). *Play:* at 3 years, most children involve themselves in peer play; by 4 years, most involved in cooperative play. *Social skills:* at 3 years, washes and dries hands and face; at 4 years, dresses with or without supervision. *Phallic stage:* both sexes have sexual fantasies about their parents for which they feel guilty; stage will last until age 6 (Freud). *Sex role and identity:* knows own sex but does not realize maleness and femaleness are permanent characteristics. *Moral development:* rules of a game are sacred and unchangeable but they tend to be applied in an egocentric manner.

**TABLE 1.5** (continued)
## Age 3–4 years

### Self-Development
**3 years:** period of acute possessiveness and egocentrism. Capable of scanning and responding to inner states (e.g., identifying mood states and changes in one's own moods).
**4 years:** beginning to understand "mineness" and "ourness" and to see self as reflected in others. If told he is cute or devilish will include these characteristics in own self-concept. Adult responses to that image give him a positive or negative image about himself.

## Age 5–7 years

### Physical Development
**5 years:** *Average size:* 41½ lbs., 43 in. tall. *Sleep:* needs 11 hrs. per day. *Perception:* development has advanced so that child can scan and focus reasonably well. *Body changes:* brain development at 90% full adult weight; average body temperature at normal 98.6 F; fewer stomachaches, digestive system more regular, fewer ear infections, distance from outer ear greater, respiratory infections lessened due to a longer trachea.
**6 years:** *Average size:* 45½ lbs., 46 in. tall. *Teeth:* at 6½ permanent upper and lower 1st molars and lower central incisors appear.
**7 years:** *Average size:* 53 lbs., 47 in. tall. *Teeth:* at 7½ permanent upper central incisors and lower lateral incisors replace baby teeth.

### Motor Development
**5 years:** catches bounding ball with elbows at sides, balances on 1 foot for 10 seconds, skips, descends large ladder, alternating feet easily, throws well, copies designs, letters, numbers, triangles, and squares, folds paper into double triangle, tries to form pictures of animals, people, and buildings.
**6 years:** can walk backwards heel to toe, running speed increases, jumping forms basis of many games and improves.
**7 years:** balance improves, more details are added to art work.

### Language Development
**5 years:** language increasingly resembles adult models.
**6 years:** average vocabulary now 2500 words.
**7 years:** can recall grammatical sentences rather than strings of words and can make grammatically consistent word associations.

### Cognitive/Piagetian Development
**5 years:** *Conservation:* beginning to understand the conservation of number. *Classification:* done largely on the basis of color.
**6 years:** *Classification:* done largely on the basis of shape discrimination using visual perception rather than touch. *Memory:* capacity is well developed and labeling aids greatly in recalling pictures.
**7 years:** beginning of *concrete operational period:* capable of certain logic so long as manipulation of objects is involved. *Classification:* uses definitions for grouping centering on one dimension, but still unable to use class inclusion. *Creativity:* drawings of the human are quite well defined and designs are very representative of reality.
**7½ years:** *Conservation:* understanding of conservation of length, seriation, and number. *Motivation:* rewards come from correct information; begins to adopt internal standards of performance. *Humor:* ability to understand riddles.

### Social Development
*Period of initiative vs. guilt:* the family is the main human relationship; children freely engage in many adultlike activities, and parents' patient answering of questions leads to initiative; a restriction of activities and treatment of questions as nuisance leads to guilt (Erikson). *Latency period:* not a stage but rather an interlude when sexual needs are relatively quiet and energy is put into learning skills—will continue until age 11 (Freud). *Aggression:* physical fighting often used as a means of solving problems or defending one's image. *Sex role and identity:* at 6 years, realizes that sex is a permanent characteristic. *Moral development:* rules in games are important as codes that must be respected, but they can be changed; children are more able to cooperate and share because they are less egocentric and develop a characteristic way of responding to others.

### Self-Development
Understands that self is part of interrelated group of others (e.g., family, friends, kinships). Develops understanding that self is a sexual person and forms preferences for own sex. Perceives self as a moral person with goals for an ideal self. Understands self as initiator of novel and creative interactions.

## Age 9–10 years

### Physical Development
**9 years:** *Average size:* 68 lbs., 53 in. tall. *Sleep:* needs 10 hrs. per day. *Teeth:* permanent upper lateral incisors and lower cuspids. *Perception:* well-developed ability to read fine print.
**10 years:** *Average size:* males, 78 lbs., 58.7 in. tall; females, 77.5 lbs., 59.2 in. tall. *Teeth:* at 10 upper and lower 1st bicuspids and upper 2nd bicuspids appear, total now 26 teeth. *Body changes:* females begin to have rounding of hips, breasts and nipples are elevated to form bud stage, no true pubic hair yet.

### Motor Development
Increased gains in vigor and balance in motor control and coordination; manual dexterity increases; greater muscular strength develops; improvement in accuracy, agility, and endurance; girls continue to run faster than boys; throwing and catching are better; jumping and climbing are done with ease and assurance; eye-hand coordination is good.

### Language Development
Acquires an average of 5000 new words in this age range. Knowledge of syntax fully developed. Has the ability to understand comparatives (longer, deeper), the subjunctive (*if I were a…*), and metaphors (*rotten egg, dirty rat*). Language has become a tool and not just words that refer only to objects. Specialized vocabularies develop for different situations (e.g., games).

### Cognitive/Piagetian Development
**9 years:** *Concrete operation period* still in effect: logic and objectivity increase; deductive thinking begins to appear. *Conservation:* understands conservation of area. *Causality:* has a firm grasp of cause-effect relationships. *Humor:* begins to appreciate use of certain metaphors in joking because of an understanding of the incongruous elements.
**10 years:** *Conservation:* understanding of the conservation of substances acquired. *Classification:* elements classified using a hierarchical construct. *Space:* able to make or interpret simple maps and distances. *Memory:* memory tasks involve use of mnemonic devices.

### Social Development
*Period of industry vs. inferiority:* has been ongoing since age 7; the neighborhood and school are now the main source of human relationships. Children are busy learning to be competent and productive using skills and tools, exercising dexterity and intelligence to gain praise for their accomplishments leading to industry. Limitation of activities, feeling inferior, criticism, and inability to do well lead to inferiority (Erikson). *Aggression:* reduction in physical fighting to defend self-image; verbal duels now become the tool. *Sex role and identity:* at 10 years, emphasizes social roles more than physical development, believing that "men should act like men and women like ladies."

### Self-Development
Develops a great variety of new skills and activities that lead to a sense of effectiveness.

## Age 13–14 years

### Physical Development
**13 years:** *Average size:* females, 99 lbs., 62 in. tall; males, 93 lbs., 60 in. tall. *Sleep:* needs 9 hrs. per day. *Teeth:* upper cuspids, upper and lower 2nd molars, and lower 2nd bicuspids appear, total number now 28. *Body changes:* average girl has had 1st menarche, pubic hair has appeared, hips have widened and shoulders narrowed, uterus becomes enlarged, vaginal lining thickens and secretion becomes acid, areola and nipples elevate to form primary breast; males, testes increase in size, scrotum grows, penis grows in length and circumference.
**14 years:** *Average size:* females, 108 lbs., 634 in. tall; males, 107½ lbs., 64 in. tall. *Body changes:* average male has had 1st ejaculation; penis, testes, and scrotum continue to grow and become larger, prostate and seminal vesicles mature, voice lowers with growth of the larynx, peak period for height spurt occurs.

### Motor Development
Boys are now able to run faster than girls, grip strength continues to increase, with boys showing greater strength. Motor awareness becomes somewhat uneven due to growth in muscles and bones, responses are now often quick, jerky motions. Balance is now quite mature. Girls tend to be better than boys in accuracy, agility, and rhythmic activities.

### Language Development
Vocabulary increases to about 50,000 words. Increased use of specialized vocabularies (lingo) for additional new situations.

**TABLE 1.5** (*continued*)
## Age 13–14 years

### Cognitive/Piagetian Development
**13 years:** *Formal operational period* has begun and will continue throughout adulthood. *Conservation:* understanding of the conservation of weight now well established. *Logical reasoning:* has firm grasp of the general laws of inverse relationship; ability to reason during a discussion becoming more highly developed; persuasion is used rather than threats.
**14 years:** *Conservation:* ability to understand the conservation of volume develops. *Logical reasoning:* solutions to problems of logical thinking involve imaginative answers and often evoke the possibility of extenuating circumstances.

### Social Development
*Period of identity vs. role confusion:* will last through adolescence: peer group and leadership models are the main source of human relationships. Individual sees self as unique and integrated person and tries to establish sexual, ethnic, and career identities; inability to establish leads to confusion (Erikson). *Genital stage:* the genitals are the focus of pleasurable sensation and satisfaction is reached through sexual stimulation. This stage will last into and throughout adulthood and its goal is a healthy life of love and work (Freud). *Sex role and identity:* at 14, adolescents emphasize psychological differences rather than physical or social differences (e.g., women cry more easily than men and are not as aggressive as men). *Moral development:* understanding of social rules (good behavior is considered behavior that pleases other people) and law and order (right behavior means obeying laws set down by those in power) established.

### Self-Development
Development of the concept of one's physical appearance, evaluation of that appearance is based on the culture's "body ideal."

## Age 16 years

### Physical Development
*Average size:* Females, 117 lbs., 63½ in. tall; males, 129 lbs., 67½ in. tall. *Sleep:* needs 8 hrs. per day. *Teeth:* upper and lower 3rd molars appear, full set of teeth present for a total of 2. *Body changes:* in females, pubic hair fully developed, breasts filled out to adult form; in males, facial and body pubic hair nearly fully developed.

### Motor Development
Slowdown in increases in height and weight allow for stabilization and reorganization of motor and muscle patterns. Boys' physical strength has doubled that found at age 12. Agility, control, and balance are greatly improved. Boys' throwing, catching, striking, and kicking have improved over girls. Endurance is greatly improved for both sexes.

### Language Development
Increase in vocabulary continues and average number of words understood is 80,300. When defining words fuller and more abstract concepts are used.

### Cognitive/Piagetian Development
*Classification:* is able to flexibly shift category criteria and can use abstract as well as perceptual categories. *Logical reasoning:* ability to use verbal transitive inference develops. *Memory:* "metamemory" improves; ability to assess own memory develops; mnemonic strategies greatly improved and used more often. *Egocentrism:* an "adolescent egocentrism" develops and adolescent will create an imaginary audience where he fantasizes how others will react to his appearance and behavior.

### Social Development
*Attachment:* bonds become basic in the development of a self-reliant, mature adult able to form stable relationships. *Moral development:* beginning to understand social contracts (rules in society exist for the benefit of all and are established by mutual agreement) and universal ethical principles (general principles that determine right and wrong, e.g., do unto others, life is sacred) are established.

### Self-Development
Development of the characteristics of adolescent egocentrism—the psychological rather than the physical world is primary. Period of search for identity, the self now the object of multiple role expectations.

# CRITICAL THINKING & YOU

**M**ark, age 7, was classified by his second grade teacher, Ms. Smith, as having an attention deficit disorder with hyperactivity. She referred him to the school psychologist because he could not sit for more than five minutes; his reading was very slow; and when he had to do work, he would get frustrated and rip his paper. He continually had to be told to stop fidgeting. He did not have friends. The teacher became especially concerned when Mark began to exhibit aggressive behavior.

**ANALYSIS:** Review this chapter to find supporting reasons that explain Mark's behavior from a:
1. biological perspective,
2. contextual perspective,
3. interactional perspective.

**SYNTHESIS:** Compare the aspects of Mark's development (for example, behavior, cognition, social interaction, emotions) that each perspective addresses.

**EVALUATION:** Which perspective do you feel best explains Mark's behavior. and how it could be used as a basis for helping Mark?

• • • • • • • • • • • • • • • • • • • • • • • • • • • • • • • • • • •

## Kenneth Johnson
*(continued from page 2)*

She felt they would never move away from the small, old tract house. In fact, Kate's children were crowded in two tiny bedrooms, close to hers and Michael's so that privacy was impossible.

On January 20, 1970, she gave birth to another child, Kenneth. All she could think of was that Kenneth represented another 18 years of worry about making ends meet. Kate, 27, asked her physician for a tubal ligation so she could not be pregnant again.

With her firstborn, George, Kate had stayed up all night nursing, and she read Dr. Spock thoroughly. But her relatives questioned the way she handled every problem. Later, after Jason and Darla were born, she was grateful for their unquestioning willingness to babysit or cook. After Kenneth was born, Kate had learned to take the best of what the relatives had to offer and to ignore the rest. She supplemented breastfeeding with a bottle, so others could feed him while she went back to work. She returned to work part-time six weeks after

Kenneth was born. When he was six months, she weaned him and began working full-time. One day she dreamed of returning to school.

Over time and with help from her husband, Kate had become a relaxed mother and liked watching Kenneth develop. He was a cuddler; smiling at seven weeks of age and sleeping through the night when two months old. She found it hard to leave him in the morning when she went to work.

By eight months, Kenny was sitting and crawling and also began to babble. Kate saw that he loved being the center of attention and got plenty of it. At his first birthday party, he walked around the living room, holding onto furniture, trying to drink from everybody else's cup. Three months later, he was walking by himself. Although he acquired the habit of sucking his thumb, Kate felt he would outgrow the habit; she did not discourage or punish him when he did so in spite of advice to the contrary give by her relatives.

Kenny slept in a crib in Darla's room until he was five years old. Then he moved in the same room with his brothers. Darla liked to play with Kenny, cooing over him and pretending she was his mother. Her gentleness was a change from his brothers' roughhousing, although sometimes his brothers would sit Kenny in front of the television explaining morning cartoons. He preferred Big Bird on "Sesame Street," calling him "Dodo!"

By the age of three, he followed his brothers into the backyard where he would try to copy them throwing a football. They laughed at him; he laughed back. Now he was good at climbing into chairs, keeping his "big boy pants" dry, and saying "no" to his parents. He often busied himself playing with his brothers' old trucks, making "vroom" noises like he heard at his grandfather's service station. When his noises became too annoying to Kate, she would give him crayons and paper. He enjoyed covering the paper with large sweeps of different colors of crayon.

Kate hated knowing Michael spanked the children. She worried he might someday go too far. Michael felt that children should do as they are told without question.

In many ways, Kate was beginning to think that Kenny was her favorite—or as she explained to him later, "One of my very favorite children ever."

At the preschool he attended, Kenny found some of his attention-getting schemes, like screaming, were not as effective as at home. At first, when he wanted to ride the tricycle at the same time as another boy, the other boy pushed him away. Kenny screamed. The boy punched him. Kenny learned he was going to have to take turns, or stay away from that boy.

Kenny's favorite time of the year was Christmas. As on Thanksgiving and Easter, all his relatives got together at Grandma's house for good food. Everybody admired Kenny and helped him play with his toys.

The first day of kindergarten, Kenny wore the first new clothes bought only for him. He smiled shyly at the teacher, skipped over to a group of children playing with trucks. "Can I be the mechanic?" he asked. By this time, he had learned to cooperate and was friendly and assertive with his friends and teachers.

At home, Kenny knew he could get a laugh by calling Kate "Toots," like his father did. But he soon learned it did not work with his teacher. "My name," she said sternly, "is Missus Simmons!"

Kenny was generally obedient with elders, having had lots of experience being bossed by his siblings and told what to do by his father and relatives. But he had trouble counting to ten and did not know his letters.

He liked school because he had lots of kids to play with. When he brought home schoolwork, his big brothers sometimes teased him. When they did, he raised his eyebrows, shrugged, and replied, "That's 'cause I'm not as big as you, but you'll see!"

Kate and Michael expected all their children to obey the teacher and do well, but they never had the time to supervise homework or to explain and help with schoolwork.

Michael bought Kenny baseball cards but worried that he still liked to watch Mickey Mouse cartoons and carried around a security blanket. He also wore one of Kate's old shiny bracelets he called "Tink," because it sent sparkles around the room—like Tinkerbell. He still played house with his sister.

Michael was irritated when Kate told the boys not to fight. He did not want to see them hurt, but he felt the boys needed to show they could not be pushed around. Despite Kate's prohibition, Kenny still got into some scuffles. But usually when he did not get his way, he pushed out his lower lip and sobbed, waves of tears streaking his face.

Kenny's great appetite helped him grow stocky, unlike his lanky brothers, who played with him less. After school, he played games in the street with the neighborhood kids. He swam at the municipal pool with friends during the summer. When they got bored, he and his friends would ride their bikes to the fancier neighborhoods and throw dirt in the backyard pools.

Kenny liked all of his friends except Troy. A year older and a head taller, Troy fought often with all the boys. Frequently, Kenny came home bruised or bleeding but refrained from fighting back because he knew his mother would punish him.

One day, Kenny's teacher called to say Kenny had beat up Troy on the playground. Disturbed that Kenny had disobeyed her, Kate asked Michael to punish him. Michael told Kenny he would be grounded for a week. But as he spoke, Kenny could see his father grinning.

When Kenny was nine years old, his paternal grandfather died. Michael took over the service station and was gone from home most of the time. Kenny became accustomed to not seeing much of his father.

Now that Kenny and Darla were old enough to stay home alone, Kate enrolled in night school. She wanted to take business classes and become an office manager. She wanted to have her work measured by dollars like the women she read about in magazines. Also, she still wanted a new home.

As his older sister grew, Kenny watched her in awe and his friends teased him about it. His friends were talking deeper, growing taller, and sprouting hair on their faces and bodies. But Kenny stayed chunky and short.

Kenny had friends who were girls, but he did not have a girlfriend. He watched the girls at school talking with the older, taller boys, the ones who shaved. He liked Karen, a girl in his English class who laughed at his jokes. He asked her to the freshman dance at school, although he did not know how to dance. Kate drove them up to the dance. To fill the silence, Kate chatted with Karen about her family. Later, Kenny complained, "Mom, did you have to talk so much?" That night he vowed to start work at his father's station to earn enough money to buy his own car. Then he could date girls without having his mother intrude. Within a week, he was working at his father's station.

Kate worried about his future. "I don't want you to work at the gas station the rest of your life," she would say. "I want you to go to college so you can have a good life. You have to study and get good grades now." She told him repeatedly, "Do your best!" One night Kate asked him about his homework, and he threw his books at her. She threw one back.

"Leave me alone!" he cried.

"Fine!" she shot back.

Kenny did not continue to laugh and enjoy his family, and he started spending more time alone in his room.

By 15 years of age, Kenny looked like a young adult. He continued to earn money working after school at the station.

At the station he met Ellen. Ellen wore designer jeans, had long, blonde hair, was beautiful, and easy to talk to. After their first date, he said to himself, "I'm in love."

They dated for one year. Then, he could not believe his ears on the night of the junior prom when Ellen did not say, "Stop." The next day he ran into the station and yelled to the other mechanics, "I made it with Ellen!"

Two months later, Kate received a call from Ellen's mother. Ellen thought she was pregnant. Kate and Michael were furious. This would ruin everything. Kenny had only one year of high school remaining. If he had to support a family, he would never rise above the life he was living and probably his life would be a greater struggle than his parents'. If Ellen was pregnant, Michael told Ken he would be fired. He would have to get married and move out.

"Fine," Ken said. "I'll leave right now!"

Ken thought he would take a bus to his brother George's apartment. He was packing some clothes when he heard his mother crying to his father. He had heard it before: She wanted him to go to college to become something better than a mechanic, and his father wanted him to go to college to learn business skills so the family service station could be expanded to support them all.

He climbed out the window and walked to the bus stop. "What right do they have to plan my life for me? I hope Ellen is pregnant, and then I can do what I want with my life," he thought.

But he could not push away the doubts. "What would we do? I don't even know what I'm good at. The money I've been saving to buy a car will now have to be spent on a baby! Where will we live? Living with her parents would be worse than living with mine. Maybe George will take us in. No, George is working two jobs and his kid drives him crazy. What will I do?"

● ● ● ● ● ● ● ● ● ● ● ● ● ● ● ● ● ● ● ● ● ● ● ● ● ● ● ● ● ● ● ● ● ● ● ● ● ● ●

## Jennifer Mason
*(continued from page 2)*

Robin and Lloyd hired a nurse for two weeks to help care for Jennifer while Robin became adjusted to staying home. When the nurse left, Robin suddenly felt out of control. This tiny infant consumed all her time. The minute Robin began to cook or take a shower, Jennifer cried. In fact, it seemed Jennifer cried continually, and Robin, frustrated, nursed her on demand and held her nearly around the clock. Accustomed to meeting problems with solutions in her job as an advertising executive, Robin did not know how to cope. Having been independent for many years, she did not want to call her mother. Besides, she was embarrassed that she could not control the situation and her child.

After four months, Jennifer began to sleep through the night, and Robin told her friends she was beginning to feel human again. Robin and Lloyd's friends, though, had begun to drift. When friends visited, Jennifer took up Robin's time and fussed if anyone else held her.

While Jennifer smiled at eight weeks, the smile was reserved for those she knew. Robin continued to nurse until Jennifer's first teeth came in at five months of age.

After six months, Jennifer started to babble, and Robin was pleased that her first word at one year was "Mama." Jennifer also sat by herself at six months and began to crawl. By ten months, she was standing, holding on, and taking a few steps.

Jennifer's development was on schedule according to the child care books: She walked at 13 months; drank from a cup at one year. Robin tried to toilet-train her at 18 months, but Jennifer refused to cooperate. Robin tried again at two years and finally succeeded at 28 months.

Lloyd took up a new hobby, photography. The bookcases now included many photo albums of Jennifer.

Robin had always planned to return to work. She and Lloyd had hired Maria, who was kind and gentle with the infant. Robin was pleased with their choice. It was their job to see that infant care was done right—they felt they did not have to do it themselves.

Robin was surprised at how left out and guilty she felt when Jennifer walked for the first time while she was at work. She bought a sackful of toys and dolls as a surprise.

Jennifer liked to color, talk to her dolls, and swing on her back-yard swing. Aside from the Mommy and Me classes she attended with Robin and visits with a one-year-older neighbor child, Jennifer had not had many opportunities to interact with other children.

When Jennifer approached the age of three, her parents agreed she should attend Montessori preschool, where teachers would encourage independent learning, autonomy, and choice. Robin knew her daughter would not understand but she explained it to her anyway.

Jennifer was timid on the first day of school and clung to her mother. However, the teacher was successful in getting Jennifer to try the many things available at the school for children. Jennifer liked setting the table with the pretty play dishes.

At preschool Jennifer learned to ride a tricycle. Lloyd bought her a new red tricycle but it was usually too dark by the time he and Robin arrived home from work for Jennifer to ride it.

Jennifer was afraid of the dark. Sometimes she screamed in the middle of the night, and Robin would rush in and explain there was nothing to be afraid of.

Robin wanted to be a good role model for Jennifer, to show her a woman could be a mother and have a successful career. Her worst fear was that Robin would become a drug-addicted, pregnant teenager, running off to live with a cowboy in a trailer.

Robin was assuming more responsibility at work and was offered a promotion. The new job would enable her to earn more than $100,000 per year, but it would mean at least three days a week traveling out of town. She turned the job down.

Jennifer watched a lot of television and listened to her parents talking so knew many things about the world and the people in it. But some things she did not understand. For example, she did not understand why people, like her friend Helen's parents, get divorced and wondered where Santa Claus lived in the summer. Many different caretakers came and went, and Jennifer kept her questions and feelings to herself.

Unaware of Jennifer's need to understand her world from her perspective, Robin and Lloyd showered her with gifts. Lloyd preferred stuffed animals whereas Robin preferred educational toys. Robin drilled Jennifer in the alphabet, labeled items in the house, and made sure she could write her name by kindergarten.

When Jennifer became one of the slower readers in first grade, Robin was dismayed and made an appointment with the principal to see what she could do for her child. The principal assured Robin that Jennifer's progress was within the normal range and that Robin should relax and let Jennifer make it on her own.

What Jennifer liked to do was to play with Barbie dolls in her room. The Barbie dolls dressed in fur, married, cooked, had children, went to dinner, and drove to the White House for a ball.

By the end of first grade, Jennifer's favorite day was Saturday when her mother took her for ballet lessons. Some mornings she forgot everything she liked about school—art projects, swings, friends—and refused to go. Her parents explained that school was important and asked her why she didn't like it. "I don't know!" Jennifer yelled. Sometimes, they promised her a new Barbie doll or a trip to an amusement park with a friend in exchange for her promise to go to school all week.

Robin had stopped reading most of the child care books bought before Jennifer was born. Instead, she talked with the school principal, friends, or her mother, who usually advised, "She'll grow out of it."

Eventually, Jennifer stopped refusing to go to school. She began to have mixed feelings about her mother's worrying about her and discussing it with everyone else. Jennifer responded by becoming an excellent student and savoring the praise of her teachers. Robin and Lloyd were proud of Jennifer's achievements. They wanted her to go to a good university. Jennifer was glad her parents had stopped hovering over her when it came to school.

Throughout elementary school, Robin and Lloyd never doubted their child was getting the best education available. The school was private and had an excellent reputation. They took a serious interest in her homework and participated as much as possible in school activities. But they were both so busy, they could not do everything. Their schedules did not allow either of them time to take Jennifer for swimming lessons, a wish she had expressed since she was six years old. Sometimes when they both were out of town, Robin would make arrangements for Jennifer's care but would forget to explain it to her before leaving.

Both Robin and Lloyd were aghast when Jennifer would howl in frustration, or when the 9 year old yelled insults. They told her they would not tolerate such behavior and sent her to her room.

She appeared to settle down when she was 10 years old. In fact, Jennifer became quiet, even bookish, and her parents were relieved and filled with pride.

With her best friends, Phyllis and Barbara, Jennifer often rode her bike to the library. Sometimes, Phyllis and Barbara went places without her and later talked about their fun times. Jennifer did not think of telling anyone how she felt about these situations. But she usually would forget about it when they started again inviting her to go skating or to the movies.

At 11 years of age, Jennifer began to menstruate. Robin congratulated her on becoming a woman and bought her a new outfit. None of her friends had started menstruating. So Jennifer sometimes wished she could stop her body from changing because she did not want to be different. The next year her breasts began to develop. She did not want to wear a bra because it felt uncomfortable, and she did not want anyone to see the outline through her blouse. Uneasy about his daughter's changing body, Lloyd asked Jennifer not to walk around the house in her underwear or her bathing suit.

Sometimes Jennifer spent afternoons watching television alone; on weekends she and Robin usually went shopping. Occasionally, Lloyd took them to a ballet. Jennifer was embarrassed by Robin's graying hair and "old-fashioned" music.

When Jennifer was in high school she began to spend afternoons with girlfriends on the telephone, talking about clothes, hair, and boys. Robin had given Jennifer lectures about sex since she was six years old, but sex did not really interest her; she only wanted to be attractive to boys. Her girlfriends met boys at the shopping mall, but Jennifer spent hours at home in front of the mirror. She felt fat and ugly.

One Saturday when her parents were gone, she raided the refrigerator, eating ice cream until she was full, then continuing to eat, finishing bags of chips and cookies. She looked around at the empty containers, went into the bathroom, and vomited. That was the only time she could remember feeling good. When she had to lie to her parents about all the consumed food—she said some girlfriends had visited—she felt deceitful and guilty, but also felt in control.

When Jennifer was 16 years old, Robin awakened late at night and heard the sounds of retching in the bathroom.

"Are you sick, honey?" she called.

"Just a little, Mom."

A week later, she heard it again. Robin did not want to think about it then. But when Jennifer's grades began to drop, Robin could no longer deny there was a problem.

Robin made an appointment with a therapist. After the first session with Jennifer, he told her she was bulimic. Jennifer was not hungry for food but hungry for confidence, the therapist said.

Shocked, Robin listened to the diagnosis—a low self-esteem that could be improved if Jennifer were encouraged to make her own choices, assert herself, and become more independent.

"What did we do wrong?" Robin asked herself.

Jennifer was bewildered. She thought, "How can I assert myself if I don't even know who I am or what I want?"

## SUMMARY

Development refers to progressive quantitative and qualitative changes over time.

- Developmental changes are orderly, directional, and stable.
- The purpose of studying human development is to understand who we are, why we are the way we are, how we got this way, and what we can do to improve ourselves.
- Developmental psychologists use theories to relate facts or events to explain past events and to predict future outcomes.
- The different theoretical perspectives can be classified into those that examine development from the perspective of forces primarily within the child, such as maturation and ethology (biological influences), forces primarily outside the child, such as learning and culture (contextual influences), and interaction between forces within and outside the child, such as psychoanalytic, cognitive, and systems (interactional influences).
- Maturationists view development as an orderly sequence determined by evolution of the species and the individual's genetic makeup.
- Ethologists view development as inherited tendencies based on evolutionary adaptation to the environment in order to survive and reproduce.
- Learning theorists who subscribe to behaviorism view development as a result of the reinforcement of behaviors that are responses to stimuli.
- Learning theorists who emphasize social cognition view development as emerging from observing another person performing actions and experiencing consequences.
- Culture refers to the concepts, habits, skills, arts, instruments, institutions, and so on of a given people in a given period.
- The influence of cultural contexts on human development can be examined presently or historically.
- Psychoanalysts view development as the result of coping with the instincts and dealing with societal demands.
- Freud's psychosexual theory focused on stages characterized by specific erogenous zones.
- Erikson's psychosocial theory focused on stages characterized by social interactions.
- Cognitive-developmentalists view development as the acquisition of knowledge resulting from acting on the environment.
- According to Piaget, development occurs in an ordered sequence of distinct stages and is characterized by an increase in complexity of thought.
- Information-processing theorists view development as what occurs when information from the environment is received, processed, and used to behave or to solve problems.
- Systems theorists view development as a joint function of the person and the environment. The environment includes both immediate settings in which a person interacts and the contexts in which these immediate settings are embedded.
- Bronfenbrenner's ecological theory provides a model of interaction of microsystems, mesosystems, exosystems, and macrosystems.
- Developmental milestones consist of significant events in a person's life, and norms are the scientifically established averages at which most normal children achieve them.

## RELATED READINGS

Bandura, A. (1986). *Social foundations of thought and action: A social cognitive theory.* Englewood Cliffs, NJ: Prentice-Hall.

Bronfenbrenner, U. (1970). *Two worlds of childhood: U.S. and U.S.S.R.* New York: Russell Sage Foundation.

Crain, W. (1992). *Theories of development: Concepts and applications.* Englewood Cliffs, NJ: Prentice-Hall.

Damon, W. (Ed.). (1990). *Child development today and tomorrow.* San Francisco: Jossey-Bass.

Erikson, E.E. (1963). *Childhood and society* (2nd ed.) New York: Norton.

Hall, C.S. (1979). *A primer of Freudian psychology.* New York: New American Library.

Ilg, F.L., Ames, L.B., & Baker, S.M. (1981). *Child behavior.* New York: Harper & Row.

Kagan, J. (1984). The nature of the child. New York: Basic Books.

Kaluger, G., & Kaluger, M.F. (1976). *Profiles in human development.* St. Louis: C.V. Mosby.

Phillips, J.L. (1981). *Piaget's theory: A primer.* San Francisco: W.H. Freeman.

Skinner, B. F. (1962). *Walden Two.* New York: Macmillan.

## ACTIVITY

Write a developmental profile of yourself from birth to adolescence using the opening vignette as a model. This can be in narrative form or a time-line. Include:
- Important developmental milestones
- Significant events
- Influential family members
- Friends
- School experiences
- Description of home and neighborhood
- Values, attitudes, hopes, and dreams

# 2

# How Is Development Studied?

*Natural science does not describe and explain nature; it is part of the interplay between nature and ourselves; it describes nature as exposed to our method of questioning.*
**Werner Heisenberg**

# ABOUT
# STUDYING
# DEVELOPMENT

Robin, Lloyd, and Jennifer sat in the psychiatrist's office completing various forms. Robin and Lloyd were asked to provide a developmental history of Jennifer from the time of Robin's pregnancy to the present. Eating, sleeping, and waking behaviors in infancy were included. Questions were asked about Jennifer's developmental milestones—when did she sleep through the night, smile, talk, and so on? How did she react to separation? Information also had to be provided about Jennifer's health. What illnesses did she have? Did she have surgeries? Did she have headaches? How did she react to stress?

Jennifer was asked to provide information about school, friends, when she menstruated, and foods she liked.

Dr. Ross finally appeared and invited the Mason family into her office. "I'm sure you must be pretty tired of answering these questions; however, your responses will enable me to construct a case history that will provide both medical and psychological information from which we can derive a treatment plan.

"Today I would like to give Jennifer a complete physical exam including blood and urine analysis to determine whether any biological causes exist to explain the current eating behavior. Then I'd like to get together with all of you next week to discuss the results of Jennifer's physical and your answers to the questionnaires. I realize you are anxious to be helped. So if you are willing, perhaps we can begin next week spending the first part doing an observed interaction task and the second part discussing the results of the tests and questionnaires."

Robin and Lloyd said, "Yes, we want to get started as soon as possible."

"And how do you feel about this, Jennifer?" asked Dr. Ross.

"Yeah, let's get this over with," replied Jennifer in a sullen voice.

"OK, then we'll meet next week. When you arrive I will give you a topic to discuss among yourselves while I videotape the interaction. Then we'll observe the tape together and see what we come up with. Do you have any questions?"

"How long will this therapy take?" asked Lloyd.

"It's hard to say at this point in time. It depends a lot on what we find out from the tests, questionnaires, the observation of your family interactional patterns, and how each of you responds to therapy. Meanwhile, I'll give you some reading material on bulimia research."

Box 2.1 offers information about bulimia.

Box 2.1   BULIMIA

Bulimia is an eating disorder involving the syndrome of binging and purging. It is characterized by a compulsive and rapid consumption of large quantities of high calorie food. Many clients report they do not have the ability to perceive a sense of fullness. Because the person has a concern about body appearance and weight, after binging, he or she purges by inducing vomiting, taking laxatives, diuretics or amphetamines, or indulging in extreme exercising. Thus, the aim of the bulimic is to eat without gaining weight.

Bulimia is more common among females than males (Thornton & De Blassie, 1989) and shows up most often in college-age youth (Lachenmeyer & Muni-Brander, 1988), although it is becoming more and more prevalent in high school females (Van Thorne & Vogel, 1985).

Bulimics often express the wish to be perfect yet they have a poor self-image, negative self-worth, are shy and lack assertiveness (Holleran, Pascale,& Fraley, 1988). They want to be attractive to the opposite sex but are preoccupied with fear of rejection (Van Thorne & Vogel, 1985).

Because of unrealistic standards and the drive for perfection, pressure builds up which is relieved through binging on food and lapses of control through purging. However, the binge-purge episode is followed by feelings of shame and guilt which contribute to the sense of low self-esteem and depression (Pyle, Mitchell & Eckert, 1981).

## RESEARCH IN REVIEW

### HOW ARE RESEARCH METHODS APPLIED TO DEVELOPMENTAL DISORDERS?

Thornton, L. P., & De Blassie, R. R. (1989). Treating bulimia. *Adolescence* , 24 (95), 631–637.

Bulimia has been recognized as a distinct eating disorder affecting a growing number of adolescent women. It is characterized by the consumption of huge amounts of food followed by some form of purging, usually vomiting to lose the gained weight. Most bulimics keep their activities secret, which makes diagnosis difficult.

Most bulimics have misperceptions and misunderstandings of the relations between food,

eating, weight loss, and dieting. The purpose of this article is to identify and discuss treatment of some of these irrational ways of thinking through the use of various intervention strategies—nutrition education, behavior modification, and emotional support.

Bulimia is more commonly found in Caucasian adolescent girls from high socioeconomic statuses. Studies of patients with bulimia have concluded that the family environment is
*(continued on following page)*

*(continued from previous page)*

entangled with a low emphasis on self-expression. It is plausible that this environment could result in some of the difficulties bulimics experience, such as helplessness, low self-esteem, and nonassertiveness.

Bulimia is a complex disorder and, therefore, should be treated from a multidisciplinary approach. The team should include a physician for the medical complications that often accompany bulimia. The high rates of depression and low self-esteem call for a mental health professional. A nutritionist is needed for education and diet counseling.

An effective treatment for bulimics has been techniques to help clients identify unrealistic and self-defeating thoughts and assumptions combined with learning how to change behavior and express emotions adequately.

Bulimics often are not knowledgeable about the requirements for a well-balanced diet. They have unreasonable expectations about food and weight reduction. They are unrealistic in goal setting. They tend to think in all-or-none terms.

They need to learn moderation is acceptable. They believe that self-worth is tied to their weight and that losing weight will make others like them more. They tend to be out of touch with their feelings; they find it difficult to assert themselves.

Being provided with nutritional information and maintaining a healthy eating pattern, the bulimic can reduce cravings stimulated by nutritional deficiencies. The bulimic needs assistance in setting realistic weight-loss goals. Maladaptive behaviors, such as irregular eating patterns and extreme dieting and exercise, can be addressed through behavioral self-control training. Bulimics should be taught to identify and express feelings through interpersonal communication. Assertiveness training helps clients to express anger without fear of social rejection.

Support from a group was found to help reinforce the nutrition education and provide a safe outlet for expressing feelings. The group also acted as a means to reduce social isolation because it served as a safe context in which to practice forming relationships.

# DEVELOPMENTAL THEORIES, RESEARCH, AND APPLICATIONS

In this chapter we will look at how theories structure the research process by identifying important questions to ask and preferred methods to collect data. We will see how theories guide the interpretation of research findings and their application to real-life situations.

*Theories* help organize, explain, and predict developmental outcomes. Research usually begins with a prediction drawn from a theory, known as a *hypothesis*. A **hypothesis** is a specific prediction that can be tested. To illustrate, several hypotheses can be derived about Jennifer's bulimia depending on the theoretical orientation—*biological, contextual,* and *interactional*.

A hypothesis derived from a *biological orientation* would be that Jennifer's bulimic behavior is a result of her brain not producing enough of the chemical that provides a sensation of feeling full. To test this hypothesis, one would do specific analyses of Jennifer's blood, as Dr. Ross recommended.

A hypothesis derived from a *contextual orientation* would be that Jennifer's bulimic behavior is a result of her feeling good when she purges. Jennifer's method of controlling her weight is reinforced when others compliment her figure. To test this hypothesis, one would use questionnaires and interviews as Dr. Ross is doing.

A hypothesis derived from an *interactional orientation* is that Jennifer's bulimic behavior is a response to her inability to live up to her parents' unrealistic expectations. To test this hypothesis, one could observe several interactions between Jennifer and her parents as Dr. Ross plans to do.

Researchers conduct studies to determine if the hypothesis is correct. If it is, then more evidence is available to support the theory. If it is not, then the theory may have to be modified to accommodate new data. Sometimes, predictions cannot be made based on a theory because little or no theory exists for that particular aspect of development. In cases where no theory exists, the researcher may begin with a question such as, "When teenagers have sex, who makes the decision to use birth control, the boy or girl?" "Are unmarried teenage mothers more likely to abuse their children than married older mothers?"

Thus, research provides a way to test hypotheses and answer questions. Such information is important to resolve some problems involving children that persist in society today, such as the high rate of teenage pregnancy or the increasing incidence of child abuse. The continuing reciprocity between theory, research, and application, provides a challenging and evolving field of study.

**Surveys and interviews are two ways in which researchers evaluate the validity of hypotheses.**

# RESEARCH DESIGNS AND METHODS USED TO STUDY CHILDREN

Theories, hypotheses, and research questions are only the beginning of scientific methodology. After a scientist has formulated a question, she must choose a method by which to study it. There are various research designs and methods available. The design that studies behaviors as they occur naturally is called the *nonexperimental design*; the design that measures the relationship between behaviors is termed the *correlational design*; and the design that manipulates behaviors to determine their cause is known as *experimental design*. Each research design can be performed by different methods.

When a scientist chooses a research design or method, he must consider its *reliability* and *validity*. **Reliability** refers to the degree to which the research design is consistent or stable in producing repeatable results. A ruler has a high degree of reliability. When you use it to measure two different tables, an inch on one table is the same as an inch on the other table, so you can be confident that the ruler has given accurate information about the table sizes. When several people observe behavior and agree on what they see, their information is reliable. When questions on a test yield similar answers among similar subjects, the test is reliable.

**Validity** refers to the degree to which the research design measures or predicts what it was intended to measure or predict. A ruler was designed to measure size, such as height and width; it was not designed to measure intelligence. Therefore, relating the circumference of a person's head to his intellectual capacity would be invalid. The Scholastic Aptitude Test (SAT) is supposed to predict the ability to succeed in college. The validity of such a test is determined by whether it actually predicts such an ability. If scores can be raised by learning techniques, then the test is not really measuring aptitude but rather achievement and, therefore, is not a valid prediction.

What kind of observable behavior is displayed between these two children?

Children usually segregate themselves by gender in their play groups.

# NONEXPERIMENTAL DESIGN

The **nonexperimental design** is a research method used to study behaviors as they occur naturally. Such a design can generate much information toward the development of theories and can stimulate further research. Charles Darwin kept a *baby biography* of his infant son. He recorded detailed behaviors during the first three years of his son's life for the purpose of scientific understanding (Darwin, 1877). Darwin documented involuntary reflexes such as sucking and voluntary behaviors such as language.

While the intent of naturalistic observation is scientific, problems sometimes occur in the interpretation. How does the observer know whether a facial expression of an infant is happiness or a reflexive reaction? Also, when parents record their own children's behaviors in infant biographies, usually bias is on the side of advanced development.

E. Mavis Hetherington (1988, 1989) explored the phenomenon of divorce and its effects on children by interviewing them. In so doing, she found variables that are important such as custody arrangements, distribution of authority, and age and gender of the child, thereby providing information for future research and practical clues on coping with family transition.

The nonexperimental design can be implemented by directly observing behavior as did Charles Darwin (*naturalistic observation* method), by asking people to describe their behavior as did E. Mavis Hetherington (*survey* method), or by examining existing records of behavior such as hospital records (*archival research* method).

## The Naturalistic Observation Method

**Naturalistic observation** involves observing and recording behavior as it occurs in the subjects' natural environment. This technique provides a situation in which investigators' interference is minimized. In other words, no effort is made to motivate or change behavior; behavior is not recorded but observed as it occurs. The researcher uses various techniques to collect information over an extended time. These techniques include direct observation, interviews, and videotaping. Sometimes everything occurring in the setting is recorded; sometimes only certain events are recorded; and sometimes events that occur during a certain period are recorded. The goal of naturalistic observation is to obtain a complete picture of how those being observed behave and interact in their environment rather than to test a previously formed hypothesis. To achieve this goal, the researchers must keep detailed notes, which can be analyzed and interpreted at the end of the study.

Examples of naturalistic observations are ethological studies of children's play conducted by Blurton-Jones (1972) and studies performed by Smith and Connolly (1972). To study play, the various types of play first have to be defined in objective terms. This is done by noting observable behaviors during play such as facial expressions, vocalizations, movements, sharing, and aggressive acts. The behaviors that occur together most often such as making a smiling face, laughing, wrestling, and running can then be categorized as a type of play; for example, *rough-and-tumble* play. Rough-and-tumble play is different from aggressive behavior, which is characterized by making a frown, pushing, grabbing, and hitting.

The naturalistic observations of Blurton-Jones as well as Smith and Connolly provide a picture of rough-and-tumble play of four-year-old and five-year-old children in preschool settings. They found that this behavior is more likely to spontaneously occur outside after the children have been released from class. Compared with girls, boys engage in more vigorous activity with more noise and physical contact. Play groups of only boys are larger than those play groups of girls. While girls engage in rough-and-tumble play, it is likely to be centered on the slide or swings. Girls appear to prefer sedentary play with toys or art materials.

Naturalistic observation is most useful when investigating complex social settings such as a preschool or a camp. It is less useful for studying simple settings such as a single family (Cozby, Worden & Kee, 1989) because not enough data can be collected to generate a hypothesis.

## The Case Study Method

A **case study** is a thorough description of a person or a setting, such as a school or community. Case studies can involve observations, interviews, or library research. As was illustrated at the beginning of this chapter, Dr. Ross was preparing a case study of Jennifer. Included were her developmental history, characteristic behaviors, reactions to situations, and symptoms.

## The Survey Method

A **survey** is an instrument that uses questions and other techniques so subjects will report on specific aspects of themselves—past behaviors, attitudes, and abilities. The census is a demographic survey that questions people about things such as gender, marital status, and race. The census is a survey conducted via a questionnaire.

Another way a survey can be conducted is via an **interview.** Interviews can be one-on-one or with a group. The interview can be specific and close-ended whereby questions call for specific answers such as yes-no, agree-disagree, multiple choice or it can be flexible and open-ended to probe for the subject's point of view as in the **clinical interview**.

The clinical interview permits subjects to express thoughts freely. This gives the researcher insight and information about the way a subject views things. Questionnaires and close-ended interviews do not provide a wide scope of knowledge.

A major weakness of the clinical interview is the accuracy with which subjects report their own thoughts, feelings, and behaviors. Some interviewers do not probe enough so a complete understanding of a subject's point of view is not revealed, causing biased responses. Sensitivity to children's behavioral cues is a necessity in interviewing children because young children do not have the verbal ability to express thoughts and feelings accurately. Also, children usually want to please the adult interviewing them so they can give answers they think the adult wants to hear.

A series of specific questions requiring specific answers would enable an adult to quickly determine the cause of this disagreement. An open-ended interview, however, would undoubtably yield different perspectives from each boy regarding how the argument started.

## The Archival Research Method

**Archival research** is the use of existing information from sources such as public records (dates of births or marriages), anthropological reports, and written records (diaries or newspapers) to answer research questions.

Archival research saves time and money because the research does not start from scratch with sample groups. Also, archival research provides a way of examining historical trends and can be used to compare cultures. The analysis, however, can be subject to the researcher's interpretation because it cannot be verified by the original people who provided the data. To reduce this problem, other research methods are used with archival research.

## CORRELATIONAL DESIGN

When a scientist is curious about the relations between specific events or behaviors, he is likely to choose the correlational design as a research method. It can be used in the various nonexperimental methods. The **correlational design** examines the relations between certain *variables*.

A **variable** is a general class or category of objects, events, situations, responses, or characteristics of a person. Examples of objects are toys and clothing. Examples of events are war and earthquakes. Situations include watching television and experiencing different parenting styles. Examples of responses are aggression, learning, and sharing. Characteristics of a person include gender, socioeconomic status, and self-esteem.

The method in which variables are used in hypotheses can be illustrated by some examples of article titles taken from a recent issue of *Child Development Abstracts*: "Differences in Reading Strategies Among 7-to-8-Year-Old Children" (variables are reading strategies and age) and "Moral Judgments by Normal and Conduct-Disordered Preadolescent and Adolescent Boys" (variables are moral judgments and conduct).

In conducting research, the investigator must decide not only on a method to study the variables but also a way to clearly define them so they can be measured. Such a definition, termed an **operational definition**, defines the variable in terms of the concrete operational techniques the researcher uses in measuring or manipulating it. For example, a reading strategy could be defined as sounding the letters of an unknown word. Such an activity is observable and, therefore, can be used as a basis for comparison. A moral judgment is more difficult to define. Moral judgments refer to the "rightness" or "wrongness" of certain acts. However, whether an act is considered right or wrong by a subject depends on other variables such as intention or whether the person doing the act will be punished. Thus, the operational definition of moral judgment provides the researcher with a *qualitative* measure, whereas the definitions of reading strategy provide the researcher with *quantitative* measures.

Once an investigator has operationally defined the variables in the hypothesis, the next step is to find whether a relation between the variables exists. As age increases, do the number of reading strategies also increase? Is moral judgment less advanced with conduct-disordered boys than with normal boys?

The most common relations found in research are a:

a. linear positive relationship

b. linear negative relationship

c. curvilinear relationship

d. situation in which no relations exist between the variables (Cozby, Worden & Kee, 1989).

These relations are illustrated in figure 2.1.

In a *positive linear relation*, increases in the values of one variable are accompanied by *increases* in the values of a second variable. For example, those who study more tend to get higher grades.

As an explorable hypothesis, there is possibly a positive relation between the amount of assistance the younger sibling gets on homework from her older sister and the improvement in grades.

FIGURE 2.1
FOUR COMMON TYPES
OF RELATIONS FOUND
IN RESEARCH

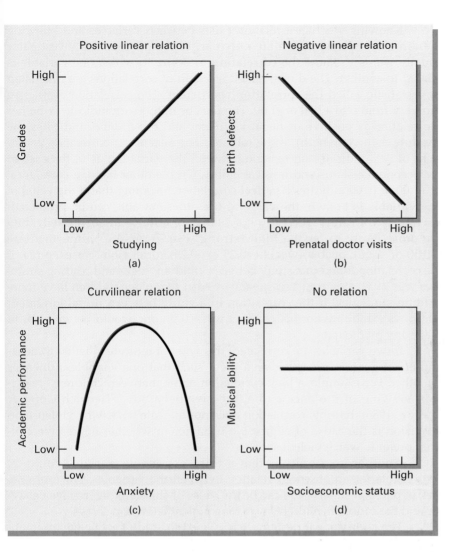

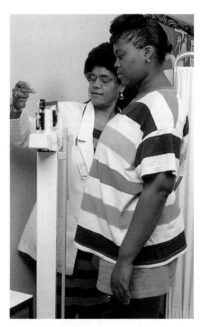

If the correlation between prenatal visits to the physician and birth defects was found to be -0.70, it would be advisable for the mother to routinely visit the physician.

In a *negative linear relation*, increases in the values of one variable are accompanied by *decreases* in the values of the other variable. For example, as the number of prenatal visits increase, the incidence of birth defects decreases.

In a *curvilinear relation*, increases in the values of one variable are accompanied by both *increases* and *decreases* in the values of the other variable. For example, increases in anxiety are accompanied by increases in academic performance but only to a point; then the relation becomes negative with further increases in anxiety being accompanied by decreases in academic performance. Thus, some anxiety helps performance, but too much hinders it.

When there is *no relation* between two variables, the graph is a straight line. For example, musical ability is not associated with an increase or decrease in socioeconomic status.

**Identical twins**

**Fraternal twins**

Knowing whether a relation exists between variables and knowing the direction of the relation are only part of the picture. The investigator usually wants to know the **correlation** or *degree* to which one variable is related to another. The direction and strength of correlations are calculated by a statistic called the **correlation coefficient**. The correlation coefficient can vary from 0 to +1.00 or -1.00. The plus or minus sign indicates whether the relation is positive or negative linear, and the number indicates the absolute value (strength) of the relation. For instance, a correlation coefficient of 0.00 indicates no relation between the variables, as in the case of socioeconomic status and musical ability. On the other hand, a correlation of +1.00 or -1.00 indicates a perfect correlation, meaning that if the value of one variable is known, the value of the other variable can be predicted. Variables are rarely perfectly correlated or totally uncorrelated; they are more likely to have a high (strong) (+0.75 or -0.75), intermediate (+0.50 or -0.50), or low (weak) (+0.25 or -0.25) correlation. For example, if the correlation found in a study between childrens' ages and reading strategies was +0.70, one could reasonably predict that older children have more reading strategies. If the correlation in a study between moral judgment and boys exhibiting normal conduct was +0.30, one would be wise not to make any prediction.

If two variables are correlated, this will not indicate whether a cause-and-effect relation exists between them such that one variable influences the other. For example, a high correlation occurs between childrens' television viewing of violence and aggressive behavior (Friedrich-Cofer & Huston, 1986), but this correlation does not indicate if viewing violence on television is the cause of aggressive behavior or whether aggressive children prefer to watch violent shows.

Another possibility is that a third extraneous variable could be responsible for an observed relation between the variables. For example, lack of parental supervision can be the cause of childrens' aggressive behavior and the cause of children's watching violent television shows.

The correlational design often is used to study genetic-environmental influences on behavior. Identical twins are genetically similar, whereas fraternal twins are not genetically similar. If the behavior of the identical twins being studied is more highly correlated than that of the fraternal twins, a genetic influence is concluded to be more influential than an environmental one.

## EXPERIMENTAL DESIGN

While the correlational design measures variables of interest in terms of direction and strength, the experimental method manipulates the variables. The **experimental design** is a research method that examines the effect of manipulating one variable on another. The variable controlled or manipulated is called the **independent variable**. The variable to be observed is called the **dependent variable** because it is affected by, or depends on, the independent variable.

The correlational design provided us with the information that children's watching television violence and aggressive behavior were related. An experiment can be designed to test the hypothesis that children's viewing violence on television causes aggressive behavior. Two groups of children are selected that are matched on the variables of gender, age, socioeconomic status, and whether or not the mother is employed outside the home. One group is exposed to a violent television show on several occasions, and the other group is exposed to a nonviolent television show. The situation (violence or nonviolence) is the independent variable. The group being exposed to the violence on television is called the **experimental group** because it is receiving the treatment. The group being exposed to the nonviolence on television is called the **control group** because it is comparable with the experimental group with the exception of receiving the treatment.

The dependent variable being observed in both groups is aggressive behavior. It can be measured by devising a situation in which only one toy is shared by two children. After the children watch the violent or nonviolent television show, each group of two children is given a toy to play with. Incidents of grabbing, not sharing, and hitting are recorded. If aggressive behavior is more prevalent in the group of children who viewed the violent television shows, we can conclude that the hypothesis was correct.

Most experiments are conducted in a *laboratory*. The laboratory provides a carefully controlled environment where the independent variable can be manipulated. Such a procedure reduces the possibility that extraneous variables will influence the results.

The problem with laboratory experiments is that they create an artificial atmosphere that can limit the generality of results. While the hypothesis that viewing television violence increases the amount of aggressive behavior in children may have been correct in the laboratory, it doesn't necessarily indicate that viewing violent television shows at home would have the same result. At home children may watch television with an adult who interprets the violence as bad, thereby reducing the likelihood that the child will copy the aggressive act. Or the child may be provoked more at home than in the laboratory to be aggressive by siblings, thereby increasing the likelihood that the child will behave aggressively.

To counter the problem of artificiality, some researchers conduct experiments in natural, or field, settings. In a *field experiment*, the independent variable is manipulated in a natural setting such as the home or school while attempting to control all extraneous variables. If a field experiment is used to test the hypothesis that viewing television violence increases aggressive behavior, the experimental and control group of children would view certain designated television shows at home alone. Like in the laboratory, the experimental group would be exposed to violent television shows and the control group to nonviolent shows. The parent would be asked to record hitting, shouting, or noncompliant incidents for a certain amount of time immediately after the designated show.

The experimental design, whether performed in the laboratory or in the field, is limited in the questions that can be addressed. For example, the experimental design cannot be used to find what kinds of child behavior elicit abusive parenting styles. First, it would be too difficult to manipulate children's behavior. Second, it would be unethical to expose children to abuse for purposes of scientific research. When the experimental design cannot be used because it would be unethical, impractical, or impossible to manipulate the variables, the correlational design is preferred.

**If the aggressive child was repeatedly represented in the experimental group, then one might conclude that violent television shows have an impact on child behavior. However, if the aggressive child was repeatedly represented in the control group then a rethinking of the hypothesis may be necessary.**

# OTHER TECHNIQUES USED TO STUDY CHILDREN

Information about the abilities of children is often learned through *standardized tests*. Information about their biological functioning and health is obtained through *physiological tests*. The research results about children in the United States can be generalized to human nature and can be examined via *cross-cultural research*. Additionally, investigators can use a combination of methods in a *multifaceted research design* to check the validity and reliability of results.

## STANDARDIZED TESTS

A **standardized test** is one in which an individual's results are compared with those of a large group of similar individuals. The scores, which are standards based on measurement, of this large sample of similar people used for comparison purposes are called **norms** (figure 2.2). The conditions under which everyone takes a standardized test must be similar. Standardization helps ensure that regardless of who gives or scores the test the results are comparable. Standardized tests can examine intellectual abilities or achievement, personality traits, and physical competence. An individual's score reflects how well she performed compared with others who took the test. For example, the Minnesota Multiphasic Personality Inventory (MMPI) includes items on a scale to assess a person's degree of rebelliousness and impulsiveness in relation to authority figures. This test can be used with adolescents to predict antisocial or delinquent tendencies compared with the norms for their age group.

**FIGURE 2.2**

The range of scores on the Scholastic Aptitude Test (SAT) is 200–800 with 450 being average. Few test takers (high school juniors and seniors) score higher than 700; those who do generally are admitted to the college of their choice.

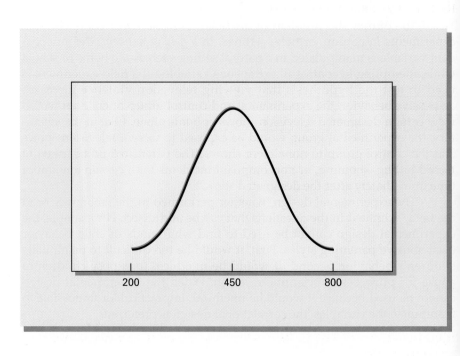

# PHYSIOLOGICAL TESTS

*Physiological tests* record various physiological responses of the body. One common physiological test is the galvanic skin response (GSR), used as a measure of general emotional arousal and anxiety. This test records changes in the electrical conductance of the skin when a person sweats. Another common test is the electromyograph (EMG), which measures muscle tension. The EMG frequently is used as a measure of tension and stress. Still another common physiological measure is the electroencephalogram (EEG), which is a measure of the electrical activity of brain cells. The EEG can be used to investigate activity in different parts of the brain when subjects are performing different tasks.

Physiological tests help us understand biological influences on development. For example, physiological tests done during pregnancy can determine certain abnormalities in the fetus.

# CROSS-CULTURAL RESEARCH

**Cross-cultural research** consists of studies that compare development in different cultures around the world. Only by examining developmental processes in a variety of contexts can generalizations and predictions about human development be made. Development studied in only modern industrialized Western societies cannot necessarily be generalized to traditional or primitive societies. Cross-cultural research is one way our understanding of contextual influences on development has been enhanced. Cross-cultural research also has been used to test the universality of certain theories. For example, Piaget's theory of cognitive development is not as universal as originally thought. Children vary greatly in the rates at which they reach Piaget's cognitive stages; and children in cultures where formal schooling is not required, rarely demonstrate formal operations as defined by Piaget (Gelman & Baillargeon, 1983). Last, cross-cultural research enlarges our perspective of human development thereby enhancing our understanding of ourselves.

# MULTIFACETED RESEARCH DESIGNS

In a multifaceted research design, the researcher first decides what he wants to discover. Then, he chooses the methods while evaluating the advantages and disadvantages of each. Because every method has problems, many investigators use more than one method to study aspects of childrens' development.

# ANALYZING DEVELOPMENTAL CHANGE

Developmental psychologists study change over time. How does a variable or aspect of development such as height or intelligence change as a function of age?

To analyze developmental change, the methods just discussed can be used in various ways—in *longitudinal studies*, *cross-sectional studies*, and *sequential studies*.

This English as a second language (ESL) class is an excellent laboratory for studying how various cultures relate to achieve a single goal: learning English.

Both preschoolers have facial expressions which may be characterized as guilt. To determine the cause of these emotional expressions, the researcher would use several methods, such as observations and interviews.

Children in grades 3, 6, 9, and 12 are tested in California for their achievement in reading, communication, and math skills. The data are used to compare same-grade children in different schools and to follow the progress of these students, thereby exemplifying a sequential study.

## THE LONGITUDINAL STUDY

In performing a **longitudinal study**, a group of people are studied over an extended period to determine developmental change in one or several aspects of development. They are examined at specified intervals.

A primary advantage is that the researcher can observe actual changes on various aspects of development occurring in the subject. Another advantage is that the research can compare early behaviors with later behaviors and analyze their relations to events occurring at the time. The main disadvantages of longitudinal studies are they are time consuming and it is difficult to maintain contact with subjects over the long term. Subjects commonly drop out, which can result in a biased sample in that the subjects who remain are the ones committed to scientific research. Also, the repetition of testing or questioning can enable the subject to perform better because of practice. A significant problem impacting the validity of longitudinal studies is the effect of sociocultural or historical change on subjects born at the same time or era. This is termed the **cohort effect**. For example, subjects born after 1950 experienced growing up with television, whereas those born in 1930 did not. The cohort effect is important to consider when evaluating research because findings based on one cohort cannot be generalizable to other children growing up at a different time. Despite the disadvantages, some ambitious longitudinal studies have followed the development of children and adults for more than a half a century and have provided valuable information.

The *Fels Longitudinal Study* began in 1929. Children were observed twice a year in their homes and twice a year in the Fels Institute preschool. In this way, records could be amassed that followed their interactions with family and peers. Occasionally, various investigators have dipped into the Fels pool of subjects to further test, interview, and observe these individuals as they have grown into adults. In this way they have, for example, observed the development of patterns of independence and dependence. The behavior patterns shown by the children ages 6 to 10, are predictive of their behavior as adults (Kagan & Moss, 1962).

## THE CROSS-SECTIONAL STUDY

In a **cross-sectional study**, a group of subjects of different ages is studied to obtain information about changes in one or several aspects of development at one point in time. For example, the cognitive development of a group of three-year-old, six-year-old, nine-year-old, and 15-year-old individuals can be compared. One advantage of comparing groups of same-aged subjects with groups of different ages is that results can be obtained quickly; one does not have to wait for the three year olds to become 15 years of age. Also, testing usually is done once or twice so the drop-out rate is minimized as are the effects of practice. A disadvantage, however, is information cannot be obtained about individual developmental change, rather, the researcher has to rely on comparisons of average performances of different-aged subjects.

Like longitudinal studies, cross-sectional studies are subject to the cohort effect, possibly influencing the validity of the study. In other words, when comparing members of different generations, such as 10 year olds, 30 year olds, and 50 year olds, it is difficult to know whether the age of the person or the era in which that person grew is responsible for the change in a particular aspect of development (Nesselroade & Baltes, 1974). For example, five-year-old children are intellectually different from children who were five years old in the 1940s. A cohort effect would be that today's five year olds have access to television, videos, and computers.

Figure 2.3 displays the cross-sectional and longitudinal studies discussed.

## THE SEQUENTIAL STUDY

To overcome some limitations of longitudinal and cross-sectional studies, aspects of developmental change can be studied by the **sequential study,** consisting of several samples of different-aged children studied in sequence over a certain period. Sequential studies combine aspects of the cross-sectional and longitudinal designs in that they compare groups of different-aged children while studying individual children over a period.

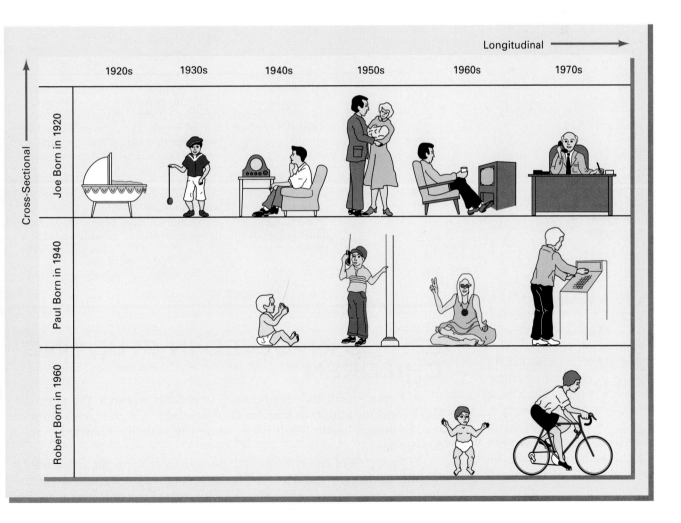

## FIGURE 2.3
## LONGITUDINAL AND CROSS-SECTIONAL STUDIES
(Fischer & Lazerson, 1984)

Children in a sequential sample are tested several times over several years. The results are analyzed to determine the differences that result over time for the different groups of children.

Table 2.1 summarizes the longitudinal study, cross-sectional study, and the sequential study.

## SUMMARY OF WAYS TO ANALYZE DEVELOPMENTAL CHANGE

### TABLE 2.1

| Study Method | Procedure | Advantages | Disadvantages |
|---|---|---|---|
| Longitudinal Study | Same individuals are observed repeatedly over time | Provides data on changes in aspects of development of individuals over a long period; can analyze relations between early and later behaviors | Time consuming, expensive, drop-out rate can lead to biased sample; repeated testing can lead to inaccurate results because of effects of practice; subject to cohort effect |
| Cross-Sectional Study | Individuals of different ages are observed and compared at one point in time | Provides quick result; inexpensive; provides information on comparing aspects of development of different ages or cultures | Subject to cohort effect, does not provide information on individual developmental change over time |
| Sequential Study | Individuals of different ages are observed sequentially and repeatedly over time | Provides means by which to study both cohort and developmental effects | More costly and time consuming than cross-sectional study; results cannot be generalized beyond groups studied |

# ETHICS INVOLVED IN STUDYING CHILDREN

Regardless of the method used to conduct research, the researcher must consider ethics, or standards of conduct: Are children's physical and/or mental health being risked to add to scientific knowledge about development?

The issue of ethics in research became more apparent as knowledge of child development increased. The more knowledge learned about children, the greater became the concern about their welfare. It was realized that children were immature and vulnerable to manipulation and, therefore, had to be protected from harmful treatment and deceitful adults.

When child psychology was in its infancy, two researchers (Watson & Rayner, 1920) set out to study how fear is learned. They conditioned, or trained, a nine-month-old infant, Albert, to fear a rat with which he previously enjoyed playing. They did this by presenting a sudden loud noise every time Albert played with the rat. Not only did Albert learn to fear the rat, he generalized his fearful response to other furry objects—rabbits, cats, fur coats. When the experiment was completed, the researchers' knowledge about how fear is learned increased, but Albert was left to cope with his fears. At that time, little knowledge was known about the long-term effects of certain experiences on development; thus, the question of ethics in conducting such experiments did not arise. However, today knowledge in developmental psychology has expanded, so much concern exists about ethics in research. Today, such an experiment would be considered unethical.

To foster knowledge about development and behavior, many types of research considered unethical with children are conducted with animals. Because of the importance of the findings to understand human development, many researchers consider it acceptable, for example, to give alcohol to pregnant rats or to deprive Rhesus monkeys of early social experience. Of course some people believe in animal and human rights and would object to any research that endangers living beings. Whenever a research project is planned, the investigators must weigh the scientific and human value of the project with the possible risks to which participants can be exposed (Rogoff, 1990).

Various professional groups such as the American Psychological Association, the Society for Research in Child Development, and government review boards such as the National Commission for the Protection of Human Subjects of Biomedical and Behavioral Research have proposed guidelines for research with children. The main purpose of these guidelines is to protect children from physical or psychological harm. These guidelines include but are not limited to those given in box 2.2.

**The younger child is seeking comfort and security from the older child. By providing comfort and security at no benefit to himself, the older boy is exhibiting altruistic behavior.**

## BOX 2.2  GUIDELINES FOR USING CHILDREN IN TESTING

- The purposes of the research and its research methods must be fully disclosed to the participating children and their parents.
- To participate in the study, voluntary consent must be given by the participating children and their parents. Parents can give consent for children too young to do so.
- Researchers cannot subject children to any harmful treatments or methods of measurement.
- Children and their parents can withdraw from the study at any time and for any reason.

Most universities, hospitals, and other institutions conducting research have review boards or peer juries to determine whether the proposed research could be harmful to children. The approval of these groups is required to obtain government funds to finance the project. Peer approval also is necessary when the researcher has to deviate from any guidelines, for example, disclosure. There are cases in which telling the subject the purposes of the experiment would ruin the results. For instance, you want to know if after watching some actors exhibit altruistic (helpful) behavior, children would help another child. You would choose two groups of similar children and observe and record their altruistic acts such as sharing toys, giving comfort when someone cries, and helping someone in a natural setting (e.g., preschool). Then you would expose the experimental group to viewing the actors help each another. The control group would not see anything. You then would observe the two groups again in the same setting to see if the experimental group's altruistic acts increased. Obviously, if subjects had been told what you were studying, the results would not be accurate. Most review groups would probably approve such an experiment even though it does not follow the disclosure guideline because increasing a child's altruistic behavior is not harmful.

# CRITICAL THINKING & YOU

In observing school-age children, you notice that some fail more often or perform more poorly on academic tasks than others. Your first thought is that these children have lower intelligence so you ask the teacher and find out this is not true.

**ANALYSIS:** List at least five possible hypotheses of why children would fail at school-related tasks (such as too much pressure from parents).

**SYNTHESIS:** Review the chapter and select various research strategies to investigate each hypothesis. State specifically how each strategy would be performed.

**EVALUATION:** Which research method(s) would be the most valid, reliable, and yield the most information about your hypotheses and why?

## SUMMARY

- Theories help organize, explain, and predict developmental outcomes. Research usually begins with a prediction, or hypothesis, drawn from a theory.
- A hypothesis can be tested via various research designs and methods.
- Some designs and methods are nonexperimental, others are correlational, and some are experimental. Researchers must consider reliability and validity when choosing a method.
- The nonexperimental method is used to study behaviors as they occur naturally.
- Naturalistic observation involves observing and recording behavior as it occurs.
- A case study describes a person or a setting and provides information about development.
- A survey uses questions to get subjects to report about themselves, their behavior and attitudes. Surveys can use close-ended questions in a written or interview format. Interviews can also be open-ended as in the clinical interview.
- Archival research is the use of existing information such as from public records, anthropological reports, written records, or computer data bases.
- When scientists are interested in the relations between specific events or behaviors, they probably will use the correlational method that examines the direction and degree of the relation between variables.
- The direction of relationships can be positive linear, negative linear, or curvilinear. The degree of relationship can vary from 0 to +1.00 or −1.00 and is called the correlation coefficient. Zero indicates no relationship, +1.00 indicates a perfect positive relationship (as one variable increases, so does the other), and a −1.00 indicates a perfect negative relationship (as one variable increases, the other decreases).
- When scientists want to manipulate the variables to determine cause and effect rather than relationship, they probably will use the experimental method.
- The manipulated variable is the independent variable, and the affected variable is the dependent variable.
- The experimental method sometimes occurs in a laboratory and sometimes in the field.
- Since developmentalists study change over time, they need to examine specific variables over a long period (longitudinal study), or compare the variables among different-aged subjects (cross-sectional study), or compare different-aged subjects in sequence over a specified period of time (sequential study).
- Regardless of design or method chosen to conduct research, ethics must be considered. Ethical standards for research have been adopted by professional groups and serve to protect children from harm.

## RELATED READINGS

Benedict, R. (1934). *Patterns of culture.* New York: New American Library.

Cozby, P.C., Worden, P.E., & Kee D.W. (1989). *Research methods in human development.* Mountain View, CA: Mayfield.

Elder, G.H. (1974). *Children of the Great Depression.* Chicago: University of Chicago Press.

Milgram, J.I., & Sciarra, D.J. (1974). *Childhood revisited.* New York: Macmillan.

Miller, S.A. (1987). *Developmental research methods.* Englewood Cliffs, NJ: Prentice-Hall.

Polakow, V. (1992). *The erosion of childhood.* Chicago: University of Chicago Press.

Wickes, F.G. (1966). *The inner world of childhood.* Englewood Cliffs, NJ: Prentice-Hall.

Observe two groups of children (at least three in each group) for at least 30 minutes each in free-play situations. Free-play is an activity chosen *by the child* and evolves through child interaction. One group should be 4–5 years old and the other 7–8 years old. If the composition of the group changes during the 30 minutes, make note of it. Although you will be observing the group as a whole, you can note individual behaviors if they are interesting. Be specific and objective in recording the following aspects of development for each group:

1. Motor coordination (poor, average, excellent)
2. Play activities (kind and duration)
3. Language (topic—give samples)
4. Social interaction (cooperation/conflict)
5. Emotional reactions (happy, angry, sad)
6. Gender differences (describe)
7. Leader–follower interactions (describe)

1. In what areas of development (motor and cognitive as exhibited by play, language, social, emotional, gender-role) did you observe the greatest difference between the age groups?
2. How were the differences exhibited? Give specific examples.
3. Based on this observation what question(s) would you investigate further?

# 3

# Heredity and Prenatal Development

*Yes—the history of a man for the nine months preceding his birth would probably be far more interesting and contain events of greater moment than all three score years that follow it.*
**Samuel Taylor Coleridge**

# ABOUT HEREDITY AND PRENATAL DEVELOPMENT

Lloyd and Robin both have brown hair; yet Jennifer has blonde hair. How can this be?

Intelligent neighbors of Michael and Kate have five sons, one of whom has a severe learning disability. Why is this so?

Lloyd's sister has twins; one is tall and thin, and the other is average in height and overweight. What is the explanation?

The answers to these situations lie in what we know about heredity and prenatal development. **Heredity** refers to all the genetic characteristics that are transmitted from parents to child at conception. **Prenatal** development refers to the period of development from conception to birth.

As you will see, the reason Jennifer has blonde hair is that both Lloyd and Robin each have a *gene* for blonde hair that was transmitted to Jennifer at conception. A **gene** is a region on a *chromosome* that carries the hereditary instructions for development from one generation to the next. A **chromosome** is a rodlike structure in the nucleus of a cell that stores and transmits genetic information.

The reason the neighbors have a retarded son is that his mother contracted rubella, commonly called German measles, when he was in the prenatal embryonic stage. Various prenatal factors can influence the development of the child.

Finally, one reason why Lloyd's twin nieces have different heights and physiques is that they are genetically different. Another reason is that one twin was in a better position to receive nourishment in the uterus. That twin was born slightly larger and more developed and had a bigger appetite.

## BIOLOGICAL INFLUENCES ON HEREDITY AND PRENATAL DEVELOPMENT

This chapter will explore biological and contextual influences on heredity and prenatal development and explain how biological and contextual influences interact to influence development.

The biological influences on heredity and prenatal development include conception, chromosomes, genes, and the different stages of prenatal development—*germinal, embryonic, fetal.*

# CONCEPTION

The development of each person begins at the moment of conception when the sperm from the father unites with the ovum, or egg cell, from the mother.

A woman is born with a lifetime supply of eggs in her ovaries. After puberty, an ovum matures about every 28 days in one of the ovaries. It then enters one of the fallopian tubes (figure 3.1).

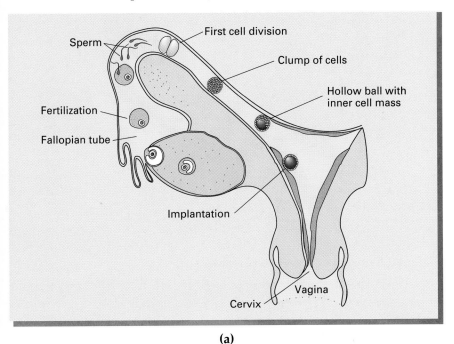

**(a)**

### FIGURE 3.1

(a) Fertilization occurs in the upper third part of the fallopian tube. By the time the fertilized ovum reaches the uterus, it has divided many times and now each layer of the cell mass will become a specialized part of the embryo. (b) Development of fetal membranes

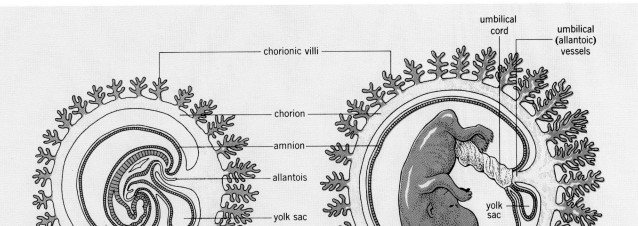

**(b)**

**Fraternal twins**

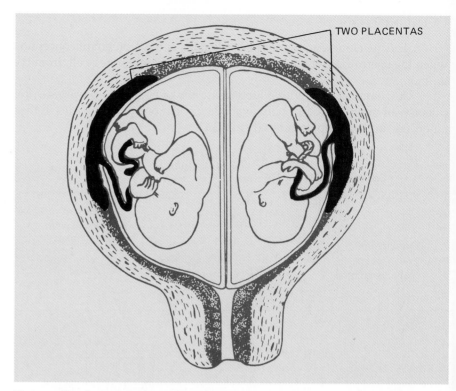

TWO PLACENTAS

**Fraternal twins: two sacs—two placentas**

**Identical twins**

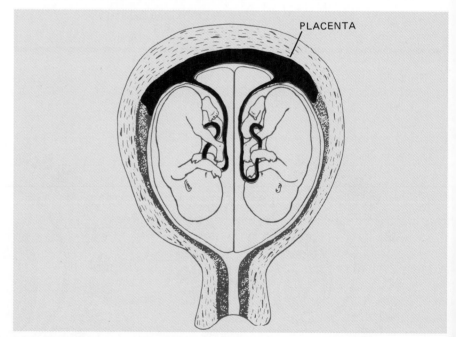

PLACENTA

**Identical twins: two sacs—one placenta**

This process is known as *ovulation*. The journey down the fallopian tube takes several days. If the ovum is not fertilized by a sperm within 24-48 hours after ovulation, it disintegrates on reaching the uterus and the female has a menses. However, if a woman has had intercourse one or two days before or after ovulation, the ovum can be fertilized by one of the 300–450 million sperm released during intercourse.

Sperm are continually produced by the male after puberty. When a male ejaculates during intercourse, the tadpole-like sperm, about 0.06 mm long contained in the seminal fluid, swim in all directions. Only a small percentage survive the long journey from the vagina through the cervix and the uterus to the upper third of the fallopian tube where fertilization occurs. Once an ovum has been penetrated by a sperm, a biochemical change (caused by the enzyme hyaluronidase) takes place and no more sperm can enter. The fertilized ovum is termed a **zygote**.

Occasionally, a woman will release more than one egg. This can occur naturally, for example, an ovum can mature simultaneously in each ovary and enter each fallopian tube or multiple ovulation can be induced by drugs to enhance fertility (box 3.1). Regardless, if more than one ovum is present when sperm are released, more than one zygote can result. If two ova are fertilized by two different sperm, **dizygotic twins**, more commonly called fraternal twins, result. These twins are no more similar to one another than are other siblings because, like brothers and sisters, they each come from different ova and sperm, hence two zygotes. They do, however, share the same prenatal environment. Lloyd's twin nieces were not genetically similar because they were fraternal twins.

## Box 3.1 ASSISTED REPRODUCTIVE TECHNOLOGY FOR INFERTILITY

*Infertility* is defined as one year of unprotected intercourse without conception (American Fertility Society, 1991). It affects approximately 7.9 percent of couples. Infertile couples are usually older with no previous children. The incidence is doubled for women age 35–44 compared with women age 30–34 (American Fertility Society, 1991).

Many infertile couples can be assisted to reproduce via surgery (for example, removing scar tissue from the seminal vesicles or fallopian tubes), hormone treatments, and/or drugs to treat infectious disease or induce ovulation. When these techniques fail or are insufficient, various technologies are employed, such as *artificial insemination*. Artificial insemination involves placing sperm in a woman's cervix at ovulation. The sperm can come from the husband or a donor. If the husband has a low sperm count, several samples of his semen are collected and frozen and then are used for insemination. If the husband is sterile or carries a genetic disease, a carefully screened (for disease) and matched (for genetics) donor can provide the sperm. If the wife is sterile, the husband's sperm can be used to artificially inseminate another woman who agrees to become a *surrogate mother* for the pregnancy and to give the infant to the natural father and his spouse after birth. In surrogacy an infant receives half of her genes from the birth mother and half from the husband of the infertile wife.

Another technology available for women who can ovulate but have blocked or missing fallopian tubes, which normally convey the

*(continued on following page)*

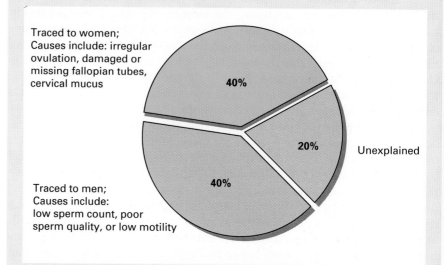

Traced to women;
Causes include: irregular ovulation, damaged or missing fallopian tubes, cervical mucus

40%

20%

Unexplained

Traced to men;
Causes include: low sperm count, poor sperm quality, or low motility

40%

FIGURE 3.2
ROOTS OF INFERTILITY PROBLEMS

*(continued from previous page)*
eggs to the uterus, is *in vitro fertilization*, or *IVF*. In IVF, one or more mature egg cells are extracted (sometimes the woman is given a drug to stimulate production of more than one mature egg) from the woman's ovaries and placed in a specially prepared laboratory dish. Sperm are added to the eggs in the dish and if fertilization occurs, the zygote or zygotes are allowed to divide until the embryo reaches a four- to eight-cell stage before being placed in the woman's uterus, which has been readied by hormone treatments. Sometimes extra fertilized egg cells are frozen and can be implanted at another time if the pregnancy fails.

IVF also can be used to assist a woman who fails to ovulate or who is at risk for passing on a genetic disease to give birth via *egg donation*. Another woman's eggs that have been extracted, screened, and frozen are fertilized in vitro by the husband's sperm. The resulting embryos then are transferred to the uterus, which has been prepared by hormone treatments. Several embryos are transferred to help ensure at least one successful pregnancy. If too many embryos continue to develop, the physician can perform *selective reduction pregnancy* by injecting a lethal chemical substance into selected embryos to improve the survival chances of the remaining embryos. The embryos that succumb are absorbed by the body. Selective reduction pregnancy is a medically and ethically controversial procedure (Roan, 1990).

Such high-tech procedures are costly and emotionally traumatic (American Fertility Society, 1991). Both partners must be able to cope with feelings about failure and infertility. Also, there is the issue of the possible biological effects of such procedures on the children involved; for example, are freezing and defrosting harmful to cell development? While the procedures appear medically safe, more research needs to be conducted to assess possible psychological consequences to parents, donors, and children.

Identical twins come from one ovum fertilized by one sperm that has undergone separation during early cell division. Because they develop from the same zygote they are called **monozygotic twins**. These twins are identical because they have inherited the same genes from their mother and father. For this to happen, the zygote divides in two and each subsequent cell undergoes cell division ultimately resulting in the development of two identical individuals.

At fertilization, the zygote is continuing its 2 to 3 day journey down the fallopian tube to the uterus.

## CHROMOSOMES

The growth and development of every living organism depend on the growth and multiplication of its cells. Every body cell in an individual has the same number of chromosomes (except the ova and sperm, or sex cells, which have half the number).

In the body cells, as distinguished from the sex cells, the chromosomes are paired, one member of each derived from one parent, the other member from the other parent. The members of each pair are alike (with the exception of the sex chromosomes), but the pairs are different. The first 22 pairs of chromosomes are called **autosomes**; the 23rd pair is called the sex chromosomes.

## Mitosis

Cells grow and multiply by division. For the body cells to do this, the chromosomes first must duplicate themselves. That way, each new cell is identical to the original cell. In other words, every time the cell divides, the hereditary blueprint is carried from the original cell to all subsequent cells. This process of **mitosis** enables a multicellular human being to develop from a single-celled zygote. Also, it is the process by which skin cells replace themselves when you have an abrasion.

As the zygote moves along the fallopian tube, development begins. The chromosomes from the sperm and the ovum have paired into 23 pairs, and each pair duplicates itself from the biochemical material in the cell. Then the cell divides into two identical cells, each having the same number of chromosomes as the original cell (figure 3.3). Mitosis continues throughout development of the many millions of cells that make up the human body.

How do the chromosomes duplicate themselves before cell division?

Chromosomes are made up of a biochemical substance called **deoxyribonucleic acid,** or **DNA**, which contains the hereditary blueprint for an individual's characteristics. The structure of the DNA molecule was discovered in the 1950s by James Watson and Francis Crick (1953). They described DNA as a double helix that resembles a twisted ladder (figure 3.4). The sides of the ladder consist of a pair of chemical bases attached to the threads and joined to each other. The chemical composition of the bases determines which one joins to another. The base *adenine* (A) joins only with the base *thymine* (T) and vice versa; the base *cytosine* (C) joins only with the base *guanine* (G) and vice versa. Even though each base has a specific complement, the pairs can occur up and down the ladder in any sequence. The sequence of A-T, T-A, C-G, G-C is significant because it provides genetic

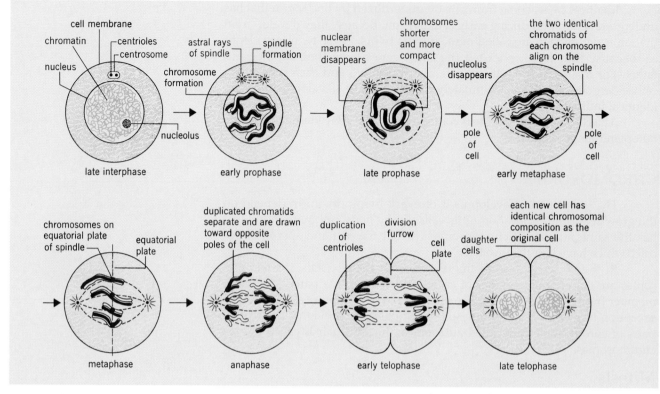

FIGURE 3.3
MITOSIS
**The major events in mitosis, the process of cellular division resulting in two daughter cells with the same number of chromosomes and containing the same hereditary code as the parent cells.**

instructions for a trait; for instance, A-T, G-C, A-T might provide one set of instructions, while T-A, G-C, C-G might provide another. The segments of the DNA molecule that have varying sequences of A-T, T-A, C-G, and G-C are the genes.

In mitosis the DNA ladder splits down the middle so that the pairs of bases forming the rungs are separated, but each side of the ladder remains intact. Each base now can pick up its complementary base from material in the cell. The newly attached bases are in the exact order as the old ones, and two new DNA ladders, each containing one new side and one old side of the previous molecule, are produced. This unique ability of DNA to duplicate itself makes it possible for the one-celled zygote to develop into the trillions of cells that make up a human being, all with the same genetic blueprint.

## Meiosis

While all the body cells have 46 individual, or 23 pairs, of chromosomes, the sex cells (ova and sperm) only have 23 single chromosomes. This occurs so that when the ovum and sperm unite, the resulting zygote will have 23 pairs of chromosomes. Thus, a process must exist by which the number of chromosomes are halved in the sex cells. This process is called

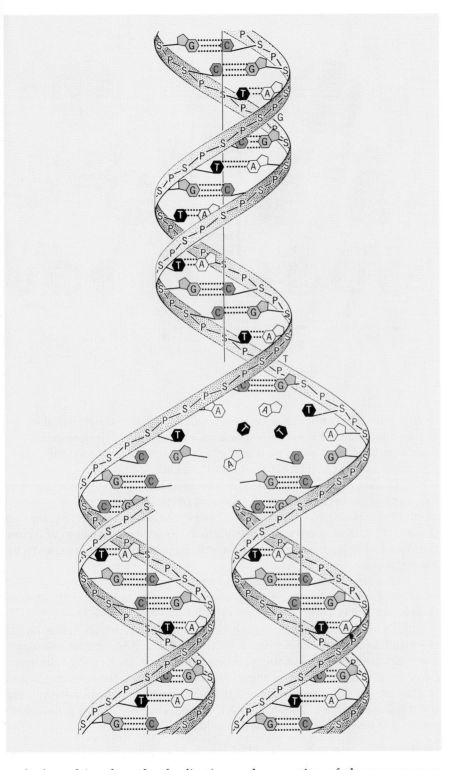

FIGURE 3.4
**DNA STRAND**
**A schematic representation of DNA. As the strands separate, two new DNA molecules are formed. DNA contains the organism's hereditary material and is located in the nucleus of every cell.**

**meiosis** and involves the duplication and separation of chromosomes so the original sex cell (ovum or sperm) divides into four cells, each having half the number of chromosomes as the original cell (figure 3.5).

In meiosis (like mitosis), the chromosomes duplicate and separate. However, unlike mitosis, two divisions (rather than one) take place, pro-

## FIGURE 3.5
## MEIOSIS

Meiosis is the process by which sex cells (sperm and ova) reproduce themselves. A primary spermatocyte produces four sperm, but only one egg results from meiosis of a primary oocyte. The polar bodies are functionless.

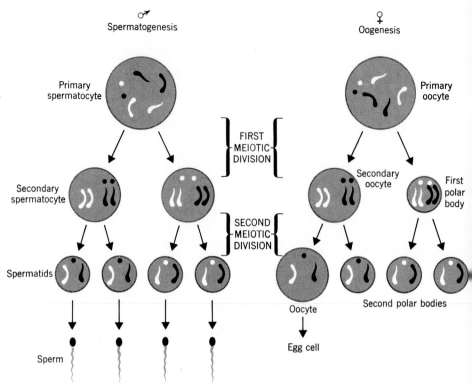

ducing four cells (rather than two) each with 23 chromosomes, half the number found in the body cells. These four cells, with 23 chromosomes each, become sperm in the male and ova in the female. Actually, only one ovum is produced in meiosis, the other three cells are cast off.

During meiosis when the chromosomes line up just before segregating, parts of them cross, break at the point of crossing, and exchange equivalent amounts of genetic material. This process is known as *crossing over* (figure 3.6). Crossing over actually alters the genetic composition of a chromosome and in so doing increases the possible combinations of genes in the sperm or ova.

Chromosomes are paired, and each member of the pair is similar. The only exception is the 23rd pair of chromosomes in the male where one is an X and one is a Y. In the female the 23rd pair would be XX.

As we see in figure 3.7 (page 72), when meiosis occurs in the female, the resulting four ova each bear an X chromosome. When meiosis occurs in the male, however, two of the resulting sperm bear an X chromosome and two bear a Y. If an X-bearing sperm fertilizes an ovum, the resulting zygote is a female (has XX chromosomes). If a Y-bearing sperm fertilizes an ovum, the resulting zygote is a male (has XY chromosomes). Thus, it is the male's sperm that determines the sex of the child.

## Chromosomal Abnormalities

When a sex cell divides during meiosis, sometimes the chromosomes do not separate from each other or sometimes a part of a chromosome breaks. This causes the resulting ovum or sperm to have too many, too few, or incomplete chromosomes. When a zygote is formed from the union of an

FIGURE 3.6
HOW CHROMOSOMES CROSS OVER

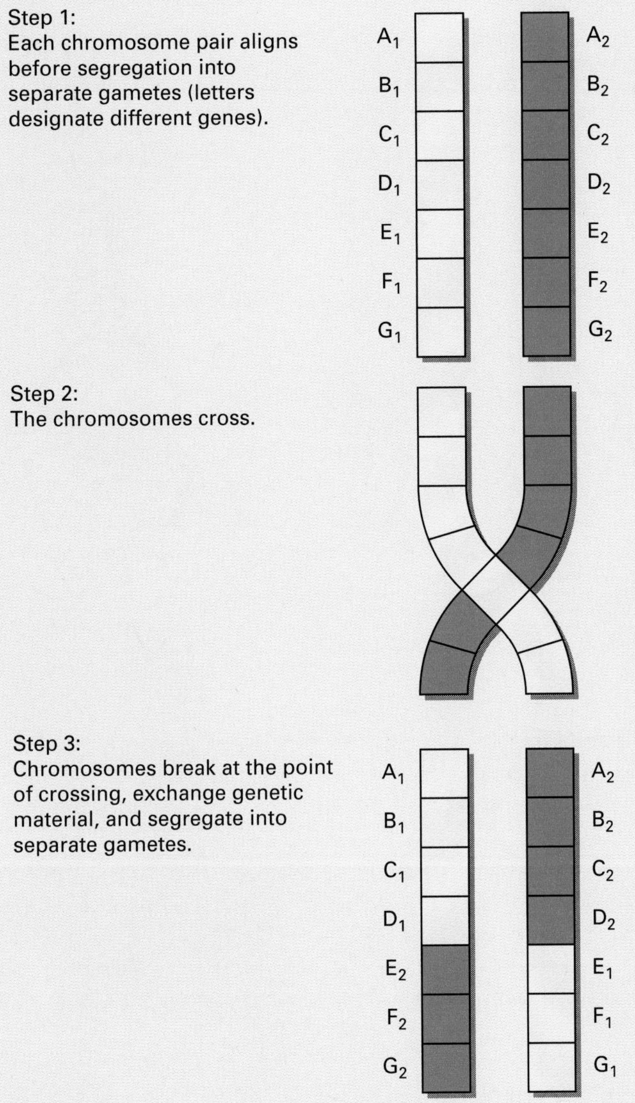
Step 1:
Each chromosome pair aligns before segregation into separate gametes (letters designate different genes).
$A_1$ $B_1$ $C_1$ $D_1$ $E_1$ $F_1$ $G_1$
$A_2$ $B_2$ $C_2$ $D_2$ $E_2$ $F_2$ $G_2$
Step 2:
The chromosomes cross.
Step 3:
Chromosomes break at the point of crossing, exchange genetic material, and segregate into separate gametes.
$A_1$ $B_1$ $C_1$ $D_1$ $E_2$ $F_2$ $G_2$
$A_2$ $B_2$ $C_2$ $D_2$ $E_1$ $F_1$ $G_1$

abnormal sperm and a normal ovum or a normal sperm and an abnormal ovum, it usually does not develop and spontaneously aborts. This is commonly termed a *miscarriage.* However, occasionally (0.5 percent) the zygote does develop, and a child is born with either one chromosome too many or one too few (Plomin, 1990). Sometimes parts of chromosomes become attached to others (Goodman, 1986).

The most common chromosomal abnormality is **Down's syndrome**, or *trisomy 21,* a condition in which the child has inherited an extra chromosome 21. Down's syndrome occurs in about 1 of 800 live births (Goodman, 1986). Children with Down's syndrome are mentally retarded, varying from

FIGURE 3.7
MEIOSIS ILLUSTRATED
WITH SEX
CHROMOSOMES

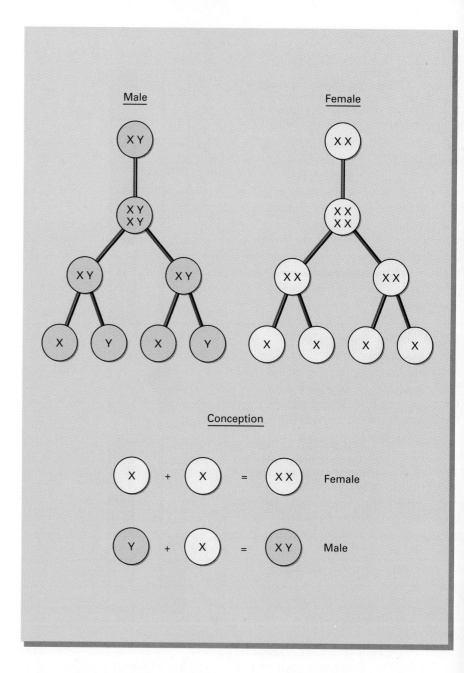

mild to severe, and have distinct physical features such as a short stocky build, flattened face, protruding tongue, almond-shaped eyes, and a unique crease across the palm of the hand. They have poor muscle tone and small hands and feet. Heart defects and hearing impairments are sometimes present. Socially, however, they are usually friendly, cheerful, and active.

The incidence of Down's syndrome rises dramatically with maternal age, and possibly paternal age because sometimes the sperm is defective (National Institute of Child Health and Human Development, 1984).

Many chromosomal abnormalities involve pair 23 of chromosomes, the sex (XX or XY) chromosomes. Occasionally, males are born with an extra X (XXY) or Y chromosome (XYY), and females are born with only one X chromosome (XO) or an extra one (XXX).

In males, the inheritance of an extra X chromosome is called **Klinefelter syndrome** (XXY). The incidence is about 1 of 1,000 male births (Goodman, 1986). Boys with Klinefelter syndrome are generally tall, and many also are overweight. They have a body fat distribution resembling that of females and have poor muscle development. They have underdeveloped testes and are sterile. In addition, they are deficient in verbal intelligence.

In males, the inheritance of an extra Y is sometimes called *supermale syndrome* (XYY). The incidence is about 1 of 1,000 male births (Goodman, 1986). Males with supermale syndrome appear normal from birth to early childhood, except for a slight increase in height. Most are fertile although some are not. They have below average intelligence and exhibit more delinquent behavior than normal males. Psychological studies indicate that certain personality traits such as infantilism, lack of emotional control, and increased impulsiveness are common among XYY males. Thus, it appears that the extra Y chromosome does lead to an increased risk of social maladjustment, but such persons can be helped by special education and counseling (Goodman, 1986).

When a female only inherits one X chromosome, she has what is known as **Turner syndrome** (XO). The incidence is about 1 of 10,000 female births (Goodman,1986). Such females are short in stature with a webbed neck and underdeveloped breasts. They also are sterile. Hormone therapy helps them appear more feminine. They score below normal on intelligence tests; however, on further analysis, many have normal verbal intelligence but below average spatial abilities.

Females who inherit an extra X chromosome (XXX) are normal in appearance but slightly taller than average, and are fertile. Therefore, many afflicted females go unnoticed. The incidence is approximately 1 of 1,000 female births (Goodman, 1986). Females with *triple-X syndrome* (sometimes called *superfemale syndrome),* like those with Turner syndrome, perform below average on intelligence tests. However, unlike females with Turner syndrome, their spatial abilities are normal while their verbal skills are retarded. In addition, they may have epilepsy, ovarian dysfunction, and behavioral problems (Goodman, 1986).

Sometimes the normal number of chromosomes are inherited but one of the X chromosomes is fragile because it is either compressed or broken in a certain area; this is termed **Fragile-X syndrome**. Fragile-X syndrome has been associated with mental retardation and certain facial features, including a prominent jaw and large ears. Males who inherit a fragile-X chromosome are more retarded than females who inherit one because males have only one X chromosome whereas females have two. If the second X chromosome in a female is normal, it can reduce or overcome the effects of a fragile-X chromosome. Fragile-X syndrome occurs in about 1 of 1,000 male births (Barnes, 1989).

## GENES

All living things receive their genetic inheritance through the chromosomes transmitted from the parents at the moment of conception. It is commonly stated that a child's appearance, abilities, or behavior are inherited, but more accurately, only the **instructions** for the formation of particular characteristics are inherited.

# F.Y.I.

For women age 20, the rate of having a child with Down's Syndrome is about 1 of 1,900 live births; for women age 30, the rate is about 1 of 900; and for women age 40, the rate is about 1 of 100 (Goodman, 1986). Scientists believe this higher incidence in older women is caused by damage to egg cells over time.

Each chromosome is made up of units called *genes*. Genes are the segments of the chromosomes where the specific sets of instructions called heredity are recorded. About 20,000 genes are in one chromosome, and they are arranged along the length of the chromosome, each with a fixed position.

Each gene carries a specification for a series of chemical processes, the results of which will ultimately be seen as some aspect of the person, such as the curve of the nose or the tendency to be shy. Some traits are determined by a single gene; others are determined by many genes.

## Patterns of Genetic Inheritance

How are genetic traits passed from parents to child?

An individual has two genes coded for each inherited characteristic or portion of it. Like the chromosomes, these genes are paired, one member of the pair, or one form coming from the mother and one from the father. These two forms of the gene for a particular trait that make a pair are called **alleles**.

The alleles for a certain trait can be similar, or **homozygous**. For example, a child can inherit alleles for blonde hair from both mother and father. Or, the alleles can hold different instructions for a trait; different alleles for a particular trait are called **heterozygous**. For example, a child might inherit an allele for blonde hair from his mother and an allele for brown hair from his father.

If the alleles are different, or heterozygous, one will usually be expressed in the individual while the other will be hidden. The expressed allele (is more powerful) is called **dominant** and the one that is hidden (is weaker) is called **recessive**. For recessive traits to be expressed, the individual must inherit two recessive alleles.

The genes expressed visibly in an individual are called the **phenotype**, whereas the hidden and expressed genes, one's total genetic endowment, are termed the **genotype**. If a child inherits an allele for blonde hair from his mother and an allele for brown hair from his father, the brown gene will be dominant and will mask the blonde gene. Therefore, the child's phenotype will be brown hair.

Table 3.1 displays examples of some phenotypes due to dominant or recessive genes.

We can figure out a person's probable genotype by doing some exercises.

Lloyd and Robin both have brown hair, yet Jennifer has blonde hair. Let:

B = brown gene (dominant allele is represented by a capital letter)

b = blonde gene (recessive allele is represented by the same letter in lower case)

BB = homozygous brown hair (trait is represented by two letters because it is the result of two genes)

Bb = heterozygous brown hair

bb = homozygous blonde hair

The phenotypes of Lloyd and Robin are brown hair. The possible genotypes are BB or Bb. Jennifer's hair is blonde. Because blonde is a recessive trait, it will be expressed only if an individual inherits two blonde genes; the only possible genotype then is bb.

## TABLE 3.1

| Dominant Traits | Recessive Traits |
| --- | --- |
| Brown eyes | Gray, green, hazel, blue eyes |
| Dark hair | Light or blonde hair |
| Curly hair | Straight hair |
| Thick lips | Thin lips |
| Roman nose | Straight nose |
| Facial dimples | No dimples |
| Normally pigmented skin | Albinism |
| Farsightedness | Normal vision |
| Normal hearing | Some forms of congenital deafness |
| Type A or Type B blood | Type O blood |
| Rh-positive blood | Rh-negative blood |
| Normal blood cells | Sickle cell anemia |
| Normal protein metabolism | Phenylketonuria (PKU) |
| Huntington's chorea | Normal central nervous functioning in adulthood |
| Normal central nervous development | Tay-Sachs disease |
| Normal respiratory and gastrointestinal functioning | Cystic fibrosis |

If both Lloyd and Robin were homozygous brown (BB), they could not conceive a blonde-haired child. To illustrate how this is determined multiply top letter by the side letter for each square. The four squares represent probable genotypes (in this case, brown hair) for each conception. The resulting genotype is determined by chance. Thus,

|     | B   | B   |
| --- | --- | --- |
| B   | BB  | BB  |
| B   | BB  | BB  |

A 100 percent chance (four of four) the child will have homozygous brown hair.

If either Lloyd or Robin were homozygous brown (BB), and the other were not heterozygous brown (Bb), they still could not conceive a blonde-haired child. That is:

|     | B   | B   |
| --- | --- | --- |
| B   | BB  | BB  |
| b   | Bb  | Bb  |

A 50 percent chance (2 of 4) the child will have homozygous brown hair; 50 percent chance the child will have heterozygous brown hair.

If both Lloyd and Robin were heterozygous brown (Bb), however, then there would be a 25 percent chance they could conceive a blonde-haired child. That is:

|   | B | b |
|---|---|---|
| B | BB | Bb |
| b | Bb | bb |

A 25 percent chance (1 of 4) the child will have homozygous brown hair; 50 percent chance the child will have heterozygous brown hair; and 25 percent chance the child will have blonde hair.

These exercises can be used as models for any dominant-recessive trait. Regardless of the number of children a couple has, the chances for the occurrence of each possible genotype refer to **each** conception. There was a 25 percent chance (1 of 4) Lloyd and Robin would have a blonde-haired child for their first-born, and there is the same 25 percent chance (1 of 4) they would have a blonde-haired child for their second-born.

## Co-dominance

The dominant-recessive pattern of expression does not always apply to every case of single-gene inheritance. In such cases it is possible for both alleles in a heterozygous condition to be expressed in an individual's phenotype. This is called **co-dominance**. An example is blood type. There are three possible alleles, A, B, and O, that can be inherited in any paired combination (A and B are dominant, O is recessive). When paired with O, the A and B alleles will determine the phenotype (AO and BO). However, when A and B alleles are inherited, the result is a combined phenotypic expression known as type AB blood in which both A and B proteins, or antigens, are present.

## Genetic Abnormalities

Generally, genetic abnormalities can be inherited by one of three ways. These categories are *autosomal dominant inheritance, autosomal recessive inheritance,* or *sex-linked inheritance* (figure 3.8).

### Autosomal Dominant Inheritance

**Autosomal dominant inheritance** refers to dominant genes that are on the first 22 pairs of chromosomes. When a defective gene for a trait is dominant, it masks the normal gene for that trait. Thus, for certain abnormalities, a person only needs one defective gene to be affected (Dn). Some examples of such abnormalities inherited this way are Huntington's disease (a progressive degeneration of the nervous system), and polydactyly (extra fingers or toes).

### Autosomal Recessive Inheritance

**Autosomal recessive inheritance** refers to recessive genes that are on the first 22 pairs of chromosomes. When two defective genes for a trait are inherited (homozygous condition), the person will be affected by the abnormality. If only one defective gene is inherited (heterozygous condition), it will be hidden by the normal gene for that trait and the person will be normal but will be a carrier of the defect (Nd). Some examples of such abnormalities are sickle cell anemia (a blood disorder wherein the oxygen-carry-

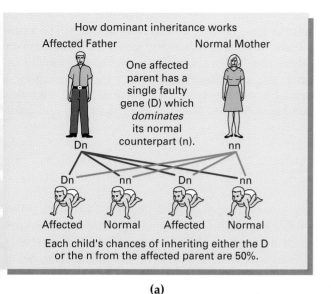

(a)

FIGURE 3.8

(a) Autosomal dominant inheritance. (b) Autosomal recessive inheritance. (c) Sex-linked inheritance . (March of Dimes Birth Defects Foundation, 1987)

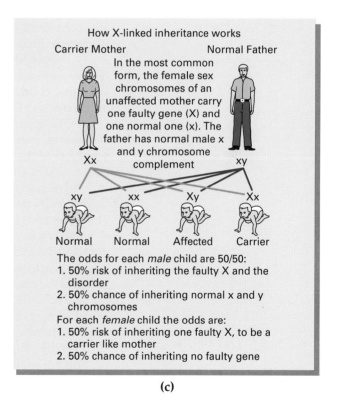

(b)                                        (c)

ing function of the red blood cells is impaired) and phenylketonuria or PKU (a metabolic disorder caused by the absence of a liver enzyme that causes mental retardation). Abnormalities inherited via autosomal recessive inheritance can be fatal.

## Sex-Linked Inheritance

**Sex-linked inheritance** refers to genes carried on the X chromosome. If a gene for a trait on the X chromosome is defective and a female (XX) inherits it, generally she will not be affected because she has another X chromosome with the normal gene for that trait. However, she will be a carrier. On the other hand, if she inherits two defective genes for a trait (one on each of the X chromosomes), then she will be affected by the abnormality. A male (XY) needs to inherit only one defective gene for a trait to be affected by the abnormality because he only has one X chromosome. Some examples of such abnormalities are hemophilia (a blood clotting disorder) and color blindness (red-green).

## GENETIC COUNSELING AND DIAGNOSTIC PROCEDURES

Genetic counseling is a medical procedure that helps couples understand their chances of having a child with a genetic disorder and assists them in making choices for the best course in having a child such as taking a chance the child conceived will be normal depending on the odds, being artificially inseminated and adopting. Making a decision to have a child knowing the chance that child will be normal involves many ethical issues. If the child is abnormal, the couple must decide to continue the pregnancy or abort. If the child is born abnormal and lives, decisions have to be made about the child's care throughout his life. Thus, genetic counseling involves not only biological issues but psychological ones as well.

People likely referred for genetic counseling are those who have a history of genetic disorders in their family, have already given birth to an abnormal child, have experienced reproductive problems such as repeated miscarriages, or are over 35 years of age.

The genetic counselor, who is trained in genetics and psychological counseling, interviews the couple and prepares a *pedigree*, a pictorial representation of the family history where affected relatives and their relationship to others are identified.

The pedigree is analyzed to determine the extent to which the couple is genetically related to a common ancestor and consequently, to each other. This is because such a common relationship increases the chances of pairing of homozygous recessive genes. Thus, if there is a defective gene present in the family, the more closely a couple is related to each other, the more likely it is that each could have one defective gene and that their child would get two genes. This is why most states prohibit first cousins from marrying.

The pedigree also is used to determine modes of inheritance and to calculate the odds that parents may bear an abnormal child using the same exercises demonstrated earlier.

If the couple decides to have a child, various prenatal diagnostic procedures are available that permit early detection of some fetal problems.

Blood tests are available for some genetic diseases to identify carriers. Other types of testing are available for other genetic diseases such as measuring the amount of salt in perspiration to identify carriers of cystic fibrosis. In cases where carriers can be identified, the probability of having a defective child can be easily determined. For example, two carriers of a recessive defect (Nd) have a 25 percent chance of having an affected child, whereas if one parent is a carrier (Nd) and the other normal (NN), there is no chance their child will be affected, although there is a 50 percent chance their child will be a carrier also.

After a high-risk pregnancy occurs, several methods can determine whether the offspring will be normal: *amniocentesis, chorionic villi sampling (CVS), ultrasound, fetoscopy,* and *alpha-fetoprotein (AFP) testing.* These procedures can diagnose a host of genetic, chromosomal, and other abnormalities. A diagnosis can ease parents' fears or alert them to the probability of serious birth defects, and allow parents the options of terminating the pregnancy or of taking both prenatal and postnatal measures to minimize the effect of the abnormality.

**Amniocentesis** involves inserting a hollow needle through the abdominal wall to the uterus and withdrawing a sample of amniotic fluid. Because the fetal cells are shed like we shed skin cells, they are present in the amniotic fluid and can be grown and cultured in the laboratory in order to analyze the chromosomes (figure 3.9). A major limitation of amniocentesis is it cannot be performed until sufficient amniotic fluid is available—at 15–16 weeks gestation. Since several additional weeks are needed to culture the cells, a diagnosis is usually unavailable until after week 18 of pregnancy.

While the risks of amniocentesis to the mother, such as hemorrhage or infection, are low, the procedure does entail some risk to the fetus, such as premature labor or death.

**Chorionic villi sampling (CVS)** is a newer technique than amniocentesis and still considered experimental (Jones, 1989). It is usually performed at 9–11 weeks gestation; some results are available five hours thereafter, while other biochemical tests take 2–3 weeks. In this procedure a tiny bit of tissue is removed from the chorionic villi, projections on the membrane surrounding the embryo that will eventually become the placenta. A catheter is inserted through the vagina and cervix to withdraw the tissue.

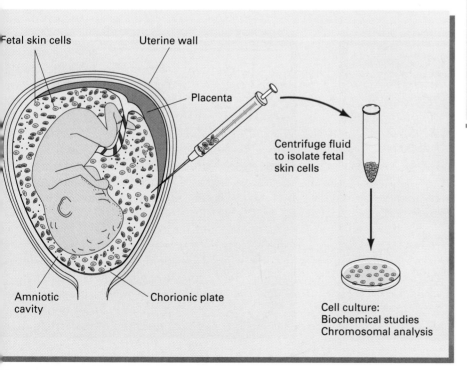

Fetal skin cells

Uterine wall

Placenta

Centrifuge fluid to isolate fetal skin cells

Amniotic cavity

Chorionic plate

Cell culture:
Biochemical studies
Chromosomal analysis

FIGURE 3.9
AMNIOCENTESIS

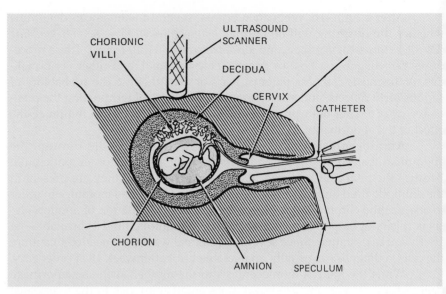

**Chorionic villi sampling at 12 weeks**

The cells obtained are then subjected to chromosomal analysis. The advantage of CVS over amniocentesis is earlier diagnosis. If the couple then decides to abort an abnormal fetus, there is less risk of complications to the mother when performed in the first trimester compared with the second trimester. The disadvantage of CVS is that a higher rate of spontaneous abortion, or miscarriage, exists after the procedure compared with amniocentesis.

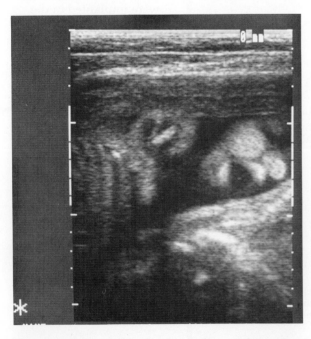

**Current ultrasound technology allows highly detailed fetal imaging.**

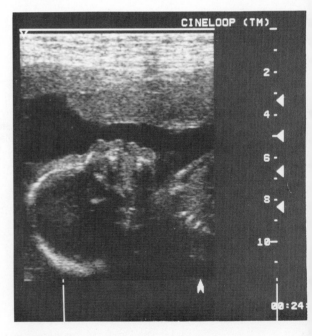

**Fetal skull**

In both amniocentesis and chorionic villi sampling, **ultrasound**, a method of scanning the womb with sound waves, is used to locate the placenta and provide an outline of the fetus so its size, shape, and location can be seen on a picture. Ultrasound imaging can show fetal malformations early in pregnancy, detect possible multiple pregnancies, and monitor fetal growth and development.

Also, ultrasound is used to support another technique, **fetoscopy**, in which a small tube with a light source at one end is inserted into the uterus to visually inspect the fetus for malformations. In addition, fetoscopy allows a fetal blood sample to be obtained, permitting prenatal diagnosis of disorders such as hemophilia and sickle cell anemia that cannot be diagnosed from the amniotic fluid.

This procedure is usually performed between weeks 16 and 19 of pregnancy. It is used when diagnosis is impossible by other means because it requires great skill to insert the instrument without causing complications, such as infection, leakage of amniotic fluid, or premature labor.

Finally, **alpha-fetoprotein (AFP) testing** uses blood analysis, amniocentesis, and ultrasound to reach a definite diagnosis of neural tube defects. The neural tube forms the spinal cord and brain. The AFP test measures the level of alpha-fetoprotein, a normal fetal liver product, in maternal blood and amniotic fluid. High AFP levels can indicate the fetus has *anencephaly*, a defective formation of the brain that invariably results in infant death shortly after birth, or *spina bifida*, abnormalities in the spinal column requiring surgical correction after birth and, possibly, also paralysis and mental retardation. All three procedures must be used to reach a definite diagnosis because the blood test alone can give false results (Willis, 1981). The blood test is usually done 15 to 18 weeks from the first day of the last menses. If the AFP is abnormal, a second test is done to confirm the level before other procedures are performed.

A new technique, **preimplantation diagnosis,** used in cases of assisted reproduction can test embryos for disease (for example, cystic fibrosis) in vitro, before implantation (Handyside et al., 1992).

## STAGES OF PRENATAL DEVELOPMENT

The processes inside the developing zygote from the moment of fertilization to the first cell division and the mechanisms transmitting genetic material have been explained. We now will examine the stages of prenatal development: the *germinal, embryonic,* and *fetal* periods.

# Germinal Period

The first phase of prenatal development includes the time from conception to implantation when the developing zygote becomes firmly attached to the uterine wall and is called the **germinal period.** This period lasts from conception to two weeks after conception.

After conception, the fertilized ovum, or zygote, travels down the fallopian tube toward the uterus. Within 24 to 36 hours, the zygote has divided by mitosis into two cells. These two cells also divide by mitosis into four cells, then eight, and so on. Within seven days these proliferating cells have formed a hollow ball-like structure filled with fluid called a *blastula*. By this time the cells have begun to differentiate. The inner layer of cells in the blastula will become the embryo; the outer layer of cells will develop into tissues that nourish and protect the embryo such as the **placenta** (organ through which the infant is attached to mother), the **umbilical cord** (organ that attaches the baby to the placenta), and the **amniotic sac** (membrane filled with amniotic fluid that surrounds the embryo by week 8 after conception). The amniotic fluid keeps the temperature constant and insulates the embryo from impacts the pregnant woman might encounter.

As the blastula approaches the uterus 6 to 10 days after conception, tiny hairlike blood vessels emerge. Meanwhile, the uterus is at a point in the woman's menstrual cycle where it is engorged with small blood vessels to provide nourishment to the embryo. When the blastula contacts the uterine wall, these tiny blood vessels attach and tap into the woman's blood supply, enabling it to receive nourishment. This is termed *implantation* and marks the end of the germinal period. At this stage, the embryo is about the size of a period on this page.

Implantation is a significant event in prenatal development because often the blastula does not implant or may implant in a place incapable of maintaining it, such as the fallopian tube (called ectopic pregnancy), and will spontaneously abort before term (Adler & Carey, 1982) or will have to be removed surgically, as in the case of an ectopic pregnancy.

## Embryonic Period

After implantation in the uterine wall, the second phase of prenatal development begins, the **embryonic period.** This period is three weeks to the end of eight weeks after conception. When the blastula implants in the uterine wall, a hormone is secreted that prevents the woman from menstruating and, thereby, shedding the uterine lining. This hormone circulates throughout the woman's body and eventually is detectable in the urine, where its presence indicates conception in a pregnancy test.

During the embryonic period, the embryo receives nourishment from the woman by means of the umbilical cord, which is attached to the placenta. The placenta is composed of both fetal and maternal cells. Many of elaborately branched projections (villi), each containing a single fetal artery and vein, make up the main fetal part of the placenta. This part originally arose from the chorionic membrane of the fetus. The testing of these chorionic villi cells makes possible the prenatal diagnostic test, chorionic villi sampling. The fetal blood vessels in the villi eventually join to form the two arteries and the vein in the umbilical cord. Within the uterine wall, maternal capillaries empty into spaces between the fetal villi, thereby permitting an exchange of gases and nutrients from the woman to the fetus and vice versa. The maternal part of the placenta originates from the uterine lining that forms during pregnancy between the maternal uterine wall and the fetal sac. The placenta is semipermeable because it allows some, but not all, substances to pass. For instance, oxygen, carbon dioxide, nutrients, and antibodies to some diseases can cross the placenta but blood cells cannot. Thus, the blood supplies of the mother and infant do not mix. The umbilical cord carries oxygen and nutrients from the woman across the placenta to the embryo and transports carbon dioxide and metabolic wastes from the embryo across the placenta to the mother where they enter her bloodstream and are expelled with her own metabolic wastes. The umbilical cord is significant to the development of the infant because it is the lifeline.

Unfortunately, it also can be responsible for developmental abnormalities in that harmful substances the woman ingests (drugs) or is exposed to (diseases) are transported through the placenta to the infant via the umbilical cord.

Rapid development occurs during the embryonic period. While the outer layer of cells in the blastula are forming the placenta, umbilical cord, and amniotic sac, the inner layer of cells are rapidly differentiating into three distinct layers. The outer layer, or *ectoderm*, will eventually become the child's skin, hair, nails, oil and sweat glands, and nervous system. The middle layer, or *mesoderm*, will form muscles, bones, connective tissue, and the circulatory and excretory systems. The inner layer, or *endoderm*, will become the digestive tract, trachea, bronchi, lungs, and other organs such as the pancreas and liver.

During the embryonic period, the groundwork for all body structures and internal systems is established and, at the end of this stage, the organism is human in form and shows signs of beginning movement. Because this development stage is closely scheduled, the embryo is extremely vulnerable to contextual influences on the prenatal environment such as disease, drugs, or chemicals.

From about 14 to 21 days after conception, the ectoderm folds to form a neural tube that soon becomes the spinal cord, the top of which swells to form a head and a brain. While the nervous system is developing, the mesoderm forms a primitive heart around day 28 that begins to pump blood around the embryo's circulatory system, and the beginnings of basic muscles, vertebrae, and ribs appear. Meanwhile, the endoderm is turning into the various digestive organs. At the end of one month the embryo is only about ¼ of an inch long.

In the second month, growth and differentiation continue rapidly, the eyes, ears, nasal organs, and jaw form. Protruding buds gradually become arms, legs, fingers, and toes. Internal organs develop further—the intestines grow, the heart develops separate chambers, the kidneys and urogenital tract appear, and the liver begins to manufacture blood cells.

At the end of the second month, sexual differentiation begins to take place. If the embryo is a male, a gene on the Y chromosome triggers a biochemical reaction that instructs the *undifferentiated gonadal tissue*, the sex cells that will become testes or ovaries, to produce testes. If the embryo is a female, the undifferentiated gonadal tissue receives no such instructions and will later produce ovaries. At 60 days after conception, the embryo is about one inch long and weighs about ½ of an ounce. It has started to look like a human being even though its head makes up almost half of the body.

## Fetal Period

The beginning of the third month until the end of pregnancy is termed the **fetal period**, the third and longest phase of prenatal development. Since pregnancy lasts for nine months, or 266 days, it is commonly divided into three trimesters. While the third month ends the first trimester, the fourth through sixth months mark the second trimester, and the seventh through ninth months mark the third trimester.

Now called a fetus, the developing organism already has formed vital parts. In the third month, the newly differentiated organs, muscles, and nervous system become organized and connected. The brain signals and, in response, the fetus kicks, bends its arms, forms a fist, curls the toes, and moves the mouth. The primitive lungs begin to expand and contract. The external genitalia become increasingly refined, so the sex of the infant is distinguishable externally by week 12 of pregnancy. Also appearing are the fingernails, toenails, hair follicles, tooth buds, and eyelids that can open and close. The fetal heartbeat is now stronger and can be heard through a stethoscope.

The second trimester also is a period of rapid growth and development. The motor activity of the fetus may be strong enough to be felt by the woman. The hardening skeleton can be detected by ultrasound. The fetus' visual and auditory senses begin to function. This is known because premature infants born 25 weeks after conception blink in response to bright light and become alert to the sound of a bell (Allen & Capute, 1986). At the end of the second trimester the fetus is about 14 to 15 inches long and weighs about two pounds.

The third trimester of pregnancy differs from the previous six months because now the fetus, if born prematurely, has a chance for survival. The longer the fetus remains in the uterus, the better chance it has, although modern technology has improved the survival rates of infants born before term. If born between 7 to 8 months, breathing is difficult because the air sacs in the lungs are not ready to inflate and exchange oxygen for carbon dioxide. Thus, the infant is susceptible to respiratory distress syndrome (hyaline membrane disease) and can die.

During the last trimester, the fetus gains about five pounds and grows about seven inches. The fetus becomes less active as the end of the prenatal period approaches. In the eighth month, a layer of fat begins to be deposited under the skin to assist with temperature regulation after birth, and in the last month the fetus acquires antibodies from the mother's blood granting temporary protection from illnesses she has had. After birth, the infant begins to produce antibodies. In the last weeks, most fetuses assume a head-down posture at the base of the uterus with the limbs curled up. Uterine contractions begin during the last month at irregular intervals. When the uterine contractions become strong and regular, birth is imminent.

Figure 3.10 illustrates the changes in body size of an embryo and fetus during development.

# CONTEXTUAL INFLUENCES ON HEREDITY AND PRENATAL DEVELOPMENT

The awareness of influences outside the womb (a disease a mother was exposed to or a drug that a mother took) that could affect the unborn child did not emerge until the 1940. Gregg (1941) described a relation between rubella (German measles) in pregnant women and cataracts in their children. McBride (1961) identified the drug *thalidomide*, which was given to pregnant women to stop nausea, as the cause of limb abnormalities. In fact, any substance a mother is exposed to or ingests that crosses the placenta may have an effect on the unborn child.

The term **teratogen** refers to an environmental agent that causes damage during the prenatal period. The modern science of *teratology* has shown that the consequences of toxic environmental agents for the unborn child are complex and varied. Effects of teratogens depend on factors such as amount and length of exposure, interaction with other teratogens, as well as the genetic constitution of the woman and unborn child, which in turn

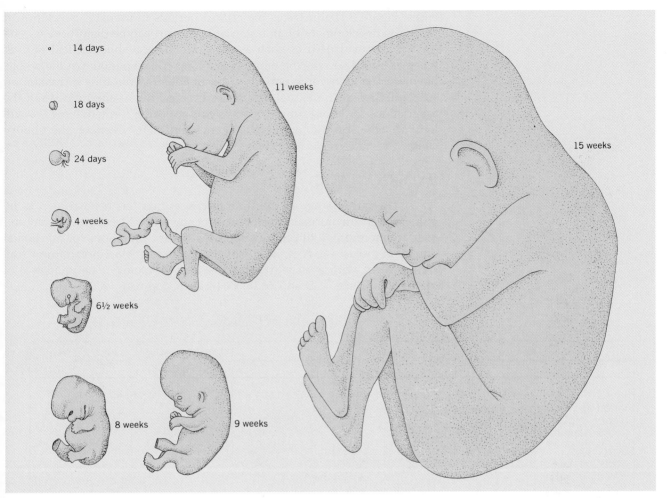

14 days

18 days

24 days

4 weeks

6½ weeks

8 weeks

9 weeks

11 weeks

15 weeks

**FIGURE 3.10**
**Changes in the body size of the embryo and fetus during development in the uterus (all figures natural size).**

affects their ability to withstand the harmful influence. Thus, not every unborn child will be affected the same way. The developmental impact of teratogens is further complicated by the fact that some consequences may not be immediately apparent. They appear later in the individual's life. An example is the link between the drug diethylestilbesterol (DES) taken by women to prevent miscarriage and the high incidence of vaginal and testicular cancer in their young adult children (Goodman, 1986). Other consequences, such as behavioral ones, can be difficult to link with the teratogen. An example is the tenuous link between hyperactivity in children and women's exposure to alcohol or drugs (Zuckerman et al., 1989; Barr et al., 1990).

Teratogens can have varied effects depending on the age of the unborn child at the time of exposure. During prenatal development, each major organ system or body part has a *critical period* when it is most sensitive to teratogenic agents. A **critical period** is the time in development that an organ system, body part, or behavior is developing most rapidly and, therefore, is susceptible to being disturbed by harmful environmental influences. Figure 3.11 illustrates the critical periods in prenatal development when the development of an organ or body part can be disturbed. As you can see, some structures such as the limbs have a short critical period, whereas others such as the brain have a long critical period. On the whole, however, the embryonic period of development is the time of maximum susceptibility to contextual influences because this is the time when the foundations for all essential body systems are being formed. Now we will look at some specific teratogenic agents and their effects on the unborn child.

## PATERNAL AGE

The father's age at the time of conception has been shown to be influential in the normal development of the fetus. Men 36 years old and over are more prone to produce sperm with new mutations for autosomal dominant diseases (Goodman, 1986). An example is Marfan syndrome (tall stature often with eye, heart, and vascular problems). The incidence of Marfan syndrome is about 1 of 16,000 births (Goodman, 1986).

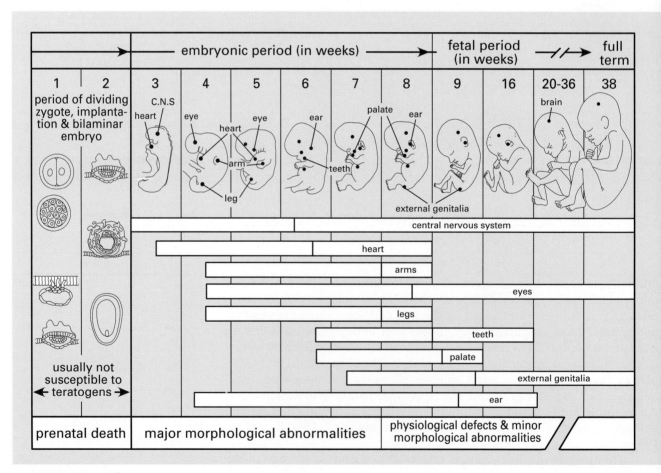

### FIGURE 3.11
**Critical periods of development for various organs and structures wherein they are most susceptible to damage by teratogens (Moore, 1983).**

## MATERNAL AGE

The age of the female influences the unborn child because more children with developmental problems tend to be born to women who are under 20 or over 35 years of age (Goodman, 1986). The inadequately developed reproductive system in women under 20 years of age and the aging reproductive system in women over 35 years of age, presumably are the causes. However, less than 20-year-old mothers are more likely to be single and do not get adequate prenatal care, which results in poor nutrition or poor health. In turn, these factors can contribute to the higher incidence of problems in those less than 20 years of age.

Females over age 35, especially over age 40, are likely to experience irregular ovulation. The occurrence of problems such as miscarriages and chromosomal abnormalities (such as Down's syndrome) increases with advancing age (March of Dimes Birth Defects Foundation, 1989).

Maternal age is significant because the number of older women giving birth has risen in recent years, as has the number of teenage births. Some reasons for the rise in older women giving birth are that many women delay motherhood until they have a career, and women who have had problems conceiving have been helped by rapidly improving technology.

The reasons the number of teenage births are on the increase are thought to be related to sexual explicitness portrayed by the media, the lack of appropriate sex education for children, the decreased availability of parental support for children, and the nature of adolescent thought and emotions in that adolescents commonly take risks (Dryfoos, 1990).

## MATERNAL NUTRITION

Because an unborn child receives nourishment from a woman's bloodstream by way of the placenta, there is good reason to be concerned about a woman's diet (March of Dimes Birth Defects Foundation, 1991).

Most knowledge about the effect of nutrition on prenatal development comes from animal studies in which the animals were fed inadequate diets (not enough vitamins, minerals, or protein) and their offspring examined and from studies of women who were severely malnourished because of poverty or famine conditions. Severe malnutrition increases the risk of spontaneous abortion, low birth weight, stillbirth, and infant mortality during the first year (Goodman, 1986).

The critical period principle appears to apply to nutrition as it does with other environmental agents in that the damage depends on the period of prenatal development during which malnutrition occurs. Research indicates that brain growth occurs in an orderly sequence, as does growth of other organs. The first-phase hyperplasia (growth by increase in the number of cells) takes place prenatally. The second-phase hypertrophy (growth by increase in cell size), in combination with hyperplasia, is the growth pattern noted during the first six months of life. Therefore, maternal malnutrition can contribute to a reduced complement of brain cells in the fetus (Bobak, Jensen & Zalar, 1989). In a study of the pregnancy outcomes of women who experienced severe famine conditions in Holland during World War II, mothers in their third trimester during the peak of the famine had infants with low birth weights and reduced head circumferences (Stein et al., 1975). Malnutrition has the greatest effect during the last trimester

**Recognizing the consequences of an increase in teen pregnancies, many school districts offer child development or parenting courses to promote awareness of what is involved in raising children. Some districts provide programs exclusively for teen mothers and their children to enable mothers to complete their education and receive parenting training.**

# F.Y.I.

**Folic Acid is one of the B-complex vitamins. It is needed to produce new DNA. It also has an impact on the development of red and white blood cells.**

**Evidence suggests that stressful pregnancies directly influence a child's irritability, restlessness, and certain physical deformities.**

because the unborn child is gaining weight, and brain cells are rapidly multiplying and increasing in size (Tanner, 1990). Thus, autopsies of infant's born to malnourished women were smaller and had fewer brain cells than babies born to adequately nourished women (Winick, 1976).

The long-term effects of prenatal malnutrition depend on the adequacy of the infant's diet after birth. While the women exposed to the famine in Holland during their third trimester of pregnancy had smaller infants with smaller head circumferences, as young men these children did not differ significantly on intelligence tests scores from children whose mothers were not exposed to the famine (Stein et al., 1975). The explanation is that after the famine the mothers and children were adequately nourished. Thus, since rapid brain growth and development continue postnatally for the first two years, it is possible that adequate nutrition during this critical time compensated for the inadequate prenatal nutrition.

It was recently found that women who take multivitamins containing folic acid during the early stages of pregnancy sharply reduce the risk of having an infant with neural tube defects (Milansky et al., 1989). Such defects, occurring at about the sixth week after conception, can cause paralysis and death. As previously stated, alpha-fetoprotein testing is used to diagnose neural tube defects.

The awareness of the relation of vitamins to birth defects emerged after World War II when a noticeably large number of infants with neural tube defects were born to malnourished women in Europe. Since then, the influence of vitamin supplements in preventing birth defects, especially in prepregnant nutrition, has been a topic of study (March of Dimes Birth Defects Foundation, 1987).

## EMOTIONAL STRESS

Although no direct connections exist between the nervous system of a woman and the unborn child, it is possible for her emotional state to affect the child (Standley, Soule & Copans, 1979). When the woman experiences emotions such as rage and anxiety her *autonomic nervous system*, the nerves that transmit impulses from the brain and spinal cord to the muscles and glands, stimulates the release of adrenal hormones into her bloodstream. The hormones cause large amounts of blood to be diverted to parts of the body involved in a defensive response: brain, heart, and voluntary muscles in arms, legs, and trunk. Blood flow to other organs, including the uterus, is diminished. Such a drop in blood to the uterus and placenta can result in a deficient supply of oxygen for the unborn infant (Stechler & Halton, 1982). Stress hormones also cross the placenta so that whenever a woman is experiencing stress, the infant also experiences stress. Fetal heart rate rises and activity level of the fetus increases greatly when women experience intense anxiety (Sontag, 1944). When stress is experienced repeatedly over a long period, birth weight and length of gestation decrease (Dunkel-Schetter, Lobel & Scrimshaw, 1990).

Generally, the impact of emotional stress on the unborn child depends on the stage of pregnancy. Severe and prolonged emotional stress early in pregnancy, can result in physical abnormalities such as cleft lip and palate or infant stomach disorders, whereas such stress later in pregnancy is more likely to result in fetal behavioral changes such as increased movement or hiccuping (Revill & Dodge, 1978).

Some researchers believe that prolonged exposure to stress hormone during the prenatal period is responsible for the increased irritability, restlessness, and digestive disturbances observed in infants born to anxious women. However, the quality of maternal interaction with the infant after birth can be equally significant in causing these difficulties (Sameroff & Chandler, 1975). For example, Field and her colleagues (Field et al., 1985) found that women who were highly anxious, depressed, or resentful during their last trimester of pregnancy usually remained so after the infant was born. These mothers were more likely to be punitive and controlling toward their children than women who did not have such stressful feelings; they also had infants who were fussier and more moody than did the non-stressed women. Thus, emotional stress in the prenatal period as well as the postnatal period affects the infant.

## DISEASE

During the 1940s the medical community recognized a link between maternal disease (rubella virus) and defects in infants. We will discuss some examples of diseases known to be teratogens.

## Rubella

In 1941, Mc Allister Gregg noticed that mothers who had contracted rubella (German measles) early in pregnancy delivered congenitally blind infants. Since then it has been established that mothers contracting rubella during the first trimester often give birth to infants with heart defects, hearing loss, mental retardation, and eye defects. Additionally, central nervous system damage and other physical abnormalities can be present (Sever, 1982). The neighbors of Michael and Kate have five sons, and one is disabled, because his mother contracted rubella when she was pregnant. He is mentally retarded, blind in one eye, hard of hearing, and walks with a limp.

The effects of the rubella virus depend on what organ or limb is in the critical stage of development when the virus is contracted. Today, physicians stress the importance of becoming vaccinated against rubella.

## Herpes Viruses

*Cytomegalovirus* (CMV) is a form of herpes that affects the salivary glands and can remain latent for years only to be reactivated during pregnancy.

Infants who contract CMV from their mothers are at risk for microcephaly (small head), hydrocephaly (large head), encephalitis (inflammation of the brain), blindness, and seizures.

Herpes simplex, one common sexually transmitted disease in the United States also can infect the fetus prenatally or more commonly during birth. No cure for this disease exists, which will kill some infected neonates and cause disabilities such as blindness, brain damage, and other neurological disorders (Hanshaw, Dudgeon & Marshall, 1985). Women with active herpes infections close to delivery are advised to undergo a *cesarean delivery*, a surgical procedure in which the infant is delivered via a uterine incision to avoid passage through the birth canal where the herpes virus manifests itself.

## Acquired Immune Deficiency Syndrome (AIDS)

*Acquired immune deficiency syndrome* (AIDS) is the result of infection by the human immunodeficiency virus (HIV), a disease that is a growing

The best defense in the spread of AIDS is a vigorous education program before children reach sexual maturity.

concern because it is fatal and because of its increase in those afflicted with the virus. It is a disease of the immune system in which the person is affected by many diseases that healthy individuals have strong defenses against. It can be transmitted through an exchange of body fluids from an infected person such as in sexual intercourse or using infected needles to inject intravenous drugs. It is currently believed that AIDS can be transmitted from female to child during the birth process when the umbilical cord separates from the placenta, allowing an exchange of blood from mother and infant (Bobak, Jensen & Zalar, 1989). At this time, the only treatment for AIDS infants is to make them comfortable and try to limit their exposure to diseases because their immune systems are deficient.

## Syphilis

Syphilis is a sexually transmitted bacterial infection. It is most harmful to the unborn child during the latter part of pregnancy since the organisms transmitting the disease cannot cross the placenta until then. Thus, if a woman is diagnosed early in the pregnancy via a blood test, she can be given antibiotics before the disease harms the infant. However, if the woman receives no treatment she runs the risk of miscarrying or giving birth to a child who has eye, ear, bone, or brain damage (Bobak, Jensen & Zalar, 1989).

## Toxoplasmosis

*Toxoplasmosis* is a common parasitic infection. The parasite is present in raw meat and cat feces. Toxoplasmosis has been linked to eye and central nervous system damage to the fetus during the first trimester (Marcus, 1983).

### DRUGS

The 1960s revealed, through the thalidomide tragedy, that seemingly unharmful drugs taken by mothers cross the placenta and can cause devastating effects in unborn infants. The specific effects depend on when drugs were taken. We will discuss some examples of known teratogenic drugs.

## Thalidomide

*Thalidomide* was a drug that was available over the counter in European countries and Canada in the early 1960s as a tranquilizer and sedative for morning sickness. Morning sickness commonly occurs during the first critical trimester of pregnancy. When thalidomide was taken from 34 to 50 days after conception, it interfered with the formation of arms, legs, and ears (Carlson, 1984).

## Diethylstilbesterol (DES)

*Diethylstilbesterol (DES)* is a synthetic hormone with properties similar to estrogen. It was given to women from the mid 1940s to mid 1960s to prevent miscarriage. The drug appeared safe at the time because infants born to women who had taken the drug appeared normal. However, in the 1970s it was found that young adult females whose mothers had taken the drug had a higher percentage of vaginal cancer than the normal population (Orenberg, 1981). Young adult males whose mothers had taken the drug were at increased risk for testicular cancer (Stillman, 1982). Later, it was discovered that DES causes abnormal development of the vaginal cells during the prenatal period in females (Johnson et al., 1979), and when these women become pregnant, they are more likely to miscarry (Barnes et al., 1980). Males who were prenatally exposed to DES have a higher incidence of abnormalities of the genital tract and some are sterile (Schardein, 1985).

## Alcohol

*Alcohol* is a drug that depresses the central nervous system. Prenatally, alcohol crosses the placenta and can alter brain development throughout gestation (McCarthy, 1983). In 1973, Jones and colleagues (Jones, Smith, Ulleland & Streissguth, 1973) described a specific cluster of abnormalities known as **fetal alcohol syndrome (FAS)** appearing frequently in the offspring of alcohol-abusing mothers. The most noticeable characteristics of FAS include microcephaly and malformations of the heart, limbs, joints, and face. An affected infant is likely to exhibit abnormal behaviors such as hyperactivity, seizures, tremors, and excessive irritability. Also, FAS babies are more likely to be mentally retarded (Abel, 1984).

Infants exposed prenatally to alcohol, even when they do not suffer from FAS, may be at high risk for many negative outcomes typically found among children of alcoholics, including hyperactivity and other behavioral and learning problems (Coles, Smith & Falek, 1987). Streissguth and colleagues (Streissguth et al., 1989) found that more than three drinks of alcohol per day during pregnancy was significantly related to an average decrease in IQ of five points.

How much alcohol is safe during pregnancy? Thus far, no minimum safe level of prenatal alcohol consumption has been established. For this reason, the United States Surgeon General has advised pregnant women to abstain from alcohol entirely and to be conscious of the alcohol content in food and drugs (Surgeon General's Advisory on Alcohol and Pregnancy, 1981). Even occasional social drinking during early pregnancy can have harmful effects on the development of the child.

## Nicotine

*Nicotine* is a drug commonly found in cigarettes. Cigarette smoking by pregnant women has been related to various consequences for the unborn child (Abel, 1984). Infants born to women who smoke are smaller and weigh less than infants of nonsmokers. Maternal smoking increases the chance of miscarriage as well as death of the infant (U.S. Department of Health and Human Services, 1983 [USDHHS]). Smoking retards growth and increases the incidence of infant mortality because smoking nicotine causes the blood vessels to constrict, thereby reducing the blood supply and consequent oxygen level to the placenta. Cigarette smoking also results in a significant increase in the amount of carbon dioxide inhaled, which also contributes to reduced oxygen in the blood. The more one smokes, the more one is likely to have a premature or a full-term, low birth weight infant who might die (U.S. Department of Health, Education and Welfare, 1979; Fanaroff & Martin, 1987). Further, prenatal exposure to nicotine has been associated with hypertension and increased nervous system excitation (USDHHS, 1983).

## Narcotics

There is evidence that marijuana and cocaine, or "crack," severely damage the offspring of pregnant animals, but the evidence for humans is unclear (Samuels & Samuels, 1986). Cocaine's teratogenic nature is due in part to the fact that it constricts blood vessels; when it constricts placental blood vessels, the supply of fetal nutrients and oxygen is reduced. Preliminary data on the regular use of cocaine during pregnancy reveal that such mothers are at risk for miscarriage or premature delivery and that their infants tend to be smaller than normal, very irritable, and susceptible to serious respiratory problems (Bartol, 1986) as well as being addicted.

Cocaine-dependent newborns often exhibit agonizing withdrawal symptoms that can last 2 to 3 weeks, including hypersensitivity to noise, poor eating and sleeping, and diarrhea. They have visual attention problems because they cannot focus on their parents' faces (Bobak, Jensen & Zalar, 1989).

Some cocaine-exposed infants can experience long-term developmental problems such as motor, sensory, and language disabilites. They also are likely to exhibit behavior problems (American Academy of Pediatrics, 1989).

Infants of heroin-addicted women also are at risk for premature birth and physical malformations, respiratory distress, and increased mortality at birth. Substitute use of methadone reduces the incidence of many complications (Cushner, 1981). However, infants exposed prenatally to either heroin or methadone become, like their mothers, physiologically addicted, and they exhibit withdrawal symptoms at birth, including tremors, vomiting, fever, and a shrill cry (Zelson, Lee & Casalino, 1973). The symptoms disappear within a few months but meanwhile these infants are difficult to care for, which can in turn interfere with the mother–child interaction, having emotional consequences (Stechler & Halton, 1982).

## ENVIRONMENTAL HAZARDS

Many potentially hazardous or harmful substances are in the environment, most of these such as fertilizers, wood preservatives, and X rays have beneficial uses and, therefore, are unlikely to disappear. Thus, we must be aware of their potential for harm and treat them accordingly.

During World War II the atomic bomb was considered beneficial to national security. However, when atomic bombs were dropped over two Japanese cities scientists realized their teratogenic effects. Pregnant women who were within one-half mile of the explosion spontaneously aborted (miscarried) or gave birth to stillborns (infants born dead). Most of those who were within one and a quarter miles gave birth to a stillborn or a severely disabled child who died soon after birth (Apgar & Beck, 1974).

Even clinical doses of radiation used in hospitals and by dentists for diagnostic purposes and cancer treatment can cause chromosomal abnormalities, spontaneous abortions, or birth defects, particularly if a mother is exposed during the first trimester of pregnancy. Thus, pregnant women are advised to avoid X rays unless necessary.

Pregnant women often encounter potentially toxic agents in their daily lives including cleaning agents, cosmetics and hair sprays, insecticides, and so on. The specific risks associated with these substances remain to be determined. It is known, however, that contact with chemical defoliants should be avoided.

It has also been found that there is a higher than normal rate of miscarriages and birth defects in women who live near water contaminated by industrial waste products (Miller, 1985).

# WHAT ARE THE EFFECTS OF PRENATAL EXPOSURE TO DRUGS?

Barr, H.M., Streissguth, A.P., Darby, B.L., & Sampson, P.D. (1990). Prenatal exposure to alcohol, caffeine, tobacco, and aspirin: Effects on fine and gross motor performance in 4-year-old children. *Developmental Psychology*, 26, 3, 339–348.

Beginning in midpregnancy, a longitudinal study was conducted, on a selected group of predominantly white, middle class, married, pregnant women. The infants were examined at delivery and followed until four years of age, when they were examined for fine and gross motor development.

The four primary drugs investigated were alcohol, caffeine, nicotine, and aspirin. Prenatal exposure levels were determined by maternal interview during the fifth month of pregnancy. The interviews were conducted before general knowledge of the deleterious effects of prenatal alcohol exposure and before any official warnings about drinking and pregnancy had been issued.

Results showed that children prenatally exposed to alcohol in early pregnancy (one drink per day) performed poorly on fine motor tasks. The more alcohol the fetus was exposed to, the slower was the child's performance. Increasing alcohol exposure in early pregnancy (about three drinks per day) also was related to increasingly poor gross motor balance.

The heavier the caffeine exposure in early pregnancy, the more errors on fine motor steadiness.

Subjects exposed to any aspirin versus those without prenatal aspirin scored slightly lower on balance; whereas those exposed to aspirin several times or more a week had lower fine motor scores.

The relation of prenatal smoking (about one pack of cigarettes per day) on child motor skills at age four was not found to be significant.

Of the four drugs examined in this study, alcohol was the strongest prediction of fine and gross motor behavior. More errors, longer performance time, and poorer balance were all effects of prenatal alcohol exposure. As infants, they all displayed signs of central nervous dysfunction including increased body tremors, increased hand-to-mouth activity, and increased head turns.

The most interesting finding of this study was that even occasional social drinking in early pregnancy affects later motor behavior.

What about potentially hazardous substances in the workplace? As more people enter the workforce and more sophisticated technology is employed, an increasing concern exists about the possible effect of certain environments on male and female reproductive systems. For example, one study found that women working with semiconductors in rooms where these computer chips are etched with acids and gases have a miscarriage rate nearly twice the national average (Meier, 1987). As a result of these findings, the American Telephone and Telegraph Company (AT&T) has banned all pregnant women from its semiconductor production lines (Sanger, 1987). This ban, however, was removed by the state supreme court in California in 1990 as being discriminatory against women.

Studies are currently under way, supported by the March of Dimes Birth Defects Foundation, to determine the risks posed by video display terminals (VDTs) on computers. VDTs emit certain types of wavelengths of low-level radiation. There is no conclusive evidence that VDTs cause permanent health problems for workers or unborn children.

In view of the sensitivity of the fetus to various substances, pregnant women should avoid potentially hazardous environmental substances.

# INTERACTION OF BIOLOGICAL AND CONTEXTUAL INFLUENCES ON HEREDITY AND PRENATAL DEVELOPMENT

Previously, we discussed hereditary traits as being passed on from parent to child. However, a more accurate description is that the *instructions* for those traits are passed on. These instructions comprise the biological influences on heredity and prenatal development. In our discussion of contextual influences on heredity and prenatal development, we focused on teratogens to illustrate how environmental substances can alter chromosomes and genes and interfere with the development of the unborn child. Thus, we know the degree to which biological instructions are carried out depends on contextual factors. To illustrate how biological and contextual factors interact to affect development, the concept of reaction range, Rh factor and disease, and the theory of genotype-environment interaction will be explained.

## REACTION RANGE

According to Gottesman (1963), one's genetic instructions, or genotype, restrict developmental outcomes. The genotype limits the range of possible phenotypes that a person can display in response to different environments. Thus, a person inherits instructions for a trait, but these instructions are within a certain range; the environment largely determines where the individual is within that range. For example, a child can inherit instructions to be mathematically talented. Where that child will be in her potential genetic range depends on contextual factors such as encouragement, teachers, ability, availability of courses or experiences to stimulate interest and further study. Box 3.2 shows the genotype-environment interaction for a range of intellectual development or abilities.

## BLOOD INCOMPATIBILITIES: Rh FACTOR, ABO

*Rh* is a genetically dominant substance found in red blood cells. Those having the factor are called Rh positive; those who do not have the factor are called Rh negative. Whether one has the factor has no bearing on health. The potential danger occurs when an Rh negative female and Rh positive male conceive a child.

Because Rh is dominant, the child will have the factor. When the factor is absent in the female and present in the unborn child, the disease *erythroblastosis fetalis*, a fatal form of anemia and jaundice, can result.

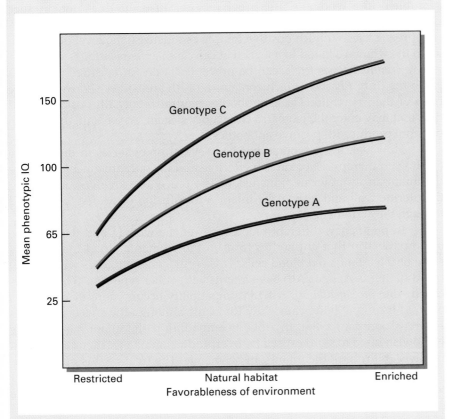

Several genotypes for intellectual development—A, B, and C—may vary in expression in more and less favorable surroundings. Depending on the environment, a person with genotype C, for example, may have an IQ phenotype of anywhere from 65 to 150, a person with genotype A one any where from 25 to 65. The range of possible scores for any genotype is its reaction range (Gottesman, 1963).

Disease resulting from Rh factor in the unborn child and absence in the women is an example of the interaction of biological and contextual fac-tors. Rh factor is biologically influenced, and whether the newborn devel-ops the disease is contextually influenced by the prenatal environment pro-vided by the woman.

For the most part, the maternal and fetal blood supplies are separat-ed by the placenta. Occasionally, however, a capillary in the placenta ruptures, which results in the mixing of a small amount of maternal and fetal blood. Likewise, some blood mixes after birth when the placenta separates from the uterine wall.

When a woman is Rh negative and the infant is Rh positive, the woman's body produces antibodies that cross the placenta and attack the infant's blood because the mother's blood "recognizes" the Rh factor in the infant's blood as a foreign substance. This condition usually does not cause a problem in a woman's first pregnancy because she does not produce enough antibodies to cause damage to the infant's blood. However, successive pregnancies with Rh positive fetuses can increase the level of antibodies in the woman's blood to a level that can cause *erythroblastosis fetalis*.

*Erythroblastosis fetalis* can be prevented if an Rh negative woman is given the drug *Rhogam*, which contains anti-Rh antibodies shortly after the birth of the first child. These antibodies neutralize any Rh positive blood cells that may enter the woman's circulatory system. As a result, the woman does not produce Rh positive antibodies.

However, if the woman has had several pregnancies in the absence of Rhogam therapy, Rhogam is ineffective and the only treatment is to give the infant an intrauterine transfusion. The procedure involves puncturing the uterine wall and giving the infant a transfusion of Rh negative blood through the abdomen.

In pregnancy, different blood types of the woman and fetus can be incompatible in that antibodies form in the woman's blood that destroy some of the infant's red blood cells. This occurs when mothers with type O blood (father is A, B, or AB) have infants with either type A or B blood; it is called *ABO incompatibility*. ABO incompatibility occurs more than twice as often as incompatibility caused by Rh factor, although the effects are not as severe (Goodman, 1986). In ABO incompatibility, the infant has jaundice (yellowish tinge to skin) caused by overproduction of a waste product from the liver (bilirubin); the infant can be anemic. The treatment is phototherapy; the naked infant, with eyes protected, is placed under a fluorescent light to break up the bilirubin that has accumulated in tissues so it then can be excreted. A blood transfusion is performed in severe cases.

## GENOTYPE-ENVIRONMENT INTERACTION

Some developmental psychologists theorize that genotypes influence environments (Scarr & McCartney, 1983; Plomin, DeFries & McClearn, 1990) in that the environment we seek depends in part on our genotypes; people make their own environments to some extent. For example, if a parent has genes to excel in reading, that parent probably will have a lot of books in the house and will read to the children.

According to Plomin and colleagues (1990), and Scarr and McCartney (1983), parents not only provide genes to children, they provide environments. Because the children inherit genes from the parents, children are more likely predisposed to be affected by the environments their parents provide. Thus, a correlation exists between the influence of one's genotype and the influence of one's environment. Three types of genotype-environment correlations are *passive, evocative,* and *active.*

**Passive genotype-environment correlations** result from the fact that parents provide both genes and environments for their offspring. Because offspring share some genes with their parents, their genotypes will correlate with the environment provided to them by their parents. Intellectually gifted parents provide intellectually stimulating environments for their children and genes for intellectual giftedness. Thus, the children's intellectually gifted genotypes correlate with their intellectually gifted environment.

**Evocative genotype–environment correlations** result from the fact that genotypically different individuals evoke different responses from their social and physical environments. Happy, extroverted children are more likely to engage others in social interaction compared with moody, shy children. Thus, they experience a warmer and more responsive environment.

**Active genotype–environment correlations**, or niche picking, result from the fact that individuals seek out environments most compatible with their genotypic predispositions. Jennifer was shy; she preferred solitary activities to group activities. When she was preschool age, she liked to draw, play with dolls and her tea set. When she was in high school, she preferred running and swimming. Thus, Jennifer, presumably influenced by her genes, chose niches while growing up, which in turn, influenced her adult personality and behavior.

According to Scarr and McCartney (1983), the importance of passive, evocative, and active gene influences changes during the course of development. Early in life the passive genotype-environment plays a significant role because activities and experiences are chosen for infants and toddlers by parents.

As children enter preschool and school and they pursue their own interests, choose friends, and are exposed to different adults, the evocative and active genotype-environments become increasingly important. The more experiences one has, the more chances one has to evoke or elicit reactions from others. In addition, the more experiences one has, the more niches one is exposed to; thus, the more likely that an individual will find the niche most compatible with his genotype.

In summary, development results from continual transactions between the person and his environment. In other words, it is the expression of our genotypes in the contexts of our environments.

# CRITICAL THINKING & YOU

**D**ennis and Kathy were heavy drug users while in their twenties. After they married, they decreased their habit, doing drugs on weekends and a few drinks during the week, so they could maintain their jobs. When Kathy turned 30, she realized she wanted a stable home and children. Dennis was tired of never getting ahead because all the profits from his business were buying drugs. So they both decided to enter a drug-rehabilitation program. They also joined Alcoholics Anonymous. Meanwhile, they had stopped using contraception, but Kathy still was not pregnant. After a year of trying to conceive, she went to the physician, as did Dennis. After many tests, it was found that Kathy did not ovulate regularly and Dennis's sperm count was slightly below normal. Kathy was given hormones to regulate menses, and Dennis's sperm was collected and frozen to artificially inseminate Kathy on ovulation. After three unsuccessful attempts, Kathy finally was pregnant. Her elation lasted two weeks when an excruciating pain on her left side forced her to the hospital. Kathy was diagnosed with ectopic pregnancy (fertilized ovum grew in the fallopian tube instead of descending to the uterus). A portion of the left fallopian tube was surgically removed.

Four months later, Kathy was pregnant. However, soon she experienced the same excruciating pain, this time on the right side. After recovering from the shock and disappointment of a second ectopic pregnancy, Kathy researched the options. Kathy was 33 and Dennis was 35. They could adopt a child, try in vitro fertilization, or Dennis could artificially inseminate a surrogate. They chose in vitro fertilization.

Kathy was given drugs to stimulate multiple ovulation. Several eggs were removed and fertilized by Dennis's sperm in a specially prepared dish. When several eggs began to divide, three embryos were selected and implanted directly into Kathy's uterus through the cervix. She had been given hormones to prepare the uterine lining for implantation. Kathy's condition was checked every week. Twelve weeks later, the physician heard two heartbeats.

**ANALYSIS:** Review this chapter and describe the risks Kathy and the infants face in this pregnancy.

**SYNTHESIS:** List the benefits of Kathy and Dennis having two healthy babies. Include available tests. Compare these benefits to the risks.

**EVALUATION:** Do you think Kathy and Dennis made a wise decision in choosing in vitro fertilization? Why or why not? (Consider the possibility of bringing two unhealthy infants into the world.)

# SUMMARY

- Heredity refers to the genetic characteristics that are transmitted from parents to children at conception. Prenatal development refers to the period of development from conception to birth.
- The life of each person begins the moment of conception when the sperm from the father unites with the ovum from the mother to form a zygote.
- The growth and development of every living organism depend on the growth and multiplication of its cells. Every cell in the human body has 46 chromosomes that come in 23 pairs. The sex cells, ova and sperm, have 23 single chromosomes.
- Body cells multiply and divide by mitosis, and sex cells multiply and divide by meiosis.
- Chromosomes duplicate themselves before cell division by adding certain chemicals to the DNA molecule. The molecule, which is a double helix, then splits.
- When a sex cell divides during meiosis, sometimes the chromosomes do not separate from each other or part of a chromosome breaks. This causes the resulting ovum or sperm to have too many or too few chromosomes. Zygotes with abnormal numbers of chromosomes usually spontaneously abort, but sometimes they develop into children who are born.
- Each chromosome is made up of units called genes. Genes are the segments of the chromosomes where the specific sets of instructions called heredity are recorded. Genes are made up of DNA.
- An individual has two genes coded for each form of inherited characteristic or portion of it. Like chromosomes, these genes are paired and are called alleles. Like alleles for a trait are homozygous; different alleles for a trait are heterozygous. When the alleles are heterozygous, one is dominant and the other is recessive. Genes expressed visibly make up the person's phenotype, whereas those that are masked and those expressed make up the person's genotype.
- Occasionally, in a heterozygous condition both alleles express themselves in the individual's phenotype. This is called co-dominance.
- Generally, genetic abnormalities can be inherited through three ways: autosomal dominant inheritance, autosomal recessive inheritance, or sex-linked inheritance.
- Genetic counseling is a medical procedure that helps couples understand their chances of bearing a child with a genetic disorder and assists them in making choices as to the best course.
- Diagnostic procedures involve blood tests, amniocentesis, chorionic villi sampling (CVS), ultrasound, fetoscopy, and alpha-fetoprotein (AFP) testing. Preimplantation diagnosis is used in assisted reproduction.
- The first phase of prenatal development is the germinal period from conception to implantation. The second phase is the embryonic period, which lasts until the end of week eight after conception. The beginning of the third month until the end of pregnancy is the fetal period.
- Any substance the mother is exposed to or ingests that crosses the placenta affects the unborn child. Teratogens are environmental agents that cause damage during the prenatal period. Teratogens can have varied effects depending on the age of the unborn child at the time of exposure.
- During prenatal development, each major organ system or body part has a critical period when it is most sensitive to teratogenic agents; the period when they are developing most rapidly and taking shape.
- Biology and context interact to influence heredity and prenatal environment in terms of reaction range, which refers to one's genotype restricting the range of possible phenotypes that a person can display in response to different environments.
- Biology and context also interact to influence development in blood incompatibilities, such as Rh factor and ABO.
- Biology and context interact to influence development in genotype-environment interactions. Genotypes influence environments in that the environment one seeks out depends, in part, on one's genotype. There are passive genotype-environment correlations, evocative genotype-environment correlations, and active genotype-environment correlations.

## RELATED READINGS

Apgar, V., & Beck, J. (1973). *Is my baby all right?* New York: Trident Press.

Bellino, J.H., & Wilson, J. (1985). *You can have a baby.* New York: Crown.

Goodman, R.M. (1986). *Planning for a healthy baby: A guide to genetic and environmental risks*. New York: Oxford University Press.

Kitzinger, S. (1985). *Birth over thirty*. New York: Penguin.

Nilsson, L., Ingelman-Sundberg, A., & Wirsen, C. (1966). *A child is born: The drama of life before birth*. New York: Delacorte Press.

Plomin, R. (1990). *Nature and nurture: An introduction to human behavioral genetics*. Pacific Grove, CA: Brooks/Cole.

Singer, S. (1982). *Human genetics* (2nd ed.). New York: Freeman.

Walters, W., & Singer, P. (Eds.). (1982). *Test-tube babies*. New York: Oxford University Press.

Watson, J. (1985). *The double helix: Being a personal account of the discovery of the structure of DNA*. New York: Freeman.

## ACTIVITY

To learn about possible genetic diseases in your family, make a family health tree. Include yourself, parents, grandparents, great grandparents.

1. Begin with yourself and work downward, filling in the spaces for parents,
2. grandparents,
3. and great grandparents.
4. Include in each person's box the information gathered about brothers and sisters. If a person is living, try to leave room for later entries. (In some cases, you may need to attach an additional piece of paper for this information.)

For each person in the tree, make a list of his siblings, parents, grandparents, and great grandparents.

For each relative write down each person's significant medical conditions or disorders using the list below as a guide.

Put each relative's information on a card and attach it to the appropriate spot on the tree.

## DISORDERS TO INCLUDE ON THE FAMILY HEALTH TREE

alcoholism
allergies
arthritis
asthma
blood diseases (*hemophilia, sickle cell disease, thalassemia, also called Cooley anemia*)
cancer (*Several forms have shown a familial relationship, most notably breast, bowel, colon, ovarian, skin, and stomach. Some evidence also suggests a familial connection in leukemia and lung cancer.*)
cardiovascular disease (*high blood pressure, atherosclerosis, heart attack, hyperlipidemia, stroke, congenital heart defects*)
congenital abnormalities at birth
cystic fibrosis
diabetes
Down syndrome
dwarfism
epilepsy
hearing disorders
Huntington disease
hypertension (*high blood pressure*)
liver diseases (*particularly hepatitis*)

mental illness (*particularly manic–depressive disorders, schizophrenia*)
mental retardation (*for example, Down syndrome, PKU*)
migraine headaches
miscarriages
multiple sclerosis
muscular dystrophy
myasthenia gravis
obesity
phenylketonuria (*PKU*)
respiratory diseases (*particularly emphysema, bacterial pneumonia, tuberculosis*)
Rh disease
sickle cell disease or trait
skin disorders (particularly psoriasis)
sudden infant death (SIDS)
suicide
systemic lupus erythematosus
thyroid disorders
Tay-Sachs disease
visual disorders (*cataracts, dyslexia, glaucoma, retinitis pigmentosa*)

# 4

# Childbirth and the Newborn

## OUTLINE

*There are but three events in a man's life:*
*birth, life and death...*

**Jean De La Bruyere**

## ABOUT CHILDBIRTH

Robin woke in the middle of the night with a slight ache in her lower back that was not unlike the sensations experienced several days before menstruation. She turned on her side to relieve the discomfort as the bulge in her abdomen prevented sleeping on her stomach. She must have dozed off, because she remembers awakening to cramps and thinking, "I can't be getting my period, I'm pregnant." Robin had no idea that what she was experiencing were uterine contractions signaling the beginning of *labor,* although she had read books and taken prenatal classes. The reason she did not suspect she was in labor was the due date was two weeks away. The due date is usually approximated to be 280 days after a woman's last menses. Not wanting to wake Lloyd with her tossing and turning, she decided to go to the other room to read. When she stood up, she felt a gush of liquid from between her legs. Her first thought was that she had lost control of her bladder, but then she realized what had happened—her baby was ready to be born because the amniotic sac had just broken. She could not contain her excitement. By the time Robin and Lloyd got into the car, the contractions were stronger and closer together. All Robin could think of was that she was finally going to meet the infant that had been growing inside her.

It took Robin and Lloyd 45 minutes to get to the hospital. Lloyd took care of registering while Robin was ushered to the examining room. She was extremely uncomfortable. She told the physician she felt tremendous pressure in the lower part of her abdomen. When Lloyd came into the room, the physician described what Robin was experiencing, "Imagine you were trying to excrete a grapefruit."

Robin's experience about the onset of labor was normal, although the amniotic sac does not break until later in many women.

**Labor** encompasses the complete birth process from the first uterine contraction to the delivery of the infant and placenta. The duration of labor can last one hour or continue for several days. It can vary according to the mother's physical condition, how many children she has had, and the size or position of the infant. The normal labor time for first births is about 14 hours.

For the infant to be born (figure 4.1), the cervix, which is the opening at the bottom of the uterus into the vagina, must thin and widen about 10 centimeters (about four inches). This is known as *effacement.* Before the onset of labor the *cervix* is thick and narrow, measuring less than two centimeters (about ⅘ inch). This opening up, or dilation, occurs in the *first stage*

**The first stage of labor**

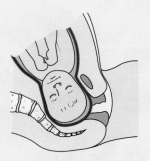 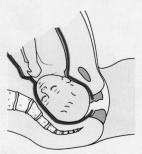 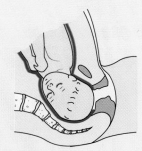

In early labor, where effacement, or thinning, has occurred and the cervix is starting to dilate.

The continuation of dilation of the cervix.

Approaching full dilation of the cervix.

**The second stage of labor**

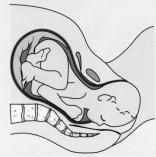 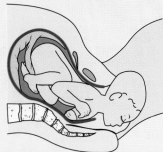

Face down, the baby's head is pressed against the perineum, which gradually stretches, widening the vaginal opening.

The baby's skull extends as it sweeps up over the perineum. The top of the skull and then the brow emerge first.

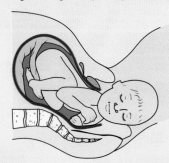 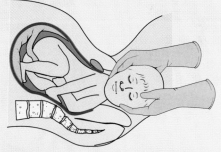

Once the head is born, the shoulders rotate on the pelvis, turning the head to left or right.

The top shoulder is born first, after which the rest of the body slides out easily.

## FIGURE 4.1
## THE FIRST TWO STAGES OF LABOR
**The first stage of childbirth begins with effacement and continues through a period of labor until the cervix is fully dilated. During the second stage of labor, which is shorter, the fetus pushes through the cervix, the vagina and its opening, and is born. (Adapted from Clarke-Stewart, Friedman & Koch, 1985)**

*of labor.* It is the longest stage, averaging about 12 hours for first births. It starts when contractions of the uterus become regular, occurring every 15 to 20 minutes and lasting from 15 to 60 seconds, and ends when the cervix is fully dilated and the connections between the pelvic bones become more flexible. Once this occurs, contractions occur about one minute apart. The infant, usually head first, pushes through the cervix into the vagina, beginning the *second stage of labor.* At this point, the woman is usually taken to a

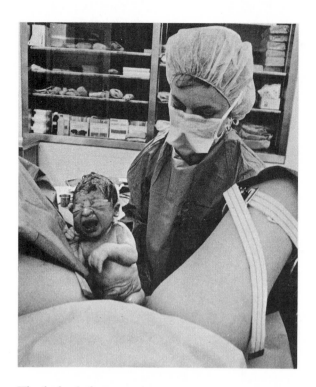

The baby is born.

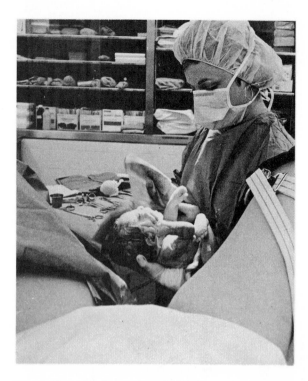

The infant is cleaned and dried.

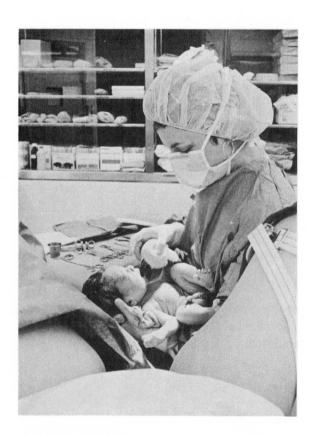

Mucus is removed from breathing passageways.

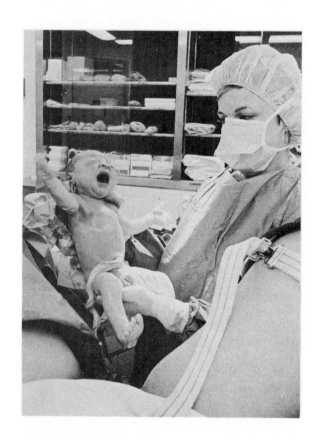

First assessment is made.

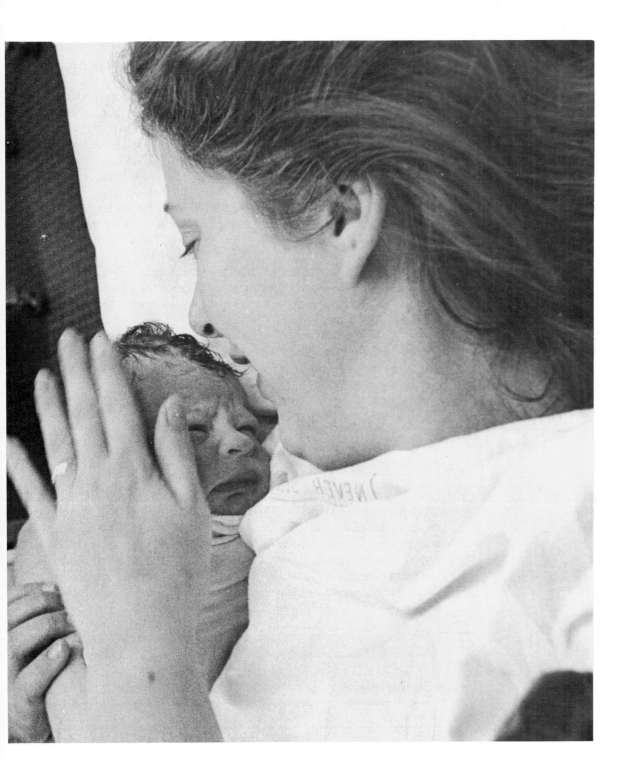

**Mother greets her newborn child.**

room specially equipped for delivery of the infant. Usually, a physician and a nurse (or two) are present.

The second stage of labor is much shorter than the first, ranging from 30 minutes to two hours. Robin was told to push. Every time her uterus contracted, she pushed. She was out of breath. Everyone kept encouraging her to push. She was dripping with sweat, feeling as though her blood vessels would burst every time she pushed, and aching like she never ached before. Finally, the head emerged. The physician suctioned mucus and amniotic fluid from the infants' mouth and nose. With another push, the shoulders emerged. Then came the shout, "It's a girl!"

Jennifer squealed as she was cleaned. The physician clamped and cut the umbilical cord as soon as it stopped pulsating. Jennifer now was on her own to breathe, circulate her own blood, excrete wastes, and adjust to a new environment.

After the birth of the infant, the placenta begins to pull away from the surface of the uterus and is expelled after several contractions. This is referred to as the *afterbirth*. This *third stage of labor* usually lasts from five minutes to 30 minutes.

While Robin was waiting for the afterbirth to be expelled, she stared at her daughter. Jennifer's functions and reflexes were being tested, and the physician said everything appeared fine. She was put in an *isolette*, a special crib in which temperature can be regulated.

While childbirth is a biological process, the moment of birth necessitates the beginning of a social process to ensure the survival of the infant. The infant must be nourished, and its needs must be met. Newborns come equipped with certain behavioral and sensory capacities that enable them to adapt to the world outside the womb. How caregivers respond to the infant's signals influences a newborn's development.

# NEONATAL ASSESSMENT

When an infant is born in a hospital, a simple test devised by Virginia Apgar (Apgar, 1953), known as the **Apgar scale**, is given one minute after birth, and again five minutes later (table 4.1). The newborn, or *neonate's*, heart rate, breathing, muscle tone, circulation, and reflexes are tested, and the neonate is given a score of 0, 1, or 2 at each measurement. If the score is between 7 and 10, the neonate is considered in good condition, which means that she is breathing well, crying, pink in color, and active. Infants who score 4 through 6 need help, usually supplementary oxygen. Infants

## THE APGAR SCALE

### TABLE 4.1

| Characteristic | 0 | 1 | 2 |
|---|---|---|---|
| Heart rate | Absent | Slow (below 100) | Rapid (over 100) |
| Respiratory effort (breathing) | Absent | Irregular, slow | Good: neonate is crying |
| Muscle tone | Flaccid, limp | Weak, inactive | Strong, active |
| Color (circulation) | Blue, pale | Body pink, extremities blue | Entirely pink |
| Reflex irritability | No response | Grimace | Coughing, sneezing, crying |

(Apgar, 1953)

who score 0, 1, 2, or 3 are generally limp, unresponsive, pale, not breathing, and possibly without a heart beat. These neonates are in critical condition.

While the Apgar scale assesses physical condition, or *physiological* responses, it does not assess *behavioral,* or adaptive, responses to the environment. The **Neonatal Behavioral Assessment Scale (NBAS)**, developed by pediatrician T. Berry Brazelton and colleagues (Brazelton, 1973; Brazelton, Nugent & Lester, 1987) is a test of newborn adaptation based on social responses and reflexes.

Usually, the NBAS is performed on the third day after birth and then repeated several days later. A total of 20 reflexes and 26 behavioral responses are tested such as response to a scratch on the foot, a light in the eyes, and reaction to a human face. The reflexes and responses tested are categorized into four dimensions of behavior: *interactive behaviors* that influence the way a neonate adapts in the home such as alertness and cuddliness; *motor behaviors* such as reflexes, muscle tone, and hand-mouth activity; *control of physiological state* such as an infant's ability to quiet himself after being upset; and *response to stress*, such as the Moro reflex. The NBAS is useful in identifying infants at risk and classifying the type of intervention necessary to optimize the infant's development.

# BIOLOGICAL INFLUENCES ON CHILDBIRTH AND THE NEWBORN

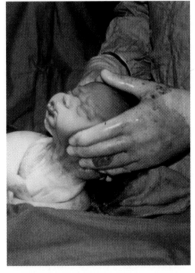

The biological influences on childbirth and a newborn pertain to the birth itself, the condition of the newborn at birth and afterward. Births that proceed normally probably have little influence on the neonate's development, but complicated births that cause stress to the woman, infant, or both can impact the neonate's development. The condition of a neonate at birth can affect how he adjusts to the world, thereby influencing development.

## BIRTHS WITH COMPLICATIONS

Some births are prolonged and complicated and, as a result, can influence development if medical intervention does not occur in time.

### Medically Assisted Births

Medical assistance can involve the use of medication, instruments such as forceps, or surgery. An example of a birth requiring medical assistance is one in which a neonate enters the birth canal in the breech position (feet or buttocks first) instead of head first, face down. Breech births can result in a prolonged and difficult labor. The physician may have to assist the birth by giving medication to the woman and using forceps to pull out the infant. Both actions can have consequences for the neonate. Studies have found that infants whose mothers received large doses of medication during the birth process were generally sluggish, inattentive, and irritable (Brackbill, McManus & Woodward, 1985). The duration of these effects is controversial because it is difficult to tell whether the infant's behavior is a result of drugs during labor or the mother's response to the infant.

Using forceps to assist delivery can cause brain damage or skull fracture to an infant. However, these consequences also could occur as a result of a difficult birth without assistance.

**According to the Public Citizen Health Research Group, no more than 12 percent of all births should be caesarean deliveries, but the rate in the United States was 22.7 percent in 1990. In 1970, it was 5.5 percent. The rate in England is less than 10 percent.**

This Hewlett-Packard medical imaging system helps cardiologists in the diagnosis and ongoing care of neonatal and pediatric patients through the use of its high quality images and annotation capabilities.

When a neonate is in the breech position, or is too large to fit through the mother's pelvis, the physician may have to perform a **cesarean section**, or surgical delivery. In a cesarean section, an incision is made in the abdominal wall, and the infant is removed from the uterus. Other conditions warranting a cesarean section are presence of maternal infection such as herpes, placental blockage (partial or complete) to the birth canal entrance, or presence of signs of fetal distress (low heart rate). Other than the risk of infection to the woman, cesarean births carry certain risks to a neonate. Infants born via cesarean section have lower levels of stress hormones than do infants born vaginally. These hormones facilitate respiration and metabolism (Trevarthen, 1987).

## Anoxia

During some births, a neonate's supply of oxygen may be obstructed before the head has emerged from the vagina, and the neonate can breathe alone. This can be due to the placenta detaching from the uterine wall or the umbilical cord becoming twisted or squeezed. **Anoxia**, or lack of oxygen, is a leading cause of brain damage in newborns and can result in *cerebral palsy*, or lack of muscle control (Apgar & Beck, 1974). The extent of damage to the infant depends on when the anoxia occurs and how long it lasts.

## NEWBORNS AT RISK

About 9 percent of all American infants are born prematurely. This percentage, rather than those of low-birth weight, account for 85 percent of newborn deaths not caused by congenital malformations (Arjavalingam, 1989). Premature, or *preterm*, infants are at risk because of immaturity of organ systems and lack of reserves. The degree of risk depends primarily on the level of maturity.

## Preterm and Low-Birth Weight Infants

Most infants are born about 280 days (40 weeks) after the woman's last menses. The time the neonate is carried in the womb is called the period of **gestation**. If the infant is one or two weeks off schedule, she usually adjusts to life outside the womb normally. However, infants born before the 37th gestational week, known as **preterm babies**, require more time to adjust and need more professional care. The most critical problem for preterm infants is respiration. Respiratory distress syndrome occurs because the air sacs in the lungs are not fully developed; they do not produce enough **surfactant**, a fatty substance that coats the air sacs and aids in transporting oxygen into and carbon dioxide out of the lungs.

If labor begins prematurely and if time permits, fetal lung maturity can be accelerated by giving the woman corticosteroids so that the fetus can be delivered safely within 48 to 72 hours. These drugs increase fetal lung maturation to a degree that would normally take several weeks in the uterus (Goodman, 1986).

Preterm babies can also be treated after birth with artificial surfactant or surfactant obtained from human or bovine amniotic fluid (Bobak, Jensen & Zalar, 1989). Oxygen therapy used to be the only treatment but was found to cause damage to preterm infants' retinas and to their lungs. Now, when oxygen therapy is necessary, the doses are carefully monitored (Bobak, Jensen & Zalar 1989).

Other problems for preterm neonates involve inability to maintain a normal body temperature of 98.6° Fahrenheit because they have not developed an insulating layer of fat, vulnerability to infection due to underdeveloped immune systems, and digestive problems due to immaturity of the digestive organs and muscle coordination involved in taking in nourishment—many preterm infants have difficulty sucking, swallowing, and assimilating what they eat. They may not suck hard enough and may spit up most of what they take in, making intravenous feeding necessary.

A common problem for preterm infants is *hyperbilirubinemia*, excessive production of bilirubin, a chemical produced by the liver during the breakdown of red blood cells. The overproduction of bilirubin and its accumulation in the tissue cells cause the infant to have a yellowish appearance, known as **jaundice**. Many normal neonates are jaundiced for the first few days of life while their livers adjust to the task of breaking down the bilirubin so it can be excreted. When the liver has accomplished its task, the infant's appearance returns to normal. In preterm infants, however, the liver often is too immature to break down the accumulated bilirubin. The danger of excessive bilirubin is that it can cause brain damage. It has been found that putting the infant under special fluorescent lights, while shielding the eyes, helps break up the excess bilirubin (Barclay, 1985). In severe cases, a blood transfusion can be performed.

The average weight of an infant at birth is 7 ½ pounds, and the average length is about 20 inches. Birth size is related to parents' size and the woman's health and nutritional status. Neonates born weighing less than 5 ½ pounds (2,500 grams) are called **low-birth weight** infants. They may or may not be preterm. Some neonates are born at term but weigh less than normal for their gestational age; they are called *small-for-dates*, and are not as developed as they should be for the amount of time spent in the womb. This may be due to maternal malnutrition, maternal disease, or medical problems. Low birth weight also can be due to multiple births and abnormalities in the placenta or umbilical cord.

Small-for-dates experience the same problems as preterm babies. Any newborn who weighs less than 3 ¼ pounds (1,500 grams) at birth faces a struggle to survive. The lower the birth weight, the less likely the infant will survive and the more likely he will suffer developmental consequences (Goldberg & DiVitto, 1983).

Developmental outcomes also depend on factors other than weight and gestational age. One factor is the availability of intensive care. When a neonate is born prematurely, some physiological systems are not developed enough to operate. The lungs may not exchange gases or oxygenate the blood effectively. The infant may not be able to take food by mouth or to properly maintain the body temperature. Most problems encountered in the early days of a preterm infant's life originate in these physiological inadequacies. If the infant's organ systems cannot function properly, then surgical, mechanical, or chemical intervention must accomplish these tasks. Examples of interventions are a respirator, intravenous feeding, and blood transfusion. Further, the infant who cannot manage these bodily functions independently also is highly vulnerable to other problems, such as infections, breakage of delicate blood vessels (especially dangerous if it occurs in the brain), and lung disease.

The other factor influencing developmental outcomes is the family environment. Prematurity has an effect on parents. Premature infants are

tiny and fragile; they are also less responsive and more irritable than fu
term infants (Brazelton, Nugent & Lester, 1987). These characteristics make
more difficult for parents initially to become attached to the infant.

Additionally, premature infants often must spend their first weeks
the hospital in isolettes that are heated and that provide protection again
infection. That means parents can only visit; they do not have enough time
learn about their infants' rhythms and idiosyncrasies in the beginning. Thu
attachment is delayed. Before the newborn is discharged from the hospit
women show less confidence in dealing with their preterm infant than
mothers of full-term infants. They are less likely to hold the infant close a
cuddle compared with mothers of full-term infants. They report being afra
of the infants' fragility (Campos et al., 1983; Field, 1990).

Despite the immediate medical problems of low-birth weight infan
long-term follow-up studies show that most have few developmental proble
(Field, 1990). Some, especially those who weigh less than 3 ½ pounds at bir
however, are more likely to have speech and hearing deficits, learning d
abilities, exhibit hyperactivity and behavior problems than normal weig
neonates, yet fall within the range of normal intellectual development (Fie
1986).

## CHARACTERISTICS AND CAPABILITIES
## OF THE NEWBORN

The characteristics and capabilities of the newborn are both interesti
and amazing. We will discuss the newborn's appearance, adaptation to t
world, reflexes present at birth, and behavior.

## Appearance

The newborn's head is large in proportion to the rest of the body.
fact, the head represents one quarter of the neonate's total size. The ne
looks short and stubby, and the arms and legs are curled up. The skin is r
and wrinkly; the nose can be flattened and the forehead can be misshape
The eyes can be swollen and puffy because of the silver nitrate drops routir
ly put into newborns' eyes to protect them from getting infected with gon
rhea, in case their mothers have an undetected case. In time, however, t
infant's features "normalize."

## Adaptations

The neonate has certain adaptations to adjust to life outside the wom
The lungs have to take in oxygen, whereas before birth oxygen was receiv
through the umbilical cord. The neonate also has to circulate her own bloc
whereas before birth the mother circulated the infant's blood. The gastroi
testinal system must prepare to accept nutrition from the mouth rather th
from the umbilical cord. Digestive enzymes begin to be manufactured
break down food into usable products and waste to be channeled out of t
body.

Still another adjustment is that of maintaining the body temperature. T
temperature of the womb was constant, the infant's new environment is not cc
stant. The layers of fat that develop during the last couple of months of fe
life enable healthy full-term infants to keep their body temperatures constar
despite changes in air temperature. Neonates also maintain body temperatu
by increasing their activity in response to a drop in air temperature.

## Circumcision

Males are born with a foreskin on the penis. **Circumcision** involves the surgical removal of the foreskin. The procedure usually involves cutting and requires that the infant be restrained. No anesthetic is used. Most male newborns in the United States are circumcised because of the belief that it facilitates hygienic care of the penis. The procedure is done on the second or third day after birth.

## Reflexes

Neonates are endowed with certain adaptive responses, or reflexes, that help them survive. These reflexes are inborn and involuntary. They are controlled by the spinal cord and midbrain. An example of a reflex that has survival value is sucking. Other reflexes, such as grasping, present in the newborn may be remnants of human evolutionary history and have had, at some time, adaptive significance (Fentress & McLeod, 1986). In evaluating reflexes, information can be gained about the maturity and function of a newborn's neuromuscular system (Fiorentine, 1973). Some reflexes gradually disappear over the first year of life as the *cerebral cortex*, the part of the brain that controls motor skills, attention, memory, language, and spatial understanding, begins to direct and control behavior. Thus, the absence or lack of disappearance of reflexes during the first year can indicate that the child's brain or nervous system is not functioning properly. Some examples of newborn reflexes are presented in table 4.2 (page 113).

## Behavioral States

When you first look at a newborn, the behavior appears to be sporadic and disorganized. The mouth moves almost constantly, the eyes flutter, the arms and legs flex and extend, sometimes the whole body quivers. If you observe a newborn more closely over time, you can see that the activities occur in regular cycles. By observing many healthy newborns, Peter Wolff (1966) was able to identify seven distinct neonatal states based on arousal or activity:

1. *Regular or quiet sleep.* The infant is at full rest. The eyelids are closed and still. There is low muscle tone and motor activity. Breathing is regular. This state is also called *nonrapid eye movement (NREM)* sleep.
2. *Irregular or active sleep.* Breathing is irregular, muscle tone and motor activity are increased, including facial grimaces and smiles. There are occasional rapid eye movements that can be seen through the eyelids. This state is also termed *rapid eye movement (REM)*, or dream, sleep and represents about 50 percent of the sleep of newborns.
3. *Periodic sleep.* The neonate alternates between regular and irregular sleep. There are bursts of deep, slow breathing alternating with bouts of rapid shallow breathing.
4. *Drowsiness.* The infant is relatively inactive. The eyes open and close intermittently; when they are open, they have a dull, glazed appearance and remain unfocused. Breathing is variable but more rapid than in regular sleep.

*(continued on page 112)*

**F.Y.I.**

Jews and Moslems practice circumcision as a religious rite. It is done eight days after birth by a specially trained religious person.

**Babinski reflex**

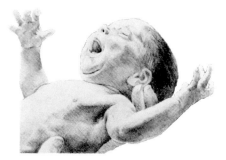

**Moro reflex**

*(continued from page 111)*

5. *Alert inactivity or quiet alert.* The infant's body is relatively inactive, quiet, and relaxed. The eyes are open, attentive, and focused. Respiration is constant in frequency and depth and is more rapid than in regular sleep.

6. *Waking activity or active alert.* The infant shows frequent bursts of diffuse motor activity of the limbs, trunk, and head. The face can be relaxed or tense and wrinkled as if the infant is about to cry, and respiration is irregular. The eyes are open but not alert or focused.

7. *Distress.* The infant enters this state by first whimpering then becoming more agitated in her cries and motor activities. The face is red and contorted into a grimace. The legs kick, and the arms flex and extend.

Knowledge of states is important because it enables caregivers to be more responsive to their infant's physical, social, and emotional needs. Infants respond to stimuli differently in different states.

Prechtl (1974) demonstrated that state affects both behavioral sensitivity and responsivity in the newborn. Whether and how newborn infants respond to actual, visual, and auditory stimuli depends on their state—in *alert inactivity*, or *quiet alertness*, for example, an infant can attend to a voice that has no effect on the infant in a period of *distress*.

Infant states also influence adults' behaviors—adults may rock and soothe crying neonates that are distressed instead of trying to interest them in other activities.

The *quiet alert* state is the optimal period for reciprocal parent-child interactions. In this state, the infant visually scans the environment and is more responsive to external stimuli than when asleep, distressed, or drowsy. This state however, is the shortest in duration. It is in this state that infants begin to extract information from and adjust to the environment both social and physical. During these moments, the infant can examine and become familiar with the features of a parent's face, or else study the mobile hanging over the crib. Most of what infants learn about objects, people, and their own abilities are acquired during periods of quiet alertness and attentiveness. Thus, developmental increases in the amount of time spent in awake and alert states permit infants important opportunities to examine and learn about the environment (Lamb & Bornstein, 1987).

Changes of state are usually caused by changing levels of stimulation—especially continuous, repetitive stimulation. Researchers have found that when a crying infant is picked up and held upright on the caregiver's shoulder, he usually stops crying, becomes alert, and begins to scan the environment (Korner & Grobstein, 1966). The change in state from distress to alertness when picked up in such a manner may be due to *vestibular stimulation*, sensations controlled by organs in the ear that register changes in body position (Gregg, Huffner & Korner, 1976). If regular soothing of this sort induces a state of visual alertness, an infant regularly picked up for crying will have earlier and more frequent opportunities to scan the environment than one who is left crying in the crib.

There are individual differences among infants in terms of states. *Temperament*, individual differences in physiological responsiveness, can have something to do with how easily a crying infant is soothed (Chess & Thomas, 1987). A neonate with a difficult temperament who is not easily

## TABLE 4.2

| Name of Reflex | Testing | Response |
|---|---|---|
| Rooting | Touch skin around cheek and mouth | Turns toward cheek being stroked |
| Startle | Sudden loud noise | Both arms thrown down and away from body then quickly returned |
| Moro | Quickly lower infant's position downward | Arms are thrown open and quickly brought back together over chest |
| Grasping | Press object or finger into infant's hand | Infant tightly curls fingers around object or finger |
| Stepping | Hold infant upright with feet touching a firm surface | Infant moves feet up and down in walking-like movements |
| Tonic neck (TNR) or "fencing position" | Infant is lying face up with head turned in one direction | Infant extends arm and leg on the side toward which the head is turned; the opposite arm and leg are flexed (pulled in toward the body) |
| Plantar | Place pressure against ball of the infant's foot | Infant will curl toes |
| Blinking | Flash light into infant's eyes | Infant will blink |
| Sucking | Place nipple-like object in infant's mouth | Infant will suck |

soothed can make the parents feel anxious, irritable, and incompetent. The parent may withdraw from the relationship by ignoring the crying or become abusive by screaming or hitting the child.

Time spent in the various states changes as the infant develops. In the first month after birth, infants sleep most of the time—on the average about 16 to 20 hours per day—with frequent, alternating periods of sleep and wakefulness evenly distributed across the day and night. By 4 ½ to 6 weeks of age, fewer periods of longer duration occur, and infants have more active states during the day and more sleep states occurring at night.

As the infant gets older, sleep and wakeful periods of similar duration become coordinated with one another. By six months of age, the longest sleep period immediately follows the longest waking period, an association that adds to the organization and predictability of a neonate's daily cycle (Coons & Guilleminault, 1984). This makes life with the infant less stressful to the parents. They can get an uninterrupted period of sleep, can play with the baby or go places while the infant is awake, and can generally settle into a fairly predictable routine of mealtimes, naptimes, playtime, bath, and so on.

Sleep patterns change as the neonate gets older, as does the type of sleep. At birth, infants spend about half their sleeping hours in **Rapid Eye Movement (REM) sleep**, a state of irregular sleep in which the eyes move rapidly beneath the eyelids with brain wave activity more typical of wakefulness than regular (Non-REM) sleep. By age six months, REM sleep becomes less frequent, leveling to about 25 to 30 percent of total sleep time.

Neonates have their REM cycle before regular sleep. For neonates it can be a source of stimulation that enables the higher brain centers to mature (Roffwarg, Muzio & Dement, 1966; Bloom & Lazerson, 1988). Perhaps the reason REM sleep declines by six months of age is that the infant is awake for longer periods of time and is being stimulated by the environment. Thus, the need for self-stimulation from the brain decreases because the infant is stimulating the self through the senses—by what is seen, heard, felt, or tasted. When an infant under one year mysteriously dies while sleeping, it is called *sudden infant death syndrome*. Box 4.1 describes what are thought to be some explanations.

## Box 4.1   SUDDEN INFANT DEATH SYNDROME

The cause of **sudden infant death syndrome (SIDS)**, the sudden and unexplained death of an apparently healthy infant who stops breathing during sleep, is unknown. Infants who score less than seven on the Apgar scale and experience respiratory distress as neonates are most susceptible. The incidence of SIDS is greater during winter among infants who are 2 through 4 months of age.

Some investigators think a virus is responsible, especially a respiratory infection. Others point out that victims of SIDS usually have irregular respiratory patterns characterized by periods of **apnea**, spontaneous interruptions in breathing, that are frequent and usually long (Steinschneider, 1975).

Still others (Lipsitt, 1979; Rovee-Collier & Lipsitt, 1987) believe that SIDS occurs most often in two- to four-month-old infants because this is when the automatic, involuntary reflexes controlled in the lower part of the brain, called the brainstem, are diminishing in strength; and voluntary responses controlled in the upper part of the brain, the cerebral cortex, are not well established yet. Consequently, if something, such as mucus, blocks the nasal passages, a two- to four-month-old infant would not struggle for breath because the innate survival reflexes are waning and the infant has not learned protective responses to discomfort, such as blowing out the mucus.

To lessen the possibility of apnea for neonates with breathing irregularities, physicians may recommend an apnea monitor, which is attached to the infant and sounds an alarm if the breathing stops for more than 20 to 30 seconds. Parents then can wake the infant, thereby coaxing her to resume breathing.

An Austrian study (Einspieler et al., 1988) identified some specific behaviors predictive of SIDS. Researchers concluded that infants exhibiting a behavioral pattern of apathy, listlessness, and lack of interest in things, and sleepiness are at risk for SIDS. Other warning symptoms include shrill crying, lack of movement, and *cyanosis*, a bluish coloration of the skin due to insufficient oxygen in the blood.

# CONTEXTUAL INFLUENCES ON CHILDBIRTH AND THE NEWBORN

Although childbirth is a biological process, it occurs in a social context influenced by religious, cultural, economic, and political factors. For example, the social context includes those present at birth—spouse, siblings, physicians, midwives—those who care for the infant immediately after birth—mother and/or healthcare professionals. The political influence involves laws and professional codes about the location of birth, assistance that can be given to a woman and infant, and those who can give it (Eakins, 1986).

## CHILDBIRTH IN THE UNITED STATES

Today most births in the United States occur in the hospital. This represents a change in cultural attitudes over the last century. Children of past generations were born at home, assisted by a midwife, a person recognized for experience in assisting in childbirth. This was a typical practice until the twentieth century.

Around the turn of the century, medicine was recognized as a respected profession. New techniques in surgery, the discovery of drugs to lessen pain, and development of antiseptic techniques all contributed to viewing childbirth as a medical procedure. In addition, the early twentieth century maternal and child welfare movement, fueled by concern about the high maternal infant death rates, encouraged the public to think of childbirth as requiring specialized care (Eakins, 1986).

# F.Y.I.

**About 1 percent of American women choose to have homebirths.**

Since the intervention of the medical profession, the lives of thousands of women and infants have been saved. In 1915, approximately 100 of every 1,000 births resulted in the death of the infant within one year, and in almost seven of every 1,000 births, the woman died (National Center for Health Statistics, 1987). By 1991, infant deaths had been reduced to approximately 9.5 of every 1,000 births. In the same year, only seven women of every 100,000 who gave birth in the United States died of causes related to pregnancy, childbirth, or after-birth complications (U. S. Bureau of Census, 1991).

While medical childbirth uses all available and necessary medical technology including drugs, monitoring machines, and surgery to ensure a safe and comfortable delivery, it has had the consequence of isolating childbirth from a family's immediate support and traditions. Birth rituals specific to the hospital were different from birth rituals at home. In the hospital, the neonate's air passageways are suctioned, the cord is cut, the infant is weighed, washed, and placed in a nursery. Usually, the spouse is present during the birth. The woman and infant remain in the hospital for several days before going home.

At home the family members and perhaps friends gather around awaiting the birth. There might be special prayers and gifts. Everyone might get to touch the infant. Food is brought, and help with household chores is given until the woman can assume them herself.

A result of isolating birth from the family is that women today know little about birth before experiencing it, unless they become educated through courses or books. Whereas up until a century ago when births occurred at home, women were knowledgeable about the process because it was likely they observed it and may have helped.

## Hospital Birth

Birth in a hospital involves a physician and nurses in attendance during the entire delivery. When a pregnant woman enters the hospital, her readiness to deliver is determined by the timing and strength of her uterine contractions and the amount the cervix has dilated. Most hospitals allow the man to remain while the woman is in labor and also during delivery. The woman can be given a regional anesthetic, which can be a spinal or epidural block to reduce the sensation of pain in the pelvic area, or a sedative for relaxation.

The woman will likely have an **episiotomy,** a surgical incision into the perineum muscle from the end of the vagina to the anus. This procedure prevents tearing of tissue and facilitates delivery. The woman is told when to push and when to relax while the physician helps pull out the infant. The vital signs of the infant and mother (heart rate, respiration, color) are monitored throughout.

## Lamaze Method

Ferdinand Lamaze, a French obstetrician, pioneered the prepared natural childbirth method (Lamaze, 1970). The **Lamaze method** involves helping the pregnant woman build stamina and cope with the pain of childbirth in an active way to avoid, or reduce, medication.

In Lamaze training, the pregnant woman attends classes with a partner, often the father, about six weeks before birth. There they learn about the birth process and receive training in breathing and relaxing exercises.

The partner becomes the woman's coach. After several weeks of practice, the partner can offer moral and physical support to the woman during delivery. Evidence indicates that the participation reduces maternal fears and improves the woman's self-worth (Wideman & Singer, 1984; Bobak, Jensen & Zalar, 1989)

## Leboyer Method

French obstetrician, Fredrick Leboyer, believes birth should be gentle, not violent (Leboyer, 1975). Leboyer feels that hospital delivery practices can create unnecessary discomfort or trauma for the infant. He criticizes the bright lights used in most delivery rooms, viewing them as irritants to the infant's eyes. Instead, he proposes using minimal light. He also feels the infant's ears are sensitive to noise and, therefore, advocates lowered voices during delivery.

The **Leboyer method** encourages patience during the delivery process. Leboyer believes the umbilical cord should be left intact for several minutes to allow the newborn a chance to adjust to breathing air. When the cord stops pulsating, then it is cut. Meanwhile, the infant is placed on the woman's abdomen so he can be caressed. After the cord is cut, the infant is placed in a bath of warm water to simulate the familiar environment of the womb, thereby making the transition to the world less stressful.

Leboyer believes that his birthing method influences children's physical and psychological development; however, little evidence supports this claim.

Despite the absence of support for enhanced development, Leboyer's method has encouraged American hospitals to modify birthing practices to consider the physical comfort of the newborn infant.

**The philosophy of an alternative birthing center is to reduce the strangeness and anxiety often associated with a hospital childbirth.**

## Homebirth

Giving birth at home has been gaining popularity among those who feel childbirth is a natural process not a medical procedure. Homebirth is an option in uncomplicated pregnancies and is usually supervised by a *certified nurse midwife,* a nurse specially trained in homebirth procedures. Certified nurse midwives generally work in close cooperation with physicians not only in homes but also in hospitals and birthing centers. If a complication arises, a physician is on-call.

The atmosphere of a homebirth is familiar and, therefore, relaxing to the woman. Compared with a hospital birth, the cost of a homebirth is less expensive. All family members can participate in the birth and have immediate contact with the newborn. The major disadvantage to homebirth is in the event of a complication, the laboring woman must be transported to an emergency facility.

## Birthing Centers

Some hospitals provide alternatives to conventional hospital delivery. *Alternative birthing centers* (ABCs) are rooms that look like home bedrooms and not like hospital rooms. Family members are welcome, and the infant can remain with the mother after birth. Medical intervention is limited to monitoring the birth so steps can be taken if complications arise for the infant or woman.

In some areas independent birthing clinics are located near and associated with local hospitals. These clinics, however, carefully screen their

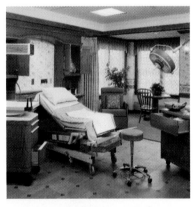

**As the second stage of labor approaches, the alternative birth center can quickly and efficiently convert into a fully equipped delivery room.**

clients to ensure they are low-risk pregnancies. Thus, most of the services consist of providing prenatal care designed to monitor pregnancies for potential problems.

## Medical Interventions

In addition to administering drugs to ease the pain of labor, other medical interventions can be necessary to ensure the safety of the woman or child. One common practice is to *induce* labor. This is done when an infant is significantly overdue or when the woman's life is at risk. Labor is induced by either rupturing the placental membranes or by giving the mother *oxytocin*, a hormone that stimulates uterine contractions. Another common procedure is cesarean section, in which the neonate is surgically removed from the mother's uterus.

## CHILDBIRTH IN OTHER CULTURES

Culture influences the experience of childbirth not only in terms of the procedures used to help the woman deliver the child, but also in the attitudes about birth. Specifically, cultures differ in values placed on children and values about marriage and childbirth. Cultures also differ in the taboos, or prohibitions, surrounding the pregnancy, birth, and care of the neonate (Clark, 1978).

## Attitudes Toward Children

The value of desiring children is illustrated by the views of the Papago Indians. Children are desired and considered a joy. To be good to young children is an obligation of adults as well as older children. Infants are passed from one person to another during visits of relatives and friends. They are cuddled and inundated with musical sounds (Aamodt, 1975).

Yet children are not valued for the sheer joy they bring in all cultures. The Ik of Northern Uganda, for example, view the birth of children as a threat to their survival. Children are regarded as useless appendages. They are not cuddled or comforted and are turned out of their parents' huts when they reach the age of three, compelled from then on to make their own way without nurturance or guidance from parents. Children are then viewed as competitors for the sacred food that exists.

## Responsibility Toward Children

In the United States when people are married and have a child, the child usually receives the father's last name, but both parents are considered legally responsible for the child's care. Paternal and maternal parents have equal status. Our system of descent, who in the family is responsible for whom and who is obligated to whom, is called **bilineal**, the descent of the child is from both maternal and paternal sides of the family. On the other hand, in other cultures, marriage has little or nothing to do with descent. The child can be regarded as descending from the mother's side or the father's side. The Hopi Indians in Arizona, for example, view the child's descent from the mother's side and so is called **matrilineal**. The mother's brother commonly is obligated to discipline and guide his sister's children, he is responsible for the children's behavior and preparation for adult life, whereas the biological father provides nurturance.

Among the Ngoni of Malawi in central Africa, the child's descent is from the father's side and is called **patrilineal**. The father's mother is

In the United States, child-rearing is traditionally and legally the responsibility of both parents.

responsible for directing the preparations for the birth and care of the child, the selection of the female to nurse the child, and the supervision of the infant care to the exclusion of the mother, who, for a time after giving birth, is isolated from the infant (Read, 1968).

## Attitudes Toward Childbirth

Childbirth is regarded in some societies as a natural event requiring no special preparation. The !Kung, a hunting and gathering society in Africa's Kalahari Desert, for example, go about their daily activities, and when the woman is ready to give birth, she does so without assistance (Shostak, 1981). The significance of treating childbirth as a natural event is that those cultures having this belief do not seek prenatal care unless something goes wrong, and then it may be too late to prevent complications for the woman or the infant. Some cultures do not interfere with nature even when woman or child is in danger.

To the Cuna Indians of Panama, childbirth is not a state of wellness but rather an illness. The expectant woman makes daily visits to the medicine man throughout her pregnancy, and she receives constant medication during labor (Stout, 1974). The significance of this attitude toward childbirth is the possible negative effect of drugs on the fetus.

Cultures all over the world have different taboos to provide protection for the woman during pregnancy and delivery as well as to provide protection for the neonate. For example, the Laguna Pueblo Indians have a naming ritual for the new infant four days after birth because the number four is considered sacred because it represents the four seasons, the four colors of the rainbow, and the four directions. Toys and charms are placed in the cradle to ensure well-being (Clark, 1978).

In the traditional Vietnamese family, the infant is swaddled in old clothes so as not to make spirits jealous and cause illness to the child (Crawford, 1968).

Thus, culture exerts an influence on the child before and after birth.

## EARLY CHILDBEARING AND ITS CONSEQUENCES

The family is the context for the development of children. A family''s ability to nurture and respond decisively to meet developmental needs of children affects how children will function as adults. The young man and woman who have children early in their lives are generally less able than their older counterparts to perform these functions because their educational attainment is shortened, their incomes are more limited, they generally have greater marital discord, and because they have more offspring (Stevens, 1980).

Compared with infants of adults, infants of teenagers begin their lives at risk. The reasons are as follows (Coalition Concerned with Adolescent Pregnancy, 1988):

The personal and social hardships of teen parenthood put both parents and infants at risk.

- Only 1 of 5 girls under age 15 receives prenatal care during the vital first three months of pregnancy.
- Increased stress and family tension lead teen mothers to attempt *(continued on following page)*

For an employed mother, the stress of returning to work, finding suitable childcare, and devoting quality time to nurturing an infant is great (Brazelton, 1985).

Support groups like LaLeche League offer assistance to women who are breastfeeding. The rationale behind such groups is to find ways of reducing emotional and physical fatigue and maximizing the joy of child rearing.

(continued from previous page)
suicide at a rate seven times greater than the national average or to more likely to be physically abusive to children compared with older childbearers.

- The lack of sound prenatal care and parenting skills is linked to the fact that children of teen parents usually have a lower intelligence quotient (IQ) and achievement test scores than the children of those who delay childbearing.
- Only half of those teens who give birth before the age 18 complete high school.
- About 54 percent of teen mothers were classified as low socioeconomic status; one-fourth currently receive Aid to Families with Dependent Children (AFDC) payment; and 61 percent of all AFDC families are headed by women who are or were teen mothers.

Thus, early childbearing makes optimal childrearing substantially more difficult. Teenage families are less likely than older parents to support the optimal development of children, especially in the early years.

## ADJUSTMENT TO PARENTHOOD AS A CONTEXT FOR CHILDBEARING

In some traditional societies, children are regarded as assets because they contribute to the survival and economic functioning of the family. Therefore, families in traditional societies, such as those in Mexican villages, are generally large. Children in these societies gradually assume adult responsibilities. For example, six-year-olds may be caring for younger children, cooking, and harvesting plants. Adjustment to parenthood in such societies is usually smooth because many family members are available to share the responsibilities of caring for a newborn and can do other family chores.

In industrialized societies such as the United States, children are generally regarded as liabilities because they have to be supported for many years before they can contribute to society. These families generally are small, and parents usually have sole responsibility for the care of their children. The length of parenting responsibilities and general lack of sharing of parental duties from other family members may be why parents have trouble adjusting to the tremendous psychological, as well as economic, burden of parenthood (Skolnick, 1987). In cases where pregnancy was not planned, the adjustment is greater.

Whether unplanned or planned, childbirth represents a major life transition. Several decades of research has shown that the transition to parenthood is a major upheaval in the lives of a couple, and it often sets the stage for increased difficulties in the marriage (Cowan et al., 1985). How parents adjust to the birth of a child affects the parent–child interaction and, consequently, a child's development.

In the first weeks of life, parents begin discovering what pleases and what distresses the baby—what stops the baby from crying, how often the baby needs to sleep, to eat, to be changed. Parents learn the skill of paying attention, of being empathetic with and responding to the baby's cues and clues. This is the way that parents answer their own questions, reduce their anxieties, and strengthen their relationship with their newborn. This skill, one which often has to be learned and relearned, underlies the entire course of parenthood (Galinsky, 1981, p. 69).

Learning to adjust to parenthood can be difficult for some people. Problems can stem from negative attitudes toward pregnancy, which can come from lack of planning or physical changes making the woman feel "ugly." They can come from feelings of parental inadequacy due to lack of experience, lack of support, and conflicting advice. Or problems can originate from an unwillingness of the female to accept role changes that accompany being a parent, including the expectation that the infant will not alter one's activities, or the unwillingness to share parenting with the spouse (Osofsky & Osofsky, 1984).

Adjustment to parenthood can be difficult because the newborn demands continual around-the-clock attention. This can cause fatigue and frustration in trying to meet the infant's demands. Other stresses involve finances and lack of time for self and spouse (Ventura, 1987).

Employed single parents have additional stresses that can ensue from not having a supporting other person (Honig, 1980; Brazelton, 1985). For example, if the woman is sick and the infant needs attention, who can help? Will the woman risk becoming more sick from not caring for herself in attending to the infant's needs, or will she attend to her own needs and ignore the infant's? What if the woman has to work late and cannot get to the babysitter's house at the designated time? Does the mother risk losing her job and leave to pick up the infant?

Ventura (1987) concludes that today's parents need more support adjusting to parenthood than they are getting. She suggests the need for support and advocacy groups in the community for families. A sampling of the mission of these groups include parent education, expansion of health care services to home care, restructuring of work, and child care services.

## CHILDBIRTH AND FATHERS

Fathers have an influence on the context of childbirth and the newborn's development. The male's biological influence on the child is well established. The father's sperm fertilizes the mother's egg, thereby contributing half of the child's genetic material. The male's contextual influence on the development of the child, however, has been recognized only recently. The interest in fathering has been partially due to changes in the composition of and individual roles in the family (Honig, 1980; Parke, 1981). The divorce rate has increased, and many fathers have custody of their children. More women are employed, and men share the role of caregiver.

Father–infant research shows that if fathers are given the chance to interact with their infants early in life, the men are sensitive to infant cues and responsive to the signals of newborns (Honig, 1980).

Men interact differently from women with their infants. While women spend more time in feeding and caretaking activities, men spend more time playing with the infant (Lamb, 1976).

With an increase in two-income households, fathers are assuming a greater day-to-day role in raising children.

# F.Y.I.

The Bayley Scales of Infant Development measure sensory-motor behaviors such as reaching, grasping, and following an object, abilities thought to be precursors of later intellectual development.

Fathers' involvement in their children's learning has been shown to be related to certain measures of the child's cognitive development.

Mothers and fathers treat female and male offspring differently.

Apparently, the additional time spent playing with infants by fathers impacts intellectual development. Infants five or six months old whose fathers were absent were compared with infants of the same age whose fathers lived with them. Using *Bayley Scales of Infant Development*, a measure of infant cognitive status, Pedersen and colleagues (1979) found that male infants whose fathers were absent got lower scores.

For female neonates, the presence or absence of the father made no difference on these measures of cognitive development. Another early indication of cognitive progress is how much interest infants show in things and events in their environment. Researchers have found that this early form of curiosity, or interest in novelty, also is related to later intellectual development.

Fathers treat male and female infants differently (Parke, 1981). In a study by Parke and Sawin (1976), fathers consistently stimulated sons more than daughters. Fathers touched sons and visually stimulated them by showing them a toy more often than daughters. Mothers stimulated daughters more frequently with the toy, also touching daughters more than sons. On the other hand, fathers were found to hold daughters more than sons, whereas mothers were found to hold sons more than daughters. Fathers also engage in more physical play, such as lifting and tossing, with male infants than with female infants, and vocalize more to girls than to boys (Kotelchuck, 1976).

Although today's fathers are interacting more with infants than fathers of the past, many traditional roles between men and women remain. Generally, women still do more of the routine care such as feeding, changing, and bathing, while men spend more time playing with infants. Of course, this is not true for all families. No single profile of the relationship between men and infants adequately portrays all fathers. Fathers can and do play a significant role in infancy, but how and how much individual men influence infants varies considerably from one family to another.

● ● ●  RESEARCH IN REVIEW  ● ● ● ● ● ● ● ● ● ● ● ● ● ● ●

## WHAT IS THE ASSOCIATION BETWEEN THE MARITAL RELATIONSHIP AND ADJUSTMENT TO PARENTING?

Owen, M.T., Lewis, J.M. & Henderson, V.K. (1989). Marriage, adult adjustment, and early parenting. *Child Development, 60,* 1015–1024.

This study was designed to investigate the relation of adult psychological and marital adjustment on parenting, considering both parent and infant gender.

The subjects in the study were 38 Caucasian married couples and the 15 female infants and 23 male infants subsequently born to these couples. The mean length of marriage for the couples at the prenatal time *(continued on following page)*

*(continued from previous page)*

husbands was 21–42 years, with a mean of 29.4 years. The age range of wives was 18–35 years, with a mean of 27.3 years. The mean family income was $35,000–39,999 per year. The mean education for husbands was 15.8 years and for wives was 15.5 years.

Data collection occurred in the family home and in the laboratory. Data were gathered using interviews, videotapes of marital interactions as well as parent–child interactions, standardized personality measures, and questionnaires.

The first visit occurred in the family home during the second trimester of the woman's pregnancy. Interviews explored the subjects' marriage, work, friendships, social networks, family of origin, and perceptions of self. The subjects also completed self-report personality measures and questionnaires.

At a later time in the laboratory, couples were interviewed about how their relationship developed, feelings about pregnancy expectations of parenthood, and plans for the future. After the interview, couples were left alone for a series of videotaped marital interaction tasks.

At three months after the birth of the child, the couples were interviewed about attitudes concerning the infant and the parenting role, perceptions of the child's development, their adjustment to the infant as a couple, and the process by which their roles had been established. They also were videotaped interacting with the infant.

During the prenatal period, subjects completed several measures to assess individual psychological health and development. Also, the couples were assessed on closeness of the marital relationship and intimacy of communication, or how much the couple confided in each other about feelings. During the postnatal period, attitudes toward parenting were rated, including the parents' delight (or expression of pleasure) in the infant, the parents' acceptance of the infant despite of its interference with the parents' autonomy, sensitivity to the infant's communications, and investment in parenting in terms of prioritizing time with the infant.

Results showed that women who had close/confiding marriages prenatally were more likely to be warm and sensitive with their three-month-old infants than mothers in less close/confiding marriages, regardless of their psychological adjustment. Men who had close/confiding marriages prenatally were more likely to hold positive attitudes toward their infants and their roles as fathers compared with men who had less close/confiding marriages, regardless of their psychological adjustment.

When gender of the infant was added to the analysis, it was found that mothers of sons had more positive attitudes toward their infants and their roles as mothers than did mothers of daughters, irrespective of the qualities of their marriages or their psychological adjustment. Fathers of sons were warmer and more sensitive and responsive with their three-month-old infants than fathers of daughters, irrespective of the qualities of their marriages or their psychological adjustments.

This study is significant because it shows that the marital relationship plays an important role in influencing the development of the parent-child relationship.

Facial expressions and emotional states of a child have a powerful influence on adults, particularly parents.

# INTERACTION OF BIOLOGICAL AND CONTEXTUAL INFLUENCES ON NEONATAL DEVELOPMENT

Now we will examine how biological factors, such as neonatal adaptive behavior to survive, and contextual factors, such as parental responsiveness, interact to influence the development of the neonate.

## SURVIVAL INSURANCE

Infants attract attention because they are cute, helpless, and responsive. They are this way to ensure their survival, according to the view of the ethologists.

Ethologists explain behavior in terms of evolution. A characteristic behavior of a species has evolved because that behavior has fostered adaptation to the environment. Thus, the appearance and behavior of infants have adapted in such a way as to attract the attention of adults to ensure survival of the human species. Konrad Lorenz (1935, 1970) observed that the young of many species manifest various characteristics considered "cute" by older individuals of their own species and even of other species. Some characteristics include rounded head shape, protruding forehead, short nose, and large eyes (figure 4.2).

FIGURE 4.2
INFANCY IN FOUR
SPECIES COMPARED
WITH ADULTHOOD
(Lorenz, 1971)

John Bowlby (1969, 1988) believed human infants have adapted certain signals, such as crying and smiling, to entice adults to approach them. When a a neonate cries, adults are highly motivated to relieve the cause of the distress. When an infant smiles at an adult, the adult is encouraged to interact.

From an evolutionary standpoint, it is understandable that various species have certain specific signals that stimulate certain responses in other members of their species. These stimuli have survival value.

# INTERACTION EQUIPMENT

In addition to appearance and possession of certain signals to ensure adult attention, human infants enter the world equipped to conduct interactions. For example, they possess certain reflexes. The rooting reflex plays a role in early infant-mother attachment in that the infant turns its head in the direction of stimulation on its cheek (Hinde, 1983).

Infants also are equipped with well-developed sensory systems at birth. Thus, they can perceive a variety of stimuli. For example, infants can see and discriminate visual patterns from birth although their *visual acuity,* or ability to focus, is not equal to that of an adult. Young infants are especially attentive to visual movement, to borders of high contrast, and to relatively complex stimuli such as a face. When face to face with infants, adults will normally present their faces at the distance where newborns are best able to focus (about eight inches) and exaggerate their facial expressions and movements. The result for the infant is a visual display with constant movement of high contrast borders. Also, adults will look into an infant's eyes to establish eye contact, and the infant usually will gaze back.

In summary neonates are biologically programmed to behave in certain ways to attract adult attention. Also, they are biologically equipped to respond to certain stimuli in their environment. Such behavior and equipment have survival value. Likewise, adults are biologically programmed to respond to neonates' appearance and behavior in a nurturing way. Such responsiveness contributes to the neonate's ability to survive.

## PARENT–INFANT INTERACTION

Most researchers agree that the biological programming of the neonate and the context or responsiveness of caregiving provide the building blocks for an interaction that influences neonatal and later development in that a basic pattern for communication, attachment, and learning is established (Stern, 1977).

Children, early in life, learn how to interact and communicate with caregivers.

## Infant Communication Via Crying

Crying is the first way in which infants communicate. At birth the cry signals that a neonate has filled the lungs with air and is breathing on his own. After birth, the cry signals caregivers that a neonate is hungry, uncomfortable, or needs comfort.

Analysis of infants' cries revealed different cries communicate various feelings. These cries differ in pattern of pauses between bursts of crying by the duration of the cry and its tonal qualities. Wolff (1969) identified four patterns of crying in young infants. One was the *basic cry,* which is usually associated with hunger but has a fundamental rhythm pattern into which all infant cries eventually end. Second was the *anger cry;* third, the *pain cry;* and fourth, the *attention cry,* which usually does not develop until about the third week after birth.

A crying infant stimulates feelings in anyone within earshot. In several studies where physiological responses such as heart rate were measured in adults while they listened to sound recordings of infant cries, intense arousal was induced in both women and men who had children (Boukydis & Burgess, 1982) as well as in adults of both genders who had no children (Murray, 1985). The powerful effect of the infant's cry is probably biologi-

According to Wolff (1969), there are four reasons a child will cry: hunger, anger, pain, and attention. Can you determine why this child is crying by his facial expression and body positioning?

Successful interaction with a child (for example, quieting a cry) provides parents with a sense of competence when it comes to "reading" the behavior of the child.

cally programmed in all human beings to ensure infants receive the necessary care and protection to survive.

Women who are breastfeeding often respond to infants' hunger cry physiologically—an increased flow of blood and milk raises the surface heat of the breasts (Lind, 1971) and, in response, women will notice milk lactating from their breasts. Parents quickly learn to respond to differences in infant cries, even though they are not always correct in interpreting the meaning of the cry; accuracy improves with experience, however (Green, Jones, & Gustafson, 1987).

It has been found that the most effective way to soothe a crying infant is to pick up the infant and provide close physical contact. A better response is to lift the crying neonate to the shoulder because this involves physical contact and motion, and the upright position causes the infant to enter the quiet alert state in which the baby is visually attentive to the environment.

Ethologists believe crying is an adaptive behavior that encourages adults to approach and nurture. Therefore, responding to an infant's cries promotes communication and closeness. Bell and Ainsworth (1972) and others (Field, 1990) found that women who delayed or failed to respond to crying had neonates who engaged in more frequent and persistent crying in the latter part of the first year. In addition, these infants had fewer communicative behaviors (facial expressions, bodily gestures, vocalizations) compared with infants who had prompt response to crying.

On the other hand, behaviorists believe that consistently responding to a crying infant rewards the crying response and results in a whiny and demanding child. A cross-cultural study of several child-rearing environments in Israel compared the crying and fussing of infants of Bedouin tribes people with Israeli infants raised by women at home and in group care by a caregiver. Bedouin mothers respond to the infant's first whimper; mothers of Israeli infants raised at home respond if the infant does not quiet down in a short time; and caregivers, because they are responsible for several children, respond when they have time. It was found that Bedouin infants, whose mothers respond at the first whimper, fussed and cried the most throughout the first year, followed by infants reared in homes. Infants raised in a group fussed and cried the least (Landau, 1982). Thus, this study provides evidence for the behaviorist view.

Best-selling author, Dr. Benjamin Spock (1968), has a different opinion. He believes a neonate cannot be spoiled during the first two months of life because her physical needs are being met; responding to crying during this time provides physical comfort for the infant. However, during the third month when infants cry for more psychologically based reasons, such as desire for attention and to express frustration or anger, Spock advises parents not to submit too easily to fussing once physical causes such as hunger, discomfort, and pain have been ruled out; otherwise, the child will become increasingly demanding for attention.

## Parental Communication Via Responsiveness

Infants' cries affect the context of caregiving. When parents or other caregivers are successful in quieting infants' cries, they gain confidence in their effectiveness. If, on the other hand, they are unsuccessful, they begin to feel helpless and consequently withdraw from interacting with the infants (Donovan & Leavitt, 1989). Susan Goldberg (1988) developed a model of parent–infant interaction to explain the significance of parental effectiveness. An adult who has experienced a successful interaction with an infant perceives the infant as "readable" and predictable and acquires a feeling of competence in further interactions. In turn, the sensitive care that results causes the infant to feel more competent at eliciting the appropriate responses and, thus, a cycle of successful interaction is established. An adult who has not experienced successful interactions with an infant, perhaps because the infant is preterm and not mature enough to give clear distress or comforting signals, experiences repeated feelings of helplessness. These feelings can be damaging to the interactive relationship in that the caregiver either stops trying to meet the infant's needs or tries too hard and in so doing overstimulates the infant, causing the infant to turn away or to fuss (Field, 1977, 1990).

## Reciprocity

The parent-infant relationship begins with the parent, most commonly the mother, initiating interaction. When the infant is born, the mother will touch it, gaze at it, and talk to it. Even immediately after birth, the infant will follow the mother's face.

Without realizing they are doing it, parents tend to structure their interactions to fit their infants' capacities. Women use position of the infants' hands and evaluate the response to touch and eye contact as cues to the type and amount of stimulation they give the infants, thereby tailoring their behavior to the infants' state. The infant is most attentive during the quiet alert state. It is during this time that a neonate will gaze at the mother. If a mother turns away to engage in another activity and the infant wants to gaze some more, the infant will whimper or fuss to regain the mother's attention. If the mother responds by gazing, the infant has learned that his actions have consequences. If the woman stimulates the infant by talking or tickling and the infant tires of the stimulation, the infant will avert his gaze and may start to fuss. If a woman stops the stimulation, she is showing the infant that she is sensitive to her infant's needs, another example of how the infant learns his actions are effective in stimulating a response. These simple interactions between infant and mother are reciprocal because they are composed of taking turns, the basis of all social interaction. As infants develop, their role in initiating and maintaining reciprocal interaction increases and that of the parents decreases (Belsky, Taylor & Rovine, 1984). Reciprocal interactions between infant and parents are significant because they form the basis of attachment or bonding and consequent emotional development.

In conclusion, many biological and contextual factors interact in a complex way to affect neonatal development. The interaction of these factors begins before childbirth. For example, the genetics of the child and the prenatal environment. The prenatal environment is, in turn, affected by factors such as the mother's health, blood type, age, and attitudes. The neonate is also affected directly by the method of childbirth and indirectly by the type of support system provided for the mother

# F.Y.I.

Mothers of blind infants report difficulty feeling close to their infants because their infants cannot look back at them (Fraiberg, 1974).

# CRITICAL THINKING & YOU

**ANALYSIS:** Assume you have total control in planning the birth of your child and postnatal (after birth) care. Return to the chapter and answer the following:

1. How would you avoid a complicated birth?

2. If your infant were at risk, how would you optimize chances for development?

3. Knowing the characteristics and capabilities of your newborn, how would you optimize development?

**SYNTHESIS:** Compare medical childbirth (in a hospital) with nonmedical childbirth (advantages and disadvantages), including the cultural context of the birth in your discussion.

**EVALUATION:** Who do you think controls the interaction between parent and infant? Is it the parent, the infant, both, neither? Support your position with evidence from this chapter.

## SUMMARY

- The first stage of labor involves regular contractions until the cervix is fully dilated. The second stage occurs when the infant pushes through the cervix into the vagina. The third stage is the expulsion of the placenta.
- The newborn's physical condition is assessed soon after birth for heart rate, breathing, muscle tone, circulation, and reflexes by the Apgar scale. The Neonatal Assessment Behavioral Scale sometimes is also used to test newborn adaptation via social responses and reflexes.
- Occasionally, childbirth involves some complications and requires medical assistance.
- Some newborns are born before term and are at risk for death or for having developmental problems later.
- The average weight of an infant at birth is 7½ pounds, and length is about 20 inches. Neonates weighing less than 5½ pounds at birth also are at risk for survival and later problems.
- Neonates have to adapt to life outside the womb to survive.
- Neonates are born with certain adaptive responses, or reflexes, that help them survive. Some reflexes do not appear to have survival value, but may be remnants of human evolutionary history. In evaluating these reflexes, information can be gained about the maturity and function of a newborn's neuromuscular system.
- Newborns' behavior, while appearing sporadic and disorganized, actually can be classified into seven distinct behavioral states based on arousal or activity.
- The social context of childbirth is influenced by religious, cultural, economic, and political factors.
- Most births today in the United States occur in the hospital whereas a century ago they took place at home.
- The Lamaze method of childbirth embraces the philosophy of preparedness to help a woman build stamina and cope with pain to avoid or reduce medication.
- The Leboyer method of childbirth embraces the philosophy that birth should be gentle and that the infant's entry into the world should be gradual, avoiding any unnecessary trauma.
- Homebirth is an option in uncomplicated pregnancies and is usually supervised by a specialized nurse.
- Some hospitals provide alternatives to conventional hospital delivery known as alternative birthing centers set aside for labor and birth and recuperation where the family is welcome.
- Culture influences the experience and attitudes of childbirth.

- The family is the context for the development of children. Its ability to nurture and respond decisively to meet the developmental needs of children affects how they will function as adults.
- Childbirth represents a major life transition. How parents adjust influences the context of caregiving for the child because the interaction between parent and child sets the course for later development.
- Men have an influence on the context of childbirth and the newborn's development. The recognition of the father's role in child development is partially due to changes in the composition of and individual roles in the family.
- Men interact differently with their newborns compared with women because they generally engage more in play rather than routine caregiving activities. They also treat male and female infants differently.
- Biological and contextual factors influence neonatal development. The infant comes biologically equipped to elicit certain responses from adults as well as interact with them.
- Adults are biologically programmed to respond to neonates' appearance and behavior in a nurturing way and can sense what stimuli are most appealing to babies.
- The parent–infant interaction is reciprocal; reciprocity leads to attachment.

## RELATED READINGS

Apgar, V., & Beck, J. (1974). *Is my baby all right?* New York: Pocket Books.

Brazelton, T.B. (1985). *Working and caring.* Reading, MA: Addison-Wesley.

Clark, A.L. (Ed.). (1978). *Culture childbearing health professionals.* Philadelphia: F.A. Davis.

Eakins, P.S. (Ed.). (1986). *The American way of birth.* Philadelphia: Temple University Press.

Field, T. (1990). *Infancy.* Cambridge, MA: Harvard University Press.

Goldberg, S., & DiVitto, B.A. (1983). *Born too soon: Preterm birth and early development.* San Francisco: W.H. Freeman.

Guttmacher, A.F., & Kaiser, I.H. (1986). *Pregnancy, birth, and family planning.* New York: New American Library.

Klaus, M.H., & Kennell, J.H. (1982). *Parent-infant bonding.* St. Louis, MO: C.V. Mosby.

Lamaze, F. (1970). *Painless childbirth.* Chicago: Henry Regnery.

Leboyer, F. (1975). *Birth without violence.* New York: Alfred Knopf.

Maurer, D., & Maurer, C. (1988). *The world of the newborn.* New York: Basic Books.

Parke, R.D. (1981). *Fathers.* Cambridge, MA: Harvard University Press.

## ACTIVITY

To better understand childbirth and the newborn, visit a local hospital.

1. Interview a nurse on the maternity ward. Ask what accommodations are provided by the hospital for childbirth. For example, is there a traditional labor room and delivery room or is there an alternative birthing center? What methods of delivery can a woman choose? What type of care is provided for the newborn?

2. Observe the infants in the newborn nursery. Describe facial expressions, body movements, fussiness. Are any infants receiving special care such as being under a bilirubin light, receiving intravenous feeding, or attached to monitors? Describe.

3. Interview a woman who has recently given birth. Ask her to describe her childbirth experiences and her reactions to the newborn.

# Physical and Motor Development: Growth and Use of the Body

**5**

*. . . tall oaks from little acorns grow.*

**David Everett**

# ABOUT PHYSICAL AND MOTOR DEVELOPMENT

Jennifer gained weight between the ages of 13 and 15. She did not like her body, especially her expanding hips and rounded thighs. She began to diet by not eating breakfast but by the time lunch arrived, she was so hungry she had to buy cookies to fill herself up. She brooded about her body, but instead of losing weight, she gained it. When she turned 16, she went out one night with her friend for a pizza. She was appalled to find she ate ¾ of it. When she went home, in desperation she stuck her finger down her throat and threw up.

When Kenneth was nine, he joined Little League. He wanted to do something his brothers had not done. However, he soon became unhappy because he could not play baseball as well as his teammates. He was smaller than the other boys, and not as strong, fast, or coordinated. When he was in the field, he often did not catch the ball when it was hit to him; when he did, he did not throw it far enough to reach the base. The other boys on the team blamed him for their losing streak and did not want him to play. He lost confidence in himself not only in baseball but also with his peers and in school.

Physical development involves the increase in size of the various body parts, and the increase in complexity of their structures and functions. Motor development refers to movement and control of the body parts. As children grow and develop, the ability to use their body parts increases in strength, speed, and coordination.

As they mature, all humans share some common principles of development. There also are *norms*, or typical patterns to account for individual differences.

## PRINCIPLES OF DEVELOPMENT

Knowing the principles of development that affect all humans enables a comparison of an individual's development to the normal course, and allows predictions about that person's future development.

Three basic principles underlie the growth and development of all body systems. These are *cephalocaudal*, *proximodistal*, and *differentiation* and *integration*.

*Cephalocaudal* means from head to tail. The principle of **cepholocaudal development** states that human development progresses from head to foot. This principle is reflected in the order in which body parts become larger and in the order in which structures and functions become more complex. Neonates' heads develop before their trunks, arms, and legs.

At birth, a neonate's head is nearer to adult size than any other body part. As an infant develops into an adult, the head doubles in size while the trunks trebles, arms quadruple, and legs grow fivefold (figure 5.1).

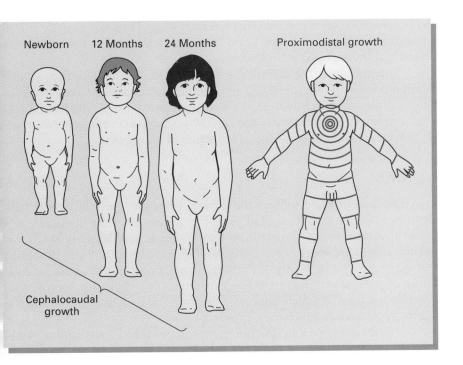

Newborn 12 Months 24 Months Proximodistal growth

Cephalocaudal growth

Not only does growth progress from head to foot but so do movement and motor ability. Infants first gain control over their head and neck muscles, then those of the abdomen and arms, and finally, the legs. Thus, infants hold up their heads before they can sit; they sit before they stand; they stand before they walk or run. Also, they control their arms (exemplified by brushing items aside with gross movements of the shoulders) long before they control their fingers (exemplified by picking up things with fine movements of the thumb and forefinger).

Physical and motor development progress from up to down and also from center outward. *Proximodistal* means "near to far." The principle of **proximodistal development** states that human development progresses from the center of the body to the extremities. Prenatally, the heart and internal organs form before the arms, hands, and fingers. Postnatally, infants learn to control shoulder movements before they direct their arms or fingers.

To illustrate proximodistal development, we follow the sequence of reaching for objects. During the first weeks of life, a neonate reaches for objects that come into view but does not grasp them because she lacks control over the hand and finger muscles. At about five months, an infant uses both hands to try to grasp objects. By six months, most infants have developed a one-handed reach, which is usually successful in brushing the object. At seven months an infant can flex the whole hand while reaching and, somewhat later, poke at the object with an index finger. Finally, at ten months an infant can grasp the object by opposing the thumb and forefinger.

The third principle of development is *differentiation* and *integration*. **Differentiation** means that infants' abilities become increasingly distinct and specific over time. For example, if an infant gets a finger caught in a zipper, the infant probably will cry and thrash his whole body. As the infant gets older and movement becomes more specific, if a finger gets caught, he will still cry but only move the affected body part. Eventually, the child will

**Developmentalists have determined that the norm for a child to begin crawling is around six months of age.**

use language to communicate what has happened. Thus, the sensory stimulation that has traveled to the brain from the caught finger becomes interpreted and transformed into language.

**Integration** is the complementary process to differentiation; simple differentiated skills are combined and coordinated into more complex skills. For example, after an infant has gained separate control of the head, neck, arm, and lower torso muscles, she can then combine several separate muscle movements into the more complex action of rolling over.

## NORMS

As development follows the general principles, specific events such as sitting, walking, talking, and skipping follow a certain sequence and occur at certain ages. Several investigators (Gesell, 1925; Griffiths, 1954; Bayley, 1956; Lenneberg, 1967; Tanner, 1990) have analyzed and described the sequence in which physical characteristics and motor skills emerge. Their investigations have resulted in **norms**, or typical patterns, that describe the way in which important attributes and skills develop and the approximate ages at which they appear.

Norms are useful in describing how most children *normally* develop. From norms it is possible to predict how the typical child progresses, thus making it possible to answer questions such as, "When do most infants sleep through the night?" and "When do most children learn to read?"

In infancy and the preschool years, pediatricians give much attention to physical and motor developmental norms. They compare a neonate's height and weight to the norm for her age (figure 5.2), and they monitor the infant's progress in motor activities such as rolling, sitting, crawling, and walking. An infant whose size or motor abilities lag behind the norm alerts a pediatrician to look for other possible problems, such as cerebral palsy or mental retardation.

## INDIVIDUAL DIFFERENCES

Although norms are valuable for comparative and predictive purposes in charting normal development, norms are *averages* and, therefore, individual children vary widely on each side of a norm. Parents tend to worry if their child is "not on schedule." However, they need to understand that norms represent ranges. For example, while the norm for walking is 11.7 months (Bayley, 1969), some children walk at eight months of age while others do not walk until they are 18 months. Also, girls and boys differ in how they follow the norms. Prenatally, girls' skeletal development surpasses that of boys', while immediately after birth boys grow faster than girls. Then, toward the end of the first year until about age four, girls surpass boys. During childhood to puberty, the growth rates of males and females are even (Tanner, 1990).

When we discuss growth, in general we usually mean height and weight. However, the child does not grow "all in one piece." Rather, the various parts and systems of the body grow at different rates. Norms exist for the various parts and systems just as there are norms for height and weight. Likewise, individual differences also are present.

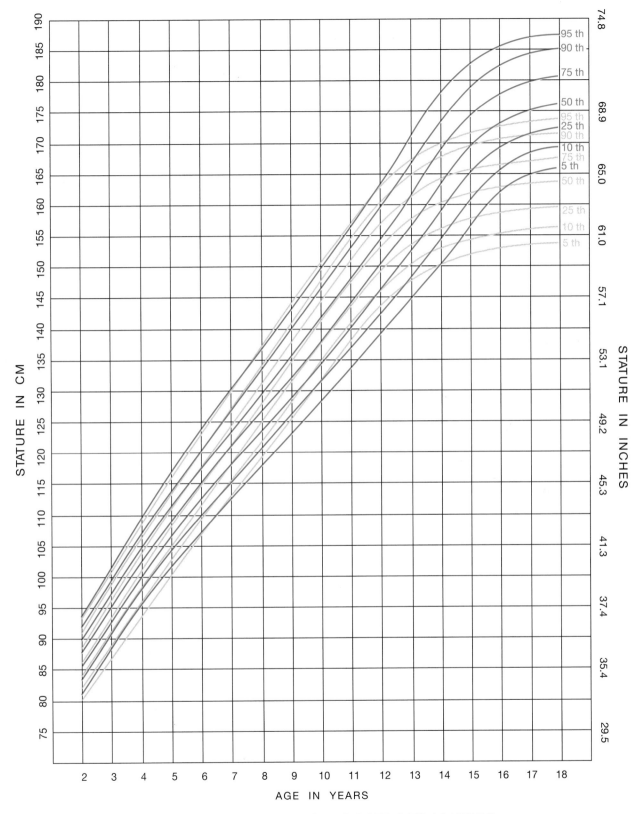

FIGURE 5.2A

GROWTH CHART FOR HEIGHT FOR BOYS AND GIRLS AGED 2 TO 18 YEARS

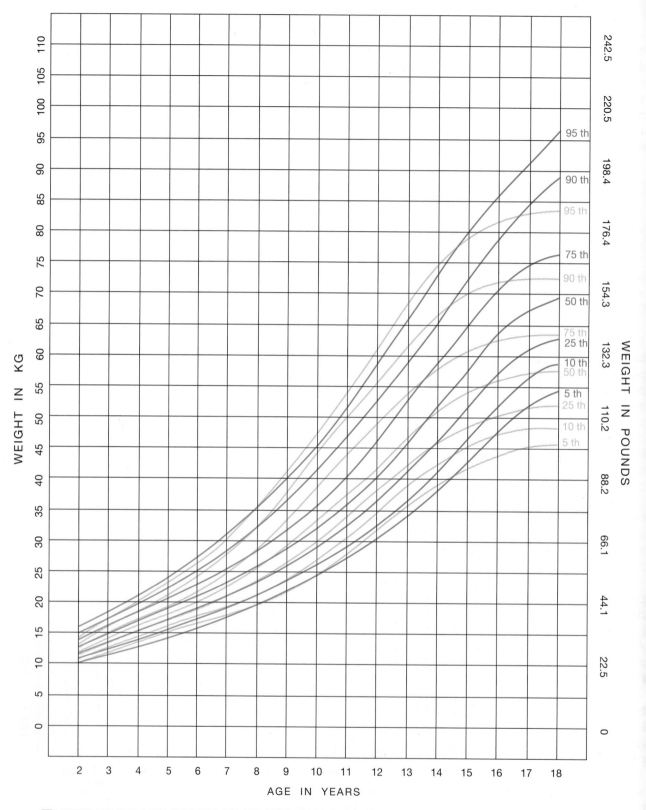

WEIGHT BY AGE PERCENTILES FOR GIRLS AGED 2 TO 18 YEARS

WEIGHT BY AGE PERCENTILES FOR BOYS AGED 2 TO 18 YEARS

FIGURE 5.2B

GROWTH CHART FOR WEIGHT FOR BOYS AND GIRLS AGED 2 TO 18 YEARS

Individual differences in physical and motor development occur for many reasons. Some biological influences are heredity, hormones, and gender. Some contextual influences are nutrition, health (physical and emotional), and exercise. Then there is the interaction between biological and contextual influences so that heredity, hormones, nutrition, and health interact to produce larger individuals who mature earlier. Heredity and exercise interact to produce differences in athletic ability; and heredity, hormones, and social context interact to produce concepts about one's physique.

## SKELETAL AND MUSCULAR DEVELOPMENT

The skeletal system, or framework of bones, provides support for the body. Bone development consists of growth in bone size, change in the number of bones, and change in their composition.

Bones grow in length at the ends. Bones grow in width by adding new bone tissue at their outer edges. When a child reaches puberty, hormones stimulate the ends of the bones to fuse with the bone shafts thereby limiting growth.

At birth, most of the infant's bones are soft, pliable, and difficult to break. The neonate's skull, for example, consists of several soft bones, separated by *fontanels* or soft spots, that can be compressed to allow the child to pass through the birth canal. During the first year of life, **ossification,** the process by which the bones harden as a result of the deposition of calcium and other minerals, begins. Ossification continues until puberty with different body parts completing the hardening process at different rates. Illustrating the principle of cephalocaudal development, the skull bones harden, closing off the fontanels by about two years of age, whereas the long bones in the legs are not completely ossified until puberty. The extent to which the bones in the human skeleton has hardened is termed as **skeletal age.**

Understanding ossification is significant because timing can influence a deformity development in a child. For example, young children's bones are soft; therefore wearing shoes that are too tight can result in foot abnormalities later. Also, if injury occurs, children's bones heal faster before ossification than they do after.

Whereas the bones provide the structure for the body, the muscles provide the strength. Muscular development proceeds in a cephalocaudal direction—muscles in the head and neck mature earlier than muscles in the trunk and lower limbs. At birth, muscle fibers are present but undeveloped. After birth, they change in size, shape, and composition. The muscle fibers grow in length, breadth, and thickness. At maturity, the muscles are at least five times thicker than at birth.

For the average person, muscle weight increases 40 times from birth to maturity. Up to five years of age, the muscles grow in proportion to the increase in body weight. Then, from 5 to 6 a rapid spurt occurs in muscle growth. After this, muscle growth slows, followed by a marked spurt at puberty.

The skeletal and muscular development that occurs between infancy and young adulthood helps explain the growth of motor skills that occurs over the same period. There is a wide range of individual differences in motor abilities in childhood and adolescence. Children who have broad, thick muscles tend to be superior in physical strength, whereas children who have smaller muscles tend to be faster and better coordinated (Eichorn, 1970).

Parents should be reminded that developmental norms are averages and may not specifically match their child's growth and development.

FIGURE 5.3

**(a) Motor neuron (b) Sensory neuron**

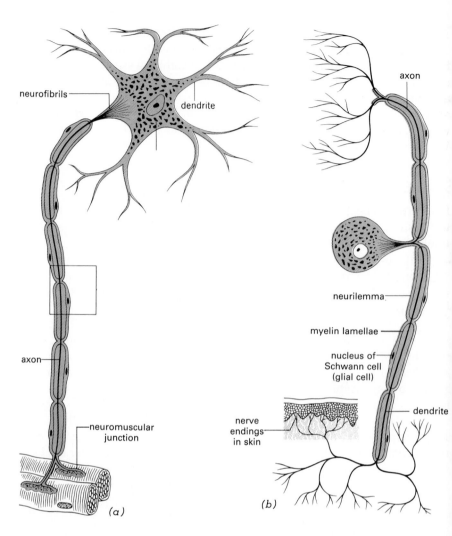

(a)

(b)

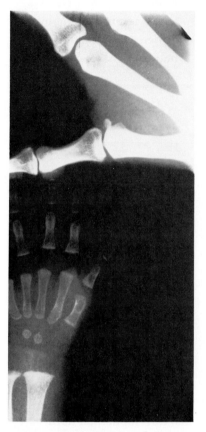

An X-ray of the hand of a 5-month-old infant. Dark areas near the ends of the bone indicate growth is incomplete. Compare this with the adult hand at the top of the picture.

F.Y.I.

There are 206 bones in the human body—28 of which are in the skull.

## NERVOUS SYSTEM

The nervous system consists of the brain, spinal cord, and peripheral nerves. The basic unit of the nervous system is the **neuron**, a nerve cell that receives and transmits impulses. The impulses result from electrical and chemical changes in and around the neuron and are transmitted across the **synapse**, or connective space between two neurons (figure 5.3).

The nervous system is divided into the *central nervous system (CNS)*, consisting of the brain and spinal cord, and the *peripheral nervous system (PNS)*, consisting of the nerves in the rest of the body. Stimuli such as sights, sounds, odors, tastes, and touch are received by neurons in the eye, ear, nose, mouth, or skin depending on the particular stimulus. These neurons, known as *receptors*, send impulses along the nerves in the PNS to the CNS where the information is recorded. Then, the brain transmits impulses to the body part affected and a response occurs. For example, when you walk out of a dark movie theater into the bright street lights, the light is received by receptor neurons in the eyes, and the signal travels along a nerve pathway from the eye to the brain. The brain records the signal and in turn transmits a signal to the eyes to adjust the pupil size to become smaller to let in less light.

## Neurons

Presently, it is thought that the production of neurons is complete at birth (Rakic, 1985). Interestingly, however, the average infant has more neurons and neural connections than the average adult. The neurons and neural connections begin to decrease postnatally and continue to do so until adolescence (Goldman-Rakic, 1987). The neural pathways used most often will survive, whereas inactive pathways will die (Greenough, Black and Wallace, 1987).

Because of the larger number of neural pathways, their lack of specialization, the various parts of a young child's brain have remarkable **plasticity**, or flexibility in structure and function. Thus, young children who suffer brain damage are more apt to recover because neurons are available to take over the functions of those damaged neurons. This is not the case with adults (Huttenlocher, 1984).

## The Brain

With age, the brain becomes more integrated and differentiated. The parts of the brain most fully developed at birth are located in the *brainstem*, such as the *medulla* and the *midbrain* (figure 5.4). The various parts of the

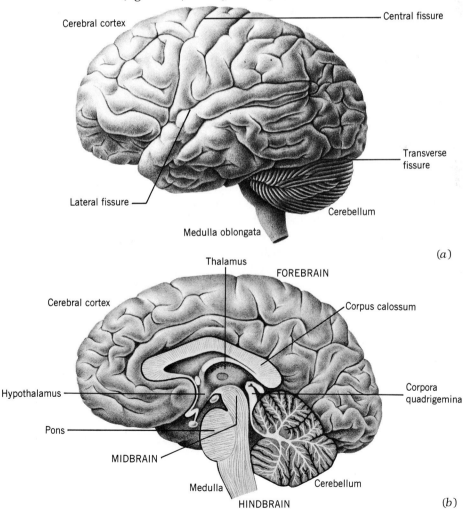

(a)

(b)

**FIGURE 5.4**

**(a) Lateral, external view of brain  (b) Lateral, internal view of brain**

brainstem regulate basic biological functions such as respiration, circulation, and digestion; behavioral states; and inborn reflexes (Bloom & Lazerson, 1988).

Surrounding the midbrain are the *cerebrum* and *cerebral cortex*. The cerebrum is the largest part of the brain. On the surface of the cerebrum is the cerebral cortex, which is characterized by many folds. The significance of the folds is that they represent an increase in surface area without an increase in volume. Thus, many neurons can fill a small space.

The first areas of the cerebrum to mature are the primary motor areas, which control simple motor activities such as waving the arms, and the primary sensory areas, which control sensory processes such as vision, sound, touch. Following the principle of cephalocaudal development, within the motor area nerve cells controlling the arms and upper trunk develop ahead of those controlling the legs and lower trunk. That is why infants can accomplish many things with their heads, necks, hands, and arms before they gain enough control over the lower trunk and legs to sit up, crawl, or walk. By six months of age, the primary motor areas of the cerebral cortex have developed so they now direct most of infants' physical activities. At this point, inborn reflexes, such as the Moro reflex and Babinski reflex, should disappear—a positive sign indicating the higher cortical centers are assuming normative control over the more primitive subcortical areas of the brain.

The cerebral cortex controls voluntary motor responses and is necessary for the development of language, abstract thinking, and all cognitive processes. It does not develop all at one time and its specific parts do not develop at the same rate.

Although infants can see, hear, smell, taste, and touch at birth, they probably cannot interpret this sensory input because other areas of the cortex involved in integrating sensory information, memory, and organizing muscular movements have not developed yet. Thus, the development of the cortex limits the child's perceptual and motor activities.

The *cerebellum*, meaning "little cerebrum" is like a small brain. It has many folds containing many neurons. Information comes to the cerebellum from the cerebral cortex, from the brainstem, and from the spinal cord. Thus, the cerebellum appears to play a role in monitoring the position of the head, trunk, and limbs. The cerebellum functions to control finely coordinated movements, such as threading a needle, as well as rapid, consecutive, simultaneous movements, such as typing (Bloom & Lazerson, 1988). The development of the cerebellum lags behind development of the midbrain, spinal cord, and cerebral cortex. The cerebellum is not completely connected to the cerebral cortex to allow control of fine motor movements until about age four (Ito, 1984). This is why preschool children have difficulty mastering tasks requiring fine motor control, such as tying shoes or cutting paper with scissors.

## Myelinization

An important process in nervous system development is **myelinization**, the process by which *myelin*, a white, fatty tissue, forms around neurons thereby facilitating transmission of impulses. Myelinization enables different body parts to communicate more effectively with the brain.

The sequence of myelinization parallels the maturation of the nervous system. At birth, or shortly thereafter, the neural pathways between the sense organs and the brain are well myelinated. As a result, a neonate's sensory equipment works well. The neural pathways between the brain and

---

# F.Y.I.

Development of the cerebral cortex is about 5 percent complete by six months, 75 percent complete by age two, and almost entirely complete by age four.

---

# F.Y.I.

Large myelinated nerves can transmit impulses at speeds of 100 meters per second (about 224 miles per hour). Smaller neurons travel at one meter per second.

he skeletal muscles myelinate in a cephalocaudal and proximodistal pattern. As this occurs, a child becomes capable of increasingly complex motor activities such as lifting the head and chest, rolling over, sitting, and eventually walking and running. Although myelinization proceeds rapidly over the first few years of life, some areas of the brain are not completely myelinated until the mid to late teens or early adulthood. For example, the *reticular formation*, a structure in the brainstem responsible for attention and consciousness, is not fully myelinated until puberty (Tanner, 1990). This may explain why infants, preschoolers, and school-age children have short attention spans and have difficulty doing tasks requiring concentration.

## Lateralization

The cerebrum is divided into two halves, or cerebral hemispheres. The two hemispheres are roughly symmetrical in appearance but have different functions. First, each side of the cerebrum receives neural impulses from and sends neural impulses to the opposite side of the body. Thus, the *right* hemisphere senses and directs action in the *left* side of the body, and the *left* hemisphere senses and directs action in the *right* side of the body. For example, when the right foot itches, the message is received in the left hemisphere of the brain; and when that foot is scratched with the right hand, it is because a message was received to do so from the left hemisphere.

Second, each side of the cerebrum controls different cognitive processes. It contains centers for speech, hearing, verbal memory, decision making, and processing of language. Among right-handed individuals, language is controlled in the left hemisphere—*Broca's* area controls speech production, and *Wernicke's* area controls language comprehension (Geschwind, 1979). Language is also located in the left hemisphere among most left-handed people, although about one third of left-handed people process language in either the right hemisphere or both hemispheres (Springer & Deutsch, 1985).

By contrast, in right-handed individuals the right cerebral hemisphere contains centers for processing visual-spatial information, nonlinguistic sounds such as music, sensations of touch, and emotional expressions.

The two hemispheres are joined by the *corpus callosum*, a massive bundle of more than a million nerve fibers. The corpus callosum facilitates communication between the two hemispheres because many kinds of information processing involve both hemispheres. To illustrate, it was found that children who suffered damage to the corpus callosum reported not seeing anything when visual images were presented to the left visual area of the eyes (Hughes, 1980). This was because the right hemisphere of the brain receives information from the left side of the body and also tells the left side what to do. Thus, if the left side of the cerebrum does not "know" what messages the right side has received the visual image cannot be interpreted.

The process by which the cerebral hemispheres specialize their functions is termed lateralization. According to Erik Lenneberg (1967), lateralization is a gradual process that begins at about two years of age and is complete by puberty. Evidence for Lenneberg's theory comes from his observations of patients who suffered brain damage to their left cerebral hemispheres. If the damage occurred before puberty, the child was likely to regain most language abilities. However, if the damage occurred after puberty, the adolescent was likely to regain few language abilities. Thus, Lenneberg believed the brain to be more plastic and less specialized before puberty than after puberty, so the right hemisphere could assume functions normally performed by the left hemisphere.

Music entering the left ear is being processed in the right hemisphere of the brain and vice versa.

Right cerebral hemisphere is processing the visual-spatial information generated by these two girls' activities.

# F.Y.I.

About 32 percent of preschoolers were consistent in their lateral preference in that they used one side of the body to do all the tasks, whereas over 50 percent of adolescents showed consistent lateral preference (Coren, Porac & Duncan, 1981).

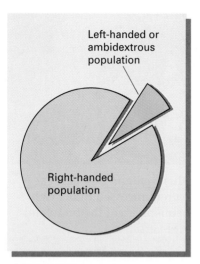

## FIGURE 5.5
**About 90 percent of the population is right-handed, with the remainder being either ambidextrous or left-handed (Bloom & Lazerson, 1988).**

**Motor development norms for infants include rapid change in behavior.**

However, later research has questioned Lenneberg's conclusions. Most psychologists believe that lateralization begins as soon as the cerebral cortex forms in the fetus (Cowan, 1979; Sperry, 1982; Kinsbourne,1989). Lateralization often is complete at an early age, and signs of dominance of one hemisphere over the other often can be observed in infants (Molfese, 1977).

Apparently, lateralization is present at birth; but as children develop, they come to rely more on one hemisphere over the other to perform specific functions. Thus, the hemispheres become more specialized (Witelson, 1987).

One indication that children rely more on one hemisphere over the other is handedness. Handedness is apparent early and is well established by 2 to 3 years of age (Ramsay & Weber, 1986, Longoni & Orsini, 1988). Figure 5.5 shows the percentage of the population that is right-handed and left-handed. Lateral preference, or specialization, becomes stronger over time (Coren, Porac & Duncan, 1981).

## MOTOR DEVELOPMENT

Motor activity, or movement, is the result of nerves carrying impulses from the central nervous system to the muscles. Motor development is exhibited in the early months of life by rapid changes in behavior. Change is evident on a weekly or even daily basis. First, infants randomly move their heads, arms, and legs. Then, they use their heads to turn in the direction of a noise, the arms and hands to grasp objects, the legs and body to roll over, and later, they coordinate all body parts to sit, crawl, and walk. These motor developments influence the nature of an infant's interactions with others as well as perceptual and cognitive experiences and development. For example, when neonates become independently mobile, they can choose what items to touch and locations to explore. Their motor development affects interactions with others in that now the parents have to constantly be aware of where the infant is moving to prevent harm. Motor development also enables infants to move to what they see or hear in the environment, thereby increasing their learning experiences.

The study and research of motor development have recently been renewed after a period of inactivity (Von Hofsten, 1989). The traditional study of motor behavior (Bayley, 1935; McGraw, 1935) was characterized by careful and detailed written observations of the progressive changes in form of different motor sequences such as reaching, crawling, and climbing. It was concluded that motor development was a reflection of a maturational process ( McGraw, 1945; Gesell, 1946). The video camera and computer have enabled researchers to record and analyze movement in more depth.

Motor development is significant because a child's motor experiences provide easily observed markers of developmental progress in infancy (Thelen, 1987). When a pediatrician assesses an infant's development, many motor items, ranging from evaluation of reflexes in the newborn to fine motor skill tasks for the toddler, are included. The reason is that motor skills reflect not only neuromuscular development but also perceptual and cognitive development.

Human movement, excluding reflexes, involves cortical areas of the brain. Whether the person is walking, which involves repetition of similar movements, or dancing, which involves learned complex sequences, muscles are recruited to perform the actions from many segments of the body. To do this, perceptual and cognitive systems must be involved (Thelen, 1987). Specific areas of the brain are involved not only in the immediate execution of motor acts but also in the planning of them (Von Hofsten, 1989). This means that motor development depends on the maturation of various physical structures such as the skeletal, muscular, and nervous systems as well as cognitive structures such as memory.

To illustrate how various physical structures contribute to motor development, Goldfield (1989) found that the onset of crawling emerges from the interaction of three developing capabilities: orientation to the support surface, kicking, and reaching (each infant has a distinct rate of development). Precrawling infants can use the eyes and heads to orient themselves in the environment, but the ability to do this in different postures develops gradually. Infants in the first weeks of life can coordinate kicking, but during the first year lateral dominance varies. While very young infants show considerable skill at reaching with one hand, they are still developing coordinated reaching with two hands. Thus, when the infant is lying face down and attempting to maintain balance while kicking and reaching to move, individual development patterns of each capability influence the specific form of locomotion. For example, the development of kicking is influenced by the increase in strength as the muscles grow and are exercised. Goldfield found that as kicking develops so does the shift from a low to a high creep that allows an infant to fully support her weight. Likewise, the release of weight bearing to start the alternation for forward crawling can be initiated by shifting strengths in lateral hand preference. Finally, when analyzing crawling, one must consider the role of motivation in that an infant usually wants to explore something beyond her reach.

In summary, motor development is influenced by the physical constraints of individual structures maturing at different rates and by the psychological constraints of the brain's ability to interpret the environment and solve problems.

## ENDOCRINE SYSTEM

While the nervous system regulates and integrates physical and motor development through electrochemical transmitters sent across the synapses between neurons, the endocrine system regulates various bodily activities by sending chemicals called *hormones* from specific endocrine glands to specific targets.

Hormones have several functions. They regulate the pace of bodily function, or metabolism; for example, the hormone secreted by the thyroid gland maintains basal or overall metabolic rate, and the hormone secreted by the adrenal glands maintains a balance of sodium, potassium, and water. Hormones also regulate growth or structural increase. Triggered by chromosomes, they establish basic sex differences, stimulate the growth of secondary sexual characteristics, and regulate reproduction. They influence the nervous system and facilitate mental processes. In short, hormones are fundamental to many life processes and are basic to life itself (Krogman 1972).

The most important endocrine glands (figure 5.6) involved in the process of physical growth are the *pituitary gland*, located at the base of the brain; the *thyroid gland*, with two lobes located on opposite sides of the windpipe; the cortex of the *adrenal gland*, located on the kidneys; and the *gonads*, or sex glands, located in the ovaries of a woman or the testes of a man (Tortora & Anagnostakos, 1990).

In the lower-central portion of the brain, a structure called the **hypothalamus** functions as a master control for the endocrine system, informing the glands when and how much hormone to secrete. The hypothalamus

Motor development affects perceptual and cognitive development in that whatever babies can put in their mouths or touch become objects to perceive and learn about.

To perform complex movements like dancing, the entire set of bones and muscles must be coordinated.

## F.Y.I.

Sodium with potassium regulates the amount of water in the cells of the body and is essential for proper transmission of nerve impulses and contraction of muscles.

## FIGURE 5.6

The endocrine glands regulate various bodily activities by transmitting hormones to different parts of the body.

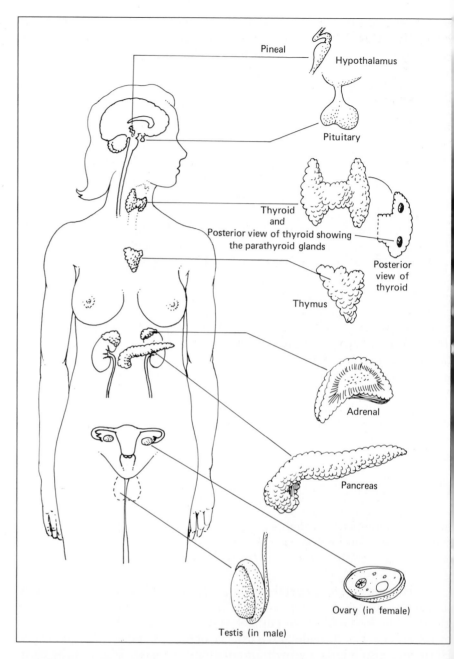

transmits messages to the pituitary. In turn, the pituitary gland stimulates and controls all other glands in the endocrine system. The way the pituitary operates is to send "messenger" hormones called *trophins* to the specific glands to secrete their specific hormones. For example, the pituitary secretes a hormone called *thyroid-stimulating hormone (TSH)*, which stimulates the thyroid to secrete a hormone called *thyroxin,* which regulates metabolism. The pituitary gland secretes a hormone that promotes breast development and milk production in the female. It also regulates the functions of the ovaries (ovulation and secretion of estrogen) and the testes (sperm production and secretion of androgen). It stimulates the cortex or outer layer of the adrenal to secrete *androgen* in both sexes. Further, the pituitary gland produces *human growth hormone (HGH)* that is responsible for size increases. The orchestration of hormones, delicately balanced, are primarily responsible for all bodily changes that occur in the 20-year growing period (Krogman, 1972) as is illustrated in figures 5.7 and 5.8 (page 146).

## Human Growth Hormone

Human growth hormone is secreted by the pituitary gland in large quantities from the time of birth until adolescence. At this time, the production of growth hormone diminishes but does not stop completely. The function of growth hormone is to promote development and enlargement of all bodily tissues. It increases the sizes of cells and also their numbers. Thus, each organ becomes larger under the influence of growth hormone.

A person whose pituitary gland fails to secrete growth hormone fails to grow. This is one cause of dwarfism (another is heredity). Dwarfism caused by a malfunctioning pituitary gland is characterized by failure of the bones to grow and a lack of sexual development. Thus, even though the individual is an adult, he remains childlike in appearance.

Human growth hormone now can be manufactured synthetically. Thus, children whose lack of growth stems from insufficient hormone can

**Dwarfism can be caused by heredity or by the pituitary gland's secreting insufficient amounts of human growth hormone.**

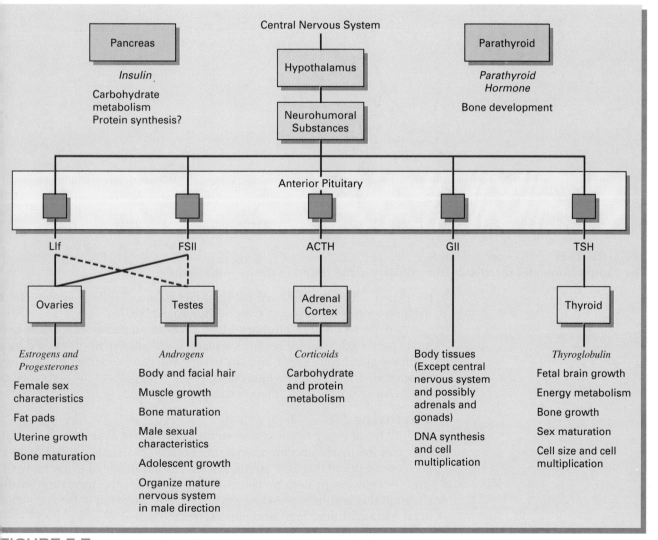

FIGURE 5.7

**The endocrine glands secrete hormones that have a profound influence on postnatal growth and development. (Smart & Smart, 1977)**

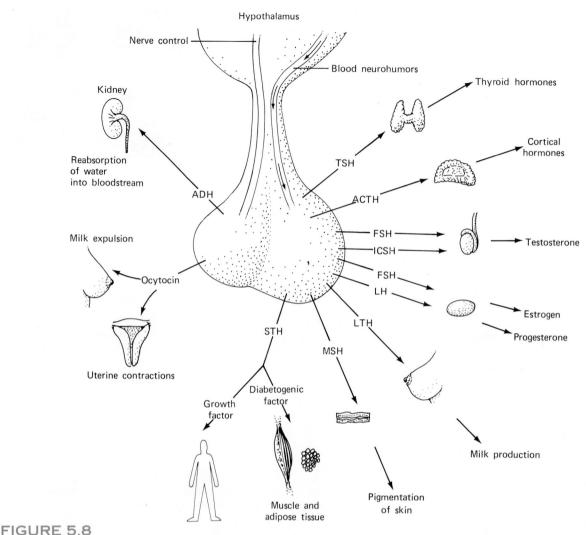

## FIGURE 5.8

**The various hormones secreted by the pituitary gland found in the hypothalamus**

be treated with large doses of the hormone although little is known abou the long-term consequences (Wilson & Rosenfeld, 1987).

A person whose pituitary gland secretes an excess of growth hor mone before adolescence becomes a giant. Giantism usually is caused by a pituitary gland tumor, but, like dwarfism, also can be caused by heredity Characteristics of giants involve enlargement of all parts of the body includ ing the skeleton, muscles, internal structures, and skin.

## Thyroxine

Almost every organ system in the body can be altered by an insuffi ciency of the thyroid hormone, *thyroxin*, because of its major effect on oxy gen consumption; that is, it stimulates the oxygen intake of every body tis sue. It promotes protein metabolism and increases the formation of the chemical that regulates muscle energy. Also, it is involved in the regulation of fat, carbohydrate, water, and mineral metabolism.

Diminished thyroxine production early in life can result in dwarfism and mental retardation. Excessive thyroxine production can result in a high basal metabolic rate, hyperactivity and nervousness, increased heart rate, and diarrhea.

# Adrenal Hormones

Adrenal hormones come from both the cortex and the medulla of the adrenal gland. The cortex produces *steroid* hormones. The medulla produces hormones that influence blood pressure and pulse rate and that act on peripheral blood vessels. Three groups of steroid hormones are:

1. hormones that maintain water, sodium, and potassium balance.
2. hormones that maintain the carbohydrate-protein balance.
3. hormones called adrenal androgens that promote masculinization and are partly responsible for the sex-related changes in puberty.

# Sex Hormones

The *gonads* or sex glands—testes in the male, ovaries in the female—play an important role in growth and maturation. The hormonal secretion of the gonads is influenced by the sex-stimulating hormone of the anterior pituitary. Male sex hormones, or *androgens*, are secreted by both the adrenal glands and testes. Female sex hormones, *estrogen* and *progesterone*, are secreted by the ovaries. In both males and females, an increase in the amount of sex hormones occurs at puberty.

Androgens promote protein synthesis, muscle development, and bone growth, and govern the growth of primary and secondary sex characteristics. A primary male sex characteristic is the male reproductive system that develops prenatally when *testosterone*, an androgen, is secreted by the testes. A secondary male sex characteristic is deepening of the voice.

Estrogens secreted by the ovaries:

1. influence protein metabolism under certain circumstances.
2. preside over linear growth and maturation.
3. regulate the timing and nature of primary sex characteristics that involve growth of reproductive system and secondary sex characteristics such as growth of breasts.
4. at puberty affect fat metabolism and, with adrenal cortical hormones, give the female body its characteristic shape.

The body's system for regulating growth is complicated. The role hormones play in physical development becomes obvious during *puberty*.

# PUBERTY

**Puberty** refers to the biological processes involved in attaining sexual maturation, or the ability to reproduce. Puberty occurs over about four years but the time varies among individuals, and between males and females—females reach puberty 1 ½ or 2 years before males.

The human body comes equipped with an endocrine system capable of initiating the process of sexual maturation at birth; however, its functioning is suppressed. Throughout childhood, both males and females produce low levels of androgens and estrogens in equal amounts. Then, in response to some unexplained biological signal, the hypothalamus stimulates the pituitary gland, which, in turn, stimulates the other endocrine glands to secrete their specific hormones.

The increase in hormonal levels has numerous results. One is the remarkable acceleration in growth of the skeletal system, leading to what is termed the adolescent growth spurt. The dramatic growth observed in adolescents is due to the rate at which their individual ultimate height is attained. At the time of boys' peak growth rate (which usually occurs at about age 14), 3 to 5 inches are added to their height in one year; for girls (whose peak growth rate usually occurs at about age 12), 2 ½ to 4 ½ inches are added (Tanner, 1990). This growth rate approximates the growth rate of a 2 year old. While growth continues after the peak, it is at a slower rate. The skeletal structure also changes so that males acquire an inverted triangular-shaped physique, with broad shoulders and narrower hips. Females' hips develop more rapidly than other areas so they acquire an hour-glass shape, with hips wider than shoulders (Tanner, 1990).

Another pubertal change is in the composition of muscle and body fat. Males are more muscular and stronger than females at all ages, but the differences are not noticeable until puberty when the increased testosterone leads to a dramatic spurt in male muscular development. Additionally, as puberty approaches, a spurt in fat growth occurs approximately one year after the beginning of the height spurt. Because of the influence of the female sex hormone estrogen, the fat layer continues to grow rapidly in females, but not in males, Thus, males actually show a decreased in thickness of fat layer and may consider themselves as skinny, whereas females are more likely to consider themselves as fat (Clifford, 1971).

The physical changes during adolescence also involve the internal organs. During the adolescent years, the heart doubles in size, and in young adulthood the circulatory system is at its peak efficiency. Increases in lung size and *vital capacity* (amount of oxygen the lungs can take in) also occur. Such changes lead to increased strength and endurance, particularly for adolescent males. For both sexes, puberty brings an increase in physical ability and motor coordination.

The most dramatic changes of puberty involve the development of the reproductive organs and the appearance of secondary sex characteristics. The internal reproductive organs enlarge and change shape for both males and females. The surge in female hormones leads to the first menses,

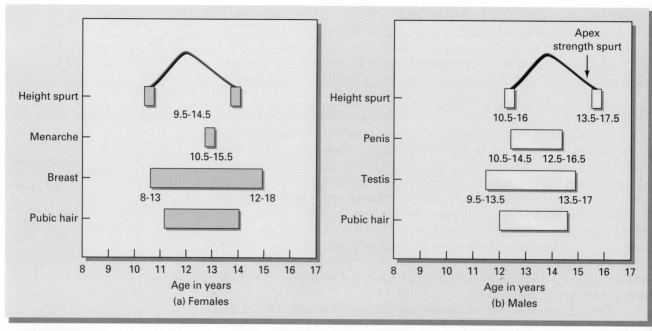

FIGURE 5.9
The developmental sequence of events at adolescence in males and females. (Tanner, 1990)

alled the **menarche**, whereas the surge in male hormones causes sperm production and the first ejaculation.

The increased hormone production also leads to a predictable pattern in the development of *secondary sexual characteristics* in males and females. This sequence of sexual development appears to follow a similar pattern from generation to generation and culture to culture, despite a wide range in the age of appearance of certain characteristics as indicated in figure 5.9.

The following is the sequence of sexual change in males (Sahler & Mc Anarney, 1981, p. 19):
1. Growth of the testes and changes in texture and color of the scrotum.
2. Initial penile growth
3. Pubic hair development
4. Accelerated penile growth and continued growth of the testes and scrotum
5. Growth of the seminal vesicles and prostate gland
6. Peak height velocity
7. Full facial hair
8. Voice change

The sequence of sexual change in females is as follows (Sahler & Mc Anarney, 1981, p. 19):
1. Broadening of the bony pelvis
2. Breast development
3. Development of the uterus, vagina, labia, and clitoris
4. Pubic hair development
5. Maximum height spurt
6. Menarche

When physical and/or motor development goes awry, physical disabilities such as those described in box 5.1 can result.

## Box 5.1  PHYSICAL DISABILITIES

A physical disability is a condition that interferes with a child's capacity to use his body. Some examples of physical disabilities are listed in table 5.1 (page 151).

Children with physical disabilities are an extremely varied population. Some disabilities can be birth defects, like cerebral palsy, and some can have been acquired later, like paralysis due to an accident. Not only does the type of disability vary but so does the degree of severity. Children with physical disabilities face the problem of public "acceptance," and many face the challenge of doing simple tasks of everyday living that most of us take for granted, like walking or writing.

Physical disabilities are not associated with a single personality type (Lewandowski & Cruickshank, 1980). How children adapt to their physical limitations and how they respond to social-interpersonal situations greatly depend on how parents, siblings, teachers, peers, and the public react to them (Hallahan & Kauffman, 1991). If others react with rejection, fear, or

The boy, who is blind and has cerebral palsy, shares a braille picture book with his sister, who can see. The book has both braille and print text and illustrations.

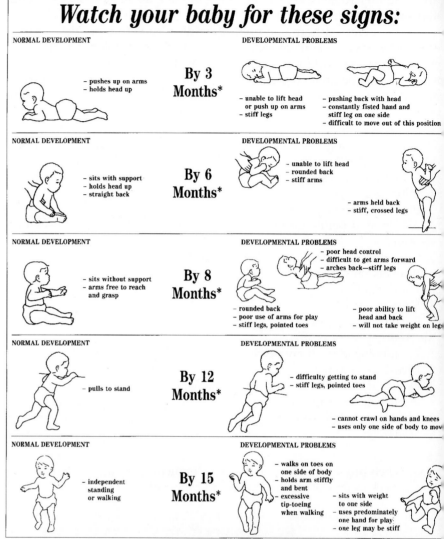

## Watch your baby for these signs:

**By 3 Months***

NORMAL DEVELOPMENT
- pushes up on arms
- holds head up

DEVELOPMENTAL PROBLEMS
- unable to lift head or push up on arms
- stiff legs
- pushing back with head
- constantly fisted hand and stiff leg on one side
- difficult to move out of this position

**By 6 Months***

NORMAL DEVELOPMENT
- sits with support
- holds head up
- straight back

DEVELOPMENTAL PROBLEMS
- unable to lift head
- rounded back
- stiff arms
- arms held back
- stiff, crossed legs

**By 8 Months***

NORMAL DEVELOPMENT
- sits without support
- arms free to reach and grasp

DEVELOPMENTAL PROBLEMS
- rounded back
- poor use of arms for play
- stiff legs, pointed toes
- poor head control
- difficult to get arms forward
- arches back—stiff legs
- poor ability to lift head and back
- will not take weight on legs

**By 12 Months***

NORMAL DEVELOPMENT
- pulls to stand

DEVELOPMENTAL PROBLEMS
- difficulty getting to stand
- stiff legs, pointed toes
- cannot crawl on hands and knees
- uses only one side of body to move

**By 15 Months***

NORMAL DEVELOPMENT
- independent standing or walking

DEVELOPMENTAL PROBLEMS
- walks on toes on one side of body
- holds arm stiffly and bent
- excessive tip-toeing when walking
- sits with weight to one side
- uses predominately one hand for play
- one leg may be stiff

\* 90% of babies do this before these ages. Remember to correct your child's age for prematurity.

discrimination, physically disabled individuals can spend much energy hiding their differences or isolating themselves. If the reaction is pity and an expectation of helplessness, the disabled person will tend to behave in a dependent manner. Thus, to the extent that other people can see children with physical handicaps as persons with certain limitations but who are otherwise normal people, disabled children will be encouraged to become independent and productive members of society (Hallahan & Kauffman, 1991).

The most powerful influence on a disabled child's image of herself is the family. The psychological effect of having a disabled child is powerful regardless of the nature or cause of the condition. The family experiences shock, disappointment, depression, and feels that life has been unfair (Roos, 1975; Lyon, 1985). Parents often experience shame and guilt over their feelings.

Having a physically disabled child in the family is a tremendous stress (Trunbull, Summers & Brotherson, 1984). Such a child almost invariably demands a disproportionate amount of the family's financial resources, energy, and time. The family can react negatively or positively. On the negative side, the parents can blame one another, neglect each other or their children, or try to deny the child is disabled. Siblings can resent

### TABLE 5.1

| | |
|---|---|
| Cerebral Palsy | Long-term condition that occurs before, during, or soon after birth. It involves damage to the brain, which causes paralysis or motion disorders of various body parts. |
| Spina Bifida | Congenital defect in spinal cord development, in which the spinal column does not close. Defect can occur at any place from the head to the lower end of the spine. Because the spinal column is not closed, the nerve fibers in the spinal cord can protrude, resulting in nerve damage and paralysis below the site of the defect. |
| Muscular Dystrophy | Group of long-term diseases that gradually weaken and waste away the muscles. |
| Osteogenesis Imperfecta | Inherited condition marked by extremely brittle bones. The skeletal system does not grow normally, and the affected bones are easily fractured. |
| Epilepsy | Seizure disorder which results in disturbance of movement, sensation, behavior, and/or consciousness. Seizure is caused by abnormal electrical activity in the brain. |
| Diabetes | Disorder of carbohydrate metabolism due to insufficient insulin. Without medical treatment, a diabetic child's system cannot obtain adequate energy from food. Eyes and kidneys can be damaged. |
| Hemophilia | Inherited disorder in which blood clotting is impaired. Internal bleeding can cause swelling, pain, and permanent damage to a child's joints, tissue, and internal organs. Blood transfusions may be necessary. |

extra care and attention the child receives. The child can be overprotected, infantilized, neglected, and denied normal experiences, or even abused.

On the positive side, the family bonds can be strengthened, and members can work together to contribute to the child's adjustment. Siblings can learn responsibility and compassion (Turnbull, Summers & Brotherson, 1984).

# BIOLOGICAL INFLUENCES ON PHYSICAL AND MOTOR DEVELOPMENT

Biological influences on physical and motor development include heredity, hormones, and gender.

## HEREDITY

While the sequence of physical and motor development is the same for all humans, one's genes influence variations in the sequence. For example, children born to tall parents will be taller than children born to short parents (Malina, Harper & Holman, 1970). Evidence for the role of heredity in physical development comes from studies of twins. Monozygotic, or identical twins from one egg, are more similar in stature than dizygotic, or fraternal twins from two eggs (Tanner, 1990).

Heredity not only plays a role in maximal growth attainment, but it affects the maturation rate as well. For example, female identical twins reach menarche generally within one or two months of each other, whereas fraternal twins differ on an average of about 12 months (Tanner, 1990).

Genes influence motor development; although the degree of inheritability is not as clear as it is for physical development. Studies of twins during infancy indicate a greater similarity for development of motor activities among identical twins than among fraternal twins (Bouchard, 1978). This also is true for middle childhood for gross motor tasks such as running, jumping, and throwing. However, for tasks requiring complex coordination, the degree of similarity among identical twins decreases (Malina, 1980).

## HORMONES

Hormones are significant in many body processes related to development. Figure 5.10 shows the glands that release these hormones. Influential hormones are released from the pituitary gland located at the base of the brain near the hypothalamus, a structure that initiates and regulates pituitary secretions. When the hypothalamus activates the pituitary gland, pituitary hormones are released into the bloodstream where they either act directly on body tissues to produce growth or stimulate the release of other growth and sex-related hormones from endrocine glands located elsewhere, including the thyroid and adrenal glands, testes, and ovaries. These growth and sex-related hormones, in turn, affect various aspects of physical maturation. The hormones that specifically influence physical development are human growth hormone, thyroxine, adrenal hormones, and sex hormones, namely testosterone, estrogen, and progesterone. Table 5.2 (page 154) summarizes the effects of hormones on growth and development.

Because hormones affect body size, body shape, muscle and bone development, metabolism, and primary and secondary sex characteristics, they have an indirect influence on motor development. For example, Parizkova (1984) found a definite relation between body build and throwing, running, and jumping tasks for preschool children with muscular children outperforming fat children.

## GENDER

The gender, or sex, differences in male and female growth patterns are due to differentiation of the specific male (XY) or female (XX) chromosomes that, in turn, affect hormonal production. For example, females usually precede males in skeletal maturity until adolescence. Also, the adolescent growth spurt in females begins earlier than in males. In females it begins at about the age of ten, reaches its maximum about two years later, and ends at about the age of 15. Among boys, the growth spurt usually begins at about the age of 12, usually peaks at about age 14, and can continue for as long as five years (Tanner, 1990).

In addition to physical growth, other differences are influenced by gender. Females have a greater proportion of fat cells and less muscle tissue

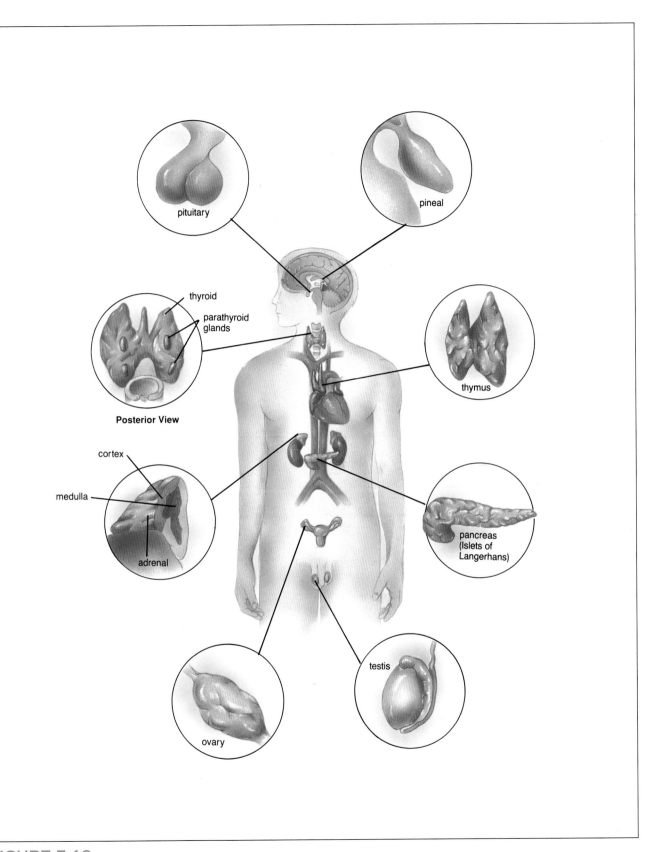

FIGURE 5.10
THE ENDOCRINE SYSTEM

## EFFECTS OF SOME HORMONES ON GROWTH AND DEVELOPMENT

### TABLE 5.2

| Endocrine Gland | Hormones | Effects on Growth and Development |
| --- | --- | --- |
| Pituitary | Trophins | Signal specific endocrine to secrete specific hormones |
| | Human Growth Hormone | Helps regulate growth from birth to adolescence |
| Adrenal glands | Adrenal Hormones | Influence sex-related changes in puberty such as adolescent growth spurt, promotion of masculinization in males, growth of axillary hair in females |
| Gonads | Sex Hormones | Development of male or female primary and secondary sex characteristics |
| Testes | Androgens | Promote protein synthesis, muscle development, bone growth, development of male reproductive system during prenatal period; trigger male growth spurt and sexual maturation during adolescence |
| Ovaries | Estrogens | Influence metabolism and body shape, regulate development of primary and secondary sex characteristics |

**From 2 to 5, girls tend to excel in tasks requiring jumping, hopping, rhythmic locomotion, and balance, while boys generally perform better in tasks requiring strength and speed.**

than males. This difference remains consistent across all ages (Smith, 1977). Males have larger hearts and lungs (Tanner, 1990), whereas females have lower basal metabolism rates, meaning they require less energy to maintain body functions compared with males (Vaughn, McKay & Behrman, 1984).

Some researchers have found sex differences in brain development and organization, specifically in lateralization. The left hemisphere of females matures more rapidly than that of males, while the right hemisphere of males matures more rapidly than that of females (Winsom, 1985). This can account for sex differences in language development, which is primarily controlled by the left hemisphere (in right-handed individuals), because females generally do better than males on verbal tasks. Males, on the other hand, generally do better than females on spatial ability, which is primarily controlled by the right hemisphere (in right-handed individuals) (Basow, 1992).

Males and females differ slightly in the development of certain motor abilities throughout childhood (Cratty, 1986). Starting at 5 to 6 years of age, males perform better in running, jumping and throwing activities, while females excel in hopping (Espenschade & Eckert, 1974).

# CONTEXTUAL INFLUENCES ON PHYSICAL AND MOTOR DEVELOPMENT

Now we will look at the contextual influences affecting postnatal development—nutrition, physical health, emotional health, and exercise.

## NUTRITION

Nutritional status is probably the most influential contextual factor affecting human growth and development. Nutritional status includes undernutrition, which is a deficiency of essential nutrients, ideal nutrition, which includes the recommended dietary allowances according to age, and overnutrition, which is an excess of nutrients. Essential nutrients include proteins, fats, carbohydrates, vitamins, and minerals. Proteins are necessary for growth, maintenance, and repair of body tissues. Carbohydrates provide fuel to meet the body's energy requirements. Fats contribute to the body's energy reserves and insulate the body against heat loss. Vitamins and minerals are required for synthesis of special structures and compounds needed by the body. For instance, vitamin D is needed for bone growth, and iron is needed to manufacture hemoglobin.

## Undernutrition

Undernourished children grow more slowly than well-fed children. If a child is undernourished for a short time and it is not too severe, the child will return to her inherited normal growth rate after assuming an adequate diet (Tanner, 1990). If, however, the undernourishment is long lasting and severe, the child will remain small throughout life. Prolonged undernutrition during the first five years of life can retard brain growth. Studies on severely malnourished children during the first few years of life show deviant electrical brain wave recordings and a reduction in the speed of motor impulses, implying an interference with myelinization (Engsner & Woldemarian, 1974; Malina, 1980).

Severe undernutrition bordering on starvation results in a disease called marasmus. **Marasmus** is caused by a diet low in all essential nutrients, resulting in emaciation: severe weight loss, muscular atrophy, and a decrease in fat. Usually, the disease occurs when, due to extreme maternal malnutrition, breast milk is insufficient for the growing infant and supplementary feeding is inadequate.

Other types of malnutrition involve *protein/calorie deficiency* that results from *insufficient* protein and/or total calories needed to sustain normal growth, or *vitamin/mineral deficiency* that results from *sufficient* food lacking one or more substances needed to maintain health and promote normal growth.

Protein/calorie deficiencies are common among children living in poor, underdeveloped countries where food resources are limited (Johnston, 1980) such as Africa, Asia, and Latin America. A disease called *Kwashiokor* results from a diet insufficient in protein. The disease is characterized by a wasted condition of the body, swelling of the face and limbs, skin rash, and an enlarged and fatty liver, leading to a swollen abdomen.

In the United States, protein/calorie deficiencies are uncommon. More common are vitamin/mineral deficiencies. For example, in one survey of lower socioeconomic preschoolers, it was found that their diets were

These children from the Congo have early symptoms of kwashiokor. Some of the typical manifestations include lethargic behavior, apathetic appearance, wrinkled skin, distended stomach, and thin, wispy, reddish-orange cast of hair.

deficient in vitamins A, C, and riboflavin (Eichorn, 1979). In another survey conducted in ten states, it was found that over 90 percent of children age 1 to 3 had diets deficient in iron (Eichorn, 1979). Iron deficiency is the most common nutritional disorder in the world, in both industrial and nonindustrial societies (Lozoff, 1988).

Vitamin A deficiency can result in eye damage, leading to blindness, and retardation in mental and physical growth. Vitamin C deficiency can impede skeletal growth and cause softening and swelling of the gums and pain in the legs. A deficiency in riboflavin can result in cracking of the skin at the angles of the mouth. Iron deficiency can result in anemia, or a reduction in the amount of blood hemoglobin, thereby impairing its ability to transport oxygen to the cells. Iron deficiency severe enough to cause anemia has been associated with impaired performance on developmental tests in infancy (Lozoff, 1989).

## Overnutrition

Undernutrition has various consequences for the developing body. Likewise, overnutrition causes problems. The most immediate effect of overnutrition is **obesity**, a weight of over 20 percent the average weight for one's age, gender, and height. There is a strong tendency for obese children to become obese adolescents and obese adults (Hughes, 1980). Obese individuals are at risk for serious medical complications such as diabetes, high blood pressure, and heart, liver, or kidney disease.

Researchers have examined early growth patterns for clues about the origins of obesity. The evidence indicates that rapidity of weight gain during the first year of life predicts overweight during the school years (Eid, 1970).

Overweight children do not only eat more, but they also are less physically active than normal-weight peers (Kolata, 1986).

In addition to potential physical problems, obesity has social and psychological consequences. Obese children may find making friends with age mates difficult. Peers are apt to tease obese children about their size and shape, thus making them feel bad about themselves. Staffieri (1967) found chubby youngsters to be the least popular in grade school classrooms.

In a review of 24 studies on the use of behavioral therapy for childhood obesity, it was found that behavioral treatment was effective in weight reduction (Epstein & Wing, 1987). Also, including parents in a child's treatment was found to result in lower relative weight for those children after five years than for children treated without the presence of parents (Epstein et al., 1987).

## PHYSICAL HEALTH

In adequately nourished children, ordinary childhood illnesses, such as respiratory infections, viruses, and gastrointestinal infections, have no effect on physical growth except for minor and temporary weight fluctuations. However, in undernourished children, disease is associated with poor physical growth (Martorell, 1980). This is probably caused by inadequate diets depressing the immune system, thereby making children more susceptible to disease (Salomon, Mata & Gordon, 1968).

In turn, disease is a major cause of malnutrition that affects growth. Illness reduces children's appetites, thereby limiting the adequacy of nutrients children consume. When illness is long term, such as tuberculosis or cancer, the impact of nutritional status can be significant. Certain parasitic diseases, such as tapeworm and malaria, draw significant amounts of nutrients for their own needs, thereby impacting the available supply for a child (Beisel, 1977).

## EMOTIONAL HEALTH

Common emotional stresses children experience, such as being frightened by a TV show or fighting with a friend, have little impact on growth (Tanner, 1990). Generally, children in families where they are given affection and support can endure a variety of emotional stresses without long-term effects. However, in families where children are maltreated (deprived of affection, are neglected, or abused) stress can cause a reduction in growth. Growth disorders called *failure to thrive* and *deprivation dwarfism* are believed to result from lack of attention and affection.

**Failure to thrive** is a condition appearing in infancy involving growth retardation with no organic or nutritional signs and symptoms. Maltreatment involving neglect or lack of response to an infant's emotional needs is the usual cause (Fontana, 1991). The syndrome appears by 18 months, and its most striking feature is a substantial reduction in weight. The loss of both fat and muscle tissue causes a neonate to have an emaciated, wasted appearance. Further, the infant is passive toward the physical environment and does not respond when picked up (Oates, 1984).

**Deprivation dwarfism** is a condition appearing in children between ages 2 and 15 involving a retardation in physical growth. Short stature is its most striking feature, but malnutrition is not the cause. Children with deprivation dwarfism often show abnormally low levels of growth hormone, and their skeletal ages, indicating the quantity of cartilage that has turned into bone, are immature. It is believed that the disorder occurs because maltreatment involving emotional deprivation (constant rejection in the form of failing to provide love and/or constant demeaning of a child through criticism or insult) affects the signals between the hypothalamus and pituitary glands. This results in a decrease in growth hormone secretion and, thus, inhibits growth. When affected children are removed from the emotionally deprived environments, their growth hormone levels return to normal and they catch up in their growth. However, if they remain in a deprived environment, dwarfism can be permanent (Oates, Peacock & Forrest, 1985).

## EXERCISE

Exercise influences physical development because it enhances or impedes bone and muscle growth. Exercise increases bone width and mineralization. The exact effects, however, of exercise on bone growth are difficult to evaluate accurately because of the interaction of other factors, including individual differences in response to exercise and hormones (Zaichkowsky, Zaichkowsky & Martinek, 1980).

Like bone, muscle tissue responds and adapts to the physical stress of exercise. Muscle mass and strength increase when one engages in a regular exercise program. Systematic physical activity affects muscle composition as well as size. Physically active children have a higher proportion of lean body mass to body fat (Parizkova, 1973).

Undoubtedly, persistent highly stressful activity results in damage to bone and muscle tissue, especially in immature individuals (Zaichkowsky,

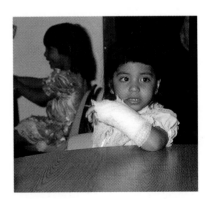

Immobilization, such as when one has to wear a cast, decreases bone mineralization.

Zaichkowsky & Martinek, 1980). For example, too much pressure on immature bones may result in chronic arm trouble such as "Little League elbow" or even arthritis later (Galton, 1980).

Exercise, or practice, also influences motor development. Motor development refers to the coordinated use of muscles controlled by the *motor neurons.* Such neurons control all the voluntary muscles in the body. Examples are grasping, crawling, and throwing.

The maturationists believe the development of motor abilities is due to maturation of the nervous system, so exercise (practice) would have little effect. Wayne Dennis (1935; 1940) confirmed this view in studies that showed motor development occurred in a predetermined course despite differences in experience. One study was on infants raised in the Hopi culture (Dennis, 1940). Hopi indian infants raised traditionally spend much of their first year of life strapped to a cradleboard that their mothers carry about as they work. Dennis compared traditionally raised Hopi infants with those raised like contemporary American infants in that they were allowed freedom of movement their first year of life. Dennis found no difference in the average age both groups of infants walked. Thus, he concluded that the maturation of motor abilities operated independently of experience.

Twenty years later, Dennis (1960) modified his views on the role of experience in motor development. He compared children age 1 to 4 raised in Iranian orphanages with American children raised at home using standard tests of motor development.

According to the Denver Development Screening Test (figure 5.11, page 160), a standard test used in the United States to assess motor development, 90 percent of all infants can sit independently before eight months of age. The children from the orphanage did not achieve this until 2 or 3 years of age. About 90 percent of infants can walk independently by 15 months of age. Unlike the children raised at home, Dennis (1960) found the orphans were left on their backs in cribs most of the day. They were deprived of experiences necessary in the sequence of developing the ability to walk. "Maturation alone is insufficient to bring about most postnatal developments in behavior" (Dennis, 1960, pg. 57).

Organized sports programs often play a role in children's development (box 5.2).

## Box 5.2   CHILDREN AND SPORTS

Sports participation for children and adolescents has served an important role in American society since the turn of the century (Weiss, 1989). Sports are not only a major form of recreation but are considered a means of achieving physical fitness. Sports also are regarded as a way for children to learn various physical skills, leadership, cooperation, loyalty, and competitiveness. The American attitude toward sports is revealed by the statistics. Approximately 20 million American children, age 6 and older, play on organized sports teams— about 2 million play Little League baseball, 1 million play organized football, and the other 17 million are involved in hockey, soccer, swimming, track, and gymnastics (Galton, 1980).

Children participate in sports for many reasons—to develop skills, demonstrate physical competence, get stronger and more physically fit, be with peers, enjoy the excitement of competition, and have fun (Gould & Horn, 1984).

Research shows that generally young children would rather play for a losing team than warm the bench for a winning team (Weiss, 1989). In some cases, the adults (coaches and/or parents) place more emphasis on winning than playing. When winning is constantly emphasized, undue pressures are placed on children (Galton, 1980). Children can perceive coaches' and parents' reactions to winning and losing games. If positive responses such as joy and excitement follow only winning, and negative responses such as disappointment and embarrassment follow losing, then children can acquire a fear of failure and will refuse to participate in sports (Gould & Horn, 1984).

Sports in American society are big business. Success in sports not only enables one to have a lucrative athletic career but also provides opportunities in the media such as advertising. These sports heroes are powerful role models for children and adolescents. In his classic study, James Coleman (1961) found that athletics and popularity were more important to adolescents than academic performance.

The pressure to succeed in sports is so great that some adolescents and young adults turn to using drugs, specifically anabolic steroids, to increase muscle size and strength. These drugs have serious side effects. In the prepubertal or pubertal male, the most significant effect is accelerated *epiphyseal* development and possible early epiphyseal closure. The epiphysis is at each end of a bone and is separated from the bone shaft by cartilage. The cartilage grows until late adolescence when it becomes bone and unites the shaft with the bone ends. If this happens early, the result would be diminished terminal height. Additional steroid effects for both females and males can include altered sex characteristics, liver damage, growth of hair, and a deepening of the voice (Zaichkowsky, Zaichkowsky & Martinek, 1980).

It is obvious from the number of spectators and the national television coverage of this Little League World Series that there is a significant interest in sports in America.

# INTERACTION OF BIOLOGICAL AND CONTEXTUAL INFLUENCES ON PHYSICAL AND MOTOR DEVELOPMENT

While biological influences (heredity, hormones, and gender) and contextual influences (nutrition, physical health, emotional health, and exercise) on physical and motor development have been discussed separately, in reality these influences interact in different combinations to produce various effects. An example of interactional effects on physical development is the interaction of heredity, hormones, nutrition, and health to produce larger individuals who mature earlier. An example of interactional effects on motor development is the interaction of heredity and exercise to produce athletic talent. Finally, an example of interactional effects on how one feels about one's physique and the use of it involves the interaction of heredity, hormones, and gender with the social context.

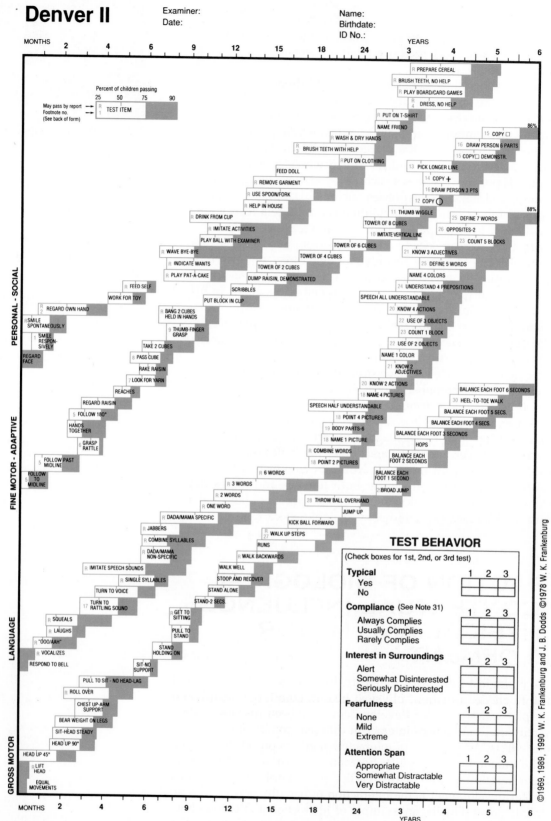

FIGURE 5.11

THE DENVER DEVELOPMENTAL SCREENING TEST

# GENERATIONAL DIFFERENCES IN GROWTH AND MATURITY

Based on historical research, developmental psychologists have found that the average adult of today is about five centimeters taller than his counterpart of 100 years ago. Similarly, foot size has increased about one size per generation over the past 100 years, and the average adult weight has increased significantly (Roche, 1979).

Based on surveys of medical records, developmental psychologists also have found that children of today mature earlier than previous generations. For example, the average age for menarche in 1840 was age 17; today it is before age 13 (Malina, 1979; Tanner, 1990). Males of today also reach puberty about 4 to 5 years earlier than they did in 1840. Today, they reach their ultimate height by age 17 or 18, whereas 50 years ago they continued to grow until age 25 or 26 ( Malina, 1979; Tanner, 1990).

In Western, industrialized societies more knowledge about diet and preventive health practices as well as more advanced and accessible medical care are available to reduce the incidence of debilitating diseases (Malina, 1979; Tanner, 1990). However, growth and maturation increases are not universal. In countries stricken by poverty, famine, or disease, there is evidence of a decrease in adult stature (Kennter, 1969; Tobias, 1975).

Tanner (1990) believes biological factors, namely genes, are also influential in the trend toward greater size. He noted that the genes for tall stature are dominant over the genes for short stature. Further, because Western society is mobile and people interbreed across all of society, the result has been an increase in the phenotype for tall stature, the cumulative effect being an overall increase in the population's height.

Some evidence suggests that generational growth increases and age of maturity are stabilizing. For example, the average height of men and women has remained stable from 1960 to the 1970s (Roche, 1979). Also, data from 1890 to 1970 show a decrease in the average age of menarche by about three months every ten years. No such decrease, however, was noted between 1970 and 1980 (Vaughn, McKay & Behrman 1984). Roche (1979) warns that unless major environmental pollutants, such as air pollution, water pollution, toxic wastes, and radiation, are controlled, they may be responsible for adverse influences on human growth and development.

## ARE ATHLETES BORN OR MADE?

Arnold Gesell, a maturation theorist, believed that development is the natural unfolding of abilities with age. He demonstrated, for example, that motor skills such as standing and walking, picking up a cube, and throwing a ball develop in a fixed sequence in all children (again see figure 5.11, the Denver Developmental Screening Test). Gesell believed the order and age at which children develop are biologically determined and unaffected by environment except under adverse conditions such as famine, disease, and poverty, which would disrupt the biologically programmed timetable.

To determine whether learning or maturation was the influential factor in motor development, McGraw (1935) conducted an experiment with identical twins. One twin was allowed to practice motor skills such as climbing stairs or stacking blocks, whereas the other twin was denied these experiences. The results showed that although one twin appeared to gain

Artistic abilities are probably a result of an interaction between biological and contextual influences.

The way children perceive their physique compared to that of others can have an impact on their self-esteem.

**F.Y.I.**

Longitudinal research on early and late maturing boys over a period of six years (Jones & Bayley, 1950; Blyth et al., 1981) found that early maturers tended to be poised and confident in social settings and held a high proportion of positions of leadership in school and also tended to be athletic stars. In comparison, late maturers were more anxious and attention-seeking and were rated as less masculine and less physically attractive than early maturers. The differences in adjustment between early and late maturing boys were long-lasting in that a low self-image among the late maturers persisted into adulthood (Jones, 1965; Clausen, 1975).

little from training in such skills as walking and climbing stairs, early training in swimming had some advantages. Training was begun with one twin at eight months. When he was 17 months old, he could swim a maximum of 15 feet without help, while his twin could not swim at all. Thus, it appears that certain basic skills, such as sitting, walking, and running, are biologically influenced, whereas more complex skills such as swimming, diving, skating, throwing, catching, and writing are contextually influenced (Hottinger, 1980). If complex skills involve strength, are athletes who execute complicated motor skills born or made? Klissouras (1976) studied identical and fraternal twins before and after training. He concluded that genetics determines the level of athletic ability, but training enables a person to reach that level.

## IMPACT OF PHYSIQUE AND MOTOR ABILITIES ON SELF-CONCEPT

Darla has naturally curly, thick hair. When she was growing up, Kate kept it cut short because it was difficult to brush and keep neat. Darla hated her hair. She wanted long, straight hair like her friends. Also, she hated her freckles. She had read that lemon juice would fade freckles, so for a time she soaked a washcloth in lemon juice and kept it on her face. The only thing she did like about herself while growing up was her nose. People said she had a cute nose and that made her feel good.

It has been found that the way children's bodies grow strongly influences how they feel about themselves (Gollins, 1984). Even a popular, outgoing 12-year-old girl who is worried about the size of her nose might avoid friends when she has to wear glasses, thereby calling more attention to her face (Brooks-Gunn & Petersen, 1983).

One wants to look like one's friends, and wants to look like the cultural ideal, the way bodies are portrayed in the media. In one study (Staffieri, 1967), children 6 to 10 years of age were shown full-length figures of thin, linear or *ectomorphic*, soft, chubby or *endomorphic*, and athletic, muscular or *mesomorphic* physiques. After stating which body type they preferred, the children were given a list of adjectives and asked to select those that applied to each body type. The children preferred the mesomorphic figure and attributed adjectives such as *brave, strong, neat,* and *healthy* to this figure while assigning adjectives such as *quiet, worrisome, fearful, lonely, sad* to the ectomorphic figure and adjectives such as *stupid, naughty, aggressive, liar, dirty* to the endomorphic figure.

The children also were asked to list the names of five classmates considered good friends and three classmates whom they did not like. A definite relation was found between body build and popularity: the mesomorphs were the most popular, whereas the endomorphs were the least popular (Staffieri, 1967; Sigelman, Miller & Whitworth, 1986).

Darla matured early. She was in the fifth grade when her breasts grew and she had menses. She did not want to wear a bra because her classmates would tease her. She wore loose shirts hoping nobody would notice. Because she felt like a freak, she withdrew from friends. Her self-concept was low and remained as such until her friends' bodies also began to change about two years later.

Studies have shown that early-maturing females are less self-confident, outgoing, and popular than late maturers; and females who mature at about the same time as their peers have the best self-images, are popular, nd hold positions of leadership at school (Jones & Mussen, 1958; Duncan et al., 1985; Aro & Taipale, 1987; Petersen, 1988). Negative outcomes associated with being an early maturer become weaker between the sixth and eighth grade because other females catch up in physical status, and the peer group as a whole develops heterosexual interests (Faust, 1960). By the time females reach adulthood, the effects of early or late maturing in adolescence do not appear to carry over (Peskin, 1973).

The cultural ideal in contemporary society for physique is muscular. When males mature, they gain more muscle tissue and become broader in the shoulders, thereby approaching this ideal. They are admired by peers for their appearance. Additionally, the increase in muscle tissue increases potential strength, so they can perform better in athletic skills. Thus, those males who attain the cultural ideal early in life generally tend to have a good self-image.

On the other hand, when females mature they gain more fat tissue, become curvy, and lose the muscular appearance they might have had in childhood. Many females feel "fat" at puberty and, therefore, have a negative self-image. Further, the development of secondary sex characteristics such as menstruation can be perceived to interfere in the lifestyle of an early maturing female who is physically active. This, too, influences her self-concept. However, when a female's interests change from physical activities to attracting attention from males, her self-concept improves, because early maturing females tend to be more attractive to older males, thus tend to be envied by their later maturing friends (Brooks-Gunn & Petersen, 1983).

Thus, biological factors involved in maturation interact with the social context of peers to influence self-concept.

# ARE THE TERRIBLE TEENS DUE TO HORMONES?

Susman, E.J., Inoff-Germain, G., Nottelmann, E.D., Loriaux, D.L., Cutler, G.B., Jr., & Chrousos, G.P.(1987). Hormones, emotional dispositions, and aggressive attributes in young adolescents. *Child Development, 58,* 1114–1134.

Puberty is a period of physical development accompanied by dramatic increases in the circulating levels of many hormones. Puberty also is a period of psychological development characterized by increases in aggressive and rebellious behavior. This study examined how these biological and behavioral changes are related.

Animal studies have shown a link between hormones and aggression, especially for males. Because children in our society are socialized to inhibit overt aggressive behavior, such as physical attacks, this study examined aggressive attributes such as irritability and rebelliousness.

The subjects were 56 boys and 52 girls, 9–14 years of age. Thus, the various stages of pubertal developments were represented. It was hypothesized that higher levels of adrenal androgens would be related to higher levels of aggression. It also was hypothesized that estrogen, also a gonadal steroid, would be negatively related to aggression.

The procedures used to assess various aspects of the adolescents' social, emotional, and cognitive development as well as family relationships involved interviews, questionnaires, and rating scales. The assessments on both biological and psychological measures took place three times at six-month intervals. Variables included in the assessment of emotional dispositions were angry–friendly mood, nervous–calm mood, happy–sad mood, and impulse control. Variables included in the assessment of aggressive attributes were delinquent behavior such as lying, cheating, or stealing, aggressive behavior such as arguing, cruelty, threats, rebellious behavior such as talking back, irritability, irresponsibility, and "nasty" behavior such as blaming others, taking advantage of others, stubbornness, and moodiness.

The findings indicated that hormone levels were related to both emotional dispositions and aggressive attributes for males, but not for females. For the emotional dispositions, the strongest relations were between hormones and sadness. For the aggressive attributes, the strongest relations were between hormones and delinquent rebellious behavior. Thus, some relation exists between hormones and certain emotional dispositions and aggressive attributes for males, but not so for females. It is difficult to speculate why the results for females were inconclusive. It is possible that the lack of findings were influenced by researchers who did not consider the phases of the females' menstrual cycles when they participated in the study. (Hormones vary during phases of the menstrual cycle.) Also, contextual influences such as family, peers, and culture play a role in mediating the influence of hormones on behavior. Perhaps such contextual influences have a more inhibiting effect on female behavior than on male behavior.

# CRITICAL THINKING & YOU

**M**ost of us have been alerted to the benefits of physical fitness. Fitness includes endurance, flexibility, strength, reaction time, coordination, and speed. Physical fitness is related to health and self-esteem. Training and physical education have proven effective in increasing physical fitness. How early should training begin? There are numerous physical education programs throughout the country such as Gymboree, a play and movement program, swim classes, dance classes, and ski classes for children under five years of age. Gymboree has classes for parents with children as young as three months of age. The parents are taught exercises to do with their infants, including bending and flexing muscles, sliding, bouncing, and providing visual and tactile stimulation. Older children are taught cooperative games played in groups. The games are noncompetitive, and various motor skills are emphasized.

**ANALYSIS:** Review this chapter and list support for such training and support for allowing children to mature at their own pace.

**SYNTHESIS:** List the advantages and disadvantages of sports training and compare with the advantages and disadvantages for early training in physical fitness.

**EVALUATION:** Including biological and contextual influences and their interactions, what is your prescription to optimize physical and motor development in children?

## SUMMARY

- Physical development involves the increased size of the various body parts and the increased complexity of their structures and functions.
- Motor development refers to movement and control of the body parts.
- Basic principles of development are cephalocaudal, proximodistal, and differentiation and integration.
- The skeletal system, which provides support for the body, develops by increase in bone size, change in the number of bones, and change in bone composition. This process occurs through the deposition of calcium and other minerals that causes bones to harden or ossify.
- Muscles provide strength for the body. Muscular development proceeds in a cephalocaudal direction.
- The nervous system consists of the brain, spinal cord, and peripheral nerves. Neurons receive and transmit impulses to and from parts of the body and the brain. With age, the brain becomes more

integrated and differentiated.
- The brain parts most developed at birth are located in the brainstem and regulate basic biological functions.
- Parts of the cerebrum control motor and sensory functions.
- The cerebral cortex controls voluntary motor responses and is necessary for the development of language and cognitive processes including abstract thinking.
- The cerebellum functions to control finely coordinated movements and rapid, consecutive movements. Its development lags behind the other areas of the brain.
- Myelinization facilitates the transmission of impulses, thereby increasing communication between the body and the brain.
- The cerebrum is divided into a right and left hemisphere, each connected by neurons to the opposite side of the body and each controlling different cognitive processes.

- The specialization of functions of the cerebral hemispheres is termed lateralization.
- The endocrine system regulates various body activities by sending hormones from specific endocrine glands to specific targets. Hormones regulate metabolism and growth increase, establish sex differences, influence the nervous system, and facilitate mental processes.
- Puberty refers to the biological processes involved in attaining sexual maturation, or the ability to reproduce. When the specific male or female hormones are released, the effects include acceleration in skeletal system growth, changes in the body composition of muscle and fat, changes in the internal organs, reproductive organ development, and appearance of secondary sex characteristics.
- Biological influences on physical and motor development include heredity, hormones, and gender.
- Contextual influences on development include nutrition, physical health, emotional health, and exercise.
- Heredity, hormones, nutrition, and health interact to produce larger individuals who mature early. Heredity and exercise interact to produce athletic talent. Heredity, hormones, and gender interact with the social context to influence self-concept.

## RELATED READINGS

Barrwtt, D. E., & Frank, D. A. (1987). *The effects of undernutrition on children's behavior.* New York: Gordon and Breach.

Bloom, F. E., & Lazerson, A. (1988). *Brain, mind, and behavior.*(2nd edit.). New York: W. H. Freeman.

Galton, L. *Your child in sports.* New York: Franklin Watts, 1980.

Ornstein, R., & Thompson, R. E. (1991). *The amazing brain.* Boston: Houghton Mifflin.

Payne, V. G., & Isaacs, L. D. (1987). *Human motor development.* Mountain View, CA: Mayfield.

Smith, D. W., (1977). *Growth and its disorders.* Philadelphia: W. B. Saunders.

Springer, S. P., & Deutsch, G. (1983). *Left brain, right brain.* San Francisco: W. H. Freeman.

Tanner, J. M. (1990). *Fetus into man: Physical growth from conception to maturity* (2nd ed.). Cambridge, MA: Harvard University Press.

## ● ● ● ● ● ● ● ● ● ● ● ● ● ● ● ● ● ● ACTIVITY ● ● ● ● ● ● ● ● ● ● ● ● ● ● ● ● ● ●

To better understand the motor development of children by age and gender:

A. Select two females and two males at two age levels (one 3-year-old girl and one 3-year-old boy; one 6-year-old girl and one 6-year-old boy).

B. Ask the children to do the following motor activities individually and rate them on a scale of 0–5. (Note: You may have to demonstrate the tasks.)

0—could not perform task
1—barely was able to perform task
2—performed task with poor coordination
3—performed task with fair coordination
4—performed task with good coordination
5—performed task with excellent coordination

### Gross Motor Items
1. Walk forward and backward for about 20 feet.
2. Run to a certain point and stop.
3. Jump forward with feet together.
4. Hop forward on one foot about ten feet.
5. Balance on one foot for five seconds.
6. Skip forward about 20 feet.
7. Catch a medium-size rubber ball.
8. Throw a medium-size rubber ball.

### Fine Motor Skills
1. Tie shoes.
2. Copy a circle.
3. Copy a cross.
4. Copy a square.
5. Copy a triangle.
6. Cut a straight line with scissors. (Draw the line for each child.)
7. Draw a house.
8. Write your name.

C. Answer the following questions.
1. What were the differences based on age?
2. What were the differences based on gender?
3. Was there a relation between the gross motor tasks and fine motor tasks for each child?

# 6 Perceptual Development: Interpreting The World

*All the mighty world, of eye and ear, both what they half create, and what perceive.*

**William Wordsworth**

## OUTLINE

# ABOUT PERCEPTUAL DEVELOPMENT

Kate had returned to work after she felt Kenny was old enough to be separated from her. Sometimes when Michael and his father had to work late at the service station, Mrs. Johnson would help Kate by having Kenny spend the night. Kenny loved to visit his grandparents, especially without his siblings, because his grandparents made him feel special.

One time when he was about four years old, he had to sleep on the couch in the living room because the upstairs bedroom was being painted. Never having slept in the living room before, he awakened in the middle of the night and became frightened. He began to scream. His grandmother rushed to his side. All he could sputter out was, "A Martian is going to get me."

His grandmother said, "Now Kenny you've just had a bad dream, go back to sleep."

"No, Gamma, it's there. See it!" He pointed to the television. His grandmother looked at the television; it had an indoor antenna. The shadow on the wall was what Kenny was pointing to. In the dark, unfamiliar environment Kenny perceived the television to be a Martian (he always watched cartoons with his brothers, so he knew what a Martian looked like). Kenny's grandmother had to leave the light on all night to convince Kenny that what he saw was only the television.

*Perception* is the process by which the brain interprets messages the body receives through its sense organs—the eyes, ears, nose, mouth, skin, body. Kenny saw the television. However, in the dark with a little light coming in from the window, it appeared different.

Kenny's experience illustrates the importance of perception—how it relates to knowledge about the environment and knowledge on how to react. This chapter will explore how information is selected from the real world to construct a perceptual world. In other words, how we represent objective reality.

Historically, infancy has been the period in which the study of perceptual development has concentrated because it is during this time that the individual contacts most aspects of the real world such as contrast, shapes, colors, distance, depth, sounds, smells, tastes, touches, and movement. How individuals perceive the real world impacts how they interact with it and think about it. Thus, perceptual development is significantly related to other aspects of development.

Because perception involves the use of the sense organs, we will discuss how each sense works before discussing each perceptual ability. We will look at biological, contextual, and interactional influences on perceptual development before discussing how the integration of perceptual abilities develops, because these influences are involved in the integration process. Finally, we will discuss how perception is involved in learning disabilities.

# SENSATION AND PERCEPTION

**Sensation** refers to the physiological process by which the senses receive stimuli from the environment, whereas **perception** refers to the process by which we represent and interpret things in the environment via the senses. The senses are systems that translate stimuli from the real world into neural activity, giving the nervous system, especially the brain, information about the world (figure 6.1). Because sensations can be interpreted at the neural level and the brain level, it is sometimes difficult to make clear distinctions between sensation and perception.

We have six major senses—sight, hearing, smell, taste, touch, and **proprioception**, the sense that informs us about the orientation of our body in space and the position of arms, legs, and other body parts when they move. Your sense of proprioception enables you to close your eyes and touch your nose.

How the bubbles are perceived to float by the children is a matter discussed in this chapter.

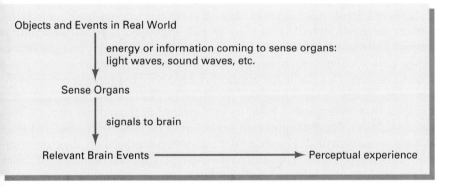

Objects and Events in Real World

↓ energy or information coming to sense organs: light waves, sound waves, etc.

Sense Organs

↓ signals to brain

Relevant Brain Events ──────────→ Perceptual experience

FIGURE 6.1
HOW THE BRAIN PERCEIVES EXTERNAL STIMULI

The senses gather information about the world through the forms of energy detected such as light, sound, odor, taste, heat, physical pressure, and movement.

Sensation and perception are the processes by which we experience, organize, and interpret our world, thereby giving meaning to what it is seen, heard, smelled, tasted, and touched. The world is full of sensory stimuli; to process everything is impossible. Thus, only certain stimuli are selected. For example, we give more attention to bright colors than dull colors.

Perceptual abilities are present at birth, but they increase as we develop. Perceptual development is affected by experience and cognitive maturity (Levine & Shefner, 1991). For example, to an infant a long, curved, brownish-black object is just that; whereas to an older child it could be a rope, a piece of hose, or a snake. Thus, because perception is an interpretation of sensory stimuli, as we interact with the world and gain more knowledge about it, our perceptions are modified accordingly. Perception relates to other areas of development. For example, visual perception is involved in many learning tasks.

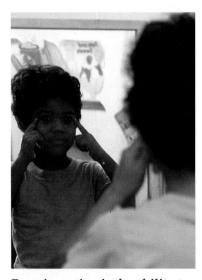

Proprioception is the ability to move the body without observing the position of its various parts. This child knows where his eyes are whether he is looking in a mirror or not.

The solution to the puzzle is available to these girls, all they have to do is differentiate between the various shapes and find the correct piece of the puzzle.

# THEORIES OF PERCEPTION

Two main views address the general processing of sensory motor information. One is known as *enrichment* theory, which focuses on the individual; the other is called *differentiation* theory, which focuses on the stimulus. Some theorists such as Jean Piaget (1969) and information-processing psychologists (Bruner, 1957) believe that each time a child perceives a stimulus, the child learns more about it. Enrichment theorists believe that perceptual development involves a child's interacting more with the world, thereby increasing associations between pieces of experiences and therefore enabling a child's perceptions to become more complex. This view of perception is termed **enrichment theory.** In other words, the child constructs his perception at each encounter, adding previous experiences retrieved from the memory to the new information about the stimulus. For example, when preschool children learn the names for colors, they initially learn the basic ones—red, blue, yellow, green, orange, and purple. As they have more experiences with colored objects, they perceive colors that cannot be accurately categorized by the basic color names they know; thus, they have to learn new names such as pink, violet, aqua, and so on.

Other theorists, such as Eleanor Gibson (1969; 1987) and J.J. Gibson (1979), believe that instead of gaining more information about a stimulus through subsequent interaction to enrich one's perception, the information already exists in external environmental stimuli available for perception; thus, the task of a child is to differentiate, or discriminate, the significant features of stimuli from the vast array of potential sensory information present in the environment. This view of perception is called **differentiation theory.** Differentiation theorists believe perceptual development involves being able to detect increasingly fine and subtle differences that exist among objects. Development occurs because humans have a natural tendency to search the environment for *invariant features,* stable aspects of a stimulus that distinguish it from its background or from other stimuli. This ability helps create order and continuity out of an initially chaotic and fluctuating sensory world. For example, infants scan objects in their environment differentiating the edges from the interior. They distinguish faces from non-faces. Later, they discriminate among faces.

Reading is a skill that exemplifies how perception is related to other areas of development, namely language and cognition (box 6.1).

# HOW PERCEPTUAL DEVELOPMENT IS STUDIED

Perceptual development involves the changes humans experience in their ability to interpret reality. Perceptual development is influenced biologically by heredity and maturation of the sense organs, and contextually by experiences.

The various techniques commonly used to examine what infants perceive are *natural observation, preference, monitoring physiological or reflexive responses, habituation, evoked potentials.*

## NATURAL OBSERVATION

Observing the natural responses of infants to various stimuli is one way of telling us what infants perceive. For example, if we observe the

BOX 6.1

# PERCEPTION, READING, AND READING READINESS

**Some visual perceptual skills involved in reading are scanning, focusing, and discrimination of forms.**

When we read, we are attaching meaning to symbols. The perceptual aspect of reading involves discriminating what is seen and relating what is seen to the language we hear. The language aspect of reading involves knowing what the words mean. The cognitive aspect of reading involves understanding the content of what is being read.

Many skills are prerequisites to reading. The accomplishment of these skills is referred to by educators as "reading readiness." Newborns scan objects in their environment and fixate on areas of contact such as edges and corners. However, they tend to stay fixed on one area of contact and not search for others until they are two months old (Banks & Salapatek, 1983). Thus, infants are born equipped with the ability to scan and fixate, but this ability develops with experience. Children who do not develop the ability to scan and fixate have reading difficulties such as omitting small words, merging ends of words into beginnings of other words, skipping sentences, not being able to copy from a book or chalkboard, or having difficulty keeping the eyes still long enough to gain information and comprehension from what is read.

Much research proved the link between language development and reading achievement (Vygotsky, 1978; Stauffer, 1980; Gillet & Temple, 1982). Language development and reading are related because some specific language skills associated with reading readiness involve both perception and cognition. These are auditory discrimination, listening comprehension, oral language expression, vocabulary comprehension, and use of contextual cues (Hillerich & Johnson, 1981).

Auditory discrimination involves the ability to hear differences in speech sounds. This ability transfers to language when one can discriminate the sound of *cat* from *hat*, *bent* from *dent*, *ping* from *ding*, and so on.

Listening comprehension involves hearing, recalling, and interpreting details from it. Children who cannot understand oral language, more specifically, literary oral language, have difficulty in understanding written language. Children who have been read to when young are more successful readers later (Wells, 1981).

Oral language expression involves the ability to use words to describe an event, a picture, a story, and so forth. For children to be successful at reading, they must be able to explain and amplify ideas (Hillerich & Johnson, 1981). They also must distinguish and understand the differences between beginnings, middles, and endings of descriptions.

Vocabulary comprehension involves the ability to name common objects. Having real experiences helps enhance vocabulary comprehension. For example, a trip to the store pointing out fruits, vegetables, cereals, and meats, can provide the groundwork for understanding those words when they are encountered in print.

*(continued on following page)*

Observing facial expressions when feeding an infant can indicate a preference of likes and dislikes for certain foods.

*(continued from previous page)*

The use of contextual cues involves interpreting the unknown word based on the setting in which it is found. For example, the word stop can be interpreted from *stop at red; go at green* by using the contextual cues of color.

Perception is only one aspect of reading. More than visual perception is involved—auditory perception also is involved. Even proprioception, awareness of the parts of one's body in relation to one another, is a component of reading in that, in English, we read from left to right, from the top of the page to the bottom, and from the front of the book to the back.

facial expressions of a neonate after presenting several substances with differing tastes or the head movement after presenting several substances with differing smells, we get an idea which ones the infant likes and dislikes. Steiner (1979) gave newborns sweet, sour, or bitter substances. A sweet stimulus evoked an expression inferred to be satisfaction as it was often accompanied or followed by sucking movements. A sour stimulus evoked lip-pursing, often accompanied or followed by wrinkling the nose and blinking the eyes. A bitter stimulus evoked an expression of dislike and disgust or rejection, often followed by spitting. Steiner also observed neonates' expressions and attempts to withdraw from odors placed on cotton swabs held beneath the nose. Butter and banana odors elicited positive expressions, while the odor of rotten eggs elicited rejection. The problem with natural observation, however, is that an infant's responses may be too subtle to notice or the stimuli may not evoke any response for various reasons (infant is asleep or crying).

## PREFERENCE

The preference method assumes that when one spends more time attending to a stimulus, one prefers this stimulus to other stimuli. Preference can occur only if a difference among stimuli is perceived.

Fantz (1961) devised a complex way to determine what infants observe. Infants were placed on their backs in a chamber. They were presented with a pair of visual stimuli simultaneously. These stimuli were cards with different patterns such as circles, lines, dots, or faces. An observer looked into the chamber through a hole in the top and watched the infant's eyes, specifically what pattern was reflected in the cornea. Because the cornea acts like a mirror, the pattern observed in it told the researcher what stimulus the infant was observing (figure 6.2). The time of each fixation was recorded. Fantz found that newborns only a few hours old had preferences among the patterns. For example, these newborns showed a preference for a bull's-eye pattern rather than a horizontal-stripe pattern.

Concluding what infants perceive is difficult if no preference between stimuli is shown because the infant may discriminate between the stimuli but find them equally interesting so show no preference. Fortunately investigators can use other methods such as monitoring physiological or reflexive responses to resolve interpretive difficulties arising from the natural observation and preference methods.

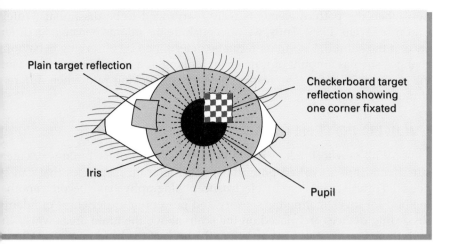

Plain target reflection

Checkerboard target reflection showing one corner fixated

Iris

Pupil

FIGURE 6.2
The eye reflecting an object off its cornea.

Theodor "Dr. Seuss" Geisel's children's book *The Cat in the Hat* was used in a 1980 study to determine if newborns can perceive differences in voices.

## MONITORING PHYSIOLOGICAL OR REFLEXIVE RESPONSES

Perception of differences between stimuli can be determined by showing an infant different objects and monitoring physiological responses such as pulse rate. When the pulse rate rises after being presented with an object, perception of difference can be inferred (Von Bargen, 1983). Similarly, perception can be inferred by monitoring reflexive responses such as sucking when an infant is shown different objects. This is known as *high amplitude sucking procedure*. Infants are given a pacifier (equipped with electric circuitry), which is connected to a slide projector or tape recorder, to suck. The electric circuitry allows an investigator to measure the rate of sucking when a stimulus is perceived on the slides or heard on the tapes. First, a baseline sucking rate is established. Then the rate of sucking is measured when different stimuli appear (Siqueland & DeLucia, 1969). If the infant's sucking increases, we can infer that the infant perceives a difference in the objects shown. For example, in one study (De Casper & Fifer, 1980), newborns could suck on a pacifier connected to a tape recorder. High amplitude sucking activated the tape on which stories were read by their mothers, and low amplitude or no sucking activated the tape in which stories were read by female strangers. The infants sucked hard when their mothers' voices were heard. They sucked harder when they heard a story (e.g., *The Cat in the Hat* by Dr. Seuss) that the mothers had read aloud during the last 6 ½ weeks of pregnancy. This experiment not only demonstrated that infants can hear but that they also can perceive differences in voices, and it is possible they can do so in utero (Kolata, 1984).

## HABITUATION

Another method that enables researchers to make inferences about the perceptual abilities of infants involves presenting a stimulus to capture a neonate's attention, observing the time required for attention to decline, then presenting another stimulus to recapture attention. The decline in responses to familiar stimuli caused by repeated exposure is termed **habituation**. The renewed tendency to respond to a new stimulus when habituation has first occurred with another stimulus is called **dishabituation**. Dishabituation signifies the ability to perceive differences. For example, infants who become habituated to two identical patterns recovered atten-

Educators must be continually on guard against children's becoming habituated to the class activity/lecture. When this happens, children lose interest in the activity, resulting in poor performance.

tion when the pattern elements were rearranged to be dissimilar (Antel Caron & Myers, 1985). Thus, we can conclude the infants perceived a differ ence in the stimuli. Habituation can be determined by observing behavior changes such as amount of time spent looking at a stimulus, or by measu ing changes in heart rate, respiration rate, or sucking rate when differer stimuli are presented.

### EVOKED POTENTIALS

With new technology in electronics and computers, brain-wave mea surements called **evoked potentials,** specific brain responses that can b detected after stimulation by electroencephalography, have become anothe method for investigating the sensory and perceptual experiences of infant Recording devices are placed on the scalp above the brain areas where th infant processes sensory information: the back of the head for visual stimu and the side of the head for auditory stimuli. Then a visual or auditor stimulus is presented, and the electrical activity in the brain is recorded t produce tracings, or an electroencephalogram. Sensing a stimulus shoul produce a response (an evoked potential); stimuli not sensed by the brai should produce no response; and two stimuli differentiated from on another should produce two different responses.

# DEVELOPMENT OF PERCEPTUAL ABILITIES

To understand how perceptual abilities develop, we will first explai how sense systems function. Then we will examine each specific sense fo lowed by perceptual abilities related to that sense.

### HOW THE SENSES WORK

Generally, all the sense systems operate similarly in that they dete certain environmental stimuli and convert them into neural impulse (Bloom & Lazerson, 1988).

A sense system begins to operate when a *stimulus* is detected by sensory neuron, the primary *sensory receptor*. There are sensory receptors fo light, for heat, for chemical odors, and so on. The sense receptor convert the detection of the physical stimulus (light, sound, odor, taste, pressure movement) into *nerve impulses*. The nerve impulses are coded into specifi forms of electrochemical activity. Specific coded information from the sens receptors travels along specific sensory neurons to the brain part, known a a *primary processing area*, responsible for that particular sense (sight, hearing smell, taste, touch, proprioception). In the primary processing area, infor mation is separated into the various qualities of the signal that are detected For example, light is seen by color and brightness. Receptor cells distir guish not only among quality of the stimulus, they also distinguish intens ties. The frequency of the impulses and the quantity of sensory receptor transmitting impulses reflect the intensity of the stimulus being sensed. brighter light means more activity in the receptor cells. The informatio about the qualities and quantities of the stimulus is transmitted from th primary processing area to other processing areas in the brain where add tional meaning from sensory stimuli is inferred. Sensations from sever processing areas and information from past experiences are integrated t

If the singing and clapping are repetitive, children are better able to integrate perceptions of the song, allowing them to learn it faster.

result in the perception of the stimulus. Then, the brain puts together all information received at a given time from the active receptor cells, thereby interpreting reality and making a mental picture of all stimuli, which becomes one's perception. For example, a touch on the shoulder can be interpreted as friendly or threatening. The perception of the touch is influenced by the actual physical pressure exerted, one's emotional state at the time, and one's attitude toward the person giving the touch. Information about the physical pressure exerted comes from receptor cells in the skin. Information about one's emotional state and attitude toward the person comes from specific areas in the brain. Thus, the senses provide the brain with raw data emotions, attitudes, and memory to interpret reality.

Table 6.1 lists the six major human sense systems, the organs that detect the stimuli, the qualities detected, and the receptor cells in each that detect the quality and quantity of the stimuli.

## BASIC PROPERTIES OF THE SIX MAJOR SENSE SYSTEMS

### TABLE 6.1

| Sensation | Sensing System | Quality | Receptors |
|---|---|---|---|
| Vision | Retina | Brightness<br>Contrast<br>Motion<br>Size<br>Color | Rods<br>Cones |
| Hearing | Cochlea | Pitch<br>Tone | Hair cells |
| Proprioception | Muscles, tendons, joints | Position<br>Movement | Proprioceptors |
| Touch | Skin, internal organs | Pressure<br>Temperature<br>Vibration | Ruffini corpuscles<br>Merkel discs<br>Pacinian corpuscles |
| Taste | Tongue | Sweet, salty<br><br>Bitter, sour | Taste buds at tip of tongue<br>Taste buds at edge of tongue |
| Smell | Olfactory nerves | Floral<br>Fruity<br>Musky<br>Pungent | Olfactory receptors |

**(Bloom & Lazerson, 1988)**

After the receptor cells convert the detection of a stimulus into nerve impulses, their response usually diminishes. They have adapted to the new stimulus. The rate and degree of adaptation to stimuli vary with each sense and with the situation. The diminishing responsiveness of the receptor cells enables new sensory information to enter the system while coping with the old information. However, if the stimuli are brief and periodic, like a siren that sounds every few minutes, then the receptor cells respond fully each time without adaptation.

The magnifying glass acts to increase the size of the image this child is observing, thus enabling him to perceive the object.

## FIGURE 6.3
## GENERAL STRUCTURE OF THE EYE
**The function of the eye as a camera.**

## SENSE OF SIGHT AND VISUAL PERCEPTION

Look out your window, you might see houses, hills, or trees. These consist of many different shapes, sizes, and colors. Some are near and some are far. How do we see and interpret such a wide variety of visual stimuli in the environment?

### How Do We See?

The receptor cells for sight are in the eyes. Their primary function is to convert light energy into neural impulses (Spoher & Lehmkuhle, 1982). The neural impulses are then carried from the eyes to the brain by the optic nerves. The image of the object seen is projected upside down on the retina (figure 6.3). This is due to the bending of light. Light enters through the **cornea**, a clear covering on the front of the eye, which bends the light as it enters. Then it passes through the aqueous humor and through the **pupil**, an opening in the **iris**, to the iris (the colored part of the eye that contains muscles to control the size of the pupil). The muscles that make up the iris control the amount of light that enters the inner eye. When you go into a dark movie theater, the pupils dilate, or become larger, so more light enters; when you leave the theater, the pupils contract, or become smaller, so less light enters.

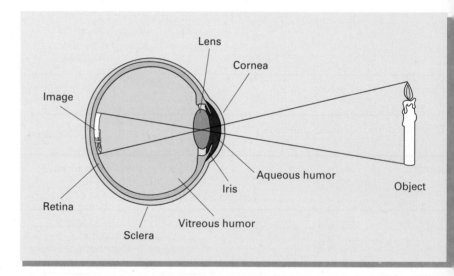

When light travels through the pupil, it passes through a **lens**, a soft transparent tissue that can stretch and get thinner or can shorten and thicken, a process called *accommodation*, to bend the light rays so they fall directly on the retina. This allows images of objects at different distances to be seen clearly. After leaving the lens, the light passes through the *vitreous humor*, a clear liquid that provides nutrients to the inner eye and cushions it against shock, and is focused on the **retina**, the thin membrane covering the back of the eyeball. The retina contains millions of receptor cells that undergo chemical reactions when stimulated by light. These chemical reactions produce small amounts of electricity that become nerve impulses, which are captured by the optic nerve and conducted to the visual receiving area of the brain located in the cerebral cortex.

The receptor cells in the retina are of two types: rod cells and cone cells. The **rod cells**, which give rise to colorless vision, are more abundant

oward the periphery of the retina, are very sensitive to light, and enable us
o see in dim light; but the images they project are poorly defined. The **cone
ells**, which give rise to color vision, are more abundant in the central por-
ion of the retina and are used for vision in bright light. They project
letailed well-defined images, and they enable us to detect color.

## How Do We Perceive What We See?

Visual perception involves the ability to see things close and far. It
lso involves the ability to:

- discriminate fine details (acuity).
- see forms.
- recognize that objects are the same, or constant, even though their
  size or shape might change according to the distance or position
  from the observer.
- see color.
- recognize faces.

This girl needs corrective
lenses because she is
nearsighted.

**Perception of Acuity.** **Visual acuity** refers to sharpness or clearness of
vision. Visual acuity is commonly measured by the Snellen chart with let-
ers of different sizes. The letters read at 20 feet are used as the reference
point. Thus, if you can read the letters that a person with "normal" vision
an at 20 feet, your vision is said to be 20/20; if you can read at 20 feet what
person with "normal" vision can read at 40 feet, your vision is said to be
20/40. Because infants cannot read or tell us what they see, the preference
method often is used to yield information on visual acuity.

The infant eye is less well developed at birth than the other sense
ystems. The center of the retina, where images are focused most sharply,
ontains visual receptors that are less mature and less densely packed than
n adult's visual receptors. This means that contrasts of light and dark con-
ours perceived by an infant are not as clear as those perceived by an adult.
'urther, the lens of the eye, which can change its shape (or accommodate)
o permit focusing of objects at different distances, does not change as
apidly and accurately in infants as it does in adults. This means an image
projected onto the infant's retina may be blurrier than that projected onto
n adult's retina. Newborns and one-month-old infants display significant
ocusing errors in that they overaccommodate for distant targets and
underaccommodate for near targets. By three months of age, the number of
cuity errors decreases significantly (Banks & Salapatek, 1983).

Using the preference method, Fantz (1961) measured infants' ability
o discriminate fine details, or visual acuity. In a cross-sectional study of
nfants less than one month in age to infants six months in age, he present-
d a black-and-white striped card and a solid-gray card (both cards were
qually bright). From a distance of ten inches, the less than one-month-old
nfants could discriminate the striped cards that were ⅛-inch thick (figure
.4); the six-month-old infants could discriminate the striped cards that
vere only ¹⁄₆₄-inch thick for the patterned cards. Because the infants showed
preferences, Fantz concluded they had the ability to perceive differences
between the two cards. Figure 6.5 is a comparison of the visual acuity of a
ne-month-old, two-month-old, three-month-old, and an adult. Thus, visu-
l acuity improves with age. The improvement is a result of changes in the
isual system, such as in the eye's ability to absorb light energy (Banks &
Bennett, 1988).

**F.Y.I.**

In order to perceive what
one sees, an individual
must use his eyes to scan
the object and its parts.
One-month-old infants
only scan one small part
of a figure, whereas two-
month-old infants trace a
larger part.

Visual acuity also involves the ability to see objects clearly at a distance. The infant eye is shorter than the adult eye in that there is less distance between the lens and the retina, which means an image size produced on the retina by a specific object at a specific distance will be much smaller (Bower, 1977). Because of this infants do not see distant objects clearly. A young infant focuses best on objects 8 to 20 inches away, about the distance from a caregiver (Atkinson & Braddick, 1982). Newborns have 20/300 vision, which means what they see at 20 feet appears similar to what a person with normal vision sees at 300 feet. An infant's vision improves to about 20/100 by about six months of age, and 20/20 by one year of age (Banks & Salapatek, 1983). Thus, an infant's ability to discriminate among objects presented at a distance improves with age.

**FIGURE 6.4**

Visual acuity was tested with these stripes: $^1/_8$, $^1/_{16}$, $^1/_{32}$ and $^1/_{64}$ inch wide. Each pattern was displayed with a gray square of equal brightness 10 inches from the infant's eyes. The finest pattern consistently preferred to gray showed how narrow a stripe the infant could perceive. Infants under one month old could see the $^1/_8$-inch stripes and the six-month-olds could see $^1/_{64}$-inch stripes.

**FIGURE 6.5**

| Visual acuity at one month (10 percent in focus). | At two months (20 percent in focus). | At three months (30 percent in focus). | As an adult (100 percent in focus). |

**Perception of Form.** Form denotes the arrangement of parts of objects to give an object its distinctive appearance. Forms can include shapes or outlines. Using the habituation method in which subjects are presented with a stimulus until attention dwindles and then are presented with a new stimulus to see if attention is renewed thus inferring discrimination, research demonstrated that by at least 12 months of age, infants can discriminate shapes by the outlines.

Form perception is significant in learning to read (figure 6.6). One must be able to distinguish among similar forms such as *F* and *E*; *M, N,* and *W*; *b,* and *d.* Eleanor and James Gibson (1955) compared the abilities of children 6 to 8 years of age, children 8½ to 11 years of age, and adults to identify a specific form; in this case the form was a curlicue.

They showed all subjects the form they were to know and then asked them to identify it every time it appeared in the context of an array of similar forms. The adults performed better than the children age 8½ to 11 years of age, who in turn were better than the children age 6 to 8 years of age. Thus, form perception improves with age.

Form perception also is significant to recognize objects from different perspectives such as a diamond and a square. Elkind (1978) showed children of different ages forms that could be interpreted in several ways. Examples are figure 6.7, which can be perceived as a tree or a head, and figure 6.8, which can be perceived as a person or a bunch of vegetables.

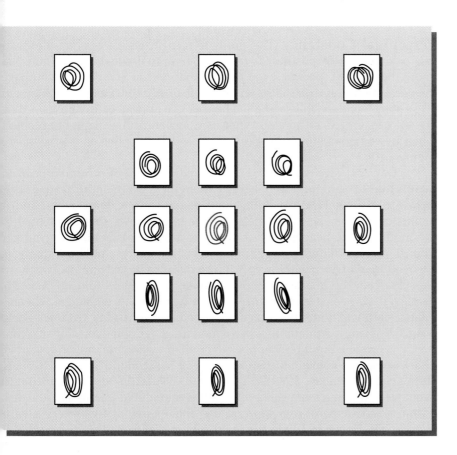

**FIGURE 6.6**
**Gibson and Gibson (1955) have found greater form perception occurs as one ages. Here the teacher may take for granted the letters she is reading, but the children are not yet able to fully perceive the forms of each letter.**

**FIGURE 6.7**
A SIMPLE ILLUSION
By about the age of ten, children usually can see both the tree and the face.

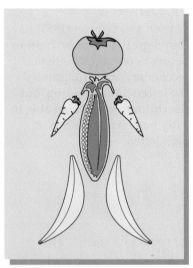

**FIGURE 6.8**
ILLUSION SIMILAR TO THAT USED BY ELKIND
Older children decenter and see both the vegetables and a "person."

In figure 6.7 adults can easily perceive both images, while children 2 to 3 years of age sometimes perceive the tree, but never the face. Children age 7 to 8 years of age frequently perceive both but may need coaching. By about age ten, children seem to have the same perceptual ability as adults to distinguish both images. Elkind (1975) believes this developmental change is due to cognitive development. That is, as children interact with the environment, they become better able to understand that objects can be identified from different perspectives. Jean Piaget termed this ability *decentering*, the ability to consider more than one aspect of a situation simultaneously. Elkind demonstrated decentering by presenting children with figures such as the one in figure 6.8. The older children could perceive the vegetables and the person simultaneously; whereas the younger children could perceive only the vegetables, although some could see the person but not the vegetables. Vurpillot (1976) explains the developmental change in perception as due to an improvement in the ability to process information. As children grow and have more experiences with reality, they develop strategies for interpreting the available stimuli. For example, figure 6.9 shows the search patterns of younger and older children in their quest to find identical pairs of houses. Four-year-old children are unsystematic in their visual searches; however, by age six they become more systematic; and by age eight, they are efficient at the task. Thus, perceptual abilities increase because children become more adept at finding similar and dissimilar features among new stimuli.

**Perceptual Constancy.** The ability to recognize sizes or shapes regardless of distances or position is termed **perceptual constancy**. When you know the size of a person, even though that person is far away, you have the perception of *size constancy*. An example of size constancy is looking out an airplane window and seeing the houses that appear as tiny boxes —they are still recognized as houses. When you recognize the shape of an object when viewed from different angles, you have the perception of *shape constancy* (figure 6.10).

Day and McKenzie (1981) presented a model of a human head to infants four to eight months of age. By changing the size of the head, its distance from the subject, or both, they set out to determine when and if infants could perceive size constancy. The infants were first habituated to the model of the head placed 3 to 5 feet in front of them. The younger infants dishabituated, or regained attention, when the head size was changed to a larger one. However, if the distance of the original size head was changed, the infants did not habituate. Four-month-old infants only displayed size constancy with respect to head distance change, whereas infants six to eight months of age displayed size constancy with respect to head size change. Apparently, by six months of age some form of size constancy is present, but it only applies to familiar objects at familiar distances. Likewise, shape constancy also appears after six months of age (Cohen, DeLoache & Strauss, 1979). Gibson and associates (1978) habituated neonates to rotating foam rubber disks. Five-month-old infants saw the disk as the same whether it rotated in front of them horizontally or vertically or at an angle. However, when the foam rubber disk was distorted so that it appeared rippled, the infants reacted as if it were a new object. Thus, the infants showed shape constancy when they had become familiar with the object. When an object was shown to them that appeared unfamiliar, they did not exhibit shape constancy.

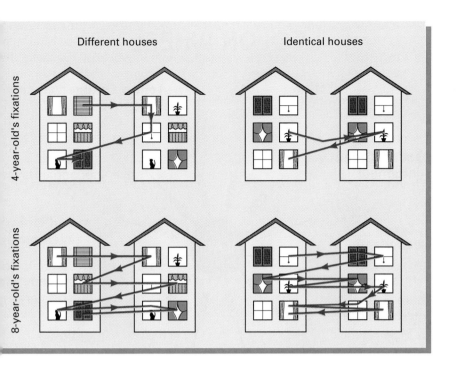

Different houses       Identical houses

4-year-old's fixations

8-year-old's fixations

FIGURE 6.9
ILLUSTRATION OF
VURPILLOT'S (1976)
RESEARCH RESULTS
This figure shows the visual
search patterns of younger and
older children in determining
whether pictures of houses
(such as those employed by
Vurpillot) are identical.

**Perception of Color.** The real world is made up not only of forms of varying sizes and shapes but it is also filled with color (figure 6.11). The basis for color perception is the selective absorption and reflection of light by objects. A surface looks red, for example, when it reflects a certain wavelength of light to the eyes. The receptor cells, or cones, in the retina are selectively sensitive to light of certain wavelengths. In this example, those receptor cells sensitive to the wavelength of light reflected by red are stimulated and carry the information to the brain. Thus, "colors" are actually the labels attached to different wavelengths of light.

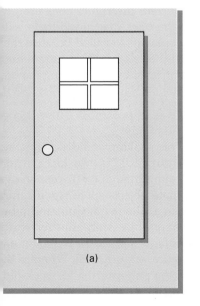

(a)

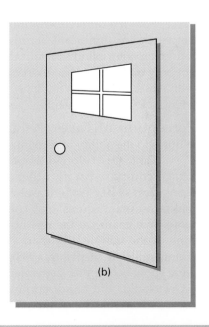

(b)

FIGURE 6.10
(a) An illustration of a door
viewed straight ahead. It is rec-
tangular in shape. (b) The same
door at a 45 degree angle. It is
now a trapezoid. However, it
still is perceived to be rectan-
gular.

FIGURE 6.11
A COLOR WHEEL

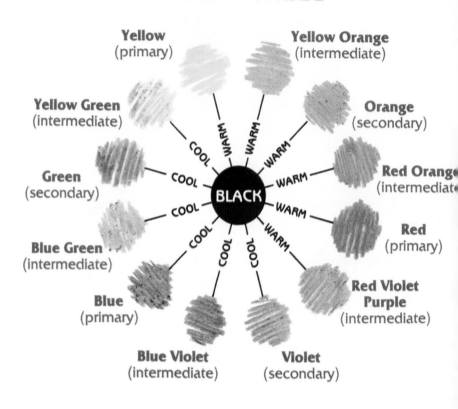

## COLOR WHEEL

Yellow (primary)
Yellow Orange (intermediate)
Yellow Green (intermediate)
Orange (secondary)
Green (secondary)
Red Orange (intermediate)
BLACK
Red (primary)
Blue Green (intermediate)
Red Violet Purple (intermediate)
Blue (primary)
Blue Violet (intermediate)
Violet (secondary)
COOL / WARM

To assess color vision status in infancy, Marc Bornstein (1976) used the habituation method with different wavelengths of light. Infants three months of age discriminated blue-green from white and yellow from green. When the wavelength was changed from the length labeled blue to the length labeled green, for instance, the infant dishabituated, thus signifying perception of a different stimulus. The sets of color discriminations used by Bornstein are significant because these are the ones that individuals with red-green color blindness fail. *Color-blind* people are so-called because they not only make color discrimination errors but they also confuse certain hues with white. Bornstein's findings have been confirmed by others using the preference method with infants as young as one month (Hartmann & Teller, 1985).

**Perception of Faces.** Perception of faces is important because it contributes to the ability to recognize and respond to others.

Fantz (1961) found that infants preferred looking at a disk depicting a face compared with other patterns (figure 6.12). In a later study (Langsdorf et al., 1983), it was found that young infants who were shown real faces, mannequins, and complex inanimate objects spent significantly more time gazing at the real human face than at the mannequin and more time at the mannequin than at the inanimate objects. In another study (Dannemiller & Stephens, 1988), groups of infants six and 12 weeks of age were shown computer-generated face-like figures (figure 6.13). Whereas the six-week-olds did not discriminate between the patterns, the 12-week-olds preferred to look at the figure most resembling a human face.

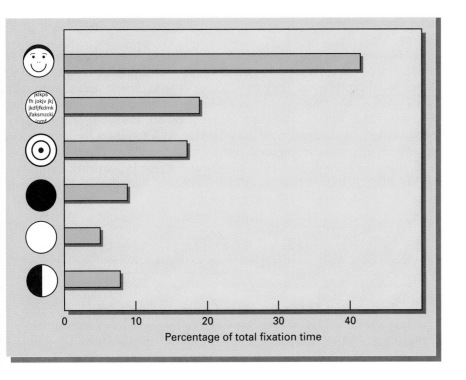

FIGURE 6.12
FIGURES FROM
FANTZ'S EXPERIMENT
**Figures such as these were
shown to infants in Fantz's
(1961) experiment. The fixation
times indicate the length of
time infants examined the various figures.**

Maurer & Salapatek (1976) recorded the eye movements of one-month-old and two-month-old infants when they were exposed to human faces. The one-month-old infants concentrated on the edges and contours of the total facial configuration and spent little time looking at the internal features such as the eyes, nose, or mouth. On the other hand, the two-month-old infants, spent more time scanning the internal features than the boundaries. By three months infants appeared to perceive the whole face as a meaningful configuration.

Infants not only perceive differences in faces, but by three to four months of age they begin to perceive differences in facial expressions. They can discriminate photos of happy faces from photos of sad or angry ones (Barrera & Maurer, 1981). However, while they may perceive differences in

FIGURE 6.13
**Computer-generated face-like
stimuli presented infants by
Dannemiller and Stephens
(1988). Figure (a) looks more
like a human face than does
figure (b).**

facial expressions, they do not yet know the emotional meaning of them (Nelson, 1987).

Between four and nine months, according to Klinnert and colleagues (1983), emotional expressions begin to become meaningful. Infants react to others' facial expressions. They smile in response to others' smiles, especially their mothers', and they express fear when others display fear. Recognizing and responding to the facial expressions of others are significant developmental milestones because now the infant can look to others for information on how to perceive an ambiguous event. This is termed *social referencing*.

Because vision is such a significant sense in learning about the world, children should have their vision checked periodically. Box 6.2 lists some ways to detect possible vision problems.

## BOX 6.2 EARLY DETECTION OF VISION PROBLEMS

According to the American Optometric Association, children should visit a doctor of optometry before they reach age three unless there are earlier indications of a problem such as the following (Merahn, 1987):

- Excessive eye rubbing
- Shutting or covering one eye
- Tilting head or thrusting head forward
- Unusual sensitivity to light
- Frequent blinking, squinting, or frowning
- Stumbling over small objects
- Eyes crossed
- Eyelids swollen or crusted
- Eyes inflamed or watery
- Child complaining of eyes itching or burning
- Child complaining of blurred or double vision
- Child complaining of dizziness, headaches, or stomachaches after close work

## F.Y.I.

Sound waves travel through the air at a speed of approximately 1,100 feet per second.

## SENSE OF HEARING AND AUDITORY PERCEPTION

While you study, perhaps the radio is playing or perhaps an airplane is flying overhead. How do humans make sense of such a variety of sounds? To explain, we will discuss the sensation of hearing to explain how we hear; then we will discuss the perception of sounds to explain how we interpret what we hear.

### How Do We Hear?

The receptor cells for hearing are in the ears. They translate **sound waves,** which are successive pressure variations in the air that vary in amplitude, wavelength, and frequency, into neural impulses. These impulses are then conducted to the auditory center of the cerebral cortex via the auditory nerve. Figure 6.14 shows the structures of the human ear. The substructures are the outer ear, middle ear, and inner ear. The outer ear consists of the *pinna*, which is the flap of skin on the side of the head enclosing cartilage, and the **auditory canal**, the part of the ear that conducts sound waves.

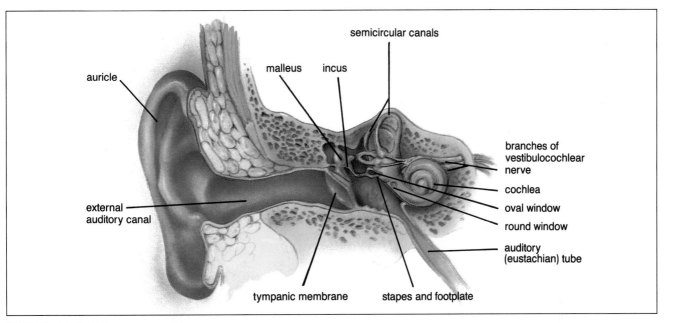

FIGURE 6.14
STRUCTURE OF THE HUMAN EAR

The pinna funnels sound waves into the auditory canal, which conducts sound to the tympanic membrane, the eardrum.

The first part of the middle ear is the *eardrum*. When sound waves encounter the eardrum, they cause it to vibrate. The eardrum is connected to three small bones arranged in sequence (the *malleus*, the *incus*, and the *stapes*). When the eardrum vibrates, it sets these three bones into motion. The motion is amplified as the vibrations move from bone to bone. The last of these three bones, the stapes, hammers against the **cochlea**, the internal part of the ear that contains the auditory nerve endings.

The cochlea is a hollow bone structure filled with liquid. When the stapes beats against the cochlea, it causes waves of the liquid to form, which travel through the cochlea and bend the tiny hairs inside the cochlea. The bending of these hairs translates the mechanical energy of the sound waves into neural impulses. The auditory nerve receives these impulses from the cochlea and transmits them to the brain.

The physical attributes of sound waves are perceived in three dimensions: *pitch, volume* (intensity), and *tone*.

Pitch is a function of frequency. Frequency is the number of vibrations, or cycles, per second of a given sound wave. Low-frequency vibrations stimulate a sensation of low pitch, and high-frequency vibrations stimulate a sensation of high pitch. Apparently, low-frequency vibrations stimulate hair cells near the apex of the cochlea; high-frequency vibrations stimulate hair cells near its base; and intermediate frequencies stimulate hair cells of correspondingly intermediate regions of the cochlea. The neurons from each region along the length of the cochlea lead to slightly different areas in the brain. When we experience pitch, it is the result of one of these areas of the brain being stimulated. Humans can hear tones ranging from frequencies as low as 20 cycles per second to frequencies as high as 20,000 cycles per second.

Volume is a function of the amplitude of vibrations. Intense vibrations cause the fluid of the cochlea to fluctuate at great extremes, thereby

The ability to perceive if a sound is high or low, soft or loud, similar or different, enables children to learn how to play musical instruments.

causing more intense stimulation of the hair cells. The result is the transmission of more impulses to the brain at one time, and consequently, the brain interprets this increased stimulation as loudness. Fewer vibrations and, consequently, less fluctuation of cochlea fluid result in less stimulation of the hair cells and fewer impulses reaching the brain, thereby causing the sound to be interpreted as soft. The intensity of sound is measured in terms of *decibels*. Zero decibels represent the absolute threshold of minimal detectable physical energy of hearing, 60 decibels represent normal conversation, 140 decibels represent the threshold of pain.

Tone is the distinctive quality of sound made by different vibrations in voices or instruments. It is reflected in the complexity or individuality of the different sound waves produced by different voices or instruments. For example, the tone heard at a particular time is the result of stimulation of hair cells in regions of the cochlea in addition to stimulation of the main region.

## How Do We Perceive What We Hear?

Perception of sound is important because of the role it plays in communication.

Determining the auditory capabilities of infants is not an easy task, and various methods have been used to gather data. Measures designed to test hearing have included reflexive responses such as eye blinking, startling reaction to a noise, behavioral responses such as head turning and crying, and physiological responses such as changes in heart rate, respiration rate, or brain wave patterns. Such methods have shown that six-month-old, 12-month-old, and 18-month-old infants have less sensitivity in low-frequency tones but have a level of sensitivity equivalent to adults at higher frequencies (Schneider, Trehub & Bull, 1980).

Auditory perception is difficult to assess. The infant's behavioral state (whether he or she is asleep versus aroused), the type of sound delivered (whether it is a click, a tone, or speech), and frequency (whether it is high or low in pitch), and the use of other senses to perceive the stimuli influence responses that researchers receive (Morse & Cowan, 1982). However, researchers have been able to identify some basic auditory capabilities in the infant such as perception of:

- location of sound
- more than one sound
- changes in sound
- speech.

**Perception of Sound Location.** Things are often heard before seen. Although visual perception enables us to identify an object when it is in our line of sight, we often look at it because our ears have told us the direction.

Morrongiello and Rocca (1987) tested the ability to locate sound in infants age 6, 9, 12, 15, and 18 months. The infants were seated in a dark room facing a semicircular arrangement of ten loudspeakers placed at different angles. Each infant received two trials—an auditory trial in which only the sound stimulus (eight clicks) was presented and an auditory-visual trial in which a light display came on in conjunction with the sound from a loudspeaker to indicate signal location. Calibration markers on infants' heads measured the angles of head turns. Comparing infants' performance when they had only the auditory cue for localization with when the visual cue also was available revealed the extent to which infants depended on visual cues in orienting toward the actual location of a sounding object in space. For all the auditory-visual trials, all the infants turned their heads in the direction of the sound; neither infant age nor loudspeaker location had n effect. However, for the auditory trials the younger infants made many errors locating the sound, whereas there was a significant decrease in error in locating the sound (as measured by the angle of head movement) from infants age six to 18 months. These and other (Hiller, Hewitt & Morrongielo, 1992) results indicate that as the infant gets older, there is a developmental change in the ability to locate sound without the help of sight.

**Perception of More Than One Sound.** The perception that sounds, which are separated by a few microseconds, are heard as a single sound although the sounds come from different directions is termed the **precedence effect** because the first sound takes perceptual precedence over the other sounds.

According to experiments in which a second sound was presented to infants from a different direction several milliseconds after presentation of a first sound, newborns failed to locate either sound correctly. They turned neither to the first sound nor to its time-delayed echo. Instead, for the time-delayed sounds coming from the right and left respectively, they behaved as if they heard a single sound coming from in front of them (Clifton et al., 1981). It is as if they averaged the localization of both sounds. Adults only localize to the first sound and ignore the second, thus exhibiting the precedence effect.

The precedence effect is important to accurate auditory perception. Without it, every sound heard would have an echo. This would be both distracting and confusing because the auditory system would be processing sounds from multiple directions. Thus, to accurately perceive a sound, the brain has to suppress the other sounds the first creates. Newborns do not have this ability. However, by about five months of age the ability to interpret precedence is no longer a problem although it is not as efficient as an adult's ability (Morrongiello, Kulig & Clifton, 1984).

**Perception of Changes in Sound.** Newborns discriminate changes in frequency and intensity (Schneider, Trehub & Bull, 1979). Infants six months and older can perceive similarity, or constancy, among complex tones that vary in intensity or duration (Erdman, 1986). Infants nine months old can detect changes in short melodies or pitch contours (Trehub, Thorpe & Morrongiello, 1987). Thus, as infants develop, they can also categorize sequences of sounds.

**Perception of Speech.** The significance of the perceptual abilities to localize sound, discriminate changes in its frequency and intensity (volume), and categorize sequences of sounds is related to an infant's ability to perceive speech. Speech consists of different frequencies of sound waves produced at different times.

The methods used to assess infant perception of speech sound boundaries are similar to those used to assess infant perception of color boundaries. The infant is first habituated to one sound. Then two sounds which are physically equidistant are presented: One sound is on the same side of the boundary as the habituated one, and the other sound is on the other side of the boundary. An increase in sucking when the sound presented is on the other side of the boundary signifies that two- and three-month-old infants perceive almost every phoneme that adults do (Eimas et al., 1971). Apparently, infants are born biologically equipped to perceive speech, but by six months they lose some ability to discriminate speech sounds not in the native language (Eimas, 1985). Thus, as children develop, there are contextual influences on speech perception.

There is evidence that pitch plays a critical role in the infant's recognition of her mother's voice (Mehler et al., 1978; Fernald, 1985).

The importance of pitch also is implied in infants' ability to reproduce speech-like sounds we call babbling, with intonation before the production of meaningful speech (Papousek & Papousek, 1981). Thus, perhaps speech has features (Eimas & Tartter, 1979) that act as cues to perception and these features are detected as configurations of frequencies and pitches similar to a musical pattern.

No child is too young for a professional hearing evaluation. Parents need to be informed about the importance of an infant's or child's responses to sounds because they are the most reliable early screeners of potential hearing impairments. Box 6.3 lists some possible indications of a hearing problem.

## Box 6.3 EARLY DETECTION OF HEARING PROBLEMS

If a child exhibits any of the following signs, he should have a professional hearing examination (Lerner, Mardell-Czudnowski & Goldenberg, 1987):
- Appearing not to respond to sounds (infants)
- Not talking (toddlers)
- Needing to have instructions repeated several times (preschoolers)
- Speaking unclearly (preschoolers)
- Speaking exceptionally loudly or softly (preschoolers)
- Exceptionally sensitive to visual clues such as movement or facial expressions (preschoolers)

## SENSE OF SMELL AND TASTE AND OLFACTORY AND GUSTATORY PERCEPTION

The receptor cells for smell line the nose, and the ones for taste line the mouth. These two senses are discussed together because the two senses are similar in that when reference is made to the taste of food, for example, the reference is actually to the experience of both smell and taste. Hot foods often appear to have more taste than cold foods because the heat makes them vaporize, thereby stimulating the smell receptors in the nasal passage, illustrating how taste affects smell. Smell, in turn, affects taste.

## How Do We Smell and Taste?

For taste or smell to be detected, chemicals must first be dissolved in the film of liquid coating the membranes of the respective receptor cells. The major difference between the two receptors is that the taste receptors are specialized for detection of chemicals present in the mouth itself, while smell receptors are specialized for detecting vapors coming to the organism from distant sources. The smell receptors are more sensitive than are taste receptors because they can detect small quantities of odors far away from the nose, while taste receptors have to be exposed to larger quantities in the mouth.

The receptor cells for taste, or **gustation**, are located in taste buds on the upper surface of the tongue and, to a lesser extent on the surface of the throat and larynx, the upper end of the trachea containing the vocal cords.

The ends of the nerve fibers are close to the receptor cells, and, when a receptor cell is stimulated, it generates impulses in the fibers.

There are four basic taste senses: *sweet, sour, salt,* and *bitter.* Apparently, all taste sensations are produced by blending these basic sensations in different relevant intensities. The receptors for these four basic tastes have areas of greatest concentration on different parts of the tongue—sweet and salt on the front, bitter on the back, and sour on the sides.

The receptor cells for smell, or **olfaction**, are located in two clefts in the upper part of the nasal passages. Unlike the receptor cells for taste, the olfactory receptors are true neurons. The olfactory bulb of the brain receives information directly from the olfactory receptor cells.

## How Do We Perceive What We Smell and Taste?

The ability to detect various odors is called **olfactory** perception and the ability to detect various tastes is called **gustatory** perception. Both olfactory and gustatory perception help us know and enjoy our environment. When food tastes abnormal, we are alerted to the fact that it might be spoiled. The smell of fresh air after a rain is a most pleasurable smell.

**Perception of Odor.** Compared with the smelling capabilities of many lower organisms, human olfactory abilities are modest (figure 6.15). However, newborns discriminate different odors and have preferences and

Learning to enjoy the taste of food is part of perceptual development.

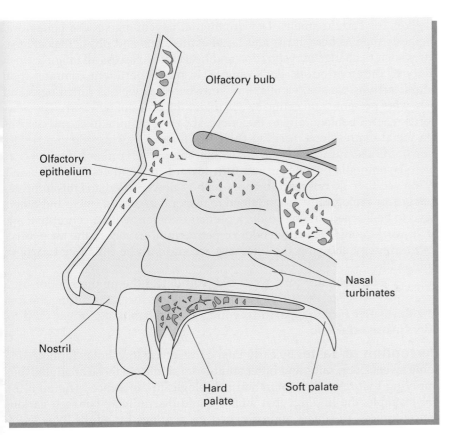

## FIGURE 6.15
**The internal structures of the nasal cavity. The receptor cells are located in the olfactory epithelium. The olfactory bulb of the brain receives information from the receptor cells.**

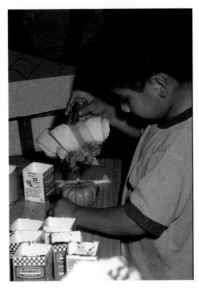

Pumpkins have distinctive odors when fresh (sweet and fragrant) and rotten (putrid).

FIGURE 6.16
**The location of certain taste receptors on the tongue.**

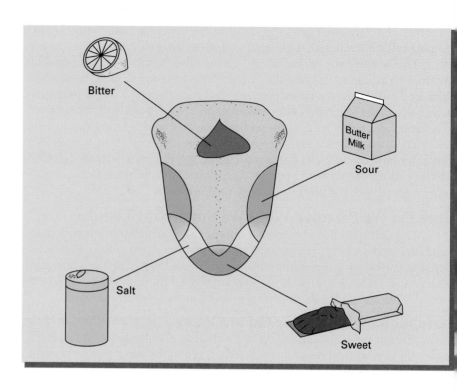

dislikes for certain smells. Developmental psychologists use behavioral methods such as head turns and facial expressions and physiological measures such as change in respiration and heart rate to assess an infant's sensitivity to different odors. For example, in one experiment common food odors, such as banana, vanilla, and strawberry, as well as rotten eggs and fish, were presented on cotton swabs under the noses of newborn. The newborns reacted behaviorally to the odors, showing definite likes and dislikes via facial expressions, turning their heads, and kicking (Steiner, 1979). Newborns also turn away or wrinkle their faces when presented with odors such as ammonia or vinegar and turn toward the mothers' scent (Russell, 1976); yet, they do not react to odors such as flowers. Perhaps this indicates that we are biologically programmed to respond to certain smells but others have to be learned. In one study, a premature infant with a conceptual age of 28 weeks could detect the odor of peppermint extract in the air (Sarnat, 1978), thereby showing the olfactory receptors to be functional early in human life.

Young neonates (one week old) can detect the mothers' odor on a breast pad (MacFarlane, 1975). Sensitivity to odors increases during the first few days after birth. Apparently, young infants habituate, or get used to, odors just as adults do.

**Perception of Taste.** By early infancy, response thresholds for detecting some sweet, sour, salty, and bitter stimuli are similar to those of adults, thus implying that taste discrimination is biologically influenced (figure 6.16). For example, the findings that infants could discriminate between various concentrations of sugars approximated the findings for adults (Nowliss & Kessen, 1976). Evidence is uncertain about infants' sensitivity to salt because they generally do not react to it as a distinct taste, whereas with sweet tastes they will suck, and with sour and bitter tastes they will purse their lips (Rosenstein & Oster, 1988).

We also have taste preferences, and these appear in the newborns who, like adults, exhibit a negative response to bitter foods and rotten odors and a positive response to sweet foods and pleasant smells. Sweetened foods are preferred over unsweetened foods throughout childhood, and evidence suggests that by the time children are toddlers, they prefer salted over unsalted food (Cowart, 1981).

It appears that newborns are equipped with mature olfactory and gustatory sensory systems. This can be because the smell and taste centers in the brain are not in the cerebral cortex (responsible for complex thinking) but rather in the lower part of the brain close to the primary sense receptors in the nose and mouth. Thus, early responses to certain smells and tastes may be more reflexive than interpretive.

## SENSE AND PERCEPTION OF TOUCH AND PROPRIOCEPTION

When you touch a hot oven and move your hand away, you have used the sense and perception of touch and proprioception. How we feel things on the skin involves the sense of touch, whereas how we sense where the parts of our body are at various times involves the sense of proprioception. Both help us experience the environment and make appropriate responses and movements.

### How Do We Feel Touch?

The sense of touch arises from a complex system of receptors in the skin. These various receptors are sensitive to touch, pressure, heat, cold, and pain. Some skin receptors are nerve endings. Others are nets of nerve fibers surrounding the bases of hairs; these fibers, which are particularly important in the sense of touch, are stimulated by the slightest displacement of the fine hairs present on most body parts. Other skin receptors are more complex, consisting of nerve endings surrounded by a specialized capsule, also called a corpuscle, of connective tissue cells (figure 6.17). These are important in sensing pressure. The energy detected and transformed into neural activity by the skin receptors is a mechanical deformation of tissue, frequently by stimulation of skin hairs. The coded information from the skin receptors is received by the brain where it is interpreted as touch, pressure, heat, cold, or pain.

Stimulation of the skin informs us what is directly adjacent to our bodies. The most sensitive areas of the skin are the fingers and hands, lips and tongue. These are the body parts most relevant to exploring the world.

The sense of proprioception, sensing where the body parts are, arises from receptors widely dispersed over the body in the muscles, tendons, and joints that receive information about the position in space of the body itself. These receptors, called proprioceptors, send impulses to the central nervous system informing it of the position and movements of the various body parts. The existence of this sense enables us, even with the eyes closed, to perform physical acts, such as getting dressed or hopping on one foot. Impulses from the proprioceptors also are extremely important in ensuring the harmonious contractions of different muscles involved in a single movement; without them complicated skillful acts such as those involved in sports would be impossible. These impulses are probably more numerous and more continuously active than any of the other senses, although we are less aware of them than any others. An idea of what life without proprioceptors

**For young children, the sense of touch in the mouth is an important way of learning about the world.**

**When an infant's cheek is touched, the child perceives that it will be fed (the rooting reflex).**

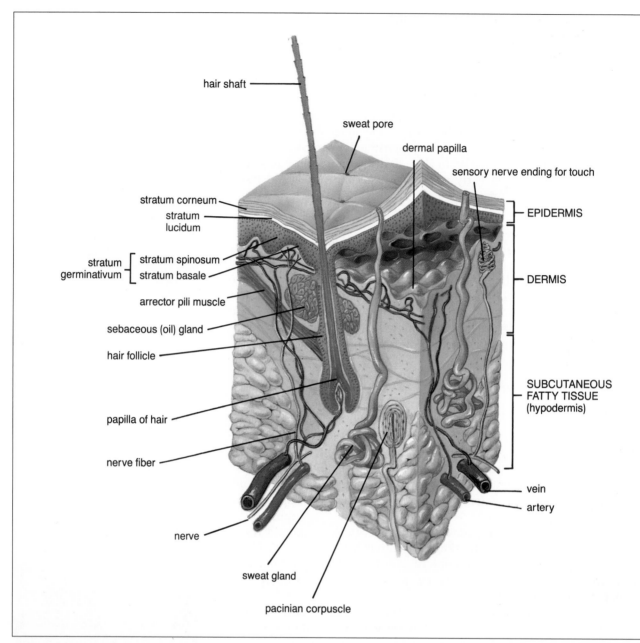

**FIGURE 6.17**
**STRUCTURES OF THE SKIN**

would be like is what is experienced when your arm or leg "falls asleep," the feeling of numbness that results from the lack of proprioceptor impulses.

**Touch and Proprioceptive Perception.** Touch perception involves the interpretation of feelings on the skin including touch, pressure, heat, cold, and pain. Proprioception involves the interpretation of where our body is oriented in space and the position of the body parts when we move. How you interpret another person's touch influences your behavior. If it is a gentle touch on your shoulder, you might interpret it as friendly and may turn to say, "hi." If it is a rough touch, you might interpret it to mean restraint and will act accordingly. How touch and body position are perceived enables us to decide how to react.

**How Do We Perceive Touch?** Newborns respond reflexively rather than cognitively to touch. For example, a touch to the lips produces sucking movements (Acredolo & Hake, 1982), and a touch to the cheek or corner of the mouth produces head turning, known as the rooting reflex. Also, it has been demonstrated that newborns sense pain and respond by crying violently (Emde et al., 1971; Anders & Chaldemian, 1974 ).

Pain sensitivity appears to increase as infants get older. Five-day-old infants cry more than one-day-old infants in response to pinpricks administered for blood tests (Lipsitt & Levy, 1959). Obviously, research cannot be done on the development of pain sensitivity, but infants who are circumcised have been observed. *Circumcision,* the removal of the foreskin of the penis, occurs without anesthetic. Male infants cry intensely while the actual surgery is in progress, and each plasma cortisol measurement, a physiological indicator of stress, is significantly higher for about two hours after the circumcision than before the procedure. Despite the trauma, circumcised infants recover quickly (Gunnar et al., 1985).

Infants learn much about the world by touching. They reach, and grasp, and try to put objects in their mouths. Thus, they learn about the shape, texture, taste of objects. They learn what is hard and soft, what can be squeezed, what can be pushed aside.

Before they are one year old, infants can recognize objects they have touched but never seen. Ten-month-old babies were given wooden objects in a dark room to play with for two minutes. Then the objects were removed. Half of the infants were given the same objects back, and the other half were given new objects to handle while still in the dark. Infants who were given the same objects handled them less than the infants who were given new objects. Apparently, the infants recognized the objects as the same and habituated, or became bored, with them (Soroka, Corter & Abramovitch, 1979).

**How Do We Perceive Proprioception?** If you close your eyes and try to touch your nose with your finger, you probably will not have much difficulty. This is because the proprioceptors in the muscles, tendons, and joints of the arm and finger inform you of the relative positions of the arm as it is approaching the nose.

Witkin (1959) examined the development of proprioceptive perception in children eight to 17 years old. He did this by seating the subject in a special chair that tilted and in a room that tilted. When both the chair and room were tilted independently, the subjects' task was to align the chair upright with gravity. Those children who relied on visual clues involving the relative position of the chair to the room, failed. Those children who relied on proprioceptive cues involving body position succeeded in positioning the chairs upright with gravity rather than to the room although doing so meant the room appeared tilted). Witkin's longitudinal study demonstrated that between the ages of eight and 17, children rely increasingly less on visual cues and increasingly more on proprioceptive ones. Proprioception plays a role in coordination of body parts and balance. Children who are slow in these perceptual/motor areas may have other developmental problems. See box 6.4 for ways that possible developmental problems are detected.

BOX 6.4 **EARLY DETECTION OF PERCEPTUAL MOTOR PROBLEMS**

The Denver Developmental Screening Test is an instrument designed to detect developmental deviation in young children from birth to six years of age (Frankenburg et al., 1975). It is used primarily by pediatricians and teachers to recommend children who may have exhibited various perceptual/motor problems and need further diagnostic testing.

The test is divided into the following sections.

- *Personal/Social:* These items measure a child's ability to take care of self and to relate to other people. Examples of tasks are playing peek-a-boo, imitating household chores, and dressing and undressing.
- *Fine Motor/Adaptive:* These items measure fine-motor dexterity, drawing ability and recognition, and manipulation of objects. It includes tasks such as building a tower with blocks, reaching for objects, and scribbling spontaneously.
- *Language:* These items measure a child's ability to perceive, understand, and express language. Examples are turning to a spoken voice, imitating speech sounds, and naming pictures.
- *Gross Motor:* These items measure the child's ability to sit, stand, walk, and jump.

The number of Denver Developmental Screening Test (DDST) items that show a child has extreme developmental delays are considered, and the child is classified as normal, questionable, or abnormal. Follow-up research shows that the abnormal category on the DDST accurately identifies over 85 percent of infants and preschoolers who continue to be developmentally delayed into the middle childhood years, most of whom experience serious learning problems after they enter school (Frankenberg et al., 1975).

## • • • RESEARCH IN REVIEW • • • • • • • • • • • • • • •

# WHEN DO CHILDREN UNDERSTAND THAT OTHERS MAY PERCEIVE THINGS DIFFERENTLY FROM THEM?

Pillow, B.H., & Flavell, J.H. (1986). Young children's knowledge about visual perception: Projective size and shape. *Child Development, 57,* 125–135.

Children's ability to understand that others may perceive things differently from them is related to understanding there is a distinction between how things appear and how they really are. Pillow and Flavell (1986) used the technique of projecting sizes and shapes of real objects to determine whether a child had the ability to discriminate a difference between the size of an object when it was near, compared with when it was far away, and the shape of an object when it was horizontal, compared with when it was vertical.

The subjects were 32 preschool children, 16 three-year-olds, and 16 four-year-old children. In one experiment, 3- and 4-year-old children were asked whether an object should be moved farther or closer to make it look larger or smaller to either themselves or another observer. A pretest was given to see if the children understood the meanings of "big" and "little." The experimenter asked, "If I put this shape close to you, will it look big or little?" "Will it *really* be little or will it just *look* little?" "If I put this shape far away, will it look big or little?" "Will it *really* be big or will it just *look* big?"

The four-year-olds performed significantly better than chance, but the three-year-olds did not. The four-year-olds clearly knew that objects appear smaller when farther away and larger when closer; and those who correctly predicted projective size changes also tended to believe these changes were apparent rather than real. Moreover, the four-year-old children's performance did not depend on whether they were required to make judgments about their own or another person's perspective or whether they were required to make the stimuli appear larger or smaller. Thus, their understanding of the projective size-distance relation could be generalized to various situations.

In a similar experiment, the three-year-old and four-year-old children were asked to indicate how a circular object should be rotated to make it appear either circular or elliptical. Like the first experiment, the three-year-olds performed near chance, but the four-year-olds demonstrated a clear understanding of the relation between an objects' projective shape and its orientation relative to an observer's line of sight. They could correctly indicate how the orientation of an object should be changed to make it appear either more circular or more elliptical. Further, this understanding was not limited to the familiar line of sight, which is horizontal; they performed equally well when asked questions about a downward, or vertical, line of sight. Thus, the four-year-olds understood that projective shape is a function of the object's orientation relative to the viewer's line of sight rather than a function of its orientation relative to the horizontal plane. They also understood that these changes were apparent rather than real. Moreover, the four-year-old children's performance did not depend on whether they were required to make judgments about their own or another person's perspective or whether they were required to make the stimuli appear circular or elliptical. Therefore, their understanding of projective shape appears sufficiently general to allow them to solve problems equally well in various situations.

The study results suggest that children begin to notice changes in projective size and shape and to understand the visual consequences for projective size and shape of certain spatial transformations of the viewer-display relation during the preschool years. Knowledge of the projective shape-orientation relation is acquired during the fourth year. Moreover, four-year-old children's understanding of the visual effects in distance or orientation changes is not limited to specific situations; instead, it is generalized, enabling them to understand another's visual perspective.

# INFLUENCES ON PERCEPTUAL DEVELOPMENT

To better understand the development of various perceptual abilities, we will discuss influences on perceptual development—biological, contextual, and the interaction of the two.

## BIOLOGICAL INFLUENCES ON PERCEPTUAL DEVELOPMENT

Evidence suggests that a neonate comes into the world equipped with some perceptual abilities, thereby implying the influence of the biological heritage of the human being. In other words, newborns can transform some information flooding their senses into something meaningful without having learned to do so. There are several examples where infants exhibit such perceptual abilities for the various senses. For instance, infants 2 to 7 days of age showed a preference for breast pads used by their mothers rather than clean pads; infants two weeks old could discriminate their mother's smell from a stranger's smell. This was investigated by presenting infants with breast pads from their mothers and strangers and observing which ones they consistently turned their heads toward (MacFarlane, 1975).

Some perceptual abilities are inborn. By the time an infant is born, the brain and sensory system are reasonably well developed. Vision and hearing are functional before birth, with hearing more developed. Myelinization of the sensory system has progressed well by birth in the subcortical areas of the brain, whereas myelinization of the cerebral hemisphere at birth is minimal and develops rapidly during the first two years of life. Thus, the wiring for certain perceptual abilities is present at birth, whereas the connections between the wires that enable perceptual abilities to increase develop over time.

*Feature detectors,* neurons in the receptor cells, respond to specific features or characteristics of the stimulus, such as direction. To provide evidence for a physiological feature detector, an experiment was done with young children to observe if they could discriminate among letters with similar features. Gibson and colleagues (Gibson et al., 1963) found that four-year-old children frequently confused *M* and *W*, *O* and *Q*, *E* and *F*, *P* and *R*, and *K* and *X*. In another experiment, seven-year-old children and college students were asked to see if pairs of letters presented simultaneously were the same or different. Reaction time, the interval between the presentation of a stimulus and the subject's response, was measured (Gibson, Shapiro & Yonas, 1968). It was found that reaction times were faster for pairs of stimuli sharing no or few features (like *M* and *O* as opposed to *M* and *Z*). Thus, perhaps humans are programmed to detect certain basic features in the environment like the computerized scanner in the grocery store that has been programmed to respond to variations in package lines on a product to identify the product and its unit price. However, if we were only programmed to respond to the basic features of environment, how could we perceive its complexities? In other words, if we only had feature detectors for horizontal, vertical, and slanted lines, how could we perceive a tree, a wheel, a painting? The connections in our basic wiring are thought to change as a result of experience, so perhaps the contexts we experience as we develop enable us to use our feature detectors in a combination of ways to perceive the complex world.

## CONTEXTUAL INFLUENCES ON PERCEPTUAL DEVELOPMENT

The contexts experienced growing up influence perceptions of the world. For example, various cultures perceive odor differently. Our culture perceives natural body odor as offensive so we use deodorants and perfumes. We can examine the role of contextual influences on perceptual

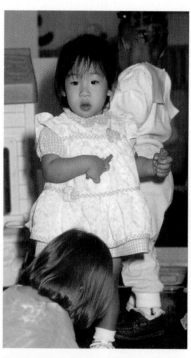

Japanese infants, until about age six months, can discriminate between sounds of the *R* and *L*; adult Japanese cannot.

development by studying the effects of restrictions and variations in early environments. To illustrate this, Blakemoore and Cooper (1970) reared kittens from two weeks to five months of age in total darkness. However, for five hours each day, the kittens were placed in cylinders in which the walls were lined with either vertical or horizontal stripes. The animals experienced only one type of stripe and wore large cuffs around their necks to ensure that other stimuli from their bodies would not interfere with their perceptions.

Recordings from electrodes attached to the kittens' heads revealed at the end of the experiment the kittens exposed to vertical stripes did not have cortical cells that responded to horizontal line orientations, whereas kittens experiencing horizontal stripes were missing cortical cells that responded to vertical lines. Thus, deprivation of normal experiences, in this case being exposed to horizontal or vertical lines, can permanently affect perceptual ability.

Other investigators (Bower, 1977; Lewis, Maurer & Brent, 1985) discuss a similar phenomenon regarding the visual perceptual abilities of infants born with visual defects, such as cataracts.

The sooner the cataract is removed after birth, the better is the infant's visual acuity. However, those whose cataracts were not removed before six months of age had great difficulty seeing patterns even though structurally they now had the capability. Thus, visual deprivation during infancy affects perceptual development later, and the effect can be permanent.

The phenomenon of "use it or lose it" also has been demonstrated with humans and the ability to perceive speech sounds. It has been found via habituation methods that infants can perceive speech discriminations (such as sound of *r* versus sound of *l* ) that are not present in the language of their parents (Werker et al., 1981; Aslin, Pisoni & Jusczyk 1983). These discriminations, however, are only maintained in adulthood if they are present in the infant's native language (Eimas, 1975). For example, Eimas (1985) reports that whereas adult Japanese can seldom distinguish sounds of *r* and *l* without special training, Japanese infants can do just as well as American infants. Apparently, exposure to one's native language emphasizes only certain sounds among all those an infant is capable of discriminating. As a result, speech perceptual abilities are decreased when sounds one is not exposed to cease to be part of one's enviroment.

## INTERACTION OF BIOLOGICAL AND CONTEXTUAL INFLUENCES ON PERCEPTUAL DEVELOPMENT

Experience can influence eventual perceptual outcomes in several ways (Aslin, 1981). Remember that experience may not be necessary where the perceptual ability would continue to mature as a function of one's genetic blueprint. First, the possibility exists that perceptual abilities are completely developed at birth before any experiences. Experience only maintains these perceptual abilities; thus, without relevant experience, these abilities are lost. Second, perceptual abilities can be only partially developed before experience. Experience facilitates further development of an ability or serves to maintain an ability; without experience, the ability, is lost. Further, an undeveloped perceptual ability can be induced by relevant experience and emerge.

## Perception of Depth

To illustrate the complexity of determining the specific ways in which biology and context interact to influence perceptual development, we will now discuss experiments on depth perception. Depth perception is a good example because it addresses the question of how we perceive the three-dimensional layout of the environment when the retina first codes only two-dimensional information. Further, depth perception is crucial to the understanding of the spatial layout of the environment and to guiding motor action.

In a classic experiment, Gibson and Walk (1960) demonstrated that chicks, turtles, rats, lambs, kids, piglets, kittens, and puppies could detect depth as soon after birth as they could move about (chicks at 24 hours, kittens at four weeks), thus implying a biological influence on depth perception. The reason animals were used in the study was that infants could not be tested until they could crawl, which is not until about six months of age. Gibson and Walk later tested infants 6 through 14 months of age and found they, too, perceived depth.

To test for depth perception, Gibson and Walk designed an apparatus known as "The Visual Cliff" (figure 6.18). The cliff consists of a board laid across a large sheet of heavy glass supported a foot or more above the floor. On one side of the board a sheet of checkerboard-patterned material is placed flush on the undersurface of the glass, giving the appearance and substance of solidity. This is termed the shallow side of the cliff. On the other side, a sheet of the same material is laid on the floor; this side of the board becomes the visual cliff.

Gibson and Walk concluded that by the time animals and humans can move they can detect depth from visual cues. The visual cue used by all subjects was **motion parallax**, a cue to depth perception that originates because visual images of distant objects are displaced less on the retina than visual images of near objects when the objects (or the observer) move. If you are driving a car, notice how objects far from you seem to move less

**FIGURE 6.18**
**THE VISUAL CLIFF**

an closer objects. Therefore, the difference in the speed of movement provides a clue to distance as well as depth. As the subjects moved along the
center board, or just as they moved their heads, the pattern on the deep side
seemed to move less or was displaced less on the retinas than the pattern on
the shallow side. This differential motion of near and far patterns was sufficient to inform them of the relative depth of the two sides. The experimenters reached this conclusion because when they replaced the patterned
cloth with a uniform gray pattern underlying the deep and shallow sides,
the subjects could no longer judge depth. This is because a patterned cloth
nearby appears larger than one farther away, thus providing a cue to depth;
uniform cloth provides no such clue. Without some pattern, motion parallax cues are ineffective.

Because animals and infants have the sensory capacities in the way
their eyes are constructed to perceive depth, it would appear that depth
perception is biologically influenced. However, as Lamb and Bornstein
(1987) showed, contextual experiences play a significant role so that depth
perception is actually the interaction between biological structures and
experience. Campos and colleagues (1970) used the visual cliff apparatus
with two- and three-month-old infants. Because these infants could not
crawl, their perception of depth was tested by monitoring the heart rates.
The researchers found the infants' heart rates did not increase, which would
have implied fear, when they were placed on the deep side. Instead, the
heart rates decreased, which was inferred to mean an indication of interest,
thus showing a detection of difference between the deep and shallow sides
of the visual cliff. If the young infants perceived a difference, why did they
not exhibit fear? Animals and older infants with depth perception become
visibly upset and their heart rates increase when they are placed on the
deep side (Campos et al., 1978). Apparently, younger infants only sense the
information about depth; they do not perceive its meaning, probably
because they do not interpret the motion parallax cue, whereas older infants
do. When older infants sense a difference in the relative motion of surfaces
in the visual field, the motion parallax cue, they perceive depth; depth
means they might fall, so the heart rates rise.

Other researchers (Bertenthal, Campos & Barrett, 1984; Lamb &
Bornstein, 1987) have shown that the extent of locomotion experience predicts the amount of fear an infant will display when placed on the deep side
of the visual cliff, thus indicating depth perception. Infants who learn to
crawl early develop the fear response early; those who learn to crawl late
develop the fear response late. Infants who were given walkers for assistance developed the fear response sooner than those not given walkers.
Thus, these experiments concluded that the experience of moving independently, without assistance results in the perception of depth; more specifically, it leads to the ability to interpret the motion parallax cue. So the structure and function of our eyes are biologically influenced, but the ability to
interpret what is seen is contextually influenced. Thus, depth perception is
the result of the interaction of biological and contextual influences.

A classic study of perceptual development by Held and Hein (1963)
supports this conclusion. Ten pairs of kittens were reared in a controlled
visual and locomotive environment. One member of the pair had visual
experiences associated with self-locomotion in that it was allowed to walk;
the other member of the pair had the same visual experiences but no self-
locomotion in that it rode in a gondola propelled by the other kitten. Figure
5.19 illustrates the apparatus designed to accomplish this experiment.

Watching the bubbles flow in different directions and at different speeds will assist in the development of depth perception.

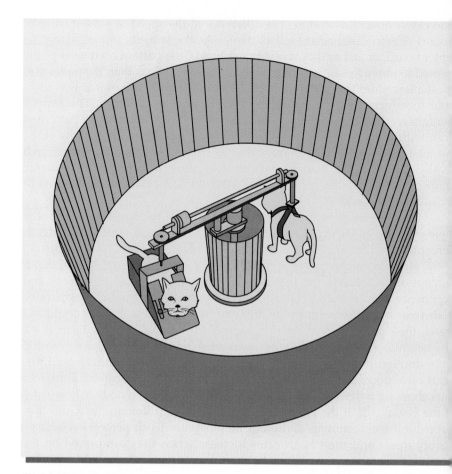

FIGURE 6.19
**Active and passive movements to determine visually guided behavior.**

The pair members spent three hours a day in the apparatus. The res
of the time, the kittens were kept with their mothers and siblings in a dark
ened cage. After experiencing 3 to 21 days of this arrangement, the pai
members were tested for the ability to perceive depth. One test was th
visual cliff. The kittens who were allowed to walk avoided the deep side o
the visual cliff every time and crossed the apparatus on the shallow side
the kittens who were confined to the gondola wandered on the deep sid
about as much as they walked on the shallow side. Thus, they were unabl
to perceive depth.

Apparently, the experience of moving about in space independentl
is crucial for developing the ability to detect depth from motion parallax
according to Campos, and Held and Hein. However, other investigator
(Walk, 1981; Acredolo, Adams & Goodwyn, 1984) believe it is visual atten
tion to cues, rather than self-locomotion, that leads to interpreting th
meaning of motion parallax. Walk (1981) suggests that movement may b
essential for visual perception development, but this movement can com
from the environment rather than being self-produced. Thus, if a child i
regularly exposed to moving stimuli that approach and recede from th
child's location in space, the child (including a paralyzed child) is likely t
become proficient at estimating depth and distance.

Regardless of whether it is self-movement or visual attention to mov
ing objects in the environment while moving that enables us to perceiv

epth, we can conclude that contextual experiences interact with biological quipment to influence visual perceptual development.

# PERCEPTUAL INTEGRATION

Most objects perceived are intersensory in that the information is vailable to more than one sense at a time. For example, we know that an range is round whether we see it or touch it. As adults, certain expecta- ons have been developed about objects in our environment. What we per- eive in one sense will have predictable characteristics in another sense.

It is well documented that young infants can detect a correspon- ence between sights and sounds (Mendelson, 1979; Spelke, 1984). lowever, little is known about the development of the ability to transfer nformation gained from one sensory mode to another, in this case, from isual to auditory. Some original work by Bower (1982) with blind infants as provided evidence that we can "see" from sound.

Bower fitted a 16-week-old boy with a sonic device that detected choes, or auditory signals, from objects in its path (figure 6.20).

After four trials, the boy was swiping at toys that were moved left nd right in front of him. Bower (Aiken & Bower, 1982) also has tried this evice on some congenitally blind infants of varying ages. He has found aat the age at which infants best learn to interpret cues from the sonic evice is four months to six months. Perhaps, a sensitive, or critical, period present whereby certain sensory inputs are converted to information.

Some researchers, such as Bower (1982) and Gibson (1969), believe nfants are born with the ability to integrate the perceptions coming from ne various senses and that the senses gradually become differentiated nrough maturation and experience. There is some support for the differen- ation view. For example, infants will look toward a sound (Wertheimer, 961; Morrongiello & Rocca, 1987), thus exhibiting auditory-visual integra- on. They also will look at what they are reaching for (Bower, 1977), thus xhibiting visual-proprioceptive integration. In addition, it has been emonstrated that neonates can translate tactile information into visual

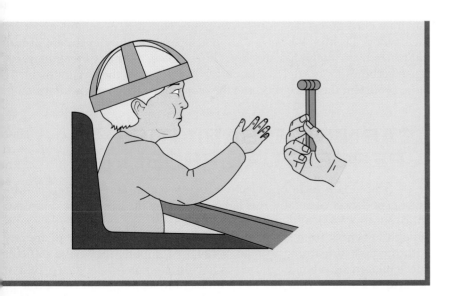

FIGURE 6.20
THE ECHO-LOCATION DEVICE

information as early as one month of age (Gibson & Walker, 1984; Meltzo & Borton, 1979). Infants were given a pacifier to suck on with either smooth surface or a rough one. After sucking the pacifiers, the infants we presented with similar ones to observe. They preferred to look at the on similar to that they had sucked, thus indicating tactile-visual intersenso perception without prior experience.

Spelke (1979) also found evidence that by four months of age infan were able to gather information via one sense (e.g., sight) and transfer it another sense (e.g., hearing) to perceive an event.

Not everyone agrees, however, that perceptual integration is inbor Piaget (1952; 1954), for example, believes that the senses are separate ar independent at birth, and perceptual integration is constructed as a result the infant's interacting with the environment, thus having various expe ences. Piaget subscribes to the enrichment theory of perceptual develo ment that says as a child increasingly interacts with the environment, pe ceptions become more complex because of the addition of information what exists in the child's memory. While the studies described earlier su ported differentiation theory, we must note that the infants were at least on month of age. Enrichment theorists thus would argue that the infa already has had some experience integrating the senses. Thus, one cann conclude that because intersensory perception is exhibited early in life th it is inborn. Piaget (1952) describes many observations of three-month-o infants reaching to touch their own hand or objects within their sigh According to Bushnell (1981), infants probably first learn that a small nun ber of highly familiar stimuli can be both seen and touched. From thes experiences, the infant eventually abstracts the more general rule that wh can be seen can be grasped and vice versa. This rule, then, is accompanie by increasingly more sophisticated reaching responses and coordinatio between three and six months of age (White, 1971). Studies of children age 5–11 years showed that visual and proprioceptive perception were not we integrated until 10–11 years old (Birch & Lefford, 1963). The ability to see a object and then trace its shape with the hand develops slowly. Such a fin ing gives support to enrichment theory.

In conclusion, there is some evidence that infants are born with th ability to integrate perception, and this ability becomes more differentiate as the child develops. Yet, there also is some evidence that the ability t integrate perceptions develops, or becomes enriched, as infants experienc their world. Perhaps the senses are not separate and independent at birt but instead, are integrated and later differentiate. As they differentiate, eac sense becomes more effective in perceiving things in the environment. Th more proficient the senses become the more they can integrate information

# LEARNING DISABILITIES— A PERCEPTUAL PROBLEM?

School is a form of objective reality which all American childre must experience. Generally, it is believed that by the age of five or six mo children are physically, perceptually, socially, and emotionally matu enough to benefit from schooling. However, when some children are face with the task of learning to read, write, or compute, they have difficult Such children are often diagnosed as having a *learning disability*. An indivi ual with a learning disability has a problem in learning that is not due pr narily to limited intelligence, to a significant emotional or social disorder, or to a sensory defect such as an impairment in seeing or hearing (Harvey, 1980).

The legal, though controversial, definition of a learning disability is as follows:

> *Specific learning disability* means a disorder in one or more of the basic psychological processes involved in understanding or in using language, spoken or written, which may manifest itself in an imperfect ability to listen, think, speak, read, write, spell, or do mathematical calculations. The term includes such conditions as perceptual handicaps, brain injury, minimal brain dysfunction (problem in the central nervous system), dyslexia (impairment in the ability to read), and developmental aphasia (failure to learn language). The term does not include children who have learning problems which are primarily the result of visual, hearing, or motor handicaps, or mental retardation, or emotional disturbance, or of environmental, cultural, or economic disadvantage (U.S. Office of Education, 1977, p. 65083).

The definition is controversial because many professionals disagree about what constitutes a learning disability. Most, however, agree with the apparent discrepancy between the child's achievement and what the child should be doing according to his age and ability in the following areas:

- oral expression
- listening comprehension
- written comprehension
- basic reading skill
- reading comprehension
- mathematics calculation or mathematics reasoning

Children with learning disabilities have academic difficulties. Reading, written expression, and mathematics are the areas in which these problems occur, with reading the most common area of difficulty (Mercer, 1983), probably because reading skills are essential to academic success (Snowling, 1988). Children with reading disabilities, known as *dyslexia*, can have trouble figuring out words, they can lose their place, or find it difficult to concentrate. They commonly reverse letters when they write or mirror-write. Thus, they perceive words differently from the norm.

Some researchers believe dyslexia, meaning poor language, to be a more complex linguistic deficiency that involves difficulty in remembering the sounds of words, poor vocabulary development, and trouble discriminating grammatical components of sentences (Vellutino, 1987). Dyslexia appears to be the consequence of limited facility in using language to code other types of information, hence its impact on learning.

Children with learning disabilities may have perceptual disorders. They may be deficient in the following (Haring & McCormick, 1990):

- Visual perception—child might have difficulty discussing a picture because of difficulty in making sensory stimuli meaningful.
- Visual discrimination—child might have a problem discriminating *ad* from *ab* because he has difficulty in perceiving the dominant

*(continued on following page)*

---

# F.Y.I.

**About 50 percent of learning-disabled individuals have language and speech problems (Marge, 1972).**

*(continued from previous page)*

features in different objects and, thus, has difficulty discriminating among them.

- Visual memory—child might have trouble remembering the sequence of letters in a word because of difficulty in recalling the dominant features of a sequence of a stimulus or the sequence of a number of stimuli presented visually.
- Auditory perception—child might be unable to follow oral instructions because she has not heard them.
- Auditory discrimination—child might have a problem distinguishing sounds such as *ba, pa, da* because of difficulty in recognizing differences between sounds and, thus, identifying similarities and differences between words.
- Auditory memory—child may forget oral instructions or have difficulty remembering the sounds of letters because of difficulty in recognizing and/or recalling previously presented auditory stimuli.

Children with learning disabilities can have memory problems, especially with visual and auditory stimuli (Torgesen, 1988). They forget a math concept they knew yesterday because it is presented in a different format.

Children with learning disabilities often exhibit attention difficulties (Hallahan & Kauffman, 1991). They find it hard to focus on a selected sound, word, line of print, or number. They get distracted because typically they cannot screen out extraneous stimuli. Some children appear intact in both visual and auditory skills when each modality is individually assessed but cannot integrate the two systems. Children who are disorganized, work slowly, rarely finish assignments, and seem confused most of the time may be presenting signs of integrative problems. While they possess the skills needed for a task, they have trouble organizing them into a coherent and useful whole (Dolgins et al., 1985).

As techniques improve for studying brain functions and perceptual abilities, more is being learned about why learning-disabled individuals process information differently than normal individuals. For example, magnetic resonance imaging (MRI) was performed on a group of children diagnosed with attention deficit-hyperactivity disorder (ADHD) and compared with a control group of nondisabled children. The MRIs of the ADHD children showed smaller corpus callosums compared with the normal control group (Hynd et al., 1991). The corpus callosum is a massive bundle of more than a million nerve fibers joining the left and right hemispheres of the brain. The corpus callosum facilitates communication between the two hemispheres, thereby influencing how stimuli are perceived and how information is processed.

**A**re perceptual abilities inborn or do they develop through experience? Information is in the chapter to support both these positions.

**ANALYSIS**: Review this chapter. Cite and describe three supports for each position (perceptions are inborn versus perceptions develop through experience).

**SYNTHESIS**: How does each position relate to enrichment or differentiation theory?

**EVALUATION**: What is your position and why?

## SUMMARY

- Sensation refers to the physiological process by which the senses receive stimulation from the environment
- Perception refers to the process by which we represent and interpret objects in the environment via the senses.
- The six major senses are sight, hearing, smell, taste, touch, and proprioception.
- Enrichment theory says that each time one perceives a stimulus, one comes to know more about it by adding the information to what already exists in the memory.
- Differentiation theory says that the information already exists in the external environment stimuli available for perception; one's task is then to discriminate the significant features of stimuli from the vast array of potential sensory information present in the environment.
- There are various methods used to study perceptual changes and development. They are natural observation, preference, monitoring physiological or reflexive responses, habituation, and evoked potentials.
- The sense systems begin to operate when a stimulus is detected by a sensory neuron, the primary sensory receptor. The sense receptor converts the detection of the physical stimulus into nerve impulses.
- The nerve impulses produced by the receptors travel along the sensory neuron to the receiving center responsible for that form of sensing, called a primary processing area. Here, the information is abstracted from the sensory impulses.

- The abstracted information is transmitted from primary processing area to other processing areas in the brain where further meaning from sensory stimuli is inferred. Sensations from several processing areas and information from past experiences are integrated to result in the perception of the stimulus.
- The basic mechanism by which we see involves light entering the eyes, being changed into neural impulses, and traveling to the brain.
- The rod cells in the retina are sensitive to light but project poorly defined images.
- The cone cells project clearer images and are also responsible for color vision.
- The basic mechanism by which we hear involves sound waves entering the ear, being translated into neural impulses, and traveling to the brain. Vibration of the eardrum causes liquid inside the cochlea to bend tiny hairs inside, thereby translating the mechanical energy of sound into neural impulses.
- The physical attributes of sound waves are perceived as pitch, volume, and tone.
- We smell and taste because of receptor cells lining the nose and mouth that detect chemicals (odors or tastes) and send neural impulses to the lower part of the brain.
- The sense of touch arises from a complex system of skin receptors sensitive to touch, pressure, heat, cold, and pain. These receptors translate physical energy into neural impulses that travel to the brain. The sense of proprioception arises from receptors widely dispersed over the body in the muscles, tendons, and joints that function primarily to receive information about the position in space of the body.

They send impulses to the central nervous system informing it of the position and movements of the various body parts.

- Biological influences on perceptual development exhibit themselves in what the newborn is capable of doing shortly after birth without any prior experience.
- There is evidence an infant comes into the world equipped with some perceptual abilities because a neonate can localize a sound, discriminate a mother's smell from that of strangers, distinguish tastes, and detect changing positions of visible objects moving in space.
- The role of contextual influences is inferred by examining the effects of restrictions and variations in early environments.
- Infants can discriminate speech sounds not present in the language of their parents, but this ability decreases when such sounds cease to be part of their environment.
- Most psychologists conclude that biological influences and contextual influences interact to produce individual differences in perceptual development. This is exemplified by depth perception experiments with the visual cliff and the accompanying explanations of motion parallax.
- Differentiation theorists believe infants are born with the ability to integrate information from more than one sense.
- Support for the differentiation view includes the findings that infants will look toward a sound, will look at what they are reaching toward, will translate tactile information into visual information, and will take in visual information and transfer it into auditory information.
- Enrichment theorists believe perceptual integration is learned through experience.
- Support for the enrichment view includes infant tested to support differentiation were at least one month old and, therefore, had a lot of experience using sensory information.
- Learning disabilities most often are displayed as a discrepancy between what a child is capable of doing in school and what a child actually achieves in school. Children with learning disabilities can have academic difficulties, language and speech problems, perceptual disorders, and/or memory problems.

## RELATED READINGS

Bower, T.G.R. (1977). *The perceptual world of the child.* Cambridge, MA: Harvard University Press.

Bryan, T.H., & Bryan, J.H. (1986). *Understanding learning disabilities.* Palo Alto, CA: Mayfield.

Elkind, D. (1981). *The child's reality: Three developmental themes.* Hillsdale, NJ: Lawrence Erlbaum.

Goldstein, E.B. (1984). *Sensation and perception* (2nd ed.). Belmont, CA: Wadsworth.

Maurer, D., & Maurer, C. (1988). *The world of the newborn.* New York: Basic Books.

Snowling, M. (1988). *Dyslexia.* New York: Basic Blackwell.

Walk, R.D. (1981). *Perceptual development.* Monterey, CA: Brooks/Cole.

● ● ● ● ● ● ● ● ● ● ● ● ● ● ● ● ● ● ● ACTIVITY ● ● ● ● ● ● ● ● ● ● ● ● ● ● ● ● ●

In dealing with what exists in the real world, we commonly integrate our perceptual abilities. Thus, it is hard for us to understand the function of each perceptual modality separately. To enable you to achieve such an understanding, you will work with a partner taking turns being blindfolded in a room under various conditions. You will need to move everything in the room next to the wall (for safety) except one chair.

*Materials:* blindfold, bag of mothballs, chair (change its position for each of the following conditions):

- **Condition 1—chair in middle of room.** Starting at one end of the room blindfolded, find the chair using touch perception. Describe the experience.
- **Condition 2—chair in middle of room being rattled by partner.** Starting at one end of the room blindfolded, find the chair using auditory perception. Describe the experience.
- **Condition 3—chair in middle of room with an opened bag of mothballs on top.** Starting at one end of the room blindfolded, find the chair using olfactory perception. Describe the experience.

Compare your use of the different perceptual modalities. Which one was most efficient? Why? Which one was least efficient? Why?

● ● ● ● ● ● ● ● ● ● ● ● ● ● ● ● ● ● ● ● ● ● ● ● ● ● ● ● ● ● ● ● ● ● ● ● ● ● ● ● ●

# Learning and Behavior: Responding to the World

*The ideal condition would be, I admit, that men should be right by instinct; but since we are all likely to go astray, the reasonable thing is to learn from those who can teach.*

**Sophocles**

## OUTLINE

## ABOUT LEARNING AND BEHAVIOR

When Jennifer was eight years old, Lloyd and Robin thought it would be fun if they all learned to ski. So when the mountains were covered with enough snow, they drove up for a weekend, rented ski equipment, and signed up for lessons. Robin never imagined learning could be so painful. First, she found the clothing to be bulky and the boots and skies cumbersome. Second, she discovered that going down a hill when you do not know how to stop is terrifying. Third, she realized falling down hurts—not to mention the chills from having the cold wind whip against one's wet clothing.

Robin finally learned to ski by following the directions of the ski instructor, by imitating and practicing the movements, and by her intense desire to avoid the negative consequence of not learning—falling down. It took her three days of practicing what she was taught to finally get down the beginner's hill without falling. Lloyd's achievement was more advanced than Robin's in that he could go down the beginner's hill faster. On the other hand, Jennifer had quickly progressed to the steeper intermediate hill. Perhaps Jennifer's learning proceeded more rapidly because as a child her body was more flexible; also, she had not developed a fear of falling as her parents had.

The following winter Robin, Lloyd, and Jennifer were able to go skiing again. Robin anticipated feeling the same fears and having the same sore muscles as she did the year before. However, once she got to the top of the hill and pushed off, all the movements she had experienced the previous year automatically were executed.

**Learning** refers to a permanent change in one's behavior that occurs over time and results from experience. Changes due to reflexes, instincts, or maturation are not considered to be learning.

Whereas, reflexes such as swallowing or breathing enable the *individual* to survive and instincts such as sexual behavior or nurturing young offspring enable the *species* to survive, learning enables both the individual and the species to adapt to the environment because it allows for flexibility. To illustrate, a swallow only "knows" one way to build a nest because that behavior is inherited rather than learned. Humans, on the other hand, have adapted many ways of building their "nests," including thatched huts, igloos, or brick mansions, according to the climate they live in and the available materials and resources.

# TYPES OF LEARNING

Learning occurs in different ways. Sometimes we become accustomed to seeing or hearing something (like a television commercial), so it no longer captures our attention. This is called *habituation*, the decline in the tendency to respond to stimuli that have become familiar due to repeated exposure. However, when what we saw or heard is slightly changed (for example, when a new character appears on the commercial), our attention is renewed. This is termed *dishabituation* and refers to the renewed tendency to respond to a new stimulus when habituation has first occurred with another stimulus. Habituation and dishabituation indicate learning has occurred.

Another type of learning is *conditioning*. This refers to the connections that are established as a result of pairing two stimuli or using reinforcement. Jennifer does not like lima beans. This is probably because she was forced to eat them when she was young. Jennifer became conditioned to not eat lima beans because their sight is associated with unpleasantness.

Still another type of learning occurs through observation and imitation or *modeling*. When Jennifer was an adolescent, she learned how to dance by watching dance shows on television.

This chapter will explore different types of learning and their applications as well as some biological and contextual influences on learning, including the interaction of these two influences.

## HABITUATION AND DISHABITUATION

In **habituation**, an individual who is repeatedly exposed to a stimulus begins to decrease his response to it. He stops paying attention. What happens is the individual recognizes and recalls the features of the stimulus so that less time is required to realize what was previously seen, heard, or touched. Habituation is considered the simplest form of learning because it indicates the person remembers the stimulus. If a person reacts to a new and slightly different stimulus with renewed attention, this means the person recognizes that the new stimulus is different from the old stimulus. This is called **dishabituation**. Dishabituation indicates an individual remembers the old stimulus and recognizes that the new one is different. It indicates the ability to discriminate among features of stimuli.

Habituation and dishabituation show a developmental trend. Infants less than four months old may require many exposures to a stimulus before they habituate, whereas four- to twelve-month-old infants exhibit habituation more readily (Bornstein & Sigman, 1986). This is probably due to the maturation of the cerebral cortex.

Also, there are individual differences in the rate at which infants habituate and dishabituate (Bornstein & Sigman, 1986). Some infants are quick to recognize an old stimulus and respond to a new one, whereas others require many exposures before they realize a stimulus is familiar and after a short time, may forget what they learned. In a review of several studies, it was concluded that infants who habituate rapidly during the first six months of life perform better on standardized intelligence tests later in childhood than do their peers who were slower to habituate as infants (Bornstein & Sigman, 1986). Some psychologists (Fagan, 1985; Berg & Sternberg, 1985) believe that the ability to detect the familiar and to retain

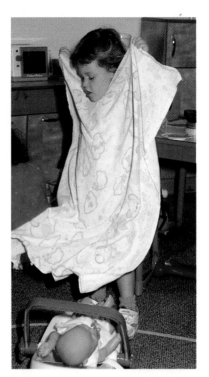

The first time this girl saw her parent folding sheets she probably was intrigued and wanted to help; however, when she was assigned to it as a chore, she quickly bored of the task.

such information is the basis for more complex intellectual processes such as analytical reasoning and problem solving.

## CLASSICAL CONDITIONING (SIMPLE LEARNING)

Ivan Pavlov, a Russian physiologist, devised a way to observe and measure canine salivary responses. During his work, he noticed that dogs sometimes salivated when no food was present. The appearance of the laboratory attendant who regularly fed them often elicited a salivary response. Thus, he devised some experiments to determine how salivation could occur in the absence of an obvious physical cause (Pavlov, 1927). First, he confirmed that a dog will salivate if some meat powder is placed on its tongue. This response was a reflex; it occurred without learning. Then, he sounded a bell (a neutral stimulus) and found the dog did not salivate. Next, he sounded the bell when the food was presented, and the dog salivated as predicted. He did this several times. Finally, he again sounded the bell alone and the dog salivated even though no food was presented. The dog had learned, or became conditioned, to salivate in response to a neutral stimulus (the bell). This process is termed **classical conditioning** (sometimes called **simple learning**), which means a reflex (innate) action or involuntary response comes to be associated with a stimulus that does not ordinarily elicit it.

Pavlov referred to the food powder as the **unconditioned stimulus (UCS)** and the salivation to the food powder as the **unconditioned response (UCR)**. The connection between this stimulus and response is unconditioned because it occurs naturally without learning. The sound of the bell was termed the **conditioned stimulus (CS),** and the salivation response to the sound was called the **conditioned response (CR)**. The connection between this stimulus and response is conditioned because it occurs as a result of repeated pairings; it is learned rather than innate.

Thus, in summary:

*Before conditioning:*
Unconditioned stimulus (UCS) ⟶ Unconditioned response (UCR)
        [food]                                [Salivation]

*Conditioning:*
Neutral stimulus   +   UCS ⟶ UCR
   [bell]                 [food]   [salivation]

*After conditioning:*
Conditioned stimulus (CS) ⟶ Conditioned response (CR)
       [bell]                             [salivation]

Classical conditioning explains why women who are breastfeeding will lactate when they hear their infants cry. When a woman initially begins breastfeeding, her infant's crying does not produce lactation; the lactating response, release of milk, only occurs when the infant sucks. Sucking is the unconditioned stimulus, and milk flow (lactation) is the unconditioned response. However, after several weeks of breastfeeding, the infant's cry becomes the conditioned stimulus for lactation that then becomes the conditioned response. Classical conditioning applies mainly to reflexes, such as salivation, or to involuntary responses, such as lactation.

Just as a response can be learned, so too can it be unlearned. After Pavlov's dogs were conditioned to salivate to the bell, he found that if he continued to sound the bell (CS) without pairing it with food (UCS), the salivation rate (CR) began to decrease, and eventually, the dogs stopped salivating to the bell. This gradual disappearance of a conditioned response by eliminating the association between conditioned and unconditioned stimulus is called **extinction**.

## Stimulus Generalization and Discrimination

Usually, after a conditioned response develops, stimuli that are *similar* but *not identical* to the conditioned stimulus also will elicit the conditioned response. This phenomenon is called **stimulus generalization**. Usually, a greater similarity between a new stimulus and the conditioned stimulus indicates the conditioned response will be stronger. Stimulus generalization enables us to adapt to the environment because we transfer what we have learned in one situation to other similar situations. For example, after we learn to drive one car, we have the ability to drive other cars. However, when a stimulus significantly differs from the original conditioned stimulus so that a response is no longer elicited, **stimulus discrimination** has occurred. Stimulus discrimination is also adaptive because it enables us to distinguish among stimuli that resemble one another. For example, a woman learns to respond to the cries of her children and to ignore the cries of other children.

Stimulus generalization is sometimes the explanation for various emotional reactions, such as fear. This was demonstrated in a classic experiment by John Watson and Rosalie Raynor (1920) who conditioned an 11-month-old child, Albert, to be afraid of a laboratory rat. When Albert was initially given the rat to play with, he showed no fear. However, as he played with the rat, the experimenters produced a very loud noise behind Albert's head, which caused Albert to cry. After several pairings of the noise and the rat, Albert exhibited fear of the rat even when no noise was sounded. Albert also showed fear of a rabbit, dog, and a sealskin coat, thereby illustrating stimulus generalization to any object with fur.

Prejudice toward an ethnic or religious group can sometimes be explained as a generalized emotional response to a negative interaction with one or more members of that group (Klein, 1987).

The anxiety evident in this young girl's face may be a stimulus generalization from past visits to the doctor's office whose lobby is similar to the one at this child care facility.

## OPERANT CONDITIONING (INSTRUMENTAL LEARNING)

**Operant conditioning**, also called **instrumental learning,** refers to learning that results when an organism operates on a stimulus in the environment and in so doing makes a response that is instrumental in getting reinforcement. For example when a dog is told to "sit," after several trials he sits, and a reward is given. After repeating this procedure several times, a dog becomes conditioned to sit when given the command because the animal has been rewarded, or reinforced, for sitting.

**Operant** refers to producing an effect. When behavior is followed by a favorable outcome (reinforcement), the probability of that behavior occurring again is increased. When behavior has no favorable outcome (if it is ignored) or has an unfavorable outcome (punishment), the probability of that behavior reoccurring is decreased. Operant methods consider the participatory role of individuals in their own learning.

Each time this boy brushes his teeth, his parents praise him. Now he enthusiastically brushes his teeth without any reminders.

## Edward Thorndike

Edward Thorndike (1898) devised a way of studying instrumental learning in animals. He set up a problem for the animal to solve and a reward for completing the task. The animal was put in a "puzzle box," a cage from which it could only escape by performing some simple action that would unlatch the door, such as pulling a loop wire or stepping on a lever. Once the animal succeeded in getting out, it was rewarded with food and then placed back inside the box for another trial. This procedure was repeated until the task was mastered. It took several trials for the cats to master the task of escaping. At each trial, the time involved in struggling decreased until finally, when put in the box, the cat immediately pressed the lever to get out and receive the reward. Thorndike explained the cats' learning as due to the **law of effect**; that is, the consequences, or effect, of a response determine whether the tendency to perform it is strengthened or weakened. If the response is followed by a reward, it will be strengthened, if it is followed by no reward, it will be weakened and eventually cease occurring (extinction).

The law of effect is applicable to children who have temper tantrums. When Jennifer was six months old, she would cry after Robin put her in the shopping cart in the supermarket. Initially, Robin would pick her up and carry her for a while, but she could not shop and wheel the cart while holding Jennifer. So Robin put her back in the shopping cart and gave her a teething biscuit. It worked; she stopped crying. Robin did not realize the behavior she was conditioning, but as Jennifer got older she always cried when they went shopping until Robin gave her something. When teething biscuits no longer satisfied Jennifer and she began demanding toys, Robin realized what had happened. Jennifer had learned, or became conditioned, to associate crying with getting a reward. Robin was faced with the very unpleasant task of reconditioning Jennifer. What Robin had to do was *not* reward Jennifer when she cried—no treats, no toys, no attention, no punishment. The law of effect partially explains why Jennifer's tantrums decreased (they were no longer being rewarded); language development played a role, too. By the time Jennifer was one year old, Robin could explain to her that no one liked to hear crying. Robin could also tell her in advance that they were going to the store, and that if she did not cry, Jennifer would receive a treat when they were done. So reconditioning involved not rewarding tantrums but instead rewarding patience.

## B. F. Skinner

B. F. Skinner (1938) expanded many of Thorndike's ideas. Skinner's primary aim was to analyze how behavior is changed by its consequences.

Skinner devised an experimental chamber that came to be known as the "Skinner box." It contained a device such as a lever or a pecking bar that an animal could operate in order to get a reward (food). Skinner also developed a cumulative recorder, a device that monitored the rate at which a particular response was given. Thus, the number of times a rat pressed the lever and the lapse of times between responses can be recorded on a graph. The animal's response in the box, such as pressing the lever, was termed the *operant*. The consequence, such as receiving a food pellet, was called the **reinforcer**. According to Skinner, a reinforcer is a stimulus event that increases the probability that the operant, or response, that immediately preceded it will occur again (table 7.1). Two types of reinforcers are positive and negative. **Positive reinforcement** is usually in the form of a

**Burrhus Frederis (B.F.) Skinner (1904-1990)**

reward, such as a toy or praise. **Negative reinforcement** involves the removal of an unpleasant stimulus; for example, allowing a child to come out of his room when a temper tantrum stops. Removal of a negative reinforcer following some response will strengthen that response's probability of reoccurring.

## TYPES OF REINFORCERS

### TABLE 7.1

1. Words—spoken and written
2. Expressions—facial and body
3. Attachment—being affectionate, or close, touching
4. Activities and privileges—allowing a child to do something she especially likes
5. Things—materials, awards, toys, food, money, tokens

**(Madsen & Madsen, 1970)**

Shaping can be useful to condition individuals to write neatly. At first anything you wrote was rewarded with praise; then only reinforced for producing approximations of numbers; then the numbers had to closely resemble the ones used as a model; then the numbers had to be written on a line, and so on.

Just as no longer pairing an unconditioned stimulus (such as food in Pavlov's experiments) with a conditioned stimulus (the bell) caused the conditioned response (salivation) to decrease and become extinguished, or disappear, when a response (such as pressing a lever) is no longer reinforced (by getting a reward of food) the response also decreases and becomes extinguished. A reinforcer to toilet-train a child is praise. When a child is put on the potty and urinates, parents usually say, "What a big boy!" or "What a big girl!" As the child continues to excrete in the potty, parents begin to expect it of the child and decrease the praise. However, if the praise is decreased too soon, that is before the child can reinforce himself by feeling proud not to wear diapers, the child is likely to have an "accident" because, inadvertently, the parents' extinguished the very response they were trying to reinforce.

**Timing of Reinforcement.** Timing is an important concept in conditioning. In operant conditioning, learning is more efficient when the interval between response and consequence is brief (Kalish, 1981). When toilet-training a child, for the reinforcement to be effective, it must come *immediately* after the child urinates or defecates in the toilet.

**Shaping of Responses.** Giving rewards for successive approximations, responses that occur with increasing frequency to the desired response, is called **shaping**. Shaping is commonly used with animals and children. For instance, shaping is used to condition circus animals to jump through hoops or walk on their hind legs.

**Extinction.** If reinforcement increases the likelihood of a response's occurring again, then removing the reinforcement should decrease and eventually eliminate (extinguish) the likelihood of the repetition of the response. *Extinction* is the gradual disappearance of a learned behavior as a result of removing the reinforcement. For example, to extinguish a habit of nail biting, a parent ignores the child when nail biting occurs, rather than telling the child to stop. Thus, the parent has removed the previous reinforcement of attention. When the child does not bite her nails for ten minutes however, the parent praises her (gives reinforcement for the desired response). Gradually, the interval between nail-biting episodes increases, with the parent praising the child for not nail biting every 30 minutes. The parent continues to ignore the child when nail biting occurs.

Extinction must be in conjunction with reinforcement to be effectiv in modifying behavior. Annoying behaviors such as tantrums, dawdling and tattling respond better to behavior modification techniques than d more complex behaviors such as aggression, stealing, or overeating.

Time-out is a popular application of extinction. **Time-out** is a proce dure in which the child is removed from an apparently reinforcing settin to one that is not reinforcing for a specified period. For example, a chil whose behavior becomes disruptive in a classroom and who is out of con trol is removed from the room for a time. This eliminates any attention th child may have received from the other children for the disruptive behavio The amount of time depends on the age of the child or the severity of dis ruption. When the child calms down and recognizes that the behavior wa inappropriate, the child returns to the classroom (aversive stimulus i removed). This technique also is used in the home. Children who exhibi temper tantrums are removed from the family setting by putting them i another room until they are ready to behave appropriately.

**Schedules of Reinforcement.** Reinforcement does not have t occur every time (**continuous reinforcement**) as a consequence for response in order for that response to be repeated. It does, however, have t occur regularly. When reinforcement is administered only some of the time it is termed **partial or intermittent reinforcement**. This reinforcement ca be based on the number or *ratio of responses that occur* (for example, a pigeo has to peck a bar ten times before receiving a reward) or the *interval of tim between responses* (for example, a rat gets a reward every 60 seconds regard less of the number of times a lever was pressed).

Both the ratio and interval schedules of reinforcement can be fixed o varied. A **fixed ratio reinforcement schedule** means that reinforcement fol lows a fixed number of responses (homework gets checked by the teache every third time). A **variable ratio reinforcement schedule** means that rein forcement varies for the number of responses although the average respons es per reinforcement is constant (homework sometimes gets checked ever other time and is checked an average of ten times per month). A **fixe interval reinforcement schedule** means that responses are reinforced at cer

**FIGURE 7.1**
**REINFORCEMENT SCHEDULE CURVES**
**The more responses per time interval, the steeper the line. These curves are typical records of responses whether the subject is an animal or human being.**

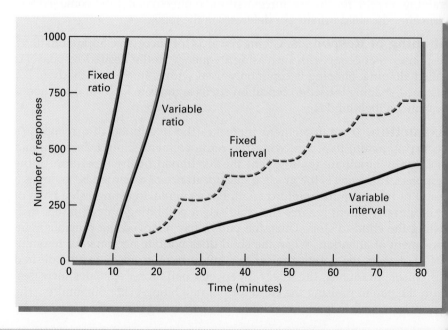

tain intervals (an allowance is given every Friday for all the chores done during the week). A **variable interval reinforcement schedule** means that responses are reinforced at different intervals although the average time between responses per reinforcement is constant (you get paid $5 for raking leaves one week and do not get paid for raking leaves for another two weeks but you get an average of $15 per month for helping with household chores). Table 7.2 is a summary of these four types of reinforcement.

Interestingly, different schedules of reinforcement produce different patterns of responding (Skinner, 1958) as shown in figure 7.1. Ratio schedules produce higher rates of response than interval schedules. Workers paid by the amount of work completed (fixed ratio) will produce more than those paid by the amount of time worked (fixed interval). Gamblers persist at trying to win because they never know when they will win (variable ratio).

With the fixed interval schedule, it does not matter how many times responses are performed during the time between rewards. As a result, the response rate drops after a reward and increases as time approaches for another reward (again see figure 7.1). This pattern is typical of how students study. They study hard before an exam and after the exam stop studying until the next exam. A variable interval schedule, however, produces responses that are slower but steadier. Thus, students with teachers

A child will persist at crying because in the past she has been picked up, so she "knows" eventually someone will come.

## SCHEDULES OF REINFORCEMENT
### TABLE 7.2

| Type | Description | Example |
| --- | --- | --- |
| **Fixed ratio** | Reinforcement follows a fixed number of responses (one reward for every ten responses) | Money earned for doing piece-work; child gets sticker for doing ten math problems correctly |
| **Variable ratio** | Reinforcement varies for number of responses even though the average remains the same (sometimes one reward for five responses; sometimes for seven; average is 1.7) | Monthly commission earned for average amount of money earned in sales, regardless of contacts made; child does not know when he will be called for raising his hand |
| **Fixed interval** | Reinforcement occurs at fixed intervals between responses (one reward for every five minutes of responding) | A weekly allowance; hourly pay; child gets praised for doing a task for five minutes |
| **Variable interval** | Reinforcement varies for different intervals between responses even though the average remains the same (sometimes one reward for two minutes of responding, sometimes for four minutes; sometimes for six minutes average is 1.4) | Commission earned for selling a certain number of products regardless of how long it takes within a set amount of time; teacher gives child individual attention two or three times during the day but the timespan differs |

who give unannounced quizzes at different times tend to study more regularly than students with teachers who give scheduled tests.

Not only do different schedules of reinforcement produce different patterns of responding, but they also have different effects on extinction. A response is harder to extinguish if it was acquired during partial rather than continuous reinforcement (Humphreys, 1939). When responses are reinforced every time, there is an expectation that a reward will follow the response; so when that expectation is not fulfilled, the responses decrease until they finally disappear. When responses are not reinforced every time, the reward is not expected every time. Therefore, when the reward is no longer forthcoming, an individual still responds as if a reward eventually will be given. Thus, it takes longer for partially reinforced responses to diminish than continuously reinforced responses.

**Token Reinforcement.** Tokens can be used with children to reinforce desirable behaviors, and the tokens can later be exchanged for rewards (material objects or privileges). Tokens can be poker chips, stickers, colored pieces of paper, stars on a chart, and so on. For example, in an after-school child-care program, children are given "bear dollars" (fake money with a picture of a bear on it) for following directions, sharing, completing homework, and so forth. At the end of the day they can trade their bear dollars for a small prize (ball, deck of cards, candy) or they can save the bear dollars for a larger prize at the end of the week (book, paint set, jump rope).

**Reinforcement Evaluated.** Walker and Shea (1980) state the conditions under which reinforcement is effective in modifying behavior.

1. The desired behavior must initially be exhibited before it can be reinforced. In training a child to defecate in the toilet, the caregiver must put the child on the seat and wait for the behavior to occur before reinforcing it. The main unresolved question accompanying the technique of positive reinforcement is how do you get children to make the desired response so they can be rewarded?
2. The desired behavior must be reinforced *immediately* the first time it occurs. If you want children to verbalize their requests rather than pointing for desired objects, they must be rewarded when they say the name of the object.
3. Initially, the desired behavior must be reinforced each time it is exhibited. Every time children verbalize requests, they should receive their requests. Every time children use the toilet properly, they should be rewarded.
4. When the newly acquired behavior is being performed, reinforcement can then become intermittent. Reward or praise can be given every few times the behavior is performed, or it can be given every few days instead of every time.
5. Because the long-range goal is self-reward, subjective reinforcers (privileges and praise) should be used with objective reinforcers (food or toys).

There are several problems in using reinforcement as a learning technique, in addition to having to wait for the desired behavior to occur. One problem is that individuals respond differently to reinforcers. For some children, a toy is an effective reinforcer; for others, adult approval is more effective. It is sometimes difficult to find the best one reinforcer. A second problem is that a child may become bored with the reinforcer, and, thus, the effectiveness of the reinforcer diminishes. A third problem with the use of reinforcement is that it is difficult for adults to constantly reward children's desired behavior even during the initial stages. If parents want to train a child to properly use the toilet, they must be present and ready to put the child on the toilet at certain intervals. They also must patiently wait for the desired behavior to occur. A final problem with the use of reinforcement as a learning technique is that adults sometimes unintentionally reinforce behaviors they want to eliminate. When children who have been toilet trained begin to urinate in their pants again and a parent says, "I thought you were a big girl," or "I thought you were a big boy," the undesired behavior probably will occur again (negative attention is better than no attention).

The child on the right is being punished by the adult for fighting with the child on the left.

## Punishment

While reinforcement increases the frequency of a response, punishment decreases it. **Punishment** is the application of an aversive stimulus that decreases the response it follows. Sometimes punishment is confused with negative reinforcement because they are both disagreeable. However negative reinforcement *increases* the response when it is *removed;* punishment *decreases* the response when it is *applied.* Punishment is getting a ticket for speeding, or being yelled at for losing books.

**Punishment Evaluated.** For punishment to be effective in modifying behavior, it must be (Parke, 1977):

1. *Timely*—The closer the punishment is to the behavior, the more effective it will be.
2. *Accompanied by reasoning*—Punishment with an explanation is more effective than punishment alone. "You cannot play outside anymore today because you went in the street. Mommy and Daddy do not want you to go in the street because we don't want you to get hurt by a car."
3. *Consistent*—If children are consistently punished for repeating a behavior, they are more likely to stop the behavior than if they are sometimes punished, sometimes ignored, and sometimes rewarded.
4. *Administered by someone to whom the child is attached*—The more nurturant the relationship between the punisher and the punishee, the more effective the punishment. A child whose parents deny a privilege for undesired behavior is less likely to repeat that behavior than if an acquaintance, such as a babysitter, administers the punishment.

The use of punishment as an effective technique in modifying behavior has been criticized for the following reasons (Walker & Shea, 1980):

1. Punishment can stop the undesirable behavior immediately, but it does not indicate appropriate or desired behavior.
2. Punishment can merely slow the rate at which the undesirable behavior is emitted rather than eliminate it entirely. Or it may *(continued on following page)*

*(continued from previous page)*

change the form in which the undesirable behavior is emitted. Children punished for physical aggression can engage in verbal aggression.

3. Punishment by an adult can have an undesirable modeling effect on the child. Parents who abuse children are likely to have been abused by their parents.

4. The emotional side effect of punishment (fear, embarrassment, low self-esteem) can be psychologically more damaging than the original behavior.

Table 7.3 is a summary of all behavior consequences previously discussed.

| SUMMARY OF BEHAVIORAL CONSEQUENCES | | |
| --- | --- | --- |
| **TABLE 7.3** | | |
| Type | Definition | Effect |
| **Positive reinforcement** | Present pleasant stimulus (give attention) | Increases desirable response |
| **Negative reinforcement** | Remove aversive stimulus (stop scolding) | Increases desirable response |
| **Extinction** | Remove pleasant stimulus (stop giving attention) | Decreases undesirable response |
| **Punishment** | Present aversive stimulus (start scolding) | Decreases undesirable response |

## Contingency Contract Programs

A popular way to apply behavioral consequences is to discuss the behavior expected of children in advance, as well as the consequences for complying and not complying. This can be done via a contingency contract. In a **contingency contract** program, the parent, teacher, or psychologist writes an individual contract with a child describing exactly what the child must do to earn a privilege or reward. Often the child participates in the process of negotiating the agreement.

## Sidney Bijou

Sidney Bijou (Bijou & Baer, 1961; Bijou, 1989) refined many aspects of behavior learning principles. The reformulated theory is called *behavior analysis*. A significant refinement specifies what constitutes a stimulus. A stimulus has been expanded to include anything physical, chemical, organismic (originating in the physiology of the individual), or social to which the individual responds. Stimuli are analyzed not only by physical dimensions but also by functional dimensions. Functional dimensions are the effects that stimuli can have on a person. The effects of a stimulus depend on the context in which the stimulus is experienced and the history of experiences with that particular stimulus. For example, if a friend touches your arm while watching a movie, the effect experienced can be one of warmth.

However, if a stranger touches your arm while watching a movie, the effect experienced can be one of fear. Also, the history of touching experiences influences how to interpret and respond to the stimulus. If experiences with touch have been pleasant, you are likely to respond in kind; however, if your experiences with touch have been unpleasant or abusive, you probably will withdraw.

Thus, behavior analysis includes unobservable behaviors such as perception, cognition, and emotion as worthy of scientific analysis, whereas traditional behaviorism considers only observable behaviors.

Box 7.1 discusses how behavioral principles are applied in the classroom.

## Box 7.1 BEHAVIORAL PRINCIPLES APPLIED IN THE CLASSROOM

The behaviorist theory of B. F. Skinner was the foundation for a model preschool program known as the Direct Instruction Curriculum (DISTAR). The curriculum, known as academic preschool, was developed by Carl Bereiter and Siegfried Engelmann (1966). Their approach assumes that it is possible to ensure learning and that the school can create readiness through behavioral principles of reinforcement and individualized instruction. In the behavioral approach to education, learning is mastery of specific content. Behavioral principles involved are the following:

- *Precise behavioral objectives*—what the learner must know at the end of a particular course of study. For example, after completion of the third grade, the learner will be able to multiply numbers one through ten correctly. Knowledge is tested by established achievement tests.
- *Sequenced material in progression*—material is presented in small, sequential steps so mastery can be reached when the progression of steps is completed.
- *Active response by the learner*—the learner makes a response at each step in the progression of sequences to be learned. The response can be speaking, writing, or pressing a button.
- *Immediate feedback*—at each step of the sequence, the learner receives immediate information about correct or erroneous responses. Correct responses are reinforced. Reinforcement is verbal praise, body language, or tokens that can be traded for privileges or small gifts.

The teacher in the behavioral setting is responsible for presenting the material in an organized, sequential, and progressive method, monitoring each child's progress and evaluating mastery.

DISTAR uses few of the play materials normally seen in many early childhood programs. The rationale is to minimize environmental distractions that could tempt the children to leave the task at hand and explore. Children are expected to be quiet and responsive.

DISTAR has been used successfully with children from low socioeconomic families. It has improved achievement test performance in the early school years (Horowitz & Paden, 1973).

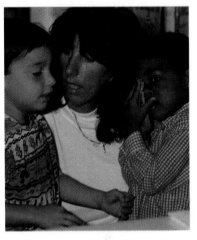

**The parents of the boy on the left have voiced their concern over the increase in aggressive behavior that he may have learned in a child care center.**

Bulletin boards are excellent places to display children's work or symbols of positive behavior. This is a method of encouraging observational learning.

# VICARIOUS CONDITIONING (OBSERVATIONAL LEARNING OR SOCIAL COGNITION)

A common complaint from some parents who send their child to preschool for the first time is that the child returns home and exhibits some unacceptable behavior, like biting or spitting. Parents wonder how and why their child learned the unacceptable behavior. The explanation is that much learning occurs not by direct reinforcement but rather by observing other people's behavior as well as by observing the consequences (either reinforcement or punishment) of that behavior (Bandura, 1977; 1989). The child who returns home from preschool and bites or spits probably observed another child doing so and receiving what he wanted from another child. Getting what one wants is reinforcement for the behavior that precedes it. So the child comes home and imitates what he has observed as an effective way of asserting his desires. Learning that occurs in this manner is called **observational learning** or **social cognition**. Technically, vicarious conditioning, learning second-hand, has taken place because by watching others the learner associates a response and its consequences (**vicarious operant conditioning**), or the learner associates a conditioned stimulus and a conditioned response (vicarious classical conditioning).

Vicarious classical conditioning can be illustrated when a person observes somebody exhibit fear while climbing a ladder. This person, as a consequence, becomes fearful when climbing a ladder.

## Imitation and Modeling

Vicarious conditioning enables us to learn many behaviors, attitudes, and emotions by imitation. Those who exhibit the behavior are called models. Models can be parents, relatives, friends, teachers, television characters, and so forth.

Modeling involves the ability to abstract information from what is observed, store it in memory, make generalizations and rules about behavior, retrieve the appropriate information, and act it out at the appropriate time. It enables one to develop new ways of behaving in situations not previously experienced. The probability that children will imitate a model, however, is a function of age, attention, level of cognitive development, motivation, and ability to reproduce the observed behavior (Bandura, 1977; 1989).

Various factors affect the extent to which children will model behavior. Models perceived as similar (physically and/or psychologically) to the observer are likely to be identified with and imitated, for example, "I have yellow hair just like Mommy." Models perceived as nurturant are more likely to be identified with and imitated, for example, "Daddy always brings me presents when he comes back from a trip." Models perceived as powerful or prestigious are more likely to be identified with and imitated (Bandura, Ross & Ross, 1963), for example, "My teacher is the smartest person in the world!"

Behavior of children also is influenced by whether the model with whom they identify is punished or rewarded. It has been demonstrated that children who see a model being punished for aggressive behavior are less likely to imitate the behavior than children who see a model being rewarded or experiencing no consequences (Bandura, Ross & Ross, 1963; Bandura, 1965).

However, children sometimes imitate a model's behavior that they have observed even if the model has not been reinforced. An experiment by Bandura (1965) illustrated this concept (figure 7.2). Some preschool children, males and females, were shown a filmed model beat up an inflated,

This young girl is modeling her mother who is, she says, "the best mommy in the whole world!"

## FIGURE 7.2
**Children will often imitate behavior which is rewarded, even if that behavior is negative.**

plastic doll called a Bobo doll in one of three situations. In the first situation the aggressor was rewarded with candy, soft drinks, and praise for the aggressive behavior; in the second situation the filmed aggressor was punished by being yelled at and spanked for the aggressive behavior; and in the third situation, the aggressor received no consequences for the behavior. After viewing the different films, each child was left alone in a room filled with toys, including a Bobo doll, where each was observed through a one-way mirror. Children who watched the films in which the aggressor was rewarded or in which the aggressor received no consequences for aggressive behavior imitated the model to a greater degree than the children who saw the film in which the aggressor was punished. Perhaps an adult's (even on film) not being punished for a forbidden behavior (aggression) is the reinforcement for a child's motivation to imitate the behavior.

In summary, for vicarious conditioning or social cognition to happen four requirements must be met, according to Bandura (1977; 1989). The first requirement is *attention:* The observer must attend to what is occurring. The second requirement is *retention:* The observer must remember the behavior seen and recall it later. The third requirement is *reproduction:* The observer must perform the behavior. The fourth requirement is *motivation:* The observer must want to imitate the behavior.

## Television Viewing
Television provides an excellent example of a context in which observational learning takes place. Much evidence indicates that children learn both prosocial and antisocial behavior by watching television (Pearl, 1982).

## CAN TELEVISION INFLUENCE CHILDREN'S LANGUAGE LEARNING?

Rice, M.L., Huston, A.C., Truglio, R., & Wright, J. (1990). Words from "Sesame Street." Learning vocabulary while viewing. *Developmental Psychology, 26* (3), 421–428.

"Sesame Street" was introduced in 1969. Its targeted audience is 3- to 5-year-olds, and its primary goal is to introduce cognitive concepts to children by dialogue. The dialogue on "Sesame Street" closely resembles that of a parent talking to the child, with simple sentences, much talk about the here and now, repeated emphasis on key terms, and an avoidance of abstract terminology. Because such speech is well suited to introducing word meanings to young viewers, the researchers predicted that viewing "Sesame Street" would contribute to preschoolers' vocabulary development.

A group of 326 children, 3 to 5 years of age, and their families were studied over a two-year period. Television viewing diaries were collected every six months, which consisted of a report of viewing by all household members.

Each television program was classified according to the intended audience (child or adult) and whether it was intended to be informative. Children's viewing frequencies were calculated for four types of programs: child audience informative, child audience noninformative, adult audience informative, adult audience noninformative. Frequency of viewing "Sesame Street" also was calculated separately from other child informative programs.

The prediction that "Sesame Street" viewing contributes to preschool children's vocabulary development was supported with the prediction that similar effects would not be evident for other kinds of viewing. Furthermore, the vocabulary enriching effects of "Sesame Street" are apparently independent of parent education, family size, child gender, and parental attitudes.

One reason for the success of "Sesame Street" as a medium for learning may be the use of certain formats and production techniques designed to elicit viewer participation and mental activity. For example, songs are often presented once with words then a second time without words so children will complete the lyrics.

## F.Y.I.

According to the 1990 Nielsen report on television, the average 2- to 5-year-olds' views about 28 hours of television per week.

*Prosocial behavior*, or altruism, is behavior that benefits another person or society, such as being helpful, or exhibiting self-control. *Antisocial behavior* is behavior that is harmful to another person or society, such as aggression or violence.

Studies on altruism agree that children who watch altruistic behavior on television become more altruistic themselves. For example, in one study (Sprafkin, Liebert & Poulos, 1975), a group of children watched an episode of "Lassie" in which the master risks his life by hanging over the edge of a mineshaft to rescue Lassie's puppy. Another group watched a "Lassie" episode without prosocial behavior, and a third group watched a "neutral" program. After watching one of the programs, five-year-old children played a game in which they could earn points toward a prize. While they were playing, they could help puppies in distress by pressing a "help" button but doing so interfered with earning points. For children who saw the prosocial Lassie program, the average time of pressing the help button was 93 seconds compared with an average of 52 and 38 seconds, respectively, for those watching the other programs.

Studies on televised violence have supported the belief that watching such programs results in an increase in aggressive behavior. For example, two independent studies by Singer and Singer (1980) examined the behavior of children three years and four years of age for one year and correlated their television viewing at home during free-play periods at daycare centers. In each study consistent associations were found between excessive viewing of violent television programs and unwarranted aggressive behavior in free-play periods.

Thus, the reason viewing behavior, whether prosocial or antisocial, on television increases the likelihood that it will be performed later is that when children see someone being rewarded for an act, they are more apt to imitate it. Usually, altruism is rewarded on television by the person becoming a hero or receiving much attention. Aggression is rewarded on television by the person "getting away with it" or getting what he wanted.

Meltzoff (1988) demonstrated that infants 14 months and 24 months who observed a television model manipulating a toy could imitate that model's actions on the same toy 24 hours later.

If young children (14 months of age) can relate two-dimensional television representations to their own actions on real three-dimensional objects, we should be concerned about television viewing and its potential influence on children's behavior.

# BIOLOGICAL INFLUENCES ON LEARNING AND BEHAVIOR

Biological influences on learning and behavior include natural instincts, maturation, and critical periods.

## INSTINCTS

Keller and Marina Breland (1972) showed how instincts limit what can be learned. The Brelands had been using conditioning techniques for years to train thousands of animals of many different species for circuses, zoos, fairs, television. While they were able to condition a raccoon to pick up one coin and let it go to get a food reward, they could not condition it to pick up two coins and let them go. The raccoon would just rub the coins together because instinct took precedent over learning.

The more similar a behavior to be learned is to a species' natural behavior, the easier it will be to learn it. Seligman (1970) refers to the predisposition to learn certain response-reinforcement relations more easily than others as **preparedness**. For example, it is easier to condition a pigeon to peck at a bar to get food than it is to condition a dog to do so because pecking is a pigeon's natural response to get food.

## MATURATION

In addition to natural tendencies or instincts influencing behavior, so may *maturation*, the unfolding of genetically predetermined traits, structures, or functions.

Arnold Gesell (1929) examined a set of identical twins to study the effects of training babies to perform a number of motor activities. One twin was trained in stair climbing, block building, and hand coordination; the other twin was not. With age, the untrained twin became just as adept at these skills as the trained twin. Gesell concluded that when children are maturationally ready to perform a skill they do so without having to learn it.

McGraw (1940) determined the effects of very early toilet training. The study involved a pair of identical twins—from the age of 2 months. One was put on the toilet every hour of every day; the other was not put on until 23 months. The twin who received early training began to show some control by 20 months and almost complete control by 23 months. The twin who was not put on the toilet until 23 months developed control shortly thereafter. This is another example of the maturational influence.

## CRITICAL PERIODS

Another influence on learning and behavior are certain biologically programmed critical periods. A *critical period* is the time during development when an event has its greatest impact.

Some evidence suggests there is a critical period for language development in humans. There is the case of Genie (Curtiss, 1977), a child who was discovered when she was 14 years old. Since she was 20 months old she had been tied to a chair, was frequently beaten, and never spoken to. She was taught some language but never mastered more than the basics ("Me go"; "House have dog"; "No take"). She could not make complicated sentences with pronouns, adjectives, prepositions, and so on.

If children are not exposed to language before 2 years of age, they have greater difficulty learning to speak later (Lenneberg, 1967). This principle has been shown by studies of deaf children and children with brain damage.

To summarize, biology plays a role in influencing what we can and cannot learn and how we can best learn. Biology possibly plays a role in a common behavioral disorder of childhood called attention-deficit hyperactivity disorder, described in box 7.2.

## Box 7.2  ATTENTION DEFICIT HYPERACTIVITY DISORDER (ADHD)

One most common behavioral disorder of childhood is attention-deficit hyperactivity disorder (ADHD) (Gelfand, Jenson, & Drew, 1988). The following are some typical parental complaints (Parker, 1988):

- "Jessie cannot sit still in a restaurant. She's four years old now and still does not know how to wait her turn."
- "Alan is in the fifth grade. We argued with him last night to do his homework. At first, he didn't remember what to do and then when we figured out what the assignment was, he didn't know how to do it. After a two-hour struggle we finally got it done. Then the teacher called to say he did not turn it in."

Children sometimes become impatient when they have to wait, especially when they are hungry. Children also occasionally have trouble getting along in school and sometimes do not know how to do their homework. However, children with ADHD almost always have problems with even routine family or school situations because of their inherent restlessness, excitability, overexuberance, impatience, and inattentiveness.

The causes of ADHD are still under investigation. Genetics may be a factor because a higher incidence of children with ADHD occurs in families with a history of ADHD or related illnesses (Cantwell, 1975). Another factor could be the structure of the brain. Children with ADHD were found to have smaller corpus callosums compared with nondisabled peers (Hynd et al., 1991). Another possible factor could be a disturbance in the metabolism of the neurotransmitters in the brain (Rie & Rie, 1980). Neurotransmitters function to send information to different parts of the brain. Certain drugs known as psychostimulants, for example, Ritalin, have been shown to affect the neurotransmitter chemicals and enable the child to better focus attention when the drugs are carefully monitored medically. Still another factor may be environmental, such as diet (Gelfand, Jenson & Drew, 1988).

The most common treatment of ADHD today is to combine medication with behavior therapy. If diet modification works, then it is employed also. Usually, the behavioral techniques include positive reinforcements for desired behavior (putting toys away, remaining seated, completeing a chore or assignment); **response cost** (a punishment procedure that results in the loss of previously earned rewards) for inappropriate behaviors such as noncompliance, incompletion of tasks, or aggression; and **cognitive-behavior modification** (therapy that tries to change habitual ways of thinking so behavior will consequently change) that trains a child to have self-control and self-reinforcement.

## F.Y.I.

Male birds generally sing a song characteristic of their particular species. They learn this song by listening to adult males of their species sing it. It has been documented that to learn the white-crowned sparrow song, the baby birds must hear an adult's song sometime between the seventh and sixtieth day of their life. The next forty days are marginal—if the baby is not exposed to the adult male song until then, it will acquire only some limited basics without all the details. If the exposure comes later, the bird will never sing normally.

It can be seen from these criteria that inattention is the central characteristic of ADHD (Weiss & Hechtman, 1986). This means a child has difficulty following instructions, staying with a task for a sustained time, and working independently. Children with ADHD may have difficulty screening out irrelevant or extraneous stimuli (Cantwell,1975) so minor events such as a truck passing can distract them from what they are doing.

Another characteristic of children with ADHD is impulsivity (Gelford, Jenson & Drew, 1988). Related to impulsivity is poor self-control, excitability, and the inability to delay gratification or inhibit urges. Examples include jumping into a pool without knowing how to swim and making tactless comments. Such impulsive behavior can be dangerous and socially isolating.

Another general characteristic is overactivity. ADHD children are frequently described as "always on the move" or "bouncing off the walls" (Gelfand, Jenson & Drew, 1988). ADHD can occur without hyperactivity, although most cases involve fidgety motor behavior.

ADHD children have learning problems in school because they cannot pay attention or sit still. These children often lose their place in reading assignments, get frustrated, and quit. ADHD children commonly have social difficulties, particularly with peers (Gelfand, Jenson & Drew, 1988). They are viewed as being immature, uncooperative, self-centered, and bossy. This is due to their inability to concentrate on games, to take turns, and to listen to others as well as energetic and often reckless behavior.

Hyperactive children may have trouble retaining friends.

**Functional families instill values, goals, and appropriate behavior in their children.**

# CONTEXTUAL INFLUENCES ON LEARNING AND BEHAVIOR

Learning and behavior occur in many different contexts. Mos research previously discussed describes learning and behavior studied in laboratory settings. We will examine how the contexts of family, school, and culture influence learning and behavior.

## FAMILY

The family is the first context in which the child is exposed to learning. Parents have certain values for their children that include how they want them to behave, the attitudes they would like them to have, and what competencies they want them to achieve. Parents instill these values by using reinforcement for desired behavior, extinction and/or punishment for undesired behavior, and by modeling, and behavioral techniques.

According to Burton White (1975), the family impacts a child's learning and consequent educational development more than school. He came to this conclusion after years of research examining how human beings acquire knowledge to get along in the world both socially and intellectually.

In a study by White and Watts (1973), the family contexts of competent and incompetent preschool children were compared. It was found that mothers of the competent children designed a safe physical environment for the children and provided interesting things for them to manipulate. Surprisingly, mothers of the competent children spent no more than 10 percent of their time deliberately teaching the children, yet they were always "on-call" when needed. They made themselves available to share in children's exciting discoveries, answer children's questions, or helping children in an activity for a few minutes while maintaining daily routines. They enjoyed their children, were patient, energetic, and tolerant of messes, accidents, and natural curiosity. They set limits on behavior and were firm and consistent in their discipline.

Mothers of the incompetent children, on the other hand, were diverse. Some spent little time with the children. Others spent a great amount of time with the children. They were overprotective and pushed the children to learn. Still others provided for the children materially (toys and other objects), but restricted the children's instincts to explore by ruling certain places and possessions out of bounds. These mothers used playpens and gates extensively.

Thus, it is the caregiving style in the family that influences a child's learning and behavior. Specifically, arrangement of the environment, shared enthusiasm with the child, setting reasonable limits following a child's developmental level, and being available as a resource when needed foster competence.

## SCHOOL

During the late 1950s and early 1960s, there was great concern about educational failure. The launching of the first satellite, *Sputnik*, into space by the Soviet Union in 1957 was one factor contributing to the concern because the United States had always regarded itself as the world leader in scientific technology. Thus, such an accomplishment by a rival power led to questions about the learning occurring in our schools. A second factor contributing to concern over educational failure was the increasing number of eople on welfare who were not equipped with enough skills to get and eep a job to support themselves. A third factor was the pressure from civil ghts groups to provide better educational opportunities for minority chil-ren so they would have an equal opportunity to succeed as adults. As a esult in 1965 President Lyndon Johnson supported the establishment of **lead Start**, an early childhood education program designed for disadvan-iged children from ages 3 to 5 to enable them to enter elementary school repared to learn. An early childhood education program is an "effort in vhich an agent, operating within a context, uses some means, according to ome plan, to bring about changes in the behavior of children between birth nd age 8 in terms of some definable criteria" (Peters, Neisworth & Yawkey, 985, p. 4). Disadvantaged children include those who are poor, those who re from ethnic minority groups and whose English speaking ability is lim-ed, those who are disabled, and those who are abused or neglected.

Head Start still exists today. Much research has been done on its ffect on the children it serves. In a review of seven studies (Berrueta-lement et al., 1984), which taken together followed the participating chil-ren at least until age nine and at most until age 20, it was found that early hildhood education has a great influence on later learning and behavior specially for disadvantaged children. Specifically, there are immediate and ositive effects on children's intellectual performance as represented by ntelligence test scores and scholastic achievement. There is also a reduction n the need for placement in special education classes.

Early childhood education programs differ in philosophy and cur-iculum but most quality preschool programs enable children to learn how o learn. Learning to learn does not refer to the teaching of reading, writing, nd arithmetic. Rather, it refers to developing a curiosity about the world nd a means to satisfy that curiosity. Having interesting activities in which hildren can become involved, such as cooking, art, building, and taking arious trips, stimulates curiosity

Specifically, different early childhood education programs have dif-erent goals and use different plans to enable children to learn. For one xample, the goal of behavioral programs (those that follow behavior-learn-ng theory) is to transmit the accumulated knowledge of the culture. What s to be learned is broken down into small, sequential steps, and children re reinforced for achievement. Participation in such programs is associated vith higher scores on intelligence tests and better performance in language nd arithmetic (Miller & Dyer, 1975; Stallings, 1975). For another example, he goal of cognitive-developmental programs (those that follow Piaget's heory) is to enable children to actively participate in their own learning because humans adapt mentally to their environments through their inter-ctions or experiences with people, objects, and events. New experiences re planned so a child can make a connection or relation to previous experi-nces. The ability to make such associations depends not only on experi-nces but on maturation. Participation in such programs was associated vith higher levels of inventiveness and curiosity, social interaction (Miller & Dyer, 1975), and problem-solving ability.

Thus, early childhood education programs tend to produce what hey set out to produce.

## CULTURE

While the basic mechanism for learning appears to be the same in all humans, what people learn, what they remember, and how they use their

**Parents who provide safe environments for play and are available to respond to and help their children while being patient, firm, and consistent in discipline, tend to raise competent children.**

**Adolescents who attended early childhood education programs such as this one were less likely to drop out of school due to more positive attitudes about learning that were fostered in preschool.**

Elardo, Bradley, and Caldwell (1975), developed an assessment scale to determine the relationship between the child's home environment and intellectual performance. This scale was known as HOME (Home Observation for the Measurement of the Environment). A high correlation was found between a child's home environment score at 6 months of age and performance on an intelligence test at 3 years of age. Thus, children who came from responsive, stimulating, interactive homes did better on intellectual tasks than children who came from other home environments.

Having adults available to answer children's questions and further stimulate the children by talking about their experiences, enables children to learn how to satisfy their curiosity because they come to regard adults as resources.

knowledge to solve problems are influenced by the cultural context in which they grow up (Cole & Scribner, 1974). For example, in some test comparing literate members of the Peace Corps with nonliterate member of the Kpelle tribe in Liberia, it was found that each group excelled at different tasks (Cole et al., 1971). In one task everyone had to estimate the number of measuring cups of rice in a bowl. The Peace Corps members estimates ranged from 6 to 20; every Kpelle tribe member estimated slightly under nine. On examining the amount of rice in the bowl, it was found to contain exactly nine cups.

In another task both groups were given eight cards, each of which was marked with numbers and red or green squares or triangles. The instructions were to sort out the cards in matching piles three differen ways. The Peace Corps members did this without errors, whereas the Kpelle tribe had great difficulty sorting the cards.

The Kpelle excelled in the rice task because they are farmers who make a living by growing and selling rice. They measure rice by the cup bucket, tin, and bag, and they know 100 cups are in a bag. Their livelihood depends on their ability to estimate accurately. On the other hand, it is unlikely that they would have had experience in sorting cards.

By contrast, the Peace Corps volunteers (all from the United States were familiar with cards as well as sorting. Many toys that they grew up with not only included games or cards but also involved colors and shapes.

Not only do experiences of people from various cultures differ but so do what particular behavior is reinforced, extinguished, and punished (Stevenson, 1983). For example, Whiting and Child (1953) studied such behaviors as nursing, weaning, and toilet training in 75 primitive cultural contexts. Examples of the differences follow:

> Kwoma infants up to the time they are weaned are never far from their mothers . . . . Crying constitutes an injunction to the mother to discover the source of trouble. Her first response is to present the breast. If this fails to quiet him, she tries something else. . . . Thus during infancy the response to discomfort which is most strikingly established is that of seeking help by crying or asking for it (Whiting, as cited by Whiting & Child, 1953, pp. 91–92).

> The Dohomean…child is trained by the mother who, as she carries it about, senses when it is restless, so that every time it must perform its excretory functions, the mother puts it on the ground. Thus, in time, usually two years, the training process is completed. If a child does not respond to this training, and manifests enuresis at the age of four or five, soiling the mat on which it sleeps, then, at first, it is beaten. If this does not correct the habit, ashes are put in water and the mixture is poured over the head of the offending boy or girl, who is driven into the street, where all of the other children clap their hands and run after the child singing, "Urine everywhere" (Herskovitz, as cited by Whiting & Child, 1953, p. 75).

Behavior expectations in a culture depend on the values in that culture. For example, studies comparing interaction patterns between mothers and infants in the United States and Japan (Caudill & Weinstein, 1969) present data that suggest American mothers rely more on verbal modes of interaction, whereas Japanese mothers emphasize more physical contact.

According to Caudill (1971), the American mother views the infant as a separate and autonomous being. Therefore, she helps the infant learn ways of expressing needs. In contrast, a Japanese mother views an infant as an extension of herself and feels she knows what is best for him or her. Thus, she has less need for encouraging verbal communication because of the constant physical proximity between the two.

Caudill (Caudill & Schooler, 1973) conducted a follow-up study of his original American and Japanese subjects when the children were two and a half and six years old. The study showed that compared with the Japanese children, the Americans were more active, independent, vocal, and assertive. Thus, Caudill and his colleagues demonstrated consistent cross-cultural differences in the behavior of children and their caregivers, which persist from infancy through early childhood. They asserted that the differences can be explained by early learning in response to differing maternal expectations and behaviors and were not due to genetic factors.

So far we have discussed how an individual's behavior is affected by outcomes, such as reinforcement or punishment. Box 7.3 explains what happens when there is *no* outcome or impact for a particular behavior—learned helplessness.

## Box 7.3   LEARNED HELPLESSNESS

When one makes a connection between behavior and an outcome, one has learned to control the environment. Infants as young as two months of age learned that if they moved their heads back and forth on their pillows they could control the movement of a mobile above their cribs (the switch that controlled the movement was in the pillow). These babies smiled and cooed at their mobiles and persisted at their behavior. Another group of infants also had mobiles over their cribs but were not provided with the control switch. Their mobiles were moved for them unrelated to any behavior of theirs. They soon lost interest in watching the mobile move (Gleitman, 1991). Thus, when one perceives she has no control over outcomes, one loses the motivation to try to perform effectively and, hence, exhibits helpless behavior that has been learned. This phenomenon has been called **learned helplessness** (Seligman, 1975).

Dweck and Reppucci (1973) found that when children believe their failures are due to uncontrollable factors in themselves such as lack of ability, their subsequent task performance deteriorates after failure. However, if children believe their failure was due to lack of effort, they try harder on subsequent tasks and often show improved performance.

Feedback is influential in whether helplessness is learned. In another study, Dweck and colleagues (1978) set up some tasks for girls and boys. One group of girls and boys were told, after doing poorly on an anagram test, "You didn't do well that time; you didn't get it *(continued on following page)*

*(continued from previous page)*

right." Another group of girls and boys were told that they did not do well and that they did not write the answers neatly enough. This feedback led the second group to believe that their poor performance was due to lack of effort. When the task was administered again, the first group gave up more easily after initial failure, while the second group tried harder. Thus, if adults enable children to realize their mistakes can be remedied by their own actions, children are more likely to reflect this opinion of themselves and behave accordingly.

# INTERACTION OF BIOLOGICAL AND CONTEXTUAL INFLUENCES ON LEARNING AND BEHAVIOR

While we have discussed some biological and contextual influences on learning and behavior separately, they actually interact. Whereas behavior can be shaped, the limits of the shaping are influenced by biological maturation and individual abilities (Sameroff, 1983). You cannot condition a three-month-old child to walk because he is not biologically mature enough to stand without support and coordinate the muscles involved in walking. In other words, a genetically programmed sequence, as well as timetable, exists for certain skills to emerge. For example, creeping occurs before crawling, and crawling occurs before walking. Therefore, training is of little advantage. On the other hand, other skills such as swimming, throwing a ball, and riding a bicycle respond well to shaping. Training for these skills occurs in the contexts of family, school, peer group, and so forth. Because of their ability to coordinate their muscles some children will learn more quickly and easily than others.

Training to learn how to play a highly complex game or an organized sport such as football is typically done with peers and coaches either in school or in the community.

Giving children a place, time, and encouragement to practice, however, enables them to improve their abilities to execute various behaviors. Depriving children of opportunities to learn can prevent children from reaching their inherited potential (Caldwell, 1970).

Thus, biology and context interact to influence learning and behavior in that maturation provides the foundation for learning to occur while opportunities for learning enhance the level of behavioral competence.

Another way in which biology and context interact to influence learning is that different characteristics of a child (appearance, temperament, gender) will trigger different responses from the environment (Sameroff, 1987). For example, a child whose birth resulted in complications, such as prematurity or birth defects, can cause an otherwise calm parent to be anxious. The parent's anxiety can cause the infant to respond by having difficulty establishing regular eating and sleeping patterns. This difficult behavior in the infant tends to decrease the pleasure that the parent obtains from the child and so less time is spent with the child, thereby affecting his development.

# BEHAVIOR-LEARNING THEORIES EVALUATED

While the early behavior-learning theorists such as John Watson and B. F. Skinner believed humans were totally malleable and their behavior was shaped by consequences experienced in the environment, we now recognize the role the individual plays in her learning. For example, for habituation and observational learning to happen, the individual has to attend to the environment, retain in memory what was experienced, and later recall it. Also, in observational learning, individuals are selective about which behaviors they imitate. Additionally, with behavior analysis, an individual's history of experiences with a specific stimulus influences her response. Apparently, individuals interpret the experiences exposed to and process the information. How this information is processed determines whether learning has occurred or whether the behavior observed will be exhibited.

The role of the individual as an information-processor is also illustrated in operant conditioning. When a behavior is followed by reinforcement, the individual will repeat the behavior only if he interprets it to be "worthwhile." Kenny's brother, Jason, would not rake leaves when he was offered $5 dollars an hour. He said that the job was not worth his time; he could earn more working at a restaurant getting tips. Interpretation of consequences also plays a role in punishment. When punishment follows a behavior, a child can feel guilty or ashamed. The association of the behavior with such negative feelings will likely stop the performance of the behavior in the future. However, if punishment is associated with being caught, then it is likely that the behavior will be performed again under less detectable circumstances. Thus, while we learn from the consequences of our behavior, what each of us learns is different.

There are many applications of behavior-learning theory. A major criticism of using this approach to modify behavior, however, is that it trains children to be reward-conscious: to behave acceptably for a reward rather than to behave acceptably because it fosters cooperation or to learn certain material for a grade rather than to learn it because it is enriching. Another criticism of the behavioral approach is that it is structured and does not use reasoning, problem solving, or creative thinking. On the other hand, behavior techniques objectify learning by setting goals, organizing what is to be mastered into small, sequential steps, and by providing feedback on progress. Each step builds upon success at the previous step.

We need to specify in which circumstances behavior-learning techniques are appropriate as well as those in which they are inappropriate.

**Behavioral techniques objectify learning by setting goals, organizing what is mastered in small sequential steps, and by providing feedback on progress. Each step builds on success from the previous step.**

# CRITICAL THINKING & YOU

**M**ost people assume children learn to read and write in elementary school. However, child developmentalists have become aware that many children have learned much about oral and written language before they enter school. For example, when parents read books to children, point out signs and letters, give children crayons and pencils and encourage them to talk about their drawings, play games with them, and encourage children to tell stories, children are learning to become literate. While elementary school provides the formal structure for learning literacy, the home environment provides the informal structure.

**ANALYSIS**: Review this chapter and discuss three specific ways children learn to read and write.

**SYNTHESIS**: Compare formal methods of learning to read or write that children might be exposed to in school with informal methods that children might be exposed to at home. Be specific—how the task is presented, how children are motivated to learn, how children are reinforced for success.

**EVALUATION**: Do you think television viewing supports or inhibits children's literacy learning? Support your position with evidence from this chapter.

# SUMMARY

Learning refers to a relatively permanent change in behavior that occurs over time and results from experience.

Habituation is when an individual who is repeatedly exposed to a stimulus begins to decrease his or her response to it.

When a new stimulus is presented that is slightly different from the one to which a person habituated and responds, dishabituation is said to have occurred.

Classical conditioning, also called simple learning, involves a reflex action or involuntary response that comes to be associated with a stimulus that does not ordinarily elicit it. Pavlov demonstrated classical conditioning.

A response can be unlearned when the association between the conditioned and unconditioned stimuli is removed. This is known as extinction.

After a conditioned response develops, stimuli that are similar but not identical to the conditioned stimulus will also elicit the same conditioned response. This is called stimulus generalization.

Stimuli that are different from the original conditioned stimulus will not elicit a response. This is termed stimulus discrimination.

Another type of learning is operant conditioning, also called instrumental learning. An organism operates on a stimulus in the environment and in so doing makes a response that is instrumental in getting reinforcement.

Thorndike studied instrumental learning. He explained learning as being due to the law of effect—the consequences, or effect, of a response determine whether the tendency to perform it is strengthened or weakened. If the response is followed by a reward, it will be strengthened; if it is not followed by a reward, it will be weakened and eventually cease occurring (extinction).

Skinner studied how responses could be shaped into desired behavior by rewarding successive approximations of a desired response.

For a response to be repeated, reinforcement has to occur within a short time after the organism makes the response. However, reinforcement does not have to occur every time for the response to be repeated.

- Different reinforcement schedules produce different patterns of responding and have different effects on extinction.
- Punishment is the application of an aversive stimulus that decreases the response it follows.
- Bijou refined many aspects of behavior learning principles into a theory termed behavior analysis. Behavior analysis includes nonobservable behaviors, such as perception, cognition, emotion, and observable behaviors.
- Learning does not always occur as a result of direct conditioning. Sometimes it occurs second-hand, or vicariously. This is termed vicarious conditioning, or observational learning or social cognition. An association is formed between a response and its consequences or between a conditioned stimulus and a conditioned response by watching others. Vicarious conditioning enables us to learn many behaviors, attitudes, and emotions by imitation.
- Those who exhibit the behavior are called models. Modeling is affected by age, attention level, cognitive development, motivation, and ability to perform the observed behavior.
- For the observed behavior to be reproduced, the observer must have paid attention, be able to remember it, be capable of reproducing it, and be motivated to reproduce it.
- Certain biological influences on learning include natural instincts, maturation, and critical periods.
- Learning and behavior occur in many different contexts such as family, school, and culture. Parents instill their values about behavior, attitudes, achieved competencies by reinforcement for desired behavior, extinction and/or punishment for undesired behavior, and by modeling.
- The school is the formal context in which learning takes place. Quality early childhood education programs have a great influence on later learning and behavior.
- The context of culture influences what people learn, what they remember, and how they use their knowledge to solve problems.
- When a person perceives he has no control over outcomes, one loses the motivation to try to perform effectively, and hence exhibits behavior that has been learned. This phenomenon is called learned helplessness.
- Biology and context interact to influence learning and behavior.

## RELATED READINGS

Aznin, N.H., & Foxx, R.M. (1974). *Toilet training in less than a day.* New York: Pocket Books.

Bandura, A. (1977). *Social learning theory.* Englewood Cliffs, NJ: Prentice-Hall.

Cole, M., Gay, J., Glick, J.A., & Sharp, D.W. (1971). *The cultural context of learning and thinking.* New York: Basic Books.

Essa, E. (1983). *Practical guide to solving preschool behavior problems.* New York: Delmar.

Farnham-Diggory, S. (1992). *The learning-disabled chil*. Cambridge, MA: Harvard University Press.

Seligman, M.E.P. (1975). *Helplessness.* San Francisco W.H. Freeman.

Seligman, M.E.P., & Hager, J.L. (Eds.). (1972). *Biologic boundaries of learning.* New York: Appletor Century-Crofts.

Skinner, B.F. (1948). *Walden Two.* New York Macmillan.

Walker, J.E. & Shea, T.M. (1980). *Behavior modification A practical approach for educators* (2nd ed.). S Louis, MO: C.V. Mosby.

## ● ● ● ● ● ● ● ● ● ● ● ● ● ● ● ● ● ● ACTIVITY ● ● ● ● ● ● ● ● ● ● ● ● ● ● ● ●

To better understand how learning theories can be applied, design a behavior learning program for a four-year-old child who continually whines in preschool. The objective is to modify behavior so she uses a normal voice when interacting with others Apply the techniques of reinforcement, shaping extinction, punishment, and modeling.

# Cognitive Development: How We Know What We Know

*A child never gives a wrong answer;
he just answers a different question.*

**Jerome S. Bruner**

## ABOUT KNOWLEDGE

When Kenneth was four years old, he learned that he could get things with money. His older brother, George, now 12, had a paper route. Kenneth would watch George put the money he collected into piles of dollar bills and coins. Sometimes George would tell Kenneth the names of the coins and give him a few pennies or a nickel. George told Kenneth that someday he would have enough money to buy a car. Every collection day thereafter, Kenneth would ask, "Do you have enough to get the car yet?"

Jason, Kenneth's other brother, now ten, sometimes would help George fold the papers for delivery in exchange for a few dollars. Unlike George, who would save most of his money, Jason spent his money as soon as he got it. When Jason babysat for Kenneth, he would take him to the store and buy baseball cards for himself and let Kenneth put his pennies in the machine to get gum or candy. Jason loved to tease Kenneth saying, "I'll give you two pennies if you'll give me a dime." Kenneth always complied—he'd rather have two coins than one, besides, a penny was bigger than a dime!

Why were George's, Jason's, and Kenneth's concepts of money, amount, and size different? Was the difference due to age, learning, or experience?

Think about how you acquired such concepts as permanence, change, equality, and so on. Do children's concepts of reality differ from those of adults? To illustrate, if you bought two packages of clay rolled one into a ball and were asked if they were equal, what would you say (figure 8.1)?

**FIGURE 8.1**
**(a) Are these equal?**
**(b) Are they still equal?**

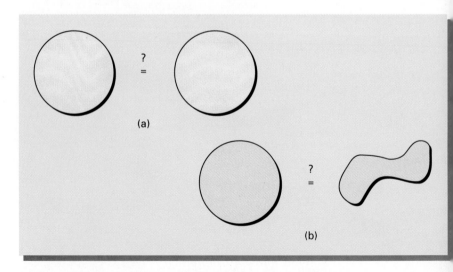

(a)

(b)

If you took one of the balls of clay and rolled it into the shape of a snake, would the two pieces of clay be equal?

Assuming you answered "equal" to both questions, how did you know? Your adult mind would reason that the amount of substance does not change by changing its shape. However, if you pose this demonstration and accompanying questions about equality to children of different ages, you will get some interesting responses. For example, a child between the ages of 2 and 7 will probably say the shapes are not equal—either the ball has more clay because it is fatter or the snake because it is longer. Children this age tend to focus on the end result rather than the process of transformation that neither adds nor subtracts any amount. Children of this age also cannot reverse their thinking on such a problem. In other words, they cannot conceptualize the original ball shape of the clay that has been transformed into a snake.

Between the ages of 7 and 11, children can mentally conceive of two dimensions at the same time. They can reason that although one shape was made longer, it still remained the same amount. They can mentally reverse a physical action to return the object to its original state. Thus, they reason that if the clay were rolled into a ball, it would be the same original size.

By adolescence a child aged 11 to 15 might answer that whether both shapes are equal depends on whether any clay sticks to your hand when the clay is reshaped. Adolescents can conceive of the hypothetical, the "if-then."

In this chapter we will explain theories of **cognitive development** that explain how knowledge is acquired—how we come to understand permanence, change, equality, differences, and similarities, causality, abstractions, and so forth. Thus, we are concerned here with the nature, or *quality*, of knowledge rather than the *quantity*.

## SIGNIFICANCE OF STUDYING COGNITIVE DEVELOPMENT

An understanding of cognitive structure at different ages is a powerful analytical tool for teachers, parents, and psychologists. Jean Piaget (1896–1980) has provided the most comprehensive view of cognitive development, although other developmental psychologists in recent years have added and refined aspects of Piaget's view.

Significant educational implications reside in the fact that a 7-year-old or 8-year-old child if shown a series of blocks differing in size can tell which is largest, medium, and smallest. However, if this child is presented with a similar problem expressed verbally (Susan is taller than Jill, and Jill is taller than Marge; who is the tallest?) the child cannot answer correctly. Adults and adolescents have no difficulty with this kind of problem. Curriculum has to be structured to be understood by children who think differently from adults.

Some adolescents think they are special and bad things cannot happen to them. Parents and psychologists who see them after they've taken drugs, become pregnant, or attempted suicide realize adolescents have not had much experience in testing reality. They often act before thinking of the possible consequences. Adults need to recognize this and talk to them to increase their awareness of the effects of their behavior.

**Preschool children cannot yet comprehend the concept of conservation.**

## F.Y.I.

That young children have difficulty taking another's point of view has implications for parents who want their children to be kind to others and share. That children confuse time and space may help explain dawdling around suppertime and bedtime. Preschoolers understand suppertime as the time when you are sitting at the table eating, and bedtime as when you are being tucked into bed. So, commands to stop playing because it's "suppertime" or "bedtime" are usually vigorously protested (Elkind, 1981).

## NATURE OF KNOWLEDGE

Jean Piaget has been the most influential scientist in establishin groundwork for many of the current beliefs about cognitive developmen He revolutionized ideas about how children think. Piaget has writte numerous books, and his ideas have stimulated countless research exper ments on infants, children, and adolescents.

Piaget attributed knowledge to mental actions on object: Knowledge is not the result of biologically inherited equipment alone or c experiences but rather of how the biological equipment acts on experience and organizes them to solve problems.

Piaget wanted to understand how knowledge developed from chilc hood to adulthood. He became curious about children's thinking while giv ing intelligence tests to children of various ages. He had been working a the Binet Institute in Paris after being involved in experimental psycholog and psychoanalysis. Before studying psychology, he did research an received a doctorate in biology. The combination of the two disciplines wa perhaps responsible for his desire to discover the nature of knowledge; h described himself as having been "haunted by the idea of discovering a so of embryology of intelligence" (Leo, 1980, p. 55).

While trying to develop standardized test questions to measure inte ligence, Piaget became intrigued with the wrong answers children gave t the questions. Not only did the answers reflect a unique sort of logic, bu the reasoning appeared consistent among children of various ages. To prob more deeply into the children's thinking, Piaget used the *clinical method*, technique of observing behavior, asking questions about the behavior, an then individualizing questions according to the responses. For example, t determine a child's conception of number, the child was given some flower and some coins. The child is asked to tell how many flowers she could bu if each flower cost a coin.

> Gui (four years, four months) put 5 flowers opposite 6 pennies, then made a one-for-one exchange of 6 pennies for 6 flowers (taking the extra flower from the reserve supply). The pennies were in a row and the flowers bunched together. "What have we done?—We've exchanged them.—Then is there the same number of flowers and pennies?—No.—Are there more on one side?—Yes.—Where?—There (pennies)." (The exchange was again made, but this time the pennies were put in a pile and the flowers in a row.) "Is there the same number of flowers and pennies?—No.—Where are there more?—Here (flowers).—And here (pennies)?—Less" (Piaget, 1952, p. 57).

Thus, the child reasoned that the row always had more than the pil because the row was spread out and, therefore, appeared to have more tha the pile.

While the clinical method reveals reasoning underlying responses t standard questions, it makes replication difficult.

## FUNCTIONS OF KNOWLEDGE

Having been trained as a biologist, Piaget viewed the acquisition c knowledge, or cognition, as a form of biological adaptation (Piaget, 1952 **Adaptation** refers to any genetically controlled characteristic that aids a organism to survive and reproduce in the environment it inhabits.

## Adaptation and Organization

Piaget believed that minds are biologically programmed to organize sensory input in ways that will improve interaction with the environment. Through biological evolution, the brain has developed mechanisms or structures to enable us to know (Forman & Kuschner, 1983). By acting on the environment (manipulating things, solving problems, having conversations), these structures are used to construct knowledge.

Adaptation may involve immediate changes or a long-term process of selection. According to evolutionary theory, certain physical structures in the human body have survived because they gradually became organized via genetics to adapt to the environment. For example, the organization of the bones and muscles of the back and legs enable us to stand upright, making us more mobile than if we had to use our arms to help us walk. According to Piaget, as physical structures are organized for adaptation, so are mental structures (Piaget, 1970). Piaget viewed intelligence as a biological adaptation to one's environment.

**Organization** refers to the tendency of behaviors or thoughts to work together as a cluster. As an individual matures, behaviors and thoughts become more organized, which permit greater adaptation to the environment. For example, in learning how to catch a ball, children must put their hands out, watch the ball, and as it approaches, grab it. Practice fosters coordination of eyes and hands, or organization of thoughts and movement.

## Assimilation, Accommodation and Equilibration

Adaptation consists of two complementary processes: *assimilation* and *accommodation* (figure 8.2). **Assimilation** is the process by which new information is incorporated into, or added to, existing structures. For example, if a child has had stories read to him about bunny rabbits and then sees one in the pet store, the child might say, "See the bunny." Thus, the child has assimilated a real rabbit into his mental structure of a picture of a rabbit. Similarly, if the child is taken to the zoo and recognizes a turtle, the child has exhibited assimilation (figure 8.3). Assimilation of the environment is part of adaptation because it is a means for increasing understanding.

To learn how to hit a baseball, the girl must organize her abilities to be able to hold the bat properly, learn how to look at the incoming ball, and learn how to swing the bat to make contact with the ball. She must do all this while blowing a bubble!

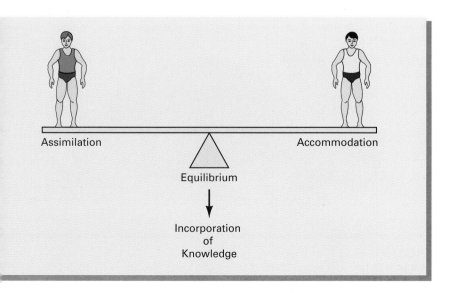

Assimilation

Accommodation

Equilibrium

Incorporation
of
Knowledge

FIGURE 8.2
ASSIMILATION,
ACCOMMODATION,
AND EQUILIBRIUM

FIGURE 8.3
(a) This a rabbit.
(b) This is a turtle.

(a)

(b)

Infants may be able to assimilate an object only through the senses of touch, taste, sight, and sound.

Older children assimilate not only via the senses but also via mental structures such as language or the ability to classify. This child can name the parts of Mr. Potato's head without actually seeing it assembled.

However, what happens if the child encounters a creature he had never seen before, as in figure 8.4?

The child now has to modify some old ways of thinking. In this case the child cannot fit the new creature into the mental categories of bunny or turtle, so he has to make up a new category ("tunny"). In so doing, the child has accommodated. **Accommodation** is the process by which mental structures are changed to incorporate new information that does not fit old structures. Accommodation is part of adaptation because it is a means to deal with unknown parts of the environment one might encounter. Accommodation is the complement of assimilation.

**FIGURE 8.4**
What is this?

Have you tried and failed to understand *new* material presented in a lecture? Piaget would say you were in a state of **disequilibrium**, or imbalance due to cognitive conflict; you could not interpret the information encountered nor could you restructure your usual way of interpreting. What do you do? Perhaps you ask a friend to help you study. Somehow, your friend succeeds in explaining the information in such a way that you now understand it. Piaget would say you were in a state of equilibrium. **Equilibrium** is the state of balance achieved through active reactions to cognitive conflict and results in the integration of new information (Piaget, 1970). Achieving balance, or equilibrium, between assimilation and accommodation fosters adaptation to the environment.

In cognitive development, the mental structures are altered and reorganized as a consequence of experience. Thus, the individual adjusts to new environmental demands thereby allowing for the understanding of more information while also becoming equipped with a more comprehensive pattern of thinking (Phillips, 1975). As an infant has experiences with more objects other than the rattle, the infant comes to know the properties that distinguish these objects from one another—a rattle rattles and a bell jingles; you shake a rattle to make it sound, whereas you strike the bell to make it sound. Thus, the infant accommodates her actions to produce different effects with different objects and, in so doing, has elaborated her supply of thinking behavior patterns.

Assimilation and accommodation occur simultaneously. The individual actively selects and interprets information, thus constructs knowledge (Flavell, 1985; Flavell, Miller & Miller, 1993). What you already know affects what new knowledge is incorporated and how it is incorporated. The new knowledge you incorporated changes what you already know and now also affects the incorporation of future knowledge.

Piaget proposed periodic reorganizations (*organization* refers to the tendency of thoughts to work together and results in greater adaptation) of a child's mental structures, each one resulting in a different more advanced form of thought. These structures are a synthesis of prior learning and genetically determined responses that provide the foundation for future development and that cause new forms of behavior.

## STRUCTURES OF KNOWLEDGE

Examining the structure of cognitive development enables us to explain how children organize knowledge out of their actions (first physical then mental) with the environment. Two basic structures are *schemes* and *operations*.

## Schemes and Operations

A **scheme** (sometimes called schema) is an organized pattern of behavior applied in various environmental situations. For example, sucking is a scheme. It is an organized pattern of behavior in that the lips purse and suction is created by the tongue and cheeks. It is also applied in situations other than for nourishment (pacifiers, thumbs, and other objects are sucked). Schemes can be combined. When learning how to serve in tennis, throwing the ball in the air is a scheme, looking at it is another scheme, and bringing the racket back is still another scheme. Combining all those schemes into a successful serve is an example of organization. Knowledge is built up via schemes.

These children know certain objects float in water and others sink. The girl, armed with this knowledge, is determining if the tennis ball is floating or sinking.

This infant is in Piaget's sensorimotor stage.

Mental activities such as naming pictures in a book can be representative of Piaget's second stage—preoperational.

An **operation** is a mental manipulation of things one has previously experienced physically. For example, adding numbers is an operation. One can do it mentally after having had experiences adding real objects. Operations are representational acts that have been organized into a functioning whole and are related to other such systems (addition is related to subtraction and multiplication). As such, they can be combined to make new operations ($4 + 4 + 4 = 4 \times 3$), to cancel other operations ($4 + 4 = 8$; $8 - 8 = 0$), or to undo other operations ($4 + 1 = 5$; $5 - 1 = 4$ and $5 - 4 = 1$). Thus, operations are mentally done, independent of physical objects or actions, and they can be reversed.

## STAGES OF KNOWLEDGE

Piaget described the qualitatively different cognitive skills children possess as they develop. He delineated four stages of cognitive development. According to Piaget, at each stage children can be observed to show a typical set of behaviors that reflect their cognitive structures and organization, or what they know and understand (figure 8.5).

These structures are a synthesis of genetically determined responses and prior learnings, which provide the foundation for future acquisition of knowledge. Each stage is the basis for the next one. The first stage (birth until 18 months to two years), **sensorimotor**, is preconceptual and behavior is physical (touching, tasting, kicking); sensing and motor activity predominate. This stage is a basis for the next because to conceptualize (a characteristic of the next stage), or to think of things mentally, one has to have had real experiences acting on things. (To conceptualize "all gone" the child would have had to have experienced drinking all the milk out of a glass.)

The sensorimotor stage ends when mental actions, or cognitive schemes, begin to replace physical actions as a way of solving problems. The second stage (18 months to two years until age seven), **preoperational**, is distinguished by the development of symbolic functions, or cognitive schemes, even though they are relatively unorganized. Symbolic functioning is the ability to make one element (or object) represent a different element that is not present.

When these cognitive schemes become more organized and operate logically, the child is said to be in the stage of **concrete operations**. This third stage (age seven until age 11 to 15) is characterized by the development of mental structures or operations, which permit children to transform a mental action or thought. For example, the child now understands that to solve $2 + x = 7$, number 2 must be subtracted from 7. However, these operations can be performed only on concrete, or real, objects (such as numbers).

When the child can perform operations on abstract and hypothetical problems, the child is said to be in the stage of **formal operations**. This fourth stage (age 11 to 15 and older) is characterized by the ability to construct contrary-to-fact hypotheses ("If I were on the moon right now,..." and reason about them. The child now has the ability to deal with the world in terms of the possible rather than just the actual. She can understand the abstract concept of government as being a system of rules, whereas a concrete-operational thinker would understand government in concrete terms of the person who leads the country.

(a)

(b)

(c)

(d)

FIGURE 8.5
SETS OF BEHAVIOR
REFLECTING VARIOUS
AGE GROUPS

**Piaget's four stages of cognitive development: (a) sensorimotor; (b) preoperational; (c) concrete operational; and (d) formal operational.**

# BIOLOGICAL, CONTEXTUAL, AND INTERACTIONAL INFLUENCES ON THE DEVELOPMENT OF KNOWLEDGE

Before we examine the stages of cognitive development and the various research studies, we will examine some factors influencing a child's progression through the stages.

According to Piaget (1964), cognitive development is influenced by *maturation, physical experience, social interaction,* and *equilibration.* Maturation is a biological influence; physical experience and social interaction are contextual influences; and equilibration results from how the child incorporates the knowledge.

*Maturation* refers to the unfolding of genetically determined functions or structures. Thus, a child's cognitive progression is based on changes in intellectual structure resulting from innate predispositions to adapt to experience and organize it in certain ways.

*Physical experience* refers to the involvement of children in manipulating and thinking about concrete objects and processes. For example, Mexican children who help their parents make pottery develop concepts of *conservation* earlier than Mexican children lacking this experience (Price-Williams et al., 1969). **Conservation** is a Piagetian term referring to the understanding that if nothing is added or subtracted from an object, the

**In social interaction, children learn how to compare and make value judgments between themselves and others, including peers, parents, and siblings.**

object remains the same even though its appearance may change. Transforming clay into pottery, then, helps children understand that altering the shape doesn't affect the amount.

Thus, from physical action a child learns the physical properties of an object. The child also derives certain principles from manipulating the objects, which become internalized.

*Social interaction* refers to talking, playing, or working with others. Through such interaction, a child learns others' viewpoints, customs, and standards.

*Equilibration* refers to the process of assimilating experience into one's existing mental framework and accommodating the structures of her framework in response to the experience. Jennifer took a tennis lesson (assimilation) and learned to make minor adjustments on her serve (accommodation) to be more consistent in placing the ball. When she could get the ball where she aimed, she felt in equilibrium.

> It seems to me that there are two reasons for having to call in this fourth factor (equilibration). The first is that since we already have three other factors, there must be some kind of coordination among them. This coordination is a kind of equilibration. Secondly, in . . . construction . . . a subject goes through much trial and error and many regulations that in a large part involve self-regulation. Self-regulations are the very nature of equilibration (Piaget, 1977, p. 10).

What actually happens is that when the child acts on the environment (physically or socially), she not only uncovers new problems thus initiating disequilibrium but also constructs a solution and attains a higher level of equilibrium. Because the child regulates the balance, or equilibrium, between assimilation and accommodation, the child is said to construct her knowledge. Table 8.1 is a summary of Piaget's key points.

## KEY POINTS FROM COGNITIVE DEVELOPMENTAL THEORY

### TABLE 8.1

1. Children view the world differently from adults.
2. Mental development is influenced by four factors:
   a. maturation
   b. experience
   c. social interaction
   d. equilibrium
3. Children's mental development progresses through a fixed sequence of stages.
4. Although the sequence of stages is the same for all children, different children move from one stage to another at different ages. Furthermore, a child may function in one stage for some concepts while functioning in a different stage for other concepts.
5. Children's mental development imposes limitations on *what* they can learn and *how* they can learn it.
6. Thought emerges from actions not words.
7. Knowledge cannot be given to children. It must be discovered and constructed through the learner's activities.
8. As children act on their environment, they are making sense of their world. This enables them to construct and reconstruct mental structures that enable them to deal with more complex information.

(Charles, 1974)

# HOW IS KNOWLEDGE CONSTRUCTED?

We now look at how children construct their own knowledge. To do so we must thoroughly examine Piaget's cognitive map outlining the four stages of cognitive development as well as some newer research supporting and questioning some aspects of his theory.

## INFANTS AND TODDLERS: SENSORIMOTOR THOUGHT

The first stage of cognitive development (birth to 18 months or two years) is called *sensorimotor* because children use their senses and motor activity to discover the environment. Children's knowledge about objects comes from their physical actions on them. These physical actions become schemes that become the basis for later cognitive, or mental, schemes. Children need to understand and organize their world through actions before they can understand and organize their world through thoughts.

In the sensorimotor stage, the infant cannot differentiate between self and objects or other people. The infant is the physical center of his world.

By careful observation of his three children, Piaget documented six levels of sequential cognitive development during the first two years (Piaget, 1952). Subsequently, the sequence of sensorimotor intelligence has been verified by other researchers (Uzgiris & Hunt, 1975; McColl, Eichorn & Hogarty, 1977).

### Reflex Activity

Piaget noticed the intent with which infants and toddlers explored the environment through touch, taste, sight, sound, and motor activity (kicking, sucking, grasping, reaching). At first, these activities are reflexive; that is, infants who come biologically equipped to use their senses to suck, cry, and blink, use their biological equipment (reflexes) to learn about their respective environments. The infant sucks the mother's breast perhaps also a pacifier or a thumb. The infant grasps a finger, rattle, ring, or crib mobile. Reflexive behaviors such as sucking and grasping are observed during the first month.

### Primary Circular Reactions

Piaget (1952) noticed that infants repeat behaviors. He called the repetitions of single actions *primary circular reactions.* A **primary circular reaction** refers to a response centered on the infant's body that is discovered accidentally and is repeated because it is pleasurable. The infant sucks a pacifier until it falls out of the mouth or until the infant falls asleep. Primary circular reactions are observed from one to four months of age.

### Secondary Circular Reactions

By four to eight months of age, the infant can repeat an action to produce a desired effect, for example grasping the ring on the crib mobile and shaking it to make the bell jingle. Purposeful actions to produce an effect are called **secondary circular reactions**. It is during this time that the infant will look for a partially hidden object. This is significant because it indicates the beginning of the development of **object permanence** (Piaget, 1954), the understanding that objects (or people) exist even though they are not in sight. Coinciding with the onset of object permanence is the disappearance of *sensorimotor egocentrism,* the inability to differentiate self from object or other persons (Elkind, 1981).

Infants are not born with an understanding of how objects exist in space and time; rather such knowledge must be constructed through their experiences. When Jennifer was five months old, leaving her with a babysitter was a difficult experience for Robin. When Jennifer was seven months old and crawling, Robin would put her on the floor with some toys. If Robin left the room, Jennifer would crawl after her. This was Jennifer's method of constructing a concept of object permanence, in this case, person permanence. By her actions and their consequences (following Robin and finding her), Jennifer began to understand that if Robin disappeared from sight, Robin existed in some other place.

## Coordination of Secondary Circular Reactions

Between 8 and 12 months of age, a child can coordinate familiar actions to produce not just the same effect all the time (grasp crib mobile and bell jingles; release grasp and jingling stops) but a new and different effect (grasp and release a plastic toy to make it squeak). The coordination of familiar actions (grasping and releasing) to achieve a new effect (squeaking) is called **coordination of secondary reactions**. During this time a child will search for a hidden object.

## Tertiary Circular Reactions

Between 12 and 18 months of age, the child not only repeats actions to produce interesting results but also varies the actions to vary the results. A common game at this time is "drop and fetch." The child experiments with dropping various things from the crib or high chair, watching them fall, and listening to their sound. The parents are supposed to retrieve whatever drops, and the game begins again. The variation of behavior, or experimentation, to produce different results is called **tertiary circular reactions**. During this time the child will search for a hidden object in more than one place when she sees the sequence of it being hidden (first in the fist, then under a blanket).

## Symbolic Representation

Between 18 and 24 months of age, the child is in transition between the sensorimotor and preoperation stages. A child can think before acting because he has developed the mental concept of representation (Piaget, 1952). Representation allows one to think about properties of objects independently of physical actions on those objects. To remove a chain from inside an almost-closed box, the child cannot succeed by acting (sticking the fingers in the box to pick up the chain) because the opening is too small. The child has to think of another way to get the chain—open the box wider. To think of such a solution, the child has to remember some mental representation of opening something (like the mouth)—the child sticks a finger in the small opening and pulls to make it wider; the child succeeds and removes the chain. The ability to perform internal symbolic actions using one element (or object) such as a word, picture, or action, to stand for another is called **symbolic representation**. During this time the child will search for hidden objects she does not find in an expected place, for example, an object was seen being hidden under a sweater. When not found under the sweater as expected, child lifts a hat that was under the sweater to locate object.

# Piaget's Object Permanence Task Evaluated

To test object permanence, Piaget observed the child's active search for an object. Some developmental psychologists have questioned whether active search is the best response to indicate object permanence because the child might have a mental concept of something before being able to demonstrate it. For example, children might know an object has permanence before they can actively search for it because active search involves eye-hand coordination, a skill they might be lacking. Or children might know an object exists but forget about it because of their limited memory span. Bower (1971) tested this latter hypothesis.

Bower tested infants 20 through 80 days of age. These infants were too young to reach for objects, so Bower used the surprise, or startle reaction, to indicate object permanence. He propped each infant to a sitting position so the infant faced a brightly colored object. As the infant looked at the object, a screen moved in front of it, hiding the object from the infant's view. The screen remained in front of the object from the infant's view from ½ to 15 seconds on different trials. Then the screen was moved away. For half of the trials, the object was visible again. For the other half, the object was not visible again. Bower watched the infants' facial expressions to see if they were surprised at seeing the object or not seeing the object after the screen was moved. He reasoned that if the infants had the concept of object permanence, they would not be surprised to see the object again after the screen was removed and, likewise, would be surprised if it were not there. On the other hand, if the infants did not have the concept of object permanence, they would be surprised to see it there after the screen was moved and would not be surprised if it were gone.

The results of Bower's experiment depended on the age of the infant and the length of time the screen hid the object. All age groups of infants were surprised when the object was gone if the screen had been hiding it for only 1½ seconds. None were surprised on the trials when the object was still present. Thus, Bower concluded a degree of object permanence is present in infants as young as 20 days if the conditions are proper (only 1½ seconds of hiding), but lack of memory prevents the infant from having a fully developed concept of object permanence. The oldest infants, however, expected the object to be present even after the longest interval of hiding.

Piaget disagreed with Bower's interpretation of these results. He said the experiment proved infants can recognize objects early, but the experiment did not confirm that the infant possessed object permanence (Piaget & Inhelder, 1976). Recognition comes from looking at an object repeatedly, whereas object permanence comes from organizing the schemes used on many objects. For Piaget, children must form a distinction between themselves as actors and the objects on which they act to actually conceptualize the permanency of an object (Gratch, 1975).

Many laboratory experiments have been done to test what Piaget observed naturally (Baillargeon, 1986; 1992; Triana & Posnak, 1986). We need to be aware that the particular task selected for the experiment to demonstrate a cognitive skill seems to affect the findings of the experiment, as illustrated above. Yet, despite disagreements regarding the age at which various skills appear, there is consensus as to their order (Wise, Wise & Zimmerman, 1974; Kagan, 1982).

**Recognition of an object comes from looking repeatedly at the object, whereas object permanence is a concept that comes from organizing the schemes used on many objects.**

## PRESCHOOLERS: PREOPERATIONAL THOUGHT

The preoperational stage (2 through 7 years) is distinguished by thinking in terms of images, symbols, and concepts (Piaget & Inhelder, 1976). The preoperational child has the ability to make one object represent a different object that is not present. A toy boat can be used to represent a real boat, or a word can represent an object or a person.

### Deferred Imitation and Symbolic Play

Piaget (1951) tells of his daughter's having watched a playmate throw a temper tantrum, stamp his feet, and howl. The next day, Piaget's daughter stood up in her playpen, stamped her feet, and howled. Her actions suggested she was trying out a new behavior. Based on this, and other observations, Piaget concluded that without a symbolic means of learning and ability to recall, his daughter could not have imitated the temper tantrum a day later. This type of imitation is called deferred, or delayed. **Deferred imitation** is the ability to produce an action after having observed it at an earlier time.

The foundation for deferred imitation is laid in the sensorimotor stage. In the sensorimotor stage, a child initially imitates a model's actions in the model's presence (waving bye-bye after having been shown). Later, simple actions are imitated in the model's absence ("making nice" to the cat). Finally, toward the end of the sensorimotor stage (between 18 and 24 months), the child can imitate a complex act in the absence of a model (dancing to music). This symbolic representation marks the transition from the sensorimotor stage to the preoperational stage. Piaget says that deferred imitation suggests that the child has progressed from representation in action to representation in thought. To imitate an action some time after it has occurred, the child must first represent it then recall the image. Because the child does not copy reality, but rather, according to Piaget, interprets it through internal structures, the resulting imitation is not an exact copy.

Deferred imitation is characteristically exhibited during the preoperational stage as symbolic play. Children treat objects as if they were something else. Symbolic play has no rules or limitations; it is completely the child's creation. He can act out fantasies, incorporate experiences, relive pleasures, resolve conflicts, and so on (Labinowicz, 1980).

### Language as a Symbol

In the preoperational stage, language begins to be used symbolically and to define the environment. Piaget (1967) believes intelligence based on manipulation of objects appears before language. The name of an object is seen as such an integral part of the object to the child that changing the name changes the object. For example:

> Four-year-old Susan was asked where she got her name. She answered "My mommy named me." "What if your mother had called you Jack?" "Then I'd be a boy." To many children, names embody certain other characteristics. If one has a boy's name, then one must have other features making one male. Susan also claimed that if the name of the sun were changed and it were called the moon, "then it would be dark in the daytime." (Ault, 1983, p. 1)

### Transductive Reasoning

Preoperational thought has certain limitations. Some obstacles to logical thought are *centration, egocentrism,* and the inability to deal with transformations.

Water tables allow children to exercise symbolic play. These children use blocks to represent boats, fish, and swimmers.

Logical reasoning can proceed from the particular to the general (**induction**) as in the following:

If A = B in one respect, then A = B in all respects.

If horses and dogs have four legs, then all horses and dogs are in the same class.

Logical reasoning can also proceed from the general to the particular (**deduction**) as in the following:

If A = B and B = C, then A = C.

If animals have four legs and horses and dogs have four legs, then horses and dogs are animals.

The preoperational child uses neither of the above but rather a type of reasoning that proceeds from particular to particular (**transduction**) as in the following:

If A = C and B = C, then A = B.

If a horse is an animal and a dog is an animal, then a horse is a type of dog.

## Centration

During the preoperational stage, children come to know the basic categories into which objects are divided; in other words, they can classify. Children who understand class properties can sort objects by size, shape, and color (figure 8.6).

Most preoperational children can choose one dimension (rather than the three dimensions illustrated in figure 8.6) to group the objects because, as Piaget observed, preoperational children cannot focus their attention on more than one dimension at a time. He called this **centration**, thinking about only one aspect of a problem while neglecting other aspects, which can be accounted for because cognitive behavior is still influenced by perceptual activities—what appears to exist rather than by rational considera-

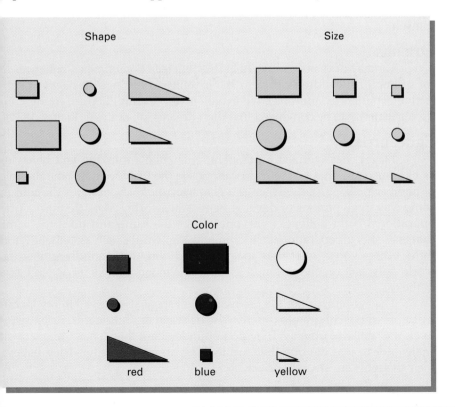

**FIGURE 8.6**
The three distinctively different ways children can group these blocks is an example of Piaget's concept of centration.

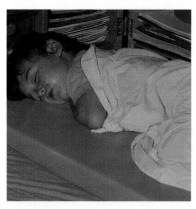

Preschoolers believe bad dreams occur because they have done something bad and that dreams come "from the night," or "from the sky."

F.Y.I.

As experiences with symbols increase and social interaction with peers increases, preoperational egocentrism subsides (Elkind, 1981).

tions (Piaget & Inhelder, 1969). Thus, preoperational thought is largely intuitive because guesses instead of logic are used to solve problems.

## Substages of Preoperations

Research suggests that preoperational knowledge develops in at least two distinct levels, or substages, the first between ages 2 and 4, the second between ages 4 and 7 (Case & Khanna, 1981). The first substage is called *symbolic thought*, or preconceptual and is characterized by a child's ability to use mental symbols for objects not present (a finger becomes a gun or an imaginary playmate is involved in a conversation). The second substage is called *intuitive thought* and is characterized by prelogical reasoning—"knowing" the answer to a question but not knowing why the answer does or does not make sense. ("What is wind?" "Someone blowing in the sky." "How do you know?" "I just do!")

## Fantasy

One characteristic of preoperational thought is the inability to distinguish between perception and reason, that is, between subjective experiences and objective events. This is exemplified in preschooler's inability to distinguish reality from fantasy. Young children believe the tooth fairy and Santa Claus are real people.

## Imaginary Companions

It is not unusual for preschool children to have imaginary companions. Sometimes they are created to meet needs for companionship or to work out feelings that cause guilt or fear. Children give such playmates names, have conversations with them, and play games with them. Adults are expected to react to these imaginary companions as though they were real. A child may blame an imaginary companion for a misdeed or may use the imaginary playmate to help deal with stressful situations such as fear. Imaginary playmates usually disappear when the child feels in control of himself.

## Dreams

Fantasy does not always help dissolve fear. Sometimes it enhances it; for example, in children's dreams the inability to distinguish between subjective experiences and objective events is also exemplified in young children's inability to be convinced that their dreams are not real (Piaget, 1951).

## Egocentrism

Piaget characterized a preoperational child's thinking and behavior as **egocentrism**. That is, the child cannot see the viewpoint or take the role of another person. Egocentrism is a characteristic that pervades thought in some way in all periods of development (Wadsworth, 1984). Because a preoperational child believes everyone thinks the same and does the same things as she, preoperational children make up words such as "elbone" and think others know what they mean. In addition, these children view the world only as it revolves around them. ("The moon follows me when I ride in the car.")

The egocentrism of the preoperational stage also is seen in the inability of preschool children to differentiate between their thoughts, or perspectives, and those of others. (They do not understand that "snail" refers to all snails, not to just the one they are looking at momentarily.) They believe their thoughts are always correct.

Piaget and Inhelder's (1967) classic mountain task experiment (figure 8.7) illustrates egocentrism. A child sits facing a table on which there are three mountains. A doll is placed on another chair, and the child is to show via a series of photos what view of the mountains the doll sees. Children in the preoperational stage always pick the photo that matches their view.

Subsequent experiments (Flavell, Shipstead, & Croft, 1978; Donaldson, 1979) have shown that by varying what is asked of the children (for example, hiding a doll behind a screen so it could not be seen by a seated adult), preoperational children could perform the tasks.

An explanation for the different findings is that the task Piaget and Inhelder chose was too abstract for the preoperational child because it was one they would not have likely experienced; whereas the task of hiding something from somebody's view was one they might have experienced.

Preschoolers cannot see causal links. For example, they may not understand that pumpkin pie comes from pumpkins and other baking ingredients.

## Transformations

A related aspect of egocentrism (in that the child does not see the inconsistencies of his reasoning) and another characteristic of the preoperational child's thinking are his inability to understand transformations, or changes. Water in a container is shown to a child. It is then frozen and then thawed while still in the same container; it is now unrecognizable to the child as the same substance. This inability to follow transformations inhibits logical thought because the child is unaware of the relation between events and things (in this case, freezing and thawing the water).

## Causality

Asking a young child what causes something, for example what causes clouds, produces interesting answers because the child's perceptions at this stage take precedence over external facts. Some explanations of causality are classified as *animism, artificialism,* and *absolute finalism* (Piaget, 1960).

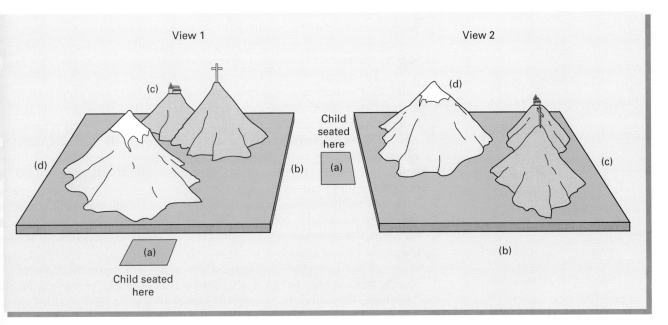

FIGURE 8.7
THE MOUNTAIN TASK EXPERIMENT

In *animism*, the child attributes life to inanimate objects. ("Why do stars shine?" "Because they're happy.")

In *artificialism*, the child believes that objects and events are made and/or caused by people. ("What is thunder?" "Somebody bowling in the sky.")

In *absolute finalism,* the result is seen as the cause. ("Why is there snow?" "For me to play in.")

Some research experiments designed to validate Piaget's observations of causality (Dolgin & Behrend, 1984; Bullock, 1985) conclude that it is children's incomplete understanding of animate and inanimate objects, rather than their general conception of the world, that causes them to make animistic statements.

The limits of preoperational thoughts about causality make it difficult for children to understand (and adults to explain) certain concepts such as illness, death, or divorce. Often, their egocentric thinking causes them to blame themselves. For example, a three-year-old child might think she is sick because she lost her sweater. Wallerstein and Kelly's research (1980) done on children of divorced parents supports the relation between egocentrism and self-blame. (My dad left because I was bad.)

A curriculum for preschoolers, based on Piaget's work and designed to enable children to derive relations between real and represented objects and events, is described in box 8.1.

## Box 8.1 PIAGET APPLIED: THE COGNITIVELY ORIENTED CURRICULUM

The theory of Jean Piaget provides the foundation for the cognitively oriented curriculum. Its purpose is to enable children to produce meaningful mental representations and to derive relations among objects and events, both real and represented (Weikart et al., 1971).

The cognitively oriented curriculum is committed to having the child first experience concepts through motor activity or physical manipulation before becoming involved verbally. For example, rolling a ball provides the basis for understanding what the word *rolling* means.

Piaget's delineation of the representation levels (*index, symbol, sign*), ordered by their degree of complexity and abstractness, is employed by the cognitively oriented curriculum to help the child develop representations.

At the *index* level, the child begins to deal with parts of objects as being representative of the whole. For example, the child can recognize that a telephone ringing represents a telephone even though the telephone cannot be seen.

At the *symbol* level, the child can deal with representations of objects that are distinct from the objects, for example, photographs, drawings, clay models, imaginative play (hopping like a rabbit or making a sound like a car).

At the *sign* level, the child can represent through words by reading and writing. While the child can understand the meaning of the spoken word at previous levels, this level requires an increasingly abstract ability. The cognitively oriented curriculum does not teach reading and writing but does provide the prerequisites.

The main premise underlying the cognitively oriented curriculum is that there are logico-mathematical and spatio-temporal relations. Logico-mathematical relations include classification, or grouping, and seriation, or ordering, of objects according to certain criteria. Spatio-temporal relations include the representation of space and the child's relation to it.

From these elementary relations, the cognitively oriented curriculum has delineated four content areas: *classification, seriation, spatial relations*, and *temporal relations*.

1. *Classification* is approached by having the child relate elements that go together because of their attributes (color, shape, size) or because they are used for the same activity (fork and spoon) or because they get their meaning from one another (hammer and nail).
2. *Seriation* is approached by having the child deal with objects by their relation in size (big or little), quantity (two or three), or quality (rough or smooth).
3. *Spatial relations* are approached through expressions of the orientation of the child's body and the orientation of other objects in space first through motor experiences then through verbal statements. ("Put the box *on* the table, *under* the table, *next* to the table.")
4. *Temporal relations* are approached through expressions of beginning and ending, understandings of what happened first, next, and last, and experiencing that time periods can vary in length. ("We stayed outside today for a *short* time because it began to rain; yesterday, we were outside for a *long* time.")

## RESEARCH IN REVIEW

# HOW DO CHILDREN COME TO UNDERSTAND THE DIFFERENCE BETWEEN REALITY AND APPEARANCE?

Woolley, J.D., & Wellman, H.M. (1990). Young children's understanding of realities, nonrealities, and appearances. *Child Development, 61,* 946–961.

Piaget found that children could not distinguish reality from fiction until they were seven or eight years old. However, recent research has shown that preschool children can differentiate reality from thought (a dog from a mental image) and reality from a misleading appearance (a rock from a sponge that looks like a rock).

In one study, recordings of children (four males and females) in natural settings were taken at ages 1–1 to 1–3 and then at 3–3 to 6–11. Noted were reality versus pretend ("You're not really dead, we're just playing."), reality versus toys ("It's not a real bowling ball."), reality versus pictorial representations ("That's not a real skunk, that's only a picture."), reality versus illusion ("They have a gun that looks real."), and reality versus fiction ("King Kong isn't real.").

The average range in age for the children when they produced their earliest use of real to assert their concept of reality was from 2–6 to 3–4.

In a second study, 23 three-year-olds (11 females and 12 males) were given tasks to test their understanding of appearance versus the real identity of toys ("Is this a real dog or a toy?"), pictures ("Is this a real banana or a picture?"), events *(continued on following page)*

*(continued from previous page)*
("Am I really brushing my teeth or pretending?"), and illusory objects (a sponge that looked like a rock).

It was found that by age three, children appropriately distinguished between reality and appearance with regard to toys, pictures, and pretend actions before they could do so with regard to illusions.

Thus, children seem to develop an understanding of the difference between reality and appearance based on their experiences (toys, pictures, pretend actions). That they have not yet had much experience with illusions (sponges that look like rocks) and that they have to deal with two realities (a sponge and a rock) at the same time might explain why they produce more errors on reality versus deceptive appearance tasks.

## SCHOOLAGERS: CONCRETE OPERATIONAL THOUGHT

The concrete operational stage (7–11 or 15 years) is distinguished by the use of operations in solving problems. Operations are mental representations that are reversible. Preoperational children can represent things mentally but cannot reverse their thinking. For example, a four-year-old preoperational child is shown two equal length rows of eight coins each. While the child is watching, one row is lengthened (figure 8.8).

The child says the two rows are no longer equal. This response is because she cannot mentally reverse the act of lengthening. She cannot maintain the equivalence of number in the face of perceptual change (lengthening the row).

Around the age of seven, according to Piaget (1967), children's thinking becomes logical in that reversibility can be observed. However, the evolution of these logical thought processes (operations) can be applied initially only on problems that exist (are concrete). After children learn from operations rather than just physical objects and actions, they can, for example, understand the sum is independent of the act of counting so they can add numbers mentally without using their fingers.

### Conservation

Piaget suggested that concrete operational children can solve conservation tasks because they can perform operations (Piaget, 1970). Conservation involves understanding that if nothing is added or taken away from an object, that object remains the same although it may undergo a change in appearance. The concrete operational child has no problem with the coin task in figure 8.8. After viewing the lengthening of the row, he says, "The rows are equal because all you did was spread one (row) out so you could put it back." The child, thus, is exhibiting that he is capable of reversing an operation. The ability to do the coin task is called conservation of number. Kamii (1982) says the concept of conservation of number devel-

**F.Y.I.**

Piaget called the move from preoperational thought to operational thought the "5 to 7 Shift" because of the ages at which it usually begins and ends.

**FIGURE 8.8**
**Are there the same number of coins?**

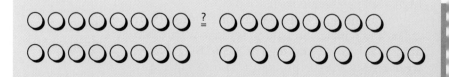

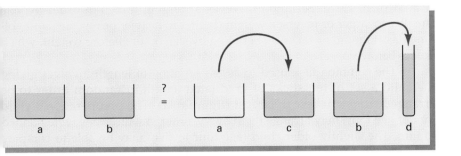

ops gradually through experience—manipulating beads, playing with blocks, finger counting, and so on are the bases for understanding number.

Another classic conservation problem involves conservation of liquid (figure 8.9). The 7- or 8-year-old concrete operational child now understands that if the amount of liquid in containers A and B were equal at the start, then when the contents were poured into C and D, the amount would still be equal. The preoperational child, however, would tell you the contents of C and D are no longer equal because she can focus only on one dimension at a time (in this case, width or height). This is an example of centration.

Piaget found that it is only gradually that children acquire the concept of conservation. Generally, 6- to 7-year-olds understand conservation of number—that the number of coins remains the same even when the row is spread out. Children age 7–8 understand that the mass of an object, such as a piece of clay, does not change when the clay is stretched into a snake, but most fail to understand that its weight and volume also remain unchanged (Piaget & Inhelder, 1969). Piaget observed that the various types of conservation are always acquired in the same order: First, the child understands conservation of number, then the conservation of mass, then the conservation of liquid, then the conservation of weight. (Which weighs more, the clay ball or the clay sausage?) Last, at about 10 or 11 years of age to about age 15, the child understands the conservation of volume (will the amount of water displaced by an object change if the shape of the object is changed?) (figure 8.10) (Piaget & Inhelder, 1941).

Other researchers have confirmed Piaget's basic findings about the sequence of this acquisition of types of conservation concepts (Uzgiris, 1964; Brainerd & Brainerd, 1972).

## Seriation

**Seriation,** the ability to arrange items in terms of greater and lesser, is one operation basic to a child's understanding of number concepts

Do you remember when you started counting in your head instead of out loud or on your fingers? What happened was that you internalized your actions and could make decisions based on what was incorporated in your cognitive structures rather than having to depend on verbal/physical manipulation.

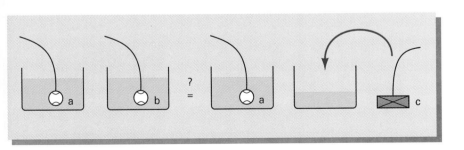

FIGURE 8.10
**Will the amount of water displaced by object C be the same as that displaced by B?**

(Wadsworth, 1978). Seriation involves arranging things in order by size (smaller to larger or reverse), weight (lighter to heavier or reverse), and volume (less to more or reverse). Seriating by size occurs before weight, which occurs before volume.

The common task used to assess seriation of length involves giving the child a set of ten sticks of graduated length in random order to be arranged from smallest to largest (figure 8.11). The preoperational child (under age four) may arrange them by the order in which they were handed to him. The slightly older child (age four to five) may be able to compare sticks in isolated pairs. The five- to seven-year-old child might align the tops of the sticks without regard to the bottom or might successfully order four or five sticks and then lose track of his strategy. The seven- to eight-year-old children successfully order the 10 sticks; however, some children do it on a trial-and-error basis, and others who have the concept of *transitivity* apply the following logic:

If A > B
and B > C
then A > C

Even though some seven- to eight-year-olds understand transitivity, they, as well as even nine- to ten-year-olds, experience difficulty in solving seriation problems that do not involve physical or concrete materials (Labinowicz, 1980), for example, "If Jane is older than Tanya but younger than Dennis, who is the oldest?"

## Classification

**Classification**, the second skill basic to understanding number concepts, is the act of grouping objects by similarities. Preoperational children can group by one property (color or size or shape) but not more than one property because they cannot hold two aspects of a problem mentally. Seven- to eight-year-old children, however, can place objects in two overlapping classes and justify their choice ("It can go in the red group because it's red, or it can go in the circle group because it's round.")

Concrete operational children understand the logical relation between a class and a subclass, or *class inclusion*.

**FIGURE 8.11**
**How sticks of different lengths are arranged by various age groups**

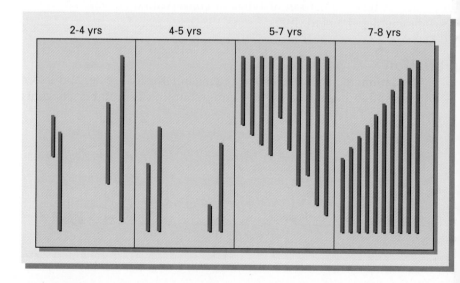

Piaget (1952) devised a task to determine whether a child has the concept of class inclusion. The child is presented with 20 brown wooden beads and two white wooden beads and asked, "Are there more wooden beads or more brown beads?" Children less than seven years of age usually respond that there are more brown beads than wooden beads. Their answer reflects the ability to compare brown and white (class to class), but not brown to wooden (subclass to large class). Thus, these children do not yet understand class inclusion. However, around age eight, children understand that the number of brown or white must be smaller than the number of total beads. Thus, they can reason about the relation between subclasses (brown beads, white beads) and classes (wooden beads).

Several studies document that the reason some children fail the Piagetian class inclusion task ("Are there more brown beads or wooden beads?") is due to the way the problem is worded. If you use one word to describe the whole class (pets) and different words to describe the subclasses (dogs, cats) children are more likely to respond—There are more pets than dogs or cats (Ahr & Youniss, 1970). If you dispense with the use of "more" and "less" and phrase the problem (three M&M's and two jelly beans) practically ("Do you want to eat the M&M's or the candy?"), even preschoolers can understand class inclusions. They demonstrate this by eating the candy (Siegel et al., 1978).

According to Piaget, the significance of the concepts of *conservation*, *seriation, transitivity*, and *class inclusion* is that they are basic to understanding arithmetic (Piaget & Inhelder, 1969). Number concepts involve equality or *conservation* (1 + 1 = 2), *seriation* ( 1, 2, 3, 4, 5 …), *transitivity* (3 > 2, 2 > 1, therefore 3 > 1), and *class inclusion* (four is part of a set that includes 1-9).

## Egocentrism versus Sociocentrism

The preoperational child's thinking was dominated by egocentrism, the inability to understand the views of others, and the lack of a need to validate her own thoughts. Egocentrism in the concrete operational stage involves a failure to differentiate between what one perceives and what one thinks. The child is unaware of the meaning of perceptions and thoughts. With the attainment of formal operations and the ability to reflect on one's own thought, this form of egocentrism diminishes (Wadsworth, 1984). Even though a lack of differentiation exists between perception and thought in the concrete operational child, we see a movement toward **sociocentrism**, an increasing awareness of the views of others and, therefore, an increase in willingness to seek validation of her thoughts.

According to Piaget, the child moves from egocentrism to sociocentrism through his interaction with peers.

**Sociocentrism makes interpersonal relationships easier to form and maintain.**

> What then gives rise to the need for verification? Surely it must be the shock of our thoughts' contact with that of others, which produces doubt and the desire to prove. …The social need to share the thoughts of others and to communicate our own with success is at the root of our need for verification (Piaget, 1928, p. 204).

The movement from egocentrism to sociocentrism makes cooperation possible because children's views can be expressed and compromises reached so they can play together. At about the age of seven or eight, children play games with rules (Phillips, 1981). To play such a game, one must be able to conceptualize the roles of the other players. In baseball, for example, the batter must understand what the pitcher, catcher, and fielders do.

## Assumptive Realities

However, egocentrism is still present in the concrete operational stage. It manifests itself when the child fails to differentiate between perceptions and beliefs. In other words, one's assumptions are treated as facts. Thus, when the child hypothesizes about something and the evidence does not support this belief, rather than change the hypothesis to fit the evidence as an adult would do, the child reinterprets the facts to fit the hypothesis. Abused children often will insist their parents are loving even though their parents have physically harmed them—the bruises providing contradictory evidence to loving behavior. Instead of saying the parent lost her temper the child changes the facts and says, "I was bad; I deserved it" in order to maintain the belief that his parents are loving. Elkind (1981) uses the term **assumptive realities** to describe the assumptions about reality that children make on the basis of limited information and that they will not change even with contradictory evidence.

Many examples exist of a particular kind of assumptive reality where the child generalizes that because he knows *some* things, he must know everything. Elkind (1981) uses the term **cognitive conceit** to describe the assumptive reality believed by many school age children that they are smarter in some cases than some adults. Many television shows ("The Simpsons") and PG movies ("Home Alone") portray children and adolescents outwitting adults.

Piaget's formal operational stage is manifested by the ability to abstract thoughts to resolve scientific problems or to debate philosophical questions.

## ADOLESCENTS: FORMAL OPERATIONAL THOUGHT

The formal operational stage (11–15 years plus) is distinguished by the ability to think beyond concrete reality. The term *formal* refers to the form or structure of statements and ideas other than the reality they represent; in other words, the order or method behind the content rather than the content itself. To the formal operational thinker, concrete reality is only one of the possibilities for thinking (Inhelder & Piaget, 1958). In the concrete operational stage, the child developed several cognitive understandings or structures from interacting with concrete materials; now she can think about thoughts, abstractions in math or metaphor in literature, and abstract concepts such as ethics, love, and justice.

### Logical Reasoning

A *proverb* is a brief common saying that expresses some obvious truth or familiar experience. For example:

*"People in glass houses shouldn't throw stones."*

A concrete operational explanation would be that people who live in a glass house should not throw stones because the glass will break, whereas a formal operational explanation would be that people should not criticize others without first looking at themselves.

What is the truth of the concluding statement of the following ?

Blonde hair turns green on St. Patrick's Day.

Brenda has colored her hair blonde.

It will turn green on St. Patrick's Day.

Many children reply that the last statement is false because blonde hair really does not turn green on St. Patrick's Day. They are thinking concretely. In other words, they are not thinking beyond the real to the hypohetical. Logic, which is characteristic of formal operations, tells us the last statement is true because it is based on the premise of the first statement.

Formal operational thinkers can construct hypotheses contrary to fact like the one above. They also can separate the process of reasoning from the specific content, enabling them to solve many such problems. Even an adolescent's thoughts and beliefs become valid objects of inquiry. He can think about his own thoughts.

Formal operations, like concrete operations, are mental representations that can be reversed. However, formal operations are more advanced because the representations can apply to potential and actual actions, and the various reversibilities can be coordinated to permit more complex thinking. Formal operations can be summarized as having three distinguishing characteristics:

1. ability to generate multiple hypotheses
2. ability to check all possible solutions systematically
3. ability to operate an operation

## Possibility Thinking

Whereas concrete operational thinkers can derive only one solution to a problem that might have several solutions, formal operational thinkers can generate many solutions. For example, thinking of ways to earn money to buy tickets to the prom.

The more possibilities that exist for the formal operational thinker, the more a systematic rather than a trial-and-error approach to testing hypotheses is needed.

## Scientific, or Systematic, Thinking

Piaget studied formal operations, or logical thought, by devising tasks or problems that involved systematic scientific principles. When he asked children of different ages to solve the problems, he noted differences in their thought processes.

An experiment by Inhelder and Piaget (1958) illustrated that formal operational thinkers examined all possible solutions, whereas concrete operational thinkers focused only on what was in front of them. Formal operational thinkers also could analyze the problem, hypothesize a solution, test it, and correct it if it was wrong. The experiment involved showing children five colorless, odorless liquids in test tubes and asking them to discover what combination of the five produced a yellow mixture. Concrete operational children attempt to solve this problem through trial and error, similar to the way they solved the task of seriating sticks. Without an overall plan or system, they soon become lost combining liquids at random; they forget which combinations have been tried and which need to be tried. On the other hand, formal operational children proceed in a more systematic fashion using some logical order. If by chance concrete operational children find a solution that works, they are satisfied they have solved the problem. Formal operational children will, however, continue testing even after one solution is found, isolating the factors relevant to the problem and discarding the irrelevant.

Formal operational thinkers apply the same rules to hypothetical problems as they would apply to concrete or real problems. They have developed a systematic approach to problem solving (operating on operations).

## Egocentrism versus Self-Centeredness and Self-Consciousness

Children enter the stage of formal operations at adolescence. Since this is the final stage of cognitive development and its characteristics enable the adolescent to reason logically about a wide range of logical problems as well as adults do, then why does the adolescent "think differently" from the adult (Wadsworth, 1984)?

Each new cognitive functioning brings a form of egocentrism. When Robin asks 16-year-old Jennifer, "Who was at the party?" and Jennifer responds, "You know—everyone," Jennifer is exhibiting a form of egocentrism in that she assumes Robin knows her thoughts. Formal operational egocentrism is concerned with the conquest of thought (Elkind, 1981).

A young adolescent in the formal operational stage is adept at distinguishing facts from assumptions. His egocentrism is characterized by new-found powers of logical thought. "In adolescent thought, the criterion for making judgments becomes what is logical to the adolescent, as if what is logical in the eyes of the adolescent is *always* right, and what is illogical *always* wrong (Wadsworth, 1984, p. 164). The egocentrism of adolescence is the inability to differentiate between his world and the "real" world, thus the adolescent is self-centered.

Adolescents see themselves as unique from adults. Their view can be termed **generational chauvinism** because they see their generation as being superior to others. As a result, adolescents are idealistic. They often become involved in naive and simplistic ways to mend the world's problems.

Formal operational thought not only enables the adolescent to conceptualize thoughts, it also permits her to conceptualize thoughts of other people. This results in what Elkind (1981) called the **imaginary audience**, the belief that one is "on stage," and that others are as concerned about the adolescent's thoughts and actions as she.

While the adolescent is self-conscious, or self-critical, due to the imagined audience, she is self-admiring, too. How long did it take you to get ready to go out with your friends when you were in high school? Jennifer allowed an hour and a half, most of which was time in front of a mirror. Gatherings of young adolescents often serve the purpose of "being seen."

While the adolescent fails to differentiate concerns about self from those of others, he exaggerates the importance of his feelings, according to Elkind (1981, p. 93), "perhaps because he believes he is of importance to so many people, the imaginary audience, he comes to regard himself, and particularly his feelings, as something special and unique." Robin was continually confronted by Jennifer with, "You don't understand. You don't know what it feels like!" These feelings of uniqueness are called the **personal fable**, the belief that one is unique or special and not subject to the system or rules by which society is governed or liable for the consequences of not following the rules (Elkind, 1981). The personal fable is one explanation of why adolescents take chances (drink and drive, or have sex without contraception) despite being educated about the consequences of certain behaviors. "It won't happen to me" is a recurring theme of the personal fable.

# Reality Testing

With formal operations the adolescent can conceptualize thought and discover the arbitrary nature of his beliefs or hypotheses. He also discovers rules for testing hypotheses against facts and, as a result, can now deal with facts and hypotheses in an experimental fashion. This leads to the recognition that many of the hypotheses are wrong and gives the adolescent a new respect for data and diminished confidence in his own ability. Through junior high school and the beginning of high school, Jennifer and her friends would borrow each other's clothes. Robin discouraged this behavior and tried to reason with Jennifer—"Your clothes will get lost," or "when you want to wear something, you won't have it." Robin tried to give Jennifer consequences—"If you don't get your clothes back, I'm not buying you any new ones"; nothing worked. Finally, at age 16, Jennifer's belief about her friends' integrity in returning clothes diminished in the face of reality—too many things were missing from her closet and Mom was not willing to replace them.

Thus, as the egocentrism of sensorimotor, preoperational, and concrete operational stages gradually diminishes, so too does the egocentrism of adolescence. It subsides when the adolescent tests his logical thoughts against reality. He discovers through social interaction and real experience that he is not on stage, is not particularly unique, and will not change the world. Therefore, when adolescents attempt to implement their beliefs and dreams in the real world, the world provides disequilibrium and provokes adjustments. "The striving to become an effective member of society is part of the motivation that activates further development" (Wadsworth, 1984, p. 168).

## Is Adolescent Thinking the Limit of Formal Operations?

Adolescent thinking is limited by egocentrism, self-centeredness, and self-consciousness. Some researchers believe that cognitive development continues beyond adolescence into early adulthood (Case, 1980; Biggs & Collis, 1982; Kuhn, 1989) and that individuals do not reach their capacity for formal operational thought until about age 25 (Fischer, Hand & Russell, 1983). Perhaps this is because young adolescents can only deal with single abstractions; they generally cannot relate one abstraction to another. For example, they can understand such concepts as society, justice, or law, but they have difficulty understanding the relationship between these concepts to form a political philosophy (Fischer & Lazerson, 1984).

Formal education has been found to influence the execution of formal thought (Greenfield & Bruner, 1966; Piaget, 1972; Cole, 1978) because it encourages the use of symbolic reasoning.

Formal operational thinking has been found to be enhanced by relating the task or situation to something familiar (Overton et al., 1987). A good teaching strategy is to use analogies from students' experiences to explain abstract concepts.

Formal operational thought often is only exhibited in certain situations (Surber & Geesh, 1984; Byrnes, 1988). Adolescents may be capable of doing algebra or physics, but may not be able to make a rational decision regarding what college to attend.

Methods for measuring formal operational thought, because abstract reasoning is involved, are not as distinct as the tasks devised for concrete operational thought.

## F.Y.I.

Individuals from undeveloped countries who are unlikely to be exposed to many problem-solving situations generally do not exhibit the level of cognitive development that individuals from urbanized societies do (Dasen, 1972; Gellatly, 1987).

# PIAGET CHALLENGED

Jean Piaget's theory of cognitive development remains the only comprehensive and integrative theory to date. It has profoundly impacted contemporary developmental psychology. Since the translation of Piaget's work, much research has been done to either confirm or refute his description of the various stages of development and their accompanying concepts.

The major criticisms of Piaget's theory involve the ages at which children display the cognitive abilities he described, the assumptions behind the tasks he devised for testing cognitive competencies, and whether knowledge develops in stages.

It has been found that many children possess certain cognitive abilities earlier than Piaget described. For example, Piaget suggested that preschool children cannot solve problems involving relative dimensions such as *smaller* or *larger*. However, 2-year-olds can think in terms of relations when it refers to something familiar to them. In one study children between 18 and 23 months of age were shown a small and a large piece of wood. They were asked which one was the infant and which one was the daddy; over half answered correctly. They even answered correctly when shown two different pieces of wood that were larger than the original ones but in the same proportions (Kagan, 1984). The language or terms used in many of Piaget's tasks can have influenced the age at which the cognitive competency was displayed.

Some developmental psychologists claim that children can have the cognitive *structure* and lack the cognitive *strategies*, such as the ability to concentrate on all relevant information and the ability to remember it all at once to solve the task (Gelman & Baillargeon, 1983). For example, Rochel Gelman (1977) demonstrated that children as young as two and three years of age can perform a simple version of a number conservation task. She showed them three checkers. Then, unseen by the children, a researcher added a fourth, or took one of the three checkers away. When viewed again by the children, they immediately noticed the addition or subtraction of the checker. When the row of checkers was spread out, the children recognized the number remained the same. The children in Gelman's experiment only had to concentrate on and remember one row of three checkers, whereas children in Piaget's experiment had to concentrate on and compare two rows of eight checkers in each. Thus, children may develop cognitive structures before developing the ability to use them in all situations.

Contrary to Piaget's assumptions, children's acquisition of cognitive concepts occurs unevenly (Fisher, 1980; Flavell, Miller & Miller, 1993). In other words, months or years can pass before a 6-year-old child who can seriate or conserve number can solve other Piagetian tasks such as class inclusion or conservation of volume. Thus, the development of cognitive concepts occurs gradually.

Another explanation of why all abilities that characterize a stage do not emerge at the same time is that performance on most developmental tasks, in particular complex tasks such as the Piagetian ones, is influenced by many sources such as the task itself, the situation, and the child's level of intelligence (Ribapierre, Rieben & Lautrey, 1991).

Most developmental psychologists recognize that although Piaget could have underestimated young children's knowledge under certain circumstances and that performance depends on the difficulty or the familiarity of the task and/or the amount of help given (Fisher & Canfield, 1986), cognitive development is qualitatively different between young children preoperational) and older children (concrete operational). More specifical-ly, certain generalizations hold true (Clarke-Stewart & Friedman, 1987): Young children depend on the way things *look* rather than the way they really *are*, whereas older children distinguish between what *seems* to be and what really *is*; young children tend to concentrate on one feature, whereas older children can attend to several features simultaneously; and young children do not understand reversibility, whereas older children do.

While Piaget viewed the child's cognitive development as an *individual* process of constructing knowledge in predictable stages, Vygotsky(1978) viewed cognitive development as a *collaborative* process emerging from social interactions within a cultural framework. Vygotsky believed that the culture in which a child grows up provides the tools for knowledge. These tools can be calculators, or fishing nets; but the most important tool for transmitting cultural knowledge to a child is language. Language is the vehicle of social interaction; language enables adults to instruct children, then children internalize the instructions and, hence, the knowledge.

Piaget judged children's level of cognitive development from their success in solving cognitive problems independently. Vygotsky (1978) believed children's cognitive level also should be judged from their success on problems that they solve under adult guidance or in collaboration with more capable peers. Most children perform at a higher level with adult guidance or peer collaboration than on their own. Vygotsky called the dif-ference between children's levels of independent learning and apprentice-ship learning *the zone of proximal development*. Vygotsky assumed that chil-dren's apprenticeship interactions with adults or peers in their culture helped children move to a higher level of cognitive development.

## CRITICAL THINKING & YOU

N ow that we know how children think at different ages and that children can be trained to develop certain concepts earlier than Piaget originally observed (if the tasks are modified to fit the language and experience of the child), does this mean we can teach any child any knowledge if it is presented so the child can understand? Can we or do we want to hurry the process of cognitive development for some children (those who are disadvantaged, for example), or even for all children?

**ANALYSIS:** Review this chapter and discuss two reasons for the position that cognitive development cannot be accelerated and two reasons for the position that it can.

**SYNTHESIS:** Choose one game to play with a child (for example, peek-a-boo, checkers) for each of Piaget's four cognitive stages. Explain why each game chosen for a particular stage would be developmentally appropriate.

**EVALUATION:** What are some historical/technological events (for example, war, television, computers) that you believe have impacted children's cognitive develop-ment? Why have these events had an impact?

## SUMMARY

- Piaget viewed the acquisition of knowledge as a biological form of adaptation, which involves organizing mental structures.
- When children interact with the environment, they assimilate knowledge and/or accommodate it to fit their mental structures, or they can accommodate the existing mental structures to account for, or assimilate, the new knowledge. When assimilation and accommodation are in balance, a child is in equilibrium and the knowledge is incorporated. When the child is in disequilibrium, however, further accommodation and assimilation have to occur.
- Knowledge is composed of cognitive structures: schemes (organized patterns of behavior that can be generalized to various situations) and operations (reversible mental manipulations on objects or experiences).
- Cognitive structures are the synthesis of genetically determined responses and prior learnings that provide the foundation for future acquisition of knowledge.
- In the sensorimotor stage (0 to 2 years), the infant or toddler acts on physical things in her environment and, therefore, builds schemes. The most significant development concept in this stage is object permanence (the understanding that things exist although they are not in sight). The form of egocentrism in this stage is that the infant cannot differentiate between objects or people and self, or between objects and her sensory perception of them.
- In the preoperational stage (2 to 7 years), the preschooler develops cognitive schemes to represent his environment. The most significant developmental concept in this stage is symbolization (the understanding that objects can be represented by words, picture, and actions). The form of egocentrism in this stage is that the preschooler cannot differentiate between symbols and their referents, nor can he differentiate between his perspective and that of others.
- In the concrete operational stage (7 to 11 years), the school-age child can perform operations on real, or concrete, things. These operations are a form of logic because they can be reversed, changed, or negated. The most significant developmental concept in this stage is conservation (the understanding that things remain the same although they can change in appearance). The form of egocentrism in this stage is that the school-age child cannot differentiate between perceptions and thoughts, or between assumptions and facts.
- In the formal operational stage (11 to 15 years and on), the adolescent can perform operations on abstract and real objects. He thinks logically in that hypotheses can be formed, tested, and evaluated. The most significant developmental concept in this stage is logical reasoning. The form of egocentrism in this stage is that the adolescent has trouble differentiating between his thoughts and actuality of the world.
- The major criticisms of Piaget's theory involve the ages at which children display the cognitive abilities Piaget described, the assumptions behind the tasks he devised for testing cognitive competencies, and whether knowledge develops in stages.

## RELATED READINGS

Cole, M., & Scribner, S. (1974). *Culture and thought*. New York: John Wiley.

Elkind, D. (1981). *Children and adolescents*. New York: Oxford University Press.

Flavell, J.H., Miller, P.H., & Miller, S.A. (1993). *Cognitive development* (3rd ed.). Englewood Cliffs, NJ: Prentice-Hall.

Labinowicz, E. (1980). *The Piaget primer: Thinking, learning, teaching*. Reading, MA: Addison-Wesley.

Piaget, J., & Inhelder, B. (1969). *The psychology of the child*. New York: Basic Books.

Rogoff, B. (1990). *Apprenticeship in thinking*. New York: Oxford University Press.

Saunders, R., & Bingham-Newman, A.M. (1984). *Piagtian perspective for preschools: A thinking book for teachers*. Englewood Cliffs, NJ: Prentice-Hall.

Wood, D. (1988). *How children think and learn*. New York: Basil Blackwell.

To better understand how different-aged children think, compare the reasoning of a preschooler (age 3–5), a school-age child (age 8–10), and an adolescent (age 15–17) on the following questions:

1. What makes the stars shine?
2. What makes it get dark?
3. What makes a car go?
4. What makes a clock tick?
5. What causes dreams?
6. What causes clouds?
7. Why do leaves fall off trees in autumn?
8. What does "birthday" mean?
9. What makes an airplane fly?
10. What causes thunder?

What relations did you find to Piaget's observations?

● ● ● ● ● ● ● ● ● ● ● ● ● ● ● ● ● ● ● ● ● ● ● ● ● ● ● ● ● ● ● ● ● ● ● ● ● ● ● ● ● ● ● ● ●

# 9 Cognitive Strategies: How We Use What We Know

*The whole of science is nothing more than a refinement of everyday thinking.*

**Albert Einstein**

## OUTLINE

# ABOUT USING KNOWLEDGE

Kenny was in the first grade and learning numbers. Some children were doing addition and subtraction, but Kenny was having trouble with numbers greater than ten. Each day Miss Torres gave out ditto sheets with fruits or animals representing a number to color. Kenny liked to color, but when he saw the number in a book or on the blackboard, he could not remember what it was.

One day Kenny brought some baseball cards to school. While the class was working on ditto sheets, Kenny was playing with his cards inside his desk. Miss Torres came over and asked why he was not doing the ditto. Kenny said, "I hate doing math; I never can remember those stupid numbers anyway."

Miss Torres said, "I think you'd better stay inside during recess."

Kenny sulked the rest of the morning. When recess time came, he had already made up his mind that he was never coming back to school.

When all the children had left the room, Miss Torres asked Kenny to show her his baseball cards. He was scared; he thought she was going to take them away. She said, "Did you ever play 'flipsies'? I used to play this with my brothers when we were little." She showed him how to flip the cards. "Now, let's start with 10 cards each; you count them and give them out. We'll each take a turn. You go first. Your card landed face up. Now I go. If my card lands face up also, I get both cards and then I flip. If my card lands words up, we leave the cards down and you go again. We keep doing this until we get a match. Whoever flips the matching card, then gets the pile."

Kenny and Miss Torres played until the first recess bell rang. She said, "That was fun; now let's each count our cards. I have 8."

Kenny said, "I have 12."

"Then you win. But before I give you my cards, I'm going to add another rule to this game. You need to tell me how many more cards you have than I do."

Kenny looked at Miss Torres's pile and then at his own. "Four," he said proudly.

"Good," said Miss Torres. "Let's write that down." She went to the blackboard and wrote $12 - 8 = 4$. "See you can work with numbers bigger than ten!"

After that day, Miss Torres played "flipsies" with Kenny several more times before involving other children in the game.

By the end of first grade, Kenny had a good understanding of numbers. His favorite job was to be scorekeeper when his class was involved in a competition sport, whether it was kickball or a spelling contest.

In this chapter we will explain how we use what we know—the strategies devised for processing information including paying attention to a stimulus, remembering it, and using it to solve a problem. How we process information can be related to how we perform on intelligence tests and how creative we are. First, we discuss using knowledge (processing information). Then we examine measuring knowledge (intelligence testing). Finally, we look at cognitive styles (impulsive-reflective, field independent/field dependent, creativity).

We all have different ways, or strategies, of using our knowledge. To illustrate, solve these analogy problems (Sternberg, 1979):

| _spouse:_ | _husband:_ | _sibling:_ | _____ |
|-----------|------------|------------|------------|
| _a. father_ | _b. uncle_ | _c. brother_ | _d. son_ |

| _water:_ | _ice:_ | _rain:_ | _____ |
|----------|--------|---------|------------|
| _a. cyclone_ | _b. snow_ | _c. hail_ | _d. dry ice_ |

When you solved these problems, you were identifying each term and retrieving it from memory (a male spouse is a husband). This process of putting information into a form in which it can be stored is called **encoding**. You also inferred possible relations between the first and the second terms of the analogy (water turns to ice when it is frozen). You then related the first term in the first half of the analogy to the first term in the second half (the third term). This process of representing the relative position of things is called **mapping** (spouse and siblings are relatives; water and rain are the same form of water). Then you _applied_ the relation between the first and second terms to the third term as well as to each answer. (A male spouse is a husband; therefore, a male sibling is a brother. Frozen water is ice; therefore, frozen rain is hail.) Then you _justified_ your answer by checking to make sure it was better than the other choices. Finally, you _responded_ with the justified answer.

If we compiled and analyzed all ways of solving the above problems, we would find individual differences in the speed with which each of us performed each of these steps, in the strategies each of us used to solve the problems, and in the contents of our memories. One way of examining how people use what they know (their intelligence) is to assess how they solve problems such as analogies. Intelligence tests do this. Young children who cannot read can be given analogies of forms (figure 9.1).

There is a developmental change with age in the strategies used to solve such problems. Young children encode few characteristics during the first step and may guess at the answer, whereas older children encode more and often solve the analogy by association. (For instance, in figure 9.1 they select by shape and size.) Adolescents can use logical reasoning (in figure

## FIGURE 9.1

Figure analogies used as intelligence tests for children

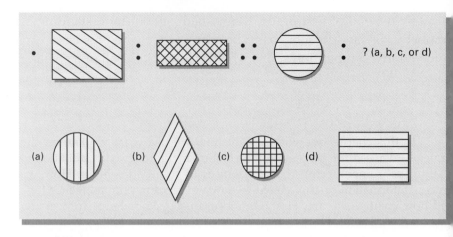

9.1 they look at the direction of the lines in relation to the different-sized shapes) thereby employing their skill of inferring relations to solve the analogy (Sternberg & Nigro, 1980).

## INFORMATION PROCESSING

**Information processing** refers to how information is taken in, remembered or forgotten, and used. Figure 9.2 is a model of what goes on inside our brains when we use what we know to either take in new information, reorganize old information, or solve problems using new and old information.

## FIGURE 9.2

A model of how the brain takes in new information, manipulates old information, and utilizes such information to solve problems.

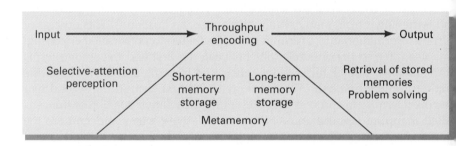

The senses are equipped to respond to stimuli in the environment. However, it is not possible for us to pay attention to everything that is going on about us; thus we only consciously attend to *some* of the available stimuli (**selective attention**). Selective attention depends on factors such as novelty of stimulus, familiarity of stimulus, strength of stimulus, number of stimuli occurring at the same time, etc. The stimuli to which we selectively attend enable us to then interpret information from the environment (*perception*). We code in our memories (*encoding*) those stimuli which we attend to and perceive. Information that we do not need to keep goes into **short-term memory** storage (such as a telephone number that must be looked up and remembered only long enough to dial); information that we want to keep goes into our **long-term memory** storage (such as how to drive a car). Most people have developed strategies for remembering things and, in the process, a knowledge for how we best remember. The knowledge of one's own memory processes is termed **metamemory**. When we have to solve a roblem, the necessary information from memory is retrieved and it is used o suit our immediate purposes.

While Piaget was concerned with the *quality* of changes in the development of knowledge, information processing theories deal more with the *uantitative* nature of developmental change—how perceptions become nore efficient and distinctive, how attention becomes more discriminating, ow strategies become more utilized and elaborate for storing and retrieving memories, how problems are solved by systematically generating and esting more hypotheses.

The information-processing approach draws on experimental evidence accumulated by many investigators working on various topics such s attention, memory, and problem solving. Attention is studied in experiments comparing a subject's reaction to a new stimulus versus one he  has ecome habituated to. Memory is studied in *recall* and *recognition* tasks. **Recall** refers to the ability to produce information from memory, whereas **ecognition** refers to the ability to identify information one has already een exposed to. Problem solving is exhibited in certain tasks on intelligence ests.

Recall is the ability to remember that one has read a specific book, whereas recognition is the ability to remember what the book was about.

## Developmental Changes in Information Processing

**Habituation and Dishabituation.** To determine the developmental hange in how children use what they know, we must begin with how they epresent what they know. With infants this is most often done by presenting a stimulus such as a picture (black straight lines on a white background) nd determining whether they are paying attention to it. Their attentiveness an be determined by measuring physiological changes (heart and breathing rate before and after stimulus presentation) or behavior changes (sucking rate on a pacifier before and after stimulus presentation) or by noting he reflection of the object in their pupils.

When an infant's attentiveness decreases (as noted by physiological hanges, behavior changes, or pupil movement), the infant is said to have xhibited habituation (become used to or bored with) the stimulus. When a ifferent stimulus is presented (black circles on a white background) and he infant's attention is renewed, dishabituation is said to have taken place.

We can then infer that the infant "realizes" a new stimulus has been resented because she has a way of representing the first stimulus in the rain, and then when presented with the second stimulus, the infant compares it to the representation and recognizes it is different, so she exhibits ttentiveness rather than habituation.

As children develop, they habituate more rapidly and dishabituate nore slowly to stimuli they recognize as familiar (Bornstein & Sigman, 986). For example, infants less than four months of age require many exposures to a stimulus before they habituate; yet after a rest they soon habituate—begin responding to the stimulus again. On the other hand, infants our to 12 months old, habituate only after a few exposures to the stimulus nd are not as likely to dishabituate even after several weeks (Fagan, 1984).

There are individual differences in the rate at which infants habituate nd dishabituate (Bornstein & Sigman, 1986). Some quickly recognize what hey have experienced and are slow to forget sensory inputs; others require epeated exposures to remember and do not retain what they have learned or very long.

Habituation is said to occur when children lose attentiveness due to boredom. The girl on the right has obviously lost her interest in participating in the same activity as the two boys.

**Selective Attention.** *Selective attention* refers to actively choosing stimuli to pay attention to while ignoring other stimuli that are present. For example, as you are reading this text some factors will immediately capture your interest (perhaps because they are new; perhaps because they are familiar; perhaps because they are boldface). Other factors will have to be reread because you were not attending the first time. Selective attention is related to habituation and dishabituation because when a new stimulus is perceived, it is more likely to attract attention than what is recognized as an old stimulus.

Although children of all ages exhibit some selective attention, the capability becomes refined with increased age. This enables the older child to eliminate certain attractive distractions (like a conversation nearby) better than the younger child. A study illustrating this was done by Higgins and Turnure (1984). Preschool, second, and sixth grade children performed either an easy or a difficult visual perception task under three conditions: quiet, continuous soft music, and continuous loud music. The younger children's performance on the tasks was impaired by the music (they often looked away from the task), whereas the older children's performance actually improved when the music was played (perhaps the distraction forced them to be more attentive).

**Memory.** Memory is the result of storing an experience or an aspect of it and then retrieving it after a period. To store something (like meat), you find a place for it (like a freezer) and then you label it (steak, fish) so you can find it when you need it. When you store something in your memory, you encode it and, knowing you'll need that information at another time, you employ certain strategies that help you remember it. Of course, not all information is deliberately encoded. In the memory system is a sensory store; storage only lasts in it for about ¼ of a second (Sperling, 1960). We also have a short-term store. The short-term store holds memories needed only temporarily (some call this "working memory," because it takes work using strategies to encode the information into long-term storage) such as remembering a price long enough to write a check. Finally, the long-term store supposedly contains all our memories (visual and verbal) of childhood, of last year, yesterday, and so on.

Like selective attention, memory is related to habituation and dishabituation because to recognize a stimulus as familiar, one has to store and retrieve it.

Is everything ever experienced recorded in our long-term memory store? We do not know, because what is there may be irretrievable. In other words, there is no way of knowing what memories are recorded in our brains if we cannot bring them forth or remember them. Thus, the way researchers study memory is by recognition and recall tasks, the methods of strategies people use to encode and retrieve memories, and by the knowledge people have of their own memory systems known as metamemory.

In a recall test, a child must search his memory for the missing fact(s) and retrieve all necessary information (for example, pictures that were removed from view). In a recognition test, a child is given both the correct and incorrect information and must select the appropriate fact (for example, the child is initially shown a group of pictures, then later shown several groups of pictures and asked to tell which were in the original group).

**F.Y.I.**

Short-term memory lasts
about one minute.

# TECHNIQUES WE USE TO REMEMBER

We all have deliberate procedures or strategies for trying to encode and retrieve memories. Some common ones are *rehearsal*, *imagery*, and organization, also called *chunking*. Strategies can be taught (as in how to repeat a vocabulary list until it is memorized) or figured out by oneself (as in picturing a physician performing surgery in a tuxedo to remember Piaget's stage of formal operations).

Cole and Scribner (1977) have shown that in different cultures the use of certain strategies to remember is correlated with the extent of formal education. People in nonindustrialized societies do not spontaneously use the memory strategies mentioned here, nor do they seem to benefit from instruction in them. Rather, to remember things in everyday life they use culturally specific clues such as stories, songs, and carved sticks. In cross-cultural research on the use of memory strategies, the repeated finding is that educated subjects remember more information than uneducated subjects (Cole & Scribner, 1977; Paris & Lindaur, 1982). This suggests that formal schooling promotes the development of memory strategies because school provides much practice in deliberate memorization as well as the motivation to do so in the form of tests and grades. Thus, the development of memory strategies is influenced by the context in which one grows up.

## Rehearsal

**Rehearsal** refers to the cognitive strategy of repeating something to remember it. Children under seven years of age do not spontaneously use rehearsal, which is one reason why their memory performance is worse than that of older children (Flavell, Beach & Chinsky, 1966). However, when young children are instructed to rehearse, they can do so, and their recall improves correspondingly (Keeney, Cannizzo & Flavell, 1967; Ornstein, Naus & Stone, 1977; Glover, Ronning & Brunning, 1990). In a laboratory experiment demonstrating performance on memory tasks by 3–7-year-olds, children were found to remember information more easily when it is useful to them. The children were required to remember a list of five words under two conditions. In one condition, they were told to simply learn the list; in the other, they played a game of grocery store and were told they had to remember the items so they could buy them. The children recalled nearly twice as many items in the grocery-store game condition than in the list-learning condition (Istomina, 1975).

## Imagery

Another strategy for remembering is **imagery**, the formation of a pictorial representation of what you are trying to remember. Like rehearsal, imagery is not spontaneously used by young children, but when an experimenter tells them to make pictures in their heads of what is to be remembered, kindergarten and even preschool children can do so, and their memory subsequently improves (Reese, 1977).

## Chunking

Still another memory strategy is **chunking**, the categorizing or organizing information into groups. For example, if a long list of vocabulary words had to be memorized, you could chunk them by their first letters (all the *a* words, *b* words, etc.), or by the grammatical categories to which they belong (nouns, verbs, adjectives). Kindergarten through third grade chil-

Perhaps children younger than formal school age do not rehearse spontaneously because they do not perceive the usefulness of such a strategy. These children may perform dance steps to a song when instructed by their teacher or they may do so spontaneously. They do not repeat the steps for the sake of helping them remember the dance.

Even though there is evidence that this child's memory will improve because of her mother's instruction, there is still a difference between the way young children and adults perform memory tasks.

F.Y.I.

Research on rhesus monkeys by Goldman-Rakic (1987) demonstrated that the number and density of synapses in the cerebral cortex reach a peak then gradually begin to decline at the time the young monkeys are able to perform Piaget's object permanence task.

dren do not spontaneously chunk items either while they examine the stimulus material or later during recall. However, with instructions on chunking ("put the things together that are alike"), even the kindergartners can do so and their memory scores improve considerably (Moely, 1977). However, compared with older children (seventh grade), young children (first grade) are more apt to categorize words by what they have seen goes together (like hat and head) rather than organize by the whole category (hat, jacket, shoes) (Bjorklund & DeMarchena, 1984).

### WHY DO CHILDREN AND ADULTS DIFFER IN MEMORY CAPABILITIES?

Even though evidence shows children's memories improve with instruction, there remains a difference between the way young children and adults perform on memory tasks. To explain developmental change, we look at biological and contextual influences and their interaction.

## Biological Influences on Developmental Changes in Memory

Some biological evidence shows that brain neurons continue to grow for as long as seven years after birth. That growth is seen in the *myeliniza-tion* of axons and branching of dendrites. **Myelinization** is the process by which the fatty substance called myelin forms around parts of the neuron and facilitates transmission of messages. It is correlated with memory (Kesner & Baker, 1980), perhaps because myelinization improves the conduction of messages from one part of the brain to another.

Also, evidence shows that synapses and consequent connections between the neurons increase until age two, then gradually decrease until about age 16, when they level to adult level (Goldman-Rakic et al., 1983). This may mean that as an individual gets older she "prunes down" the connections because of experience. That is, those connections used are maintained, whereas those *not* used disappear while the superfluous neurons die (Goldman-Rakic, 1987; Bloom, Lazerson & Hofstadter, 1988). Perhaps the use of strategies to encode and retrieve information is a selective pruning process whereby the person becomes more efficient at using her knowledge.

## Contextual Influences on Developmental Changes in Memory

Researchers have concluded that involuntary memory develops before voluntary memory (Smirnov & Zinchenko, 1969). They observed the natural physical activities of infants and preschoolers in the contexts of home and school. These natural activities induced them to perform cognitive activities such as labeling and classifying, which provided a framework for cognitive strategies to emerge later. For example, when young children play, they label and classify things based on their limited experience. When labeling and classifying are practiced during play, these strategies involuntarily or unconsciously become part of a child's cognitive repertoire to be deliberately, or consciously, used later (Meacham, 1977). Memory becomes a byproduct of the child's natural activities (Paris & Lindaur, 1982); experience results in knowledge storage.

**Socialization** by adults, the process by which the child is taught the ways of society, contributes to the child's development of deliberate memory from involuntary memory (Vendovitskaya, 1971). The adult says, "That's a kitty." "See the kitty." "Look, there's a kitty," and so on until one day the child points and says, "kitty."

Even if involuntary memory is accepted as a precursor to voluntary memory, empirically it is difficult to distinguish which memories possessed were encoded involuntarily and which ones were voluntarily encoded. However, most researchers agree that a child's rapidly developing storehouse of knowledge (probably stored involuntarily) can be crucial for memory development and for the deployment of increasingly successful memory strategies (Siegler, 1983; Flavell, Miller & Miller, 1993). In other words, you cannot recall or retrieve something not stored. To illustrate the significance of knowledge storage, or involuntary memory, Chi (1982) taught a kindergartner to use a chunking strategy—to alphabetize the names of children she knew in her class. After successful performance on this task, she had great difficulty using the same memory strategy to retrieve a set of names of people she did not know.

Adults label things in the environment and repeat the labels until the child learns to do so on his own.

## Interaction of Biological and Contextual Influences on Developmental Changes in Memory—Metamemory

As children get older, their information processing abilities appear to become more conscious and deliberate. This is likely due to maturation of neural connections as well as their increasing number of experiences. Metamemory exemplifies their interaction between biological maturation and contextual influences. Metamemory consists of four categories: One category is *sensitivity*, which involves knowing when to exert an effort to retrieve information or prepare for some future retrieval—"I had better reread the chapter so I can remember it better for the test." A second category is *person variables*, which involves knowing how you compare to yourself at other times in situations requiring remembering—"I had better write the report on what was said at the meeting before I go to sleep, otherwise by morning I will have forgotten the details." A third category is *task variables*, which involves knowing what is to be memorized and the best way to memorize it—"I need to study those formulas; I'll write them down repeatedly." Finally, a fourth category is *knowledge strategies*, which involves knowing what helps one remember best—"I have a great memory for pictures so when I have to remember words or theories, I always use imagery." Metamemory improves in all four categories from the preschool years to the school years. Improvement is due to the interaction of maturation and learning. An individual's comprehensive understanding, however, of how the categories work together is not achieved until toward the end of elementary school (Kail, 1990, Flavel, Miller & Miller, 1993).

Sensitivity in children (and adults) as to what to remember can be enhanced by telling them in advance for example, "Remember to let the cat out before you leave." Even three-year-olds profit from such reminders (Wellman, Ritter & Flavell, 1975; Kail, 1990).

Regarding person variables, young children think they remember better than they actually do. Five-year-olds overestimate their memory spans (Flavell, Friedrichs & Hoyt, 1970). This must be why when a kindergartner is told to remember to bring his jacket home after school, he arrives home empty-handed. During the elementary school years, predicted and actual memory span come closer together (Flavell, Friedrichs & Hoyt, 1970).

Regarding task variables, by kindergarten children know it is easier to remember familiar things than unfamiliar things (Schneider, 1985). Yet, it

# HOW DO CHILDREN DEVELOP MEMORY STRATEGIES OF PAST EVENTS?

Friedman, W.J. (1991). The development of children's memory for the time of past events. *Child Development, 62,* 139–155.

According to memory organization theories, memory is organized by the order in which information is stored. Thus, it would follow that memories of events that occurred a long time ago would not be as easy to recall, or possess as many details, as memories of events that occurred recently. According to *memory reconstruction* theories, to recall a past event the time must usually be constructed by relating information associated with what was happening at the time; for example, recalling a presidential election campaign in progress. *Memory organization* theories focus on *distance,* the amount of time that has elapsed since an event, whereas memory reconstruction theories focus on *location*, the linkage between an event and a point in some autonomous time pattern. These two senses of memory are strongly interactive in adults.

This study was designed to test the distinction between time memory as distance and time memory as location and to provide information about age changes in children's sense of a chronological past.

Children of four, six, and eight years of age were asked to order a pair of events that had taken place seven weeks and one week earlier. The event that occurred seven weeks before the children were tested on their recall ability was a videotaping session during recess followed by a lecture on how videotaping works by a researcher. The event that

occurred one week before was a several minute lecture and demonstration of proper toothbrushing technique by the regular class teacher. The testing session asked the involved children if they remembered "these two things." Each child was shown two cards, one depicting a tooth and toothbrush and the other a television with a running child and swing set on the screen. Each child was asked which event happened a *long* time ago and which one happened a *short* time ago. The children also were asked if they remembered the day of the week these events occurred and how they knew, what time of day (morning, afternoon, evening) and how they knew, what month it was and how they knew, and what season it was and how they knew.

The first and third grade children's accuracy in ordering the one-week-old event was nearly always correct, whereas in the preschool group about 30 percent of the children reversed the order.

The preschoolers seemed to judge the distance of past events without reference to their locations in time. By age six, however, children begin to share with adults the ability to reason about locations in the past on scales longer than a day. Six-year-old children have a general time knowledge of days of the week, months, and seasons that enables them to structure the past by location and distance.

In conclusion, children's development of memory strategies for past events is influenced by their development of a general time sense.

is not until third to fifth grade that children realize learning a story verbatim is more difficult than learning the theme that studying helps recall, and that having to learn more items hinders recall (Kreutzer, Leonard & Flavell, 1975; Kail,1990). Also, there are individual differences in the way children use their existing or familiar knowledge to remember, or store, new information. Some children (usually those who perform well in school) draw on old knowledge when presented with new information, while others (usually those who perform poorly in school) make little use of their knowledge base when faced with having to learn a new task (Bransford, et al., 1981).

Regarding strategies, older children can think of more ways to remind themselves than can younger children (Kreutzer, Leonard, & Flavell, 1975; Kail, 1990). According to Fabricus and Wellman (1983), several years are required for children to understand how to use available strategies. For example, many of the first-graders studied believed that a memory aid (a reminder-note) would help them remember something even if they saw it *after* they were supposed to do the task. The older children realized memory aids had to be seen *before* the task, but it was not until fifth grade that children realized a memory aid used too far in advance was of little help.

## PROBLEM SOLVING

Problem solving encompasses all the previously discussed components of the information processing system (selective attention, perception, encoding, metamemory, retrieval).

To determine how a child uses the information he possesses to solve a problem, the problem must first be analyzed into all its component steps, somewhat like computer programming.

The progress from unsuccessful to successful problem solving is what developmental psychologists study. Outlining the program, or the plan of solution, helps pinpoint where the child might get stuck in the process of solving a problem.

When children recognize a problem is to be solved, they must generate a solution or a set of solutions and evaluate the success of the solution they select. Young children are less systematic in the approach to problem solving than are adolescents. They also have less experience and knowledge about the workings of the world, so they have fewer resources for solutions.

Siegler (1978) describes a method by which he could assess children's problem-solving strategies. The approach is based on the assumption that children's problem-solving strategies are governed by rules; that with age these strategies progress from less sophisticated to more sophisticated. Siegler used a variation of one of Piaget's tasks, the balance scale problem. The apparatus (figure 9.3) had a fulcrum on which both sides had four equally spaced pegs on which metal weights could be placed.

## F.Y.I.

Flow charts also are useful to show what one needs to know, as well as where one is lacking in being able to solve a problem. Pinpointing areas of difficulty is educationally valuable because a teacher can then provide appropriate experiences to enhance a child's level of understanding, hence performance.

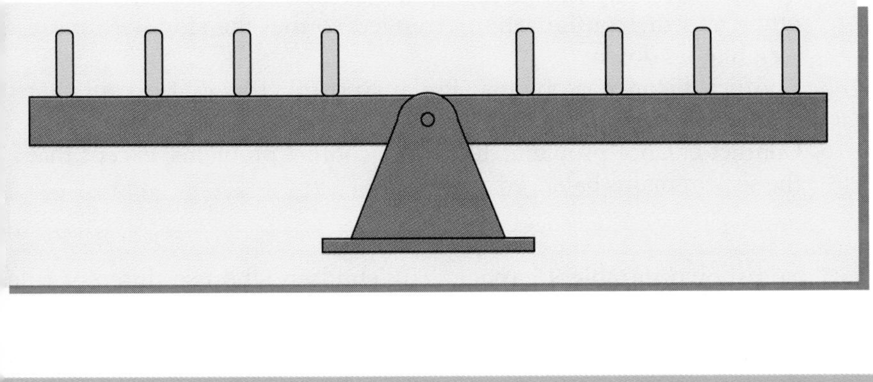

**FIGURE 9.3**
**Balance scale apparatus**

The arm of the balance could tip left or right or remain level depending on how the weights were arranged. The child's task was to predict which (if either) side would go down if a lever that held the scale motionless was released.

Siegler's analysis of Piaget's work (Inhelder & Piaget, 1958) and his findings led to the conclusion that there are four possible strategies or rules children of different ages use to solve problems. Three-year-old children did not appear to use rules. About half of the four-year-old children used Rule I. Nine-year-old children used both Rules II and III; 13-year-old and 17-year-old children almost always used Rule III. Rule IV was used by a minority of college students.

A child using Rule I considers only the numbers of weights on each side of the fulcrum: If they are the same, the child predicts that the scale will balance; otherwise, she predicts that the side with the greater number of weights will go down. A child using Rule II also employs Rule I; but if the weights are equal on both sides, then the distance between them is considered (the side whose weights are farther from the fulcrum is considered heavier and will go down). A child using Rule III considers both weight and distance in all cases. (If weight and distance are equal, the scale will balance; if weight is equal, then distance determines which side is heavier or vice versa; if both weight and distance are unequal, the side with the greater value based on both weight and distance is heavier and will go down; however, if one side has more weight and the other has greater distance between the weights, the child guesses.) A child using Rule IV computes torques (combination of forces to produce the movement) on each side by multiplying the amounts of weight on each peg by the peg's distance from the fulcrum. (Weight times distance equals torque.) The side with the greater torque is the heavier and will go down. Figure 9.4 shows the models of the four rules.

To determine which, if any, of these rule models accurately characterized a child's knowledge about the scale, Siegler constructed the following six problems and examined percentages of correct and incorrect answers related to the balance problem:

1. Balance problems with the same configuration of weights on pegs on each side of the fulcrum
2. Weight problems with unequal amounts of weight equidistant from the fulcrum
3. Distance problems with equal amounts of weight different distances from the fulcrum
4. Conflict-weight problems with more weight on one side and more "distance" (i.e., occupied pegs farther from the fulcrum) on the other, and the configuration arranged so that the side with more weight goes down
5. Conflict-distance problems similar to conflict-weight except that the side with greater distance goes down
6. Conflict-balance problems like other conflict problems, except that the scale remains balanced

As shown in table 9.1 (page 280), children who use different rules produce different response patterns of these problems. Those using Rule

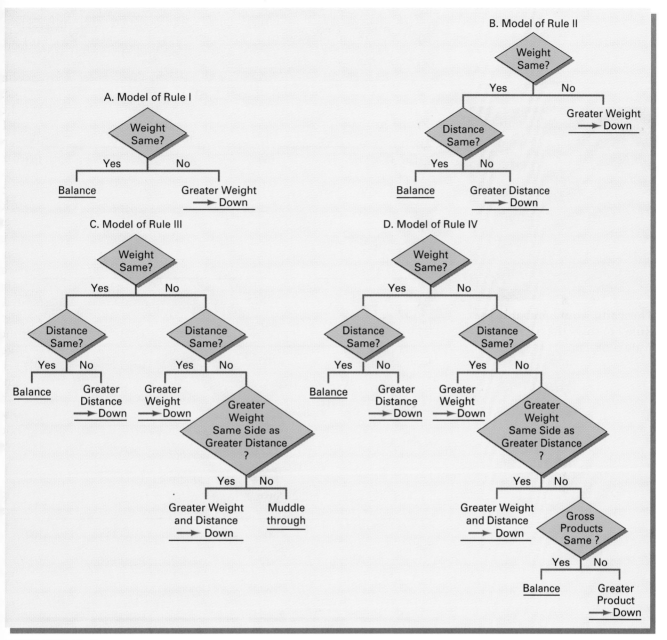

**FIGURE 9.4**
Decision tree model (flow chart) of rules for performing balance scale task. (Siegler, 1978)

would consistently make correct predictions on balance, weight, and conflict-weight problems; they were never correct on the other three types of problems. Children using Rule II would have similar predictions, except they could also solve distance problems. Those following Rule III would consistently make accurate predictions on weight, balance, and distance problems and would perform on a chance level (be unpredictable in their responses) on all conflict problems. Those using Rule IV would solve all the problems.

## TABLE 9.1

| Problem-Type | Rule | | | |
|---|---|---|---|---|
| | I | II | III | IV |
| Balance | 100 | 100 | 100 | 100 |
| Weight | 100 | 100 | 100 | 100 |
| Distance | 0 (Should say "Balance") | 100 | 100 | 100 |
| Conflict-Weight | 100 | 100 | 33 (Chance Responding) | 100 |
| Conflict-Distance | 0 (Should say "Right Down") | 0 (Should say "Right Down") | 33 (Chance Responding) | 100 |
| Conflict-Balance | 0 (Should say "Right Down") | 0 (Should say "Right Down") | 33 (Chance Responding) | 100 |

**(Siegler, 1978)**

This child would probably use Rule I to solve the balance scale problem.

There was a developmental pattern in children's use of various rules. As children get older, they use different rules going from simple (Rule I) to complex (Rule IV). In particular, Siegler (1976) examined five-year-old, nine-year-old, 13-year-old, and 17-year-old children's existing knowledge about balance scales. The rule model fits 90 percent of children of all ages.

Five-year-old children most often used Rule I; nine-year-old children most often used Rule II or III; and 13-year-old and 17-year-old children most often used Rule III. Few subjects used Rule IV.

These results demonstrate how analysis of correct and incorrect responses can denote individual children's knowledge. Siegler's rule-assessment approach has been applied to assessing understanding of other concepts such as conservation, probability, time, and speed. In all cases, the patterns of correct and incorrect answers have identified partial under-standings that children have before they master the total concept (Siegler, 1983). This is an improvement over Piaget's theory in that one of the criticisms of his theory was that he did not account for partial understandings of concepts.

How can the developmental changes in rule use be explained? Piaget's explanation was that younger children do not yet have the logical structures to reason in a formal scientific manner as exemplified in Rule IV. It may be that adolescents have the logical structures or competency to use Rule IV but do not execute their ability because of their egocentrism. Case's (1974) explanation is there are three prerequisites for solving formal operational problems: Sufficient memory capacity, exposure to situations that would promote disequilibrium, and the personality trait of *field independence*, a cognitive style in which a person can analyze a problem independent of the context presented. Thus, to use Rule IV, these prerequisites would have to be met. Siegler (1976), however, explains the developmental difference in the use of rules as due to differences in sophistication of encoding abilities. His evidence comes from another assessment measure where older children could encode both weight and distance, whereas younger children could only encode weight. (Piaget said young children *centrate*, they can only focus on one aspect of the problem whereas older children consider all aspects.) When the younger children were trained via experience to encode both dimensions they could do the conflict problems that previously could not be done.

Thus, according to Siegler and other information-processing theorists, there are educational implications to how one processes available information. If we could pinpoint what cognitive activity the individual was not using in solving problems, perhaps we could provide appropriate experiences whereby she could improve her attention, encoding, memory strategies, or metamemory and enable an improvement in performance of problem-solving tasks.

## INFORMATION-PROCESSING THEORIES EVALUATED

There are advantages of information-processing theories for understanding how we use what we know. Information processing enables us to find out what information children get from a problem and how they use it to solve the problem. By analyzing a particular task and breaking it down into specific components, we can form specific hypotheses about how children reason (e.g., Siegler's four-rule hypothesis for problem solving) and then test these hypotheses on children of various ages to get a developmental picture of knowledge. This is more accurate than classifying a child by stage (as in Piagetian theory) because a stage classification does not provide knowledge of what *aspects* of the child's performance caused him to be assigned to the particular stage (Siegler, 1978).

The strength of the information processing perspective (breaking the use of knowledge into its components) is also its weakness. Information-processing theorists have had difficulty integrating the parts into a broad comprehensive theory like Piaget's. Although information processing has outlined basic developmental changes in the areas of perception, selective attention, memory, and problem solving, little is known about how these facets of knowledge are put together and used from childhood to adulthood.

Information processing researchers have identified effective performance factors in school-related tasks. Box 9.1 shows how teachers can use this knowledge to improve children's learning (Dembo, 1988).

---

## Box 9.1   INFORMATION PROCESSING APPLIED: IMPROVING TEACHING EFFECTIVENESS

**To focus attention:**
1. Arrange the environment so distractions are minimized.
2. Inform students of the lesson goals. When students know why it is important to learn something or how it relates to them, they are more likely to attend.
3. Emphasize important information. Repeat, write on the board, tell students what is important because learning how to distinguish essential from nonessential information is a valuable learning skill.
4. Teach students self-monitoring and self-control techniques so they can resume attending to the lesson when distracted.

**To reveal students' cognitive processes:**
1. Ask students to show all their work.
2. Ask students questions about their thought processes—"How are you going to solve the problem?" "Why do you think you are having difficulty?"

**To enhance memory strategies:**
1. Present material at a pace that does not overwhelm short-term memory (short-term memory lasts for about one minute or less).
2. Teach and prompt rehearsal, imagery, and chunking strategies.
3. Teach students to monitor their thought processes—"How do you remember best?" "What makes you get stuck on these problems?"
4. Provide discussion whereby students can share their learning strategies.
5. Teach students how to underline important information, take notes, summarize, paraphrase, relate new information to old, and make predictions based on information.

---

# ABOUT MEASURING KNOWLEDGE

Whereas knowledge refers to the storehouse of information, it is measured in terms of how that knowledge is retrieved and used. This brings us to the concept of intelligence.

## WHAT IS INTELLIGENCE?

While there is little consensus among psychologists about the specific nature of intelligence, most agree that intelligence reflects an ability to adapt to one's environment, to think abstractly, and to solve problems effectively (Sternberg & Berg, 1986). Psychologists measure intelligence by assessing the degree of success in using these abilities to perform certain tasks. The ranch of psychology concerned with measuring mental abilities is called **psychometrics**. Psychometric theories are based on the study of individual differences among people on several factors that compose intelligence. The number of factors in the theories range from 1 to 150 (Sternberg, 1985).

At the low end of the factor scale is a general factor of intelligence ($g$) proposed by Spearman (1923). Individual differences in $g$ might be understood in terms of the differences in people's abilities to comprehend experiences, to elicit relations, and to determine correlations. For example, lawyer:client, as physician:? (Sternberg, 1985). Comprehension refers to encoding, or perceiving information and understanding it. Thus, you would have to know what a lawyer, client, and a physician do. Eliciting relationships refers to knowing the connections between events, people, or objects. Thus, you would have to know that a lawyer provides legal services to clients. Determining correlations refers to applying a connection between two objects to others. So you would extract the connection of service between lawyer and client and apply it to physician, and your answer to the analogy would be "patient." Because analogies embody the aforementioned principles of general intelligence as outlined by Spearman, and subsequently many others (Sternberg, 1977), analogies are frequently used in intelligence tests.

At the middle of the factor scale is Thurstone's (1938) seven primary mental abilities:

The demonstration these children are observing is a basic analogy between colored water and the syringe and the human circulatory system. Can you complete the analogy? Red water is to the syringe as _____ is to the heart.

1. *Perceptual speed*—measured by tests requiring rapid recognition of symbols (*b* and *d* or *g* and *p*)
2. *Memory*—measured by tests of recognition or recall
3. *Spatial visualization*—measured by tests requiring the ability to picture two- and three-dimensional objects in space by manipulating given symbols or geometric designs
4. *Verbal comprehension*—measured by vocabulary tests and reading comprehension
5. *Verbal fluency*—measured by tests that involve usage of words (telling stories in your own words)
6. *Number*—measured by arithmetic problems involving adding, subtraction, multiplication, division, as well as some reasoning
7. *Reasoning*—measured by tests of analogies, completions, logical problems

At the upper end of the scale in delineating the number of factors composing intelligence is Guilford, who identified 150 mental abilities (Guilford, 1982; 1985), although all of the projected factors have not yet been demonstrated methodologically. See figure 9.5 for the three-dimensional structure of intellect proposed by Guilford. Guilford's model has been useful in designing measures to identify the creative aspect of intelligence.

## HOW IS INTELLIGENCE MEASURED?

The first intelligence test was developed in France by Alfred Binet and Theodore Simon for the purpose of identifying slow learners in order to give them special education. Binet and Simon theorized that slow learners think like normal children of a younger age (a slow eight-year-old might

FIGURE 9.5

**Guilford's structure-of-intellect model (Wolman, 1985 )**

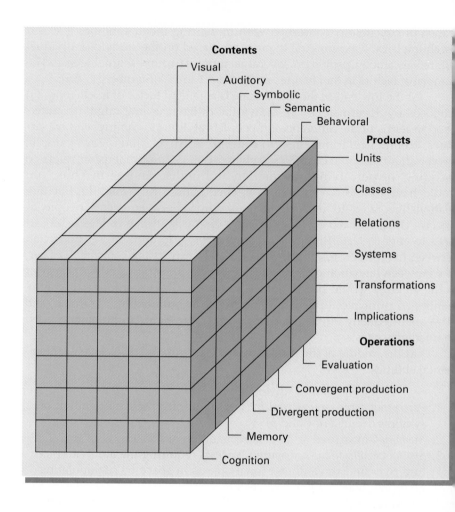

be able to answer the same questions as a normal five-year-old). Thus, they came up with the concept of **mental age** to denote a child's level of intellectual functioning as compared to others. This concept was based on their observations that knowledge and reasoning improve with age.

In 1916, the Binet-Simon scale was brought to the United States and revised by Lewis Terman and his colleagues at Stanford University. The adapted test became known as the *Stanford-Binet Intelligence Test*. The latest revision occurred in 1986, and like earlier versions, is suitable for testing individuals age 2 through 18 years of age, but is more ethnically sensitive. Performance is measured by a formula known as the intelligence quotient (IQ) which is equal to one's mental age (MA) divided by one's chronological age (CA) and multiplied by 100.

$$IQ = \frac{MA}{CA} \times 100$$

Mental age is calculated by asking the child **standardized** age-graded questions (questions determined to be answerable by most children of a certain age based on tests of large representative samples).

The test is administered individually to each child in a private setting by a psychologist who asks the child each question. When the child starts missing more than half of the questions designated on the test for a particular age, that is considered to be the child's mental age and the test stops.

If a child has a chronological age of five and can answer most of the seven-year-old questions, but not the eight-year-old questions, her mental age is seven and her IQ is figured as follows:

$$IQ = \frac{7}{5} \times 100 = 140$$

The average IQ of the general population is 100, designated as such because an individual is expected to be able to answer the questions for her age group—so the IQ of a five-year old child who answers the five-year-old questions but not the six-year-old ones, equals ⅘ x 100 or 100. The distribution among the general population is outlined in figure 9.6.

The important concept about IQ is that it is merely a measure of how well an individual performs relative to others of the same age at the time of taking a particular test; it is not a fixed label (like on a cereal box) that tells how much intelligence one has.

Other intelligence tests widely used today were developed by David Wechsler. Originally developed to measure adult intelligence (*Wechsler Adult Intelligence Scale*, or *WAIS*), there now are forms for school-age children ages 6 to 16 (*Wechsler Intelligence Scale for Children*, or *WISC-R* ), as well as for younger children, ages three to eight (*Wechsler Preschool and Primary Scale of Intelligence*, or *WPPSI-R*).

Unlike the Stanford-Binet Intelligence Test, which is organized by age levels, the Wechsler scales are organized by the information or skill being tested. The subtests are divided into two main categories, verbal and nonverbal (or performance).

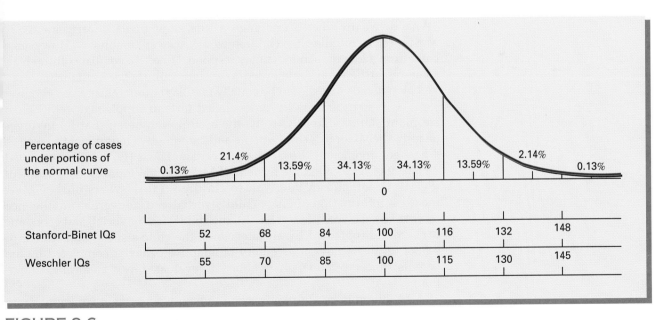

## FIGURE 9.6
**The bell-shaped curve represents the distribution of IQs among the general population.**

An intelligence test based on information processing skills, called the *Kaufman Assessment Battery for Children* or *K-ABC*, is designed to measure the intelligence of children from ages 2½ –12. The specific abilities tested are **sequential processing**, which refers to the capacity to solve problems in a stepwise fashion, and **simultaneous processing,** which involves the ability to elicit meaning from various stimuli at the same time.

# INTELLIGENCE TESTS EVALUATED

Intelligence tests such as the Stanford-Binet and the Wechsler predict school success fairly well; that is the purpose for which they were originally designed. However, they do not predict creativity (Gardner, 1983), or success on the job (McCall, 1977). A major criticism of IQ tests is that they are not a fair representation of a person's supply of intelligent behaviors; for example, they do not measure how a person acquires and uses new knowledge, a significant skill in effectively adapting to one's environment (Sternberg, 1983, 1985, 1986).

The positive aspect of IQ tests is that they have identified gifted and retarded children who otherwise may have missed special educational services. Also, they have prevented children from being placed in special classes because of behavioral or emotional problems.

The negative aspects of IQ tests are they have been used to label children from minority groups as retarded (Mercer, 1972), and they have caused teachers to act on the **self-fulfilling prophecy**, the process by which one's initial belief, prediction, or impression elicits behavior that confirms the belief, prediction, or impression; thereby children with different IQs are treated differently (Rosenthal, 1973).

IQ tests have been criticized as being culturally biased (although recent revisions have tried to be more sensitive to ethnic minorities). **Culture** refers to the knowledge, beliefs, art, morals, law, customs, and traditions of a group of people. Thus, individuals from non-Western cultures may not be able to answer correctly some items on an IQ test because they have never had experiences related to the item. For example, take the question, "What do we use when it's raining—a cane, an umbrella, a scarf, or a tree ?" Most Western middle-class children would answer "umbrella." However, a child from a low class in India may respond, "tree." To combat cultural bias, some researchers have attempted to design "culture-fair" tests using nonverbal materials that should be equally familiar or unfamiliar to everyone.

Other researchers have developed tests to supplement rather than supplant standardized IQ tests; the assumption being that IQ involves adaptive behavior in a child's home and community environment as well as school environment. For example, Mercer and Lewis (1978) have assembled a battery of tests called the System of Multicultural Pluralistic Assessment (SOMPA), which can be given to children 5 to 11 years old. SOMPA includes information about a child's verbal and nonverbal intelligence assessed by the Wechsler (WISC-R), the child's family, social, and economic background (obtained by an interview), the child's social adjustment to school (evaluated by an inventory of adaptive behavior completed by the parents), and the child's physical health (evaluated by a medical examination).

With an increasing knowledge of how we use what we know, more valid and more encompassing assessments of intelligence will soon be developed. For example, work is being done in **neurometrics**, the measurement of brain waves by a computer (Karmel, Kaye, & John, 1978). A child is given various sensory, perceptual cognitive tests while his brain is connected to a computer screen via electrodes taped to areas of the head. The computer evaluates the evoked potentials (brain waves) of the child, comparing them with average reactions. The Neurometric Battery of tests can deter-ine whether a child's brain is functioning normally and can pick up some pecific learning disorders. Some psychologists, however, remain skeptical bout the Neurometric Battery's reliability to pick up learning disorders.

To summarize, the problem with intelligence tests is that each one measures what it was designed to measure by its creators. In other words, ntelligence tests measure different things by how the designers of the test efine intelligence; and because there is disagreement as to the specific ature of intelligence, designing a test to encompass all the definitions is ifficult.

# DOES INTELLIGENCE CHANGE OVER TIME?

It used to be believed that IQ was fixed, that it was an indication of ne's native intelligence and, therefore, could not change (Burt, 1937). Yet, measurements of intelligence do show changes over time.

Most psychologists agree that intelligence tests are more **achievement tests** (measure what one already knows) than they are **aptitude tests** measure what one is capable of knowing); thus, we can attribute the hange in scores over time to greater learning and experience. Remember, Q scores come from a comparison with age-mates, so the child having more experiences, or more motivation to learn, or better teachers may test etter than her peers at any particular time.

Since scores on intelligence tests given in infancy (before age two) ear little resemblance to IQ scores later (Wohlwill, 1980), tests given to nfants need to be compared with those given to older children. Bayley 1955) points out that infant tests measure sensorimotor abilities (reaction to stimuli, coordination, recognition of differences), whereas childhood tests measure verbal ability and cognitive skills.

The Bayley Mental and Motor Scales are one of the most widely used measurements of infant development. They measure the infant's adaptive responses to the environment—attention to stimuli (visual and auditory), grasping and manipulating objects, holding head up, sitting, crawling, standing, walking, showing memory, exhibiting object permanence (looking for a hidden toy), understanding language, and so on (Bayley, 1970), as illustrated in table 9.2.

There is, however, recent evidence showing a relation between an infant's response to novel stimuli (looking at a green circle after having been shown a red one several times), cognitive functioning at age two, and performance on verbal intelligence tests at age three (Fagan,1984; Berg & Steinberg, 1985) and even age six (Rose & Wallace,1985). Perhaps psychologists then can detect a continuity in intelligence from infancy to childhood if they use the appropriate measure. Fagan (1985) suggests that an ability to detect similarities among otherwise different or diverse stimuli is a basic intellectual process that underlies not only recognition memory (recognizing the red circle as the old stimulus by pairing it with a new stimulus, a green circle) and the understanding of similarities and differences but also the ability to do analogies. If intelligence includes the ability to respond quickly and successfully to new situations, then perhaps testing an infant's response to new stimuli is a valid predictor of intelligence.

If IQ tests were more achievement-oriented than aptitude-oriented, then IQ scores would probably increase as one is coached or learns more.

## ILLUSTRATIVE ITEMS ON THE BAYLEY SCALES OF INFANT DEVELOPMENT

### TABLE 9.2

| Age (months) | Mental Scale | Motor Scale |
|---|---|---|
| 2 | Visually recognizes mother | Elevates self by arms; prone |
| 4 | Turns head to sound of rattle | Head balanced |
| 6 | Looks for fallen spoon | Sits alone 30 seconds or more |
| 8 | Uncovers toy | Pulls to standing position |
| 10 | Looks at pictures in book | Walks with help |
| 12 | Turns pages of book | Walks alone |
| 14 | Spontaneous scribble | Walks sideways |
| 16 | Builds tower of 3 cubes | Stands on left foot with help |
| 18 | Initiates crayon stroke | Tries to walk on walking board |
| 20 | Differentiates scribble from stroke | Walks with one foot on walking board |
| 22 | Names 3 pictures | Stands on left foot alone |
| 24 | Names 3 object | Jumps from bottom step |
| 26 | Train of cubes | Walks down stairs alone: both feet on each step |
| 28 | Understands 2 prepositions | Jumps from second step |
| 30 | Builds tower of 8 cubes | Walks on tiptoe, 10 feet |

(Sattler, 1982)

## BIOLOGICAL INFLUENCES ON INTELLIGENCE

A general biological influence on the development of intelligence involves evolution of the brain. A specific biological influence on the development of intelligence is heredity in that it is significant in determining individual differences in intellectual competence.

### Development of the Human Brain

According to Jerison (1982), throughout history several periods existed in which the brain evolved. The first was during the Mesozoic Age, commonly termed the age of the dinosaurs (about 200 million years ago). The main change was in the ability of the mammalian brain to coordinate smells with auditory and visual information. Fish and amphibian still have "smell brains" that concentrate on the sense of smell, whereas reptiles, birds, and mammals exhibit more neural association in their cerebral cortexes, which coordinate various sensations (Simpson & Beck, 1965).

The second major step in the evolution of the brain occurred about 50 million years ago after dinosaurs became extinct and when other animals inhabited the earth. The mammalian brain could not only coordinate sensory information, it could relate it to past and present experiences. This ability was the beginning of thought (Konner, 1982).

The third evolution of the brain occurred about one million years ago when ancestral humans developed language (Jerison, 1982). Language enabled humans to label experiences and communicate with one another. In turn, communication laid the foundation for culture. Culture created an environment in which those individuals who had a greater ability to learn and to solve problems were more adaptive and therefore had a greater chance of surviving and reproducing (Scarr, Weinberg & Levine, 1985).

The human brain in its current form (large with many interconnected nerve cells folded and wrinkled) has been passed on from one generation to another. Even though human brains resemble each other in structure and function, each human exhibits individual differences with respect to how he uses the brain. This is due in part to heredity, the contexts to which a person was exposed while developing, and the interaction of biological and contextual influences.

## Heredity

There is evidence that the more closely related two people are, the more closely their scores on intelligence tests correspond. These correlations between identical twins (developed from a single fertilized egg cell), fraternal twins (developed from two fertilized egg cells), siblings (brothers and sisters), parents and their children suggest a genetic influence on intelligence (Bouchard & McGue, 1981; Bouchard et al., 1990). Identical twin IQ correlations are about .85, whereas that of fraternal twins is about .60 (Dunn & Plomin, 1990).

Another piece of evidence supporting the genetic influence on intelligence comes from adopted children. One study (Horn, Loehlin & Wellerman, 1975) done on two hundred children who were adopted immediately after birth, found the correlation between their IQs and those of their biological mothers (whom they had never seen) was greater than the correlation between their IQs and those of their adoptive mothers (who provided the interaction and the environment while they were growing). The correlation of adopted-away offspring and their biological parents has been found to be about .25 (Dunn & Plomin, 1990).

Still another piece of evidence supporting the genetic influence of intelligence comes from a study comparing identical and fraternal twins on the specific abilities measured by the WISC-R (other studies only used general IQ scores). Thus, according to Segal (1975), who did the study, as well as others (Dunn & Plomin, 1990) not only may the general level of intelligence be inherited, but so may the specific factors such as verbal, spatial, and reasoning ability.

## CONTEXTUAL INFLUENCES ON INTELLIGENCE

Contexts that influence a child's intelligence are family (including birth order, interaction patterns, social class), school (including teacher expectations and peer expectations), and intervention programs. To determine the effects of various contexts on the development of intelligence, we have to rely on performance measures such as IQ tests or achievement tests while keeping in mind that these measures do not tap all possible intellectual abilities.

## Family

Birth order seems to affect intellectual performance. First born children usually have higher IQs than siblings born later (Zajonc & Markus, 1975; Zajonc, 1983). Zajonc, Markus & Markus (1979) explain that this is because first-born children have more adult interaction than do later-borns.

Discussion and feedback are interactive patterns between parents and children that can increase a child's intelligence.

Children from lower socioeconomic environments have been shown to have lower scores on IQ tests.

However, other researchers ( McCall, 1984; Rodgers, 1984) dispute this explanation on the grounds that older siblings often become models or tutors to their younger brothers or sisters, thereby compensating for the decreased adult interaction common with later-borns.

Interaction patterns within a child's home environment were studied to assess the relation to intellectual development. An assessment scale, called HOME (Home Observation for the Measurement of the Environment), was developed to determine the quality of the home environment for children under the age of three (Elardo, Bradley & Caldwell,1975; Bradley, Caldwell & Rock, 1990). This assessment scale contained 45 items in the following six areas:

1. Emotional and verbal responsiveness of the mother (mother responds to child's vocalizations with physical or verbal response)
2. Avoidance of restriction and punishment (mother does not interfere with child's actions or prohibit them more than three times during the observation)
3. Organization of the physical and temporal environment (child's play environment is safe and accessible to child)
4. Provision of appropriate play materials (child has toys that are safe, are age appropriate, and stimulate play)
5. Maternal interaction with the child (mother keeps child within visual range and looks at, touches, or talks to child often)
6. Opportunities for variety in daily stimulation (mother reads stories or plays games with child)

The HOME assessment included fathers and other caregivers even though the six areas listed above refer only to the mother. The assessment was administered through observations and interviews. The HOME score was found to be positively correlated with IQ scores at six months, at three years, at four-and-one-half years, and at six-and-one-half years (Elardo, Bradley & Caldwell, 1975; Bradley & Caldwell, 1976; Bradley & Caldwell, 1984).

Social class has been shown to be related to intellectual achievement. Children from lower social classes consistently score 10 to 15 points lower on IQ tests than do children from middle to upper classes. One explanation is that the home environments are different. According to Bradley and Caldwell (1976), there is more disorganization of where things are and when events occur in the lower-class home; the child often does not know what to expect. There is less opportunity to explore, fewer items to explore, more physical punishment, and fewer explanations in regard to discipline (Bronfenbrenner, 1958).

Jensen (1969; 1980) has long been a proponent for a genetic explanation of differences. However, other researchers (Scarr & Weinberg, 1976) have criticized Jensen's methods and conclusions. For example, after comparing the IQs of African-American and Caucasian children from families of similar social classes, Nichols and Anderson (1973) concluded that the difference between average African-American and Caucasian IQ scores is more due to social class rather than ethnicity because a higher number of African-Americans are in the lower class. This would explain why African-Americans as a group score lower than Caucasians. Jensen did not consider this fact.

## chool

Rosenthal and Jacobson (1968) demonstrated that teachers' expecta-
ons influence students' achievement. They administered a nonverbal intel-
ence test to all children in an elementary school. The teachers were told
e test was to predict who would be an academic "bloomer" by the end of
e year. The participating teachers were provided with a list of "bloomers"
ctually the list was selected randomly and had nothing to do with the
st). Eight months later all the children in the school were retested with the
me IQ test and the designated bloomers actually demonstrated an
crease in scores. The results with the younger children were more dramat-
than with the older children.

Good and Brophy (1984) explain the phenomenon of the self-fulfill-
g prophecy. The teacher expects a certain level of achievement from a stu-
ent. Because of this expectation, the teacher treats the student differently
erhaps giving more attention, giving more approval for achievement and
isapproval for lack of achievement). This differential treatment influences
e student's motivation to achieve and her self-confidence.

Not only do teacher expectations influence intellectual performance
ut so do peer expectations. Coleman (1961) surveyed ten Midwestern high
hools and found that peer values, rather than intelligence, influence
hool achievement. Thus, if one's peers valued athletics or popularity over
cademics, one did not work hard in academics. In a replication of
oleman's research, Eitzen (1975) found that athletic achievement was still
ore important to males than academic achievement and popularity was
ore important to females.

## ntervention Programs

Intervention programs are designed to interfere with the negative or
otential negative effects of certain home environments. The purpose of
tervention is to prevent or compensate for the disadvantages that impede
hievement in public schools. Because it has been demonstrated that chil-
ren from lower social classes do not perform as well on IQ tests as children
om middle or upper classes, children from disadvantaged families are the
rgets for such programs. Minority cultural groups and children with special
ducational needs (mentally, physically, emotionally disabled) are also targets.

The rationale for early intervention partly comes from the writings of
unt (1961) and Bloom (1964), both of whom stressed the importance of
rly experience for intellectual development.

There are various government-supported intervention programs;
ome occur in a child's home (*Project Home Start*), others in day-care centers
*Project Head Start*), still others in elementary schools (*Project Follow Through*).
lost of these programs were implemented in the 1960s to compensate for
e disadvantage some children in low income and ethnic minority families
ce in being ready to learn when they enter elementary school.

Home Start programs send trained visitors to the homes of qualified
amilies to teach parents of children under three years of age how to opti-
ize their child's development. Project Head Start is a preschool program
or 3- to 5-year-old disadvantaged children. It provides social and academic
xperiences for the children as well as social and health services for the
amilies. Parents of enrolled children are required to participate—to attend
arent education classes, to work in the classroom, and to participate in pol-
cy decisions for the program. Project Follow Through extends Head Start's
ervices through the third grade by working with the public schools.

**School is a primary setting in which children develop their knowledge base.**

In a longitudinal study, Lazar and Darlington (1982) examined th long-term effects of government intervention programs begun in the 1960 They compared children who had participated in 12 infant and preschoc intervention programs with children from the same community who ha not participated. They also followed these children through elementar school. On analyses of their data, the results showed that program childre achieved more in school; they were less likely than those who did not pa ticipate in a program (the control group) to be assigned to special educatio classes; and they were less likely to be held back a grade. In addition, th IQs of the participating children surpassed their controls for up to thre years after the program ended.

One explanation of why the IQs of the experimental group did nc consistently remain higher than the control group is that the interventio was not long enough to have had a permanent effect on IQ. Another expla nation is that disadvantaged children, whether or not they have had inte vention, are more likely to attend the same schools and be affected by pee influences. A third explanation is that no amount of intervention will con pensate for a disadvantaged home life if the home environment is no improved as part of the program.

In addition, IQ tests do not measure all possible aspects of intelli gence. This was shown by documented changes in the participating chi dren that were not measurable by tests. Their attitudes toward school wer more positive and their mothers reported more satisfaction with their chi dren's school performance and had higher aspirations for them than th mothers of control children.

In conclusion, intervention programs do have an influence on intelli gence. However, the extent of that influence reflects one's definition c intelligence—the kind measured by IQ tests, which relate to school succes or a broader kind that encompasses adaptation to life.

## INTERACTION OF BIOLOGICAL AND CONTEXTUAL INFLUENCES ON INTELLIGENCE

If we think of the concept of **reaction range,** the limits within whicl the effects of genes can vary depending on changes in environments, ther we can understand the effect of poor versus excellent environments on IC We have two children who initially score average on an IQ test (about 100) One is raised in a poor environment (no one to provide enriching real expe riences, read books, be a role model), and the other is raised in an excellen environment (plenty of discussions and explanations, many stimulatin; toys and books, much socialization). After several years, the average chilc raised in the intellectually excellent environment will likely outperform th child raised in the poor environment, thus reaching the height of his intel lectual reaction range; in other words, reaching maximum intellectua potential (Scarr & McCartney, 1983).

A stimulating environment that provides experiences should influ ence the biological development of the human brain and in turn affect intel ligence. Experience interacts with biological development because to grov and maintain their contacts, nerves need to be stimulated, otherwise thei connections regress or die out (Leonard, 1986). Neuroscientists believe thes changes in brain structure represent learning. Synapses increase in the human until age two and then begin to decrease (figure 9.7). Since early experience affects the increase in synapses, more neural pathways are available when the number of synapses begins to decrease. The decrease in synapses represents more efficient nerve communication and, hence, information processing.

In reviewing the literature on early experience, relative plasticity (ability to be molded), and cognitive development, MacDonald (1986) states that brain development and subsequent behavior may be relatively plastic. However, he also points out that there are age differences in susceptibility to contextual influences, as well as individual differences in an organism's ability to respond to the influence of a given stimulation. Thus, more specific models are needed to account for critical periods in learning, different types of stimulation, and individual responses to various types of stimulation.

## ABOUT COGNITIVE STYLES

There are many different ways of approaching problems, taking tests, and showing knowledge. Some pick the first solution that comes to mind; others think through many solutions before choosing one. Some can solve a problem without having to know its relation to people, places, or objects; others can solve it only by its context. Some can think of many solutions to a problem; some can barely think of one solution. These differences are known as cognitive styles. To illustrate this concept, *impulsive-reflective, field independence/field dependence,* and *creativity* will be explained.

**An identical twin raised in a nurturing environment will outperform the other twin raised in a poor environment on intelligence tests.**

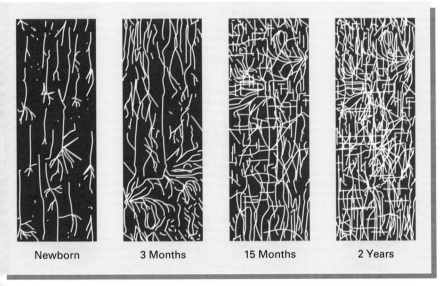

| Newborn | 3 Months | 15 Months | 2 Years |

### FIGURE 9.7

**The development of neurons in the cerebral cortex from birth to 2 years of age. The neurons grow both in size and in number of connections between them (Conel, 1939, 1959).**

## IMPULSIVE-REFLECTIVE

Solve the Matching Familiar Figures Test (figure 9.8). Did you jump right in and guess, or did you compare each teddy bear with the standard and each tree with the standard? If you leaped to a solution, your cognitive style is called **impulsive**; if you took time to evaluate the problem, considering various strategies and changing your solution after evaluation, then your cognitive style is called *reflective*. *Impulsive* thinkers value speed over accuracy; *reflective* thinkers value accuracy over speed.

The way one approaches problems affects performance on tasks. For example, reading errors are more numerous among impulsive children (Kagan, 1965). Impulsive children also make more errors on a variety of

**FIGURE 9.8**
**THE MATCHING FAMILIAR FIGURES TEST**

If we knew when a child was most receptive to learning art and how the child responds to various teaching techniques, then we could probably structure the context in which the child was exposed to creative concepts to enhance artistic ability.

nductive reasoning tasks (Kagan, Pearson & Welch, 1966). Reflective chil-ren pay more attention to fine details (Zelnicker et al., 1972). This general-y places them at an advantage in academic situations except in timed tests here too much attention to detail slows one down. Kagan and colleagues 1964) believe that impulsiveness or reflectiveness is a consistent and stable ersonality trait that is evident by the time a child is two years old.

## IELD INDEPENDENT/FIELD DEPENDENT

Another dimension of cognitive style is *field independence/field depen-ence*. Take the Hidden Figures Test (figure 9.9). If you had difficulty per-eiving the parts separate from the whole (the field), you are likely to be **ield dependent**; whereas if you could easily analyze the whole into its arts, you are likely to be **field independent**. Each cognitive style pproaches problem solving from a different perspective. Field indepen-ence is related to the ability to restructure problem elements and arrive at solution; whereas field dependence is related to the ability to focus on the ntire problem and quickly identify a solution.

Field independent individuals can organize unstructured situations. hey probably can solve problems without explicit instructions and guid-nce. Field dependent individuals, on the other hand, have greater difficulty arning unstructured material and may need explicit instructions on how to olve problems and use memory aids. They are good at interpreting social ues and have a better memory for social information (Witkin et al., 1977).

On a social and emotional level, field independence is associated ith self-direction; whereas field dependence is related to other-direction

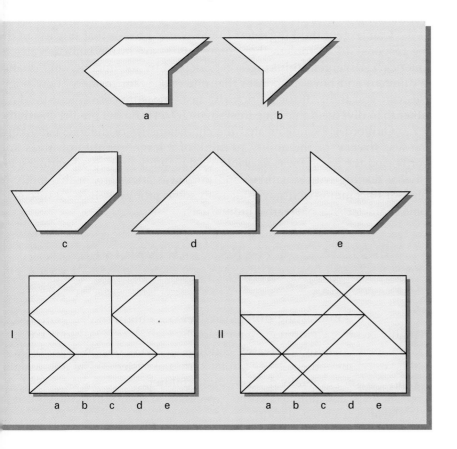

FIGURE 9.9
THE HIDDEN FIGURES
TEST

(Witkin & Moore, 1974). Children whose cognitive style is field independent tend to be more task-oriented; whereas children whose cognitive style is field dependent tend to be more people-oriented.

Cognitive style is related to socialization practices (Witkin, 1967). Children who are raised to respect authority, tradition, and close family ties tend to be more field dependent perhaps because they are trained to look to others for approval and direction. Also, field independence has been observed to increase with development, but individual differences do exist.

## CREATIVITY

Sir Francis Galton was the first to examine creativity. He studied the families of famous scientists, poets, artists, musicians, politicians, and athletes. He found many of these prominent British citizens had equally prominent relatives. He, himself, was related to Charles Darwin. He concluded that creative genius was genetically determined (1869).

Most psychologists agree that **creativity** is a unique mental process whereby a novel end product is developed and valued (Young, 1985). Thus, if you have never painted a picture before and you do so and are pleased with the result, that would be considered a creative process for you, even though others might not think of your product as particularly creative. The key components of creativity, novelty and value, are interpreted individually and with reference to the larger society.

Guilford (1950; 1959; 1985) developed a model for studying components of intelligence including creativity. Guilford believed that intelligence was not one dimensional. He distinguished between *convergent* and *divergent* thinking.

**Convergent thinking** refers to the mental process that singles out the one response to a problem (how many states are in the United States of America?). **Divergent thinking** is represented by the quantity and quality of different and novel responses that one makes, for instance, how many uses can you think of for a brick? IQ tests measure convergent thinking rather than divergent thinking; this is why IQ tests do not predict creativity.

Guilford (1959) delineated the characteristics of divergent thinking; one was *fluency*, or the ability to think of a large quantity of ideas and words, and the second was *flexibility*, or the ability to think of various new ways of dealing with situations, and third was *originality*, or the ability to think of uncommon and novel ideas to solve problems. Box 9.2 discusses some characteristics of creative individuals.

A child who is able to play a musical instrument probably exhibits some creativity when he performs.

## Box 9.2 CHARACTERISTICS OF CREATIVE INDIVIDUALS

Some interesting differences between highly intelligent and highly creative children were revealed by Getzels and Jackson (1962). They found that highly creative children tended to be nonconforming; they question and challenge adults and "the system." The following characteristics generally describe these children:

- They are not inhibited in the expression of their opinion even if it deviates from the majority.

- They fantasize, imagine, and enjoy intellectual playfulness.
- They accept disorder and are not interested in details.
- They generate a large number of ideas or solutions to problems.
- They display humor.
- They may be thought of as silly, but they do not fear being different.
- They rely more on their own evaluations than those of others.

In examining the differences in cognitive styles between intellectually gifted and creative children, Shaw (1985) found a link between the ability to imagine and creative thinking.

## Measuring Creativity

Building on the work of Guilford, Torrance (1966b; 1974), and others (Getzels & Jackson, 1962; Wallach & Kogan, 1965) have developed a variety of tests for measuring divergent, or creative, thinking. Figure 9.10 gives samples from various creativity tests. Table 9.3 illustrates how an item is scored. Generally, most creativity tests score fluency, flexibility, and originality of responses.

One study of creativity in elementary school children (Wallach & Kogan, 1965) and another of adolescents (Getzels & Jackson, 1962) concluded that creativity is independent of intelligence. It was assumed by many educators and psychologists that creative thought was possible only above a certain IQ; however, these studies found this assumption not to be valid. For example, Getzels and Jackson (1962) identified a group of adolescents who scored in the top 20 percent on measures of creativity but who were not in the top 20 percent in measures of intelligence. These they labeled

### F.Y.I.

Researchers studying children and adults have found little relationship between creativity and intelligence as measured by IQ tests (Kogan, 1983; Kersher & Ledger, 1985; Ruth & Birren, 1985).

## SAMPLE ANSWERS AND SCORING PROCEDURE FOR ONE ITEM FROM A CREATIVITY TEST

### TABLE 9.3

| Item: | How many uses can you think of for a nylon stocking: |
|---|---|
| Answers: | * Wear on feet |
| | §* Wear over face |
| | * Wear on hands when it's cold |
| | †* Make rugs |
| | * Make clothes |
| | §†* Make upholstery |
| | †* Use as a sling |
| | †* Tie up robbers |
| | §†* Cover broken window panes |
| | †* Use as ballast in a dirigible |
| | †* Make a fishing net |

| Scoring | | | |
|---|---|---|---|
| * | Fluency: | 14 | (total number of different responses) |
| † | Flexibility: | 9 | (number of shifts from one class to another) |
| § | Originality: | 5 | (number of unusual responses—responses that occurred less than 5 percent of the time in the entire sample) |

(Lefrancois, 1992)

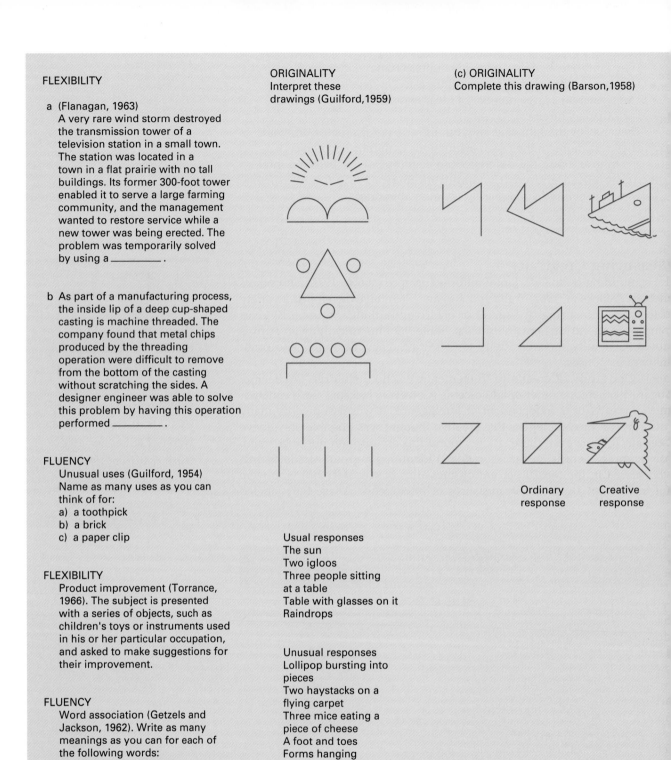

**FLEXIBILITY**

a (Flanagan, 1963)
A very rare wind storm destroyed the transmission tower of a television station in a small town. The station was located in a town in a flat prairie with no tall buildings. Its former 300-foot tower enabled it to serve a large farming community, and the management wanted to restore service while a new tower was being erected. The problem was temporarily solved by using a _____ .

b As part of a manufacturing process, the inside lip of a deep cup-shaped casting is machine threaded. The company found that metal chips produced by the threading operation were difficult to remove from the bottom of the casting without scratching the sides. A designer engineer was able to solve this problem by having this operation performed _____ .

**FLUENCY**
Unusual uses (Guilford, 1954)
Name as many uses as you can think of for:
a) a toothpick
b) a brick
c) a paper clip

**FLEXIBILITY**
Product improvement (Torrance, 1966). The subject is presented with a series of objects, such as children's toys or instruments used in his or her particular occupation, and asked to make suggestions for their improvement.

**FLUENCY**
Word association (Getzels and Jackson, 1962). Write as many meanings as you can for each of the following words:
a) dock       c) pitch
b) sack       d) fair

**ORIGINALITY**
Interpret these drawings (Guilford,1959)

Usual responses
The sun
Two igloos
Three people sitting at a table
Table with glasses on it
Raindrops

Unusual responses
Lollipop bursting into pieces
Two haystacks on a flying carpet
Three mice eating a piece of cheese
A foot and toes
Forms hanging

**(c) ORIGINALITY**
Complete this drawing (Barson,1958)

Ordinary response          Creative response

**FIGURE 9.10**
**A variety of creativity tests. (Lefrancois, 1992)**

"highly creative." Similarly, they identified a group of adolescents wh scored in the top 20 percent on measures of intelligence but were not in th top 20 percent on measures of creativity. These they labeled "high IQ." Th average IQ of the highly creative group was 23 points lower than the average IQ of the high IQ group; it was even lower than the average IQ of the entire student population in their school.

We can regard creativity tests as being valuable for understanding how individuals use and apply their knowledge.

## Biological Influences on Creativity

Recent evidence points to biology as a determinant of certain creative talents. For example, you might not think of mathematical talent as creative because the lower levels of addition, subtraction, multiplication, and division are based on convergent thinking. However, the higher levels of mathematics such as calculus require divergent thinking. Stanley and Benbow found that mathematical talent was biologically influenced (McKean, 1987). They had collected data on children who, before the age of 13, score 700 or better on the math Scholastic Achievement Test (the minimum score on the SAT is 200 and the maximum is 800). The surprising discovery was that among the 292 high scores on the math test, males outnumber females 12 to 1! Even though it has been well documented that in math males do better than females at age 17 (the usual age at which students take the SAT), that difference has been attributed to the fact that males take more math classes than females. Stanley and Benbow's findings at age 13 were surprising because the amount of math taken by females and males in elementary and junior high school is the same.

It appears there are some biological influences on creativity, specifically on mathematical talent. We now discuss contexts that influence creativity and how these contexts interact with biology.

## Contextual Influences on Creativity

There is evidence that creativity can be enhanced by the contexts of home, school, and community. MacKinnon (1962) studied the home environments of creative architects. He found that the mothers of these men provided continued opportunities and encouragement for their sons' intellectual growth.

According to Feldman (1982), more than innate creative talent is required to produce a genius. First, the field (architecture, music, science) has to exist. Second, the person must be exposed to the field at the proper time (taking a child to a concert when the child is curious or motivated). Third, the person must have continuous, careful instruction (a nine-year-old violinist and composer who is given lessons in violin and piano as well as music theory and composition). Last, community forces have to be ready to accept the creative contribution of the person (an African tribe is unlikely to appreciate a computer whiz).

Bloom (1985) and colleagues found that among the 120 Olympic athletes, concert pianists, sculptors, theoretical mathematicians, and research neurologists interviewed, all reported needing encouragement, help and support of others to "make it." Parents and teachers were critical to their success. Not only did the parents provide encouragement and financial support for lessons, they removed obstacles to their children's progress (for example, they drove children long distances to take lessons from a certain teacher). Generally, the child's first teacher was reported as having been inspiring, admired what the child was doing, and was excited about the child's progress. The second teacher stressed hard work and precision. The third teacher was a role model who had high achievements and drove the

Some studies suggest that creativity is biologically determined, but encouragement of family, friends, and role models probably sustains an interest in various creative activities.

## F.Y.I.

Researchers, by modifying adult spatial tests, found an early advantage in spatial performance reliably appearing in males by age 10 and the maintaining of that advantage through age 18 (Johnson & Meade, 1987). They explain their findings as possibly due to gender differences in the sensitivity to and preference for visual versus auditory stimuli observable in infancy, with males preferring visual, and females preferring auditory (McGuiness, 1976).

Our culture encourages creativity by its respect of innovativeness.

child toward excellence. The child, too, played a part in his success. H invested hours of time and hard work to practice the talent.

## Interaction of Biological and Contextual Influences on Creativity

If certain talented families are observed such as the Jacksons, Fondas and Kennedys, one might assume creativity is inherited. However, some times creative geniuses "pop up" in seemingly ordinary families. For exam ple, the famous pianist Arthur Rubenstein came from a family that, in hi own words, "lacked the slightest musical gifts" (Gardner, 1983, p.113).

Because creativity is not exhibited until a child is of school ag (sometimes preschool age) because of certain mental prerequisites (a certai amount of knowledge; the ability to analyze, synthesize, and evaluate infor mation; ability to communicate), it is impossible to separate the biologica from the contextual influences on creativity. For example, while creativit can be enhanced through training, those more creative before trainin remain so (Kogan, 1983).

A strong relation appears to exist between divergent thinking an play (Lieberman, 1977). Dansky (1980) found children's ability to fantasiz linked with high performance on divergent thinking tasks. What play mate rials stimulate fantasy or make-believe? Pepler and Ross (1981) gave group of three- and four-year-old children different types of toys. One group wa given a form board and different colored and shaped pieces, which fit int holes on the board (a *convergent* task because only one piece fits into on hole). The other group was given toy animals, vehicles, and different shaped blocks (a *divergent* task because many things could be done with th toys provided). The children were then tested on convergent and divergen tasks that were different from the play situations. The results showed tha divergent play enhanced the uniqueness of responses on the divergent thinking tasks; this was not true of the children who were in the convergen play set-up, nor was it true of the control groups where there were no pla materials. Divergent play even enabled the children to do better on the con vergent tasks because they could expand their problem-solving strategie On the other hand, convergent play only seemed to enhance performanc on convergent-thinking tasks similar to the play set-up.

Although this experiment showed exposure to certain types of pla materials enhanced divergent thinking, other research studies have show that those who initially score high or low on divergent thinking tasks may individually, do better after intervention, but their relationship to others i the group who were exposed to the same intervention remains the sam (Kogan, 1983). Box 9.3 discusses how creative thinking can be enhanced.

## Box 9.3  ENHANCING CREATIVE THINKING

It has been documented that training requiring fluency, flexibility, and originality enhances creative thought in school-age children, high school students, and college students (Glover & Gary, 1976; Glover & Sautter, 1977; Glover, 1980). Based on the research on creativity and training studies, some suggestions follow (Glover & Bruning, 1987):
1. Encourage all questions. Ask the child, "What made you think of that?"

2. Find something positive in all ideas.
3. Reward creativity—praise ideas, display children's work, give points for the *most* ideas or most *original* ideas, and so on.
4. Expect creativity—"I'm sure you can think of another way to do this problem."
5. Model creativity—be fluent (increase the number of ideas related to what is being discussed), flexible (talk about differences among ideas being discussed), and original (come up with something brand new) whenever possible.

# RELATION BETWEEN INFORMATION PROCESSING, INTELLIGENCE, AND CREATIVITY

Many of Gardner's intelligences can be identified in this photo: verbal, logical-mathematical, spatial skills, social skills, and self-knowledge.

Sternberg (1983) proposed a triarchic theory of intelligence that incorporates divergent and convergent thinking and also includes using these skills effectively in one's environment. Sternberg suggests that intelligence includes not only the abilities measured on IQ tests (such as problem solving) but also the ability to deal with novelty and *automatize* (make automatic) mental processes as well as to adapt to one's environment. The ability to deal with novelty involves thinking about new kinds of concepts and only the familiar ones (compare this to Piaget's concept of *accommodation*). When Robin bought a computer, learning to use the word processing program was very novel. It took her a while to think like the computer. The ability to automatize involves doing things without conscious thought thus requiring minimal mental efforts to add new information (compare this to Piaget's concept of *assimilation*). Thus, according to Steinberg, novelty and automation trade off with each other; the more efficient a person is at one, the more resources are left for the other (compare this to Piaget's concept of *equilibration*). The more intelligent person can automatize novel tasks quickly. For example, speed is often a factor on most tests, so the more automatized one's responses are on the easy questions, the more time one can spend on the difficult (novel) ones.

If Sternberg is right in his assumption that more intelligent people automatize novel tasks quicker, this might explain why an infant's response to novel stimulation is significantly correlated with later IQ ( O'Conner, Cohen & Parmelee, 1984; Rose & Wallace, 1985).

Sternberg's theory is concerned with the practical application of intelligence in real world situations. Some people do well on IQ tests but are not creative; others are creative but do not do well on IQ tests. Success in society depends on knowing how to use one's cognitive abilities to the best advantage in the world. Thus, intelligence and creativity need to be examined within sociocultural contexts (Helms, 1992). What is considered intelligent or creative in one context may not be so in another context. Writing books can be an intelligent and creative pursuit in our society; however, in a culture that has no written language, writing a book might be considered folly.

Gardner (1983) hypothesizes that at least seven broad categories of intelligence exist. Three are conventional in that they encompass convergent abilities and have been tested. They are verbal or linguistic, logica[l,] mathematical, and spatial skills. The other four are unconventional in th[at] not only do they encompass divergent abilities but they have not been tes[t-]ed or documented empirically as has intelligence. They are musical abilit[y,] bodily or kinesthetic skills, social or interpersonal skills, and intraperson[al] or self-knowledge. Gardner defends his categories of intelligence with th[e] following rationale: Each of the seven can be destroyed by brain dama[ge] because they are located in different areas of the brain; each shows up [in] highlighted form in the talents of gifted people or **idiots savants** (individ[u-]als who have low IQs, yet possess extraordinary talent in some area), a[nd] each involves unique cognitive skills.

Gardner's theory includes not only Western definitions of intel[li-]gence, but also those of other cultures. For example, in the Puluwat cultu[re] of the Caroline Islands, intelligence may be defined as the ability to nav[i-]gate by the stars. However, some feel Gardner has inappropriately include[d] creative talents in his definition of intelligence because some of the abiliti[es] Gardner has identified as intelligence, such as musical or athletic talent, a[re] not significant in adapting to the real world. The one thing psychologis[ts] have agreed on about the definition of intelligence, however, is that [it] involves the ability to adapt to one's environment.

## CRITICAL THINKING & YOU

ome people believe that intelligence is a general capacity that each human possesses to a greater or lesser extent and that it can be measured.

**ANALYSIS:** Review this chapter; give two reasons that support the preceding statement and two explanations that refute it.

**SYNTHESIS:** Define intelligence and creativity and compare their applications in terms of success in school and life.

**EVALUATION:** How is information processing related to intelligence and creativity?

# SUMMARY

- Information processing involves individual differences and developmental changes in how we use knowledge, our storehouse of information.
- Generally, we selectively attend to certain stimuli that we perceive in the environment.
- We encode our perceptions into our memories.
- Then we retrieve them as needed to solve problems.
- Attention is studied via novelty and habituation observations.
- Memory is studied via recall and recognition experiments. Problem solving is studied via analogies, and science and math experiments.
- Selective attention involves actively choosing stimuli to attend to while ignoring other stimuli.
- Memory involves storage and retrieval of information.
- Memory strategies involve rehearsal, imagery, and chunking.
- Some biological influences on developmental changes in memory are myelinization, and the increase and subsequent decrease of synapses in the cerebral cortex.
- Some contextual influences on developmental changes in memory are play and socialization.
- Problem solving involves generating a solution or set of solutions and evaluating their success.
- Intelligence is the ability to learn from experience; the ability to acquire and retain knowledge; the ability to respond quickly and successfully to new situations; and the ability to use reason in solving problems.
- Tests have been developed to assess intelligence; the most common ones used are the Stanford-Binet and the Wechsler. Both assess intelligence by how an individual differs from the average.
- The formula for figuring one's IQ (intelligence quotient) is to divide mental age (MA) by chronological age (CA) and multiply by 100 (IQ = MA/CA x 100).
- The main criticism of intelligence tests is that they are culturally biased. Some alternatives have been developed.
- The Bayley Mental and Motor Scales are one of the most widely used measurements of infant development.
- One biological influence on intelligence is evolution of the brain.
- Another biological influence on intelligence is heredity.
- Contextual influences on intelligence are family (birth order, interaction patterns, social class), school (teacher expectations, peer values), and intervention programs.
- Impulsive learners are quick to select a solution to a problem.
- Reflective learners think about many possible solutions before choosing a solution.
- Field-dependent learners rely on the context of the problem to solve it.
- Field-independent learners can analyze the complete problem into parts to arrive at a solution regardless of the context.
- Creativity is a unique cognitive style in which a novel (new) end product is developed and has value.
- Creativity does not appear to correlate with scores on IQ tests because IQ tests measure convergent thinking processes and creativity involves divergent thinking processes.
- Divergent thinking involves fluency, flexibility, and originality.
- Sternberg feels that divergent and convergent thought, and the ability to use these skills effectively in one's environment are the components of intelligence and that the strategies one uses to deal with novelty and automatize mental processes enable one to effectively adapt to the environment.
- Gardner feels intelligence is composed of divergent and convergent thought, which includes linguistic or verbal, logical-mathematical, and spatial skills. However, he includes musical ability, bodily-kinesthetic skills, interpersonal or social skills, and intrapersonal or self-knowledge under divergent abilities.

## RELATED READINGS

Bloom, B.S. (1964). *Stability and change in human characteristics*. New York: John Wiley.

Bloom, B.S. (Ed.). (1985). *Developing talent in young people*. New York: Random House.

Gardner, H. (1983). *Frames of mind: The theory of multiple intelligences*. New York: Basic Books.

Getzels, J.W., & Jackson, P.W. (1962). *Creativity and intelligence: Explorations with gifted students*. New York: John Wiley.

Hunt, J. McV. (1961). *Intelligence and experience*. New York: Ronald Press.

Kail, R. (1990). *The development of memory in children* (3rd ed.). New York: W.H. Freeman.

Segal, J., & Segal, Z. (1985). *Growing up smart and happy*. New York: McGraw Hill.

Sternberg, R.J. (Ed.). (1982). *The handbook of human intelligence*. New York: Cambridge University Press.

Sternberg, R.J. (Ed.). (1985). *Human abilities: An information-processing approach*. New York: W.H. Freeman.

## ACTIVITY

To compare how different-aged children problem solve and remember, interview a five-year-old, a ten-year-old, and a 15-year-old.

1. Record their solutions to the following problem: *Pretend you lost the key to your house and you could not get in without it. How would you try to find it?*
2. Compare the strategies each used to solve the problem. Note a disorganized versus organized approach and a random versus systematic approach.
3. Then ask what each child would do in the future in order to remember where the key was placed. Record the answers.
4. Compare the strategies each used to remember.
5. Finally, ask each to name as many different places they can think of to hide a key so no one else could find it. Record their responses.
6. Compare the number and originality of responses.

# Language Development: How We Communicate

*Every vital development in language is a development of feeling as well.*
**Thomas Stearns Eliot**

# ABOUT LANGUAGE

One day at the end of fourth grade as Kenny walked down the street toward his house, he could be seen talking to himself. Every once in a while he would laugh and then start all over again. When he bounced in the door he yelled, "Darla, where are you? I have a joke to tell you." Darla came out of the kitchen and Kenny said, "When I say something you answer, OK?"

Darla said, "Yeah, yeah, I know. Go ahead."

"Knock, knock."

*"Who's there?"*

"Lettuce."

*"Lettuce who?"*

"Lettuce in; it's cold out here!"

Kenny burst into giggles. Darla smiled and said, "I've got one for you."

"Knock, knock."

*"Who's there?"*

"Amos."

*"Amos who?"*

"A mosquito bit me!"

Kenny laughed and Darla laughed with him. Kenny, like his peers, had just discovered how to play with words. To do that Kenny had become aware that words have more than one meaning depending on the context. Kenny asked Darla to teach him her joke so he could tell it to his friends. By the end of the school year, Kenny and his friends had a huge supply of jokes.

That summer when it was not raining, Kenny and his friends would gather at someone's house. The house was chosen on the basis of whose mother was not home. Kenny and his friends would take turns calling people up and, in their most adult voice, they'd ask, "Is your refrigerator running?" When the person said, "Yes," they would say, ""Then you'd better go catch it!" and then they would hang up laughing hysterically.

Preschool and young schoolage children who are in the stage of pre operations, one of Piaget's stages of cognitive development, cannot understand the incongruities that make these jokes humorous, because the language skills of four- to seven-year-olds are not extensive enough nor have children of this age gathered enough information about the world. Schoolage children and young adolescents who are in the stage of concrete operations can have the concept of reversibility, so they can go back and forth between the meanings of words depending on the context.

adolescents and adults in the stage of formal operations can deal with abstractions so they not only enjoy puns, or plays-on-words, but absurdities as well.

In this chapter we will discuss the significance of language, its components, and the sequence of language development. Also, we will examine biological, contextual, and interactional influences on language development.

*Language* is the expression or communication of thoughts and feelings by means of vocal sounds and combinations of such sounds to which meaning is attributed. **Linguistics** is the study of language.

An infant enters the world with only one means of communication—the cry—yet by the time she enters kindergarten she knows more than 8,000 words as well as how to put these words to work in comprehensible sentences.

Language development follows a pattern. Although an infant's first words and the eventual combination of them into sentences appears haphazard, all children throughout the world learn a language in the same order: They cry, coo, babble, say their first word, combine two words together, and utter a sentence. They learn the word for *in* and *on* before *under*. When they get to the two-word stage, they ask for more of something ("more juice") or say "no" to something ("no shoes") before they use verbs as in "Mommy eat." English-speaking children tag *ing* onto the end of verbs before they tag *ed*. "Why" questions do not surface until well after a toddler asks the first "what" question. Even mistakes in grammar, such as saying "bringed" instead of "brought," are predictable and occur at a specific point in a child's language development.

Some have argued that the universal order of language development indicates that language development is innate and will evolve unaided, like crawling or walking. Others say that learning is responsible, because children learn to talk by imitation and because talking is rewarded. Still others say that biology predisposes and experience exposes. Psychologists and linguists agree more on the sequence of language development than on how the process of language acquisition occurs. At this point, however, it is safe to say that although an infant might be born with certain innate qualities that help language development, such as the ability to distinguish between human sounds, a child will not learn to speak unless guided by other speaking people.

One influence on language development over time was the biological evolution of the brain, nervous system, and vocal apparatus. The brain has specialized areas for language. Another influence on language development was the cultural evolution wherein humans began to work together in groups and share resources to survive. Thus, the physical capacity to communicate plus the environmental need to do so provided the adaptive conditions for humans to acquire language.

## SIGNIFICANCE OF LANGUAGE

The earliest prehistoric communications were related to survival—a warning of danger, a request for help, a discovery of food, an indication of a desire to mate. When humans began to use tools, communication functioned as a means to teach others; language became the vehicle by which knowledge could be passed on, making first-hand experience or "reinventing the wheel," unnecessary. Thus, language played a significant role in the advancement of humankind from prehistoric times to today's modern technology.

Some psychologists say the ability to learn language depends on one's cognitive development.

# F.Y.I.

The human species acquired language some 10,000 to 100,000 years ago (Swadish, 1971).

Language also is significant in what it does for the individual. To illustrate, Halliday (1973), a linguist, observed the development of language in his son. He could distinguish the following seven different functions of language:

1. *Instrumental*—language is a means of satisfying wants and needs.
2. *Regulatory*—a child discovers language is a means by which others try to control his behavior and by which he can control the behavior of others.
3. *Interaction*—a child realizes language is a means to establish and maintain social contact.
4. *Personal*—language is a way of asserting oneself and expressing individuality.
5. *Heuristic, or learning*—language is a means by which one can ask questions and get information about the world.
6. *Imaginative*—the child discovers she can create images and pleasurable effects by talking.
7. *Representation*—the function of talking to inform.

Thus, language is significant to the individual in that it is a means of
- expression
- relating to others
- learning
- creating

## COMPONENTS OF LANGUAGE

Language is composed of four segments: *phonology, semantics, grammar,* and *pragmatics*. **Phonology** is the study of speech sounds and involves how one understands and produces the speech sounds of one's language. The basic units of sound in a language, or **phonemes**, range from about 10 to 70 depending on the particular language; English has about 40 (Reich, 1986). Some examples are the *b*, the *ah*, the *d* in the word *bad*. Phonemes are the building blocks for an expandable set of words because they can be combined in many ways as in *bat, bit, cat, cab*. When phonemes change so do word meanings. Neonates cannot distinguish between phonemes shortly after birth, and they begin producing them when they start to coo at about two months. *Cooing* involves mostly vowel sounds produced in the back of the throat. At about six months infants combine consonants and vowels ("ba, ba, ba, ba") by using their lips and tongue in what is known as *babbling*. Phonology then gives some insight into how children learn language.

**Semantics** is the study of word meaning and involves how concepts are expressed in words and word combinations. The significance for language development is that it enables us to comprehend how children understand the meaning of different words and sentences and how children learn to use words correctly to communicate. For example, young children might use the word *doggie* to signify any animal with four legs and a tail. As children get older, they refine the meaning of *doggie* to refer only to dogs and use other words to refer to different animals such as *cow*.

**Grammar** is that part of the study of language which deals with the form and structure of words termed **morphology** and with the rules that govern their customary arrangement in phrases and sentences, called **syn-**

ix. The smallest unit of a language that by itself has a recognizable meaning is called a **morpheme**. For example, *pet* is one morpheme, whereas *pet-ed* and *petting* are two; *ed* is a morpheme because it signifies the past tense. The ending "ing" also is a morpheme signifying present tense. Studying how children use morphemes gives a clue to their understanding of word usage in their language. When children combine words into sentences applying syntactic rules, they are exhibiting linguistic creativity rather than imitation. Each language has specific syntactic rules for expressing possession ("my book"), negation ("no milk"), inquiry ("What is that?"), and standard word order (subject-verb-object, as in "She rode the bike"). The acquisition of syntax is usually accomplished by the child at age four or five.

**Pragmatics** is the study of rules governing how language is used in different social contexts. It involves taking turns, maintaining relevancy in a discussion, and using gestures and tone of voice to command meaning.

By studying pragmatics we can learn how children learn to take turns, how to adapt to talking about one topic while remaining concentrated, how they adjust their speech to converse with younger children or to communicate in different social settings (school versus playground).

# EARLY LANGUAGE DEVELOPMENT

Early language development consists of the development of prelinguistic skills, phonology, semantics, grammar, and pragmatics.

## PRELINGUISTIC SKILLS

Preparation for language development occurs long before the child utters what we recognize as words. For one, physical and brain maturation are taking place. The oral cavity is becoming larger, and the infant is gaining control over the tongue, jaw, and lips (Sachs, 1985). Until such control occurs, speech production is impossible. Neural connections are developing rapidly in the area of the brain which specializes in language. The growth of these connections is most rapid during the first two years (Goldman-Rakic, Isseroff, Schwartz & Bugbee, 1983), which is a time of rapid language development.

A second precursor to language growth is auditory perceptual abilities that enable infants to distinguish speech from other sounds, and to distinguish between phonemes. By the time infants are one month old, they can tell the difference between most language sounds (Aslin, Pisoni & Jusczyk, 1983). Understanding speech, or receptive language, occurs before productive language.

For a third precursor to language development, children must have the opportunity to interact with others by hearing language and using it. Infants begin interacting with caregivers by crying, smiling, gazing, and looking away. The more responsive caregivers are to infants' signals, the more infants sense they are effective in communicating. As they grow, their motor development enables them to visually track objects, to point and touch. These are considered prelinguistic speech acts in which the communication is intended to help the neonate achieve some goal (Bruner, 1983).

A fourth precursor to language is the ability to understand one's world. Until several cognitive advances occur, a child cannot use words meaningfully. For example, a basic understanding of the world involves the concept that people and objects exist on a permanent basis, that they exist although one cannot see them at the time. This concept is called *object permanence*. A child who cannot remember the existence of vanished objects cannot attach labels to objects with any consistency and so cannot speak

Another part of social interaction that precedes speech is turn-taking. Peek-a-boo or hide-and-seek is an example where the adult shows her face or an object, then hides, then shows it again.

about them. Most children begin to communicate with words toward the end of the first year, corresponding to the sensorimotor period, the time when they exhibit object permanence (Harding & Golinkoff, 1979).

Obviously, the first vocal communication is crying. Crying communicates distress. Another communication that occurs at about two months is cooing. Cooing is associated with contentment and can be described as vowel-like sounds from the back of the throat. The various sounds infants produce in early cooing are thought to be limited by the physical configuration of their mouths and the lack of voluntary control over the tongue and lips (Reich, 1986).

## PHONOLOGY

By the time the infant is between four and nine months, reduplication of syllables composed of consonants and vowels occurs, such as "baba." When this begins, the child is said to be in the **babbling** stage. During this stage greater numbers of clearly articulated vowels and consonants are formed. Also during this time, intonation patterns similar to those of adult speech appear so it sounds as if the infant is carrying on a conversation. Thus, during the babbling stage, the infant exhibits the basic repertoire of speech sounds he is capable of making.

While babbling appears to be an exercise in using the vocal apparatus and supply of speech sounds, it does not symbolize or refer to anything. Prior to uttering their first word, close to their first birthday, infants begin to use different sounds to refer to different objects or actions. Reich (1986) call these sounds *idiomorphs* because they are created by the child, and the child consistently uses them until they are replaced by standard words. Interestingly, children do not learn these from caregivers; rather, caregivers have to learn them from children. Some examples are *dah* signifying "gimme that," or "I want that one," or "bottle"; *wuh wuh* signifying dog, or horse, or cow. Kenny used the idiomorph *goy goy* to refer to his pacifier. Michael and Kate figured out what it meant because Kenny would look at it and point to it while saying "goy goy." He kept using the term long after he understood the word *pacifier*. At this like every other stage of language development, children understand more than they can express. When asked, "Where is mommy?" many one-month-old infants will look in her direction, or when told,"Wave bye-bye," will open and close their hand. Thus, idiomorphs indicate the child has reached a certain level of cognitive development, specifically, mental representation, wherein vocalizations, gestures, or both are used to communicate thoughts. To do this, a child has to have established the concept of object permanence indicating the ability to mentally represent something in its absence. When Kenny could not find his pacifier, he would say, "goy goy" between his cries.

## SEMANTICS

*Semantics* involves the meanings of words and how words are used.

### First Words

At about one year of age, most children produce their first word. It is only with consistent and spontaneous use with understanding that a word can be said to be acquired. The first words a child speaks are usually the words that are most important, familiar, and functional to the child. Nelson

Nelson found that most early words were general labels for categories of objects—such as *ball, doggie,* or *juice.*

1973) enlisted 18 families to keep a diary of everything their infants said during the months they were acquiring their first words. Some common categories of early words were specific labels for particular objects such as *Mommy*, action words (*bye-bye, want*), modifiers (*hot, dirty*), and words that express feelings or relationships (*no, mine*).

The first words acquired are significant clues to what the child is thinking because they are closely linked to objects the child can act on and to those objects that produce a change or movement (Greenfield & Smith, 1976). For example, the words *shoes, socks, toys*, and *cars* are more common than words denoting objects that are "just there" such as *tables, store*, or *trees*. Children also tend to use words at the moment when objects are changing and moving, suggesting a link between words and actions in a young child's mind (Greenfield, 1982). Yet, the object words are produced more often than the action words (Schwartz & Leonard, 1984).

Children's first words often mean different things compared with adults when they use the same words. There are characteristic ways that children treat early words. One is that they use a single word to mean many different things. This is termed **overextension**. For example, *birdie* is commonly overextended to refer to butterflies, bees, airplanes, or other flying objects. Children's early overextensions appear strongly influenced by perceptual features of the items named and by the way that the things named function in children's actions (Clark, 1973).

Children also commit the error of **underextension**, restricting the meaning of a word. For example, *car* can only be used to refer to those vehicles that look like mommy's van.

As children learn their first words, they use facial expressions, gestures, and intonation to communicate meaning. Looking at Daddy with hands outstretched, obviously conveys they want to be picked up by daddy. The use of a single word to convey a whole thought is called a **holophrase**. Some theorists believe these early one-word utterances, which stand for whole sentences, are the bases for later more differentiated language capacities (McNeill, 1970).

Other theorists (Greenfield & Smith, 1976) interpret the one-word utterance differently. They believe the single word does not stand for a whole sentence but rather for only a particular element of the situation the child is communicating. To these theorists, the single word is not a holophrase; it is simply one part of the total communication that includes nonverbal actions that help express the whole thought.

It is difficult to decide between competing theories of children's linguistic understanding at the stage of single-word utterances because a child cannot correct our assumptions. Certainly, adults respond as if a child's single-word utterances are meaningful. For example, a child says "car" and a parent responds by saying, "Oh, you want to go for a ride in the car." How much of this meaning is the child's and how much of it is the adult's interpretation of the utterance based on information gleaned from the context in which the child speaks? It is difficult to determine where a child's word leaves off and the adult's interpretation begins. Although this problem of interpretation never completely disappears, it becomes less vexing when the child begins to string words together.

## Two-Word Combinations

About seven months after children produce their first word, they begin to put words together to form two-word statements (Reich, 1986); this usually occurs between 18 and 24 months of age. The two-word stage is significant because it indicates an advance in children's ability to code their mental understanding in linguistic terms and to project their ideas into communication. It begins when children can process two words at a time without running out of space in their short-term memory.

When children combine two words, they can convey much meaning, such as the following (Slobin, 1972, p. 73), although they still rely on facial expressions and gestures to help them:

*Identification*: "See doggie."
*Location*: "Book there."
*Repetition*: "More milk."
*Nonexistence*: " All gone."
*Negation*: "Not wolf."
*Possession*: "My candy."
*Attribution*: "Big car."
*Agent-action*: "Mama walk."
*Action-direct-object*: "Give papa."
*Action-instrument*: "Cut knife."
*Question*: "Where ball?"

One interesting factor about this list is that the same pattern is used by children throughout the world. The examples are taken from utterances in English, German, Russian, Turkish, and Samoan (Slobin, 1972).

A child's two-word utterance differs substantially from adult word combinations. Beginning with two-word utterances and continuing until grammar is mastered, early sentences appear much like telegrams in that they contain nouns and verbs and convey meaning without the grammatically functional words such as articles and prepositions. These utterances are called **telegraphic speech**. If you were on a trip and your wallet was stolen, you might send a telegram home saying, "Wallet stolen. Send $500. Thanks." Because each word costs money, only the essential ones are included in the telegram.

Children in the two-word stage appear to be using a consistent pattern in their construction of these early sentences. This pattern is called *pivot grammar* (Braine, 1963). Although the child may have a vocabulary of 50 or more words, the first two-word sentences appear to originate from a small set of words. These were termed **pivot class words**. The other words in the sentence come from the remaining words in the child's vocabulary. This larger set of words is termed **open class words**. For a word to be designated as a pivot word, it has to appear frequently and its position must be fixed; that is, it has to appear *only* in the first position or only in the second position in a two-word combination. Pivot words as a class are small in number and are slowly added to children's vocabularies compared with words of the open class. The open class contains many words, words are added to it rapidly, and its constituents occasionally occur alone. Some examples are (Braine, 1963):

pivot-open order:    *No* bed
                     *More* cereal
open-pivot order:    Shoe *off*
                     Bunny *do*

As the pivot-order classification was applied in linguistics research, it was discovered that it failed to capture completely the system in children's early language. Although some words fit the pattern and always ppear to be either pivot or open words, many others are inconsistent Maratsos, 1983).

Investigators (Bloom, 1970; Bowerman, 1973; Brown, 1973) found that English-speaking children produced utterances that could be analyzed by the following patterns:

1. *Agent-Action*: A word denoting an action can be preceded by a word denoting the being, or agent, that performed the action, as in "Tommy hit"
2. *Action-Object*: A word denoting an action can be placed before a word denoting the recipient of the consequence of the action, as the object in "hit ball"
3. *Agent-Object*: A word denoting the initiator of an activity can be placed before a word denoting the recipient of the consequence as in "Mommy, lunch"
4. *Possessor-Possessed Object*: As in "mommy sock"
5. *Action-Location*: A word denoting an action can be placed before a word denoting the place or end point of the action as in "walk street"
6. *Located Object-Location*: A word denoting an object can be placed before a word denoting the location of the object as in "sweater chair," meaning the sweater is on the chair
7. *Attribute-Object*: A word denoting an attribute, or characteristic, of an object can be placed before the word denoting the object as in "big train"

Brown (1973) also noted the common use of what he called **referential operations**, the way in which children name or call attention to objects in their two-word utterances. Referential operations include:

1. *Nomination and Named Object* ("that book")
2. *Notice and Noticed Object* ("hi Mommy")
3. *Recurrence* ("more milk")
4. *Nonexistence and Nonexistent* ("no toy")
5. *Disappeared Object* ("no more juice")

Table 10.1 summarizes the milestones in language development.

# GRAMMAR

*Grammar* involves rules for word formation and word combination in sentences. Rules are a short cut to learning. If we know the rule, we can apply it to new situations rather than learning each time. For example, if you know the grammatical rule for making plurals, you just add "s" to *dog*, *cat*, and so on rather than memorizing separately each newly formed word.

To combine two words requires that the children analyze aspects of the situational meanings of words to account for how they may be ordered with respect to each other. According to Brown (1973), word usage and word order during the two-word stage correspond to the general cognitive concepts a child is developing at the time. Because of the child's changing

The reason researchers are so intensely interested in discovering a pattern to children's early speech is that it provides a clue to analytical capabilities in that once the child makes two-word utterances, the child is expressing relations. This has a bearing on language and cognitive development later in childhood.

## MILESTONES IN LANGUAGE DEVELOPMENT

### TABLE 10.1

| Age | Response |
| --- | --- |
| Birth | Crying |
| 1 month | One-syllable vocalization; attends to speech |
| 2 to 3 months | Cooing |
| 3 to 4 months | Vocalizes to social stimulation |
| 4 to 6 months | Babbling (*da, ma, di*) |
| 7 to 9 months | Reduplication of syllables (*mama, dada*); use of intonation |
| 9 months | Understands gestures and responds to "bye-bye" |
| 10 to 12 months | Responds to simple commands |
| 11 to 14 months | Says first word |
| 15 to 18 months | Says five or more words |
| 16 to 20 months | Understands "no" and simple commands ("Show me your eyes") |
| 20 months | Repeats things |
| 21 to 24 months | Uses two words in combination |
| 23 to 24 months | Uses first pronoun, phrase, sentence |
| 23 to 25 months | Understands prepositions "in" and "under" |
| 24 months | Vocabulary of more than 50 words |
| 24 to 30 months | Asks names of objects and repeats answers |
| 30 to 36 months | Vocabulary of about 1,000 words; understands most of what adults say |

(McCarthy, 1954; Lenneberg, 1967; Bayley, 1969

notions of the permanence of objects, for example, one could expect a child to be interested in the recurrence and disappearance of objects. The child is also likely to be interested in actions on objects and in possession of objects.

Grammar requires more than just a single word to be evident in children's speech. A major controversy in the area of grammatical development concerns how early children develop an appreciation of adult grammatical categories, such as subject-verb-object ("Baby drink milk" or "Daddy give toy"). Evidence for an early grasp of grammar leads one to believe language development, or acquisition of grammar, is biologically influenced. On the other hand, findings indicating grammar is not present in children's early word combinations leads one to believe other factors, such as context or the interaction of biological and contextual factors as exhibited in cognitive abilities, account for the acquisition of grammar.

Between the ages of two and three, children begin to use more than just two words in their sentences. Sentence length is measured for analytical and comparison purposes in terms of **mean length utterances (MLU)** which averages the number of morphemes rather than words per utterance. For example, "The boys are playing" has four words but six morphemes. The words are *the, boys, are, playing*, while the morphemes are *the , boy, s, are, play, ing*. Counting morphemes rather than words provides an index of a child's total potential for expressing meaning in a particular utterance. Brown (1973) proposed that MLU is a good index of a child's language maturity.

## Acquisition of Morphological Rules

Transition from two- to three-word sentences is gradual, sometimes with an insertion of a word as in "Mommy is eating," or an insertion of a morpheme as in "Mommy's lunch." This is the beginning of grammatical acquisition. Several years are required for the grammatical rules of one's native language to be used consistently in conversation (Maratsos, 1983).

As children make the transition from two-to three-word sentences, the morphemes they acquire appear to follow a regular pattern (Brown, 1973; de Villiers & de Villiers, 1973; Kuczaj, 1977). The sequence is displayed in table 10.2.

## ORDER OF ACQUISITION OF ENGLISH GRAMMATICAL MORPHEMES

### TABLE 10.2.

| Morpheme | Example |
| --- | --- |
| 1. Present progressive *ing* | "He *sing*ing." |
| 2. Preposition *in* | "*In* box." |
| 3. Preposition *on* | "*On* table." |
| 4. Plural *s* | "Two dog*s*." |
| 5. Irregular past tense | "It *broke*." |
| 6. Possessive | "Adam*'s* ball" |
| 7. Uncontractible use of "to be" | "Eve *is* girl" |
| 8. Articles *a* and *the* | "That *a* truck;" "That *the* dog." |
| 9. Regular past tense | "Adam *walked*." |
| 10. Third person, regular present tense | "He *walks*." |
| 11. Third person, irregular present tense | "She *has* cookie;" "He *does* hit." |
| 12. Uncontractible auxiliary verb *to be* | "We *are* eating." |
| 13. Contractible use of *to be* | "That*'s* Mommy." |
| 14. Contractible auxiliary verb *to be* | "Doggie*'s* eating." |

**(Brown, 1973)**

The morpheme likely to appear first is *ing*. (This form is called the present progressive verb case.) This verb form allows children to describe their ongoing activity. Morphemes indicating location, possession, and number make their appearance next. Children have many opportunities to use these words in the course of play with toys; dolls go *in* their cribs; blocks are stacked *on* top of one another, and a little girl's lunch belongs to *her*. Morphemes that mark complex relations, such as "I'm going" (which codes a relation between the subject of the action and the time of the action), are generally slower to emerge.

The appearance of grammatical morphemes is a strong indicator that children are implicitly beginning to distinguish parts of speech, at least nouns and verbs, because their speech conforms to rules about which morphemes should be attached to which words in a sentence. Children demonstrate their intuitive grasp of the rules for using grammatical morphemes because they do not apply a past-tense morpheme to a noun ("girled"), nor do they place articles before verbs ("a walked"). By the time they are five or six years old, most children will have command of all the standard parts of speech they will use as adults.

## Overregularization of Morphological Rules

After children have mastered a morphological rule (how words are formed, as in adding *ed* to the past tense, *s* to make plurals), they progress through a period when they use the rule even when an exception is the

By the time the child is five or six years old, she returns to using the correct morphological rules in speech.

norm; for example, they will say "foots" instead of "feet." It is as though the strategy is to "avoid exceptions" so the rule will be better learned (Slobir 1973). By **overregularization**, the application of a morphological rule to all cases, including the exceptions, a child is attempting to make language more systematic.

Overregularization is significant in language development because it indicates the child has figured out the structure and formation of words in her native language. Interestingly, before age three, when overregularization begins, a child uses the correct form of the word in exceptional cases. For example, a child will say, "My feet hurt," whereas after the child figured out how to put verbs in the past tense and pluralize, she says, "My *foot* hurt."

To assess the development of morphological rules, Berko (1958) showed 32 preschool children and 61 first graders pictures of objects and actions that had nonsensical descriptions. She wanted to see if the children could supply the correct form of the noun or verb even though these were nonsense words they had never heard. For example, "This is a *wug*. Now there is another one. There are two of them. There are two ____." Another example is, "This is a man who knows how to *rick*. He is *ricking*. He did the same thing yesterday. What did he do yesterday? Yesterday he ____." Even the preschoolers could supply the correct morphemes to many of the nonsensical descriptions. For example, they said "wugs" and "ricked." Berko's findings show that children construct mental rules for morphology when they use language; they do not learn the rules by imitating adults.

## Acquisition of Syntactical Rules

Children construct morphological rules and they construct syntactical rules (how words are organized into sentences). For example in English adjectives are placed before nouns, such as "big boys," and the word order in a question is different from that in the answer ("What is the girl doing?" versus "The girl is skipping.") Applying syntactical rules correctly is crucial to communication. For example, in the sentences "John hit Bob" and "Bob hit John," the words are identical but the word order tells who did what to whom.

Syntax develops gradually because it is an extremely complex task. To illustrate, the development of the ability to ask questions will be traced (Brown, Cazden & Bellugi, 1969). There are two types of questions in the English language—*yes/no questions* (Did you put your toys away?) and *wh questions* (begin with what, where, when, why, who, how).

To form a yes/no question, the word order of a statement has to be changed: "Daddy is cooking," becomes, "Is Daddy cooking?" Two-year-old children have not learned how to change the word order of a declarative statement to form a question, so they raise their intonation at the end of a sentence when they want to ask a question: "Daddy cook?" At around three years of age when children speak in longer sentences, they add auxiliary, or helping, verbs to sentences and move them as required to communicate what they want to say: "Is Daddy cooking?" Also they use more complicated yes/no questions such as ones with a negative: "Can't you fix this?" Questions with a tag ending ("I can play, can't I?") do not appear until after age four.

*Wh* questions are harder to form than yes/no ones, which is why young children often make errors doing so. To form a *wh* question ("Where is Daddy going?"), the order of subject (Daddy) and auxiliary verb (is) must be inverted from the declarative ("Daddy is going to the store.") and a *wh* word must be placed at the beginning of the sentence. Young children learn early where to put the *wh* word, but they require more time to learn the auxiliary inversion (Kuczaj & Brannick, 1979). Thus, it is common to hear preschool children asking such questions as "What Mommy is doing?"

The acquisition of *wh* questions occurs in a certain order. *What, where,* and *who* questions that ask about concrete objects, places, and people appear first. *When, how,* and *why* refer to more difficult concepts such as time, manner, and causality, and they appear later. These questions also are more difficult to construct than are *what, where,* and *who* questions (Tyack & Ingram, 1977; de Villiers & de Villiers, 1979).

Although most English grammar (morphology and syntax) is acquired by age five, subtle forms of syntax pose problems for the child until about age ten. For example, in the sentence, "John told Bill to shovel the driveway," most five-year-olds understand who told whom to do what. However, in the sentence, "John promised Bill to shovel the driveway," the meaning is more subtle. Most five-year-olds will interpret it as John telling Bill to shovel the driveway.

Chomsky (1969) studied five- to ten-year-old children on their knowledge of subtle syntax by showing them a big doll and asking "Is the doll easy to see or hard to see?" Even the youngest said the doll was easy to see. When Chomsky put a blindfold on the doll and asked the same question, 78 percent of the five-year-olds and 57 percent of the six-year-olds said that the doll was "hard to see."

Thus, as children's language ability develops, they learn to go beneath the surface features of the sentence to figure out the true relation it codes.

*What is this?* **A toy school bus.** *Where does it go?* **To school.** *Who rides in it?* **Children on the way to school. These are the first series of questions children are likely to ask before:** *When does it take children to school? How does the bus take them?* **and** *Why does it take them?*

## PRAGMATICS

Language is more than an application of grammatical rules; it is expressive and it is social; it serves to communicate feelings and needs and to respond to feelings and needs. *Pragmatics* involves how language is used in social contexts.

To communicate effectively, one must consider the listener. For example, when a teacher is lecturing and sees blank looks on students' faces, the teacher either should ask if there is a question about the information or should rephrase what was said in a more simple way. Likewise, to respond effectively, one must understand what is being said. One can indicate understanding by nodding. One can indicate confusion by a facial expression or by saying, "Huh?"

Children learn language pragmatics early. Some evidence that children consider the listener can be observed in two- or three-year-olds' use of "baby talk" when addressing younger children or dolls and their use of a deeper voice to give commands to dogs or cats. Also, when playing the role of teacher or doctor, their language becomes more formal (Rice, 1984).

Four-year-old children were found to use shorter sentences, speak more slowly, and use simpler vocabulary and syntax when explaining the rules of a game to younger children (Shatz & Gelman, 1973).

Young children appear to understand that when you talk, you take turns. In her extensive study on children's talk, Garvey (1984) observed that among three-year-olds only 5 percent of their turns at talking overlapped; when they did, the overlap was brief and involved only one or two words.

**Communication involves eye contact, turn-taking gestures, and language.**

## Egocentric Speech versus Social Speech

Findings on children's use of pragmatics present a challenge to Jean Piaget's (1926) hypothesis about egocentrism. Piaget said children under the age of seven were egocentric because they could not take the perspective of their listener. The egocentric child "does not bother to know to whom he is speaking nor whether he is being listened to…. The talk is egocentric because he does not attempt to place himself at the point of view of his hearer…. He feels no desire to influence his hearer nor to tell him anything." (Piaget, 1955, p. 32). The following example illustrates the lack of collaboration in a common activity. The children are drawing pictures, and each one is talking about his picture (Piaget, 1955, p. 77):

Lev (5, 11): "It begins with Goldilocks. I'm writing the story of the three bears. The daddy bear is dead. Only the daddy was too ill."

Gen (5, 11): "I used to live at Saleve. I lived in a little house and you had to take the funicular railway to go and buy things."

Geo (6, 0): "I can't do the bear."

Li (6, 10): "That's not Goldilocks."

Lev: "I haven't got curls."

Garvey and Hogan (1988) explain that while they observed many instances of *egocentric speech* in three and a half- to five-year-old children's play situations including monologues, muttering, self-answered questions, and self-guidance on tasks, they also observed mutually responsive speech or *social speech*, that is, speech adapted to the talk or nonverbal behavior of their partner. Thus, children who are given opportunities to play together move from egocentric speech to social speech to facilitate mutual engagement. An example of mutual engagement follows (Garvey & Hogan, 1988, p. 201):

Child A: "If I grow up my voice will change and when you grow up your voice will change. My mom told me. Did your mommy tell you?"

Child B: "No, your mommy's wrong. My voice, I don't want it to change. Oh, well."

Child A: "Oh, well, we'll stay little, right?"

Child B: "What?"

Child A: "We'll stay little."

Child B: "No, I don't want to. I *want* my voice to change. I don't care if it changes."

Child A: "I care."

However, playing together is not enough to foster communicative speech. Nelson and Gruendel (1988) believe it is shared knowledge of social scripts—how things are done, what to expect next, who plays what role—that serves to overcome egocentrism. The following example illustrates a shared script. There is a toy model of a schoolroom, and toy people are used as props. Both children had similar knowledge of the school day on which they could share. (G-1 is girl #1; G-2 is girl #2.)

*Part I*    (Rings the bell)

G-1:    "Stop!! The school is open!"(rings bell)
        "School is open. Walk, walk, walk, walk in.
        Whoops!"

G-2:    "You shut up this end."(Closes the front flap of the
        school house.)

G-1:    "Yeah, shut up this end and let's get all these things
        ready."

G-2:    "Yeah, it's night-time. We have to go home now."

G-1:    "Yep. Now where's the other person? Put it, put it
        on, now, yeah." (Brings people out of school.) "Now
        close this up."

G-2:    "They have to go home! Why do you think they
        have to stay in school! They have to go home!"

G-1:    (Laughs.)

G-2:    "And the teacher has to go home, too. What do you
        think she's in there. She likes to sleep in a school.
        Nobody sleeps in a school."

G-1:    "Nooo."

*Part II*

G-2:    "OK. Here's her house and she's sleeping right here.
        She's in here. OK. Here comes…She's right next to
        the school" (walks teacher to school). "Right here.
        She doesn't have to walk too far."

G-1:    (Rings bell) "School's open!"

G-2:    "Ding, ding! Go in."

G-1:    "Having snack."

G-2:    (Rings bell loudly)

G-1:    "Having snack, no. I want to ring the bell for snack."
        (rings it)

G-2:    "Here, here."

G-1:    "What's that?"

G-2:    "In case she sits right there." (Puts people in chairs
        at tables.)

G-1:    "Whoops. School is closed."

G-2:    "All the people out." (Moves them out).

G-1:    "School is closed." (Rings the bell)

G-2:    "Walking home! Walking home!" (Both sing-song
        this way as they move people around the room.)

G-3:    "Back at school, back at school!" (Rings the bell)

G-2:    "Walking home, walking home."

G-1: "School is ready."

G-2: "School is ready! Uh-oh, ba sketti-oh!"

G-1: "The door's closed, because it's not locked up. But you can walk in this door." (Walks person in.) "Not snack time, yet. First, you take your coat off."

G-2: "Hee, I come to school, walk. The Teacher!" (Walks teacher into school.)

G-1: "Then, then you play, then you play."

G-2: "This is the teacher. This is the teacher. She's looking out the window."

G-1: "These guys are playing outside now. Now people are playing outside."

G-2: "No, they're taking a nap now. Put' em in! They're going to take a nap now. Teacher, the teacher's rubbing her back."

G-1: "This is the teacher, and she's walking outside to get something from her car. Ba-doop, ba-doop." (Walks teacher to pretend car.) "Get something out from her car." (Laughs, walks back inside)

G-2: "Her mother's car is broken, so let's ride in the teacher's car."

G-1: "Yeah. Rubbing your back, rubbing your back." (Makes teacher rub children's backs.) "Ooops, school's closed!"

G-2: "School's closed! Wake up everybody. Time to go outside, time to go outside. Whee!!!" (Everyone is moved outside the school.)

*Source: Nelson, K. & Gruendel, J. M. (1988). At morning it's lunchtime. A scriptal view of children's dialogue. In M.B. Franklin & S. S. Barten (Eds.), Child Language: A Reader. New York: Oxford University Press, pp. 272-273.*

Thus, pragmatics involves knowledge of social situations. When the child lacks the knowledge, the speech is egocentric. Likewise, for adults to converse they must establish and maintain a shared context based on a mutual understanding of situation and script. Adults differ from children in that when they do not understand how to respond in a situation, they usually keep quiet.

## LATER LANGUAGE DEVELOPMENT

During the early school years, words are understood and used on a concrete level ("sharp" is what a knife is), whereas in the later school years approaching adolescence, words are understood and used on an abstract level as well (His memory is "sharp" as a tack.). Children by the age of 11 understand that words and what they represent are different entities

# HOW DO WE COME TO UNDERSTAND THE MEANING A SPEAKER INTENDS TO CONVEY?

Abbeduto, L., Davis, B., & Furman, L.(1988). The development of speech act comprehension in mentally retarded individuals and nonretarded children. *Child Development*, *59*, 1460–1472.

Language comprehension involves understanding the intent of the speaker. Sometimes what is spoken can be interpreted as either a question or a directive. For example, if "Would you open the telephone book?" is interpreted as a question, the listener would answer either "yes" or "no." If it is interpreted as a directive, the listener would open the telephone book. Comprehending such sentences, called speech acts, requires that the listener use clues not only provided by the speaker's utterance but also clues provided by the context in which the utterance is spoken. In addition, listeners need to know certain conversational rules, such as the response to an utterance is related to what the speaker said or asked. Listeners also know the rule that the speaker does not ask a question if the answer is already known. This is called the *answer obviousness rule*.

The purpose of this study was to examine the development from childhood through adolescence of retarded and nonretarded persons' use of the answer obviousness rule. Retarded and nonretarded individuals at the nonverbal mental ages of five, seven, and nine years were studied. Mental age was assessed by a standardized test of nonverbal cognitive maturity. Subjects were also assessed on ability to understand language by a standardized test providing a developmental index of receptive linguistic competence. By comparing the receptive linguistic competence between retarded and nonretarded subjects who were matched for their mental ages, the researchers concluded there is strong support for the existence of learning mechanisms unique to grammar that are different from those involved in cognition.

The subjects were tested individually. The experimenter explained that the subject's task was to do or say what the speaker wanted. The questions referred to objects placed in front of the subject (table 10.3). The compatible condition could be easily performed, whereas the incompatible condition would be difficult, but not impossible, to perform.

The questions posed by a *could you?* sentence ask about a listener's ability to perform the action named. For example, the answer to "Could you roll the clay into a ball?" is an obvious "yes" because the action is easily performed. However, the answer to "Could you squeeze the air out of the ball?" is nonobvious in that it could be "yes" or "no," depending on the motivation of the subject.

The questions posed by a *would you?* ask about a listener's willingness to perform the action named. While subjects are usually cooperative, the answers are generally nonobvious. A *would you?* question was interpreted as a *directive more often* and as a *question less often* than *could you?* Compatibility did not have as much of an effect as it did in the *could you?* questions.

The questions posed by a *do you think?* ask about a listener's opinion of the ability to perform the action named. A listener's opinions on this matter are, presumably, least obvious to another. This appears to be the reason that *do you think?* was interpreted as a *directive less often* and as *question more often*.

Thus, whether an interrogative is interpreted as a directive or a question depends on how it is worded (*could you?*, *would you?*, *do you think?*), and whether the answer is *(continued on following page)*

*(continued from previous page)*

obvious. Obviousness depends on compatible versus incompatible contexts.

Retarded subjects at all developmental levels studied were found to interpret the experimental interrogatives as questions most often and as directives least often, under conditions in which answer obviousness was thought to be low. Of the three interrogative forms, they responded to *would you?* as a directive most frequently and *do you think?* as a question most often. It appears that by the time retarded persons have reached a developmental level of five years, they have acquired some form of the answer obviousness rule.

The normally developing children also reached a question interpretation most often and a directive interpretation least often in precisely those conditions for which answer obviousness could be assumed to be low.

This suggests that the answer obviousness rule is normally acquired by the age of five. However, other rules of conversation, such as a listener's response must follow a speaker's utterance and the response must be relevant to a speaker's utterance, are not acquired until age six or seven.

The reason the answer obviousness rule is acquired first is that it involves only one linguistic form, the interrogative, whereas other conversational rules are broader and involve many linguistic forms.

In this study, nonretarded and retarded individuals could use the linguistic interrogative form as a basis for deciding between a question and a directive interpretation in compatible and incompatible contexts. The study thus shows that we come to understand the meaning a speaker intends to communicate by recognizing both linguistic and contextual properties.

## EXAMPLES OF STIMULUS MATERIALS BY INTERROGATIVE TYPE AND CONTEXT TYPE

### TABLE 10.3
### Example Sentence (and Object)

*Would you?*

|  |  |
|---|---|
| Compatible | Would you open the scissors? (standard children's scissors) |
| Incompatible | Would you tear the telephone book in half? (2-inch-thick telephone book) |

*Could you?*

|  |  |
|---|---|
| Compatible | Could you roll the clay into a ball? (small, flat piece of clay) |
| Incompatible | Could you squeeze the air out of the ball? (standard, inflated soccer ball) |

*Do you think?*

|  |  |
|---|---|
| Compatible | Do you think you could roll the pencil? (standard lead pencil) |
| Incompatible | Do you think you could scoop up the salt with the fork? (dinner fork, mound of salt) |

(Osherson & Markman, 1975)—that the word *giraffe* would still exist even if giraffes became extinct.

An example of complex grammar that is not mastered until middle childhood is the passive voice. In the passive voice, the subject of the sentence is acted on by the verb as in "Mary was kissed by John" (Sudhalter &

Braine, 1985). Another example is the ability to understand the difference between the agent and object of an action as in "John is eager to please" in which "John" is the agent of "please" and "John is easy to please" in which "John" is the object of "please" (Karmiloff-Smith, 1979).

As children develop, their conversations are longer and more coherent, and they build topically on what was previously said. Compare the two following conversations, the first took place among second graders and the second among fifth graders:

*Second Graders* (Dorval & Eckerman, 1984, p. 55)

1. "Well, we…uh…have paper plates…with turkey on it and lots of (unintelligible). You know."
2. "Doo-doo-doo-doo-doo" (singing)
3. "I don't know what you're talking about."
4. "You know what? My uncle killed a turkey."
5. "Not frying pan?"
6. "No."
7. "I seen a frying pan at Hulen's store!"

*Fifth Graders* (Dorval & Eckerman, 1984, p. 22)

1. "Be quiet! Start off, Billy. What if you was the teacher?"
2. "OK. if I was the teacher, I'd give us less work and more time to play. And I'd be mean to y'all, too."
3. "OK. Ann" (meaning that it is her turn).
4. "If I was the teacher, I'd do work…um. I'd sit around and watch TV. I wouldn't assign no papers…umm…"
5. "I'd let y'all watch TV stories!"
6. "I'd turn the TV on Channel 4 at 9:30 to watch Popeye!"

Adolescents often use conversation to get another person's perspective ("What did you think of that guy?") (Dorval & Eckerman, 1984). Remember your conversations with friends when you were in high school and the time you spent comparing your perspective with that of your friend's on peers, teachers, clothes, and parents.

It is common for adolescents to have a special vocabulary of their own. Linguists refer to the special language of a particular group as *argot*. The use of argot by teenagers serves to distinguish their generation from that of adults. Teenage argot or slang is always changing because many words are eventually adopted by the older generation. The following list is a representative sample of language of affluent suburban youths in the Detroit area (Tobias, 1980):

- *Bummer*—a bad deal or situation
- *Gross*—someone or something distasteful or awful
- *Jungle patching*—driving a car across a suburban lawn or golf course and spinning the tires, leaving bare patches

Slang also is part of the college students' vocabulary. Various campuses have their own argot, although not much has been studied scientifically. To contribute to the scant literature on college slang, Munro (1989) with the help of students compiled a dictionary of slang words and expressions used at a university. For example, among the words for being drunk are *blasted, blitzed, bombed, buzzed, ripped, shredded, slaughtered, toasted, blown, tattered, tanked,* and *polluted.* Demeaning epithets include *animal* (a wild, crazy person), *airhead* (a dumbell), *beddy* (a promiscuous woman).

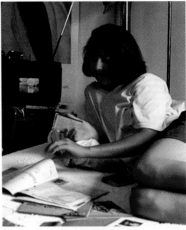

While most children understand and use language effectively by age five, language development continues through adolescence: Vocabulary increases, grammar becomes more complex, and conversational skills become more sophisticated.

# BIOLOGICAL INFLUENCES ON LANGUAGE DEVELOPMENT

Evidence indicates that other species also communicate. For example, honeybees have a dance that communicates the location of a food supply. Other species' communications are related to survival because knowing the location of food helps ensure that members of the species will survive and reproduce. Such communications are biologically influenced in that they are evidence of adaptation. Unlike animals, humans communicate for many reasons other than survival, for example, to express feelings and thoughts.

Evidence supporting a language acquisition device is that children, on acquiring a sufficient vocabulary, can combine words into novel but grammatically consistent utterances and are able to understand the meaning of the language they hear.

## DO WE HAVE A LANGUAGE ACQUISITION DEVICE?

Some linguists such as Chomsky (1968; 1980) and McNeill (1970) believe humans are biologically programmed to acquire language (perhaps because initially language had an adaptive function). In other words, a **language acquisition device ( LAD),** which represents a universal grammatical structure underlying all human languages enabling us to combine words so they are understood, is programmed into our genes. This universal grammar consists of rules for producing sounds, meaning, and structure. Major observational evidence for the existence of an LAD comes from the universality of the sequence of language development. Children throughout the world acquire language in the same order: crying, cooing, babbling, one word, two words, telegraphic speech, complex phrases and sentences (Brown, 1973).

Evidence indicates language processing is controlled in the left hemisphere of the brain. Further, studies of brain-damaged persons show that *Broca's area* (area of brain near front of the left hemisphere) is important for producing speech, and *Wernicke's area* (area of brain near back of the left hemisphere) is important for understanding speech (Slobin, 1979).

Evidence suggests the left hemisphere can perceive language from birth. In electromyegraphical studies, or evoked potentials, speech sounds generally elicit more electrical activity from the left side of an infant's brain, while music and other nonspeech sounds produce greater activity from the right side (Molfese, 1977). Also, an infant can discriminate among certain speech sounds (Eimas, 1982), implying that the neonate comes into the world prepared to understand and produce speech.

According to Witelson (1987) in a review of the literature on neurobiological aspects of language in children, regions in the left hemisphere appear specialized for mediating speech and language processes from the first few months of life, probably from birth. Although inconclusive, the available evidence indicates that brain hemispheric specialization is functionally present in the neural system from the beginning. Such evidence may eventually support Chomsky's theory of a human language acquisition device.

Strong evidence supporting a biological predisposition to communicate comes from research by Goldin-Meadow (1979; Goldin-Meadow & Mylander, 1983). The gestural language of ten congenitally deaf children between the ages of one and four was studied. These children had not been taught sign language because their parents had wanted them to communicate orally; so they were taught to lip read and speak in a special school. Despite the efforts, little success was achieved in oral language understanding or acquisition. Instead, the children had spontaneously devised gestures to communicate with one another.

When Goldin-Meadow and colleagues analyzed the children's manual communication, they found two gestures that were spontaneously produced by the children. One was a *pointing gesture* that served to indicate people, places, and objects to which they referred. The other was a *characterizing gesture* that served to simulate an action or a specific object being referred to, such as a twisting motion with the hands to indicate a jar being opened.

When the developmental course of the gestures was followed, it was found to parallel the developmental course of language acquisition in hearing children. Specifically, when the gestures began, they singularly referred to familiar objects and actions just as hearing children use one-word and two-word utterances to refer to familiar elements in the environment. About the same time as hearing children combine words into two-word utterances, the deaf children were using two-gesture sign combinations. Further, between two and three years of age (slightly later than when hearing children produce verbal sentences of three words and longer), the deaf children began to produce more complex manual sentences.

It is significant that deaf children produce a system of communication in the same order as hearing children acquire language because it illustrates the powerful biological influence in humans to use language. Even though humans may be biologically programmed to acquire language, language acquisition will not occur without exposure to language. The deaf children in the studies by Goldin-Meadow were not exposed to sign language, but they were exposed to oral language. Thus, they may have assumed gestures were easier for them than lip reading or speech, so they applied their biological programming in a manner more efficient and adaptive for them.

## F.Y.I.

Some children (at one and two years of age) learn as many as 20 new words every week (Goldfield & Reznick, 1990).

## IS THERE A CRITICAL PERIOD FOR LANGUAGE ACQUISITION?

The brain grows rapidly during the first five years of life. At birth, the brain of a child is about 25 percent of its adult size; by age two, it is about 75 percent; and by age five, it is about 90 percent (Tanner, 1990). Growth is uneven, with a major growth spurt occurring by about the age of two, and another between ages three and five (Fischer & Pipp, 1984). Interestingly, the spurts in overall brain growth seem to correspond with developmental changes in language development, determined by studying the myelinization of nerve cells located in specific areas of the brain (Lecours, 1975).

Before birth until infancy, myelinization is rapidly occurring in the brainstem and limbic system, which appears to be associated with babbling. Between birth and about three-and-one-half to four-and-one-half years of age, myelinization is rapidly occurring in certain areas of the cerebral cortex responsible for speech. At the same time, speech is developing from the one-word stage to sentences. Meanwhile, myelinization is taking place in other areas of the cortex associated with intelligence; the maturation of these association areas corresponds to the critical period for acquiring language, which according to Lenneberg (1967; 1973), is age two to puberty.

Lenneberg (1967) believed the ability to speak and understand language to be an inherited species-specific characteristic of humans.

Lenneberg (1967) stated that language development does not occur in a vacuum; exposure to language is necessary for the maturational "unfolding" of language to take place.

Language is based on highly specialized biological mechanisms including the articulatory apparatus specific in brain centers and a specialized auditory system that processes speech sounds differently from other sounds. Lenneberg associated language development stages with milestones in motor development such as sitting and walking.

Support for Lenneberg's critical period hypothesis of language development comes from the fact that before puberty a child can become fluent in more than one language without special training, whereas after puberty learning a second language is difficult. Languages learned after puberty retain the accent of the native language, whereas languages acquired before puberty do not (Krashen, 1975).

Additional evidence supporting the critical period of language development comes from case studies of children deprived of exposure to language. The following case of Genie, a neglected girl who grew up in almost total isolation serves as an example (Curtiss, 1977; 1980).

Genie was discovered in 1970 when she was 13 years old. She had been confined to a small room away from the living quarters in the house from the time she was an infant. She had been fed and cleaned but not spoken to. The only sounds she was exposed to were her father's growling noises, which he made to frighten her whenever she vocalized. When Genie was found, she weighed 60 pounds, spoke no language, seemed to understand a few simple commands, and was emotionally disturbed.

Eight months after being placed in a foster home with parents who cared for her and provided a normal language environment, she mastered most English phonemes, had a vocabulary of 200 words, and had begun to generate two-word utterances. The sequence of her language development followed that of normal children. Genie's language continued to develop over the years, but even after a decade she never reached normal development. She continued to have articulation problems and problems with syntax. She used proper names instead of pronouns and had difficulty incorporating auxiliary verbs into her sentences.

Genie's case supports some aspects of the critical period hypothesis for language development because she never could achieve full language proficiency because she was not exposed to language or allowed to talk before puberty. However, the case also refutes some aspects because Genie did succeed in learning to basically communicate after puberty. One can argue Genie learned language because she was biologically prewired but that genes programmed for language are not enough; a context for hearing and speaking language must be provided.

# CONTEXTUAL INFLUENCES ON LANGUAGE DEVELOPMENT

Most psychologists and linguists agree that language development occurs in a context; that is infants must be exposed to language and must have opportunities to use language to communicate. That context is important in language development was illustrated by Coley and Gelman (1989) in their study on children's interpretations of the word *big*. Previous research indicated that preschool children have difficulty interpreting *big*

*big* can refer to relative height, width, area, or overall dimensions). Coley and Gelman showed each of 40 children, ages three and five, 35 pairs of items and, for each pair, asked them to point to "the big one." The types and orientation (vertical or horizontal) of objects were varied. The older children consistently relied more on height compared with younger children. All children relied on area more often in the horizontal condition than in the vertical condition. The younger children relied more on height when judging the bigness of people than for rectangles that matched the people in size. Thus, children's understanding of the meaning of words depends on the context in which the word is used, in this case the orientation of the object more so than the object itself, as well as the cognitive development of the child. In this experiment, there was an increasing effort between three and five years of age to impose a consistent interpretation onto the word *big*.

That hearing language spoken is important for language development is supported by research comparing vocal development in deaf and hearing infants. Specifically, well-formed syllable production is established in the first ten months of life during the babbling stage by hearing infants but not by deaf infants, indicating audition plays an important role in vocal development (Oller & Eilers, 1988). Deaf infants babble, but the articulation patterns of the speech sounds differ from those of hearing infants. Generally, they soon stop using their vocal apparatus to communicate.

Some theories explaining contextual influences on language development will now be discussed.

This infant is in the babbling stage. Because she can hear herself "speak," her language development will differ from that of infants who have a hearing disability.

## BEHAVIOR LEARNING THEORY

B.F. Skinner, a leading proponent of behavior learning theory argued that language is a verbal behavior and is acquired in the same way as any other behavior—by reinforcement (Skinner, 1957). Skinner as well as Bijou and Baer (1965) explained that because caregivers usually talk to infants while feeding, playing with, or cleaning them speech becomes reinforcing in that it is associated with something pleasant. As neonates begin to vocalize on their own, cooing and then babbling, the vocalizations become self-reinforcing. Also, when infants babble, adults will respond by smiling, touching, or talking back. These too are reinforcers. Behavior learning theorists believe that as an infant's babbling increases, adults only reinforce the sounds that approximate words, thereby shaping the infant's vocal responses to conform to the adult's language. For example, "ju" might be shaped into "juice" or "duh" into "dog."

When a child says words, she is reinforced by attention and a response ("You want some juice?") or by a tangible reward, the actual object (a glass of juice).

According to recent research about the acquisition of vocabulary words, reinforcement (attention, praise, compliance with requests) plays a significant role. A group of two- and three-year-old English-speaking children was exposed to toys in a naturalistic environment. Likewise, a group of Spanish-speaking children of the same age was taught English words for the same toys in a naturalistic environment. Those children who were reinforced in the foreign language used the words they were taught when they requested the toys, whereas those children not reinforced used their native tongues when they wanted the toys (Whitehurst & Valdez-Menchaca, 1988).

## SOCIAL COGNITIVE THEORY

Social cognitive theorists such as Bandura (1977; 1986) propose that observation and imitation play a major role in language acquisition. Parents and others in the child's environment serve as models for a child to listen to and imitate ("That's a plane," says mother pointing to an airplane).

Whitehurst (1982) explains that children imitate the patterns of words, called *grammatical frames*, so that they can put the words they know into sentences different from ones they have heard. Bandura (1986) proposes language is acquired through a kind of imitation called *abstract modeling* wherein the child abstracts general linguistic principles from specific utterances the child hears. A child who has repeatedly heard sentences such as "Look at the bird; oh, look, there are lots of birds," abstracts the plural form of the noun and can add *s* whenever talking about more than one.

## MOTHERESE

Throughout the world, caregivers speak "baby talk" to infants. Baby talk, or **motherese**, is a special form of language that includes simple sentences with exaggerated intonation, high pitch, and slow and clear pronunciation (Gelman & Shatz, 1977). Some linguists prefer to call it *child-directed speech* (Snow, 1986).

Of all traits identified in mothers' speech to infants, the most obvious is the change to a higher pitch and its melodic "sing-song" quality (Papousek, Papousek & Bornstein, 1985). Infants only a few days old can discriminate between differences in pitch, and they seem to respond to certain frequencies more readily.

The enunciation, or sounds of words, in child-directed speech is different from adult language. There is a deemphasis of consonants and a corresponding stress on vowels to produce an exaggerated effect. Syllables are commonly duplicated as in "choo-choo" for train and "ni-ni" for good night.

Sentences in child-directed speech are short and simple. For example, pronouns are eliminated so that instead of "Give me a kiss," the parent says, "Give Mommy a kiss." Usually, motherese consists of questions and commands ("What's that?" "No touch!"). Much of what is said is repeated (Reich, 1986). All of this probably helps a child label the environment and become socialized.

As a child becomes able to combine words into two-word utterances (about 18 months), sentences in child-directed speech gradually become longer and more complex but only slightly above the child's comprehension (Shatz, 1983; Bohannon & Warren-Leubecker, 1985).

Some of these longer sentences take the form of **expansions**, elaborations of a child's speech by adults. For example, an infant says "Daddy eat" and the parent says, "Yes, Daddy is eating." Thus, through expansion the adult has modeled the correct grammatical form of the child's primitive sentence. Another way the adult makes child-directed sentences longer is by **recasting**, or restructuring. The adult might respond to "Daddy eat," with "What is Daddy eating?" or "Yes, Daddy is hungry." Through recasting the adult provides the child with new words and related concepts.

Not all researchers believe child-directed speech is beneficial in helping children learn the structure and rules of language (Gleitman & Wanner, 1982; Schieffelin & Ochs, 1983). For example, in certain cultures such as Samoan it is believed that children cannot understand anything until they re 18 months old so they are not spoken to directly. When they become 18 months old, they are talked to in adult language. Apparently, they have no problems in acquiring language. However, there is much evidence that child-directed speech speeds language acquisition and later language growth ( Roe, McClure & Roe, 1982; Bornstein & Ruddy, 1984; Hoff-Ginsberg, 1986).

Also, it was found that the structure of a mother's speech to two-year-olds predicted later language growth, particularly the use of auxiliary verbs and other markers for verb tense (Hoff-Ginsberg, 1986). Child-directed speech and the manner in which adults talk to children (for example, pointing out objects in the environment and labeling them) influence language development. Baldwin and Markman (1989) found that by 10 to 14 months of age, infants are more attentive to unfamiliar objects that have been labeled than those objects that have not been labeled, even after the labeling occurred. Thus, when adults label things, they are encouraging infants to take the first step in establishing word-object relations: the step of noticing and remembering the correspondence between the word and the object.

# INTERACTION OF BIOLOGICAL AND CONTEXTUAL INFLUENCES ON LANGUAGE DEVELOPMENT

Today most psychologists and linguists agree that the child is an active participant in acquiring language. A child arrives biologically equipped to understand and produce language. A child can perceive, conceptualize, store, and access information and vocalize. A child also is exposed to language in a social context—an infant is spoken to by others, and the infant observes others talking to each other. Neonates understand that language is a social exchange. They begin to participate in social exchanges when they return their parents' gazes and later when they vocalize. Both biological endowment and a rich communicative environment interact to influence a child's discovery of the functions and regularities of language (Bates & MacWhinney, 1982; Bohannon & Warren-Leubecker, 1985).

According to the interactional viewpoint, biological maturation of the brain and central nervous system provides the cognitive basis for language development to occur. As the brain develops, the child can better understand the environment. For example, a child forms concepts such as object permanence, can remember things, and can symbolize. A certain basic level of cognitive competence is required for language to be acquired. A child has to have not only a level of cognitive competence but must also have experience in actively participating in human interaction. Prelinguistic interaction occurs with another person and includes joint attention, mutual gazing, and taking turns. From such experience the child builds a linguistic system that relates the form and content of language to its social meaning.

## CHOMSKY'S VIEW ON LANGUAGE AND THOUGHT

Chomsky (1965) believed language develops independently of thought. In his view, linguistic categories are "hard-wired" in the human

Infants prefer listening to child-directed speech more than they do to adult speech because of the patterning of sounds and intonation (Fernald, 1985; 1987).

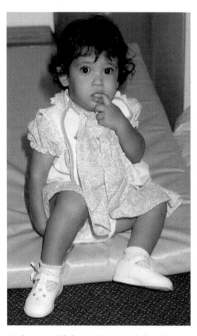

Is it possible to have thought without language or vice versa?

brain as a result of evolution. Exposure to language is what triggers the language acquisition device (LAD) with which every human is innately endowed. Language is not learned but rather unfolds given contextual stimulation. Evidence for Chomsky's view is that regardless of the language, children show great consistency in the order in which words and grammar are acquired.

## PIAGET'S VIEW ON LANGUAGE AND THOUGHT

Piaget (1970) viewed language as a reflection of thought, or more specifically, nonlinguistic knowledge. Children begin with a sensorimotor understanding of the world and then try to find linguistic ways to express that knowledge. Sensorimotor knowledge determines the forms of language. The development of thought occurs before language acquisition; as language develops it simply "maps onto" previously acquired cognitive categories and structures.

Evidence exists to support Piaget's view. To see which occurs first, the linguistic category or the cognitive understanding, Sinclair-de Zwart (1967) taught four-, five-, and six-year-olds the correct meanings of comparative adjectives (*more* and *less, short* and *fat*) by using different-sized clay balls and different amounts of beads. Although the children appeared to understand how to use the words appropriated in the training sessions, they could not apply them to a cognitive test requiring conceptual understanding of quantity. Thus, the advancement of these children linguistically was insufficient to stimulate advancement cognitively.

Other evidence that supports language as a reflection of thought is the finding that what children understand and express linguistically is based on prior nonlinguistic experience with objects, actions, and events (Clark, 1977). For example, children will say "Daddy," or "juice" before they will say "pencil," or "sun," words with which they have no direct experience.

Thus, Piaget and those who support his views maintain that linguistic categories such as verb and noun are only attainable after the child has mastered parallel nonlinguistic knowledge (Piaget, 1980).

## WHORF'S VIEW ON LANGUAGE AND THOUGHT

Whorf (1952) claimed that language determines thought. Linguistic patterns structure thought in that they affect an individual's perception of the world. The word *red* tells what that color looks like, and the word *blue* tells what a different color looks like. According to Whorf, language is a shaper of ideas rather than an expression.

The rationale for Whorf's view comes from cross-cultural linguistic studies. Speakers of different languages objectify reality in different ways. For example, in English the flow of time is treated as if it were an objective entity "like a ribbon with spaces marked off denoting past, present, and future" (Cromer, 1979). According to Whorf this is due to the structure of English, which requires the encoding of verb forms into tenses. By contrast, the Hopi Indian language of North America has no tenses for its verbs. Further, it has no words, grammatical constructions, or expressions that refer directly to what we call time. A Hopi thinks about events in *both* space and time, for neither is found alone in the Hopi view of the world. Thus, Hopi language is adequate without verb tenses (Cromer, 1979).

Children are more likely to understand that a sentence does not make sense or is incorrect semantically ("The horse rode the boy.") than that a sentence is incorrect grammatically ("The boy rided the horse.").

# VYGOTSKY'S VIEW ON LANGUAGE AND THOUGHT

Interactionist theorists believe that language and thought depend on each other. The most influential interactionist view is that of Vygotsky (1962).

Vygotsky believed that early in life language and thought develop separately. There is *prespeech intellect* that occurs in infants as in sensorimotor schema, and there is *preintellectual speech* that also occurs in infants (crying or babbling). At the point when a child begins to acquire first words and name objects, the developmental paths of language and thought begin to merge. By about age two, speech begins to reflect thoughts and thoughts begin to be verbal. Thus, while thinking and language have different origins, once they combine they mutually influence each other (Elliot, 1981).

The union of language and thought is marked by a child's curiosity about words ("What's that?") and by a rapid increase in vocabulary. As children's vocabulary increases, they begin to talk to themselves. At first they may describe what they are doing ("Go bye-bye"). Later, they may say what they plan to do ("I'm gonna hit you"). Vygotsky calls this thinking aloud, **inner speech**, or private speech. Inner speech is critical to the organization of thought. Words that children have acquired and their associated meanings influence how children classify unfamiliar objects. For example, *kitty* might be associated with a furry four-legged animal with a tail. When the child sees a rabbit, the child might call it a *kitty*. Inner speech differs from **social speech**, which refers to speech used to communicate. Social speech occurs when people have conversations.

After language and thought join, a child's way of perceiving and learning about the world changes. Language becomes a tool for thought. For example, words such as *in, under,* and *after* structure reality. Words such as *run,* and *jump,* describe actions. Words such as *vegetable* and *mineral* classify objects. Thus, language helps one reason, and the ability to reason motivates language development (figure 10.1).

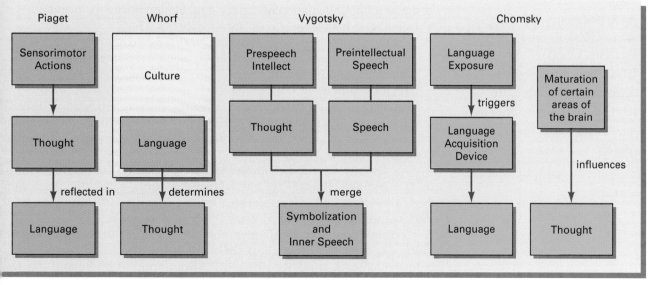

FIGURE 10.1
THEORIES RELATING THOUGHT AND LANGUAGE

# LANGUAGE DISORDERS

A language disorder is the abnormal acquisition, comprehension or expression of spoken or written language. The disorder may involve all, one, or some of the phonologic, morphologic, semantic, syntactic or pragmatic components of the linguistic system. Individuals with language disorders frequently have problems in sentence processing or in abstracting information meaningfully for storage and retrieval from short and long term memory (ASHA, 1980, pp. 317–318).

A language disorder can involve only speech (phonology) with normal language usage. Speech disorders include articulation problems (a person who lisps) and fluency problems (a person who stutters). A mentally retarded individual may speak clearly but have a problem with word meaning or complex sentences. Autistic individuals who parrot the speech of others have a language disorder because they do not communicate with eye contact or responsiveness in conversations. Language disorders can involve both speech and language problems (a person who is deaf). As a result, people with this problem have difficulty articulating sounds and gleaning the meaning from words; thus, a person's ability to communicate is impaired.

Several factors can contribute to language disorders in children (Chaney & Frodyma, 1982). These are:

1. Structural abnormalities of the speech mechanism
2. Hearing impairments
3. Mental retardation or brain damage
4. Environmental deprivation or abuse

Structural abnormalities of the speech mechanism or hearing impairments result in articulation disorders. Articulation disorders include:

- *omission* such as saying "cool" for "school"
- *substitution* of sounds such as saying "train" for "crane"
- *distortion* of sounds as a lisp such as saying "thleep" for "sleep"
- *addition* of sounds making comprehension difficult, such as saying "hamber" for "hammer"

Articulation disorders vary in severity. A severe articulation disorder that interferes significantly with intelligibility is as debilitating a communication problem as many other disorders but is not always easy to diagnose (Emerick & Haynes, 1986).

Mentally retarded children are slow to develop language, and their understanding and usage are limited by their mental capacities. Brain damage called *aphasia* is characterized by the inability to formulate, or to retrieve, and to decode the arbitrary symbols of language.

Environmental deprivation and abuse can result in children's not being exposed to language or their not being rewarded for efforts to communicate. A child who has little stimulation at home and has few chances to speak, listen, explore, and interact with others will probably have little motivation for communication and may develop disordered language patterns. The same is true of the child who is punished for talking, gesturing, or making other attempts to communicate (Heward & Orlansky, 1992).

Procedures to identify infants at risk for language disorders begin at birth. Birth defects such as cleft palate, deafness, and cerebral palsy indicate speech therapy will probably be needed.

Observation of developing children is important in the assessment of speech, language use, and communication skills (table 10.4).

## FIVE STAGES OF LANGUAGE DEVELOPMENT DURING THE PRESCHOOL PERIOD

### TABLE 10.4

| Stage | Attainments |
|---|---|
| Approx. age: 12–26 months | *Speech.* Produces some words consistently but varies others greatly; limits initial words in number and type of syllables; gradually comes to be governed by phonological rules<br>*Language.* Uses single-word utterances naming specific objects and classes of objects (animate and inanimate) or expressing a relational meaning (existence, nonexistence, disappearance, recurrence); uses successive single-word utterances; uses two-word combinations to express existence, negation, recurrence, attribution, possession, location, agent-action, action-object, agent-object<br>*Communication.* Uses gestures to express intentions; uses gestures plus vocalizations to communicate desires and direct the behavior of others; uses multiword utterances to perform a range of functions |
| Approx. age: 27–30 months | *Speech.* Begins to follow phonological rules that provide for consistent speech performance<br>*Language.* Begins producing morphemes; *in, on*, present progressive (*-ing*), regular plural(*-s*), irregular past tense, possessive (*'s*), uncontractible copula, articles, regular past (*-ed*), irregular third person, uncontractible auxiliary, contractible copula, contractible auxiliary; produces some pronouns (*I, you, them, they, he/she, we, it*)<br>*Communication.* Responds to a conversational partner and engages in short dialogue; uses terms such as *here* and *there* to direct attention or to reference |
| Approx. age: 31–34 months | *Speech.* Articulates all English vowels and the majority of consonants<br>*Language.* Continues to experiment with and modify simple declarative sentences; begins to produce negative, interrogative, and imperative sentence forms<br>*Communication.* Learns to become a better conversational partner, taking turns and using contingent queries and questions; uses a greater variety of forms to attain desired objects and services; can take the perspective of the conversational partner |
| Approx. age: 35–40 months | *Speech.* May reduce or simplify words and consonant clusters<br>*Language.* Produces questions in the adult form; produces embedded sentences and other complex constructions; uses negative contractions including *isn't, aren't, doesn't*, and *didn't*; uses the modal auxiliaries *could, would, must*, and *might* in negatives and questions<br>*Communication.* Seems to have a better awareness of the social aspects of conversation; uses some indirect requests |
| Approx. age: 41–46 months | *Speech.* Produces a few consonant clusters and blends<br>*Language.* Has mastered regular and irregular past tense in most contexts; uses the third person singular and the contractible copula; inverts auxiliary verbs appropriately in questions; uses *and* and, later, *if* to conjoin clauses<br>*Communication.* Switches codes (produces simplified utterances) for younger children; uses most deictic terms correctly; can talk about feelings and emotions; produces indirect requests in which the goal is embedded in a question or statement |

**(Haring & McCormick, 1990)**

By the time most children with normal language development enter school, they can make all the phonological discriminations necessary for word identification and production (Menyuk, 1983). Articulation errors in the primary grades are reason for referral for speech assessment. The assessment process can be accomplished through imitation tasks, such as imitation of hand-clapping patterns, imitation of syllable sequences, words, and phrases. Another assessment method is to present pictures to the child to get him to produce consonants in different positions ("cat," "tack"). Articulatory proficiency is judged by comparing a child's omissions, substitutions and distortions, and additions with norms for his age.

Usually, school children have a large supply of language use and communication strategies. They know how to participate in conversations—share information, ask and answer questions, acknowledge, and request information. Many formal assessment devices are available to evaluate phonology, morphology, syntax, semantics, and pragmatics.

Children with language disorders appear *not* to grow out of their problems when they reach adolescence (Donahue, Pearl & Bryan, 1982; Wiig & Semel, 1980). Wiig (1984) notes significant delays and differences in concept formation, semantic development, acquisition of syntax, and memory when language-disordered adolescents are compared with normal peers. Further, they seem to differ from peers in three aspects of communicative competence (Donahue, Pearl & Bryan, 1983):

1. Adapting communicative intentions to listener and situational characteristics
2. Conveying and comprehending information
3. Initiating and maintaining cooperative conversational interactions

With intervention, language and communicative abilities improve over time. However, the gap between skills of language-disordered individuals and those of normal individuals does not seem to narrow (Haring & McCormick, 1990). Box 10.1 provides examples to enhance a child's language development.

## BOX 10.1 ENHANCING CHILDREN'S LANGUAGE DEVELOPMENT

1. **Expose infants to language**—Talk and sing to infants and play games with them involving gestures and taking turns. Describe what you are doing. Although infants cannot understand *what* is being said, they will begin to associate language with various activities.
2. **Encourage infants' communication**—Respond to crying, be sensitive to facial expressions and gestures, and label what an infant points to and ask what the infant wants.
3. **Read to young children**—Read to children as soon as they seem interested in words (in the latter part of the first year) and do it often. Material read should be slightly above children's stage of language development.
4. **Encourage young children's communication**—Ask children to describe their experiences and listen to them, prompting them when needed; be responsive to questions, and ask them to tell stories or to draw pictures about what they see.
5. **Encourage children to read**—Take children to the library and let them choose books; limit the amount of television they watch; let them see you reading.
6. **Encourage children to write**—Ask children to write letters, a diary, or stories about pictures they see.

# CRITICAL THINKING & YOU

oes language code experience, or does language elaborate experience? Information is in the chapter to support both positions.

**ANALYSIS:** Review this chapter and describe three supporting reasons for each position.

**SYNTHESIS:** What are the similarities and differences among the three supporting reasons you have chosen for each position?

**EVALUATION:** What is your position and why? Based on your position, what experiences or activities would you suggest to enhance a child's language development?

## SUMMARY

- Language is the expression or communication of thoughts and feelings by means of vocal sounds and combinations of such sounds to which meaning is attributed.
- Linguistics is the study of language.
- Language development follows a pattern from crying to cooing to babbling to first words to two-word combinations to telegraphic speech to grammar.
- Language is composed of phonology, semantics, grammar (morphology and syntax), and pragmatics. For language to be produced, brain and physical maturation must occur. A second precursor is auditory perception. A third precursor to language development is the opportunity to interact with others. A fourth precursor is cognitive, the ability to understand one's world.
- Children produce their first words at about one year of age. Before this, they have exercised their vocal apparatus in babbling and they have used idiomorphs, intonation, facial expressions, and gestures to communicate.
- About seven months after children produce their first word, they begin to put them together to form two-word statements.
- Grammar involves rules for word formation and word combination in sentences.

- Grammatical rules appear in the use of morphemes, such as adding *ing* to a word. The acquisition of morphological rules follows a regular pattern—present progressive verb case, location, possession, and number.
- Grammatical rules also appear in the use of syntax, how words are organized in sentences. Applying syntactical rules is crucial to communication.
- Communication involves eye contact, taking turns, gestures, and language.
- While syntax takes a long time to develop, pragmatics seems to develop early because children take turns speaking and they adjust their speech to the listener.
- Egocentric speech diminishes as the child becomes more knowledgeable about social situations.
- Language development continues to adolescence.
- Biological influences on language development are thought to involve the unique genetic programming of the human brain.
- Some linguists believe humans are equipped with a language acquisition device (LAD) that represents a universal grammatical structure underlying all human languages, enabling humans to combine words so they are understood.
- Some linguists believe there is a critical period between age two and puberty for language acquisition. There is some evidence that myelinization of nerve cells located in specific areas of the brain corresponds to the period of language acquisition.

- Exposure to language probably is necessary for the maturational unfolding of language to occur.
- Behavior learning theorists believe verbal behavior is like other behavior and, therefore, is influenced by reinforcement.
- Social cognitive theorists propose that observation and imitation play a role in language acquisition.
- Child-directed speech (motherese) includes simple sentences with exaggerated intonation, high pitch, and slow and clear pronunciation. There is evidence that children whose mothers spoke to them with child-directed speech were more advanced in language development than children whose mothers spoke to them like adults. Child-directed speech attracts attention, simplifies, exaggerates, and expands language, apparently making it easier for the child to acquire it.
- Most psychologists and linguists today agree that the child is an active participant in acquiring language. As the brain develops, the child can better understand the environment. A certain basic level of cognitive competence is required for language to be acquired. Active participation in human interaction is necessary.
- Psychologists and linguists disagree on the relationship between thought and language. Some believe language develops independently of thought, whereas others view language as a reflection of thought. Some believe language determines thought, whereas others view language and thought as independent entities developing separately early in life but whose paths cross when the child says the first words.

- Language disorders can involve phonology, semantics, morphology, syntax, pragmatics, or a combination.
- Factors contributing to language disorders include structural abnormalities of the speech mechanism, hearing impairments, mental retardation or brain damage, and environmental deprivation or abuse.

## RELATED READINGS

Brown R.W. (1973). *A first language: The early stages.* Cambridge, MA: Harvard University Press.

Bruner, J.S. (1983). *Child's talk.* New York: Norton.

Curtiss, S.R. (1977). *Genie.* New York: Academic Press.

de Villiers, P.A., & de Villiers, J. G. (1979). *Early language.* Cambridge, MA: Harvard University Press.

Garvey, C. (1984). *Children's talk.* Cambridge, MA: Harvard University Press.

Lane, H. (1979). *The wild boy of Aveyron.* Cambridge, MA: Harvard University Press.

Lenneberg, E.H. (1967). *Biological foundations of language.* New York: Wiley.

Reich, P.A. (1986). *Language development.* Englewood Cliffs, NJ: Prentice-Hall.

Schickedanz, J.A. *More than the ABCs: The early stages of reading and writing.* Washington, D.C.: National Association for the Education of Young Children.

Vygotsky, L. (1962). *Thought and language.* Cambridge, MA: MIT Press.

● ● ● ● ● ● ● ● ● ● ● ● ● ● ● ● ● ● ● ● ● ● ACTIVITY ● ● ● ● ● ● ● ● ● ● ● ● ● ● ● ● ● ● ● ●

To better understand how language develops, briefly describe the context and then record a five-minute language sample for each of the following:
- 1½- to 2-year-old
- 3- to 4-year-old
- 5- to 7- year-old
- 10- to 12-year-old
- 14- to 16-year-old

Focus on just one individual in an interaction. Analyze each sample for:

1. **phonology** (how are the words being used pronounced?)
2. **semantics** (how are the words used in the particular context to communicate meaning?)
3. **grammar** (what form of the words is used and how are the words arranged in sentences?)
4. **pragmatics** (how effective is the individual in communicating in the particular context—taking turns, staying on the topic being talked about or relating to it, adapting speech to the listener?).

● ● ● ● ● ● ● ● ● ● ● ● ● ● ● ● ● ● ● ● ● ● ● ● ● ● ● ● ● ● ● ● ● ● ● ● ● ● ● ● ● ● ● ● ● ● ● ●

# 11 Emotional Development

*Emotion is the chief source of all becoming—conscious.
There can be no transforming of darkness into light and of
apathy into movement without emotion.*

**Carl Gustav Jung**

# ABOUT EMOTIONS

When Jennifer was 17, she and Robin had a dramatic argument. Jennifer ended it by storming out of the house and speeding away in her car. Robin's heart was beating rapidly, and she was breathing in short gasps. Robin stomped around the house, and finally her heart rate and breathing returned to normal. Then Robin was able to put the situation in perspective and could understand (even though she disagreed with) Jennifer's response to flee. However, with understanding came new sensations. Robin's heart now seemed to skip a few beats and her stomach contracted. She thought, "Jennifer left so fast, what if she has an accident?" Robin was frightened. She began to call her friends to find out where Jennifer went. Emotions, rather than logic, were directing Robin's actions.

**Emotions** can be defined as physiological changes in arousal levels expressed subjectively by various responses. Emotions affect us physically (Robin's anger left her with a headache; her fear, with a loss of appetite), cognitively (Robin's anger disabled her from logical thinking; her fear caused her to imagine), and psychologically. (Robin's fear caused her to mobilize into action by calling Jennifer's friends.)

While Robin's response to the argument was to "fight," Jennifer's response was to flee. While Robin's emotional release was to stomp and then make phone calls, Jennifer's release was to stay at a friend's. Thus, the expressions of emotions are subjective in that they are individualized. Emotions are difficult to measure and classify scientifically. While there are relations of physiological measures such as heart rate, electroencephalographic (brain cell) activity and electromyographic (muscle cell) activity with changes in expressive behaviors (Strayer, 1985), labeling the distinct emotions as interest versus surprise or distress versus grief is uncertain.

One method for measuring emotion devised by Izard (1979, 1982) is the Maximally Discriminative Facial Movement (MAX) system. This system classifies facial expressions by movement of the eyebrows, forehead, eyes, nose, cheeks, and mouth. For example, fear might be identified by slightly raised eyebrows, enlarged eyes, cheeks lowered, and an opened, tense mouth (figure 11.1). MAX identifies facial patterns that include anger-rage, interest-excitement, enjoyment-joy, fear-terror, sadness-dejection, discomfort-pain, disgust, and gaze aversion. Infants' responses to various events, such as having a toy taken away, were videotaped. The infants' expressions were then coded by researchers who were unaware of what event was experienced.

Another way to classify emotions is by measuring changes in the voice (Scherer, 1979). For example, when a person is happy, the voice tends to have a loud high pitch with a fast tempo; when a person is sad, the voice tends to have a soft low pitch with a slow tempo.

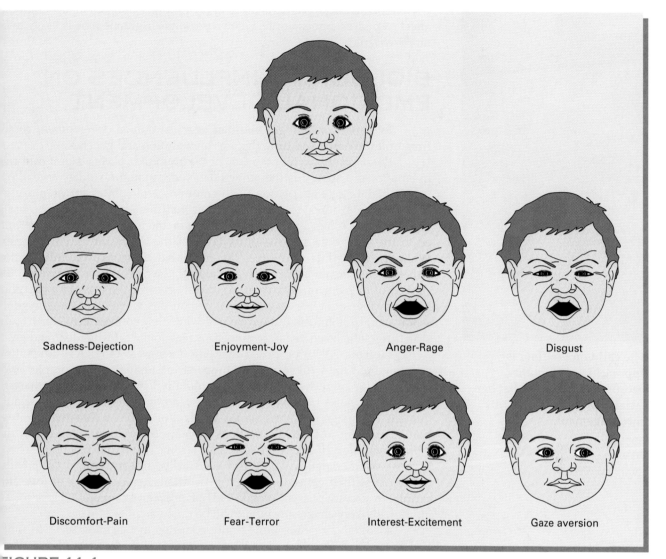

FIGURE 11.1
Maximally Discriminative Facial Movement (MAX) System (Izard, 1979).

Faces labeled: Sadness-Dejection, Enjoyment-Joy, Anger-Rage, Disgust, Discomfort-Pain, Fear-Terror, Interest-Excitement, Gaze aversion

## SIGNIFICANCE OF EMOTIONS

Emotions are important because they serve as forms of communication (Hetherington & Parke, 1986). They are the means by which feelings, desires, and needs are shared with others. They are the means by which infants become attached to parents. Neonates who have not formed emotional ties are likely to have personality and social problems in childhood and adulthood.

Emotions not only communicate internal states, they also regulate social distance—a smile beckons, a frown sets up a barrier—and provide a clue as to how to behave. For example, a parent's display of fright during a tornado warning will elicit a fear reaction in her child.

Emotions also are significant in that they influence what one attends to in the environment thereby affecting what one perceives (Campos et al., 1983). They also influence the processing of information. For example,

> ## F.Y.I.
>
> The amygdala is a small, almond-shaped structure located in the lower part of the brain.

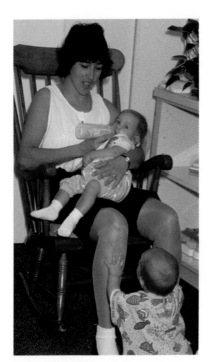

The child on the floor is approaching his mother because he perceives that her facial expression represents encouragement.

when a person is angry, he is more likely to forget things. Finally, emotions affect responses. For example, when a person is frightened, he is likely to be more reticent.

# BIOLOGICAL INFLUENCES ON EMOTIONAL DEVELOPMENT

Evidence for biological influences on emotional development comes from brain research and from theories of evolution and genetics.

Research shows that the area of the brain that plays a significant role in emotional response is the amygdala. Neuroanatomy studies reveal that the amygdala acts as a gateway to emotions and a filter for memory by attaching significance to the information that the senses send to the brain (Patlak, 1991). When a person hears a scream, the information heard is routed to the amygdala and the outer layer of the brain, the cerebral cortex. While the amygdala scrutinizes the emotional content of the information (whether the scream is frightening or joyful), the cerebral cortex assesses the context of the scream. (For example, did it occur in response to a gun shot or a sporting event?) If an emotional response is warranted, the amygdala sends signals along the numerous pathways that connect it to other brain structures, which can generate numerous reactions, including fear and joy.

Plutchik (1980) proposed that emotions are a biological adaptation enabling the successful survival of humans and animals. For example, emotions such as anger and fear are accompanied by physiological changes (increases in pulse rate, blood pressure, secretion of hormones) that enable humans to engage in a struggle for survival or to flee a threatening situation. According to Plutchik, millions of years of evolution resulted in the natural selection of ancestors who had strong emotional reactions. Those with weak emotional reactions did not survive threats, and, consequently, did not pass their genes to the next generation. Emotions such as love and caring are also adaptive (Plutchik, 1983). For example, a parent's love for an infant will likely ensure the infant will be nurtured.

Also, emotions are biologically adaptive in that they seem to function as a signal for other emotions to respond. By extensive observation, Wolff (1969) was able to distinguish different types of infant cries to denote hunger, pain, or anger. Sensitive parents learn by experience to interpret these cries. Some researchers (Campos et al., 1983) believe emotions presuppose social interactions and relationships. The infant's emotions (distress or fear) are likely to elicit crying. A parent can respond by picking up the infant and soothing her. When an infant is calm, the infant may gaze into the parent's eyes. The parent may smile and say, "You recognize your daddy." By the second or third month, an infant's contentment might cause her to smile back. Thus, a reciprocal social interaction is set up. Both parent and child stimulate each other and respond to each other. This is termed **interactive synchrony** (the coordination between individuals whereby each responds to subtle verbal and nonverbal cues of the other). As infants approach their first birthday, they take on an increasing share of the social interaction (Belsky, Taylor & Rovine, 1984). If the infant is gazing at the parent and the parent looks away, the infant might whimper to get the parent to look at her again. And when the parent does, the infant smiles. When the parent is too stimulating in the interaction (too chatty) the infant may look away to reduce the interaction. As the infant becomes more aware of the effect of her part in this reciprocal interaction, she assumes a greater role using emotions to direct the transactions (Sroufe, 1979).

That emotions are basic to the human species has been demonstrated across cultures. People in both literate industrial societies and preliterate tribal societies were asked to demonstrate and identify pictures of emotional expressions usually associated with certain events, such as death. The subjects produced identical expressions and agreed on identifications of happiness, sadness, disgust, and anger (Ekman & Friesen, 1972). This agreement lends credibility to a biological., rather than contextual., basis of emotions.

**Differential emotions theory** proposes that certain primary emotional expressions such as joy, anger, surprise, fear, and distress are innate, each having a distinctive neurological system (Ekman & Friesen, 1978; Izard, 1982; Plutchik, 1983). These discrete emotions are based on separate innate neurological programs and are set to emerge when such emotions become adaptive in life. For example, smiling, fear, and distress are present at birth, whereas anger appears between four and six months when the infant can push or kick away a restraining stimulus (Izard, 1982).

Other researchers support **differentiation emotions theory**, which states that emotions are differentiated as a function of maturation and cognitive development from genetically similar routes, beginning with a general increase in arousal level and becoming more specific and differentiated throughout development (Strayer, 1985).

Sroufe (1979) described the course of human emotions. He traced the **endogenous** smile appearing at birth that is elicited by internal or physical stimuli to joy and the **exogenous** smile appearing at about three months that is elicited by external or social stimuli to laughter at seven months, elation at 12 months, and pride and love at 36 months. Negative emotions were differentiated from rage as exhibited by newborns to disappointment at three months, anger at seven months, defiance at 18 months, and guilt at 36 months.

Emotions are difficult to measure. Therefore, it becomes perplexing to evaluate emotional development as a *differential* or *differentiation* process.

**Both father and daughter are expressing fear of a medical procedure about to be administered to the child.**

# CONTEXTUAL INFLUENCES ON EMOTIONAL DEVELOPMENT

Emotional reactions are contagious. This was demonstrated in 1992 when riots involving shooting, looting, and burning of buildings occurred in Los Angeles as a reaction to the Rodney King police brutality case. Thus, emotional reactions in others can influence emotions in ourselves.

## SOCIAL REFERENCING

A dramatic study with one-year-old children using a modified visual cliff demonstrated the influence of context on emotional expression (Campos et al., 1983). When one-year-old infants attempting to cross the visual cliff apparatus to mothers on the other side were faced with an apparent four-foot dropoff they avoided crossing. When there was no apparent dropoff they crossed without checking the mothers' expressions. However, when the dropoff on the deep side was set at an intermediate level—somewhat fear-provoking, but not enough to prevent crossing—the infants looked to the mothers; if the mother had a fearful expression on her

# F.Y.I.

Differentiation emotions theory is analogous to the growth of a tree from a young sapling. The sapling has a few roots when first planted. As it grows taller, the root system expands and grows more branches. When the leaves appear in the Spring, the tree has a distinct shape.

face, they did not cross; if she had a happy expression, they crossed. Thus the emotional expression of the mother regulated the infant's behavior. The infant used the mother as a social reference. **Social referencing**, then, refers to looking for cues from others about how to behave in an unfamiliar situation.

When a mother and child interact, each affects the other's emotions. Cohn and Tronick (1983) showed that infants adopt their behavior by reading mothers' emotional signals. The researchers demonstrated this by having one group of mothers of three-month-old neonates act normally and another group act depressed (kept their face expressionless, talked low and slowly, minimized touching the infant). Infants of normally acting mothers played, smiled at their mothers, and rarely acted wary. On the other hand, neonates of the "depressed" mothers protested, reacted warily, and only smiled slightly.

Social referencing begins early and is not exclusively directed toward mothers or caregivers. This was demonstrated in a study by Klinnert et al. (1986). They found that infants look to adults other than their mothers for emotional clues. In the presence of their mothers, a group of one-year-old children were confronted with an unusual toy (a robot) where an experimenter familiar to the infants posed happy or fearful expressions. The mothers were instructed not to provide facial signals. More than 80 percent of the infants referenced the familiarized experimenter. Once the adults' facial expressions were perceived, the infants approached the toy accordingly: Fear signals resulted in significantly more infants approaching the mother, whereas smiles resulted in more infants approaching the robot toy.

Social referencing continues throughout development. Teenagers will often seek out how their friends feel about a person or an event before committing themselves to an opinion. Adults, too, who are unsure of themselves in a situation will look for social cues.

## LEARNING

As children develop, their emotional expression is often regulated by social or culturally defined contexts for the appropriate display of certain emotions. For example, American children learn early to curb displays of anger. Also, females and males are socialized differently with respect to the display of emotions: Expression of anger is more tolerated in males than it is in females, whereas the expression of fear is more tolerated in females than in males. In other cultures certain emotions may be absent or repressed. For example, in Tahiti because grief is not allowed, no label for the emotion exists.

Behavior learning and social cognitive theories provide evidence for certain learning contexts influencing emotion. The learning contexts we will discuss are classical conditioning, operant conditioning, and social cognition.

Classical conditioning involves the following steps:

1. An unconditioned eliciting stimulus, such as food, elicits an unconditioned or reflexive response such as salivation.
2. A neutral stimulus such as a bell that is paired with the unconditioned stimulus (food) elicits the unconditioned response (salivation).
3. After many pairings, the neutral stimulus (bell) becomes a conditioned stimulus, eliciting the response (salivation) on its own. Thus, the response (salivation) becomes a conditioned response.

Classical conditioning explains some fears of children and adults; for example, being afraid of a doctor because of receiving a painful shot in the past.

The younger child is demonstrating social referencing by providing emotional comfort to his older sibling.

Lamb and Malkin (1986) have shown that by the age of one month, infants develop conditioned associations between showing distress by crying and being picked up and comforted. By four to five months, they develop cognitive expectations about social responses. For instance, when they smile, they expect a smile back. When their expectations are violated, they exhibit protest and turn away. Thus, classical conditioning can be viewed as part of the total picture of emotional development.

Another type of conditioning is operant conditioning. Operant conditioning involves a voluntary response that can be repeated because it is reinforced or can be eliminated because the reinforcement is removed. Operant conditioning plays a role in explaining emotional development. When Jennifer was about eight months old, she began to whimper when Robin answered the telephone. To quiet her, Robin gave her plastic containers from the kitchen to play with. Then, every time the telephone would ring, Jennifer would whine until Robin gave her a toy. Inadvertently, Robin reinforced her negative display of emotions. Robin should have removed Jennifer from the room until her whining subsided and then provided her a toy, thereby rewarding the control of rather than display of negative feelings.

Joy

According to learning theory, responses can be generalized. For example, if a child experiences joy at seeing her mother, this feeling may later be generalized to other adults. Responses also can be subject to discrimination. A child may feel joy at seeing only familiar adults, whereas the child may feel frightened when seeing unfamiliar adults.

Finally, another type of learning that can be applied to how emotions are expressed is social cognition, which states that we observe and imitate those models we admire. Kate found a picture of Kenny when he was about three years old kissing a crying friend's knee. Kate was sure this empathetic behavior occurred because whenever Kenny fell down and hurt himself, she or Michael would say, "I'll kiss it and make it better."

# INTERACTION OF BIOLOGICAL AND CONTEXTUAL INFLUENCES ON EMOTIONAL DEVELOPMENT

So far we have analyzed separately the biological and contextual explanations of emotional development. However, Campos and colleagues (Campos et al., 1983) believe emotional development results from an interaction between biological and contextual influences and has the following features:

Anger

1. There is a set of differentiated core emotion states (joy, anger, sadness, fear, interest) present throughout life. These emotions are based on biological goals (e.g., survival).
2. As cognitive development proceeds in a child, such complex and coordinated emotions as shame, guilt, envy, and depression appear. These emotions are based on socialized goals.
3. As a child develops, different circumstances have different effects in eliciting specific emotions.
4. The relation between the expressions and experience of emotions changes as a person develops. Infants can manifest an emotion

*(continued on following page)*

Interest

(continued from previous page)
(such as a smile or angry expression) that does not correspond to the underlying emotional state. This is probably a result of neurological immaturity.

5. Coping responses to emotions change as the individual develops in terms of cognitive and motor development. An infant, for example, can be frightened by the approach of a stranger. However, when the infant can crawl away from the stranger or crawl to the mother, interest rather than fear may be exhibited.

6. The expression of emotions is socialized into acceptable forms. Culture can dictate the circumstances in which emotions are experienced (it is appropriate in Western culture to cry at a funeral). Culture also socializes us to have certain emotions toward certain individuals and to express them in certain ways. (Children are taught to love their parents; for example, American children are taught to express their love by giving a kiss.) In addition, the labels given to emotional states and how emotions are managed are culturally influenced. (For example, American children are socialized to curb angry responses.)

## F.Y.I.

A study by Harlow and Zimmerman (1959) showed that infant monkeys raised in cages with "surrogate mothers" made of wire mesh and "surrogate mothers" made of wire mesh but covered with terry cloth, spent more time clinging and chattering to the cloth mothers even though they were fed by the wire mothers. When they were frightened they went to the cloth mothers for comfort.

As a person develops, his receptiveness to others' emotional expression changes (table 11.1). For about the first six weeks of life, an infant does not attend to facial details (such as eyebrows, eyes, mouth) that give clues to emotional expression. From about six weeks to four or five months, an infant scans the face and can discriminate among emotional expressions even though the meaning of the expression is not understood. From about four or five months to about nine months, an infant reacts with a positive or negative expression according to the perceived facial expression. An infant now can deliberately search for emotional information in another person's face, voice, and gesture when a situation is ambiguous. This is called social referencing. As children get older they become more sophisticated in communicating and understanding emotions. However, children cannot understand that people can feel more than one emotion (sometimes opposite emotions) at the same time until children are nine or ten years old. Box 11.1 is a summary of the different and important milestones of emotional development.

## EMOTIONAL TIES

The development of emotional ties is considered the cornerstone of normal social and personality development. For example, when you love another person, you depend on that person for comfort, for affection, and for sharing feelings.

Bowlby (1958; 1969; 1973; 1980; 1988) developed a theory to explain an infant's tie to the mother. According to Bowlby, emotional ties or attachments result from evolved adaptive behavior to seek proximity to the parent. There are certain infant responses such as crying, smiling, clinging, sucking, and following that result in eliciting parental care and protection. These responses then are important for species survival because they ensure contact between parent and child. The parent, usually the mother, is biologically programmed to respond to the infant's eliciting stimuli (e.g., crying

## GENERALIZED SCHEMA FOR PREDICTING ELICITATION OF MORE COMPLEX EMOTIONS

### TABLE 11.1

| Emotion | Goal | Appreciation | Action tendency[a] | Adaptive function[b] |
|---|---|---|---|---|
| Shame | Maintenance of others' respect and affection, preservation of self-esteem | Perception of loss of another's respect or affection; perception that others have observed one doing something bad | Like those of sadness, anger (at self), and fear | Maintenance of social standards |
| Guilt | Meeting one's own internalized standards | Anticipation of punishment because one has not lived up to an internalized standard | Like those of fear and anger | Encouragement of moral behavior |
| Envy | Obtaining a desired object | Perception that an object cannot be had because another has it; one's deficits prevent oneself from attaining the object | Like those of sadness and anger | Motivates achievement so as to obtain similar goods |
| Depression | Having the respect and affection of both others and one's self | Perception of lack of love or respect from both others and one-self; perception of lack of possibility of attaining any significant goal | Like those of sadness and anger (at self) | Elicits affection and nurturance from others; conservation of energy |

[a]Action tendencies for complex emotions are specific forms of action tendencies of component emotions.
[b]Any of these emotions can become maladaptive if severe or prolonged.

**(Campos, Barrett, Lamb, Goldsmith & Stenberg, 1983)**

## Box 11.1 IMPORTANT MILESTONES OF EMOTIONAL DEVELOPMENT

According to Greenspan (1985), six milestones of emotional development emerge from the special relationship between infants and caregivers (interactive synchrony). After birth, infants have two challenges:

- To feel regulated and calm
- To use all senses to be interested in the world.

1. *Self-Regulation and Interest in the World*—occurs within the first three months of life. It involves gaining the ability to organize the senses—

*(continued on following page)*

*(continued from previous page)*

to feel calm about new sights, sounds, and touches while also actively seeking them out.

2. *Falling in Love*—occurs between two and seven months. It involves becoming interested in the world. An infant who shows no interest or is frightened of sights and sounds, however, probably will not progress to this second stage where contact with humans is enticing and exciting. A three- or four-month-old infant in this stage exhibits joy when you look at her and when she hears your voice. This stage is usually indicated by the appearance of the smile.

3. *Developing Intentional Communication*—can be observed from three to ten months. It involves human interaction in the child's world. A child responds to parents' expression of emotions, and the child's responses then lead to reactions from parents and others. When a parent tries to remove an object from the child, the child may protest in anger. This in turn may cause the parent to soothe the child or to return the object. At the latter part of this stage, infants often initiate the interaction (dropping a toy off the high chair and laughing).

4. *Emergence of an Organized Sense of Self*—occurs between nine and 18 months. It involves connecting feelings with actions. Anger can involve more than crying; it can be accompanied by throwing a toy.

5. *Creating Emotional Ideas*—can be observed between 18 and 36 months. It involves constructing ideas to express emotions (connecting feelings to ideas). The child can now picture an object or a person in his mind when the object or person is not present and he can construct an emotion associated with that object or person.

6. *Emotional Thinking: The Basis for Fantasy, Reality, and Self-Esteem*—occurs between 30 to 48 months. It involves using emotions to relate to the rest of the world. This involves the ability to distinguish between one's feelings and the feelings of others—what makes the child happy can upset parents. In fact, a popular activity often observed in preschool settings is fantasy play, which usually occurs in a corner of the room set up like a house. The children generally dress up like Mom or Dad with available clothes. Usually the play involves acting out feelings—Mom or Dad going to work (distress), child being put to bed (anger) or going to the doctor (fear).

Acting out feelings in various roles leads to the capacity to be empathetic. Children this age now understand the feelings of others because they have experienced those same feelings.

Children not only act out feelings, they now have become more skilled in controlling them. Controlling feelings is important in relating to others. For example, one learns to express anger verbally rather than physically. The ability to relate to others in turn influences one's self-esteem.

and smiling). As a result of the interaction between the infant's and mother's genetically based behavior, attachment develops between the two.

While Bowlby primarily attributed attachment to proximity-seeking behavior, his theory also emphasized that attachment figures served two related functions for young infants. One was to provide children with secure bases for exploration of the environment, thereby facilitating cognitive growth. A child who knows her mother is available if she needs her will feel free to explore the environment. The second was to give children safety when encountering threats, thus permitting children to regulate their level of stress. (A child is less likely to be frightened by a stranger if he is being held by the mother).

Other researchers (Ainsworth, 1973; Sroufe & Waters, 1977; Ainsworth et al., 1978) have expanded on these functions. The notions of the caregiver as a secure base for exploration and a place of safety helped stimulate the development of a model that has become the most popular procedure for assessing infant–adult attachments. This model procedure, devised by Ainsworth and colleagues (1978), is called the *Strange Situation*. The Strange Situation involves observing a 12- to 18-month-old child in an unfamiliar room with the parent, alone, and with an unfamiliar adult. According to Bowlby (1969), because fear and distress elicit attachment, the strange situation has been effective in assessing individual differences in attachment. Attachment is assessed by measuring the extent to which a parent is used as a secure base for exploration when the child is permitted to play with toys in the unfamiliar room and as a haven of safety when a stranger enters the room. Separation distress (which also signifies attachment) is assessed when the parent leaves the child all alone and alone with the stranger. A child's reaction to the return of the mother is observed, and, finally, the child's ability to be soothed by the stranger is compared with the child's reaction when soothed by the parent.

Ainsworth and colleagues (1978) classified children's attachment by three types:
- avoidant
- secure
- ambivalent

The avoidant, or "anxiously attached," group (22 percent of the sample studied) avoided the parent during the reunion episodes, failed to cling when held, and tended to treat the stranger the same way as or sometimes more positively than the parent. The secure, or "securely attached," group (66 percent of the sample) tended to seek proximity to and contact with attachment figures, particularly during reunion episodes. Moreover, such infants manifested clear preferences for their caregivers over the stranger. The ambivalent, or "ambivalently attached," group (12 percent of the sample) tended to resist interaction and contact with their caregiver, yet they also manifested contact- and proximity-seeking behavior.

## ANTECEDENTS OF DIFFERENT TYPES OF ATTACHMENT

Infants have different response patterns to mothers' interactions for various reasons such as their prematurity or their *temperament*. *Premature,* or *preterm,* refers to infants born after less than 35 weeks gestation who weigh less than 2,500 grams at birth. **Temperament** refers to the characteristic way one emotionally responds to objects and people including one's mood, activity level, and reaction intensity. Temperament is usually classified as *easy, difficult,* or *slow-to-warm up.*

The effect of prematurity is illustrated by the facts that full-term infants as compared with four-month-old preterm neonates vocalize less (Field, 1980), are fussier, avert gazes from mothers more frequently (Field, 1979), and remain somewhat less responsive during their first year (Goldberg, Brachfeld & DiVitto, 1980). Thus, as a result of his neurological immaturity, the infant may interfere with an optimal infant–parent interaction for attachment.

## F.Y.I.

It has been found that mothers are more responsive to cuddly (easy) infants (Schaffer & Emerson, 1964) and less responsive to irritable (difficult) infants (Wolff, 1969).

Because the infant is not responsive, the parent reduces her initiating efforts at interaction, or overreacts and stimulates the infant too much. Both scenarios, understimulation and overstimulation, reflect a lack of sensitivity to what the infant is feeling; thus, the risk of impaired attachment exists.

Mothers have different response patterns to infants' interactions. Studies (Clarke-Stewart, 1973; Ainsworth et al., 1978; Bowlby, 1988) have shown that attachment patterns and the attachment intensity are related to patterns of mothering; that is, securely attached infants have mothers who are the most responsive to their infants. These mothers tend to notice infants' signals, to accept the necessary tasks of caring for infants, to have concern and respect for infants' activities, and to be available.

Mothers who are unresponsive, neglectful, or abusive have children whose attachments are insecure and anxious. Egeland and Sroufe (1981) compared two groups of mothers and children in regard to the quality of care and attachment. One group consisted of mothers who provided high-quality care in feeding, health, and safety. The other group consisted of mothers who provided low-quality care in that they were unresponsive to the children's need for physical protection (a child was often left unsupervised) and these mothers were often violent or abusive. The children's attachment was assessed at 12 and 18 months. Seventy-five percent of the children who received high-quality care were securely attached compared with only 38 percent in the low-quality care group. The earlier an infant's maltreatment had begun, the more likely the infant's attachment to the mother was insecure.

## RESEARCH IN REVIEW

### DOES THE INFANT'S TEMPERAMENT INFLUENCE THE QUALITY OF ATTACHMENT?

Izard, C.E., Porges, S.W., Simons, R.F., Hayes, O.M., Hyde, C., Parisi, M. & Cohen, B. (1991). Infant cardiac activity: Developmental changes and relations with attachment. *Developmental Psychology, 27* (3), 432–439.

Temperament is viewed as a psychobiological construct in that it represents differences in physiological reactions, which come to be exhibited as individual behavioral differences.

In this study the relations between heart rate and attachment were investigated over the first 13 months of life. The subjects were 88 Caucasian infants from middle-class families. They were seen periodically from 2.5 to 63 months of age. Heart rate data from this study were obtained during the 3-, 4.5-, 6-, 9-, and 13-month visits, and the attachment classification was obtained during the 13-month visit using the Ainsworth strange situation (Ainsworth et al., 1978).

A child's behavior during each episode was recorded using Ainsworth's standardized method. A judgment was then made based on the number and intensity of certain behaviors (such as proximity- and contact-maintaining behavior, resistant behavior, avoidant behavior, search behavior, and distance interactions) as to whether the child demonstrated a secure or insecure attachment (insecure/avoidant or insecure/resistant) to the mother. A secure child responds positively to the mother, seeking and maintaining contact with her, and receiving comfort at reunion. These children exhibit little or no resistant behavior and can use their mothers as a secure base from which to explore the environment. Insecure/avoidant children show little or no tendency to seek proximity or contact with mothers, even during reunion episodes. These children may ignore mothers or exhibit more salient avoidant behaviors such as turning or looking away or withdrawing from mothers. Insecure/avoidant children typically demonstrate few search behaviors and little or no distress at separation. Insecure/resistant children tend to display angry resistant behaviors toward their mothers. These children demonstrate limited exploration of their surroundings, and they are difficult to soothe after separation.

It was found that infant measures of heart rate variability taken over time were significantly related to insecure attachment. The meaning of the positive relation between heart-rate variability and attachment insecurity is not yet clear. While the behavior of insecure/resistant children is negatively expressive, the behavior of insecure/avoidant children is not. Perhaps avoidant children react physiologically but suppress negative emotion expressions as an early coping mechanism to stress. Thus, while insecure/avoidant children have a high heart rate variability, they differ from secure and insecure/resistant children in how they express emotion or respond to physiological changes.

# FATHERS AND ATTACHMENT

Evidence shows that infants become attached to fathers as well as mothers when their fathers hold them, respond to their cries, vocalize, and play with them (Lamb, 1977a; Parke & Sawin, 1980). Fathers' styles of interaction are different from mothers'. Generally, men tend to engage in more physically stimulating and unpredictable play while women tend to be more verbal and predictable in that they play the usual infant games (such as Peek-A-Boo) (Power & Parke, 1982). However, women and men tend to stimulate same-sex infants more than opposite-sex infants. For example, mothers visually and tactually stimulated their three-week-old and three-month-old girls more than they did their boys, while fathers of 15- to 24-month-old boys were observed to vocalize to their sons more than their mothers (Lamb, 1977a; Lamb, 1977b).

Thus, fathers play a significant role in the development of emotional ties. The early differential treatment of female and male infants by their mothers and fathers may even play a part in gender-role development.

Children become attached to each of their parents although each parent generally treats male and female offspring differently.

# DAY CARE AND ATTACHMENT

Kagan and colleagues (1978) compared infants who spent five days a week in a day-care center from three months of age on with infants of the same socioeconomic and ethnic backgrounds who were cared for at home primarily by their mothers. The ratio of adults to children at the center was one to three for infants and one to five for toddlers. The caregivers played with each child individually several times a day. This study found no significant differences between day-care and home-care children in emotional., social., or intellectual development. Both groups were similarly attached to their mothers.

Apparently, *quality* day care generally does not weaken an infant's attachment to the mother. However, if day care starts before a child's first birthday and the day care is unstable (several changes occur in the supplementary caregiver), there is likely to be a disruption in the emotional ties with the mother (Vaughn, Gove & Egeland, 1980).

Belsky and Rovine (1988) reviewed studies done in the 1980s comparing infants with and without day-care experience in the first year of life.

Children enrolled in quality child care programs usually do not weaken attachments to mothers.

Children who feel emotionally secure feel safe in exploring their environment, which in turn contributes to intellectual competence.

They concluded that experiencing extensive nonmaternal care is associated with increased avoidance and insecurity in the relationship with the mother. Their own investigation showed when mothers are employed more than 20 hours per week and infants are cared for by someone else (not a parent) during their first year, there is likely to be an insecure attachment to the mother. When mothers are employed more than 35 hours per week, sons are likely to exhibit an insecure attachment to their fathers as well. However, not all infants exposed to extensive day care during their first year succumb to this risk. Temperament plays a role. The infants in Belsky and Rovine's sample who were classified as having an insecure attachment were more likely to be males and to be characterized as fussy or difficult by their mothers. The mother's sensitivity to her infant's needs also is responsible. Mothers of insecurely attached infants were career-oriented, expressed less satisfaction with their marriages, and reported limits to their sensitivity. Finally, the father's participation in the care of his infant influences the security of the attachment. The infants in Belsky and Rovine's sample who developed secure relationships with their mothers were more likely to be cared for by their fathers.

It is not the mother's employment during the infant's first year of life that impacts the child's attachment, but how the child generally responds to her, how she feels about combining work and family, and what the father's role is in caregiving.

## SIGNIFICANCE OF EMOTIONAL TIES

The development of emotional ties is significant because it provides a foundation on which other areas of development can build, such as social competence. For example, one study showed that infants who were securely attached at 12 or 18 months approached problems presented to them as two-year-olds with greater enthusiasm and interest than did avoidant or resistant children (Matas, Arend & Sroufe, 1978).

A study (Slade, 1987) of mothers and toddlers examined from 20 to 28 months of age showed that secure children had longer episodes of symbolic play than their anxious peers. Also, the mothers of the securely attached infants and the mothers of anxiously attached infants behaved differently in the experimental situation. The mothers of the secure children were more involved in their play, whereas the mothers of the anxious children were more passive in their participation.

One study (Lewis et al., 1984) found a relation between insecure attachment at age one and maladjustment and behavior problems at age six. This relation was found for the males in the sample but not for the females. The investigators concluded that although attachment is an important influence on later development, secure attachment does not prevent the later development of emotional problems and insecure attachment does not ensure it.

## DEVELOPMENT OF SPECIFIC EMOTIONS

Most researchers agree that infants possess the musculature to display a variety of emotions. Some emotional expressions appear at birth while others occur in reaction to particular external events. The earliest displays of emotion are generalized. That is, the infant feels OK or not OK. Feeling OK usually elicits pleasure, and feeling not OK usually elicits distress, wariness, or rage. Later displays of emotion are more specific. A smile may be reserved only for parents. The development of some specific emotions to understand how expressions change as a child matures will now be explained. Table 11.2 shows the emergence of some emotions that will be discussed.

## EMERGENCE OF SOME HUMAN EMOTIONS

### TABLE 11.2

| Month | Pleasure-Joy | Wariness-Fear | Rage-Anger |
|---|---|---|---|
| 0 | Endogenous smile | Startle/pain | Distress due to: covering the face, physical restraint, extreme discomfort |
| 1 | Turning toward | Obligatory attention | |
| 2 | | | |
| 3 | Pleasure | Wariness | Rage (disappointment) |
| 4 | Delight Active laughter | | |
| 5 | | | |
| 6 | | | |
| 7 | Joy | | Anger |
| 8 | | | |
| 9 | | Fear (stranger aversion) | |
| 10 | | | |
| 11 | | | |
| 12 | Elation | Anxiety, Immediate fear | Angry mood, petulance |
| 18 | Positive valuation of self-affection | Shame | Defiance |
| 24 | | | Intentional hurting |
| 36 | Pride, love | | Guilt |

[a] The age specified is neither the first appearance of the effect in question nor its peak occurrences; it is the age when the literature suggests that the reaction is common.

(Sroufe, 1979)

Males who have avoidant or ambivalent attachments later showed depressive and withdrawal tendencies.

## JOY

Smiling appears in the newborn. When it first occurs, it reflects moderate arousal. Usually, it is seen during *REM sleep* (rapid eye movement sleep, usually associated with dreaming). By about the third month, the smile is elicited not by an internal stimulus such as sleep state but by an external one such as a familiar face. The recognition or mental assimilation of the familiar face elicits the smile (Sroufe, 1979). We can thus infer the infant is probably experiencing pleasure.

When the infant is about four months of age, laughter appears (Sroufe, 1979). At first, it occurs in response to physical stimulation, such as tickling. Later, as the infant can process meaning onto events, he will laugh at incongruous, or silly, things such as a parent sucking on a bottle. Still later, the infant experiences joy in anticipation of things, such as a parent

**FIGURE 11.2**
## CHILDREN'S FEARS
**(Jersild & Holmes, 1935)**

**Joy is being able to dance and laugh with a friend.**

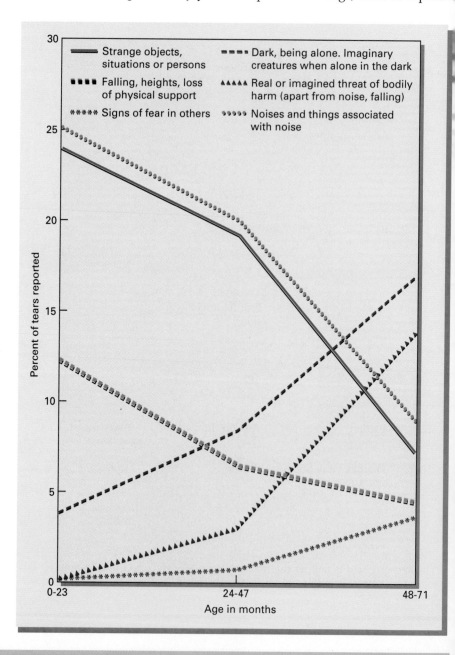

eturning. Finally, a child experiences joy when the child accomplishes what he set out to do.

In early childhood, joy is experienced based on outcomes—getting presents or being taken some place special, and so on (Weiner & Graham, 1984). Later in childhood, being with a friend is often cited as a source of pleasure (Jersild, 1968). Adolescents cite being with friends, extracurricular activities, travel, and self-improvement as giving them pleasure (Jersild, 1968).

## FEAR

Wariness is a negative reaction to the unfamiliar or unknown and appears during the first six months; whereas fear, which is a more specific negative reaction to a particular stimulus, does not appear until about nine months (Sroufe, 1979). Fear can be caused by anticipation or awareness of danger. The danger can be physical or psychological.

Bronson (1972) observed wariness in young infants when they looked at an unfamiliar face with an immobile expression. After about 15 to 30 seconds, the infant would frown and cry. Bronson attributes this reaction to the infant's inability to assimilate the face of the stranger.

As children develop, their fears change in intensity and what they fear changes (figures 11.2 and 11.3).

One fear commonly observed in infants is the fear of unfamiliar people, also known as stranger anxiety. This, in part, is due to cognitive maturity. The infant recognizes that the stranger is not "known." It is possible that

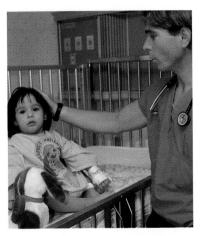

**This child has an obvious and understandable expression of fear.**

FIGURE 11.3
VARIATION IN
CHILDREN'S FEARS
(Barnett, 1969)

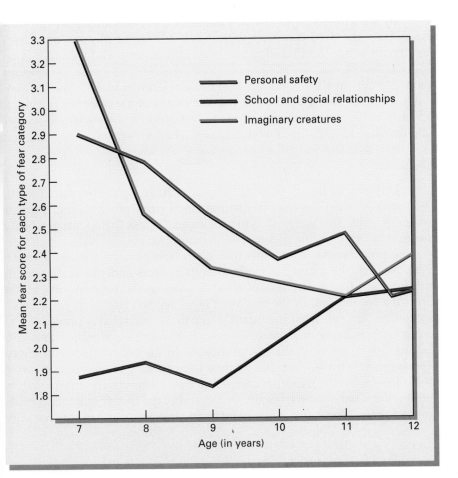

Adolescents fear falling short when compared with peers.

for some infants, strangers are perceived as aversive (especially if they are intrusive) and thus elicit fear. Stranger anxiety is the means by which researchers assess the quality of attachment. In general., the more securely attached an infant is to its mother, the greater is the stranger anxiety, which exhibits itself between four and six months of age and peaks in intensity by the end of the first year (De'carie, 1974; Sroufe, 1977). The intensity of stranger anxiety, however, is also influenced by whether the infant is in a familiar environment.

Other common fears in infancy are loud noises, unfamiliar situations, sudden movements, flashes of light, shadows, and a feeling of falling (Jersild & Holmes, 1935).

Preschoolers have difficulty distinguishing between reality and fantasy. A three-year-old may wake up terrified after having dreamed about a witch because he is convinced that a witch is in the closet. Even after the light is turned on and the closet door is opened, the child may still be afraid to go to sleep because he believes that closing the eyes will cause the witch to return.

School-age children generally have fears about school, for example, worries about grades and fears of teachers. They also have fears about social relationships, being teased and bullied, and not being liked (Jersild, 1968).

Some more contemporary fears exhibited by school-age children are losing a parent through divorce (Brozan, 1983) and nuclear war (Beardslee & Mack, 1986). As children approach adolescence they fear sexuality, abortion, suicide, and disabled children (Miller, 1983).

By the time a child reaches adolescence, fears focus on the self-image. How the child compares with peers in terms of physical attractiveness, competence, and intelligence is a real concern. The teenager is no longer afraid of witches, but pimples, dandruff, and fat cause tremendous emotional upheavals (Kellerman, 1981). When Jennifer was 15, she suddenly refused to go to the beach. She was not afraid of the water or of getting cancer from too much sun exposure; she was afraid someone would see her cellulite. Box 11.2 explains how to deal with children's fears.

## ANGER

Differences in the cries of newborns have been observed (Wolff, 1969) with a "mad" cry being distinguished from other crying, such as hunger or pain. This can be due to prolonged distress (being hungry, being uncomfortable, not being picked up and comforted).

A precursor to anger, other than distress, is physical restraint (Sroufe, 1979). At first, the infant responds to both distress and physical restraint without cognitive awareness of what is causing the rage. As the infant enters the second half of the first year, however, she begins to perceive an association between what the infant wants to do and what is preventing it. Anger is then becoming more specific. For example, Stenberg and colleagues (1983) observed that seven-month-old infants reacted with angry expressions when a teething biscuit they were sucking on was pulled out of their mouths by the experimenter; their expressions were angrier when their mothers removed the biscuit. By the end of the first year, anger is often directed against the source of restraint or frustration. Anger is now not only

## Box 11.2 DEALING WITH CHILDREN'S FEARS

- **Respect a child's fear**. A child's fear is real. Do not make fun of or trivialize it, or shame the child for having it. Children have a different perception and understanding of reality from adults.
- **Realize a child will outgrow most fears**. As a child gains experience, people, objects, and activities become less strange, and, therefore, less frightening. Also, as a child gains confidence in the ability to control herself and her environment, fears diminish.
- **Be familiar with fears children naturally experience at different ages**. Knowing a fear is common for a certain age is comforting, and, therefore, enables one to effectively deal with a child. For instance, saying the following shows a child understanding and also gives credibility for offering a solution: "Many children your age are afraid of the dark. I was, too, when I was your age. I took my teddy bear to bed to cuddle; what would you like?"
- **Allow a child to adjust to a fearful situation gradually**. For example, do not throw a child who is afraid of the water in a pool even if someone catches him. Rather, spend time watching others having fun in the pool. When that is comfortable, sit at the edge of the pool or on a step, and kick the water commenting on how much fun it is. Gradually, move toward the water letting the child allow you to hold him in the water. Always be positive and reinforce every adjustment. Put a life-jacket on the child so he can enjoy the water while learning to swim. When you and the child feel ready, remove the life-jacket, always being there to supervise (Ilg, Ames & Baker, 1981).

expressed as crying but also shows up as batting away objects, hitting, kicking, or pushing (Sroufe, 1979).

The manner in which anger is expressed changes with age. Angry outbursts have been found to peak at two years, especially undirected temper tantrums ( Goodenough, 1931; Jersild, 1968), which involve crying, screaming, hitting, and kicking. By age three, anger becomes more focused; it is more retaliatory and revenge-seeking. Grabbing someone's toy who earlier had done the same thing to the victim is common. Threats such as "I'll break your head" or "I'm gonna tell" are also quite common between ages three and five. Scolding ("You're not nice") and insulting ("I hate you") are other ways children often express anger.

As children get older, the physical manifestations of anger (crying, hitting, kicking) decrease and the verbal manifestations (tattling, name-calling) increase.

## F.Y.I.

Males use more physical responses to express anger throughout development than do females (Jersild, 1968).

From about age five through adolescence, the ability to understand causes of frustration and distress matures and, therefore, influences the expression of anger. A five-year-old, for example, can be angry with a parent for being delayed on a business trip and missing the child's birthday party. A nine- or ten-year-old will still be angry but will likely attribute the cause to his parent's boss, the airplane, or the weather. Thus, as children's cognitive abilities improve, anger responses become less frequent and more realistic (Weiner & Graham, 1984).

Anger responses change as the child develops, and so do what triggers them. Infants and toddlers become angry at parents' efforts to socialize them—eating on a schedule, going to sleep, wearing certain clothes, holding their hand in a store, and so on (Feshbach, 1970). Preschoolers (age three to six ) appear to direct most anger at peers—for not sharing toys, not taking turns, being interrupted, and other infringements on their rights (Feshbach, 1970). School-age children become angry when they are teased, treated unfairly, or when things do not work as they expected. Adolescents are angered at unsolicited advice, being accused unfairly, being contradicted, being interrupted in activities, and failure (Jersild, 1968). Box 11.3 discusses some methods to deal with anger.

## Box 11.3 DEALING WITH ANGER

Anger is best dealt with when it first appears, usually at the age of two in the form of a temper tantrum. Anger that is not appropriately confronted can become either suppressed, and emerge later as aggressiveness or depression, or can become controlling. Some children scream until the parent gives them what they want.

The first step in dealing with the initial display of anger is to understand it from a child's point of view. The child feels frustrated and helpless because she cannot do something or get something. Because the young child's ability to reason is limited, talking to the child is not an option.

Understanding that the tantrum is a child's method of releasing tension does not imply giving in to it. Most professionals agree that the best reaction is to ignore the outburst. This may mean letting the child scream while you leave the room or it may mean removing the child from the situation. Unfortunately, temper tantrums do not always occur at home or school; they are more likely to occur in public places. However, ignoring tantrums eventually causes inappropriate displays of anger to be replaced by acceptable behaviors.

When older children hit or yell to express anger, it is best to confront them with their feelings and discuss how they might deal with the situation next time. If children have trouble learning to verbalize anger, you can try to get them to redirect it.

Thus, dealing with anger involves acknowledging or understanding it and allowing for its release in an acceptable way (talking about feelings) rather than in an unacceptable way (screaming in public).

# WHEN EMOTIONS GET OUT OF CONTROL

Many complicated reasons explain why emotions get out of control, many of which are not thoroughly understood. Some explanations are biological., some contextual., and some interactional. We will examine *anxiety*, including phobias and obsessive compulsions, *autism,* and *depression*.

## ANXIETY

Some children exhibit **anxiety**, a psychological state characterized by tension and apprehension. It is an emotional reaction to fear that has gotten out of control. The emotional reaction can manifest itself as a *phobia* (the fear is attached to a person, event, or object) or as an *obsessive* or *compulsive* behavior. (The fear is dealt with by rigidly prescribed behaviors.)

## Phobias

Fear is regarded as a common emotion; it is an adaptive response to warn us to avoid potentially dangerous situations. At different ages children tend to be afraid of different things such as strangers and the dark. Most fears usually disappear and do not interfere with a child's functioning. However, when fears become so exaggerated so they prevent a child from relating to others or experiencing his environment, then the child is said to have a **phobia.**

A well-known phobia in both children and adolescents is school phobia. Children who are school phobic try to avoid going to school by crying or having a tantrum. Some develop physical symptoms such as nausea, vomiting, and abdominal pains. The most common reason for the anxiety is the belief that something will happen to the parent while the child is at school (Wenar, 1982). Such concern may have emerged from an anxious attachment.

After being confronted by a stranger after just having awakened, these children are clearly exhibiting some anxiety.

## Obsessive Compulsions

**Obsessive compulsiveness** is a disorder in which persistent and irrational thoughts and uncontrollable, repetitive acts occur as a defense against anxiety. Some children have rituals that they employ regularly, such as a kiss goodnight or sleeping with a certain toy. Though these behaviors can last for a long time, they usually do not interfere with a child's activities or interactions. In contrast, obsessive-compulsive behavior, like washing one's hands several times after touching anything and showering several times a day, does interfere with one's daily life. *Obsessions* are recurring involuntary thoughts that pervade the consciousness. *Compulsions* are apparently irresistible urges to repeat an act or engage in ritualistic behavior. Obsessions and compulsions are often found together in the same person because the recurring thoughts lead to anxiety-reducing behavior patterns.

About 2 percent of children who are seen by professionals for emotional disturbances have obsessive-compulsive behaviors (Hollingsworth et al., 1980). These children tend to be of normal or above-normal intelligence, feel guilty about imagined (or real) wrong-doings, and exhibit active fantasy lives.

## F.Y.I.

About 1 percent of school-age children suffer from school phobia (Yule, 1981).

# AUTISM

Infantile or childhood **autism** is a severe disorder affecting about four of 10,000 children (DeMyer, Hingten & Jackson, 1981). This disorder appears in early childhood and affects how the individual relates to objects and people in the environment. By 30 months it is obvious these children are different (Rutter, 1978). They appear aloof and disinterested in the people around them. They tend to look through people rather than make eye contact. When they speak, which they rarely do, they often echo or parrot what has been said to them. They sometimes have their own words to describe common items; for example, "door" might be called "dark hole" (Apter & Conoley, 1984).

Autistic children exhibit many ritualistic behaviors such as repetitive body rocking, head banging, and scratching. They appear to require sameness, and they react violently to changes in their environment such as rearranging furniture. While their memories for routine information appear intact, they have difficulty learning concepts such as "larger than" (Hermelin & O'Connor, 1970).

The cause of autism is unknown. It was believed that autism was caused by emotional deprivation, and researchers blamed parents for being cold and distant (Kanner, 1965). More recently, however, most researchers (Chess, 1971; Ornitz, 1974; Coleman, 1976) agree that biology is more involved than context. No commonality exists among parents of autistic children, whereas a likeness in the behaviors of many autistic children exists. Also, there is a preponderance of males diagnosed as autistic, and finally, numerous children diagnosed as autistic develop seizure disorders in later adolescence (Apter & Conoley, 1984).

# DEPRESSION

**Depression** is a state of deep and pervasive dejection and hopelessness, accompanied by apathy and a feeling of personal worthlessness. Recently, depression has been recognized in children with increased frequency. Some believe it affects about 2 percent of the general child population and 15 to 20 percent of children seen by professionals (Kasahni et al. 1981). The reason depression was not usually recognized in children is that it is often masked by other symptoms such as *conduct disorders* and *psychosomatic ailments*. **Conduct disorders** are marked by persistent acts of aggressive or antisocial behavior. **Psychosomatic ailments** are physical disorders in which psychological factors play a major role.

Another reason depression was not usually recognized in children is that young children have difficulty talking about feelings. However, it is well known that depressed children, like depressed adolescents and adults, feel unworthy, powerless, and tend to blame themselves (Garber et al. 1985).

Some researchers use biological explanations for the cause of depression. For example, some adults and children respond to drug therapy, which may indicate that depression is a biochemical reaction (Puig-Antich, 1982). However, it is unknown if biochemistry promotes depression or depression changes biochemistry.

Other researchers look to contextual influences to explain depression. For example, Bowlby (1980, 1988) has suggested that a major disruption in

tachment due to such events as death, illness, divorce, or other separation
an cause depression. For another example, severe emotional neglect by
arents can lead to depression (Kaufman & Cicchetti, 1986). It may be that if
child's emotions are not responded to because of separation from the
tachment figure or neglect by the attachment figure, the child not only
ecomes sad but also gives up hope of attracting a response and, conse-
uently, feels unworthy of receiving one.

## UICIDE

Suicide is the ultimate reaction to emotions that for some reason got
everely out-of-control so that death is the only solution.

Suicide is the second leading cause of death for people aged 15 to 24;
ar accidents are the first cause of death (Jones, 1988).

Suicidal adolescents tend to come from families with problems
Grueling & DeBlassie, 1980). Such problems include divorce, negative or
ejecting attitudes toward the child, economic stress, early parental physical
r emotional deprivation, illness, death, or abandonment by the father.

Suicide attempters often state they do not feel emotional ties with
ny adult and have a sense of detachment from their peers (Jones, 1988). A
pical comment is "There is no one to turn to when I need to talk to some-
ne" (Teicher 1973).

Another frequent component of suicide is depression (Tishler &
IcKenry, 1983). This can be displayed by crying spells, lack of motivation,
arelessness, changes in sleep patterns (increase in sleep or insomnia), and
icrease in drug or alcohol use.

Adolescents who attempt suicide appear to have a limited capacity
support themselves emotionally; they rely greatly on relationships with
thers and seem to lack enough self-worth to feel in control of themselves
Topol & Reznikoff, 1984). They also do not know how to deal with nega-
ve emotions such as those associated with failure (Jones, 1988). When an
idividual fails, she can blame herself or blame others. If one blames one-
elf, one can choose to rectify the failure. Suicidal adolescents blame them-
elves and do not rectify anything; rather, they give up.

Some other emotional components of suicide are guilt or anger.
nding a romance or becoming pregnant have been reported as factors in
uicide-attempting girls (Teicher, 1973).

To summarize, the symptoms of suicidal risk are a "dangerous triad
f emotions: feelings of worthlessness, helplessness and hopelessness"
Jones, 1988, p. 1).

## EMOTIONAL ABUSE AND NEGLECT

When a child is severely rejected or emotionally deprived so that
ndangerment to the child's emotional or mental development results, that
s called **emotional abuse** or **neglect** (Maidman, 1984). Emotional abuse can
ccur when parents are inconsistent in talk, rules, or actions; when they
ave unrealistic expectations of children; when they belittle and blame their
hildren. Emotional neglect occurs when parents do not respond to their

## F.Y.I.

According to a commis-
sion formed by the
American Medical
Association and the
National Association of
State Boards of Education,
about 10 percent of
teenage boys and 18 per-
cent of girls try to kill
themselves at least one
time.

## F.Y.I.

A mother who was report-
ed to the police by a pediatrician for emotional
neglect (the infant failed
to thrive) explained, "I
have never felt loved; so
when I had this baby, I
thought he'd love me; but
when he cried all the
time, it meant he didn't. I
couldn't cope, so I left
him to cry it out in his
crib."

infants' cries, smiles, or fears; when they are not interested in a child's activities; when they never praise the child (Garbarino, Guttman & Seely, 1986).

Emotional abuse or neglect is difficult to document and prove, but its effects can be crippling, not showing up until years later when the symptoms become obvious and professional help is sought (Kempe & Kempe, 1978). Some behavioral indicators in children who are emotionally abused are (School Safety Center, 1981):

- Withdrawn, depressed, apathetic behavior
- Antisocial, destructive, or aggressive behavior
- Comments such as, "My parents always tell me I'm stupid," or "My parents wanted a boy."

The physical effects of emotional neglect are seen in children who lag in development. They may fail to thrive, be mentally retarded, be susceptible to illness, and have speech disorders (Spitz, 1946; Bowlby, 1969, 1973, 1988). Some behavioral indicators are (School Safety Center, 1981):

- Habit disorders such as lip sucking
- Constantly "seeking out" or "pestering" other adults for attention and affection
- Antisocial, destructive, or aggressive behavior
- Sleep disorders
- Behavior extremes such as compliant/demanding or passive/aggressive
- Anxiety, phobias, obsessive/compulsiveness
- Attempted suicide

Emotionally abusing or neglecting parents are likely prompted by their own psychological problems rather than by something a child did or did not do. They are likely to have suffered emotional deprivation themselves (Kempe & Kempe, 1978; Garbarino, Guttman & Seely, 1986).

When an emotionally abusive family is identified to child protective services, usually by the child's teacher or physician, the family can be required by the court to have psychological counseling and parent education.

ne stereotype associated with females is emotionality. Is the difference in the expression of emotions between males and females caused by biology or socialization?

**ANALYSIS:** Review this chapter and find three supporting reasons for a biological basis and three reasons for a contextual basis for emotions.

**SYNTHESIS:** Apply both the biological and the contextual positions to explain the stereotype that females are more "emotional" than males.

**EVALUATION:** Do you agree or disagree with the emotionality stereotype for females? Give reasons for your position.

## SUMMARY

Emotions are defined as physiological changes in arousal levels expressed subjectively by various responses.

Emotions are difficult to measure and classify scientifically. One method is the Maximally Discriminative Facial Movement (MAX) system, which classifies facial expressions by movement of the eyebrows, forehead, eyes, nose, cheeks, and mouth.

Emotions can be the result of a biological adaptation that enables the successful survival of a species. Anger can motivate a fight response, fear can motivate a flight response, and love can motivate a nurturing response.

Differential emotions theory proposes that primary emotional expressions such as joy, anger, surprise, fear, and distress are innate, with distinctive neurological subsystems for each. These discrete emotions are based on separate innate neurological programs and are set to emerge when such emotions become adaptive in life.

Differentiation emotions theory states that emotions are differentiated as a function of maturation and cognitive development from genetically similar routes, beginning with an increase in arousal level and becoming more specific and differentiated throughout development.

- Evidence indicates that infants' behavior is influenced by the emotional expression on their mothers' faces. They also use other adults' expressions as social references. Social referencing continues throughout development.

- Emotional development has been observed to go through six milestones based on the interactive synchrony of infants and caregivers. These are self-regulation and interest in the world, falling in love, developing intentional communication, emergence of an organized sense of self, creating emotional ideas, and emotional thinking.

- Emotional ties or attachments are thought by some to result from evolved adaptive behavior to seek proximity to parents.

- Attachment figures provide children with a secure base for exploration of the environment and a place of safety when stress is encountered. Children's attachments can be classified as avoidant or anxiously attached, secure or securely attached, and ambivalent or ambivalently attached.

- The attachment level is influenced by how an infant responds to the mother, which in turn can be influenced by his prematurity or his temperament.

- The attachment level also can be influenced by how a mother responds to the infant.
- Evidence indicates that infants become attached to fathers as well as mothers when fathers hold them, respond to their cries, vocalize, and play with them.
- Some researchers claim that quality day care does not impair the attachment relationship. Other researchers have found, however, that when a mother is employed full-time and an infant is cared for by another caregiver, the infant may form an insecure attachment to both parents depending on the infant's temperament and the mother's feelings about her work.
- Emotions develop from the general to the specific.
- Sometimes emotions get out of control. Examples are anxiety, including phobias and obsessions-compulsions, autism, and depression. The extreme is suicide.
- Emotional abuse or neglect refers to the emotional rejection or deprivation of affection leading to the endangerment of a child's emotional or mental development.
- Emotional abuse occurs when parents are inconsistent, have unrealistic expectations, or when they continually belittle or blame their children.
- Emotional neglect occurs when parents do not respond to the infant's needs or distress, interests, or excitement.

## RELATED READINGS

Bowlby, J. (1988). *A secure base: Parent-child attachme  and healthy human development*. New Yor  Basic Books.

Cicchetti, D. & Hess, P. (Eds.) (1982). *Emotional deve  opment*. San Francisco: Jossey-Bass.

Dunn, J. (1977). *Distress and comfort*. Cambridg  Harvard University Press.

Greenspan, S. & Greenspan, N.T. (1985). *First feeling  Milestones in the emotional development of yo  baby and child*. New York: Viking.

Harris, P.L. (1989). *Children and emotion: The develo  ment of psychological understanding*. New Yor  Basil Blackwell.

Izard, C., Kagan, J. & Zajonc, R. (Eds.) (1984  *Emotions, cognitions and behavior*. New Yor  Cambridge University Press.

Jersild, A.T. (1968). *Child Psychology* (6th ed  Englewood Cliffs, NJ: Prentice-Hall.

Lewis, M. & Michaelson, L. (1983). *Children's emotio  and moods*. New York: Plenum.

Lewis, M. & Saarni, C. (Eds.) (1985). *The socialization  emotions*. New York: Plenum.

Parke, R.D. (1981). *Fathers*. Cambridge: Harvar  University Press.

Stern, D. (1977). *The first relationship: Infant and mothe  Cambridge: Harvard University Press.

## • • • • • • • • • • • • • • • • • • ACTIVITY • • • • • • • • • • • • • • • • • • •

To better understand the role of emotions in social interaction, observe an adult and an infant (under six months) engaged in an interaction (interactive synchrony). This can be done in a child's home, in a day-care center, in a store, in a physician's office.

1. Note who starts the interaction (infant or adult) and the immediate response.
2. Describe the continued interaction in terms of facial expressions, vocalizations, and body language.
3. What emotions did you observe in the infant (us  Izard's classifications of facial expressions)?
4. What conclusions do you have about the expres  sion of emotions (facial expressions, vocalizations  and body language) on the part of the infant an  communication with the adult?

# 12 Social And Personality Development

*No man is an island, entire of itself; every man is a piece of the continent, a part of the main....*
**John Donne**

## OUTLINE

# ABOUT SOCIAL AND PERSONALITY DEVELOPMENT

Kate had to take Kenny to the physician for an earache. While she was sitting in the waiting room, a friend whom she had not seen since several years after high school walked in with a toddler. "Shelly, how are you? Do you still live in town?"

"Kate! Well, no. I moved away when Tom and I married. He's in the Navy, so we move every couple of years. Right now he's over seas so I'm spending time with my mother."

"Well, you have not changed. How many kids do you have?"

"Three. This is Tracy. She's two. Tara is six, and Joe is nine."

"I have four. This is Kenny; he's seven. Darla is ten, Jason is 13 and George is 15."

Kenny smiled and went over to the corner to play with the toys. He did not want to listen to his mother and her friend chatter away. His ear hurt.

Shelly said, "Tell me about your family while we're waiting."

Kate began. "Michael still works at his father's service station. Sometimes Jason and George help out. They are so different. George couldn't wait for his father to ask him to help out. He likes finding out how things work so when Michael has to take an engine apart George is right there. Jason could care less. Working at the station for him is a big inconvenience; he only does it to earn money. He'd much rather be playing ball with his friends. George is a quiet boy and likes to be by himself. He is slow to warm up to people. Jason is noisy and always likes to be around people. He was a difficult baby, crying all the time. And now he's a difficult teenager, arguing all the time.

"Darla, the only girl, is a big help around the house. When Kenny was a baby, she loved to play with him. She likes being the little mother. She likes to please and is very sensitive. She gets good grades in school. She's the only one of the kids who likes to read, maybe because the boys are always hogging the TV.

"Kenny is a charmer. He knows how to get what he wants with that cute grin. He was an easy baby. He eats anything you give him, likes to play with whomever is around, and likes to make you laugh.

"It's amazing how kids from the same family can be so different! How about yours?"

"Same here," said Shelly. "Each one has a different personality. Things come easy to Joe. He likes school, and he's the best batter on his Little League team. Maybe because he's the only boy, his dad gives him a lot of attention. Tara has a hard time with everything. She is having trouble learning to read. She's always losing some hing at school, whereas Joe keeps his things in order, Tara is sloppy. She is shy with strangers and would rather watch other kids than play with them. The other two were more independent. I don't understand it, we've taught them the same things."

The discussion between Kate and Shelly about the different characteristics of their children is typical. Not only parents but psychologists, too, ponder about how children develop the unique characteristics we call *personality* and exhibit these characteristics in their interactions with things and people in their environment. **Personality** refers to the sum of physical, mental, and emotional traits and behaviors that characterize an individual.

Most psychologists agree that personality emerges from biological predispositions and social interactions with others in various contexts (figure 12.1). An individual is affected by others and in turn affect others. Others affect one through the process of **socialization**, the process by which individuals acquire the knowledge, skills, and dispositions that enable them to participate as more or less effective members of groups and society (Brim, 1966). Socialization begins at birth; it teaches one the ways of the society in which one lives, such as how to behave, dress, eat, speak, and conduct business. A person affects other people according to his personality. If one is friendly and helpful, others want to interact. If one is belligerent and argumentative, others want to either fight back or avoid the person. Thus, reciprocity is between individuals and others. Biological and contextual influences are analyzed separately and then how they interact to produce different effects on individual children is explained.

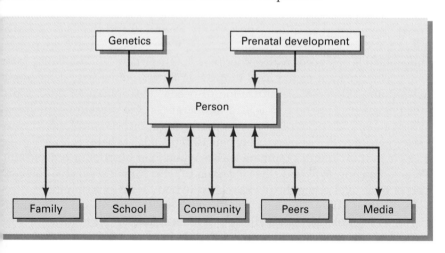

FIGURE 12.1
FACTORS THAT
INFLUENCE
DEVELOPMENT OF
PERSONALITY

# THEORIES OF SOCIAL AND PERSONALITY DEVELOPMENT

Many theories try to explain why we behave the way we do, for example, behavior learning, social cognitive, and self-theories. The theories discussed in this chapter, however, are developmental; that is, they explain progressive changes over time in the way we behave. Sigmund Freud emphasized infancy and early childhood as the significant periods in which personality develops, influenced by how a child comes to balance biological

An example of id is to eat when one is hungry.

needs and social pressures in dealing with reality. Erik Erikson, on the other hand, emphasized eight stages during life in which critical psychological conflicts occur that must be resolved for a healthy personality to emerge and reemerge with an increased sense of inner unity, good judgment, and capacity to do well according to standards of significant others (Erikson 1980).

## PSYCHOANALYTIC THEORY OF SIGMUND FREUD

Sigmund Freud (1856–1939) was a physician who specialized in neurology. His theory of personality development emerged as a result of his work with people who had problems. He felt personality disorders could be treated by bringing them out of the unconscious mind into the conscious mind. The techniques he used are known as **psychoanalysis**, the process of analyzing the unconscious aspects of the mind. Thus, Freud's theory is called psychoanalytic.

Freud believed that thoughts, feelings, and behaviors are fueled by energy from the basic instincts—the instinct to live and the instinct to die. The instinct to live is exemplified by hunger, thirst, and the desire to reproduce. The instinct to die is exemplified by aggression. Throughout life we focus on gratifying these basic instincts by behaving so that energy from these instincts is released. When the energy is repressed, one feels tension and anxiety (Freud, 1935).

As we develop so do parts of our personality that serve the purpose of handling instinctual drives in different ways. According to Freud, the first structure to develop is called the **id**, from the Latin word for "it," the part of the personality that represents unconscious drives and needs. The id has no organization, and it operates in illogical and uninhibited ways. Freud thought that an infant's personality was all id and that even when an infant grew to adulthood, the id remained a permanent part of the personality, which is balanced by the other personality structures developing later.

The function of the id is to provide for the immediate discharge of tension and immediate gratification of needs. This release of energy provides pleasure. Thus, the id is said to operate on the **pleasure principle**: it avoids pain and seeks pleasure, or gratification of needs. Infants cry and kick when they are hungry or in pain; infants suck whatever they can get into the mouth; infants eliminate wastes when their bladder or bowel is full. Thus, according to Freud, the id serves to help humans survive the early part of their lives when the needs related to body functions dominate.

As the infant develops, the "real world" begins to make demands. Crying is less tolerated; everything put in an infant's mouth does not serve to nourish; feeding times become scheduled rather than demanded; pressure is exerted to delay the urge to eliminate until the infant is seated on the toilet. According to Freud, the second personality structure to develop is called the **ego**, from the Latin word for "I," the part of the personality that represents conscious awareness of reality. To illustrate, as children gradually learn to delay gratification of some instinctual needs and learn to master impulses, they are also becoming aware that a difference exists between their desires and the desires of others. The ego then is the part of one's personality that carries on transactions with the real world. According to Freud, the ego operates on the **reality principle** in that it postpones the gratification of a need until an appropriate object that will satisfy the need is found.

Dealing with the real world is not sufficient; one also has to behave by societal rules, which distinguish right behavior from wrong behavior. People cannot hit others if they are in the way; one should say "thank you" or "excuse me"; in our society, one must wear clothes in public. According to Freud, the third and final personality structure to develop is called the **superego**, meaning that which rises above the ego, the part of the personality representing the morals and ideals of society. The superego represents the *ideal* rather than the *real*. Thus, the superego operates on the **ideal principle** in that it strives for perfection rather than for reality or pleasure. It does this by having an **ego-ideal** (one's conception of what is morally good that should be rewarded) and a **conscience** (one's conception of what is morally bad that should be punished).

After the three structures have developed, which usually occurs about age five, they compete with one another to satisfy needs.

When the ego cannot handle conflicts between itself, the id, and the superego, the result is anxiety. Because anxiety inhibits the ability to act, the ego has several *defense mechanisms* to deal with conflicts unconsciously, thereby protecting the conscious mind from stress so it can conduct transactions with the world. **Defense mechanisms** are processes by which the ego keeps unacceptable impulses and thoughts in the unconscious, thereby preventing them from becoming conscious. Defense mechanisms distort reality or deny it in some way. Table 12.1 (page 368) lists some common defense mechanisms.

## Psychosexual Stages of Personality Development

Freud believed that as children develop they progress through distinct stages marked by maturation, specifically sexual drive maturation. Freud focused on the **erogenous zones**, areas of the body that are the focus of pleasure—mouth, anus, and genitals—to delineate the stages. Thus, these stages are termed *psychosexual*. The adult personality is affected by what one experienced during these stages, known as the oral, anal, and phallic.

**Oral Stage (birth-1 year).** When an infant is born, the mouth is the focus of activity as exhibited in sucking, swallowing, and grimacing. According to Freud, for normal development to occur, an infant has to receive optimal oral stimulation—not too much or too little. If the neonate experiences too much or too little oral stimulation, the infant may get **fixated**, or "stuck," at this stage and continue to seek oral gratification throughout childhood and adulthood; for example, by smoking.

**Anal Stage (1-3 years).** During the second to third year of life, a child's activities center around toilet training. The muscles in the bowel and bladder have matured so the child has voluntary control. Sexual energy can now be released through the anus. According to Freud, for normal development to occur the child should be allowed to experience pleasure and curiosity regarding excretion while gradually being trained to meet adult expectations during this anal period.

**Phallic Stage (3-5 years).** When the child is about three years of age, he becomes aware of pleasure from the genitals; masturbation is common. It is during this phallic period that males view their mothers as a love-object and females similarly view their fathers. The desire to possess the parent of the opposite gender usually causes intense anxiety, according to Freud. To avoid such uneasy feelings, males try to become like their fathers by imitat-

If toilet training is too lax or too harsh, a child can get fixated at the anal stage and can exhibit sloppiness or compulsiveness as an adult.

## TABLE 12.1

| Defense Mechanism | Definition |
|---|---|
| Repression | Tendency of the ego to push anxiety-producing situations into the unconscious. Thus, a person nondeliberately forgets. For example, incidents of sexual abuse are commonly repressed so the conscious mind does not have to deal with them. |
| Reaction formation | Repressed thoughts from the unconscious appear in the conscious part as opposites. For example, a woman who did not want to get pregnant has a child and becomes overprotective. |
| Regression | Under stress, a person may revert to using a tactic that was useful in reducing stress at an earlier age. For example, children will often suck their thumbs when faced with a situation they cannot accept. |
| Denial | The ego shuts itself off from certain realities that cause stress. For example, if a friend is killed in a car accident, a first reaction is "No, it couldn't have happened." |
| Projection | The tendency to see a disliked or guilt- and shame-producing aspect of oneself in another person. For example, the child who arrives at a hospital might say, "I have to hold my teddy bear tight because he's scared." The child wanted to be held by the parents but consciously knew bravery was required. Thus the child's unconscious desire was projected to the stuffed animal. |
| Rationalization | Presenting an excuse or justification for an action or behavior in which guilt or shame was felt. It occurs when the real motive for behavior is not accepted by the ego so an altered, less anxiety-producing motive is offered. For example, a student explained why he did not go to class for two days. One day he was ill. On the next day, the student was allowed by a parent to continue sleeping because the parent thought the student was still ill. When the student finally woke up it was late and the class would have been disrupted by a late arrival. |
| Displacement | A feeling, often anger, is transferred from its original threatening source to a safer, less powerful person or object. For example, one can be angry at a boss but fail to exhibit the feeling. Thus, the person goes home and yells at her spouse. |

ing their behavior, a process called **identification**, in which one assumes th characteristics of another. Likewise, females try to become like their moth ers, to be loved by the opposite-sex parent. If the feelings are not resolve egarding possessing the opposite-sex parent and identification does not occur, then a child risks having sexual problems as an adult, according to Freud.

**Latency Stage (5-12 years).** Freud regarded latency as an incubation period, a time when the first three personality stages have had their influence on development but the effects of that influence have not yet emerged. It is during the latency period that a child is involved with school and friends of the same sex. Thus, identification with the same-sex parent is extended to friends, coaches, and teachers. According to Freud, a significant event during this time is the development of defense mechanisms to cope with anxiety. No fixations occur at this stage.

**Genital Stage (12-18 years and older).** The child enters the genital stage when she reaches puberty, or sexual maturity. People of the opposite sex now become the focus of interest. However, if conflicts from earlier stages have not been resolved, mature heterosexual love, which is normally the outcome of the genital stage, is unlikely to occur, according to Freud.

## Freud's Theory Evaluated

Freud made a tremendous contribution to psychology. His study of the unconscious aspects of human behavior opened many avenues of inquiry. His emphasis on the vulnerability of the early childhood period influenced child-rearing practices so that flexibility and permissiveness were allowed rather than the traditional strict discipline. His concept of defense mechanisms provided new insight into understanding personality.

However, Freud's ideas have not gone without criticism. His emphasis on the sex drive is seen by most psychologists as being too pervasive. It is generally believed that social interactions rather than the sex drive are the influential factors in personality development (Adler, 1927; Sullivan, 1953; Erikson, 1963). Also, Freud's notion that the first five years of life were most significant in shaping the adult personality has been disputed by psychologists who view *events* as being influential in personality development. For example, in studying the effects of early child-rearing practices (feeding, weaning, and toilet training said by Freud to be responsible for forming a child's personality), Caldwell (1964) found few demonstrable links to later behavior.

Freud's theory was criticized on scientific grounds. First, the structures of personality (id, ego, superego) were questioned because they could not be observed, nor could their functions be used to predict behavior; rather, they explain behavior that has already occurred. Second, because Freud's theory was generated from the memories and fantasies of his neurotic adult patients, the generalization the theory to healthy individuals is questionable. Finally, Freud's theory was based on the societal norms of European culture in the 1900s, which were male-dominated and valued sexual repression. Thus, the theory could not be generalized to other cultures or times.

## PSYCHOANALYTIC THEORY OF ERIK ERIKSON

Erik Erikson refined and expanded Freud's psychoanalytic theory. He agreed with critics of Freud who claimed that Freud had focused only on neurotic personalities and, consequently, had neglected to define the nature of healthy personalities or to trace their pattern of development.

# F.Y.I.

**Born in Germany in 1902, Erik H. Erikson emigrated to the United States in the 1930s. He authored** *Childhood and Society* **2nd ed. (1963) and** *Identity: Youth and Crisis* **(1969).**

Thus, Erikson began by identifying the characteristics of a healthy personality and studying how the healthy personality develops. Erikson believed that personality development continued throughout life and emerged from the progressive resolution of conflicts between a person's needs or instincts. Resolution resulted from maturation and societal expectations or demands. He delineated eight stages from birth to death, each of which had conflict or crisis (table 12.2). While Freud focused on the unconscious mind, Erikson focused on the conscious mind, especially the search for identity (Erikson 1968; 1980).

## ERIKSON'S PSYCHOSOCIAL STAGES

### TABLE 12.2

|  | 1 | 2 | 3 | 4 | 5 | 6 | 7 | 8 |
|---|---|---|---|---|---|---|---|---|
| **I INFANCY** | Trust vs. Mistrust | | | | Unipolarity vs. Premature Self-differentiation | | | |
| **II EARLY CHILDHOOD** | | Autonomy vs. Shame, Doubt | | | Bipolarity vs. Autism | | | |
| **III PLAY AGE** | | | Initiative vs. Guilt | | Play Identification vs. (Oedipal) Fantasy Identities | | | |
| **IV SCHOOL AGE** | | | | Industry vs. Inferiority | Work Identification vs. Identity Foreclosure | | | |
| **V ADOLESCENCE** | Time Perspective vs. Time Diffusion | Self-certainty vs. Identity Consciousness | Role Experimentation vs. Work Paralysis | Anticipation of Achievement vs. Work Paralysis | Identity vs. Identity Diffusion | Sexual Identity vs. Bisexual Diffusion | Leadership Polarization vs. Authorization Diffusion | Idealogical Polarization vs. Diffusion of Ideals |
| **VI YOUNG ADULT** | | | | | Solidarity vs. Social Isolation | Intimacy vs. Isolation | | |
| **VII ADULTHOOD** | | | | | | | Generativity vs. Self-absorption | |
| **VIII MATURE AGE** | | | | | | | | Integrity vs. Disgust, Despair |

(Erickson, 1980)

According to Erikson, identity emerges as a result of inner and outer conflicts, or crises, that the healthy personality confronts. One's identity reemerges from each crisis with an increased sense of inner unity, with an increased sense of good judgment, and an increased capacity to do well by the person's own standards and the standards of significant others. In other words, how one resolves the eight crises, or stages, that one encounters in a lifetime determines how one's personality develops. At each stage the crisis involves the individual interacting in a social environment; hence, these stages are termed *psychosocial*, whereas Freud's were psychosexual.

## Psychosocial Stages of Personality Development

At each psychosocial stage, a crisis needs to be resolved. Typically, there are two opposing tendencies operating at the time of each crisis, one tendency is positive (for example, *trust*) in that it promotes development; the other tendency is negative (for example, *mistrust*) in that it retards development. The crisis at each stage must be resolved before one can effectively deal with the next conflict. That is, one must lean toward the positive tendency of each crisis while understanding that some negative tendency remains (Erikson, 1980). For example, while having *initiative* in the United States is considered to be a positive attribute, exercising it without regard for others' rights is cause for disapproval; having *guilt* serves to prevent initiative from becoming "pushiness."

When a crisis is resolved, an outcome results. The positive outcomes, or goals, of the psychosocial stages are hope, willpower, purpose, competence, fidelity, love, care, and wisdom (Erikson, 1963). Regardless of the success at resolving a particular crisis positively, one still must progress through each goal because biological maturation and the related societal expectation propel one to move from one stage to the next. For example, by age two, a child has matured enough to be able to walk, talk, and manipulate objects. Due to these new abilities, society now expects the child to become increasingly autonomous, such as to begin self-feeding.

Erikson's theory emerged from his experience with disturbed people as well as healthy people. He studied Western culture and other cultures, and he found that different cultures face the same crises throughout life yet have different values about crisis resolution. For example, the Sioux provide their children with a long and indulgent period of nursing to enable children to trust others and become generous themselves (Erikson, 1963). In American society, by contrast, nursing beyond a year is discouraged. Children are taught not to be too dependent or too trusting of others. Thus, the American value for a healthy outcome in the first stage is to have trust tempered with some distrust. Now we will discuss the eight stages delineated by Erikson.

**Basic Trust versus Basic Mistrust (birth–1 year).** During the first year of life, infants depend on their caregivers to meet their needs. If those needs are met consistently and with love, the infant develops a sense of trust. On the other hand, if the care is inconsistent, unloving, or neglectful, the infant develops a sense of mistrust. How the conflict between trust and mistrust is resolved sets a pattern for later relationships.

**Autonomy versus Shame and Doubt (2–3 years).** By the second year of life, children can control their own muscles and begin to assert their individuality. At the same time, parents begin imposing demands on a child

A search for one's identity and social role is the basis of Erickson's eight stages.

to conform to socially acceptable behavior, especially in controlling elimination of wastes. The crisis during this stage is whether the child develops feeling of autonomy or self-control over his actions or develops a feeling c shame and doubt because of being unable to control his own bodily func tions and behavior.

**Initiative versus Guilt (4–5 years).** Four-year-old children are mas ters of their own bodies. Now, they can try out ideas and take the initiativ in reaching goals—go for a ride on the tricycle or ask questions. During thi time, children are not only dealing with ideas but also are dealing with cor flicting feelings about the opposite-sex parent. If a child can overcome feel ings of powerlessness about controlling ideas by successfully initiatin activities, and controlling feelings by identifying with the same-sex paren this stage will have a positive outcome for the child. On the other hand, the child is continually prevented from initiating activities, then this stag will have a negative outcome for the child. The child will feel guilt for hav ing ideas and feelings and, thereby, will feel powerless to control her envi ronment.

**Industry versus Inferiority (6–12 years).** During the middle year of childhood, children are involved in activities in school. Achievement i intellectual, physical, and social activities becomes important. Children ar expected to develop certain skills, such as reading, riding a bike, and get ting along with peers. Children are evaluated by adults and evaluate them selves by comparisons with others. The positive outcome of the conflic between industry and inferiority during this stage is a sense of productive ness and competence; whereas the negative outcome is a sense of unpro ductiveness and inferiority. How the conflict is resolved affects a person' attitude toward work and achievement throughout life, according t Erikson.

Erickson's industry vs. inferiority is characterized by competition among peers and evaluation by adults. Is the purpose of the competitive game to have fun or to win?

**Identity versus Role Confusion (13–18 years and older).** Whil at earlier stages unresolved conflicts affect resolution of the crisis, adoles cence is the time during which one must come to terms with earlier conflict if they were not successfully resolved (Erikson, 1980). One must establish a identity—a gender identity and an occupational identity. Adolescents als pass through all the previous conflicts again in this stage, except on a differ ent level. They must deal with trusting or mistrusting their friends an adults; they must reestablish control or autonomy over their bodies an emotions after progressing through puberty while often feeling shame an doubt; they are expected to show some initiative in getting a job or they ar made to feel guilty; they are expected to compete in school and with th opposite sex or else they feel inferior. Therefore, if a child progresse through this stage with an identity (knowing who you are) and goals (wha you want to be), then he can plan a life and achieve personal goals. Th danger in this stage is confusion of purpose, specifically about making com mitments to others or to an occupational role. Expectations are ill-defined Erikson (1980) clarifies that while the end of adolescence is the stage o overt identity crisis, identity formation neither begins nor ends at adoles cence; it is a lifelong process.

**Intimacy versus Isolation (young adulthood).** The young adult i expected to have a job and form an intimate relationship with a member o the opposite gender. Real intimacy means a commitment to a relationshi that involves compromise and sacrifice. You have to know who you are hough, before you commit to another. The conflict in this stage centers on being able to give of oneself to a relationship without losing oneself in the process versus not being able to give of oneself to another thereby risking isolation.

**Generativity versus Stagnation (middle adulthood).** Adulthood is the time when people have children, are productive in their work, and have an opportunity to be creative. *Generativity* involves being concerned with the next generation. It can include child-rearing or contributing to society in a way to benefit others. These are the positive outcomes of this stage. The negative outcome is stagnation, which comes from self-absorption and doing nothing for the next generation.

**Ego Integrity versus Despair (late adulthood to death).** Late adulthood is a time to reflect on one's life. Integrity involves a sense of coherence and wholeness, being able to "put it all together." The positive outcome of this stage is wisdom. The negative outcome, however, is despair, a feeling of futility in existence. This results from not having resolved earlier conflicts and now questioning the worth of one's life. Table 12.3 provides some examples of healthy and unhealthy psychosocial behaviors.

## HEALTHY AND UNHEALTHY PSYCHOSOCIAL BEHAVIOR

### TABLE 12.3

**Infant**
**Trust:** relates well to caregivers; knows parent will return

**Mistrust:** cries at being left with caregivers; distances self from caregivers or is clingy

**Toddler**
**Autonomy:** begins to control bodily functions and emotions; takes pride in doing things for self; is assertive

**Shame/Doubt:** difficulty in controlling self; exhibits helplessness; is withdrawn

**Preschoooler**
**Initiative:** asks questions; exhibits imagination

**Guilt:** exhibits passive behavior; is conforming

**School-ager**
**Industry:** enjoys achieving and producing; meets challenges confidently

**Inferiority:** is discouraged; avoids challenges

**Adolescent**
**Identity:** exhibits self-confidence; is cooperative; can confront problems and ask for help

**Role-Confusion:** exhibits self-doubt, excessive conformity, or rebelliousness; avoids confronting problems (e.g., substance abuse, delinquency, running away, suicide)

## Erickson's Theory Evaluated

Erikson's contribution to the field of developmental psychology was his emphasis on the role of society in the development of personality. His theory can be adapted to cultures other than Western European cultures. He recognized that if a conflict was not completely resolved satisfactorily in one stage, the person could continue to work on it in another stage, perhaps moving toward a more positive outcome. This led to a more optimistic view of the role the person plays in her own mental health. Also, his focus on the development of personality throughout life has led us to recognize the significance of certain events in our lives, such as going to school, falling in love, getting a job, as influencing a change in behavior and attitude. Erikson has given us an appreciation of how social factors enter into the various stages.

Like Freud's theory, Erikson's is general; it lacks specific hypotheses to test and predict future behavior. This is so because it, like Freud's, is based on clinical experience rather than empirical research. However, it does provide a flexible framework from which investigators can get ideas. For example, Marcia (1966; 1991) was interested in the crisis of identity versus identity or role confusion. To determine the status of college students, Marcia developed an interview technique. The interview involved questions about occupational choice and religious and political beliefs and values. The students were classified by whether they had gone through an active decision-making process, called a "crisis of choice" and the degree to which they had made a commitment to an occupation and set of beliefs. Marcia delineated four identity statuses: *identity achievement, identity foreclosure, identity moratorium,* and *identity diffusion.*

The students in the status of *identity achievement* had gone through considerable decision making and had as a result developed some commitments: for example, someone who takes courses in several areas before finally deciding on a major.

The students in the status of *identity foreclosure* were those who had passively accepted others' goals, usually parents, for themselves and had made a commitment without having gone through the decision-making process on their own: for example, a student who takes over a family business without considering any alternatives.

The students in the status of *identity moratorium* were those who were in identity crisis—they were struggling with occupational or ideological issues, trying to make a choice among various alternatives: for example, a student who cannot decide on marriage or medical school.

The students in the status of *identity diffusion* were those who avoided making decisions and commitments—students who changed values or goals according to peers, students who took easy courses instead of challenging ones, or students who changed majors without a goal.

Thus, it appears that Erikson's theory can generate empirical research. Marcia's work has shed some new light on Erickson's stage of identity versus role confusion.

## BIOLOGICAL INFLUENCES ON SOCIAL AND PERSONALITY DEVELOPMENT

Biological influences on social and personality development include heredity and temperament. The precise effect of such biological influences is difficult to determine because in reality heredity and temperament interact with contextual influences to affect development. To foster understanding, biological, contextual, and interactional influences are discussed separately.

## F.Y.I.

Genetic influences can be studied by comparing identical twins raised together in the same environment with identical twins raised in different environments. The Minnesota Twins Study has found a 30 to 60 percent influence of heredity on certain personality traits such as orderliness, conformity, and paranoia (Tellenger et al., 1988).

# HEREDITY

One way to examine the influence of heredity is to study *identical* twins and *fraternal* twins. Identical twins come from one egg and, therefore, have all genes in common. Fraternal twins come from two eggs and, therefore, have only some genes in common. If the identical twins are more like each other than fraternal twins in certain personality traits, we can assume genetics is responsible, at least initially. As children get older, they elicit differences in parental treatment (Scarr & McCartney, 1983) and then it becomes more difficult to pinpoint whether it is the child's genes, the parent's behavior, or the interaction between the two that is most influential in social and personality development.

Several studies evaluate how personality is the same and different between twins.

One theory of personality development proposed by Buss and Plomin (1975; 1984) takes the approach that certain personality traits exhibited early are genetically influenced. These traits are *emotionality, activity,* and *sociability*. Emotionality refers to distress, or the tendency to become upset easily and intensely. Activity includes energy level and how quickly one responds. Sociability refers to the preference to be with other people; the avoidance of contact with others is shyness.

The data from various twin studies of identical twins and fraternal twins that used different measures such as observing the infants (Matheny, Dolan, & Wilson, 1976), interviewing the parents about the infants' behavior (Matheny et al., 1981), and giving the parents information to list aspects of the infants' behavior (Goldsmith & Campos, 1982) consistently supported the hypothesis that differences in emotionality in infancy are affected by genetic factors (Plomin, 1990).

The trait of activity also yielded evidence for genetic influence (Goldsmith & Gottesman, 1981; Matheny, 1983) as did sociability and shyness ( Plomin & Rowe, 1979; Matheny, 1983).

Biology appears to be a predisposition for social and personality development, but the flourishing, stagnation, or deterioration of certain tendencies appears to depend on interactions with the environment. Research on temperament supports this view.

# TEMPERAMENT

If you visit a newborn nursery in a hospital, you will notice that some neonates are quiet and relaxed while others are tense and active; some are responsive to being held while others seem to resist it. To explain such variations in behavior, Thomas, Chess, and Birch (1968; Chess & Thomas, 1984; 1987) point to individual differences in biological composition called *temperament:*

> Two children may each eat skillfully or throw a ball accurately.... Yet, they may differ with respect to the intensity with which they act, the rate at which they move, the mood that they express, the readiness with which they shift to a new activity, and the ease with which they will approach a new toy, situation, or playmate (Thomas, Chess & Birch,1968, p. 4).

**Temperament** refers to individual differences in physiological responsiveness to various experiences. However, psychologists do not agree on the specifics of the definition. Some focus on differences in behavioral style, some on differences in reactivity and self-regulation, some on differences in emotion and arousal, and some on differences in heritable traits appearing in the first year. Psychologists do agree that expression of temperamental dispositions is purest during early infancy after which it becomes increasingly subject to context and experience (Goldsmith et al, 1987).

Thomas, Chess, and Birch (1968) hypothesized that differences in infants' temperaments might influence the way in which their parents interacted with them, and, consequently, infants' early and later years of development would be affected. To test this hypothesis, they began the New York Longitudinal Study (NYLS) in 1956 with 133 middle- to upper-class children whom they followed from infancy to adulthood (Chess & Thomas, 1984). Other children from the lower class and ethnic minority groups later were added to the sample. The children were seen by trained observers and given standard psychological tests, and the parents were interviewed at regular intervals about how their children behaved in specific situations. When the children reached school age, their teachers also were asked to report on specific behaviors (Thomas & Chess, 1977; 1980).

The researchers found that newborns differed in the nine qualities listed in table 12.4 (page 378) when responding to various situations. These differences sometimes continued into childhood.

The researchers also found that certain temperamental qualities tended to occur together. These clusters of characteristics fell into three types—*easy* infants (about 40 percent of the sample), *difficult* infants (10 percent of the sample), and *slow-to-warm-up* infants (15 percent of the sample). The remaining 35 percent of the children did not fit easily into one of these types but instead had varying combinations of the nine qualities. The easy infants were cheerful, adaptable to new situations, had low to mild responses, and were regular in eating and sleeping. The difficult infants generally were cranky, had hard times adapting to change often withdrawing, had intense responses, and were irregular in body functions. The slow-to-warm up infants were low in activity levels, tended to withdraw in new situations, and had mild responses. The NYLS found that the children most likely to have problems with their parents, school, and friends were those classified as difficult infants.

Thus, Thomas, Chess, and Birch's (1970) most significant contribution to explaining social and personality development was that infants vary in their responses to people and situations. Consequently, an infant's temperament affects the way adults treat him. For infants to develop optimally, they require adults who understand their temperaments. If a neonate is difficult or slow to warm up, parents need to be patient and understanding instead of trying to change the infant. Thomas, Chess, and Birch used the term *goodness-of-fit* to explain the relation between temperament and environmental demands that contribute to healthy development. "If the two influences are harmonized, one can expect healthy development of the child; if they are dissonant, behavioral problems are sure to ensue" (Thomas, Chess & Birch, 1970, p. 108).

Healthy social and personality development occurs when there is goodness-of-fit, or compatibility, between the temperament of the individual and the demands and expectations of the environment. Impaired social and personality development occurs when there is a poorness-of-fit, or incompatibility, between the individual and the environment (Chess & Thomas, 1986).

While Thomas and Chess primarily focused on the child's temperament and how parents respond to it, Barker-Cohen and Bell (1988) examined the relation between temperament and social adjustment to peers. They were concerned with a child's introduction to preschool as perhaps setting the tone for later peer relationships. Using Thomas and Chess's dimensions of temperament, they found that children who scored high in activity, high in approach, and low in sensitivity were more socially responsive toward peers as reported by teachers. When the temperamental dimensions were clustered into easy, difficult, and slow-to-warm-up groups, the researchers found that easy children were the most responsive to peers, difficult children were intermediate, and slow-to-warm up children were the least responsive. However, over time these differences among the groups were no longer significant. Thus, perhaps with the guidance of a sensitive teacher, the children were enabled to become accustomed to peer relationships in preschool so their initial temperamental reaction to a new situation was modified over time by a goodness-of-fit.

Some evidence suggests that early temperamental differences persist throughout childhood and adolescence (Carey & Earls, 1988). For example, certain infant temperament variables such as fussiness and low adaptability have been shown to be highly predictive of physical noncompliance in later childhood (Himmelfarb, Hock & Wenar, 1985).

# CONTEXTUAL INFLUENCES ON SOCIAL AND PERSONALITY DEVELOPMENT

As a person develops, that person experiences many contexts that influence her social and personality development, such as the family, school, peers, community, and media. Interactions occur in these contexts (except the media, which is experienced passively) with significant others, such as parents or friends that influence a person's behavior, morals, and self-esteem. These significant members of society influence social and personality development by a process called *socialization*, whereby individuals acquire the knowledge, skills, and character traits that enable them to participate as effective members of groups and society. We will examine how socialization occurs in the contexts of family, school, peers, community, and media.

## FAMILY

To understand a child's social and personality development, we need to look at the primary context in which a child develops, the family. The family is the child's first experience with social relationships, and it sets the tone for all later ones. The loved and nurtured child will feel confident and will trust others. The neglected or abused child will lack confidence and will mistrust others. In the family a child is first exposed to values, attitudes, morals, role models, and norms. Thus, the family serves as the most significant socializing agent for the child.

Families have different structures. For instance, some families include brothers, sisters, or other relatives; others have two parents and some have one parent; some families include a stepparent and/or stepsiblings.

To understand the influence of the family's structure on the social and personality development of the child, the effects of siblings, which

## TABLE 12.4

| Temperamental Quality | Rating | 2 Months | 6 Months |
|---|---|---|---|
| 1. Activity level (Tendency to be in motion) | High | Moves often in sleep. Wriggles when diaper is changed | Tries to stand in tub. Bounces in crib. Crawls after dog |
| | Low | Does not move when being dressed or during sleep | Passive in bath. Plays quietly in crib and falls asleep |
| 2. Rhythmicity (Regularity of biological functions) | Regular | Has been on 4-hour feeding schedule since birth. Regular bowel movement | Is asleep at 6:30 every night. Awakes at 7 A.M. Constant food intake |
| | Irregular | Awakes at a different time each morning. Size of feeding varies | Variable length of nap. Variable food intake |
| 3. Distractibility (Degree to which extraneous stimuli alter behavior) | Distractible | Will stop crying for food if rocked. Stops fussing if given pacifier when diaper is being changed | Stops crying when parent sings. Will remain still while clothing is changed if given a toy |
| | Not Distractible | Will not stop crying when diaper is changed. Fusses after eating even if rocked | Stops crying only after dressing is finished. Cries until given bottle |
| 4. Approach-withdrawal (Response to something new) | Positive | Smiles and licks washcloth. Has always liked bottle | Likes new foods. Enjoyed first bath in a large tub. Smiles and gurgles |
| | Negative | Rejected cereal the first time. Cries when strangers appear | Cries at strangers. Delays playing with new toys |
| 5. Adaptability (Flexibility of response) | Adaptive | Was passive during first bath; now enjoys bathing. Smiles at nurse | Used to dislike new foods; now accepts them well |
| | Not Adaptive | Still startled by sudden, sharp noise. Resists diapering | Does not cooperate with dressing. Fusses and cries when left with sitter |

| 1 Year | 2 Years | 5 Years | 10 Years |
|---|---|---|---|
| Walks rapidly. Eats eagerly. Climbs into everything | Climbs furniture. Explores. Gets in and out of bed while being put to sleep | Leaves table often during meals. Always runs | Plays ball and engages in other sports. Cannot sit still long enough to do homework |
| Finishes bottle slowly. Goes to sleep easily. Allows nail cutting without fussing | Enjoys quiet play with puzzles. Can listen to records for hours | Takes a long time to dress. Sits quietly on long automobile rides | Likes chess and reading. Eats very slowly |
| Naps after lunch each day. Always drinks bottle before bed | Eats a big lunch each day. Always has a snack before bedtime | Falls asleep when put to bed. Bowel movement regular | Eats only at mealtimes. Sleeps the same amount of time each night |
| Will not fall asleep for an hour or more. Moves bowels at a different time each day | Nap time changes from day to day. Toilet training difficult because of unpredictable bowel movement | Variable food intake. Variable time of bowel movement | Variable food intake. Falls asleep at a different time each night |
| Cries when face is washed unless it is made into a game | Will stop tantrum if another activity is suggested | Can be coaxed out of forbidden activity by being led into something else | Needs absolute silence for homework. Has a hard time choosing a shirt in a store because they all appeal to him |
| Cries when toy is taken away and rejects substitute | Screams if refused some desired object. Ignores parents' calling | Seems not to hear if involved in favorite activity. Cries for a long time when hurt | Can read a book while television set is at high volume. Does chores on schedule |
| Approaches strangers readily. Sleeps well in new surroundings | Slept well the first time he stayed overnight at grandparents' house | Entered school building unhesitatingly. Tries new foods | Went to camp happily. Loved to ski the first time |
| Stiffened when placed on sled. Will not sleep in strange bed | Avoids strange children in the playground. Whimpers first time at beach. Will not go into water | Hid behind parent when entering school | Severely homesick at camp during first days. Does not like new activities |
| Was afraid of toy animals at first; now plays with them happily | Obeys quickly. Stayed contentedly with grandparents for a week | Hesitated to go to nursery school at first; now goes eagerly. Slept well on camping trip | Likes camp, although homesick during first days. Learns enthusiastically |
| Continues to reject new foods each time they are offered | Cries and screams each time hair is cut. Disobeys persistently | Has to be hand led into classroom each day. Bounces on bed despite spankings | Does not adjust well to new school or new teacher; comes home late for dinner even when punished |

**TABLE 12.4** *(continued)*

| Temperamental Quality | Rating | 2 Months | 6 Months |
|---|---|---|---|
| 6. Attention span and persistence (Length of time activities are maintained and tolerance for difficulty) | Long | If soiled, continues to cry until changed. Repeatedly rejects water if wanting milk | Watches toy mobile over crib intently. "Coos" frequently |
| | Short | Cries when awakened but stops almost immediately. Objects only mildly if cereal precedes bottle | Sucks pacifier for only a few minutes and spits it out |
| 7. Intensity of reaction (Energy level of response) | Intense | Cries when diaper is wet. Rejects food vigorously when satisfied | Cries loudly at the sound of thunder. Makes sucking movement when vitamins are administered |
| | Mild | Does not cry when diaper is wet. Whimpers instead of crying when hungry | Does not kick often in tub. Does not smile. Screams and kicks when temperature is taken |
| 8. Threshold of responsiveness (Intensity of stimulation required to produce a response) | Low | Stops sucking on bottle when approached | Refuses fruit he likes when vitamins are added. Hides head from bright light |
| | High | Is not startled by loud noises. Takes bottle and breast equally well | Eats everything. Does not object to diaper being wet or soiled |
| 9. Quality of mood (Proportion of happy, friendly behavior to unhappy, unfriendly behavior) | Positive | Smacks lips when first tasting new food. Smiles at parents | Plays and splashes in bath. Smiles at everyone |
| | Negative | Fusses after nursing. Cries when carriage is rocked | Cries when taken from tub. Cries when given food she does not like |

# BEHAVIOR ILLUSTRATIONS FOR RATINGS OF THE VARIOUS TEMPERAMENTAL ATTRIBUTES AT VARIOUS AGES

| 1 Year | 2 Years | 5 Years | 10 Years |
|---|---|---|---|
| Plays by self in playpen for more than an hour. Listens to singing for long periods | Works on a puzzle until completed. Watches when shown how to do something | Practiced riding a two-wheeled bicycle for hours until he mastered it. Spent over an hour reading a book | Reads for two hours before sleeping. Does homework carefully |
| Loses interest in a toy after a few minutes. Gives up easily if he falls while attempting to walk | Gives up easily if a toy is hard to use. Asks for help immediately if undressing becomes difficult | Still cannot tie her shoes because of giving up when not successful. Fidgets when parents read to him | Gets up frequently from homework for a snack. Never finishes a book |
| Laughs hard when a parent plays roughly. Screamed and kicked when temperature was taken | Yells if feeling excitement or delight. Cries loudly if a toy is taken away | Rushes to greet parents. Gets hiccups from laughing hard | Tears up an entire page of homework if one mistake is made. Slams door of room when teased by younger sibling |
| Does not fuss much when clothing is pulled on over head | Looks surprised and does not hit back when another child hits him | Drops eyes and remains silent when given a firm parental "no" | When a mistake is made on a model airplane, corrects it quietly. Does not comment when reprimanded |
| Spits out food he or she does not like. Giggles when tickled | Runs to door when parents come home. Must always be tucked tightly into bed | Refuses milk if it is not ice-cold | Rejects fatty foods. Adjusts shower until water is at exactly the right temperature |
| Eats foods she likes even if mixed with disliked food. Can be left easily with strangers | Can be left with anyone. Falls asleep easily on either back or stomach | Does not hear loud, sudden noises when reading. Does not object to injections | Never complains when sick. Eats all foods |
| Likes bottle; reaches for it and smiles. Laughs loudly when playing peekaboo | Plays with sibling; laughs and giggles. Smiles when she succeeds in putting on shoes | Laughs loudly while watching television cartoons. Smiles at everyone | Enjoys new accomplishments. Laughs when reading a funny passage aloud |
| Cries when given injections. Cries when left alone | Cries and squirms when given haircut. Cries when parents leave | Objects to putting on boots. Cries when frustrated | Cries when unable to solve a homework problem. "Weepy" if not getting enough sleep |

(Chess & Birch, 1970)

complicate the family's structure, and the effects of divorce, which disrupt the family structure, have to be examined. Because many people who divorce remarry (Hetherington & Camara, 1984), divorce also may lead to a restructuring of the family by adding a stepparent and/or stepsibling (Hetherington, 1991; Hetherington & Clingempeel, 1992).

Families differ in the way they perform their functions. The functions of a family are reproduction, socialization, and support, both economic and emotional. In some families the father performs certain functions or roles, for example, economic support, and the mother performs other roles, for example, emotional support. In other families both parents share various roles. In some families where there is one parent, the children may have to contribute to the functioning of the family, perhaps economically, or even in the emotional support of the parent.

To understand how the performance of roles within the family influences the social and personality development of the child, we examine research that has been done on the effects of employment of mothers. Employment of mothers may involve a shift in roles performed in the family. Fathers or children (especially in single-parent families) have to assume household and child-care responsibilities. A mother's employment may mean day care for a young child and, perhaps, self-care for an older child.

Within these various family structures and ways of performing the family functions, there are individual *parenting* styles. **Parenting** refers to implementing a series of decisions about the socialization of the child—how fighting, performance in school, imparting values and morals, and so on are handled.

To understand the influence of parenting styles on social and personality development, three general types—*authoritarian*, or adult-centered; *permissive*, or child-centered; and *authoritative*, or democratic—will be discussed.

## Siblings

Siblings increase the size of the family. The more children in a family, the more interactions occur within that family. However, more children mean fewer individual parent-child interactions (Dunn, 1985). This means less time for adults to become involved in children's activities, schoolwork, and problems. As family size increases, parenting styles become more strict and punitive because of lack of time to explain every rule (Elder & Bowerman, 1963). As family size increases, resources increasingly have to be shared. Larger families usually have smaller economic resources compared with smaller families. Thus, the greater parental responsibility and stress combined with fewer economic resources are believed to contribute to the greater amounts of antisocial behavior and delinquency appearing in large families (Wagner, Schubert & Schubert, 1985).

The birth order of the siblings also affects the parent-child interactions (Dunn,1985; Dunn & Plomin, 1990). First-borns have been found to receive more attention, affection, and verbal stimulation than later-born siblings. They also are coerced more by their parents. More mature behavior is expected of them than of siblings. Second-born children have been found to receive more protection and "babying" after age three (Lasko, 1954).

The relationships siblings establish with one another is equally if not more important in influencing social and personality development than interactions with parents (Dunn & Plomin, 1990). Children learn many

The number of children in a family affects the quality and quantity of parent-child interactions.

interactional skills from their siblings. Later-born children have been found to be more popular with peers than first-born children (Miller & Maruyama, 1976). Perhaps this is due to having to get along with older siblings, and in so doing younger siblings learn to negotiate. Older children usually are more nurturant than younger children perhaps because they are given the task of caring for younger siblings (Bryant, 1982).

There is a wide range of differences in the quality of the relationship between siblings in terms of affection, cooperation, aggression, imitation, hostility, and empathy (Dunn, 1985). In some families, interactions are warm and affectionate, while in other families, interactions are ambivalent. Family interactions set the tone for the relationship between siblings. Evidence shows that the quality of the relationship between siblings is linked to each child's relationship with the parents (Dunn, 1985). Talking to each child about the other, explaining feelings and actions, emphasizing consistently the importance of not hurting the other all appear to be linked to the development of a more harmonious relationship. In the early years, hostility is often more common between siblings of different gender, whereas with young siblings there is often a greater amount of friendly, helpful interaction and imitation between same-gender siblings. Research on sibling relationships has shown that sibling conflict increases when one sibling is emotionally intense or highly active (Brody, Stoneman & Burke, 1987).

Thus, siblings exert an important influence on development, both directly through the relationships siblings establish with one another, and indirectly through the effects that the presence of another child has on the parenting style.

## Divorce

Divorce is a stressful time for parents and children. It is not a single event but rather a multistage process of radically changing family relationships (Wallerstein, Corbin & Lewis, 1988). The process begins with a failing marriage and may include separations before the legal divorce. Evidence indicates that during the first two years after the divorce is a time of emotional distress and poor parent-child relationships (Hetherington, Cox & Cox, 1982; Hetherington, 1988; 1989). Most children and many parents experience psychological., health, and behavior problems. Disruptions in family functioning, problems in adjusting to new roles, relationships, and life changes associated with the altered family situation occur.

The parent with custody experiences role-overload. The custodial parent must assume the tasks of the other parent to keep the family functioning (Hetherington, Cox & Cox, 1982). This can mean a decrease in availability to meet the needs of the child.

Single-parent families headed by the mother often experience financial strain. Women, regardless of marital status, still earn less than men. Sometimes men do not continue to provide financial support to the family, despite legal requirements.

A change in the financial status of a family may mean the family has to move, and the mother may have to seek employment. These changes cause additional adjustments for children.

Joint custody is a contemporary solution in divorce cases where both parents want custody. Joint custody legally requires shared decision-making authority for the child in areas such as education, medical care, and discipline. Sometimes physical custody is shared where the child spends a cer-

Siblings provide companionship, competition, serve as role models, and provide emotional support.

tain time living in each parent's home. The positive aspect of joint custody is that it requires both parents to prioritize the child's welfare above their own (Bowman & Ahrons, 1985). The negative aspect is that the parents are usually divorcing because they can no longer communicate or cooperate; so when legally required to do so, the child is exposed to more conflict and therefore, risks more psychological damage (Johnston, Kline & Tschann, 1989).

Recently, psychologists have become interested in the role of support systems for families (Vanderslice, 1984; Hetherington, 1989). Relatives, neighbors, and community services play critical roles in the functioning of families undergoing adjustments and stress, especially low-income families (Coletta, 1978). Support systems are important as shown by research findings indicating that single-parent households who lack support also can have problems in child rearing. In families where a man was the authority figure and now has become the noncustodial parent, the woman has difficulty assuming authority and power in the newly structured family, especially with boys. Boys exhibit more noncompliance and lack of self-control after the divorce (Hetherington, Cox & Cox, 1982; Hetherington, 1988, 1989). While girls do not exhibit the behavior problems that boys do, adolescent girls are more troubled than adolescent boys (Wallerstein, Corbin & Lewis, 1988).

Finally, the divorce and custody arrangements influence gender-role typing. Research findings suggest that males may adapt better socially in father-custody homes, whereas females may develop better in mother-custody homes (Santrock & Warshak, 1979), although this may be more true of younger children than of adolescents (Hetherington & Clingempeel, 1992).

Children in families where a remarriage has occurred can show adjustment problems, especially when the remarriage brings children to the newly structured step-family (Hetherington, Cox & Cox, 1982; Hetherington, 1988; 1989; 1991). Interestingly, while males exhibit more antisocial behavior than females after divorce, two years after remarriage their behavior was found to be no different from that of males from nondivorced families (Hetherington, 1989). It may be that for females, a step-father is an intrusion on the relationship with the mother, whereas for males the step-father is a support and a role model ( Hetherington & Clingempeel, 1992).

Thus, how the family restructures itself after divorce affects females' and males' social and personality development. The long-term affects of divorce and remarriage are related more to a child's developmental status, gender, and temperament, parenting styles, and support systems available to parent and child than they are to divorce and marriage (Hetherington, Stanley-Hagan & Anderson, 1989). Box 12.1 explains children's reactions to divorce.

## Mother's Employment

The proportion of children with mothers in the labor force has grown dramatically over the last two decades. For children under six years of age, the proportion has increased by nearly 80 percent; for school-aged children, the proportion grew by nearly half. The proportion of children under age 18 with mothers who worked full-time nearly doubled, with the greatest growth occurring among those whose youngest child was under two years. By the time the youngest child is two years of age, about 60 percent of today's married mothers are in the labor force (Rogoff, 1990).

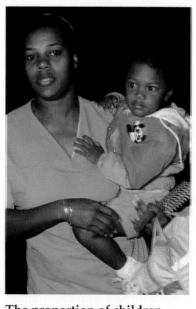

The proportion of children with employed mothers has increased substantially over the last couple of decades.

How the divorce is explained to children mediates its effect. A child's efforts to handle the stress of a divorce are strengthened when he understands the divorce as a serious and carefully considered remedy for an important problem, when the divorce appears purposeful and rationally undertaken, and indeed succeeds in bringing relief and a happier outcome for one or both parents (Wallerstein & Kelly, 1980). In contrast, a divorce that occurs without warning or explanation can leave children bewildered and shaken in their trust of parents.

The age of the child at the time of the divorce is an important factor in determining its impact on the child (Wallerstein & Kelly, 1980; Wallerstein, Corbin, & Lewis, 1988). Young children may blame themselves and fantasize the reconciliation of the parents. They also may distort the outcomes of the divorce. For example, in preschoolers (up to age five) the fear of abandonment is common and is expressed in various ways—fear of the dark, clinginess, and regression in behavior. In young school-age children (six to eight years) the anxiety about abandonment can be communicated through overeating, pleading for gifts, or fantasies about special trips.

Older school-age children (9 to 12 years) begin to recognize their lack of control over what has happened in their family. They may argue with parents to try and gain control, or they may divorce themselves from the conflict by becoming involved in outside activities. Adolescents (13 to 18 years) tend to see their parents in terms of their own immediate developmental needs—either as weak, fallen idols or powerful, idealized figures (West, 1984). Adolescents can feel they are being hurried, asked to participate in adult problems and assume adult responsibilities prematurely. At this age, anger is often directed at both parents for being selfish and insensitive for putting their own needs first.

For all children, contact with the noncustodial parent appears to be an important aspect of the post-divorce adjustment (Wallerstein & Kelly, 1980). In general, outcomes for children are more favorable when expartners can set aside their differences and function together as parents.

When both parents are employed, the role of the mother may be perceived by the child as similar to the role of the father, not only because the mother works outside of the home but also because the father is likely to share more child-rearing tasks (Pleck, 1984; Zaslow, 1987).

Some evidence indicates that employed mothers use different child-rearing practices than do nonemployed mothers, especially in independence training. Generally, employed mothers encourage self-sufficiency, such as caring for self and belongings and participating in household tasks at an early age. However, opposite situations, for example prolonged dependence, sometimes occur when mothers feel guilty about working (Hock, 1978).

Children who attend child care programs have been found to be more outgoing, aggressive, and independent than children reared exclusively at home.

The developmental consequences of being a latchkey child are in dispute—some argue that the child will be stressful because of the burdens prematurely thrust upon them; others argue that the child will become self-sufficient.

The major concern about the effects of a mother's employment on children's development is alternative child-care. After reviewing studies of children in alternative care arrangements, Clarke-Stewart and Fein (1983) concluded that these children remain attached to their mothers. Although infants in day-care form an affectionate relationship with an involved and stable caregiver—a relationship that is similar to their attachment to their mothers—they still overwhelmingly prefer their mothers to the other care giver. This is evidenced in that they go to their mother for help, stay close to her, approach her more often, and go to her when distressed or bored in assessment situations. Belsky (1988) disagrees. On the basis of reviews of many studies, he concludes that extensive infant day-care experience (defined as when mothers work for more than 20 hours per week during the first year of an infant's life) is associated with insecure attachment during infancy and heightened aggressiveness during the preschool and early school-age years. Belsky acknowledges that the heightened insecurity and aggressiveness in those children who experience extensive infant day-care may be due to a child's temperament, experiences at home, and the child care settings.

Clarke-Stewart and Fein (1983) found that children who attend day care programs interact more with peers, both positively and negatively, and that they are less cooperative with adults than children cared for at home. Specifically, children attending early childhood programs compared with those who do not, are more self-confident, more outgoing, less fearful, more assertive, and more independent of parent or teacher. Also, they were more verbally expressive and more knowledgeable about the social world, for example about gender roles, emotional labels, and problem solving. They were more comfortable in new or stressful situations and more realistic about their achievements. On the other hand, the children in early childhood programs compared with those who were not, are observed to be less polite, less agreeable, less respectful of others' rights, and less compliant with maternal or teacher demands. They were more assertive, louder, more aggressive, rebellious, bossy, belligerent, irritable, and hostile. Apparently, these findings appear regardless of the type of child-care program.

Children who care for themselves before or after school, known as "latchkey" children because they carry their own house key to open the door, often are fearful (Long & Long, 1982). Young school-age children regularly left alone are vulnerable to hazards that supervised children are not. Neighborhood crime, medical., and other emergencies are ever-present dangers (Meredith, 1986). According to Elkind (1981), less commonly recognized is the social and emotional harm to which these children are subjected. They are responsible for themselves and sometimes for younger siblings often before they have the maturity to handle such responsibility. According to Elkind, this premature granting of responsibility produces undue stress with a characteristic response of anxiety not attached to any specific fear. Coping with premature responsibility increases the chances of later social and emotional problems.

All researchers do not agree with Elkind. Some researchers contend that children left to their own resources acquire a sense of independence, self-competence, and earlier maturity. For example, Vandell and Corasaniti (1988) studied 150 third-grade children from predominantly middle-class, suburban families who returned home to their mothers, attended child-care centers, stayed with sitters, or took care of themselves after school. The atchkey children proved socially, academically, and emotionally as well adjusted as those who went home to their mothers or to sitters. Interestingly, of the four groups, the children who went to child-care centers were rated lowest on both social skills and academic grades. These outcome differences were apparent in both divorced and intact families.

A mother's employment affects the roles played by the family members. How well the family adjusts to these new roles influences the impact of a mother's employment on the child's development.

## Parenting Styles

Research has shown that parenting styles have an impact on children's behavior. Baumrind (1966; 1967; 1971), for example, studied parenting styles by observing the behavior of preschool children aged three and four. She rated their behavior by degree of impetuosity, self-reliance, aggressiveness, withdrawal., and self-control. The children were classified into three groups:

1. *competent children*—happy, self-reliant, self-controlled
2. *withdrawn children*—usually sad, rarely approaching other children, engaged in solitary activities
3. *immature children*—usually lacking self-reliance and self-control

The parents of these three groups of preschool children were observed and interviewed to determine how their parenting styles differed. Baumrind found that parents of the children who were most self-reliant, self-controlled, explorative, and contented were controlling and demanding while also being warm, rational., and receptive to the child's communication. She labeled this combination of high control and positive encouragement of the child's autonomous and independent strivings "authoritative." The components of the **authoritative parenting** style include (Baumrind, 1968; 1971):

1. Setting clear standards and expectations for mature behavior
2. Firmly enforcing rules and standards using commands and prohibitions when necessary but sharing reasons behind policies
3. Encouraging a child's autonomy and individuality
4. Having open communication between parents and children
5. Recognizing rights of both parents and children

Parents of the children who were relatively discontented, withdrawn, and distrustful were detached, controlling, and somewhat less warm than the other parents. Baumrind labeled this group "authoritarian." The components of the **authoritarian parenting** style include (Baumrind, 1968; 1971):

1. Attempting to shape, control, and evaluate behaviors and attitudes of children by absolute standards

*(continued on following page)*

*(continued from previous page)*
2. Valuing obedience, respect for authority, work, tradition, and preservation of order
3. Favoring punitive, forceful measures to curb child's self-will when in conflict with parents
4. Discouraging verbal give and take between parent and child

Parents of the children who were the least self-reliant, explorative and self-controlled were noncontrolling, nondemanding, and relatively warm. Baumrind labeled this group "permissive." The components of the **permissive parenting** style include (Baumrind, 1968; 1971):

1. Accepting a child's impulses, desires, and actions
2. Consulting with a child on policy decisions
3. Demanding less for responsibility and orderly behavior
4. Avoiding exercise of control

Baumrind (1966, p. 105) concluded that, "authoritative control can achieve responsible conformity with group standards without loss of individual autonomy or self-assertiveness."

It must be remembered that parents rarely fit into a given style all the time. The styles previously discussed are simply dominant patterns that distinguish certain parents from other parents. Children of these parents differ in their behavior. In Baumrind's studies, children of authoritarian parents showed little independence and scored in the middle range on assessments of social responsibility. Children of permissive parents conspicuously lacked social responsibility and were not independent. Children of authoritative parents were independent and socially responsible.

According to Baumrind, both the authoritarian and permissive parents had unrealistic beliefs about young children. Whereas the strict, or authoritarian, parents thought the child's behavior must be constrained, the permissive parents tended to regard the child's behavior as natural and refreshing. Neither group considered the child's stage of development—for example, the desire in early childhood to model parental behavior or the inability in early childhood to reason when given a parental command. Thus, Baumrind endorsed the authoritative parenting style in which parents consider children's needs, as well as their own, before deciding how to handle a situation. Authoritative parents exert control over children's behavior when necessary, yet they respect children's need to make their own decisions. Reasoning is used to explain parenting policies, and communication from children is encouraged.

After reviewing the literature on parenting styles, Maccoby and Martin (1983) suggested that most parents are characterized by how demanding or controlling they are with their children and how responsive or accepting they are (table 12.5). *Demanding* parents exert much control

Discipline takes many forms. If this parent used punishment to exert control, the parenting style would be classified as authoritarian. If, however, the parent used reasoning, the style would be classified as authoritative.

over their children; *undemanding* parents let children do as they please. *Responsive* parents tend to accept their children and to see their children's needs as primary; *unresponsive* parents tend to reject children and to see their own needs as primary.

## A TWO-DIMENSIONAL CLASSIFICATION OF PARENTING STYLES

### TABLE 12.5

| | *Accepting Responsive Child-centered* | *Rejecting Unresponsive Parent-centered* |
|---|---|---|
| *Demanding, controlling* | Authoritative-reciprocal High in bidirectional communication | Authoritarian Power assertive |
| *Undemanding, low in control attempts* | Indulgent | Neglecting, ignoring, indifferent, uninvolved |

**(Maccoby & Martin, 1983)**

Maccoby and Martin referred to Baumrind's authoritarian style as *authoritarian-power assertive* because that parent exercises considerable control over the child and is demanding, rejectory, unresponsive, and parent-centered. They referred to Baumrind's authoritative style as *authoritative-reciprocal* because that parent is demanding, controlling, accepting, responsive, and child-centered. They found two subcategories of Baumrind's permissive style: the *permissive-indulgent pattern*, parents who are highly involved in children's lives but who allow them much freedom and who do not control negative behavior, and the *permissive-indifferent* pattern, parents who are uninvolved in children's lives and who have minimal interaction with them. The permissive-indulgent pattern is associated with children's being impulsive, aggressive, and lacking independence or ability to take responsibility. The permissive-indifferent pattern is associated with children's demanding behavior, noncompliance, and aggressiveness. The authoritative or authoritative-reciprocal style of parenting is significant in that it facilitates psychosocial competence.

Dornbusch and others (Dornbusch et al., 1987; Steinberg, Elmen & Mounts, 1989) found that authoritative parenting is positively correlated with adolescent school performance whereas authoritarian and permissive parenting are negatively correlated. Authoritative parenting influences how a child behaves in the early years and also how a child deals with responsibility, as exhibited in adolescence.

# WHAT ARE THE EFFECTS OF PARENTS' MARITAL PROBLEMS ON CHILDREN'S ABILITY TO REGULATE EMOTION, PEER RELATIONSHIPS, AND HEALTH?

Gottman, J.M. & Katz, L.F. (1989). Effects of marital discord on young children's peer interaction and health, *Developmental Psychology, 25, 3,* 373–381.

It has been shown that children from divorced families have more behavior problems, at least for the first two years after the divorce, than do children from intact families.

This study hypothesized that marital discord adversely affects the functioning of a child's nervous system which, in turn, influences the child's ability to regulate emotion, which, subsequently, affects peer relationships and overall health. The investigators defined emotion regulation as the ability to inhibit inappropriate behavior related to strong negative or positive feelings, the ability to soothe oneself after being physiologically aroused by strong feelings, and the ability to refocus attention and become organized in action to pursue a goal.

The study subjects were 56 families; 24 had a male and 32 had a female four- to five-year-old child. The families were interviewed to assess marital satisfaction. The sample represented a large range from highly satisfied to highly dissatisfied (marital discord).

Parent–parent interaction was assessed by observing the couple in a high-conflict task, which consisted of discussing two problem areas in their marriage. Physiological variables also were measured.

Parent–child interaction was assessed by having the parents get information from the child about a story that was read to her as well as having the parents teach the child a specific task. Parenting style was coded on such dimensions as warmth-coldness, presence or lack of structure, persistence or lack of persistence in limit setting, parental anger/displeasure-happiness, and unresponsiveness-responsiveness. Physiological variables in the child were also measured.

The researchers found that couples who were maritally distressed and physiologically underaroused had a parenting style that was cold, unresponsive, angry, and low in limit setting and structuring and that this interaction style may be related to anger and noncompliance in the children and high levels of stress-related hormones. Children from such homes tended to have fewer interactions playing with peers, more of which were negative than positive, and have worse health. The researchers also found that maritally distressed couples seem to have children who are under a high level of chronic stress, which appears to be related to their efforts to avoid peer interactions in play, causing conflict.

Thus, children who are highly stressed in their families can have a reduced ability to play at a complex interactional level involving conflict resolution with a peer. Children without this problem have opportunities to learn social skills, such as assertiveness or compromise in conflict situations; children who avoid conflict never get a chance to rehearse with friends. Lacking such social skills can cause these children to later be rejected by peers and can eventually influence emotional health.

## SCHOOL

The school influences social and personality development in that it is the setting in which significant cognitive and social experiences occur. It is where children develop the skills, knowledge, interest, and attitudes that characterize them as individuals and that shape their abilities to perform adult roles (Morrison & McIntyre, 1971). Considering the amount of time children spend in school, it is no surprise that school is a significant socialization agent.

The influence of the school's physical setting, its educational program, and the teacher interaction on the child's development will be discussed.

## Physical Setting

There are differences in children's social behavior in various school settings. For example, in a study of preschool children Smith and Connolly (1981) varied the space, size of group, and play equipment. They found that aggression increased when the available space per child was reduced to less than 15 square feet. They also found aggression to increase when group size increased but play equipment did not.

The significance of the impact of school size on later social and personality development can be seen in the data on school dropouts, substance abuse, teenage pregnancy, suicide, and depression because youths at risk for these problems are less likely to be involved in school and extracurricular activities. Thus, schools having an appropriate ratio of activities to students are more likely to have increased student involvement, identification with the school, sense of responsibility, personal control, and importance, thereby reducing the likelihood of having students with personal problems (Linney & Seidman, 1989).

## Educational Programs

Educational programs differ in their goals for children's basic academic skills, creativity, and social and emotional growth. They also differ in their methods of motivating learning and in the techniques implemented for performing their goals. Learning is motivated in some programs by positive and negative reinforcement (grades) and in other programs by individual interest. Techniques used involve those that foster competition, where children work individually to be best in the class, or cooperation, where children work together to complete a project.

Elementary school programs are usually divided into *traditional* and *modern*, or open (Minuchin et al., 1969; Minuchin & Shapiro, 1983). Traditional programs, also called teacher-centered, usually subscribe to the philosophy that the functions of the school are to impart basic factual knowledge, such as reading, writing, arithmetic, and to preserve the American cultural heritage. Those who support this philosophy believe that education should include homework, tests, memorization, and strict discipline. They view the school as a place where hard work and obedience are expected. The teacher structures the curriculum. Subjects chosen are based on the teacher's, school's, or community's goals.

Open programs, also called learner-centered, usually subscribe to the philosophy that the function of the school is to develop the whole child; that is, not only a child's cognitive and language skills but physical., social., emotional., and personal skills as well. Curriculum emerges from the child's interests and abilities. Those who subscribe to this philosophy believe learning occurs spontaneously and is best when children can interact with materials and people in their environment. Learning materials may be grouped in various centers where children explore. Children are given opportunities for inquiry and discovery. They become involved in their own learning by making choices about what they will learn. Subject matter is integrated into student activities.

Small class sizes tend to offer a greater opportunity and challenge to students than large class sizes.

These children, by interacting with computers, are experiencing a learner-centered curriculum. They discover and learn rather than being lectured to as in a teacher-centered curriculum.

Parent-teacher-child conference

Children in open programs reported a more positive attitude toward school (Horwitz, 1979). Regarding patterns of social interaction, many studies have documented the wider variety of interactions in open classrooms and the existence of more varied bases for forming friendships and achieving popularity (Minuchin & Shapiro, 1983). This is explained by the fact that in traditional programs teachers teach to the whole class and children work individually, whereas in open programs there are many opportunities for group work and a cooperative work ethic is developed.

## Teacher Interaction

Teachers provide the environment for children's learning. They understand children's needs, interests, and abilities and empathize with children's fears of failure. The teacher has the ability to encourage children to explore, to satisfy their natural curiosity, and to enjoy learning. The teacher also plays a major role in helping children learn to deal with positions of authority, to cooperate with others, to cope with problems, and to achieve competence. What the teacher does and the emotional climate affect student achievement (Brophy, 1986).

Teachers affect children's behavior by their expectations. Different children elicit different expectations, and teachers respond accordingly (Minuchin & Shapiro, 1983). The most widely known study by Rosenthal and Jacobson (1968) demonstrated that what teachers expect from children influences how they treat them and that this affects how the children actually perform. Rosenthal and Jacobson gave teachers phony data on children who were designated intellectual bloomers. These children actually demonstrated significant intellectual growth at the end of the year even though their designation was contrived. Rosenthal and Jacobson's study generated much controversy because of methodological weaknesses and the inability of others to replicate the original results. However, studies observing actual teachers' behavior in the classroom have shown similar effects of expectancy. The explanation is that because teachers expect certain kinds of behavior from high achievers and different behavior from low achievers, they treat them differently and thereby sustain the patterns. For example, high achievers are given more opportunities to participate in class and more time to respond, whereas low achievers are given fewer opportunities and less time to respond (Cooper, 1979).

Teachers also treat males different from females (Minuchin & Shapiro, 1983). It has been found (Serbin et al., 1973) that teachers are more responsive to the disruptive behavior of males than females and more likely to reprimand males. When children request attention, teachers usually respond to males with instructions and to females with nurturance. In addition, females receive more attention when they are close to the teacher, whereas males are given attention from a distance.

Also, it has been found that the feedback received by females and males on the intellectual quality of their work is different. Males receive considerable criticism for failing to obey the rules while females receive criticism related to their performance. This impacts males' and females' perceptions of their ability to do the required work. Males attribute their failure to do well to lack of effort; females attribute their failure to do well to lack of ability (Dweck et al., 1978).

In conclusion, while school influences social and personality development, no classroom provides a uniform context for all children. The physical setting, the educational program, and the teacher interaction all form different social experiences for individual children.

## PEERS

*Peers* are equals in status; they are about the same age, and they have similar amounts of social power in relation to adults. The peer group is where children interact with their friends and experience independence and learn cooperation.

Peers are significant in influencing a child's social and personality development, specifically, in the child's capacity to relate to others, in the development of social controls, and in the acquisition of social values and roles (Hartup, 1983). Peer interaction and influence change as a child develops. The interaction moves from loosely coordinated exchanges to complex coordinated interaction. When children begin to interact with peers, they have a primitive awareness of the needs of others. As children gain in peer experiences, they not only become more aware of others' needs but they have a greater knowledge of social norms and have better communication skills. Two-year-old children will play next to each other enjoying each other's company but not really engaging in a mutual exchange. They are unaware of the social norm of taking turns in speech or behavior. Also, their language and cognitive development are not mature enough to enable them to express all their thoughts. Four-year-olds cooperate, take turns, and play roles. School-age children understand rules and organize their own games. Adolescents consider rules and the feelings of the group when engaging in peer activities.

As children develop, they spend more time with peers so that by adolescence time spent with peers exceeds time spent with parents or teachers (Medrich et al., 1982). The time children spend with peers is significant because much of what children learn about the world, they learn from other children and practice with other children.

## Significance of Peer Group

Humans without normal peer relations are later affected in emotional development (Hartup, 1983; Parker & Asher, 1987). The long-term effects of poor peer relations during childhood have been studied and have been shown to be linked to the later development of neurotic and psychotic behavior and to a greater tendency to drop out of school (Roff, Sells & Golden, 1972). Psychologists actually find that **sociometric measures**, measures of patterns of attraction and rejection among members of a group, taken in the elementary grades predict adjustment in later life better than other educational or personality tests. "The child's peer group seems to be a sensitive barometer of current and future adjustment problems" (Asher, 1982, p. 23).

Peers are influential in setting norms for achievement. A research study on aspirations in junior high school showed that the peer group played a large role in determining whether students later enrolled in college preparatory curricula. Students with friends who modeled high aspirations and achievement were more likely to later enroll in a program preparing them for college (Alexander, Cook & McDill, 1977).

Peers reinforce gender-stereotyped behavior; boys are encouraged by their friends to play with blocks and trucks, while girls are encouraged to play house and color (Fagot & Patterson, 1969; Jacklin, 1989).

**Peers are significant socializing agents because they provide emotional security; set norms for behavior; teach various cognitive, motor, and social skills; provide opportunities for play; and help children adjust to life (Asher, 1978).**

# Play

Play is a pleasurable activity engaged in for its own sake. Play is one major function of peer groups because children spend much time playing with other children, from the make-believe of preschoolers to the formal games of schoolagers. Different kinds of play contribute in different ways to development, especially to social and cognitive development.

Play can be classified by the social interactions that occur; experiences in social interaction influence social development. The following stages outlined by Parten (1932), which were based on observations of preschool children engaged in free play, illustrate a developmental progression:

1. **Unoccupied play**: Child is not engaging in play as commonly defined but rather may stand in one place and observe, or randomly wander around looking at others engaged in play

2. **Solitary play**: Child may play with toys by himself. Two- and three-year- olds engage in this play more commonly than older children.

3. **Parallel play**: Two or more children simultaneously use similar toys or play next to each other but do not interact. They may, however, mimic each other. A running commentary but no shared conversation can ensue. Two- and three-year-olds often engage in this play.

4. **Associative play**: Children interact socially, but with little or no organization. They are more interested in being with each other than in what they are doing. Some leading and following but no set rules occur. Preschoolers often play associatively.

5. **Cooperative play**: Children interact, share toys, or take turns. Cooperative play usually involves some purpose, such as playing house, and division of roles, such as "You be the mommy, and I'll be the baby" (Hartup, 1983). There is an organization, such as rules about turn-taking and sharing or formal games involving competition aimed at winning. This type of play, rarely seen in the preschool years, is the forerunner of games played in middle childhood.

Play also can be classified by the activities children engage in; activities can both influence and reflect cognitive development. That children's play becomes more complex and interactive with age was observed by Sutton-Smith (1971) and others (Rogers & Sawyers, 1988; Garvey, 1990):

1. **Practice play**: Children repeat behavior while learning new skills or improving coordination. In infancy, the kinds of practice play exhibited follow Piaget's description of sensorimotor thought (an example would be repeatedly shaking a rattle). In the school-age years, the kinds of practice play exhibited are those involved in games, such as running, jumping, and throwing.

2. **Symbolic play**: Children transform physical objects, action, or events into substitute ones. A preschool child might push a block

Solitary play

Cooperative play

along the floor making noises like a fire engine. Symbolic play marks the beginning of representational thought (Rogers & Sawyers, 1988). It coincides with Piaget's stage of preoperational thought and reflects the language development of the child.

3. **Games**: Children engage in activities for pleasure with rules and often compete with one another to win. Game-playing increases in the school-age years when playing with peers assumes an increasingly important role. Game-playing coincides with Piaget's stage of concrete operations when cause and effect and rules can be understood.

Play is a vehicle whereby children test themselves—physical-motor, interpersonal and cognitive skills. Through play children discover capacities. They compare themselves with others. ("I bet I can run faster than you.")

Thus, play influences children's social development in that it is a vehicle by which children learn appropriate behavior by real consequences—if they take a toy from someone, they may get hit. It influences children's cognitive development in that it is a way in which children can try various activities, learn from others, and compare themselves with others to find their strengths and weaknesses.

## Friendship

Like play, children's social relationships and friendships also become more complex and interactive with age (Rubin,1980). Selman and Selman (1979) interviewed more than 250 people between the ages of three and 45 to get a developmental perspective on friendship patterns. They delineated the following five stages:

1. *Momentary playmateship*: Most children under age four and some older children are in this stage. They cannot consider the views of others and can think only about what they want from the friendship. Friends are defined by how close they live; so friendship is momentary.

2. *One-way assistance*: At about age four until about age nine, children are more capable of telling the difference between their own perspectives and those of others. Friendship, however, is based on whether someone does what the child wants that person to do ("He's not my friend anymore; he didn't want to play cars"). Thus, friendship is viewed as a one-way affair.

3. *Two-way, fair-weather cooperation*: Children aged 6 to 12 acknowledge that friendship involves give and take. They see friendship, however, as mutually serving individual interests rather than mutually cooperating toward a common interest ("We are friends. We do things for each other"). At this age, children emphasize similarities between friends, as well as equalities and reciprocities ("We all like to collect baseball cards. We trade them and give doubles to

*(continued on following page)*

**Momentary playmates**

*(continued from previous page)*

our friends who are missing those."). Children of this age are beginning to recognize that friendship is based on getting along—sharing interests, ideas, and feelings.

4. *Intimate, mutually shared relationships*: Children aged 9 to 15 can now view a friendship as an entity. It is an ongoing, committed relationship that incorporates more than doing things for each other; it tends to be treasured for its own sake and may involve possessiveness and jealousy ("She is my best friend. How can she go to the movies with Susan?"). Thus, friendship is intimate in that it involves mutually shared feelings and loyalty. It also is mutually exclusive in that friends are not supposed to be friends with anyone but each other.

5. *Autonomous interdependent friendships*: About age 12, children are capable of respecting their friends' needs for both dependency and autonomy ("We like to do most things together and we talk about our problems, but sometimes Jason just likes to be by himself. I don't mind."). Friendship is viewed as a special relationship, but not a mutually exclusive one.

## Acceptance/Rejection by the Group

Effective relationships with peers impact later life adjustment. It has been demonstrated that there are consequences of rejection by the peer group. For example, isolated children were more likely to drop out of school (Ullman, 1957) and they were more likely than accepted children to have later emotional problems or to become juvenile delinquents (Roff, Sells & Golden, 1972; Kupersmidt & Coie, 1990). It was interesting that of all the data gathered in a study (Cowen et al., 1973) on third grade children including school attendance, grade-point averages, IQ scores, teacher ratings, school-nurse referrals, self-concept scores, anxiety-test scores, and peer ratings, the one that best predicted mental health status 11 years later was peer ratings. Of course, peer relationships are not totally responsible for one's mental health, but they do influence social and personality development.

A child's acceptance by peers and successful interactions with them depend on willingness to cooperate and interact positively with other children (Asher, Gottman & Oden, 1977; Dodge, 1983). Children who are popular with peers tend to be healthy and vigorous, capable of initiative, and are poised. They also are adaptable, conforming, dependable, affectionate, and considerate (Hartup, 1983). Children are rejected by peers because of the child's inappropriate behavior, such as aggressiveness (Dodge, 1983). Additionally, children who do not know how to initiate a friendship, who have difficulty communicating, and who rarely praise their peers are not readily accepted by the group. Also, children who are poor losers are not welcome in most children's groups. Finally, a child's physical appearance and manner of dressing or speaking can cause rejection by peers (Asher, 1982).

**Unpopular children are often teased by their peers.**

# Conformity

Children learn from each other. How conforming children are to the group depends on many factors such as age, particular situation, and perception of one's status in the group. Experiments show that children become most susceptible to peer influence in middle childhood and become less conforming in adolescence (Constanzo & Shaw, 1966; Berndt & Perry, 1990 ) (figure 12.2).

Even when an action or behavior is known to be wrong, middle-years children still conform with the majority opinion of the group. In a study by Berenda (1950), 90 children aged 7 to 13 were asked to compare the lengths of lines on 12 pairs of cards. They had already taken this same test in school. However, this time the children participating in the experiment were tested in a room with the eight brightest children in their class. Answers were given out loud. These eight children had been instructed beforehand to give seven wrong answers out of 12. The results pointed to the power of group influence. While almost all subjects had given correct answers to the seven critical questions in the original test taken in school, only 43 percent of the 7- to 10-year-olds and only 54 percent of the 10- to 13-year-olds gave correct answers on the second test in the group setting. The rest changed their former answers to match the group's, which were incorrect.

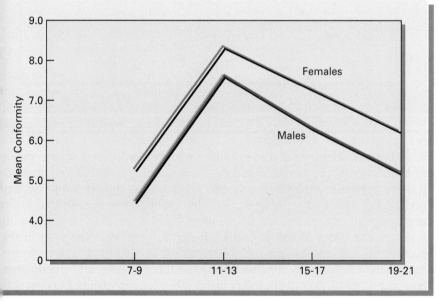

**FIGURE 12.2**
Children become most conforming in preadolescence—sixth to ninth grade (Constanzo & Shaw, 1966).

Such conformity is more apparent in ambiguous situations where children are unsure about what they should do or are supposed to do (Hartup, 1983). For example, Berndt (1979) gave a questionnaire to students ranging from third to twelfth grade, asking how they would respond to various hypothetical *prosocial., neutral.,* and *antisocial* situations. A question exemplifying a prosocial situation asked the students whether they would help a classmate with a report if asked by peers, instead of doing what they wanted to do, which was helping another classmate operate the film projector. A question exemplifying a neutral situation asked the students whether they would go to a movie if asked by peers even if they were not particular-

## F.Y.I.

Children not readily accepted by peers can be coached in social skills. A year after learning to participate, communicate, and cooperate more effectively, a group of unpopular children showed more sociability and acceptance by peers than the control group of unpopular children who were not coached (Oden & Asher, 1977; Coie & Koeppi, 1990).

ly interested in that movie. A question exemplifying an antisocial situation asked the students whether they would steal candy if a peer wanted help in doing it.

One of Berndt's (1979; Berndt & Perry, 1990) findings was that conformity to antisocial behavior and neutral situations peaked in the ninth grade and then dropped to previous levels. Another finding was that conformity to prosocial behavior peaked in the sixth grade and then dropped. In general, the sixth to ninth graders exhibited the most conforming behavior. The results are plotted on figure 12.3.

**FIGURE 12.3**
**Conformity to prosocial and antisocial behavior in children in grades three through twelve. (Berndt, 1979)**

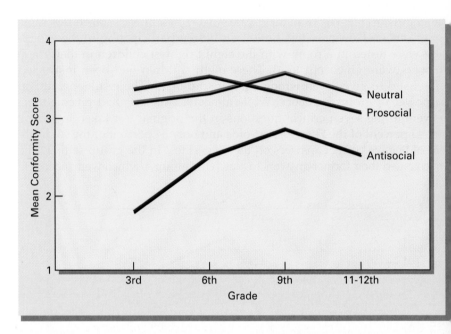

Berndt also found that whether people conformed to the group depended on the particular situation—how good or bad they felt about it. Students were more likely to conform to situations they did not feel bad about. Thus, personal standards affect the likelihood of conforming to the peer group.

On the basis of these studies, it can be seen that the peer group becomes an increasingly powerful socializing agent during the period of development between early childhood, age three to five, and pubescence about age 11 to 13. A concern today is the role peer conformity plays in substance use and abuse (box 12.2).

## BOX 12.2    SUBSTANCE USE AND ABUSE

The most common reason cited by high school students for using alcohol and marijuana is that their friends do (Santrock, 1993). Some adolescents try drugs or alcohol because they want to have a new experience. For others it represents an exhibition of independence from adults. For still others, the feeling of relaxation and escape from tensions are the attractions. When use of drugs or alcohol becomes a dependency, a need to function in situations, then its *use* becomes *abuse*.

**Substance abuse** refers to the excessive and harmful use of alcohol and drugs.

From a personality perspective, alcohol abusers have been described as aggressive, impulsive, anxious, depressed, having low self-esteem, and lacking in success (Hawthorne & Menzel, 1983). From a social perspective, adolescent substance abusers have been found to value independence over academic achievement and are more influenced by their peers than by their parents (Penning & Barnes, 1982). They tolerate deviant behavior more than nonabusing peers. Compared with nonabusing adolescents, abusers more often come from single-parent homes, have learning disabilities, attempt suicide, and have close relatives who abuse drugs (Kite, 1980).

According to Spoth & Rosenthal (1980), the attractiveness of alcohol or drugs comes from personality needs that demand satisfaction. For example, alcohol may be used as a means of coping with personal problems or to facilitate social interaction while drugs may be used to reduce loneliness, anger, and parental pressure (Segal, 1983; Newcomb & Bentler, 1989).

Many studies have explored genetic factors involved in alcohol abuse and have found a familial pattern (Goodwin, 1981; Mathews, 1981; Saunders, 1982). For example, in studies of adopted children, a higher incidence of alcoholism was observed in the biological children of alcoholics than in the adopted children (Goodwin, 1981). Also studies of twins indicate genetic factors in alcoholism (Goodwin, 1979).

There appears to be a genetic predisposition to substance abuse, but there are also personality and social factors involved that stem from relationships with family, peers, or school. In one study, it was found that adolescents who were more insecurely attached to parents were more likely to drink to facilitate social contact than securely attached counterparts (Kwakman et al., 1988). It is difficult to specify exact causes of substance abuse, especially because substance abuse itself causes changes in personality and social behavior.

Substance abusers tend not to explore their capacities nor do they develop coping skills to deal with problems.

## COMMUNITY

The term *community* is derived from the Latin word for fellowship. It refers to the affective relationships expected among closely knit groups of people having common interests. It also refers to people living in a particular geographical area who are bound together politically and economically.

The shared organization of ideas, including intellectual., moral., and esthetic standards prevalent in a community is termed **culture** (LeVine, 986). Culture affects the way one perceives the world, behaves, learns, and

The community influences social and personality development in that it provides a sense of belonging and friendship, and contributes to the socialization of children.

relates to others (Hall, 1959; 1966). For example, some cultures stress the importance of the group while others stress the importance of the individual. Some cultures make status distinctions among age, gender, or position in society; for other cultures such distinctions are less important. Thus, the community is a significant socializing agent via the culture it transmits to the developing person.

In a cross-cultural, longitudinal study spanning six years, personality development in Mexico and the United States was compared (Holtzman, 1982). Using various personality tests, significant differences were found between Mexican and American children from grades 1 through 12. These differences were attributed to socialization practices in the particular cultural communities. To illustrate, a basic Mexican value is the primary importance and solidarity of the family. Mexican children play with the sibling rather than the schoolmates or neighborhood children as American children do. The Mexican father has undisputed authority and is expected to be obeyed. The Mexican mother is the primary source of affection and care. The emphasis on family affiliation socializes the Mexican child to achieve so her family is proud. In contrast, the American child, whose family is more loosely structured and more egalitarian in relationships, is socialized to achieve for himself. Mexican children exhibit more differences in expectations for male and female behavior than do American children. Mexican children exhibit a passive coping style whereas American children exhibit an active one. This means that Mexican children are more passively obedient and adapt rather than trying to change stresses in the environment. American children, on the other hand, tend to be more actively independent and to struggle for a mastery of problems and challenges in the environment rather than accept them as unconquerable.

Thus, while there are individual personality differences within cultural communities, the Holtzman study has shown that culture has a profound influence on personality development in children.

Whiting and Edwards (1988) investigated the cultural similarities and differences in the social behavior of girls and boys 2 to 10 years old who lived in communities in India, Okinawa, the Philippines, Mexico, Kenya, and the United States. They documented the powerful influence on children's behavior of their relationship to the people with whom they interacted. Specific dimensions affecting the influence of children's interactions with others were age, gender, and cultural community. These dimensions were significant because they determined children's assignment to or choice of settings such as home or school, activities such as caring for siblings or doing errands, and social companions. Different cultural communities varied their expectations of behavior by age. In some cultures 6-year-olds were expected to learn the ways of their culture by taking on household responsibilities and caring for younger siblings, while in others, 6-year-olds were expected to go to school. They also varied their expectations of behavior by gender. Some cultures had different scripts for males and females and assigned children to settings or activities accordingly. Boys were allowed more autonomy and were expected to exhibit more dominant behavior with others, while girls were kept in close proximity and expected to engage in more nurturing activities with younger siblings.

Thus, according to Whiting and Edwards, cultural forces in the community "modulate social development and lead to increasing differences in the kinds of behavior which adults expect in children" (Whiting & Edwards, 1988, p. 266).

MEDIA

Television has become an integral part of everyday life. It appeals to visual and auditory senses and attracts our attention. Infants as young as six months of age gaze at it, and, if allowed by parents, small children sit in front of it for hours. Television helps determine not only how we spend our time but also what we learn and what we think about things (Condry, 1989). It helps shape our behavior (Pearl, 1982; Huston, Watkins & Kunkel,1989). Television has a more profound effect on children than it does on adults because children come to television knowing less about the physical and social world than do older viewers and the adults who create television content (Dorr, 1986). Therefore, children's transactions with television are less informed and less critical than adults. Specifically, children may not completely understand the program content and may accept the program as true information without considering the motives for broadcasting it. Thus, television exerts a significant socializing influence.

**Television provides models for behavior and affects behavior such as emotional sensitivity, aggression, and prosocial behavior (Comstock & Paik, 1991).**

## Observational Learning

Children learn from television by observation. Researchers also have analyzed specific issues about observational learning, also known as social cognitive theory (Bandura, 1965; 1974; 1989). Social cognitive theory states that role models act as stimuli to produce similar behavior in the observer of the role model. The behavior is learned first by being observed then imitated. Imitation is affected by how the observed act is reinforced. If children see someone rewarded for doing certain things, they are more likely to imitate these acts. Thus, if children see a television character rewarded for aggressive behavior, they will probably act out that behavior. If the actor is punished, the children are less likely to imitate the aggressive behavior. Observed reinforcements thus influence the behavior's occurrence. The persistence of the behavior, however, appears to be related to whether the children are rewarded or punished (Parke & Slaby, 1983).

Observational learning can be related to age (Collins, Berndt & Hess, 1974). Some investigators say that by the time children reach their teens, behavior is no longer significantly affected by observational learning. Young children, however, who do not see the relation between aggressions and motives, are more prone to imitate the aggressive behavior. Children start to imitate what they see on television when they are young, some as early as two years of age.

## Emotional Sensitivity

Children show a wide range of emotional reactions to television. While children can learn to be more empathic and to express or understand emotions from television presentations with guidance from adults, the data on heavy viewing suggest that they tend to be less empathic. For example, Drabman and Thomas (1976) exposed one group of third grade children to a violent detective program and another group to a baseball game. To assess whether exposure to television violence affected children's reactions to real-life aggression, they assigned the two groups of children the task of watching younger children play via a television monitor. The third graders were told to seek adult help if they saw younger children having a problem. When teasing, arguing, and finally pushing, shoving, and crying took place, the third graders who had watched the violent television program took longer to seek adult help than did the children who watched the baseball game. Thus, it appears as if exposure to television violence can breed apathy or decreased sensitivity to real-life violence.

## Aggression

Numerous studies have been conducted to assess the effects of television violence on children. The research is based on social learning theory wherein the behavior is first learned by observation then is imitated depending on how it is reinforced. For example, two independent studies by the same investigators (Singer & Singer, 1980) followed three- and four-year-old children over one year and correlated television viewing at home with the various behaviors displayed during free-play periods at day-care centers. In each study consistent associations were demonstrated between excessive television viewing of violent programs and unwarranted aggressive behavior in free-play. It was concluded that for these preschool children watching television violence was a cause of heightened aggressiveness. The effects of television violence have been investigated more thoroughly than any other aspect of television. Experts have repeatedly concluded that a small but reliable causal effect of television violence on aggressive behavior exists (Friedrich-Cofer & Huston, 1986; Huesmann, 1986; Comstock & Paik, 1991).

## Prosocial Behavior

Mister Rogers meeting with children and discussing behavior, play, and interests.

Just as aggressive behavior is influenced by observational learning, so is *prosocial behavior*. **Prosocial behavior** refers to helping, sharing, or cooperating. Research suggests that children can learn constructive social behavior such as helpfulness, cooperation, and friendliness from television viewing, especially if adults help them grasp the material or reinforce the program content ( Pearl,1982; Huston, Watkins & Kunkel, 1989 ). For example, in a study by Friedrich and Stein (1975) preschool children were assigned to five groups. One group saw "neutral" programs about nature. The other four groups saw four programs from "Mister Rogers Neighborhood," a television series stressing cooperation, sharing, sympathy, affection, and friendship. When children who saw the prosocial program were asked questions such as "How do friends show they like you?," they answered with more ways of showing affection than the children who saw the neutral shows. This was true in situations like those in "Mister Rogers Neighborhood" as well as others. Another interesting finding was that if children saw the prosocial program and also were given direct training by adults in role-playing, they were more helpful than if they received only the training or only saw the prosocial programs. Thus, exposure to prosocial television increases knowledge about prosocial behavior. When exposure is combined with other reinforcing activities such as role-playing, then helping behavior will probably increase even in situations different from what was originally seen on television.

## INTERACTION OF BIOLOGICAL AND CONTEXTUAL INFLUENCES ON SOCIAL AND PERSONALITY DEVELOPMENT

While we have discussed biological and contextual influences on social and personality development separately, in reality they interact in complex ways. The most extensive explanation of how biological and contextual influences on social and personality development interact is Urie Bronfenbrenner's ecological approach to studying human development. **Ecology** is the science of the relationships between organisms and their environment. According to Bronfenbrenner (1989, p. 188):

> The ecology of human development is the scientific study of the progressive, mutual accommodation, throughout the life course, between an active, growing human being, and the changing properties of the immediate settings in which the developing person lives, as this process is affected by the relation between these settings, and the larger contexts in which the settings are embedded.

## ECOLOGICAL SYSTEMS THEORY OF URIE BRONFENBRENNER

Urie Bronfenbrenner (1979; 1989) believes that developmental processes and outcomes vary as a joint function of the characteristics of the person and the contexts that the person experiences. For example, effects on one's social and personality development can be triggered by events within the person, such as puberty, or within the context of family, such as divorce. Despite the origin, the significance of such events is that they alter the relationship between the person and the context thereby creating the potential for developmental change. The timing of puberty can affect self-esteem; late-maturing males had a lower self-esteem than males who matured early. Divorce can affect gender-role typing, with males adapting better if raised by fathers and females by mothers.

Bronfenbrenner's ecological systems theory provides a means to study humans in their various social contexts and serves as a guide for future research on the complicated process of socialization. According to Bronfenbrenner's theory, four systems are arranged in a hierarchical structure (figure 12.4, page 404).

The first basic structure, the **microsystem**, refers to the activities and relationships experienced by a developing person in a particular context such as family, school, peer group, or community. A child's development is affected in each of these contexts not only by the child's relationships with others in the family, school, peer group, or community but also by interactions between members of the particular microsystem. For example, a father's relationship with the mother affects her treatment of the child (Clarke-Stewart, 1978).

The second basic structure, the **mesosystem,** consists of linkages and relationships between two or more of a developing person's microsystems, such as the family and school, or the family and peer group.

The impact of mesosystems on the child depends on the quantity and quality of relationships. Bronfenbrenner (1979) uses the example of the child who goes to school alone on the first day. This means there is only a single link between family and school—the child. Where little linkage exists between family and school in terms of values, experiences, objects, and behavioral style, there also tends to be little academic achievement for the child. In contrast, where all these links are strong, as when the family supports school values by supervising homework, meeting with teachers, and so on, academic competence is likely to be present. The more numerous the qualitative links or relationships between the child's microsystems, the

FIGURE 12.4
BRONFENBRENNER'S
ECOLOGICAL
SYSTEMS

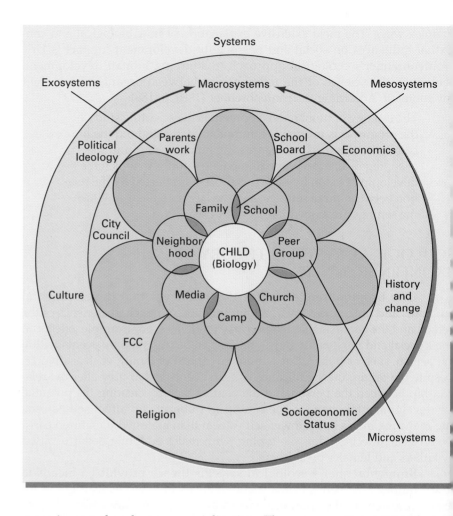

**Interaction between parent and teacher is an example of Brofenbrenner's mesosystem.**

more impact they have on socialization. Thus, mesosystems provide support for activities occurring in microsystems. For example, when parents invite a child's friends to their home, the socialization impact of the peers is enhanced through parental support.

The third basic structure, the **exosystem**, refers to settings in which children are not active participants but that affect them in one of the microsystems—for example, parents' jobs, school board, city council. The effects of exosystems on the child are indirect via the microsystems. To illustrate, when both parents work, child care must be found. Job stress is sometimes brought home to impact family interaction, particularly between parents and children. An illustration of exosystem effects is when the local government approves an air traffic pattern over a school; socialization is impacted in that noise interferes with learning.

The fourth basic structure, the **macrosystem,** consists of the developing person's society and subculture with particular reference to the belief systems, lifestyles and options, and patterns of social interchange. Examples of macrosystems are the United States, the middle class, and Spanish ancestry. Macrosystems are viewed as patterns, or sets of instructions, for exosystems, mesosystems, and microsystems. Democracy is the basic belief system of the United States and so is considered a macrosystem. Democratic ideology affects the world of work, an exosystem—for example employers cannot discriminate in hiring. Democratic ideology affects how schools communicate with families; school-family interaction is a mesosystem, for example, schools must inform parents of policies and parents have the right to question those policies. Changes in a macrosystem can result in changes in the other systems.

Chess and Thomas focused on the microsystem level of the child in the context of family. After studying temperament for over 30 years, Chess and Thomas (1987) concluded that differences in temperament in newborns and young infants are biologically determined, but then the infants' temperaments are influenced by their interactions with their parents, which may either intensify or modify their original temperaments.

Sometimes analyzing behavior on only one level, the microsystem, does not completely explain it. For example, in the NYLS, Thomas & Chess (1977) found that low regularity or rhythmicity in infancy and early childhood years predicted later adjustment problems in the primarily Jewish middle-class children in the sample, but not in the Puerto Rican working-class children. Lerner (1983) explains that the cultural contexts, or macrosystems, in which these children grew up were different. Low regularity or rhythmicity in the Puerto Rican families did not cause any concern or conflict between parents and children, whereas it did in the Jewish families.

Analyzing the behavior on *both* a macrosystem and microsystem level enables researchers to discover that cultural and familial expectations influence how the parent responds to a child's temperament thereby affecting the interaction.

## Bronfenbrenner's Theory Evaluated

Bronfenbrenner (1979; 1989) has criticized the experimental design of, in particular, laboratory studies of children's behavior as being very limited. He claims that the experimental design implemented in the laboratory sacrifices much valuable information for the sake of experimental control and scientific analysis. To understand how children actually develop, Bronfenbrenner believes it is necessary to observe their behavior in natural settings, such as family, school, peer group, and community, over prolonged periods.

Bronfenbrenner's ecological systems theory has provided a means for studying issues relevant to real people in the real world. He has provided a comprehensive model for analyzing the various contexts that influence development as well as the role of children themselves. Bronfenbrenner has called attention to the various links involved in development. He has provided a challenge for the reform of research procedures in developmental psychology. His theory provides a useful model for both basic research and its translation into policy and practice. However, the very comprehensiveness of his theory makes it problematic to implement. Bronfenbrenner admits having oriented his research too heavily on the contextual aspect of the theory and negating the developing organism. To formulate a research methodology is difficult because the theory deals with a changing organism in changing contexts, which in turn impact each other.

With more sophisticated computer technology and consequent accessibility to statistical analysis, determining interactional relationships between biological and contextual variables changing over time will be facilitated.

# CRITICAL THINKING & YOU

**P**aul was born into a middle-class family. Both parents had advanced college degrees; they lived in a new home in a suburban neighborhood. Paul's birth was normal and a welcome event because his father had wanted a boy. His three-year-old sister enjoyed helping her mother care for him.

Paul's motor development was slower than his sister's. He did not walk until he was 18 months old. He was content to play by himself, which relieved his mother because that allowed her to be attentive to his sister, who was more demanding. Paul's father was trying to build his medical practice so he was rarely at home.

The mother's parenting style was permissive. When the children were hungry, they were fed; when they were tired, they were put to bed. The mother never raised her voice to the children, nor was she very warm or affectionate. The father, on the other hand, was structured but also affectionate. He criticized his wife for not making demands on Paul at age three to be toilet-trained and to eat regular meals. His wife would try to be more organized and assertive, but eventually she would revert to old ways. The inconsistency did not affect Paul's sister, but it did affect Paul. Paul refused to use the toilet, would throw temper tantrums when his will was thwarted, and ignored demands. His language development was slow, so he would scream and kick to get his way rather than express himself verbally.

Paul attended preschool at age three for a few days a week. He would get into fights with the other children usually over toys. The teachers referred to his behavior as stubborn. He preferred to play by himself or watch television. About this time his parents were divorced. Paul's behavior regressed—his tantrums increased, and he refused to comply with any demands. The parents sought counseling. The divorce was blamed for Paul's behavior. Paul's father visited the children three times a week, spending more time with them.

By the time Paul was in first grade, the tantrums had decreased. Occasionally, he would make strange noises, and the other children would laugh. They did not want to play with him, so Paul had no friends. He often would refuse to do the classroom work and, on several occasions, walked out of the room. He was having problems learning to read and was not as well coordinated as his peers. The school psychologist diagnosed Paul as having a learning disability and an attention-deficit disorder.

**ANALYSIS**: Name at least one biological, contextual, and interactional influence on Paul's social and personality development. Review this chapter and find supportive reasons for each influence.

## SUMMARY

- Most psychologists agree that personality emerges from biological predispositions and social interactions with others in various contexts.

- Freud's psychosexual theory of personality development emphasized infancy and early childhood as the significant periods in which personality develops. The three components of personality are the id, the ego, and the superego. To deal with conflicts between the id and the superego, the ego develops defense mechanisms. Freud outlined five stages of personality development—oral, anal, phallic, latency, and genital—delineated by the development of the erogenous zones (mouth, anus, and genitals).

- Erikson's psychosocial theory of personality development emphasized a person's social interaction throughout eight significant stages of life. At each stage the person has a conflict to resolve: trust versus mistrust, autonomy versus shame and doubt, initiative versus guilt, industry versus inferiority, identity versus role confusion, intimacy versus isolation, generativity versus stagnation, ego integrity versus despair. Positive resolution of the conflict or crisis enables the person to move to the next stage and deal with that crisis effectively; negative resolution retards development in that it impedes resolution of the next crisis.

- Biological influences on social and personality development include heredity and temperament. Certain traits such as emotionality, activity, and sociability are believed to be genetically determined.

- Temperament refers to individual differences in physiological responsiveness to various experiences. These individual differences in activity level, rhythmicity, distractibility, approach-withdrawal, adaptability, attention span and persistence, intensity of reaction, threshold of responsiveness, and quality of mood influence parent–child interaction.

- Some contextual influences on social and personality development are the family, school, peers, community, and media.

- Parenting styles within a family (authoritarian, permissive, authoritative) have been shown to be related to various personality traits in children.

- The school influences social and personality development in that it is the setting in which significant cognitive and social experiences occur. The physical setting has been shown to affect activities and interactions. The educational programs (teacher- or learner-centered) affected attitudes toward school. Teacher expectations also influenced children's performance.

- Peers are significant in influencing social and personality development, specifically in the capacity to relate to others, in the development of social controls, and in the acquisition of social values and roles.

- The community and its shared organization of ideas, termed culture, influence how children are socialized. Culture affects the way one perceives the world, behaves, learns, and relates to others. Different cultural communities have different expectations for children's behavior.

- The media help determine how we spend our time, what we learn, and what we think about things. It has been demonstrated that television affects children's observational learning, emotional sensitivity, level of aggression, and prosocial behavior.

- Biology and context interact to influence social and personality development as is explained in Bronfenbrenner's ecological systems theory. The child's development is affected by the mutual accommodation throughout life between him and microsystems, mesosystems, exosystems, and macrosystems.

- Microsystems are the immediate settings in which the developing person participates.
- Mesosystems are the interactions that occur between microsystems.
- Exosystems are those settings in which the child does not participate but that affect her, such as the parents' work or the local school board.
- Macrosystems represent the belief system of the child's society, culture, religion, or socioeconomic status.

## RELATED READINGS

Asher, S.R. & Coie, J.D. (Eds.). (1990). *Peer rejection in childhood.* Cambridge, England: Cambridge University Press.

Berndt, T.J. & Ladd, G.W. (Eds.). (1989). *Peer relationships in child development.* New York: John Wiley.

Berns, R. (1993). *Child, family, community* (3rd ed.). Fort Worth, TX: Harcourt Brace Jovanovich.

Best, R. (1983). *We've all got scars: What boys and girls learn in elementary school.* Bloomington, IN: University Press.

Bronfenbrenner, U. (1979). *The ecology of human development.* Cambridge, MA: Harvard University Press.

Brophy, J. & Thomas, G. (1974). *Teacher-student relationships: Causes and consequences.* New York: Holt, Rinehart & Winston.

Chess, S. & Thomas, A. (1987). *Know your child.* New York: Basic Books.

Dorr, A. (1986). *Television and children: A special medium for a special audience.* Beverly Hills, CA: Sage.

Dunn, J. & Plomin, R. (1990). *Separate lives: Why siblings are so different.* New York: Basic Books.

Elkind, D. (1981). *The hurried child: Growing up too fast, too soon.* Reading, MA: Addison-Wesley.

Erikson, E.H. (1980). *Identity and the life cycle.* New York: W.W. Norton.

Farnham-Diggory, S. (1990). *Schooling.* Cambridge, MA: Harvard University Press.

Fraiberg, S.H. (1959). *The magic years.* New York: Charles Scribner & Sons.

Garbarino, J. (1992). *Children and families in the social environment* (2nd ed.). New York: Aldine de Gruyter.

Garvey, C. (1990). *Play.* Cambridge, MA: Harvard University Press.

Parke, R.D, (1981). *Fathers.* Cambridge, MA: Harvard University Press.

Plomin, R. (1986). *Development, genetics, and psychology.* Hillsdale, NJ: Lawrence Erlbaum.

Whiting, B.B. & Edwards, C.P. (1988). *Children of different worlds: The foundation of social behavior.* Cambridge, MA: Harvard University Press.

● ● ● ● ● ● ● ● ● ● ● ● ● ● ● ● ● ● ● ● ● ● **ACTIVITY** ● ● ● ● ● ● ● ● ● ● ● ● ● ● ● ● ● ● ● ●

To understand the developmental progression of friendship:

1. Select a boy and girl from each of the following age groups: preschoolers (aged 4–5), second or third graders (aged 7–8), fifth or sixth graders (aged 10–11), eighth or ninth graders (aged 13–14), and eleventh or twelfth graders (aged 16–17).

    Ask:

    a. "Who is your best friend?"

    b. "What kinds of things do you do together?"

    c. "What is it about your friend that makes him or her your best friend?"

    d. "What is it about you that makes you a best friend?"

3. Record the answers.

4. Discuss and explain the developmental progression of friendship including things friends do together by age.

5. Was there a difference in the developmental progression of friendship and things friends do together by gender? Explain.

● ● ● ● ● ● ● ● ● ● ● ● ● ● ● ● ● ● ● ● ● ● ● ● ● ● ● ● ● ● ● ● ● ● ● ● ● ● ● ● ● ●

# 13 Gender-Role Development

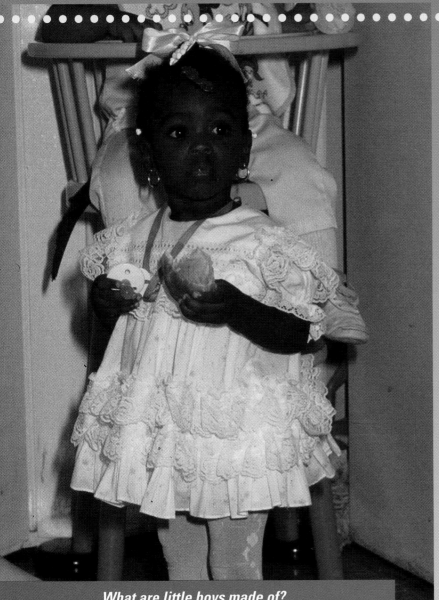

*What are little boys made of?*
*Frogs and snails and puppy-dog's tails.*
*What are little girls made of?*
*Sugar and spice and all things nice.*
**English nursery rhyme**

## ABOUT SEX AND GENDER

When Jennifer was born, Robin and Lloyd agreed they would optimize her development by providing traditionally male activities, such as sports or a chemistry set, as well as traditionally female ones, such as sewing skills or dolls.

When Jennifer's grandmother bought her a tea set for her second birthday, Robin bought her a set of blocks. Lloyd took Jennifer to his college football game and to the ballet.

Before Jennifer was old enough to go to preschool, she amused herself by imitating Maria, the housekeeper and caretaker. Jennifer would dust everything within reach and move her plastic vacuum cleaner around the house.

Lloyd liked to play blocks with Jennifer; after all, he was an architect. It was hard for him to let her build what she wanted; sometimes he would show her how things should look.

During Jennifer's early years her playmate was Nancy, a neighbor who was one year older. Nancy and Jennifer liked to play with their dolls, watch television, and color.

When Jennifer was six, Robin and Lloyd enrolled her in soccer and ballet lessons. After a few months of trying to learn to kick the ball run, and remember the rules, Jennifer decided she did not like soccer because, "It was too rough." But she loved ballet. She loved to wear her pink leotard, and she adored her teacher, "She's so beautiful, I want to be just like her when I grow up."

Thus, despite Robin and Lloyd's intention to remove gender stereotypes in raising Jennifer, Jennifer sought them out in the process of forming a gender identity and developing a gender role.

Whereas an *identity* has to do with self-perception and categorization, a *role* has to do with a socially expected behavior pattern, usually determined by an individual's status or position in a particular society. Thus, **gender roles** involve "a constellation of qualities an individual understands to characterize males and females in his or her culture" (Block, 1973, p. 512). They also involve relationships with one's own sex and the opposite sex. In American society, the stereotype for masculinity includes aggressiveness, independence, strength, and dominance, whereas the stereotype for femininity includes nurturance, gentleness, submissiveness, and sensitivity.

The terms sex and gender often are used interchangeably. However, an increasing number of authors are beginning to distinguish between the terms. *Sex* is used when referring to **biological** differences of males and females—people are classified as male or female based on chromosomes, hormones, and genitalia. *Gender* is used when referring to **psychological** differences—people's perceptions and feelings of maleness and femaleness (Archer & Lloyd, 1982). Because it is often difficult to separate biological and psychological influences, this text uses the terms synonymously.

Looking at the adult roles that men and women perform in our society, we find that women dominate the nursing and secretarial fields while men dominate engineering and carpentry (Bureau of Labor Statistics, 1990). What attracts men and women to different fields? Are they biologically programmed to excel in certain activities? Nursing requires nurturing skills; secretarial work requires attention to details; engineering and carpentry require spatial and mathematical ability. Are men and women socialized into various roles so society will function smoothly? Or does some biological predisposition (such as physical strength or verbal skills) attract males and females to certain activities, which society reinforces through approval consequently producing men and women who have developed different competencies?

To understand how we develop particular gender roles, we will first explain the similarities and differences between males and females, then we will discuss the influences of biology and context and their interaction on these similarities and differences.

## PHYSICAL SIMILARITIES AND DIFFERENCES

Both males and females have 23 pairs of chromosomes. In the female, each member of each pair is the same; in the male this is also the case, except with the 23rd pair. The female's 23rd pair of chromosomes is XX and the male's is XY. Male, female, or ambiguous genotype is determined at the moment of conception.

About six weeks after conception, the gonads begin to differentiate from a single structure into male and female structures. **Gonads** are the reproductive organs that produce sexual hormones and reproductive cells (sperm or egg). Male gonads are the testes; female gonads are the ovaries. Both testes and ovaries produce hormones called androgens, estrogens, and progesterones, however in different amounts. The testes produce more androgens, and the ovaries produce more estrogens.

After hormonal activity begins, the reproductive anatomy of males and females begins to differentiate. This includes the development of the internal anatomy diagrammed in figure 13.1 (page 412) and the external genitalia diagrammed in figure 13.2 (page 413).

During early development we all have the rudimentary internal ducts or structures for our own sex and for the opposite sex. At about three months after conception, these structures for our own sex enlarge, whereas those for the opposite sex degenerate. In a male, the *Müllerian* structure degenerates completely, and the *Wolffian* structure develops into the structures (*epididymis, vas deferens,* and *seminal vesicles)* for carrying sperm from the testes and secretions from the prostate. In a female, the *Müllerian* structure differentiates into *fallopian tubes, uterus,* and the upper portion of the *vagina,* and the Wolffian structure degenerates. Later, we will discuss cases where an error happens in differentiation and/or degeneration, and, consequently, a child is born with an ambiguous sex.

The final step in sexual differentiation is the development of the external genitals. These, like the gonads, develop from structures that are unisex at the outset (the genital tubercle, genital fold, and genital swelling).

# F.Y.I.

Examples of ambiguous genotypes are Klinefelter's syndrome (XXY genotype) and Turner's syndrome (XO genotype).

FIGURE 13.1
INTERNAL
REPRODUCTIVE
ANATOMY

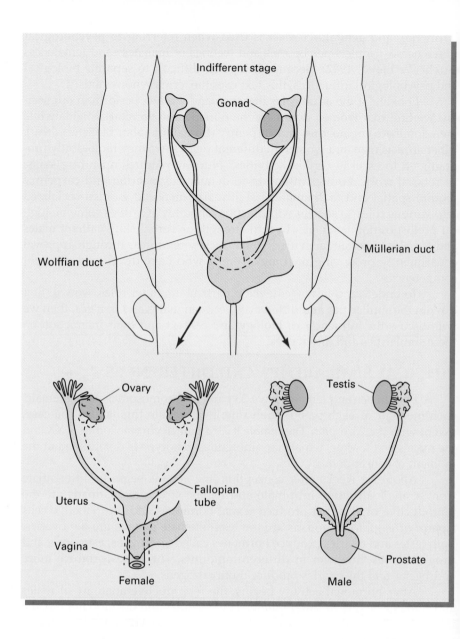

Androgen promotes development of the male *penis* and *scrotum*. The absence of this hormone leads to the development of the female *clitoris* and *labia*.

Hormones, not only influence the development of the external genitalia but they also act on the developing fetal brain causing the hypothalamus to signal the pituitary gland to release chemicals termed *gonadotropins*. In turn, these are responsible for the cyclic production of gonadal hormones in the female, which accounts for the monthly menstrual cycle involving production of estrogen and progesterone and release of an egg, and the acyclic, or continuous, pattern in males that accounts for the constant production of testosterone and, in turn, sperm. Both patterns make their appearance at puberty.

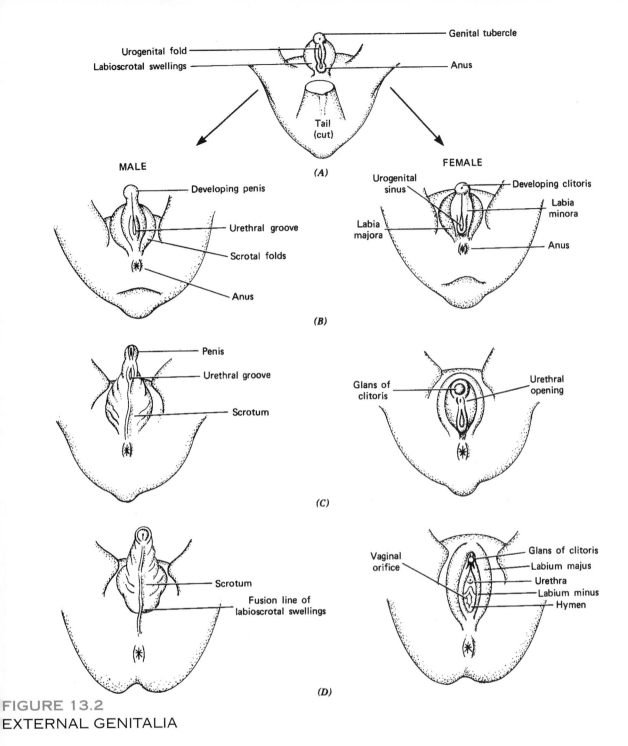

FIGURE 13.2
EXTERNAL GENITALIA

Thus, before birth four biological events that differentiate males and females have occurred:

1. chromosomal makeup (XX for females, XY for males)
2. gonadal structure (ovaries for females, testes for males)
3. internal structure and reproductive tracts
4. external genitalia

From birth onward (except for a few years between ages 11 and 14) males tend to be larger than females. Men have larger bones than women and male bones are arranged differently. "Men have broader shoulders and a narrower pelvis, which enables them to stride out with no waist motion. A woman's wider pelvis, evolved for childbearing, forces her to put more movement into each step she takes with the result that she displays a bit of a jiggle and sway as she walks" (Brothers, 1982). It is easier for a man to climb a ladder or stairs or a mountain than it is for a woman because of the angle at which his thigh is joined to his knees.

Males and females also have different maturational rates. Prenatally, on the average, females are about four weeks ahead skeletally (Tanner, 1990). They grow faster and reach puberty an average of two years before males, and they stop growing earlier. Females on the average also are more coordinated from birth (Tanner, 1990). Generally, male infants are more irritable than females in that they exhibit more frequent crying and less frequent sleeping (Moss, 1967). This may be due to their relative immaturity and higher incidence of birth complications (Tanner, 1990).

Other physical differences between males and females occur at puberty, triggered by the hormone testosterone in the male and estrogen and progesterone in the female (figure 13.3).

In males, testosterone produces several changes: the voice deepens, sweat gland activity increases, body hair distribution changes, and muscular development increases, particularly in the neck, chest, and shoulders (Glucksmann, 1974). Testosterone also promotes growth in the skeletal system, and it increases the size of the heart and lungs, the capacity of blood to carry oxygen, and the body's ability to neutralize the waste products of muscular exertion (Archer & Lloyd, 1982).

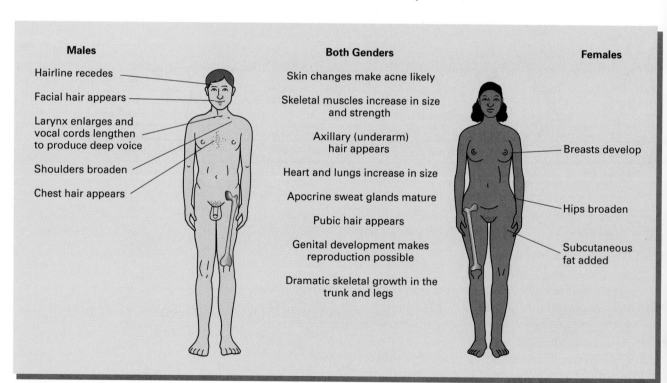

FIGURE 13.3
MALE-FEMALE DIFFERENCES AT PUBERTY

In females, the rise in estrogen levels leads to breast development, fat redistribution, and the beginning of the menstrual cycle. Estrogen and progesterone show cyclic fluctuations during the menstrual cycle, with estrogen levels rising during the earlier phase and progesterone increasing during the later phase.

## SOCIAL AND EMOTIONAL SIMILARITIES AND DIFFERENCES

Some people believe that females are more sociable and emotional than males. However, according to Maccoby and Jacklin (1974), males and females are more similar than different in their sociability. That is, infants of both genders show visual preferences for people rather than objects, children of both genders are about equal in friendliness to others, and adults of both genders seem to have similar needs for affiliation even though they exhibit those needs differently (Tavris & Wade, 1984; Basow, 1992).

In the first year of life, males and females play with the same toys and do the same amount of banging and cuddling. In the second year, differences begin to appear (O'Brien & Huston, 1985; Caldera, Huston, & O'Brien, 1989). By the beginning of the third year, males spend more time with guns, blocks, and trucks; females with stuffed animals, dolls, puzzles, and pegboards. By the end of the third year, gender differences in toy play are firmly established (Maccoby & Jacklin, 1974).

When playing, males engage in more rough-and-tumble play (fighting, wrestling, and chasing) than do females (Humphreys & Smith, 1984). Also, males are more aggressive physically and verbally (Maccoby & Jacklin, 1974), and they are involved in conflict situations more often than females. When conflict occurs, males tend to use threat and physical force significantly more often, whereas females tend to attempt to mitigate or diffuse the conflict significantly more often, especially when interacting with other females (Miller, Danaher & Forbes, 1986).

As children move from preschool to elementary school, the rough-and-tumble and fantasy play give way to more organized rule-governed games. Segregation of playground activities by gender is marked during the middle-school years.

Not only does social development begin similarly in females and males and become differentiated as they grow but emotional development follows a similar pattern. Young children of both genders are similar in dependency, fear, and anxiety (Basow, 1992). However, as females approach adulthood they begin to rate themselves as more dependent, fearful, and anxious than males. As males approach adulthood, they report more of an attraction to physically risky recreations and occupations (Hetherington & Parke, 1986).

## COGNITIVE SIMILARITIES AND DIFFERENCES

Tests of intellectual and developmental abilities indicate that although females may have a slight advantage up until about age seven, males and females generally are not found to differ in average ability (Maccoby & Jacklin, 1974; Basow, 1992). However, they do differ in specific abilities. From about age 10, males exhibit an excellence in visual-spatial ability. This includes such tasks as manipulating objects in two- or three-dimensional space, reading maps, or aiming at a target. From about age 12, males show a superiority in mathematics (Hetherington & Parke, 1986).

For boys, gender-preferred play includes transportation toys, building blocks, construction toys, and mud play.

For girls gender-preferred play includes art activities, play in the kitchen, play with dolls, and dress-up (Fagot, 1977).

While females' achievement in school exceeds males, males do better on the Scholastic Aptitude Test (SAT) and the National Merit Scholarship Test (Basow, 1992).

# BIOLOGICAL INFLUENCES ON GENDER-ROLE DEVELOPMENT

To determine the extent of biological influence, researchers examine animals because they are not subject to the contextual and cognitive influences that humans are and also because it is possible to do experimental manipulations of hormone exposure (inject with androgen or estrogen) and anatomical structures (castrate or remove ovaries) that would be considered unethical in human subjects. Human subjects are studied when a biological error occurs with their development.

Research has demonstrated that through programs of prenatal and postnatal hormone regulation, female birds can be induced to sing male songs, and female monkeys will refuse to "present" themselves to males who want to copulate. By the same token, prenatal castration of male animals and later treatment with estrogen and progesterone can induce behaviors in males that are typically female. For example, male rats given progesterone after castration early in life will build nests and care for the young (McGraw, 1987).

Studies on laboratory rats show that when hormones have been manipulated prenatally, alterations in adult sexual behavior and aggression occur (Huston, 1983). Animals exposed to androgen during the critical prenatal period of sexual development (differentiation) show the male pattern of mounting in adult sexual behavior. Animals of both sexes who are not exposed to masculinizing levels of androgen in the prenatal period tend to show the feminine pattern of passive receptivity rather than aggressive mounting in adult sexual behavior.

Similar experiments on monkeys have shown that when a pregnant mother carrying a female fetus is injected with testosterone during the middle part of the gestation period, the infant is born with masculinized genitalia. In one study, these masculinized females showed more aggressive play and more threatening gestures than normal females but less than normal males (Goy, 1975).

Such studies give support to the idea that testosterone organizes the brain and nervous system during a critical period of prenatal sexual development so that the behavior of males and females is differently primed (Timiras, 1982). However, other studies have found that if male hormones are injected into normal female monkeys after birth but preceding puberty, the females also become more assertive, sometimes even attaining the prime dominance status in the monkey troop (Hetherington & Parke, 1986). Hormones released during puberty also affect behavior.

We can deduce that manipulating the biochemistry of certain animals affects sex-role behavior.

## HUMAN STUDIES

Although human behavior is less responsive to hormone levels than nonhuman behavior, some evidence links prenatal exposure to androgens with male-like behaviors in humans. Much of this evidence comes from

**Beginning in infancy, females are superior in verbal abilities, and this superiority increases markedly into adolescence. This includes vocabulary, reading comprehension, and verbal expression.**

ase histories recorded by Money & Ehrhardt (1972) of women prenatally exposed to androgens One group of women had a condition called *adrenocortical hyperplasia* in which the adrenal glands (on top of the kidneys) secrete androgens. This secretion begins prenatally and has a masculinizing effect on gonadal tissue. Unless treated postnatally with cortisone on a regular basis, the masculinization continues as the child develops and the child may look like a male even though she is genetically a female (XX). The other group of women were those whose mothers had taken the drug *progestin* during pregnancies to prevent miscarriage. *Progestin* produces a similar androgen-like effect and results in the same prenatal genital and brain masculinization as occurs with adrenocortical hyperplasia.

These two groups of women were compared with normal women matched for age, IQ, race, and socioeconomic status. The women who were exposed to androgens and progestins prenatally were more tomboyish and energetic in play and aggression than the matched sample of normal women. The findings of Money and Ehrhardt support the study discussed earlier of female monkeys exposed prenatally to androgens who exhibited more aggressive play than normal females.

Biology may play a role not only in the way males and females behave but how they think. Evidence indicates that the brain structure and the cerebral organization of males and females differ. A study of the brains of four-year-old children who had died found that the right hemisphere was at a more advanced state of maturation in males, the left hemisphere in females (Levy, 1980). This could be ascertained by the amount of myelinization of the nerves. Such maturation is related to the ability of each hemisphere to execute specific functions. For 95 percent of the human population, the left side specializes in language functions, and the right hemisphere specializes in spatial functions. In the remaining population, these functions are reversed, and the cognitive sex differences also are reversed (Levy, 1980).

Some researchers believe that sex differences in visual-spatial skills, with males exhibiting superiority to females on various tests, might result from a sex-linked recessive trait (Harris, 1978). Because a male has only one X chromosome, a recessive gene on that chromosome will be expressed, whereas a female would have to receive two recessive genes (one on each X chromosome) to have the trait fully expressed. Because this hypothesis has not been statistically validated its supporters explain that some prenatal hormonal exposure may be essential for the activation of the gene.

Another explanation of the male and female difference in visual-spatial skills is that adult males have more cerebral hemispheric specialization of their brains than females (Bryden, 1982). In other words, in most right-handed adults, the left cerebral hemisphere is specialized for verbal and analytic processing of information. The right hemisphere is specialized for visual, spatial, and global processing of information; male cognitive functioning tends to follow this pattern. Females, however, are more likely to process information bilaterally; that is, they tend to use verbal modes of processing for spatial problems, and this method is less efficient.

Differences in spatial abilities of females and males show up in their understanding of horizontals and verticals. In a study by Liben and Golbeck (1980), the understanding of horizontalness was assessed by asking children to anticipate the position of liquid in tipped containers; the understanding of verticalness was assessed by having children show the position of plumb lines, for example a light bulb on a cord hanging from a ceiling

**Males have been found to exhibit better visual-spatial ability than girls.**

hook of a van (figure 13.4). Apparently, males have a more integrated spatial processing system.

Some theorists believe that at a critical period in prenatal development sex hormones determine the potentials for hemispheric specialization and brain organization. This brain organization, in turn, influences how information is processed by males and females. That is, prenatal hormones sensitize the brains of females to be more effective processors of verbal information and those of males to be more effective processors of spatial information (Hetherington & Parke, 1986; Basow, 1992).

**FIGURE 13.4**

**Sex differences in children's understanding of horizontal and vertical relations. (Hetherington & Parker, 1986)**

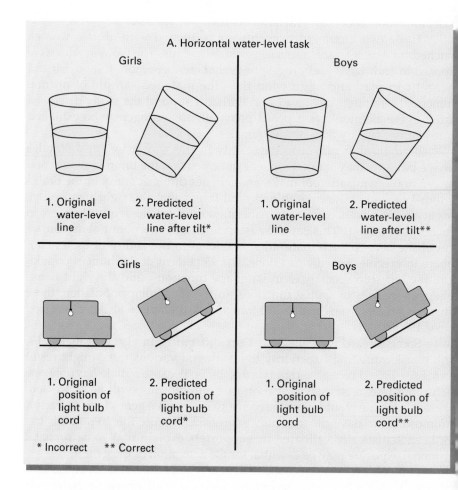

# THEORIES OF SEX-ROLE TYPING

**Sex-role typing** refers to an individual's taking on the societal or cultural characteristics (masculine or feminine) of his sex. There are four major theories of sex-role typing, each with a different perspective:

- *Psychoanalytic theory* explains sex-role typing from an emotional perspective (how one comes to feel like a male or female).
- *Social cognitive theory* explains it from a behavioral perspective (how one comes to behave as a male or female).

- *Cognitive developmental theory* provides an intellectual perspective (how one comes to think of self as a male or female).
- *Gender schema theory* explains sex-role typing from an information-processing perspective (how one comes to process gender-linked information and perceive self as male or female).

# PSYCHOANALYTIC THEORY

Sigmund Freud's theory of sex-role typing is part of his psychosexual theory of personality development. The theory assumes that the degree to which the sexual desires (sucking, expulsion of feces, masturbation) can be gratified at each stage determines the extent to which they influence later adult personality characteristics. Whereas, the first stage *(oral)* may have implications for adult dependent behavior and the second *(anal)* may have implications for adult compulsive behavior, the third *(phallic)* has implications for adult sex-role behavior.

The phallic stage centers on the *Oedipus Complex*. The **Oedipus Complex** is a psychoanalytic term referring to a boy's desire to possess his mother.

Because the Oedipus Complex takes the form of an initial desire to sexually possess the mother, the father is viewed as a rival. Freud believed the male was afraid of the possible loss of his penis at the hands of his father; he referred to this fear as "castration anxiety." Partially responsible for castration anxiety is the boy's belief that girls have already been castrated for something terrible they have done (Freud, 1925).

Eventually, the boy realizes that he will never possess his mother so he represses this desire. He does this by identifying with and taking on the characteristics of his father. Identification with the father involves not only the acquisition of masculine behavior and characteristics but also the development of the superego, or conscience. Thus, the resolution of the Oedipus Complex in males results in the ultimate internalization of social and moral norms (the father's standards) and the development of a sex-role identity (masculinity).

In females, the desire for a penis ("penis envy") is what causes the identification with the father as a love-object, according to Freud. Eventually, the female discovers that she cannot have her father nor can she have a penis so she identifies with her mother, replacing her wish for a penis with a wish for a child. In so doing, females begin to take on the feminine characteristics of their mothers. However, because they are not threatened with castration anxiety, females never attain a fully developed superego according to Freud (1925).

Freud's theory has been criticized because it was developed through the treatment of neurotic adults who reconstructed their childhood experiences during psychoanalysis. Making universal generalizations from specific cases, especially abnormal ones, is not considered scientific. Also, Freud did not test his theory by observing random samples of children at different ages. Finally, Freud's theory reflected a societal bias (Brooks-Gunn & Matthews, 1979). Most of Freud's patients were unhappy women. Freud attributed their problems to unresolved sex-role conflicts during the genital stage. He did not consider that the Victorian society in which these women lived was oppressive to females.

# F.Y.I.

The name comes from Greek mythology wherein Oedipus unwittingly kills his father and then marries his mother, unaware of the incestuous relationship.

Social cognitive theory says that children observe the behavior of those around them and imitate those whom they perceive as similar to themselves and whom they admire.

Children learn about gender differences usually based upon outward appearance such as physical size, clothing, and length of hair rather than on genital differences.

Another criticism of Freud's theory comes from the fact that research has shown young children age three to six (Freud's genital stage) do not identify sex by genitals but rather by hair and clothing (Katcher, 1955). This does not necessarily imply that young children do not notice genitals but rather that they do not use them cognitively as cues to gender identification (Thompson & Bentler, 1971). Thus, children do not emphasize their genitals as much as Freud believed.

## SOCIAL COGNITIVE THEORY

Theorists such as Bandura (1969; 1986) and Mischel (1970) disputed Freud's theory that to develop a sex-role identity, a child had to identify with the same-sex parent and internalize parental standards and personality characteristics. They believed a sex-role identity is the consequence of being rewarded (and punished) for certain sex-typed behaviors that are imitated. Socializing agents (parents, teachers, coaches, and peers) either encourage or discourage an individual's behavior through approval or disapproval. Smiling at a little girl for dressing in her mother's clothes while admonishing her brother for doing the same is one example. Social cognitive theory also says that children observe the behavior of those around them and imitate those whom they perceive as similar to themselves and whom they admire.

Social cognitive theory explains masculine sex-typing as resulting from the son's attachment to his father, who is the most powerful provider of rewards and punishments. Attachment to the father leads to identification with him and, consequently, imitation of his behavior. In turn, imitation leads to a generalized masculine sex-role identity. A similar process occurs for girls and their mothers.

However, children do not exclusively imitate same-sex models. In a study by Bandura, Ross, and Ross (1961) on modeling behavior, it was shown that children will imitate an aggressive adult model whom they have observed live or on film beating up a doll. The sex of the model did not seem to affect whether or not females and males would imitate the behavior as much as whether the behavior was reinforced.

## COGNITIVE DEVELOPMENTAL THEORY

Kohlberg (1966) applied Piaget's ideas about cognitive development to sex-typing. He proposed that the basis for sex-typing is a child's cognitive organization of the social world in a manner that parallels the cognitive organization of the physical world. The first step in this organization is **gender identity**, one's perception and consequent self-categorization of being a boy or a girl, which then serves as an organizer of incoming information and attitudes. Gender identity arises from the awareness that males and females are different.

Gender identity emerges in most children by age three (Huston, 1983) and is manifested by verbal labeling of "boy" and "girl" or "mommy" and "daddy." At about age four or five children realize genders are permanent. The concept that gender is permanent is termed **gender stability**. The development of a complete concept of gender as a constant, unchanging attribute, however, does not emerge until age seven or eight.

**Gender constancy**, the concept that gender remains the same despite superficial changes in appearance or behavior, parallels a child's thinking about the physical world. As children learn that the identity of objects remains the same even though the appearance may change, they come to understand that females remain females even if they cut their hair short.

As children are in the process of developing the concept of gender constancy, they tend to have rigid stereotypes for gender role behavior (Huston, 1983)—"only girls iron clothes." However, once the concept is established (in the stage of *concrete operations*) and the child understands that appearances cannot change gender, then the child begins to be more flexible in accepting or displaying "opposite-sexed" behaviors. Females may go fishing; males may help bake cookies.

According to cognitive developmental theory, after children have established concepts of gender constancy, they learn societal gender roles by observing the behavior and social roles of males and females around them and imitating them accordingly. By valuing same-sex people and activities and sharing their behavior, children come to identify with their same-sex parent.

That children value same-sex people, objects, and activities was demonstrated by Thompson (1975). He told a group of preschool children that some pictures were male things and others were female things. At a later time, the same children were asked which objects they liked best. Even the three-year-olds chose those things that were congruent with their gender.

One limitation of the cognitive developmental approach, however, is that it does not account for individual differences in sex typing, that is, in the degree to which children adopt or conform to gender-role norms in their society (Serbin & Sprafkin, 1986; Basow, 1992).

## GENDER SCHEMA THEORY

Information-processing theorists believe that a child uses gender to categorize people and objects and that the child is influenced by societal stereotypes. After children categorize their genders, they learn by observation what behavior is appropriate for males and females in their society. They then judge themselves by how close they can match the cultural stereotype of maleness or femaleness.

Gender schema theory (Bem, 1981a; Martin & Halverson, 1981) explains the process by which children code new information in terms of gender roles. The basis for coding information is the *schema*, a cognitive structure or conceptual framework that individuals build up as a result of past experiences and that helps individuals assimilate new information.

As children develop, they observe male and female behavior. They form a stereotype of what a male is and what he does as well as what a female is and what she does. These stereotypes serve as schemas to organize and evaluate other social information. For example, a little girl may prefer helping her mother bake a cake rather than helping her father change the oil on the car because she has "tuned-in" to what is appropriate for her because she is a girl. She then becomes more knowledgeable about baking than about cars. Thus, her schema of female influences what information gets processed. Furthermore, her self-concept may eventually become assimilated into her gender schema such that self-evaluation becomes orga-

Children form stereotypes about the roles of males and females.

nized around the degree to which she perceives herself as congruent with her gender schema. In this case, she is likely to feel good about herself because she selected an activity related to her gender schema for female. There are, however, individual differences in the prominence or functional importance of gender-related schemas. For highly sex-typed people, gender is a dominant schema applied to many situations in everyday life; for people who have less stereotypical schemas for gender, these schemas are less dominant in the individual's overall set of social constructs—for example, a telephone repair person who is female. For these individuals, self-evaluation is not based on a stereotypical gender schema.

Some studies support the view that children process information on the basis of gender. For example, males exhibit a better memory recognition for masculine-type toys and objects, whereas females remember feminine-type toys and objects better (Cann & Newbern, 1984). For another example, children seem to remember sex-stereotyped behavior better than cross sex-typed behavior. One group of five- and six-year-old boys and girls were shown sex-stereotyped pictures of boys playing with trains or sawing wood and girls cooking or cleaning. Another group was shown the opposite sex engaged in these activities. A week later when the children were asked whether a male or female had performed the pictured activity, the group exposed to the cross sex-stereotyped pictures replied incorrectly more often (Martin & Halverson, 1983).

Apparently, as soon as children can correctly label men and women (between ages two and three), they adopt certain sex-typed behaviors such as aggressiveness and play with same-sexed peers (Fagot, Leinbach & Hagan, 1986) .

# CONTEXTUAL INFLUENCES ON GENDER-ROLE DEVELOPMENT

The contextual influences on gender-role development are family, school, peers, and media.

## FAMILY

Evidence shows that parents describe newborn daughters as smaller, softer, and more fragile than sons, and sons as stronger, more coordinated, and alert than daughters (Rubin, Provenzano & Luria, 1974). They play with them differently, too. Fathers in particular engage in more rough-and-tumble play with sons and more cuddly play with their daughters (Lamb, 1977; Maccoby & Jacklin, 1974). Parents buy different toys for their sons and daughters (Rheingold & Cook, 1975; O'Brien & Huston, 1985). Males are given army toys and sports equipment. Females are given dolls and doll houses.

As children grow older, parents encourage males in active, gross motor, and manipulative play; they encourage females in dependent behavior and feminine sex-typed play, with fathers more stereotypical than mothers (Huston, 1983). Males also are allowed to take risks (play in an empty

t) and are left unsupervised more often and earlier than females (Huston, 983; Basow, 1992). Finally, in achievement contexts, parents expect and emand more of males while they provide help more readily for females Huston, 1983; Basow, 1992).

Fathers are the more influential agent of sex-role socialization than mothers (Langlois & Downs, 1980). Fathers reward sex-typed play (trucks or males, dolls for females) and punish cross-sexed play (soldiers for emales, pots and pans for males).

Physical play (such as tickling, chasing, and playing ball) is an important vehicle for differential socialization of females and males into appropriate sex roles, and fathers tend to engage in more physical play than mothers (MacDonald & Parke, 1986). Also, males receive a more intensive and prolonged exposure to physical play than females.

Children from father-present and father-absent homes were matched in age, IQ, social class, sibling constellation, and so on. Boys from father-absent homes generally obtained less-masculine scores than boys from father-present homes on measures of sex-role orientation and preference for sex-typed activities (Hetherington, 1966; Drake & McDougall, 1977). However, ability to interact with other significant males (grandparent, uncle, teacher) would probably ameliorate these effects. Males in father-absent homes exhibit more behavior problems, especially aggressiveness (Hetherington, Stanley-Hagan & Anderson, 1989).

There are few immediate effects of father absence on sex-typed behaviors in females (Hetherington, 1972). However, adolescent females from father-absent homes have problems in social interactions with males. Females aged 13 to 17 of divorced women were flirtatious and sexually precocious, whereas females of widows were withdrawn and avoided interacting with males. In addition, the daughters of divorcees married earlier than the other groups and continued precocious heterosexual interaction patterns (Hetherington & Parke, 1986).

Because common practice today is to give fathers custody in divorce cases when the situation warrants, we are seeing more children growing up in mother-absent families. A study by Santrock and Warshak (1979) showed that females' sex-typing and social maturity are affected by maternal absence more than males. Father-custody girls were rated as less feminine, less independent, and more demanding than mother-custody girls. On the other hand, father-custody boys were rated as more socially mature and competent than mother-custody boys (Hetherington, Stanley-Hagan & Anderson, 1989).

Thus, it appears that the absence of the same-sex parent has some pervasive effects on a child's personality development in addition to sex-typing.

Maternal employment often changes parental roles in the family. While employed mothers still perform most child care and housekeeping chores, husbands of employed mothers participate more than husbands of nonemployed mothers (Scanzoni & Fox, 1980; Hoffman, 1989). Thus, children whose mothers are employed have less stereotypical role models than those whose fathers are "breadwinners" and mothers are "bread bakers" (Gardner & LaBrecque, 1986).

## F.Y.I.

One consistent finding in the research done over the last 20–25 years is that children's concepts about sex-typing are less stereotyped when their mothers are employed than children with nonemployed mothers (Huston, 1983; Hoffman, 1989).

# HOW DO PARENTS INFLUENCE CHILDREN'S PLAY WITH GENDER-RELATED TOYS?

Caldera, Y.M., Huston, A.C., & O'Brien, M. (1989). Social interactions and play patterns of parents and toddlers with feminine, masculine, and neutral toys. *Child Development, 60,* 70–76.

Many children display sex-stereotyped toy preferences by age two. While parents select toys for children, the researchers wanted to find out how parents responded to child's play with stereotyped toys for the same gender and the opposite gender as well as with gender-neutral toys.

The rationale behind examining the influence of toys on gender-role development is that toys have properties that elicit particular behaviors in children; play with sex-typed toys can be the source of some observed behavioral gender differences. For example masculine toys, such as trucks and adventure figures, promote motor activity.

This study addressed three questions:

1. Do parents encourage sex-typed toy play and discourage cross-sex play?
2. What types of parent-child interaction are promoted by sex-typed toys?
3. Do fathers and mothers respond differently to sex-typed toys?

Forty parent-child pairs (20 mothers and 20 fathers) were studied. Half of the sample was observed with a daughter, the other half with a son. The children ranged in age from 18 to 23 months. Toys were selected to represent feminine, masculine, and gender-neutral categories based on earlier studies. The feminine toys were dolls and a kitchen set. The masculine toys were trucks and a set of blocks. The neutral toy sets were two puzzles and two shape sorters. Because parents did not know which toys were in the boxes until they were opened, their initial responses (very excited, mildly excited, not excited) were recorded.

The level of involvement for the child was recorded as rejecting, minimal involvement, active involvement. The level of involvement for the parent was recorded as noninvolvement, low involvement, high involvement.

Parental verbal behaviors were scored as they occurred: directives (guiding the child's play), questions (asking specifics about the targeted toys), teaching statements (instruction on appropriate play), praise, fantasy, or animated statements (pretending to speak for the doll), negative comments, corrections (not related to the target toy—for example, "Don't touch the door"), and general comments (any statement not relating to the child's play with the targeted toy).

Study results confirmed that many children display sex-stereotyped toy preferences before age two. Even when no alternative toys were available and the parents' involvement was statistically controlled, toddlers showed less involvement with toys stereotyped for the other gender than with those stereotyped for their own gender, and they rejected cross-sex toys more than same-sex or neutral toys.

Parents showed subtle tendencies to respond more positively to and be more involved with same-sex than with cross-sex toys. They did this by becoming involved in play with same-sex toys rather than with cross-sex toys when their child's interest flagged.

The major finding was that sex-stereotyped toys had definite effects on the nature of the parent–child interaction, regardless of the gender of parent or child. Masculine toys, especially trucks, were associated with relatively low levels of questions and teaching and with low proximity between parents and children. When playing with masculine toys, especially trucks, parents made a lot of animated sounds rather than statements to elicit information from the child. They also corrected children frequently; perhaps this was due to the lower proximity evoked by the masculine toys and the subsequent need to use verbal corrections for behavior.

By contrast, play with feminine toys elicited close proximity and more verbal interactions in the form of general comments and questions.

The neutral toys elicited more positive and informative verbal behavior from the parents than did either the feminine or masculine toys. Sex-stereotyped toys elicited fantasy play and general conversation.

These patterns of interactions were similar for boys and girls as well as fathers and mothers.

Thus, the researchers concluded that gender differences in behavior arise partly from differences in the toys with which females and males typically play. The toy effects observed were probably both due to physical qualities of the play materials and to the parents' beliefs or scripts for play with each toy.

## SCHOOL

The influence of school in sex-typing is implemented by the teacher, classroom structure, and curriculum.

Actual observations of teacher behavior in both preschool and elementary school classes indicate that males receive more disapproval, scolding, and other forms of negative attention from teachers than females (Serbin et al., 1973; Cherry, 1975; Sadker & Sadker, 1985; Basow, 1992).

Findings for positive responses to children, on the other hand, are mixed. Some studies show teachers give more positive attention to females (Fagot' 1973, 1981; Gold, Crombie & Noble, 1987), whereas other studies show that males get more positive attention (Serbin et al., 1973). This discrepancy may be explained in terms of the activities that elicit attention. In observations of preschool classrooms, teachers gave positive attention to females when they stayed close; males got positive responses when they solicited attention regardless of where they were located (close or far) (Serbin et al., 1973).

In a study of junior high school students by Buxton (1973), it was revealed that teachers have sex-stereotyped attitudes for good male and female students. "Good" male students were active, assertive, curious, energetic, enterprising, independent, and inventive; "good" female students were conscientious, appreciative, considerate, cooperative, mannerly, sensitive, dependable, poised, obliging, efficient, and thorough. Teachers are often unaware of how their own expectations contribute to sex-role stereotypes and the development of different academic abilities and behaviors of male and female students (Serbin, 1983; Sadker & Sadker, 1985). This is often referred to as the "hidden curriculum."

Evidence also suggests that children's sex-typed behavior is influenced by adult reinforcement. By reinforcing independent task persistence and ignoring help-seeking and proximity, teachers affected how children sought attention. Also, how teachers introduced new toys and activities (labeling them boy or girl activities, or giving them to a boy or girl to model), influenced the participation of children in sex-typed activities (Huston, 1983). According to Jacklin (1989), most teachers are unaware of the influential gender expectations they communicate to children.

Researchers have observed that teachers treat boys and girls differently. This differential treatment may influence development according to which behaviors get attention.

Males are often encouraged to go to the "block corner."

Females are often encouraged to go to the "housekeeping" or art areas.

Schools encourage sex-typing by separating curriculum into male and female activities (Marland, 1983; Basow, 1992). In elementary school, males are encouraged to do tasks that require physical activity or mechanical skill such as setting up and running the movie projector while females are encouraged to do more sedentary tasks such as grading papers. In high school, the separation gets more formalized—females into home economics and males into shop. More significantly, enrollments in advanced high school and college math courses reveal most are males (Sadker & Sadker, 1986). Moreover, this differential enrollment may explain the segregation found in engineering and other science-related fields, such as medicine.

Texts, which are a major part of the school curriculum, influence gender roles through various forms of bias—women being invisible, female roles being stereotyped, the imbalance of male and female representation, the unrealistic portrayal of equality, and language (sexist words such as "mankind" ignore that 51 percent of the population is female) (Sadker & Sadker, 1991). Professional associations such as the American Psychological Association have provided nonsexist guidelines for publishing companies and school districts.

## PEERS

Children impact each other's behavior through reinforcement and modeling. As early as age three, children who play in sex-typed activities tend to be rewarded for doing so by peers, while those who play in cross-sex activities tend to be criticized by their peers or left to play alone (Fagot, 1977; Hartup, 1983; Martin, 1989).

Studies of older children who play in cross-sex activities reached the same conclusion. Males with feminine play and behavior patterns are rejected by peers and spend a considerable amount of time playing alone. Females with masculine play interests experience some disapproval from peers but not complete rejection (Huston, 1983; Basow, 1992).

As children progress through elementary school, gender segregation in play groups becomes more noticeable. The play of girls' and boys' peer groups was shown by Lever (1978) to be significantly different. Fifth-grade children, mostly white and middle-class, were observed in three schools. Lever discovered that boys' play was more complex than girls' play on all of the following dimensions:

- Size of group—Is it large or small?
- Role differentiation—Do the players have the same role, as in checkers, or different roles, as in baseball?
- Player interdependence—Does a player's move affect another's, as in chess, or does it have no influence, as in hopscotch?
- Explicitness of goals—Is playing merely a cooperative venture with no winners or end point, as in "playing house," or is the purpose of playing a goal, such as scoring the most points or until a certain end point is reached?
- Number and specificity of rules—Are there a few vague rules, as in tag, or many specific ones, as in baseball?
- Team formation—Does the play require teams?

Lever observed that males typically engaged in team sports with 10 to 25 players; females typically played tag, jump rope, or hopscotch, usually involving two to six participants. Males' play often involved multiple roles, whereas females' play rarely involved role differentiation. Females commonly engaged in activities in which they all played the same role, as skating, or two roles, as in jump rope (the jumper and the turner). Males' play involved more interdependence, which required decision making. Females' play tended to require less interdependence, but when it did, play was of a cooperative nature. Males' games were found to have more elaborate rules—often interpretations and discussions ensued. Finally, males were more often involved in team play.

According to Lever, males' play reinforces the ability to deal with diverse actions simultaneously, coordinate actions to foster group cohesiveness and work for collective goals, engage in competition, cope with impersonal rules, and engage in strategic thinking. Females' play, on the other hand, reinforces cooperation, spontaneity, imagination, flexibility, and empathy.

## MEDIA

The media provide models of female and male behavior. Males not only appear with greater frequency on television than females, they also are portrayed in a greater variety of occupations with higher-status jobs than females. For example, the attorneys, physicians, and store owners are usually men, while the secretaries, nurses, and teachers are usually women (Pearl, 1982; Signorielli, 1989). Even in television commercials, males are often portrayed as the authorities and are used in the voice-over comments about the merits of products; women are usually shown as believing demonstrations of a product's superiority. However, women are shown as experts in ads for food products, laundry soap, and beauty aids (Hetherington & Parke, 1986; Basow, 1992).

That television has the potential for influencing sex-role stereotyping (Comstock & Paik, 1991) was illustrated by an investigation by Miller and Reeves (1976) in which males and females were interviewed to determine how often they watched certain television programs and how they felt about males and females having certain occupational roles. Those who frequently watched programs in which women were portrayed in nontraditional female roles more often reported that they felt it appropriate for women to have such occupations than did those who did not watch such programs often.

That television can actually shape perceptions about sex roles was illustrated in a study by Johnston and Ettema (1982) who evaluated over 7,000 children (aged 9 to 12) in seven different sites across the nation. The children watched a series of thirteen 30-minute episodes of "Freestyle," a federally funded program designed to broaden perspectives about stereotyped sex roles. Children who viewed the shows in their classroom with a discussion showed the most change in stereotypical attitudes, but even children who viewed the shows at home were affected.

It must be noted that children's prior attitudes about gender roles influence the impact of what they see on television. Children with highly sex-stereotypical attitudes attend to traditional role portrayals, whereas children with low sex-stereotyped attitudes attend equally well to both traditional and nontraditional role portrayals (List, Collins & Westby, 1983).

Models of sex-role stereotypes appear in the print media as well a television. Studies of magazine advertising show that females are portraye more as decorative, while males are portrayed more as instrumental (Basov 1992).

# INTERACTION BETWEEN BIOLOGICAL AND CONTEXTUAL INFLUENCES

The topics we will examine that involve the interaction between bio logical and contextual influences on gender-role development are physica differences and social responses to them, the interplay of chromosome hormones, and context (prenatal and postnatal), and the influence of cu ture on gender roles.

## PHYSICAL DIFFERENCES AND SOCIAL RESPONSES

The response of people within a culture to physical sex difference between males and females illustrates how biological and contextual force interact to affect gender-role development.

Beginning at birth, males and females are distinguished from on another in a culture by physical differences. The genitals signal what t name and how to dress an infant. These physical differences even promot differential treatment from parents in the manner infants are held, talked t and played with.

As the child gets older, physical differences provide a rationale fc differences in social roles between the two genders. For example, averag differences in size and strength are used as reasons for restricting wome from certain occupations (Archer & Lloyd, 1982; Basow, 1992). Men pre dominate in police and fire services and in certain sports.

After puberty, sex differences in reproductive function are used a the basis for rationalizing differences in social roles—women bear and such le children, therefore, they stay home and care for them (Archer & Lloyc 1982; Basow, 1992).

## CHROMOSOMES, HORMONES, AND CONTEXT (PRE- AND POSTNATAL)

Money and Ehrhardt (1972) describe the biological and contextua sequential and interactional components of male-female gender-identit differentiation. The first step in the process is that the sperm bearing an X c Y chromosome unites with the egg bearing an X chromosome. The result either a male (XY) or a female (XX). Next, the XY or XX chromosomal con bination programs the undifferentiated fetal gonad to determine its destin as a testes or ovary. Thereafter, the sex chromosomes have no known dire influence on subsequent sexual and psychosexual differentiation.

When the undifferentiated gonad differentiates into either a testes c ovary, it begins to secrete hormones. Testicular hormones (androgens) a imperative for the continuing differentiation of the reproductive structure of a male; in their absence, a fetus develops as a female (even though it ha XY chromosomes). Likewise, if a fetus has XX chromosomes and is expose to androgens (from a malfunctioning organ or from ingestion by the mother, who may have taken drugs to prevent miscarriage), the embryo develops as a male.

The presence or absence of androgens accounts not only for the shape of the external genitals but also for certain patterns of organization in the brain, especially via the hypothalamus, that in puberty influence certain aspects of sexual behavior.

According to Money and Ehrhardt, as a result of being affected by prenatal hormones, the brain and central nervous system influence the individual to exhibit behavioral traits classified by others as predominantly boyish or girlish. If the traits exhibited are traditional in a child's context for her biological sex, then they will be reinforced. If, on the other hand, the traits exhibited are cross-sex traits, they will be ridiculed (called "sissy" or "tomboy"). Money and Ehrhardt believe that gender identity differentiation is predominantly influenced by those who rear the child and regularly reconfirm the child's sex. Once differentiated, gender identity is further confirmed by hormonal changes in puberty and acceptance of one's gender role. Gender role includes a public display of feminine or masculine behavior and an attraction to the opposite sex. Figure 13.5 (page 430) is a diagram that illustrates the sequential and interactional components of gender-identity differentiation.

To illustrate how child rearing complements the shaping of gender identity and gender role, Money and Ehrhardt (1972) tell of a father's interaction with his two children. The older one was a normal boy, the younger was a genetic male *hermaphrodite* with ambiguous genetalia. (His phallus was the size of a clitoris.) A **hermaphrodite** has both male and female organs.

At age 15 months, the younger child was reassigned the gender of female. The father reported that both children enjoyed a rowdy kind of solo dancing (rock-and-roll) to music; the younger child copied the older one. However, after reassignment the father felt the impulse to dance close, as a couple, with the younger child. Soon, the girl began to prefer the daughter role with her father to copying the rowdiness of her brother. Thus, the girl's gender stimulated certain behavior in the parent that, in turn, stimulated certain behavior in the child.

The child's gender reassignment from male to female was explained to her three and a half-year-old brother by saying the physicians had made a mistake; he had a baby sister rather than a baby brother. The older child accepted the explanation and, as his father reported, began to treat her differently. Now he was more gentle and protecting.

As the child approached the age of three, she began to imitate her mother's activities. She also liked to play games with the boys.

Another one of the cases described by Money and Ehrhardt (1972) is of a boy who was referred because, at age 11, his breasts had developed. The boy was in fact a genetic female with *androgenital syndrome*. **Androgenital syndrome** is a type of pseudohermaphroditism in which a genetic female has masculine sex organs due to prenatal exposure to androgens. The decision was against reassignment of gender because the child's gender identity was male. He shared interests with his father such as fishing and hunting. He also had a girlfriend with whom he experienced erotic arousal. It was decided to perform a mastectomy and hysterectomy and to prescribe androgen replacement therapy. Thus, biological genital identity was matched to contextual gender identity.

FIGURE 13.5
**The sequential and interactional components of gender-identity differentiation.**

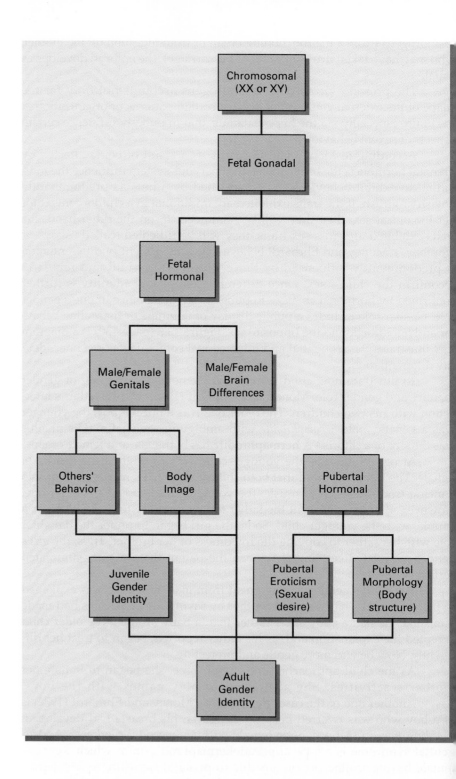

Money's studies of females with androgenital syndrome found that if the reassignment of the child to her correct feminine gender role occurred after the first few years of life, inadequate sex-typing and poor psychological adjustment occurred. If early reassignment occurred, normal psychosexual development in most of the subjects followed. This finding led the authors to conclude that a critical period for the establishment of gender role occurs between 18 months and three years.

Not all researchers agree with Money and Ehrhardt about the critical period for gender-role development. Imperato-McGinley and colleagues (1979) studied 37 children from the City of Santo Domingo in the Dominican Republic who had a rare genetic disorder that can result in a change in gender at puberty. The dysfunction disrupts testosterone metabolism so male genitals are not properly formed during prenatal development. The children are born with penises that look like clitorises. At puberty, however, hormones cause the genitalia to grow.

Of the 37 children studied, 17 had been thought to be girls and were raised as such; the other 20 were thought to be boys. At puberty, the activation of male hormones in these children caused masculinization of the genitals and the development of male secondary sexual characteristics—the "girls" turned into boys. Apparently, despite normal female socialization in their childhood, these young males adjust to their male gender identities in terms of activities and sexual interests. Thus, in this society, the biological exhibition of sex influences the gender role individuals are expected to assume.

## CULTURE AND GENDER ROLES

In some societies masculine and feminine behavior are not related to the genitalia. Margaret Mead's study of sex and temperament in three primitive societies (1935) illustrates that there is no universal male or female gender role. According to Mead, gender roles are malleable; they are determined by culture, not by biology or cognition. The three New Guinea tribes she studied were the Arapesh, the Mundugumor, and the Tchambuli. There was little sex-role differentiation in the Mundugumor and the Arapesh. However, the Arapesh men and women exhibited behaviors similar to what our culture stereotypes as feminine, and the Mundugumor men and women exhibited behaviors that we stereotype as masculine. The Arapesh were passive, cooperative, and unassertive; the Mundugumor were hostile, aggressive, cruel, and restrictive. Arapesh mothers and fathers both were actively involved in raising infants.

In the Tchambuli, Mead found a reversal in roles for men and women of what our culture stereotypes as masculine and feminine. The men were socially sensitive and concerned with the feelings of others, dependent, and interested in arts and crafts. The women were independent and aggressive and played the controlling role in decision making.

The social and economic organization of a culture determine the daily routines of adults and children, the individuals who frequent the same settings, and the activities performed (Whiting & Edwards, 1988). For example, in the industrial societies such as the United States, adults go to work and children age six and older go to school. In agricultural societies such as some African communities, adults work around the home or in the fields and children over age six help with family tasks; for example, females wash dishes and shell maize while males drive oxen and milk cattle.

When children are performing routine tasks in various settings, they observe and model adults, and receive direct instruction. Thus, cultural scripts in many communities set females and males on a different course by giving different responsibilities in different settings. When males and females are given time to play, they segregate themselves by sex, according to Whiting and Edwards (1988), to further learn and practice culturally approved sex-role behavior. Thus, differences in gender roles occur because children have been given different responsibilities as they mature, and they develop different skills and preferences for companions, accordingly.

In some cultures, the female may be taught to serve the male.

In other cultures, males serve the females.

Table 13.1 is a summary of male and female characteristics. Box 13. explains how to be free from sex-role stereotypes.

## MALE AND FEMALE CHARACTERISTICS

### TABLE 13.1

| Characteristic | Male | Female | Explanation |
|---|---|---|---|
| **Biological:** Chromosomal composition | XY | XX | At conception, an unborn child's sex is determined by whether the father's sperm cell contains an X or a Y chromosome; if it is a Y chromosome, child will be a boy. |
| Gonads | Testicles | Ovaries | |
| Hormonal composition | Androgen, etc. | Estrogen, progesterone, etc. | These hormones operate before birth to differentiate male and female fetuses and again at adolescence to produce secondary sex characteristics —e.g., deep voices, beards, and body hair in men; breasts and menstruation in women. |
| Internal accessory organs | Seminal vesicles and prostate gland | Vagina, uterus, and fallopian tubes | |
| External genitalia | Penis and testicles | Vulva | |
| **Contextual:** Gender identity | I am a male | I am a female | The basic sense of one's social identity. |
| Masculinity-femininity | I am a masculine or effeminate male | I am a feminine or mannish woman | This refers to the person's conformity to the sex-role standards of the particular culture; it involves certain interests, attitudes, fantasies, ways of moving and speaking. |
| Sex-objective preference | | | Whether one is aroused by members of one's own sex or the opposite one. |

(Skolnick, 198?

Box 13.1 **BECOMING FREE FROM
SEX-ROLE STEREOTYPES**

A **sex-role stereotype** is a standardized mental picture of behavior expected of males and females commonly held by members of a group representing an oversimplified attitude or perception. Beliefs about the behavior of males and females may partly determine that behavior and vice versa (Hargreaves, 1987; Basow, 1992).

Characteristics assigned to males and females are often a clue to stereotypical attitudes. Bem (1974) asked university students to rate a list of traits as to their desirability for males and females.

## TRAITS FROM THE BEM SEX-ROLE INVENTORY
### Classified by Dimension

| *Feminine* | *Masculine* |
|---|---|
| Affectionate | Acts as a leader |
| Cheerful | Aggressive |
| Childlike | Ambitious |
| Compassionate | Analytical |
| Does not use harsh language | Assertive |
| Eager to soothe hurt feelings | Athletic |
| Feminine | Competitive |
| Flatterable | Defends own beliefs |
| Gentle | Dominant |
| Gullible | Forceful |
| Loves children | Leadership abilities |
| Loyal | Independent |
| Sensitive to others' needs | Individualistic |
| Shy | Makes decisions easily |
| Soft-spoken | Masculine |
| Sympathetic | Self-reliant |
| Tender | Self-sufficient |
| Understanding | Strong personality |
| Warm | Willing to take a stand |
| Yielding | Willing to take risks |

**(Bem, 1974)**

It is possible to help children become free from society's sex-role stereotypes. Suggestions for parents and teachers follow:

**Parents:**
- Model flexibility—women can use a screwdriver, and men can do domestic chores; women can be assertive, and men can be sensitive; both participate in decision making.
- View domestic chores as a necessary part of family life; do not delegate chores based on tradition, rather, rotate them so all family members can take turns at what needs to be done.
- Instill self-confidence and independence in both males and females. One way is to not do for them what they can do for themselves. Another way is to praise efforts and encourage success by pointing out what a child does correctly and what needs improvement.
- Allow both males and females to express emotions and discuss feelings.

*(continued on following page)*

*(continued from previous page)*

- Buy creative toys that stimulate play and can be enjoyed by both females and males (for example, puzzles and tricycles).
- Encourage both genders to play games of logic, such as chess, and to learn music or art.

**Teachers:**

- Have a family corner rather than a doll corner; include tools, kitchen equipment, and dishes.
- Have a "pretend corner" with blocks, dress-up clothes, a cash register, transportation equipment, stethoscope, and so on to enable children to create any setting and play any role.
- Choose books that have dominant female roles and those that have dominant male roles.
- Encourage children to help each other and make cross-sex friends.
- Deal with male and female misbehavior in a consistent manner.
- Encourage physical activity and achievement in both genders.
- Encourage both genders to be independent.

Until recently, athletic events such as track and field have been dominated by males. The aggressive and competitive nature of athletics is no longer considered incompatible with traditional feminine attributes.

# ANDROGYNY

**Androgyny** refers to the extent to which an individual displays both masculine and feminine psychological characteristics. According to Bem (1974; 1981b) and others (Spence, Helmreich & Stapp, 1975; Spence & Sawin, 1985) certain attributes are considered more masculine or feminine than others. Examples of masculine attributes are aggressiveness, dominance, and ambitiousness; examples of feminine attributes are nurturance, compassion, and submissiveness.

Until recently, in our culture masculinity and femininity were regarded as opposite extremes with females on one side and males on the other; anyone falling between the two was regarded as having a deviant gender-role identity. Now, however, many psychologists and developmentalists believe that children have both masculine and feminine characteristics and that having both allows for more adaptability (Block, 1973; Bem, 1974; Spence, Helmreich & Stapp, 1974; Spence & Helmreich, 1978). In other words, one can be nurturant if a situation calls for care or competitive if situation warrants winning. To measure the extent to which individuals are masculine or feminine, Bem (1974; 1981b) created the Bem Sex Role Inventory (BSRI) and Spence and colleagues (Spence, Helmreich & Stapp, 1974) developed the Personality Attributes Questionnaire (PAQ). A special PAQ inventory was adapted for children (Spence & Helmreich, 1978) to assess androgyny. Items on the inventories include independence, dependence, dominance, passivity, aggressiveness, compassion, affection, self-reliance, achievment, and so on.

The concept of androgyny as a healthier psychological state than masculinity or femininity was the zeitgeist of the 1970s. The 1960s was a time of great social upheaval and demand for civil rights, which included the Feminist Movement. As part of the quest for equality, feminists sought to change attitudes about the superiority of masculine traits. Thus, research that showed feminine traits had value, would enhance men's personalities and also that men's traits would enhance women's was popular.

However, as people were adopting the concept of androgyny and applying it to themselves, research in the 1980s was showing that androgenous personalities were not necessarily healthier than sex-typed personalities, especially those that were masculine (Basow, 1992). For example, one study (Lubinski, Tellegen & Butcher, 1983) found that individuals who score as masculine or androgenous have the highest self-esteem, lowest stress, and greatest social effectiveness. Another example showed that masculine scores for middle adolescents, especially for females, were related to high levels of self-esteem, which included general self-worth and social and physical competence (Cate & Sugawara, 1986).

Bem, who popularized androgyny in the 1970s, modified her position in the 1980s to advocate a gender-free world rather than an androgynous one (Bem, 1981a; 1983; 1989); that is, a world in which sex-typing is downplayed rather than a world in which both sexes become psychologically the same. Bem says that we are socialized for more than behaving like males or females in our society; we are also socialized to perceive the world in terms of a male-female dichotomy. Our socialized perceptions then become cognitive structures or gender schemas on which future information is categorized or coded. For example, we categorize clothes, jobs, and behavior patterns as male or female. Until recently, hurricanes were given only female names; we now see male names. Such male-or female-designated categories reinforce traditional sex stereotyping and, hence, gender schema even more.

Bem believes that even though our society is based on gender schema, children can be raised free of a gender schema that programs perceptions and behavior. Bem (1989) suggests parents teach their children that differences in genital anatomy are for reproductive purposes, not behavioral patterns. She also suggests that parents mediate what children read and see on television so children are exposed to both gender-typical and gender-atypical activities. Parents should discuss their expectations about men and women, explaining that not everyone shares a belief in nonsexism but rather that some people are more comfortable with traditional gender roles.

# DEVELOPMENT OF SEXUALITY

Gender-role development involves sexuality. **Sexuality** is the acceptance of a sexual role as male or female and the consequential attraction to the opposite sex, called *heterosexuality*. The development of sexuality into heterosexuality, homosexuality, and teenage pregnancy will be discussed.

## HETEROSEXUALITY

**Heterosexuality** refers to sexual attraction to the opposite sex. According to Rice (1990), achieving heterosexuality involves three stages of development:

*autosociality*
*homosociality*
*heterosociality*

In infancy and preschool years, children are **autosocial**: their main pleasure and satisfaction come from themselves. Two-year-olds who enjoy playing in the company of others but who do not interact with them are typical of this state. An untypical example of this stage would be an adolescent who does not have friends and is a loner.

As children approach school age (about three to seven), they seek the companionship of other children regardless of sex. Then, about age 8 to 12, they become more exclusive in their desire for same-sex friendships. This, according to Rice, is termed the **homosocial stage** because a child's pleasure and satisfaction come from being with others of the same sex for companionship (not sexual purposes). Some adolescents, however, remain in this stage throughout adulthood and get sexual satisfaction from same-sex relationships.

By adolescence (age 13 to 18), although boys and girls retain some same-sex friendships, they begin becoming interested in the opposite sex. The **heterosocial stage** involves an individual's pleasure and friendship from both sexes. At first, females and males are awkward in this new interest. Males are likely to tease females, and females are likely to watch the males play and to giggle at them. By high school many males and females do activities in groups (movies and parties); some pair off to form exclusive dating relationships.

The onset of puberty and its hormonal changes are often accompanied by an interest in sexual activity. At first it is self-centered. Adolescents are concerned about their changing bodies and how they appear to others. Slowly, they become aware of their developing sexual feelings and drives. Most adolescents begin some experimentation by touching themselves and may experience their first orgasm by self-manipulation. Gradually, adolescents become more interested in sexual experimentation with others. Part of this behavior is motivated by the desire for sexual stimulation and release and also by a need for love and acceptance from another person (Peplau et al., 1977). As adolescents gain in heterosexual experience, they seek an intimate relationship—one that is close and enduring that involves love and commitment (Orlofsky, 1976). Society expects this will lead to marriage and a family, thereby fulfilling one's sexual role.

## HOMOSEXUALITY

**Homosexuality** refers to sexual attraction to those of the same biological sex. Evidence shows that some homosexuals differ from heterosexuals in hormonal levels. Some lesbians have been found to have a larger amount of the male hormone testosterone. Some males who are exclusively homosexual have been found to have lower testosterone concentrations than heterosexual males (McCrary & McCrary, 1982).

There is also evidence from postmortem examinations of homosexual men who died from AIDS that the brain region governing sexual behavior, the anterior hypothalamus, had the anatomical form usually found in women rather than the form typical of heterosexual men (Barinaga, 1991).

A 15-year longitudinal study correlated males' early "feminine" behavior with later development of homosexuality (Green, 1987). "Feminine" behavior included cross-dressing, dislike of rough-and-tumble play, and attention to mothers' fashions. This association between boyhood "femininity" and manhood homosexuality can be explained both biologically and contextually.

The biological explanation involves neural organization, possibly due to genetics, that affects prenatal hormonal output. Hormonal levels modify the central nervous system to become sexually aroused in the female pattern (attraction to males).

The contextual explanation can be within a psychoanalytic framework or social cognitive one. Psychoanalysts would say that incomplete sychological separation of the male child from the mother results in excesve feminine identification by the male. This interferes with progression rough the Oedipal phase with its normal psychosexual outcome, identifiation with the father, and the later pursuit of other females as sexual parters. Social cognitive theorists would say that a male's interests, attitudes, nd behaviors are shaped by all females in his environment. Thus, females nd not males become role models. As the male matures along this femalepe developmental track, his erotic patterns are like those of his female ssociates; he seeks males.

Green (1987) explains homosexuality development as a complex iteraction between biology and context. He found that mothers of "femiine" boys tended to have had distant relationships with their own mothers nd, during pregnancy, had wished for a girl. These mothers also reported leir boys to have been "beautiful" infants. They did not discourage their ons' early cross-gender behaviors, nor did they react negatively during readolescence and early adolescence to their sons' feminine behavior.

Some fathers of "feminine" boys were less masculine in their boyood and did not discourage their sons' early cross-gender behavior. athers who wanted daughters during the pregnancy spent less time with leir sons, and by midchildhood these boys exhibited "feminine" behavior. hen during preadolescence and early adolescence, these fathers did not ncourage their sons' masculine behavior.

Thus, a child's biological appearance can remind the parent of the ish to have a girl, and the parent then reacts to the child as if he were a irl. This involves reinforcing feminine behavior and not providing a male lodel of behavior (father distances himself). These feminine behaviors set le child apart from peers, who tease him for being a sissy. The increased olation from males and the distance from his father make sexual experinces with males in adolescence and adulthood appealing because these exual experiences provide the affection and companionship from males lat the boy has lacked throughout his development.

Thus, the question remains: Do atypical hormonal and brain develpment cause homosexuality or do atypical early experiences direct horlonal and brain development?

## EENAGE PREGNANCY

Premarital adolescent sexual activity in the United States has been icreasing. Sexually active individuals who do not use contraception risk nplanned conception and disease.

When young people become involved in an unplanned pregnancy, le situation can mean the emotional dilemma of considering abortion or doption, dropping out of school, leaving home, or depending on welfare. also can mean health risks for a woman due to her immature reproducve system or health risks to the infant such as low birth weight, prematuri/, and congenital malformations (Children's Defense Fund, 1989).

By the time females reach age 19, three-quarters of unmarried romen and 86 percent of unmarried men are sexually active (National ommission on Children, 1991). While contraceptive use, especially conoms, has increased in recent years, still only one-third of sexually active 5- to 19-year-olds reported they and their partners used condoms (NCC, 991).

Sexuality is a selling medium on television. Sexuality pervades conmporary music and movies. Despite the bombardment of sexual imagery,

Each year, over one million girls under age 20 become pregnant and almost half give birth (National Commission on Children (NCC), 1991).

# F.Y.I.

Each year more than 1 million girls under age 20 become pregnant and almost half give birth (National Commission on Children, 1991).

teenagers are ignorant about the scientific facts of reproduction. Some prevailing myths are that pregnancy cannot occur the first time during intercourse or if standing (Wallis et al., 1985).

Teenagers often think contraception is "uncool" (Planned Parenthood, 1986). Being prepared is considered unromantic—"doing it" does not get you a bad reputation but "wanting to" (indicated by a contraceptive device) does.

Some adolescents believe in the *personal fable*—that they are special and that bad things cannot happen to them. Thus, adolescents feel they can have intercourse without becoming pregnant.

Some adolescents select pregnancy, rather than drugs or alcohol, to solve some problem in their family life. Perhaps it is an unconscious attempt to become independent or a belief that an infant will give the love they did not get from the family (Westoff, 1976).

Evidence shows that teenagers are more likely to become pregnant and deliver infants when their lives seem pointless and the doors to the future seem closed (Schorr & Schorr, 1989). They are likely to seek self-esteem by having an infant.

Box 13.2 has some suggestions to help adolescents accept their sexuality.

## Box 13.2  HELPING ADOLESCENTS DEAL WITH THEIR SEXUALITY

Sexual feelings are normal. Adolescents need to accept their feelings but should be aware of the consequences of a lack of control.

What can be done?

- If your children are not asking, answer anyway. Robin asked Jennifer when she was 15 if she knew when a girl could become pregnant. Jennifer took a few guesses, and then Robin took the opportunity to tell her that one can usually conceive in the middle of the menstrual cycle, but because many teens are irregular, it is hard to know the exact time of fertility. Robin also told her how conception could be prevented and shared her feelings about premarital sexual activity.

- Teach decision-making skills. Adolescents have begun to experience independence from parents but as of yet have little experience in planning and making decisions. Teens need to learn the difference between short-term decisions, such as deciding what clothes to wear, and long-term decisions that have irreversible consequences.

Teens should be allowed to make decisions such as how to use their money and to experience the consequences.

- Help your child feel good about becoming a man or woman. Girls who are complimented on achievements and appearance and boys who are praised for sensitivity to others and athletic prowess are likely to grow into well-adjusted adults who put sex in perspective. On the other hand, males who are encouraged to prove their "masculinity" through sexual experience and females who are taught to use their "femininity" to attract males are likely to view sex as a means toward self-esteem.

If a child chooses homosexuality, it is best for parents to realize that it was probably a decision considered for a long time.

# CRITICAL THINKING & YOU

omen dominate of the nursing and secretarial fields, while men dominate engineering and carpentry. Why is this so? What attracts men and women to different fields?

1. Are they biologically programmed to excel in certain activities?
2. Have they been socialized into various roles so society will run smoothly?
3. Does some biological predisposition, such as physical strength or verbal skills, attract males and females to certain activities that then are reinforced by society consequently producing men and women with different competencies?

**ANALYSIS**: Review this chapter and cite two research studies supporting each position (biological, contextual, interactional).

**SYNTHESIS**: Four theories for gender-role development were discussed. Choose one for each position (biological, contextual, interactional) and explain.

**EVALUATION**: On the basis of what you have learned, why do you think men and women pursue different careers?

# SUMMARY

- Gender roles involve the qualities an individual understands to characterize males and females in culture. In our culture masculine traits are stereotyped to include dominance, strength, and aggressiveness whereas feminine traits are stereotyped to include submissiveness, gentleness, and nurturance.

- Males and females have like pairs of chromosomes with the exception of the sex chromosomes. These sex chromosomes direct a different pattern for differentiation of gonadal tissue in females and males because of the different prenatal hormones released. In males, the gonads are the testes; in females, the gonads are the ovaries. Male hormones lead to the development of a penis and scrotum; female hormones lead to the development of a clitoris and labia.

- Males and females differ in bone size and arrangement.

- Females mature physically earlier than males.

- Males and females are similar at birth and in early childhood in social and emotional development. Between two and three years of age, there are gender differences in preferred toys and in the type of play in which children are engaged. By school age, sex-segregated activities are more the norm and girls' and boys' games differ markedly.

- Males are superior in spatial skills, and females are superior in verbal skills.

- Biologically, hormones influence masculine and feminine behavior. This has been demonstrated in humans by accidents of nature whereby the fetus, genetically a female, was exposed to androgens from malfunctioning adrenal glands or to progestin (which produces an androgen-like effect) from a drug taken by mothers.

- Psychoanalytic theory deals with a child's identification with the parent of the same sex due to fear of retaliation for loving the parent of the opposite sex.

- Social cognitive theory deals with a child's observing and modeling of the same-sexed parent's behavior due to reinforcement.

- Cognitive developmental theory deals with a child's mental understanding that she is a girl and then choosing same-sexed models to imitate.

- Gender schema theory also concerns a child's mental understanding of self as a boy and then choosing same-sexed activities accordingly. However, the theory also says a child builds a schema of masculinity and femininity, and this schema affects how the child processes new information.

- For highly sex-typed people, gender is a dominant schema applied to many situations; whereas for less stereotypical people, gender is less prominent in helping process information.

- Some contextual influences on gender-role development are family, school, peers, and media.

- Parents, especially fathers, treat females and males differently in terms of the way they engage in play, select toys, and the activities they encourage.

- Children in families where the mother is employed tend to have less sex-stereotyped views of male and female roles than children in families where the mother is the homemaker and the father is the primary earner.

- Teachers treat females and males differently. Males receive more negative attention than females. Activities are separated into male and female activities, and children are directed into them accordingly. Teachers encourage independent behavior from males, but encourage help-seeking behavior from females.

- Children impact each other's behavior through reinforcement and modeling. Feminine play is encouraged for girls; masculine play for boys. Cross-sex play is discouraged and may result in peer rejection. By school age, children usually play with their own gender exclusively.

- The media provide models of female and male behavior both visually and in print. Males are portrayed more often as active, independent leaders and in jobs with high status. Females are portrayed more often as dependent, helping, pleasing, and in jobs with low status.

- People of different cultures respond to physical sex differences between males and females differently.

- Biological and contextual interaction occur sequentially beginning with chromosomes and prenatal hormones impacting brain development that, in turn, influences behavior and stimulates various contextual responses that leads to gender identity.

- A sex-role stereotype is a common standardized mental picture of behavior expected of males and females by members of a group and represents an oversimplified attitude or perception.

- Androgyny refers to the extent to which an individual displays both masculine and feminine psychological characteristics.

- Sexuality is the acceptance of a sexual role as male or female and the consequential attraction to the opposite sex. Achieving heterosexuality involves the autosocial stage, homosocial stage, and the heterosocial stage.
- Homosexuality refers to sexual attraction to those of the same sex. Evidence indicates that homosexuals differ from heterosexuals in hormonal levels and brain structures. Other evidence shows that the interaction of contextual and biological influences is responsible.

## RELATED READINGS

Basow, S.A. (1992). *Gender: Stereotypes and roles* (3rd ed.). Pacific Grove, CA: Brooks Cole.

Brooks-Gunn, J. & Matthews, W.S. (1979). *He & she: How children develop their sex-role identity.* Englewood Cliffs, NJ: Prentice-Hall.

Hargreaves, D.J. & Colley, A.M. (1987). *Psychology of sex roles.* Cambridge: Hemisphere.

Maccoby, E.E. & Jacklin, C.N. (1974). *The psychology of sex differences.* Stanford, CA: Stanford University Press.

Marland, M. (1983). *Sex differentiation and schooling.* London: Hernemanns.

Money, J. & Ehrhardt, A.A. (1972). *Man and woman, boy & girl.* Baltimore: Johns Hopkins University Press.

Savin-Williams, R.C. (1990). *Gay and lesbian youth: Expressions of identity.* New York: Hemisphere.

Tavris, C. & Wade, C. (1984). *The longest war: Sex differences in perspective* (2nd ed.). New York: Harcourt Brace Jovanovich.

## ACTIVITY

To better understand influences on gender-role behavior, observe a group of preschool children (aged three to five) engaged in free-play in a center for one hour. Note the following:

1. List the toys the girls played with and those played with the most.
2. List the activities of the girls and those engaged in the most.
3. List the toys the boys played with and those played with the most.
4. List the activities of the boys and those engaged in the most.
5. Describe how the teacher interacted with the girls—how did the teacher suggest activities, intervene when problems occurred, reinforce desired behavior, use body language, and so on.
6. Describe how the teacher interacted with the boys—how did the teacher suggest activities, intervene when problems occurred, reinforce desired behavior, use body language, and so on.
7. Was there an age difference between the younger and older children you observed in what and whom the girls and boys played with and how the teachers responded to them?
8. What can you conclude about the interaction of biological and contextual influences on sex-related behavior in the preschool children you observed?

# Moral Development: How We Know Right From Wrong

*Morality is not properly the doctrine of how we make ourselves happy, but how we may make ourselves worthy of happiness.*
**Immanuel Kant**

## OUTLINE

# ABOUT MORAL DEVELOPMENT

Kenny was faced with a moral dilemma. He had sexua[l] intercourse with Ellen and now she is pregnant. Is h[e] responsible for marrying her? Should he let her handl[e] the problem because she was equally responsible[?] Should he pay child support? Should he convince her to have a[n] abortion or put the baby up for adoption? How could he know fo[r] sure that he was the father? Kenny's parents had taught him t[o] always take responsibility for his actions. So, naturally he fe[lt] responsible and guilty for Ellen's condition.

Kenny's brother George had married because his girlfrien[d] was pregnant; he was doing all right. Kenny remembered, though[,] how his parents yelled at George for cutting off future options whe[n] he told them he was getting married. Michael and Kate expecte[d] Kenny to go to college. If he married Ellen and they had a child, h[e] would be responsible for supporting a family; he would have n[o] time or money for college.

Kenny's friends told him to forget about Ellen. It was he[r] problem if she did not use birth control. Yet, if Kenny did not marr[y] Ellen and she gave the baby up for adoption, how would he dea[l] with the guilt of not knowing what kind of life his child would expe[-] rience? On the other hand, if Ellen kept the baby how would he con[-] tribute to its support? If he went to college, he could not earn enoug[h] money to support himself and a child. The child would still hampe[r] his future goals.

What if he makes a decision and Ellen does not agree? Mayb[e] she does not want marriage. Maybe she wants an abortion. Mayb[e] she wants to give up the child. Maybe she wants to keep the chil[d] but to forget about Kenny.

How Kenny resolves his moral dilemma will involve his emo[-] tions, thoughts, and behavior.

**Morality** has to do with the concept of right and wrong in dealin[g] with others. Sometimes morality is a one-to-one situation (Kenny and Elle[n] for example); sometimes morality involves oneself and the immediat[e] group of family or friends (Kenny and his parents, for example). Sometime[s] morality involves oneself and the larger society (Kenny and his church, fo[r] example). Sometimes, one is guided by external rules such as parents['] approval, convention, or the law; sometimes one is guided by internal rule[s] such as self-approval or self-condemnation. In life one is usually confronte[d] with moral conflicts. Kenny's situation is a good example. The moral con[-] flicts involved Kenny's future goals versus reality and his responsibility t[o] Ellen and the child versus his responsibility to himself and his family.

Generally, the ability to distinguish and act on right and wrong depends on many factors, such as the ability to understand the rules, the ability to empathize with others, the ability to take another's perspective, one's need for approval, one's level of guilt, and the particular context.

Studying morality is complicated because what is considered right and wrong depends not only on the individual's perspective, but also on social, societal, and historical contexts. For example, most religions and cultures believe that it is wrong to kill. However, when countries go to war, killing is right.

Thus, morality is an individual construct that develops out of the necessity for people to get along with one another. It involves obeying society's rules for daily living such as not stealing, not assaulting, not maligning another's character, and so on. It also involves obeying one's conscience, or personal rules, for interacting with others, such as being kind, cooperative, and helpful.

Sometimes the rules of society and personal rules conflict. Freud would have explained this conflict in terms of the impulses of the id versus the ideals of society, as represented by the superego. Kohlberg explained it in terms of how a person reasons about herself in relation to humankind. Learning theorists explain the resolution of the conflict in terms of what is the better pay-off for the individual.

The girl who is "stealing" blocks from the boy is too young to know right from wrong.

As children develop, their morality changes. Infants and toddlers do not distinguish right from wrong and are therefore considered by most psychologists to be *amoral*. Preschoolers and young school-age children consider right and wrong to be black and white (either/or). Older school-age children (about age 9 or 10) start to see shades of gray in rightness and wrongness and that behavior is not always totally right or totally wrong, but that one's motivation can influence the degree of rightness or wrongness.

Morality involves feeling, reasoning, and behaving. To address feeling, we will examine psychoanalytic theory dealing with conscience development and research on empathy and guilt. To address reasoning, we will explore theories of moral judgment and reasoning and some research on social cognition. To address behavior, we will discuss learning theories and research on prosocial and antisocial behavior. Also, we will look at biological and contextual influences on moral development including their interaction.

Moral behavior partly depends on one's understanding of what is considered right and wrong in one's society.

# PERSPECTIVES ON MORAL DEVELOPMENT

Moral development can be viewed from three perspectives: moral feeling, moral reasoning, and moral behavior.

### MORAL FEELING

The perspective on moral development that focuses on moral feeling includes Freud's psychoanalytic theory and Hoffman's theory of empathy and guilt.

### Psychoanalytic Theory—Freud's View

Freud was the first theorist to explain how children develop a sense of morality. He believed young children are impulsive creatures who want every desire immediately gratified and who become angry and aggressive when frustrated. He also believed children have strong feelings toward parents: erotic feelings toward the parent of the opposite sex and hostility toward the parent of the same sex. Because children fear punishment and the loss of parental love for expressing such feelings, they become anxious and repress the feelings. To avoid anxiety and maintain repression and to avoid punishment and maintain parental love, children curb their impulses and adopt their parents' rules and prohibitions, which generally represent the moral norms of society. Freud referred to this process as *identification*. When children violate these norms, the previously repressed feelings for their parents now turn against themselves and are experienced as self-punishment, or guilt. Guilt then becomes a powerful motivating force in a child's moral development.

The process of internalizing parental standards (identification) and punishing oneself for noncompliance (guilt) is accomplished by age five or six. Freud referred to it as the formation of the superego, or conscience, motivated largely by a child's fear of losing parental love.

Contrary to the psychoanalytic prediction, research on parental discipline techniques (Hoffman & Saltzstein, 1967) showed that withdrawing love from a child did not promote internalization of morality. However, identification with parents appeared to be linked with some forms of moral behavior, such as helping or making moral judgments about others (Hoffman, 1988).

## Empathy and Guilt—Hoffman's View

There is considerable empirical evidence that the feelings of empathy and guilt function as moral motives (Hoffman, 1982; 1988). Empathy involves the experiencing of another person's emotional state (Hoffman, 1982). Empathy is often the motive that impels us to do right even if some sacrifice is required and to refrain from doing wrong because it may harm another. When one does not do right and another is distressed or harmed, one is likely to experience guilt.

Psychoanalytic theorists hold that empathy develops from the earliest infant-caregiver interactions because the caregiver's moods are communicated to the infant by touch, tone of voice, and facial expressions (Mussen & Eisenberg-Berg, 1977).

Learning theorists believe that empathy develops through conditioning as one comes to associate pleasure with another's corresponding feelings, or associating the pain or distress of another with one's own painful past experiences (Aronfreed, 1968). To illustrate empathetic distress, consider a one-year-old child who has cried several times a day for one year. The sound of crying has repeatedly been associated with distress. By association when the child hears crying from another, distress is evoked, which would be described as empathy. Learning theorists also believe guilt is conditioned as the child comes to associate her actions with another's distress. ("Look what you did, you made Patty cry!")

Hoffman (1988) believes simple conditioning is only part of the explanation of the development of empathy and guilt. A cognitive component also exists, which involves perspective-taking.

Hoffman believes that for the first year infants do not distinguish between themselves and the person in distress. Psychoanalytic theorists agree. Hoffman describes an 11-month-old girl who saw another child fall and cry. The infant girl, looking as if she were about to cry herself, put her humb in her mouth and buried her face in her mother's lap—her customary reaction to distress.

At about age two when children have developed the concept of object or person permanence, they begin to consider others as physically distinct from themselves and that the observed distress is not their own. However, they assume the person in distress feels exactly as they do.

After age two, children develop an awareness that other people may have different responses than they do to a situation. As they move away from egocentrism they can put themselves in another's place. They then, however, can respond in ways to relieve the other's distress rather than their own.

Later in childhood (between age six and nine), children develop the ability to appreciate others' feelings that go beyond the immediate situation; they begin to understand such things as poverty, oppression, and incompetence. As they develop cognitively, they go beyond empathizing with individuals to comprehending the plight of groups such as the economically disadvantaged and cultural minorities. They can even experience guilt if they feel their inaction or their society is responsible for the inequities in the world. Thus, Hoffman's theory views empathy (and guilt) in a developmental perspective, changing with age and advancing cognitive capacities. An initial feeling based on one's own experience culminates as a feeling based on the ability to understand the experience of others. Parallel with this view is one's ability to understand the relation between one's actions and another's distress. That empathy and consequent perspective-taking ability are related to moral development in terms of prosocial behavior is supported by research. For example, in one study (Rubin & Schneider, 1973) children's perspective-taking ability was assessed in a game whereby the child and experimenter were separated by a screen. Each was given an identical set of cards, and the goal was to match as many as possible. This was done by having the child describe the cards so the experimenter behind the screen could understand which card was being discussed. This communication involves the ability to put oneself in another's place so the appropriate information is given. In subsequent tasks, children with a high capability of taking the experimenter's point of view donated substantial amounts of their candy to poor children and gave a lot of help to a younger child assigned a difficult task. Children with low perspective-taking ability donated little of their candy and gave little help to younger children who needed it.

Even though empathy and its cognitive component of perspective-taking ability are powerful motives to behave prosocially, all moral situations cannot be explained on the basis of empathy. Cognitive developmental theorists show that certain moral dilemmas based on competing claims to right and wrong can only be explained in terms of logical thought or judgment, which sometimes is impeded by empathy. For example, when Kenny told his mother about his moral dilemma, her empathy for Ellen began to cloud her logic. "She's the one who has to go through the pregnancy and the birth; how do you think she will feel about giving the baby up for adoption? After giving birth to you, I could never give you up."

After age two, children develop an awareness that other people have different responses than they do to a given situation. As they move away from egocentrism, they can put themselves in another's place.

## MORAL REASONING

The moral reasoning perspective is assumed by Piaget, Kohlberg, and other theorists.

Children at this age (two to six) are following rules of play but are not attempting to win.

# Cognitive Developmental Theory—Piaget's View

Piaget (1932) believed a person's morals depended on his cognitive understanding of various situations. Piaget's theory of moral development describes how reasoning about moral situations changes as children develop. Because morals are based on standards of right and wrong and these standards are implemented in the rules or laws by which we live, Piaget studied children's morals by observing and questioning them about how they followed the rules of games they played. In particular, he observed children playing marbles.

Piaget discovered that children below the age of two have no rules because they cannot play the game; children merely manipulate the marbles. From about age six until age 10, children attempt to follow the rules but their complete understanding of the details differs according to the individual child. However, children this age regard the rules as emanating from an external authority. For example, they believe the rules for Monopoly came from the manufacturer (Parker Brothers) and cannot be changed. The combination of their individual conceptions of the rules and their beliefs in the sacredness of them may be why children this age often accuse one another of cheating.

From about age 10 to 12, children's understanding of the details of the rules becomes more common. Children of this age also begin to understand that rules are made so the game will be played fairly and that, if the players agree, they can change the rules to better suit them. For example, many children develop a method to shorten the game of Monopoly.

Piaget (1965) not only wanted to know about how children follow the rules but how they reasoned about rules being broken. He developed pairs of stories about various childish transgressions, such as clumsiness or stealing, and asked children from age 6 to 12 to explain which action was naughtier. Younger children usually replied that the act of doing more damage was naughtier than doing less damage. They did not consider intentions, for example, that the child who did greater damage did so by accident while trying to be helpful. They considered only outcomes. Older children, on the other hand, considered both intentions and consequences before judging the naughtiness of an act.

On the basis of his work, Piaget distinguished two stages of moral development. The first stage, referred to as morality of constraint or *heteronomous morality* is usually seen in children from ages four to seven. **Heteronomous morality** refers to the view that rules are absolute and unquestionable. In this stage children feel an obligation to comply with rules because rules are sacred and cannot be changed. They view behavior as either totally right or totally wrong and think everyone else is of the same opinion. They judge the rightness or wrongness of an act on the basis of the magnitude of its consequences and whether it conforms to established rules. They also believe in **imminent justice,** that is, bad deeds are punished if not by some authority then in the form of a physical accident or some misfortune. For example, a child may believe he suffered a broken arm because he lied to his parents.

Piaget's second stage of moral development, termed morality of cooperation or *autonomous morality* is usually seen in children older than 10 years of age. **Autonomous morality** refers to the understanding that rules are arbitrary agreements that can be questioned and changed with consensus. Children aged seven to ten are in a transition period between the stages of heteronomous and autonomous morality and exhibit some features of each. In the more advanced stage of autonomous morality, rules are understood to be formed and maintained via reciprocal agreement among individuals and therefore subject to change as needed. At this stage, children understand viewpoints other than their own. Their judgments of right and wrong stress intentions and consequences. They now believe punishment should be related to the misdeed rather than arbitrarily administered by an authority. For example, someone who breaks a window should work to earn money to replace it rather than get spanked by her parents. Finally, duty and obligation are no longer defined in terms of obedience to authority but in terms of conforming to peer expectations. This involves putting oneself in another's place and considering others' welfare.

Piaget believed both cognitive development and social experience are involved in the transition from one stage to the next. Interaction with peers provides the opportunities to move away from egocentrism and learn the value of perspective-taking, reciprocity, and cooperation.

## Kohlberg's View

Using Piaget's work as a basis for his theory of moral development, Kohlberg (1976) proposed a series of six qualitatively distinct stages of moral reasoning (table 14.1). Kohlberg's theory evolved from interviewing children, adolescents, and adults from different cultures spanning over 20 years using a series of stories depicting moral dilemmas. He was interested in the reasoning, rather than the decision, of his subjects.

A significant component of Kohlberg's theory is that regardless of culture all individuals go through the stages in the same order, varying only in how quickly and how far they move through the stage sequence (again see table 14.1). The stages are constructed by individuals as they try to make sense out of their own experience, rather than being implanted by culture through socialization. In addition, progress always moves forward not backward through the stages. Kohlberg viewed the development of moral thinking as related to the development of logical thinking outlined

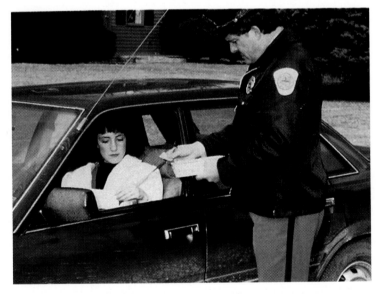

**F.Y.I.**

One of Kohlberg's (1969) stories follow:

A woman was near death from a rare type of cancer. The doctors thought one drug, a form of radium that a druggist in the same town had discovered, might save her. The druggist was charging ten times the cost of making the drug. The sick woman's husband, Henry, could borrow only half the money required. He told the druggist his wife was dying and asked him to sell the drug for the amount of money he had or let him pay later. The druggist refused. So Henry broke into the store to steal the drug for his wife.

Should he have done so? Why or why not?

**F.Y.I.**

The Golden Rule is to do to others as you would have others do to you.

Most people understand and accept the consequences for violating traffic laws, provided the laws are not arbitrarily administered and are open to repeal. This is an example of advanced autonomous morality.

## TABLE 14.1

| Level and Stage | What Is Right | Reasons for Doing Right | Social Perspective of Stage |
|---|---|---|---|
| Level I: Preconventional Stage 1: Heteronomous morality | To avoid breaking rules backed by punishment, obedience for its own sake, and avoiding physical damage to persons and property. | Avoidance of punishment, and the superior power of authorities. | *Egocentric point of view.* Does not consider the interest of others or recognize that they differ from the actor's; does not relate two points of view. Actions are considered physically rather than in terms of psychological interests of others. Confusion of authority's perspective with one's own. |
| Stage 2: Individualism, instrumental purpose, and exchange | Following rules only when it is to someone's immediate interest; acting to meet one's own interests and needs and letting others do the same. Right is also what's fair, what's an equal exchange, a deal, an agreement. | To serve one's own needs or interests in a world where you have to recognize that other people have their interests, too. | *Concrete individualistic perspective.* Aware that everybody has his own interest to pursue and that these interests conflict, so that right is relative (in the concrete individualistic sense). |
| Level II: Conventional Stage 3: Mutual interpersonal expectations, relationships, and interpersonal conformity | Living up to what is expected by people close to you or what people generally expect of your role as son, brother, friend, etc. "Being good" is important and means having good motives, showing concern about others. It also means keeping mutual relationships, such as trust, loyalty, respect, and gratitude. | The need to be a good person in your own eyes and those of others. Your caring for others. Belief in the Golden Rule. Desire to maintain rules and authority that support stereotypical good behavior. | *Perspective of the individual in relationships with other individuals.* Aware of shared feelings, agreements, and expectations, which take primacy over individual interests. Relates points of view through the concrete Golden Rule, putting oneself in the other guy's shoes. Does not yet consider generalized system perspective. |
| Stage 4: Social system and conscience | Fulfilling the actual duties to which you have agreed. Laws are to be upheld except in extreme cases where they conflict with other fixed social duties. Right is also contributing to society, the group, or institution. | To keep the institution going as a whole, to avoid the breakdown in the system "If everyone did it," or the imperative of conscience to meet one's defined obligations (easily confused with stage 3 belief in rules and authority). | *Differentiates societal point of view from interpersonal agreement or motives.* Takes the point of view of the system that defines roles and rules. Considers individual relations in terms of place in the system. |
| Level III: Postconventional, or Principled Stage 5: Social contract or utility and individual rights | Being aware that people hold a variety of values and opinions, that most values and rules are relative to your group. These relative rules should usually be upheld, however, in the interest of impartiality and because they are the social contract. Some nonrelative values and rights like *life* and *liberty*, however, must be upheld in any society and regardless of majority opinion. | A sense of obligation to law because of one's social contract to make and abide by laws for the welfare of all and for the protection of all people's rights. A feeling of contractual commitment, freely entered upon, to family, friendship, trust, and work obligations. Concern that laws and duties be based on rational calculation of overall utility, "the greatest good for the greatest number." | *Prior-to-society perspective.* Perspective of a rational individual aware of values and rights prior to social attachments and contracts. Integrates perspectives by formal mechanisms of agreement, contract, objective impartiality, and due process. Considers moral and legal points of view; recognizes that they sometimes conflict and finds it difficult to integrate them. |
| Stage 6: Universal ethical principles | Following self-chosen ethical principles. Particular laws or social agreements are usually valid because they rest on such principles. When laws violate these principles, one acts in accordance with the principle. Principles are universal principles of justice; the equality of human rights and respect for the dignity of human beings as individual persons. | The belief as a rational person in the validity of universal moral principles, and a sense of personal commitment to them. | *Perspective of moral point of view from which social arrangements derive.* Perspective is that of any rational individual recognizing the nature of morality or the fact that persons are ends in themselves and must be treated as such. |

(Kohlberg, 1978)

y Piaget. Therefore, to attain the highest level of moral reasoning, one has ɔ think abstractly, in other words, to be in the stage of formal operations.

The six stages are classified into three basic developmental levels of noral reasoning distinguished by what defines right and wrong. At the **preconventional level** the individual seems to be motivated by the person-l consequences of the behavior: How will I be affected? In stage 1, people ᴥehave morally to keep from being punished. In stage 2, people behave norally to gain a favor in return. At the **conventional level** the individual an look beyond personal consequences and consider others' perspectives ᴥcluding the law: What will they think of me? Conventional moral reason-ng focuses on maintaining the social order and fulfilling the expectations of ᴥthers. In stage 3, people behave morally to appear good in the eyes of hemselves and others or because they care about other people. In stage 4, ᴥeople behave morally because they believe rules and obligations are neces-ᴥary for a stable society. At the **postconventional level**, the individual con-iders and weighs the values behind various consequences from various ᴥoints of view: How would I respect myself if I did such and such? Such easoning emerges from principles and standards that have universal rather han a personal or societal logical validity. A sense of justice prevails at this evel that enables one to determine the legitimate moral claims of people in ᴥ situation and to balance these claims in a way that best handles the per-ᴥpectives of all contending parties. In stage 5, people behave morally ᴥecause the will of the majority demands it. The will of the majority in our ᴥociety is expressed in democratically derived laws that protect everyone's velfare and guarantee certain rights. These laws are a contract that one ᴥgrees to uphold as part of being a citizen. One may not always agree with he law, but one abides by it because it has a rational function for society. In ᴥtage 6, people behave morally because they are following self-chosen inter-ᴥalized principles that they believe are universal. They are aware of the mportance of law and contract, but when forced with a conflict between he law and their principles, they will choose their principles.

Like Piaget, Kohlberg believed cognitive development and interac-ion with peers are a critical influence on a child's progression through the ᴥtages. Cognitive development can be enhanced through discussions about noral issues that expose children to reasoning at levels higher than their ᴥwn (Berkowitz & Gibbs, 1983).

## Views of Other Researchers

Kohlberg's theory, while contributing to understanding the progres-ᴥion of moral thought in children, adolescents, and young adults, has not ᴥone unchallenged. The concerns include the connection between moral thought and behavior, Kohlberg's research methods, possible sex bias in the ᴥample, and his basic assumption that the highest universal moral principle ᴥnvolves justice or fairness.

While there is a significant relation between moral judgment and ᴥehavior, in reviewing 75 studies Blasi (1980) found the relation not to be ᴥtrong because of the number of inconsistencies in behavior. The studies examined a wide range of behavior including antisocial (delinquency, cheating) and prosocial (helping, showing empathy). Inconsistencies ᴥetween moral reasoning and behavior can be explained in terms of the complicated nature of any decision making, moral or otherwise—what one ᴥught to do, whether one is capable of doing it, and what the rewards or ᴥonsequences are. Research (Haan, Aerts & Cooper, 1985) has shown that

Peer interaction enhances moral development because the interactions impose give-and-take responses that require one to take the perspective of another. Playing provides opportunities to generate rules democratically.

whether a person behaves morally in any particular situation depends on how stressful the situation is, how much the person has to give up in order to act morally, and what the person's cognitive assessment of the situation is (what are alternative solutions and which is most practical?).

Turiel (1983) addressed Kohlberg's conception of morality. He distinguished *moral* thinking from *conventional* thinking, whereas Kohlberg viewed them as the same. According to Turiel, *moral* rules serve the function of regulating the behavior that affects other people's rights or well being, whereas the function of *conventional* rules is to promote behavioral uniformities that coordinate interactions within a social group. He found that school-age children will break a conventional rule when an authority tells them it is OK to do so—"Today you can paint without your smock"—but will not break a moral rule when likewise given permission—"Today you may hit other children." Thus, moral and conventional reasoning operate in different domains.

The criticism that Kohlberg's research was sex biased emerges from the fact that Kohlberg's original sample of subjects whom he followed for 20 years was all male. Gilligan (1982) points out that when Kohlberg's stages are applied to females, their responses to the dilemmas are usually categorized as stage 3, a lower stage of moral development. She claims that the feminine view of morality is different from the masculine view and therefore, Kohlberg's view of morality should be reformulated. Kohlberg's view of morality is one of *justice* or rights; Gilligan's is one of *care* or responsibility. According to Gilligan, women traditionally have been taught to equate goodness with helping others; they tend to see moral problems as arising from conflicting responsibilities. In Kohlberg's theory, moral problems arise from competing rights, so women who base reasoning on compassion, responsibility, and obligation are automatically classified at a lower level of moral development.

Others (Hoffman, 1984) besides Gilligan have criticized Kohlberg's basic assumption that the highest universal moral principle involves justice. Simpson (1974) believes Kohlberg's theory is not universal because it is culturally biased toward constitutional democracies in that it focuses on issues of equality, rights, and justice. Also, its highest level of morality is based on the highest stage of cognitive development—formal, abstract reasoning,—which many cultures do not teach.

In response to his critics, Kohlberg and associates (Colby et al., 1983; Colby & Kohlberg, 1987) revised the scoring system, switching its emphasis from reasoning to structural moral features. One effect is to evaluate people (often women) who focus on interpersonal concerns from stage 3 to a higher stage. Another effect is the elimination of stage 6 because none of the people in Kohlberg's study reach that stage by the new scoring system.

Despite the criticism, Kohlberg's theory has stood the test of time. Most psychologists agree that morality, regardless of perspective, is developmental; that is, children universally progress through stages of understanding, and even though the timing of the progression and highest stage reached are individual, the sequence of stages is the same.

## Social Cognition: Perspective-Taking

Because morality is centered around dealings with others, a basic task in the development of morality is to differentiate between one's perspective and others' perspectives. This task not only relates to understanding others' rights, it also relates to understanding when others are in disress and need help as well as understanding what behavior might hurt or offend others. These understandings are considered social cognition. There is empirical evidence for the assumption that perspective-taking ability facilitates prosocial behavior and in many situations inhibits aggression (Hoffman, 1988).

To examine the development of perspective-taking in children, Selman and colleagues (Selman & Byrne, 1974; Selman, 1976; Selman, 1980) presented groups of children, aged four, six, eight, and ten, with filmed stories depicting moral dilemmas such as the following:

> Holly is an eight-year-old girl who likes to climb trees. She is the best tree climber in the neighborhood. One day while climbing down from a tall tree she falls off the bottom branch but does not hurt herself. Her father sees her fall. He is upset and asks her to promise not to climb trees any more. Holly promises.
>
> Later that day, Holly and her friends meet Sean. Sean's kitten is caught in a tree and cannot get down. Something has to be done right away or the kitten may fall. Holly is the only one who climbs trees well enough to reach the kitten and get it down, but she remembers her promise to her father (Selman & Byrne, 1974).

On the basis of answers to questions about the dilemmas, Selman distinguished the following levels of perspective taking:

- Stage 0: *Egocentric perspective-taking* (about ages four to six). The child does not distinguish her own perspective from that of others. Thus, in responding to the story of Holly, a child who thinks it is important to get the kitten down from the tree is likely to think the father is thinking about this, too. This stage corresponds to what Piaget and Kohlberg referred to as premoral.
- Stage 1: *Social information perspective-taking* (about ages six to eight). A child now recognizes that different people can have different interpretations of the same social situation. However, the child has great difficulty in simultaneously maintaining both perspectives. The child may focus on Holly's desire to get the kitten down or on her father's expectation that she will keep her promise. The child may not recognize these two perspectives conflict. This stage corresponds to Kohlberg's stage 1 (punishment and obedience orientation).
- Stage 2: *Self-reflective perspective-taking* (about ages eight to ten). A child is able to see himself from another's perspective and is aware that the other person can do the same thing. This permits the child to anticipate and consider the thoughts and feelings of others. This stage corresponds to Kohlberg's stage 2 (instrumental orientation).
- Stage 3: *Mutual perspective-taking* (about ages 10 to 12). A child can understand her own perspective and that of another, can be aware the other person can do the same thing simultaneously, and can view this mutual perspective from the position of a third person. Thus, the child can think of how someone else (a teacher or a friend) can view both persons' perspectives. This stage corresponds to Kohlberg's stage 3 (orientation to maintaining mutual expectations).
- Stage 4: *Social and conventional perspective-taking* (about ages 12 to 15 and older). The adolescent can understand the perspectives of whole systems, like society in general, or particular ethnic groups. This stage corresponds to Kohlberg's stage 4 (orientation to society's perspective).

The changing levels of perspective-taking imply that children of different levels will have different understandings of the same moral injunction. Therefore, when examining moral development, one must consider a child's level of social cognitive development.

Lickona (1983) synthesized the theories and research on moral reasoning into six developmental profiles for children of normal intelligence growing up in supportive moral environments. These profiles are explained in box 14.1.

## Box 14.1 STAGES OF MORAL REASONING

**Stage 0—Egocentric Reasoning (preschool years–about age 4)**
**At Stage 0 of moral reasoning, kids:**
1. Begin to express their independence in moral terms ("It's not fair!"), but think "fair" means getting their way.
2. Are highly egocentric, especially in conflict situations, seeing things only from their point of view.
3. Take an "I want it, it's mine" approach to property.
4. Do everything they can to try to make the world conform to their wishes, including manipulating parents, telling "lies," and "cheating" at games, without understanding why these behaviors are wrong.
5. Often break rules, show off, use bad language, or engage in other provocative, out-of-bounds behavior, all as part of a pattern of experimentation and self-assertion.
6. Can, like children at other moral stages, understand moral reasoning that is at a higher level than the reasoning they can produce on their own.
7. May show spontaneous helping or compassion in situations where their desires don't conflict with someone else's.
8. Show individual differences in social-moral behavior that reflect differences in kids' total moral personality.

**Stage 1—Unquestioning Obedience (about kindergarten age)**
**At Stage 1 of moral reasoning, kids:**
1. Swing away from self-assertion toward greater obedience and cooperation.
2. Can take the viewpoint of another person but think that only one viewpoint is right—that of adults.
3. Respect your authority and believe that:
   • What's right is to do what grown-ups say;
   • The reason to obey is to avoid getting punished.
4. Think that adults are all-knowing and always manage to catch kids when they're naughty.
5. Think that if something bad happens to them, they must have done something bad to deserve it.
6. Tend to tattle a lot, because they see adults as the sole source of morality.
7. Have trouble holding two things—two viewpoints, for example—in mind at the same time.

8. Even though they think they *should* follow rules often don't when grown-ups and the threat of punishment aren't present because they don't yet understand why rules are needed.

## Stage 2—What's-In-It-For-Me Pairness (early elementary grades)

### At Stage 2 of moral reasoning, kids:

1. Swing back toward independence and individuality.
2. Believe that everybody has his own point of view and that what's right is to:
   - Follow your own point of view ("Do your own thing") and look out for yourself ("What's in it for me?");
   - Do unto others exactly what they do unto you (both good and bad).
3. Think of themselves as the moral equal of adults ("Kids have rights!").
4. No longer think adults should "boss kids around."
5. Have a rigid, tit-for-tat sense of fairness.
6. Understand the two-sidedness of relationships, and think of their relationship with you as a kind of a deal ("Kids should obey parents so parents will do nice things for them").
7. Tend to sneak it they can't negotiate for what they think is fair.
8. Make constant comparisons ("He's got more than me!") and demand equal treatment.
9. Have a new potential for meanness that stems from their greater assertiveness, reduced fear of adult authority, and insensitivity to the feelings of others.
10. May fail to see an action as wrong unless they can see the harmful results (and so often see nothing wrong with lying or cheating).
11. Get into more fights and exchanges of name-calling because they believe they have to pay everything back.\

## Stage 3—Interpersonal Conformity (middle to upper elementary grades and early to mid-teens)

### At Stage 3 of moral reasoning, kids:

1. Believe that:
   - Being a good person means living up to your internalized image of what a "nice person" does;
   - You should be a nice person so others will think well of you (social-approval) and you can think well of yourself (self-esteem);
   - You should treat others the way you would like them to treat you (the Golden Rule).
2. Can think of what others need, not just what's in it for them. When they put themselves in the other guy's shoes, they're capable of good deeds.
3. Are more forgiving and flexible in their moral judgments. They can consider extenuating circumstances; mercy tempers justice.
4. Have a concept of character. During the childhood years, unless adults and television have made them cynics, they generally
   *(continued on following page)*

*(continued from previous page)*

accept the idea that grown-ups are wise and good and that following their advice will help a kid be a good person.

5. Think of a good relationship as one where people help and trust each other. They're capable of being more responsible family members because they can see things from a group perspective.

6. Are relatively easy to get along with as children, but during the early teens may seem to "regress." Feeling insecure about themselves, they become highly critical of others and seem to need peer approval like a drug to feel good about themselves.

7. Have a true conscience, but one with a terrible flaw: it's inner-directed and outer-directed at the same time. It's inner-directed because it has internal standards, but outer-directed because it depends on others to define what those standards should be.

In childhood, if parents make the effort, they can largely determine a child's moral standards. But in adolescence, the peer group moves in as a major competitor for a child's conscience. And because of their intense emotional needs, fragile self-concept, and immature moral reasoning, Stage 3 teens may have a tough time bucking peer pressure. "If everybody's doing it," they reason, "can it be so bad?" But they can, with help, learn to resist that pressure

**Stage 4—Responsibility to "The System" (high school years or late teens)**

**At Stage 4 of moral reasoning, kids:**

1. Believe that being a good person includes carrying out their responsibilities to the social systems they feel part of.

2. Believe that the reason to fulfill their social responsibilities is to help keep the system going and to maintain self-respect as "somebody who meets my obligations."

3. Are more independent of peer pressure than they were at Stage 3, because being a responsible person is now a higher priority than pleasing people around them.

4. Can see the ripple effects of an action like stealing, cheating, or lying by thinking, "What if everybody did it?"

5. Care about people in their system that they don't know personally as well as those they do know.

6. Believe that cooperation is essential for the survival of society.

7. Have a need for a creed that gives them answers to questions about life, society, and their role in it.

8. Understand what it means to be a good citizen.

**Stage 5—Principle and Conscience (young adulthood)**

**At Stage 5 of moral reasoning, kids:**

1. Believe that what's right is to show the greatest possible respect for the human rights of every individual person, and to support a social system that protects those rights.

2. Believe the reason to be good is the obligation of conscience to be faithful to the principle of respect for all human beings.

3. Can mentally stand outside their social system and use the principle of respect to judge the morality of the system's actions.
4. Value democracy as a way to seek liberty and justice for all.
5. Don't impose their personal values on others but do hold every individual responsible for respecting the rights of others.
6. Feel a Good Samaritan obligation to be concerned about the welfare of all members of the human family.
7. Believe the end doesn't justify the means.
8. Understand that respect for persons requires keeping commitments.
9. Believe that all persons, no matter what their status, deserve to be treated as moral equals.

(Lickona, 1983)

## MORAL BEHAVIOR

The moral behavior perspective is generally expressed by learning theory and specifically by theories of *prosocial* and *antisocial* behavior.

## Learning Theory

Learning theory deals with moral behavior that has a prosocial component representing what is right and an antisocial component representing what is wrong. **Prosocial behavior** includes respecting others' personal and property rights and being kind and helpful. **Antisocial behavior** includes disregard for the rights of others and being mean and hurtful. Those interested in moral behavior study conditions under which a child of a given age is likely to behave in a particular way.

Children who are too young to have internalized moral standards or are too young to reason about moral concepts of right and wrong can still learn to respect others' rights (not take things that belong to other people) and to avoid hurting others (not hit people). Learning theorists believe that children learn moral behavior as they learn any other behavior: through experiencing the consequences of their actions and by observing others they admire. Thus, children discover that when they do "right" (something for which their parents or other significant adults approve of), they generally receive affection. Thus, prosocial behavior is reinforced and becomes associated with feelings of self-approval. On the other hand, when they do "wrong" (something that is disapproved of), they generally are punished; punishment can be in the form of love withdrawal. Thus, the antisocial behavior becomes associated with feelings of self-reproof. So, young children learn to behave morally even when significant adults are not present to provide consequences. This is usually called self-control. Part of self-control is the ability to resist temptation, an ability researchers can test in the laboratory under various conditions.

A common method used to test children's abilities to resist temptation is to show children some toys and tell them that the toys belong to someone else or that the toys are fragile and must not be touched. The children may then be given a variety of experimental influences—they might be punished by being yelled at for touching the toys in the presence of the experimenter; they may be given a thorough explanation about respecting other's property; they may be told how disappointed the experimenter

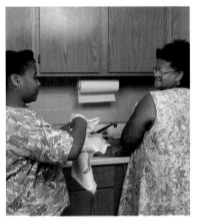

Prosocial behavior is often reinforced by parents and other adults.

would be if they did touch the toys; they might be exposed to a model who either resisted touching the toys or who succumbed to the temptation. Then the experimenter leaves for several minutes, leaving the children alone with the toys. The children are observed through a one-way mirror to see whether the temptation to play with the toys is resisted.

Research shows that children who were punished for touching the toys were more able to resist touching them when the experimenter left the room than children who were not punished (Aronfreed & Reber, 1965; Parke, 1977). Giving children a rationale for their behavior (without any punishment) proved to be considerably more effective than punishment (Maccoby, 1980). However, the combination of punishment and reasoning was the most effective method (Parke, 1974).

Children not only learn from their own experiences, they also learn from the behavior of others. If a model is warm, powerful, and competent, his behavior is likely to be imitated. In addition, if the model is rewarded, the child is likely to copy the behavior and expect a reward, too. If the model is punished, however, the child is unlikely to copy the behavior because she would expect to receive a similar consequence. Research shows that children who observe a model resist temptation and receive approval for doing so will be likely to forgo temptation even when it means having to continue working on a boring task (Grusec et al., 1979). Interestingly, research also shows that absence of expected punishment can act as a reinforcement for the behavior. An experiment by Walters and Parke (1964) showed that children who observed a model play with forbidden toys and not get punished were likely to succumb to temptation and likewise play with the forbidden toys in the experimental situation.

One criticism of learning theory's explanation of moral development is that it cannot generalize about an individual's morality from specific behaviors observed in the laboratory. The findings on the relation of punishment to resisting temptation support this criticism. While punishment influences the likelihood the child will resist temptation, studies of the effects of punishment administered repeatedly by parents at home have shown that parents who use power assertion (physical punishment, yelling, threats) have children with weak self-control who have difficulty resisting temptation in various situations (Maccoby, 1980).

It is difficult to generalize about an individual's morality. This was demonstrated in a study by Hartshorne and May (1928) that showed children were likely to succumb to temptation especially when it was easy and unlikely to be detected. They examined 11,000 schoolchildren for antisocial behavior as exemplified by cheating, stealing, lying in numerous contexts such as home, school, and with friends. They found that most children cheat some of the time and that knowing a child has cheated in one situation does not allow prediction as to whether the child will cheat in another situation. Cheating and lying were not related. Moreover, a child who lies to the teacher is not necessarily the child who lies to peers.

However, Burton (1984), when reanalyzing the results of Hartshorne and May found strong evidence for a general factor of moral behavior. Burton concluded that children have general predispositions for moral behavior depending on their learning experiences; however, when the context deviates from the original learning situation, the child is also likely to deviate from the established sense of self-control. Situational variables that influence behavior are fear of detection, peer support for deviant behavior, and pressure for achievement.

## Antisocial Behavior (Aggression)

In socializing children, a goal of adults is to enable children to learn to inhibit antisocial behavior. Antisocial behavior refers to actions intended to harm or do disservice to another person or group of people often coupled with the intent to achieve personal goals (steal another's toy or cheat to get a better grade) (Patterson, 1984).

Aggression is an example of antisocial behavior. Some theorists believe aggression is a natural human instinct. Some believe it is a response to frustration (any interference with a goal-directed activity). Others believe it is learned; and still others believe it occurs because of the way information is processed (a tap on the back is interpreted as hostile or friendly).

Aggressive behavior can be observed at an early age. Usually it is instrumental; that is, its purpose is to get a toy or reclaim a possession. For example, in a study of pairs of 21-month-olds, it was found that most engaged in at least one conflict during four 15-minute play sessions. Most of these physical confrontations (grabbing, pulling) involved contested objects (Hay & Ross, 1982).

As children approach preschool age (four to six years), physical aggression appears to decrease whereas verbal aggression increases (Goodenough, 1931) but it still is instrumental. Children aged six and seven exhibit more person-oriented or hostile aggression such as name-calling, ridicule, and verbal disapproval (Hartup, 1974). This is partly due to their ability to understand the motives of those that do them harm so they retaliate against the attacker rather than his possessions.

With increasing age, elementary-school children become more adept at distinguishing accidental versus purposeful provocations. However, some children, especially ones who are highly aggressive, still have trouble discerning between unintentional and intentional acts when cues about the motive are ambiguous (Dodge, 1985).

## Prosocial Behavior (Altruism)

In socializing children, another goal of adults is to enable children to learn to behave prosocially—"Prosocial behavior refers to actions that are intended to aid or benefit another person or group of people without the actor's anticipation of external rewards. Such actions often entail some cost, self-sacrifice, or risk on the part of the actor" (Mussen & Eisenberg-Berg, 1977).

Altruism is an example of prosocial behavior. It includes helping, comforting, rescuing, defending, or sharing with others. Young children have been shown to exhibit altruistic behavior even though they do not have a cognitive perspective.

Learning plays a large role in the development of altruistic behavior. Parents can often directly encourage, elicit, and shape these behaviors or act as models from which children can learn new prosocial acts. Zahn-Waxler, Radke-Yarrow, and King (1979) found that mothers' reactions to their children's antisocial behavior influenced subsequent displays of altruism. Mothers who gave explanations like, "Sally's crying because you pushed her," or who accompanied the explanations with an emotional overtone, "You must never bite anyone, people won't be your friend!" were more likely to have children who showed concern when someone else was distressed.

Children not only model parents' prosocial behavior but other people they admire, for example, television characters. In one study (Freidrich

Altruism, as exhibited by these Girl Scouts who are planting trees, is a project without reward other than feeling good about helping the environment.

& Stein, 1975), children aged five and six watched either a prosocial television program ("Mister Rogers' Neighborhood") focusing on understanding the feelings of others, expressing sympathy, and helping, a neutral program. Those who watched the prosocial show not only learned the specific content but could apply what they learned to other situations involving children.

Table 14.2 summarizes perspectives on moral development that have been discussed.

**TABLE 14.2**

| Perspective | Theorist | Mechanism | Process | Evidence |
|---|---|---|---|---|
| Moral Feeling | Freud | Superego, guilt | Identification | Psychoanalysis of patients |
| | Hoffman | Empathy, guilt | Conditioning, cognitive capacities for perspective-taking and relating one's actions to another's feeling of distress | Observation, laboratory experiments |
| Moral Reasoning | Piaget | Cognitive understanding (rules) | Maturation and interaction with environment | Observation, interviews |
| | Kohlberg | Cognitive understanding (justice) | Maturation and interaction with environment | Interviews |
| | Selman | Cognitive understanding (perspective-taking) | Maturation and interaction with environment | Interviews |
| Moral Behavior | | Behavior (pro- or antisocial) | Conditioning, modeling | Laboratory experiments |

# BIOLOGICAL INFLUENCES ON MORAL DEVELOPMENT

Some theorists believe there is a biological basis for both prosocial and antisocial behavior. Prosocial behavior in the form of helping, empathy, cooperation, and altruism is beneficial for nurturing the young and forming attachments. It is also beneficial to the survival of the group. On the other hand, antisocial behavior in the form of aggression plays a role in the survival of the human species. According to some, the aggressive instinct protects us from attack by others. It also enables the strongest and fittest to survive. Both altruism and aggression show consistency over time.

Antisocial behavior has been the subject of study for a long time, while prosocial behavior has only recently received attention. Because much of children's moral development is involved with inhibiting antisocial behavior, we will discuss the biological influences on the most common type of antisocial behavior, aggression, first. Then we will explain the biological influences on prosocial behavior, exemplified by altruism. Finally, we will explore the interaction of biological and contextual influences on antisocial and prosocial behavior.

## AGGRESSION

Freud (1927) proposed that humans had both a life instinct, called *eros,* and a death instinct, called *thanatos.* Freud linked these instincts to biological processes. Freud believed that it was the life instinct that prevented the death instinct from being turned inward to cause self-destruction and, instead, caused it to be turned outward in the form of aggression toward others. Freud's view, however, is not supported by empirical evidence.

Ethologists, for example Lorenz (1966), believe that aggression is an instinct and that aggressive energy builds up in a person until an external environmental stimulus causes the energy to be released. Such a stimulus is known as a *releasing stimulus.* In an animal species the releasing stimulus might be a color. In humans some releasing stimuli are thought to be threats, insults, and frustration. When some individuals get frustrated, they tend to lose their tempers at the slightest provocation.

Lorenz believes aggression is functional for the human species in that it serves to adjust the population level to the natural resources in the environment. It also results in the selection of the best animals for reproduction because those who cannot defend themselves die. Finally, it results in the protection of the young to ensure survival.

A common explanation of the role that biology plays in aggression is hormones. Olweus (1980) and colleagues, studying 16-year-old males, found a significant relation between plasma testosterone levels and self-reports of physical and verbal aggression, particularly aggressive responses to provocation and threat. There also was a significant correlation between testosterone and self-reports of frustration tolerance. Males with higher levels of testosterone tended to be habitually more irritable and impatient than males with lower testosterone levels. The precise role hormones play in influencing aggressive behavior is unclear. For one reason, hormones may influence body build and that may be the more direct influence on behaving aggressively. For another reason, the act of behaving aggressively can increase hormonal levels.

Another explanation of the role biology plays in aggression is genetics. It is difficult to separate the role of genetics from that of the early environment because research shows that parental treatment differs among various infant temperaments. For example, infants who are perceived to be difficult by their parents are felt to need more control (Patterson, 1982; Lee & Bates, 1985).

## ALTRUISM

In comparison with the work on human aggression, there is less empirical research related to the biological bases of human altruism. There is, however, evidence from animal species that points to a genetic base for altruism. According to Wilson (1975) altruism among animals can be seen in the behavior of some female birds who protect their young from predators

This volunteer candy striper exemplifies altruistic behavior in that she likes to make people who are confined to a hospital bed feel better.

by pretending they are injured and can, therefore, be captured easily. When a mother bird spots a predator nearby, she may go some safe distance from the nest, fluttering her wings or stumbling so the predator's attention is drawn away from the young. When the predator has been lured far enough away from the babies, she will try to fly back, sometimes getting caught in the process. Her actions and, in some cases, her self-sacrifice enable the young to survive.

In Wilson's view, altruism has evolved because helpful individuals pass altruistic genes to offspring who are the ones being helped to survive and that generation passes them on to the next, and so on.

Although Wilson extrapolated his animal observations to humans, saying that human social behavior, including altruism, can also be influenced by genes, critics say human research on the genetic nature of altruism is still only suggestive. For example, in twin studies, adults' self-reports of altruism, nurturance, and empathy have been found to be more similar among monozygotic (one egg) than dizygotic (two eggs) same-sex pairs of twins (Rushton et al., 1986). More work on the biological bases of social behavior needs to be done.

# CONTEXTUAL INFLUENCES ON MORAL DEVELOPMENT

The contextual influences on moral development supported by empirical research are family (especially parenting styles), peers, school, culture, and media.

## FAMILY

Parents begin teaching children about right and wrong early in life. One study showed that parents attempted to change children's behavior by two years of age on an average of about once every six to seven minutes (Minton, Kagan & Levine, 1971).

Parents differ greatly in child-rearing techniques. The ways in which children are disciplined affects the ways they think about themselves and others, thereby influencing moral development. When a parent disciplines a child, a certain kind of behavior is being modeled. A parent who uses physical force or threats is acting as an aggressive model and at the same time is showing the child that aggression is a useful method to reach a goal. For example, Patterson (1982) found that the aggressive children referred to his clinic came from coercive family environments. They were punished for misbehavior, and often for no reason. Thus, punishment did not have the expected suppressive effect on these children's behavior; rather, it had the reverse—aggressiveness increased.

On the other hand, a parent who reasons with a child, pointing out the "rights" and "wrongs" of the child's actions as well as the consequences, is likely to model consideration for others and empathy. For example, in a study of generosity among preschool males, it was found that those who shared the most with friends portrayed their fathers as warm, nurturant, and models of generosity, sympathy, and compassion (Rutherford & Mussen, 1968).

Martin Hoffman and colleagues (Hoffman & Saltzstein, 1967; Hoffman, 1970) examined the relation between child-rearing practices and conscience development. They interviewed seventh-grade children (matched for intelligence and socioeconomic status) as to which method of discipline their parents ordinarily used. They also asked the parents which method they had used when their child was five years old. Three categories of disciplinary techniques related to moral development were identified:

1. *Power assertion*: refers to control by physical power or material resources. This type of discipline is exemplified by physical punishment, deprivation of material objects or privileges, force, or the threat of these. This technique relies for its effect on a child's fear of punishment and does not appeal to the child's inner resources.

2. *Love withdrawal*: refers to direct but nonphysical expression of anger, disappointment, or disapproval when a child misbehaves. This type of discipline is exemplified by ignoring, isolating, refusing to speak to the child, or even threatening to leave the child.

3. *Induction*: refers to reasoning with a child, explaining the consequences of the child's act to herself and others. This technique appeals to the child's inner sense of empathy and understanding of another's perspective.

The children were rated for conscience development along several dimensions:

- Severity of guilt, as expressed in story completions
- Acceptance of responsibility for wrong-doing as judged by teachers
- Tendency to confess misdeeds as reported by mothers
- Judgment of right and wrong independent of rewards and punishment
- Consideration for other children as judged by classmates

Results showed that discipline by power assertion was associated with low ratings on conscience development; discipline by induction was associated with high conscience ratings; and discipline by love withdrawal was not significantly associated with conscience development.

According to Hoffman (1970), children of parents who are punitive tend to have *externally oriented consciences* (a description that generally corresponds to Kohlberg's stages 1 to 3). Children who have externally oriented consciences are "good" in order to receive praise, avoid punishment, or please others. Children of parents who are warm and affectionate tend to have *internally oriented consciences* (generally corresponding to Kohlberg's stages 4 to 6). Children who have internally oriented consciences are "good" in order to fulfill their duty or conform to their own standards.

## PEERS

To illustrate the significance of peers in moral development, Youniss (1980) studied how children aged 6 to 12 conceptualized kindness and unkindness in relationships. He found that children recognize need in others sooner in regard to peers than in regard to adults. They also expect reciprocation for kindness from a peer but not necessarily from an adult. Youniss also found children's concepts of friendship change over time from a person who shares toys to a person who shares thoughts and feelings. Thus, as children get older and have more peer group experiences, they discover the importance of cooperation, reciprocity, and principles that serve mutual ends.

Peer interaction, however, does not always have a positive influence on morality. Children's peers are influential in the development and maintenance of aggressive behavior. Aggression, like cooperation or altruism

Children of mothers who explained why certain behavior is wrong ("you made Doug cry; it's not nice to bite.") act altruistically when someone is in distress more often than do children of mothers who only give verbal prohibitions ("stop that!") (Zohn-Waxler, Radke-Yarrow & King, 1979).

among peers, is a reciprocal process. A child who is aggressive toward another usually elicits a retaliatory aggressive act from the other (Parke & Slaby, 1983). Studies of free play in preschools show frequent conflict (usually over possessions), ranging from 2 to 24 incidents per hour, with an average of about nine incidents (Hay, 1984). These conflicts are usually brief and end when the aggressor wins (the other child gives in). Getting what she wants via aggressive means likely reinforces the aggressive behavior. In addition, a child who observes the aggressor and the victim tends to model the dominant child (Grusec & Abramovitch, 1982). If the aggressor is not punished (hit by the victim or reprimanded by an adult), the likelihood of the observing child behaving aggressively is increased even more (Hoffman, 1977).

Apparently, children modify behavior according to the group norms. For example, less cheating occurs in schools that operate by an honor system (therein expecting internalized control) than in schools where tests are closely monitored (therein exercising external control) (Bonjean & McGee, 1965). Also, there is greater cheating among fraternity and sorority members than among nonaffiliated students (Hetherington & Feldman, 1964). For another example, a study (Pope, 1953) found more aggressive behavior among lower class males because it was valued in their group, whereas less aggression was seen among higher socioeconomic levels because it was rejected by their group.

## SCHOOL

School influences moral development through teachers and curriculum. Teachers create the atmosphere for modeling responses. Research has shown that modeling has a positive effect on moral development (Harris, 1970). Teachers who model compassion, honesty, altruism, and justice are likely to have students who exhibit similar behavior.

Certain activities incorporated into classroom programs have been found to foster moral development. For example, research has indicated that group discussions on moral issues can raise the level of moral reasoning (Lockwood, 1978). Group discussions can deal with various problems in the classroom, such as how certain transgressions (fighting) should be handled (Good & Brophy, 1986).

Giving children roles to play and discussing them enhance moral development (Staub, 1971). Through role-playing children learn to view events from various viewpoints. They learn what it feels like to be helpless, what it feels like to be helped, and what it feels like to be the helper.

How children are organized in the classroom for achievement influences children's attitudes about competition, cooperation, helping, and empathy. In their view of educational research, Johnson and Johnson (1974, 1991) describe three educational organizations:

- *cooperative*—students work together to accomplish shared goals
- *competitive*—students work against each other to achieve goals that only a few students can attain
- *individualized*—one student's achievement of the goal is unrelated to other students' achievement of the goal

According to Johnson and Johnson, each organizational structure promotes a different pattern of interaction among students. A cooperative structure promotes positive interpersonal relationships such as sharing, helping, trust, and acceptance. A competitive goal structure promotes comparisons and mistrust. An individualized goal structure promotes student-teacher interaction and responsibility for oneself.

Thus, since children spend a high proportion of their time in school, characteristics of the school environment that contribute to moral development must be recognized.

## MEDIA

Most research on the influence of media on moral development has centered around television and aggression. The National Institute of Mental Health Summary Report on Television and Behavior (Pearl, 1982) concluded that, "violence on television causes aggressive behavior in children and teenagers who watch the programs." In one of the studies discussed in the report that occurred over a five-year period and involved 732 children, several kinds of aggression (conflicts with parents, fighting, and delinquency) were all positively correlated with the total amount of television viewing.

Laboratory experiments have shown that children exposed to a live or filmed model behaving prosocially or antisocially are apt to behave like the model shortly afterward (Hoffman, 1977; Comstock & Paik, 1991). For example, televised models, as shown on "Mister Rogers' Neighborhood" or "Sesame Street," who exhibit prosocial behavior are imitated by viewers (Coates, Pusser & Goodman, 1976). Likewise, violent models affected the imitative behavior of viewers (Comstock & Paik, 1991). Singer and Singer (1980) followed a group of 3- and 4-year-old children over one year, correlating television viewing at home with the various behaviors the children showed during free-play periods at day-care centers. They found consistent associations between excessive television viewing of violent programs and unwarranted aggressive behavior in free-play. According to Comstock and Paik (1991), antisocial behavior is more likely to be modeled than prosocial., especially by young children, because aggressive acts are more concrete and simpler to understand than helpful acts.

Television is not only a source of models but a provider of information. Many television dramas are stories with moral messages. According to Stein (1972),

> Aggression and illegal actions are often portrayed as successful and morally justified. . . . Law enforcement officers and other heroes use violence as frequently as villains and often break laws and moral codes as well. In both adults' and children's programs, these socially disapproved methods of attaining goals are more often successful than socially approved methods. . . . While criminal and illegal activities frequently escape punishment, goodness alone is rarely sufficient to achieve success. . . .The fundamental philosophy manifest in most current television programming is that the end justifies the means and the successful means are often immoral., illegal or violent.

Because young children attend primarily to the consequences of acts and not to intentions, they are unlikely to understand moral messages of programs, even when messages are explicit. Thus, their television-viewing experiences leave them with the impression that it is all right to do bad things as long as you can get away with them.

The characters on Mister Rogers' Neighborhood exhibit prosocial behavior.

## F.Y.I.

Potter and Ware (1987) found that during prime-time television antisocial acts were prevalent not only on the part of villains but of heroes as well. The antisocial acts were presented as justifiable ways to achieve goals.

## CULTURE

Cultures stress different aspects of morality. Our urbanized culture places more emphasis on individual rights for fairness and justice (the type of morality Kohlberg discussed), whereas other cultures such as rural ones place more emphasis on caring and responsibility for others (the type of morality Gilligan discussed).

Madsen and Shapira (1970) found cultural variations in children's tendencies to cooperate or compete. Using a game that could be changed so that either the most competitive player won or the most cooperative player won, they found that children reared in traditional rural subcultures and small, semiagricultural communal settlements cooperate more readily than children reared in modern urban subcultures. They even cooperate in competitive conditions—when rewards are given for individual performance. Specifically, school children in Mexican villages and small towns were found to be more cooperative than their urban middle-class Mexican, Mexican-American, African-American, or Caucasian peers. Similarly, Israeli children reared on a *Kibbutz*, a rural cooperative where work and profits are shared, and children from Arab villages were more cooperative than Israeli urban children (Shapira & Madsen, 1974).

Apparently, children raised in traditional rural subcultures and small, semiagricultural communal settlements have been socialized to have close personal ties, concern with others' welfare, reciprocity, and readiness to lend a helping hand; whereas children raised in urban subcultures have been socialized to have more impersonal ties, competitiveness, obligations based on contracts (payment for services), and behavior for personal advantage.

Whiting and her colleagues (Whiting & Whiting, 1973; 1975; Whiting & Edwards, 1988) confirmed that the cultural variable most closely associated with altruistic behavior was the extent to which children in the six cultures they studied were given responsibility to perform chores related to the family's functioning and economic security.

Summarizing the influence of context on moral development, we find child-rearing practices such as parental warmth combined with inductions, the modeling of positive behaviors, and the provision of opportunities to cooperate, take another's perspective, and to assist others appear to be associated with the development of prosocial behavior, thereby enhancing moral development. On the other hand, a pattern of coercive family interactions and inconsistent discipline, the modeling of negative behaviors, and the provision of opportunities and lack of opportunities to cooperate and be helpful, appear to be related to the development of antisocial behavior, thereby inhibiting moral development.

## RESEARCH IN REVIEW

### WHAT ROLE DO PARENTS PLAY IN CHILDREN'S MORAL REASONING DEVELOPMENT?

Walker, L.J. & Taylor, J.H. (1991). Family interactions and the development of moral reasoning. *Child Development, 62,* 264–283.

The purpose of this study was to address the relation between parents' and children's levels of moral reasoning development. Parents' level of moral reasoning and interaction styles used in discussion of moral issues with their child were used to predict a child's moral development over a subsequent two-year interval. Participants were 63 family triads (mother, father, and child) with children drawn from grades one, four, seven, and ten.

The participants responded individually to a moral reasoning interview and then as a family discussed both a hypothetical and real-life moral dilemma.

In addition to individual interviews of parents and children, family members participated in a group discussion to attempt to reach consensus on one of the hypothetical moral dilemmas and the child's real-life dilemma. (The child was asked in advance if what was discussed individually with the experimenter could be shared in the session with parents. Most children were willing to reveal their dilemma.)

The entire procedure (interviews and family session) was repeated two years later.

Interactional styles in the discussions were categorized as:

1. *Operational* (speeches that operate on the reasoning of another)—critique, competitive request, counter consideration concession, clarification
2. *Representational* (speeches that elicit or represent the reasoning of another)—paraphrase, request, comprehension check
3. *Informative* (speeches that entail sharing of opinions)—opinion, agreement, disagreement, request for change, intent for closure
4. *Supportive* (speeches that indicate positive affect and encouragement to participate)—encouragement, listening responses, humor
5. *Cognitively interfering* (speeches that interfere with sustained and coherent discussion)—distracting, refusal, devalue task, distortion
6. *Conflictual* (speeches that indicate negative affect)—resist/threaten, hostility
7. *Miscellaneous*—unclear, incomplete statements whose meaning could not be discerned

Results indicated that parents accommodated to their child's level of moral rea-soning when in actual dialogue. In other words, parents lowered their level of moral reasoning in the real-life dilemmas presented by the child but kept their reasoning level in the hypothetical ones. Distinct differences in interaction styles were found between the hypothetical context and the real-life one. When discussing the real-life dilemma, which was recalled by the child, the parents were less operational (challenging) and more representational (i.e., questioning and paraphrasing) and supportive than when discussing the hypothetical dilemma. Thus, these differences between the two types of family discussions illustrate the importance of context in assessing interaction patterns.

The parental interaction style that predicted the greatest moral development in children entailed a high level of representational and supportive interactions. The representational category includes behaviors such as eliciting the child's opinion, asking clarifying questions, paraphrasing, and checking for understanding. The children of parents who relied on an operational and informative discussion style developed minimally. This operational style is one in which the child is directly challenged; counter considerations and critiques of the child's position are presented. In the context of a discussion of the child's moral problem, such heightened cognitive conflict can be perceived as hostile criticism and thus arouse defensiveness. Similarly, an informative style is one in which parents are providing their opinions. In this context, it can be seen as something of a "lecturing" style and, therefore, is less effective.

In conclusion, this study suggests that parents play an influential role in children's moral development in contradiction to views implied by cognitive developmentalists, such as Piaget and Kohlberg. Children's moral development was predicted by a parental interaction style that involved supportive interaction, eliciting and paraphrasing of children's opinions, and presentation of higher level moral reasoning.

# INTERACTION OF BIOLOGICAL AND CONTEXTUAL INFLUENCES ON MORAL DEVELOPMENT

Biological and contextual influences on moral development in terms of prosocial and antisocial behavior have been separately examined. We will now examine their interaction. Two models, one for prosocial behavior and one for antisocial behavior, have been proposed to illustrate the complex nature of how biology and context interact to influence moral development. First we look at an adaptation of Parke's model (1982) for aggression.

## ANTISOCIAL BEHAVIOR

A study of infants rated as difficult at six, 13, and 24 months showed them to be high in hostility at age three (Bates, 1982). While temperament is generally regarded as biologically influenced, how it leads to aggression usually involves contextual influences. Parents eventually adopt different child-rearing practices with infants of differing temperaments, which in turn may contribute to the later emergence of aggression. In support of this, Bates found that mothers of temperamentally difficult and easy infants interacted differently. Mothers of difficult toddlers used more prohibitions, warnings, and restraints than mothers of easy toddlers. Despite their mothers' increased control, the difficult toddlers were less compliant and expressed more negative behavior.

## PROSOCIAL BEHAVIOR

Eisenberg's model (1986) of prosocial behavior (figure 14.1) illustrates the indirect relation between socialization and a child's level of sociocognitive development (perspective-taking skills, for example), two factors that may be biologically influenced.

Usually we think of socialization as being contextually influenced. Socialization, however, may be biologically influenced, as in terms of temperament whereby parents adjust child-rearing styles accordingly. Because of the relation between high self-esteem and prosocial behavior among preschoolers, which persists in elementary school and high school (Mussen & Eisenberg-Berg, 1977), one wonders what roles biology and context play in the process.

Sociocognitive development is biologically influenced by a child's maturation or brain development as pointed out by Piaget and others. Maturation and experiences in social interactions lead to an increase in sociocognitive understanding. For example, a two-year-old child cannot understand the concept of sharing, but a four-year-old child can. The two-year-old child is too cognitively immature to understand the word *share*. As the child has experiences with other children in fighting over toys and an adult intervening and demonstrating what share means, as the child approaches four years of age, an awareness of what it means and feels like to share occurs.

Whether a child will behave prosocially in a given situation not only is influenced by the child's temperament and maturation but also depends on the child's assessment of the situation. (Will I get approval? Will my deed be reciprocated? Am I acceptable?) Box 14.2 explains how altruistic behavior can be nurtured.

Coercive child-rearing practices by a parent or teacher can exacerbate inherently difficult behavior (Patterson, 1982).

Evidence indicates that children who have had their own needs and feelings nurtured tend to model similar comforting behavior with others in distress (Staub, 1971).

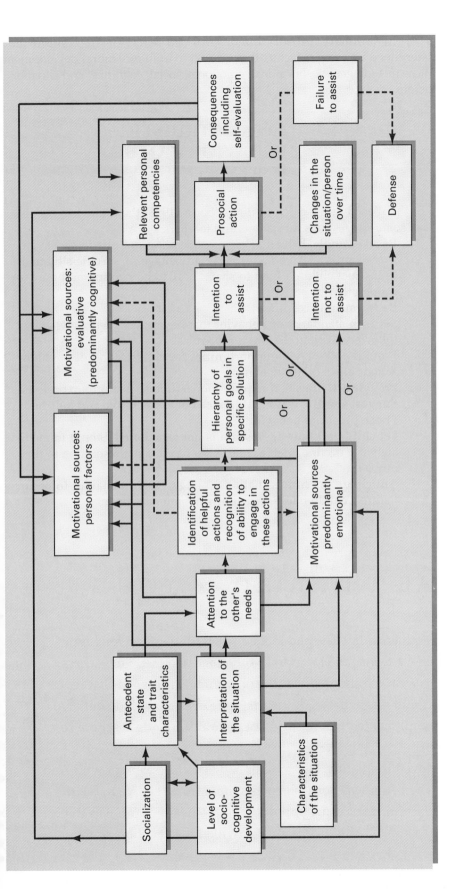

FIGURE 14.1
A MODEL OF
PROSOCIAL BEHAVIOR
(Eisenberg, 1986)

In summary, prosocial and antisocial behavior are complex and determined by various factors that interact to influence moral development. These include genetic, hormonal, emotional, social, cognitive, and situational factors.

---

### BOX 14.2 HOW ALTRUISTIC BEHAVIOR CAN BE FOSTERED

Based on research findings (Berns, 1993) the following is a list of some suggestions for parents and teachers:

1. **Be an example.** Exhibit helping, cooperating, and sharing behavior.
2. **Preach prosocial behavior.** Take advantage of specific situations to instruct children how to share, how to be helpful, and how to cooperate.
3. **Be warm and accepting.**
4. **Set firm standards of behavior** that have consequences when not followed. Explain reasons for the rules.
5. **Provide role-playing opportunities** for children and discuss how actions affect others' feelings.
6. **Provide activities that require cooperation** such as group projects.
7. **Suggest specific ways children can be cooperative and helpful.**
8. **Praise prosocial behavior.**
9. **Let children know aggression is not sanctioned.** Stop it immediately if it occurs. Enable children to figure out a resolution to their problem.
10. **Anticipate possible situations for aggressive behavior to occur.** Redirect children into an activity that interests them.

---

## CRITICAL THINKING & YOU

Today is Ann's thirteenth birthday. She had looked forward to it for a long time; fantasizing about being a teenager. Her grandmother had sent her a new dress, which she decided to wear to school. It was the only thing she owned that represented what she had seen in fashion magazines. For the first time ever, a few kids initiated conversation; a few teachers complimented her. She did not have any friends at school so this attention was great.

Growing up, Ann had moved frequently. Her mother had become pregnant with Ann before finishing high school. When Ann was born, she was shifted from relative to relative while her mother finished school and worked to support them. By the time Ann was three, her mother had met and married a man. Ann's stepfather provided the affection Ann craved. However, occasionally he would come home drunk and beat Ann's mother and abuse Ann. In fact, his alcoholism was the primary reason the family moved so much—he would either get fired or quit in a fit of rage.

Not having friends while growing up, Ann watched a lot of television and fantasized. She had a younger brother who was seven years old whom she often had to care for after school while her mother slept. Her mother worked the night shift as a telephone operator.

After school was dismissed, Ann was still ecstatic. It was the first time she thought school could be fun for now she had friends. As she skipped up the driveway to her house, she saw her stepfather standing with his hands on hips in the doorway. His look chilled her happiness. She lowered her eyes and said, "Hi Dad," but he did not move. He grabbed her wrists and threw her to the floor; her books and papers scattered all over the living room. As she raised herself to pick them up, he kicked her and yelled, "What are you doing going around all gussied up, you whore!"

"But Dad," she stammered through her sobs, "my grandma sent me this dress for my birthday."

"Oh she did, did she," he snarled, and with one swift motion he grabbed the neckline and ripped the dress.

A feeling erupted in Ann that she had never before experienced because she had learned to repress her emotions. She began to scream. Her stepfather laughed, "This will calm you down," he said as he exposed his genitals.

Ann was screaming "You'll never touch me again," as she ran to the kitchen. Her stepfather was right behind her when she grabbed the butcher knife and plunged it into his belly.

When Ann's mother returned from picking up her brother at school, Ann was huddled in the corner clutching her dress.

Ann's stepfather soon died because his body was weak and diseased from 20 years of alcoholism.

**ANALYSIS:** Did Ann commit murder? If you were the judge of Ann's case, what circumstances would you consider in making a decision? Review this chapter to find supportive evidence to discuss three factors such as age, family, background, available models, reasoning ability, emotional state, situation and so on.

**SYNTHESIS:** Compare how theories of moral feeling, moral reasoning, and moral behavior would explain Ann's case.

**EVALUATION:** What is your decision about Ann's behavior and why?

# SUMMARY

- Morality has to do with the concept of right and wrong in dealing with others. As children develop, their morality changes: Infants and toddlers are amoral; preschoolers and young school-age children's morality is objective, inflexible, and based on consequences; older school-age children's and adolescents' morality is more subjective, flexible, and based on group, societal., or universal consequences.
- Morality involves feeling, reasoning, and behaving.
- The psychoanalytic perspective deals with the feeling component.
- The cognitive developmental perspective deals with the reasoning component.
- The learning perspective deals with the behavioral component.
- The psychoanalytic perspective of Freud views moral development as a function of the superego, which is formed by identification with the parents. The parents represent the moral norms of society. Because children love their parents and fear losing their love, they internalize their parents' morality and in doing so punish themselves by feeling guilty for deviating from parental expectations. Guilt then becomes a powerful motivating force in a child's moral development.
- Empathy and guilt function as moral motives.
- Piaget's cognitive developmental view of morality explains how children understand rules. Children's moral understanding changes from heteronomous to autonomous morality, a change from understanding that rules are made by authorities and cannot be changed to understanding that rules are made by the individuals who live by them and therefore can be changed by them.
- Kohlberg proposed a series of six qualitatively distinct stages of moral reasoning categorized in three levels: preconventional., conventional., and postconventional reasoning. One advances through the stages in sequence, although not all individuals reach the highest stages in adulthood.
- Kohlberg's work has been criticized for several reasons: relation of moral reasoning to moral behavior, research methods, possible sex bias, and basic assumption that the highest universal moral principle involves justice or fairness.
- Social cognition is a basic component of moral development, specifically, the ability to take another's perspective.
- Learning theorists view moral development in terms of prosocial and antisocial behavior that develop as consequences of conditioning and modeling. The techniques of punishment, reinforcement, and observation of both prosocial and antisocial models are effective influences on children's consequent display of altruism and/or aggression.
- Biological influences on moral development have been examined in terms of aggression and altruism.
- Contextual influences on moral development involve family, peers, school, culture, and media.
- A family's influence is primarily implemented in child-rearing practices.
- Peers influence children's moral development because among peers there is an absence of power differentials thereby enabling children to experience empathy, taking another's perspective, cooperating, reaching consensus, and making decisions for the benefit of the group. Peers are also models for aggressive and altruistic behavior.
- Schools influence moral development through teachers and curriculum. Teachers create the atmosphere for modeling responses and providing activities that enhance reasoning.
- The mass media, especially television, influence children's aggressive and altruistic behavior through modeling and providing information.
- Culture influences moral development in that behaviors considered right and wrong are often culturally determined. Some cultures stress individual rights for fairness and justice; other cultures stress caring and responsibility for others.
- Biology and context interact in complex ways to influence moral development. Some interactive variables operating in aggressive behavior are a child's temperament, activity level, premature status, intellectual and social skills with the family, school, community, and culture. Some interactive variables operating in prosocial behavior are a child's socialization and level of sociocognitive development, traits, motivations, and goals, characteristics of the situation, interpretation of the situation, and competencies.

## RELATED READINGS

Damon, W. (1977). *The social world of the child.* San Francisco: Jossey-Bass.

Eisenberg, N. & Mussen, P.H. (1989). *The roots of proso-cial behavior in children.* New York: Cambridge University Press.

Ekman, P. (1989). *Why kids lie: How parents can encour-age truthfulness.* New York: Penguin Books.

Gilligan, C. (1982). *In a different voice: Psychological the-ory and women's development.* Cambridge, MA: Harvard University Press.

Lickona, T. (1983). *Raising good children.* New York: Bantam.

Maccoby, E.E. (1980). *Social development: Psychological growth and the parent-child relationship.* New York: Harcourt Brace Jovanovich.

Patterson, G.R.(1982). *Coercive family processes.* Eugene, OR: Castilla Press.

Piaget, J. (1965). *The moral judgment of the child,* (M. Gabain, trans.). New York: The Free Press.

Selman, R.L. (1980). *The growth of interpersonal under-standing.* New York: Academic Press.

Turiel, E. (1983). *The development of social knowledge, morality and convention.* New York: Cambridge University Press

Whiting, B.B., & Edwards, C.P. (1988). *Children of dif-ferent worlds: The formation of social behavior* Cambridge, MA: Harvard University Press.

Zahn-Waxler, C., Cummings, E.M. & Lannotti, R.J. (1986). *Altruism and aggression.* New York: Cambridge University Press.

● ● ● ● ● ● ● ● ● ● ● ● ● ● ● ● ● ● ● ● ACTIVITY ● ● ● ● ● ● ● ● ● ● ● ● ● ● ● ● ● ● ●

To better understand moral development from a moral reasoning perspective, interview two six-year-old children and two 12-year-old children about the following stories and questions. Work with each child alone to get an unbiased spontaneous response.

*Story situations.* You say, "I am going to read two stories about some children, and I want you to answer some questions about the stories when I finish."

**STORY 1:** Mark was excited that his mother's birthday was today. His older sister had six glass plates for the birthday cake stacked on a table by the cabinet. Mark decided to help and get the napkins for his mother's party. He went to the drawer by the sink where the napkins were kept. As he opened the draw-er, it bumped the table and the plates crashed to the floor. Five plates broke.

**STORY 2:** It was Jane's mother's birthday, too. When Jane came into the kitchen, she saw that her older sister had everything ready. There were six glass plates on the cabinet for the birthday cake. Jane was too hungry to wait for the cake so she decided to get some cookies to eat. She climbed on the cabinet to get the cookies, but she slipped and knocked one plate to the floor and it broke.

A. Ask each child separately:
1. What did Mark do?
2. What did Jane do?
3. Some children think Mark was more wrong than Jane, and some think Jane was more wrong. Do you think one of the children did more wrong than the other?
4. Which one?
5. If you were the dad or mom, which one would you punish most?
6. Why did Mark break the plates?
7. Why did Jane break the plate?

B. Contrast the answers of the younger children with the older ones.
1. Do young children consider intentions?
2. Do the older ones?
3. How did the different-aged children view the amount of damage done in relation to intent?
4. Assess your results in terms of Kohlberg's stages of moral development—at what stage(s) were the children reasoning?

● ● ● ● ● ● ● ● ● ● ● ● ● ● ● ● ● ● ● ● ● ● ● ● ● ● ● ● ● ● ● ● ● ● ● ● ● ● ● ● ● ●

# Development Of The Self: How We Achieve An Individual Identity

*It is a peculiar sensation, this double-consciousness, this sense of always looking at one's self through the eyes of others.*

William Edward Burghardt DuBois

## OUTLINE

## ABOUT
## THE SELF

I n Chapter 1 we left Kenneth and Jennifer at critical times in their lives, with Kenneth having possibly impregnated Ellen, and with Jennifer having been diagnosed as bulimic. Now, both face the task of achieving an individual identity, a self-concept. No longer can either of them totally depend on their parents to continually nurture and advise, to make choices or decisions, to help them avoid consequences. How Kenneth and Jennifer resolve their particular dilemmas and emerge as healthy adults depends on the interaction of biological and contextual influences thus far in their lives. Their resolutions also are influenced by their individual perceptions of themselves at this point. The perception of self begins at birth.

**Self-concept** refers to a person's perception of his identity as distinct from others. It emerges from the understanding of self as being separate from others.

When you were born, your parents named you and may have sent out announcements to relatives and friends signifying that a new individual had entered the world. While everyone else treated you as a separate being, you still were unaware of where your environment ended and you began.

As the months passed and you had some experiences using your senses, you noticed that when you touched your hand you felt something in your fingers and hand, whereas when you touched your mother's hand you only felt sensation in your fingers.

Gradually, as people met your needs, you realized they existed even when you could not see them. As you developed language, you learned objects have names and so did you, and each had an independent existence. Language enabled you to describe and compare. Sometime around 15 to 18 months you put it together and understood that you are you. You could recognize yourself in a mirror. You could assert your wants ("Me do it!"), especially when you perceived someone else was controlling you.

As you got older, your concept of self—your identity, your understanding of who you are—was influenced by significant others. If your needs were met consistently and you were given opportunities to discover things on your own, you developed a sense of autonomy, or *self-control*. If, on the other hand, your needs were not met consistently and you did not get to explore your environment, you developed a sense of doubt. A sense of autonomy versus doubt is influential in identity achievement. These significant others also acted like a mirror. Your teachers and friends provided constant feedback on your achievements and failures. Thus, in developing a self-concept, or identity, you also develop *self-esteem*, an evaluative judgment of yourself and how you compare with others.

As you entered adolescence, your self-concept included how you related to others. Being a member of a group was important to your identity. In the later part of adolescence, your self-concept expanded to include how you related to the larger community. Self-concept involves not only "who am I?" but "where am I going?" and "how will I get there?"

This chapter will examine how different aspects of the self emerge over time and the influences on them. For example, in our society it is expected that one achieve an identity by the end of adolescence to the beginning of adulthood. The expectation manifests itself in the most commonly asked question of high school seniors, "What are you doing next year?" and likewise the most commonly asked question of college seniors. Thus, by the time you are in your twenties, you are expected to be independent of your parents, to be able to relate to the opposite sex, to pursue a career to support yourself, and to have developed a philosophy of life (Havighurst, 1972). These expectations are called **developmental tasks**, or what society expects of individuals at certain points in development.

Since we expect identity achievement by young adulthood, we put certain pressures on children to prepare for this as they develop. In our culture we immediately put infants in their own beds, while in other cultures, it is common for infants to sleep with their mothers until they are weaned. We also encourage children to drink from a cup and feed themselves as soon as they can control the thumbs in opposition to the fingers. However, we do not have a consensus on when the developing child should be formally recognized as an independent self. You can vote and go to war at age 18, but in all states you cannot drink. In Georgia you can marry without parental permission at age 16, whereas in Rhode Island you have to be 21. Later in this chapter we will discuss the ways in which other cultures recognize selfhood. We will also see that who you are is a biological phenomenon influenced by the context in which you develop as well as how you and those contexts interact.

# DEVELOPMENT OF SELF-CONCEPT

Self-concept includes your perception of your body as distinct; knowledge about your abilities, wishes, beliefs, and actions; personal ethical code; and feelings about self. Thus, self, or identity, encompasses all areas of development we have thus far explored. First we look at how it emerges; then we will discuss influences on its development.

## INFANTS AND TODDLERS

The first task in developing a self-concept is the recognition that one is a separate being who initiates and controls her actions. Lewis and Brooks-Gunn (1979) studied infants and toddlers aged 5 to 24 months to see how and when the sense of self emerges. They found that between five and eight months infants react to their image in a mirror by smiling, gazing, touching themselves, or making hand motions, thus showing interest in themselves. However, they give no indication that they know they are the cause or initiator of these actions. Between nine and 12 months, they use their mirror image to guide their reaching movements, thus indicating they understand they have some control over their movements. Between 15 and 18 months an infant will touch his nose when a mirror image shows a spot is on it. Some infants point to and even refer to pictures of themselves by name, thus indicating they can distinguish themselves visually as separate beings. By 21 to 24 months, toddlers can use their own name and personal pronouns for themselves and for others ("mine," "Mommy's," "yours"), thus showing they understand they and others are unique beings who can be labeled with words. Infants' ability to recognize themselves in a mirror appears to develop with the concept of *object permanence* (Bertenthal & Fischer, 1978). This makes sense because to be aware of one's identity as being permanent, one must be aware that objects and people continue to exist even when they are not in sight.

Lewis and Brooks-Gunn propose that the key to the process of developing a self-concept is an infant's experiences of connecting her actions with the outcomes. Thus, gradually an infant discovers that shutting the eyes makes the world dark, putting the thumb in the mouth provides an object to suck, shaking the rattle makes a sound. Such connections between action and outcomes are applied to interactions with people (notably the mother), such as crying and being picked up, making a noise or a face and being imitated, and so on. Therefore, an infant gradually learns his actions are separate from others' actions. Later, the infant will learn her perceptions are separate from others' as are thoughts and feelings.

Mahler and colleagues (1969; Mahler, Pine & Bergman, 1975) have a psychoanalytic explanation of the development of self, dealing with feelings rather than thoughts. Mahler believes the process by which the infant separates itself from the mother occurs by gradually internalizing an image of the mother as a source of sustenance, comfort, and love. The image allows the infant to separate and gradually become an individual. The individuation-separation process takes about three years. At first there is no differentiation between self and other. Then between 5 to 10 months differentiation occurs. The infant distinguishes mother from other people by smiling at her or being quieted sooner by her when crying. It is inferred that this distinction also applies to infant and mother. Between 10 to 16 months while the infant is practicing motor skills and exploring the environment, he is experiencing separation. Mahler infers that the infant can do this because an image of the mother as a source of comfort is being established in the infant in her absence. Between 16 to 24 months there is a conflict, between needing to be attached and needing to be separate; thus temper tantrums are common. Mother is a source of not only comfort but also control. By 25 to 36 months a child's internal representation of the mother has stabilized and the child can engage in activities independent of the mother. It is thus inferred that the child perceives herself as a separate being from the mother.

Erikson's (1983) psychoanalytic explanation of the sense of identity lies in an infant's formation of a sense of trust rather than a sense of distrust. The consistency and continuity of care from the mother provide an inner certainty and an outer predictability, the ingredients (according to Erikson) of a rudimentary sense of ego identity.

Building on a sense of trust is a sense of autonomy rather than a sense of shame and doubt. An infant with a sense of trust is more likely to explore her environment thereby establishing a sense of self by separating from the mother. On the other hand, an infant who has a sense of distrust is not as likely to leave his mother. Parents who allow children opportunities to be autonomous (to take the wrapping paper off the present, or to put on their own pants) are encouraging the development of a child's self. Parents who overly control children, by declaring behavior unacceptable or who do

Although it may be tempting to cut up this child's food and feed him in order to avoid a mess, doing this repeatedly may stunt his development of self.

for children what they can do for themselves, foster a sense of shame and doubt thereby inhibiting individual identity development.

## PRESCHOOLERS

The concept of self continues to develop and become more refined during the ages two to six. Children understand not only that they are separate beings with names but also that they are boys or girls, big or little, good at some things and poor at others. Throughout the preschool years, children perceive of themselves in terms of concrete attributes, such as gender, age, personal appearance, behavior, and possessions. When asked to describe themselves they reply: "I'm Joe." "I'm four." "I can pick things up." (Keller, Ford & Meacham, 1978). These descriptions correspond to their cognitive developmental level, what Piaget called the *preoperational stage*.

According to Erikson (1963), a child's developing selfhood is exhibited in terms of initiative versus guilt. A child's realization that he is an autonomous person with an independent will and developing physical and cognitive abilities enables the child to plan and perform various activities (ride a tricycle, color a picture, ask questions). When this sense of initiative is carried to extremes (when Kenny was three, he took apart the vacuum cleaner to see how it worked), parents are likely to reprimand and a child feels guilty. Too many reprimands inhibit a child's sense of initiative and foster her sense of guilt. To help children develop selfhood, parents need to give children opportunities to do things while at the same time protecting them with guidance and firm limits. This leads to the ability in adulthood to enjoy life while remaining a responsible person. Conversely, too many limits and too much guilt lead to psychological problems in adulthood such as inhibition and psychosomatic illnesses.

A sense of initiative balanced with enough guilt to inhibit antisocial behavior yet not restrict curiosity and interactions with others, allows children to enlarge the concept of self by relating it to the world. Having made themselves separate and distinct, they integrate their self-concept by trying on different roles (playing mother, police, teacher).

Children's mastery of language enables them to elaborate and refine their senses of self. An indicator of a child's growing sense of separateness from others is the acquisition of the pronouns *I, me,* and *you* (Maccoby, 1980). The proper use of the pronouns *you* and *I* requires an inversion of point of view. The child must realize that she is "you" to others and not "you" to herself. The child usually figures this out by hypothesizing "I" means whoever is speaking and "you" means whoever is spoken to (Clark, 1976). Thus, correct pronoun usage depends on a child's ability to take the perspective of others toward himself and to understand that the self can be a "you" to others in the same way that others are "you" to self.

In addition to language, art is another vehicle of expression by which the child can exhibit the sense of self. As a child's cognitive and physical abilities develop, the child becomes increasingly able to execute her perception of self in art (figures 15.1–15.5, pp. 480–481). When children draw themselves, families, or the world around them, they are putting together a more complex representation of how they see things than the simple lines and unsophisticated style of the picture might indicate to the untrained eye (Hofman, 1984). For example, figure 15.5 shows how Jennifer, a four-year-old, perceives herself in relationship to her family. She has drawn herself as the largest. Children in the preoperational stage are egocentric, so Jennifer's

**A child's healthy development of self includes initiative, independence, and responsibility.**

**FIGURE 15.1**
Tammy (age three years and two months)

**FIGURE 15.2**
Gregory at age four years

**FIGURE 15.3**
A Mad Gregory (age three and one half)

**FIGURE 15.4**
Part of the self-concept is gender. These drawings were done by a five-year-old boy. PS stands for the penis of the male (left) and VA stands for vagina on the female (right).

FIGURE 15.5
**My Family By Jennifer (age four)**

concept of herself as the focus of her family is normal for her stage of development. Children with a poor self-image might not include themselves in the picture or they might draw themselves small or in the corner (Hofman, 1984).

## SCHOOLAGERS

When children reach schoolage, about six or seven to 11 or 12, they begin to describe themselves in terms of personal qualities—"I'm smart," "I'm a good worker." The significance of this is that they have changed from describing themselves in terms of specifics (name, age, gender) to general qualities applicable in many situations, thereby signifying an advance in cognitive development. According to Piaget, they are in the *stage of concrete operations*. The following excerpt from research by Montemayor and Eisen (1977) illustrates how classifications of appearance, intelligence, and personal likes and dislikes become part of the self-concept:

*9-year-old* : My name is Bruce C. I have brown eyes. I have brown hair. I love sports. I have seven people in my family. I have great eye site. I have lots of friends. I have an uncle who is almost 7 feet tall. My teacher is Mrs. V. I play hockey. I'm almost the smartest boy in the class. I love food. I love school. (Montemayor & Eisen, 1977).

Montemayor and Eisen collected data from 262 boys and girls age nine to 18 by asking them to give 20 different answers to the question, "Who am I?" The answers from the nine-year-old and 10-year old children included concrete facts as was exemplified by Bruce's previous description—name, age, gender, where they lived, and so on. After age 11, however, especially among the females, more personality traits (good, helpful, trustworthy) and how the child related to others appeared in the descriptions. For example, an 11 ½-year-old girl gave the following answer to "Who am I?"

*11 ½-year-old:* My name is A. I'm a human being…a girl…a truthful person. I'm not pretty. I do so-so in my studies. I'm a very

"I'm shy," says the girl. "I'm still hungry," says the boy. These statements show an advance in cognitive and self-development.

good cellist. I'm a little tall for my age. I like several boys. I'm old fashioned. I am a very good swimmer....I try to be help-ful....Mostly I'm good, but I lose my temper. I'm not well-liked by some girls and boys. I don't know if boys like me. (Montemayor & Eisen, 1977).

Thus, after age 11 the self-concept begins to include more abstract qualities applicable to various situations.

According to Erikson (1963), a child's self-concept is influenced by whether he has a sense of industry versus inferiority. A sense of industry is established by having one's desire to produce things rewarded—"Your written composition was good; your printing was straight, and your ideas were so interesting. Next time you can work on your spelling." A sense of inferiority is established by having one's products continually criticized—"Your written composition was not acceptable; you had too many erasures and spelling errors; I couldn't read it."

School-age children primarily derive a sense of industry or a sense of inferiority from school; however, activities engaged in outside of school with friends also contribute to the self-concept. When children are chosen or not chosen for teams, their concepts of self are affected. By age seven or eight children begin to evaluate themselves by comparing their own and others' behavior—"I can ride my bike better than my brother" (Secord & Peevers, 1974).

Ruble and colleagues (1980) gave different-aged children a task to perform and then told the children how the work of their peers on the same task compared with theirs. In evaluating themselves, first-graders did not consider their peers' performance. A few second-graders and almost all of the fourth-graders were influenced by how their performance compared with peers'. Newfound perspective-taking skills equip the school-age child with the ability to imagine what other people are thinking and, in particular, what they are thinking of her (Harter, 1983). Cooley (1902), considered to be one of the founders of sociology, explained the development of a self-image as a "looking-glass self"; another famous sociologist, Mead (1934), called it a "generalized other."

Rosenberg (1979) explains that the ability to take the perspective of others is necessary before one can incorporate the evaluative judgment of others into one's self-concept. He writes:

It is only when the child is able to get beyond his own narrow view of the world that he can succeed in seeing himself as an object of observation by others, as one who arouses in other people's minds a definite set of thoughts and feelings. By taking the role of others, the individual comes to define himself in terms of the reactions he rouses in the minds of others—as well-liked, popular, easy to get along with, and other looking glass traits (Rosenberg, 1979).

## ADOLESCENTS

In adolescence, the concept of self changes qualitatively; that is, it becomes more flexible, more encompassing, and more precise, and more abstract terms are used to describe it (Livesley & Bromley, 1973). Comments such as the following illustrate the increase in self-knowledge by early adolescence:

*14-year-old*: I am a very temperamental person, sometimes, well *most* of the time, I am happy. Then now and again I just go moody for no reason at all. I enjoy being different from every-body else, and like to think of myself as being fairly modern. Up till I was about 11, I was a pretty regular churchgoer but since then I have been thinking about religion and sometimes I do not believe in God. When I am nervous I talk a lot, and this gives some important new acquaintances a bad impression, when I am trying to make a good one. I worry a lot about getting married and having a family, because I am frightened that I will make a mess of it. (Livesley & Bromley, 1973).

The following excerpt illustrates the individuality and level of abstraction utilized in late adolescence:

*17-year-old:* I am a human being…a girl…an individual…I am a moody person…an indecisive person…an ambitious person. I am a big curious person….I am lonely. I am an American….I am a Democrat. I am a liberal person. I am a radical. I am con-servative. I am a pseudoliberal. I am an Atheist. I am not a classifiable person (i.e., I don't want to be) (Montemayor & Eisen, 1977).

What Piaget described as entry into the *stage of formal operations* explains the change from focusing on concrete observable aspects of the self, such as physical attributes and behaviors and later, to traits focusing on abstract psychological processes, such as thoughts, attitudes and emotions. In addition, as children get older they become more sophisticated at pro-cessing information. They also become more aware of what they know and how they know it. This applies to self-knowledge and general knowledge. They are thus more aware of internal components (thoughts and feelings) being part of the self-concept as well as external components (looks, behavior).

As the concept of self develops so does self-consciousness, the con-cern about what others think. Elkind (1981) explained the egocentrism of adolescence as a belief that others are equally preoccupied with one's thoughts and therefore always notice one's appearance, behavior, and actions. He referred to this belief as the imaginary audience. Rosenberg (1979) explains adolescent self-consciousness as due to the changing nature of adolescent thought. Adolescents can now form hypotheses and what was unquestioned before about the self now is given careful scrutiny.

Self-consciousness diminishes as one approaches adulthood. Elkind and Bowen (1979) studied children in fourth, sixth, eighth, and twelfth grades by asking them what they would do in certain potentially embar-rassing situations like going to a party and noticing their clothes were stained. They found self-consciousness shows a developmental trend and peaks in the eighth grade. Females in this study were more self-conscious than males in every age group possibly because females learn to take oth-ers' perspectives sooner than do males.

Still another explanation of the heightened self-consciousness in ado-lescence, especially early adolescence, has to do with physical changes. On the average it takes about two years for the body to reach puberty, or sexual maturity. Females reach puberty from age 9 to 14 years of age and males reach puberty from 11 to 18 years of age (Chumlea, 1982; Tanner, 1990). In the rapid growth stage of puberty, legs grow faster than the trunk—one becomes clumsy. When males' voices deepen, they may not know whether a soprano or alto voice is going to emerge when they speak. When females' hips widen, they find themselves not fitting into their clothes. The hormon-al changes in both genders cause mood swings.

These adolescent girls take great care in their physical appearance. Self-consciousness is part of the development of self.

This boy has decided that having an athletic physique and athletic abilities is important to his self-image.

Physical changes in puberty impact the self-image. Not only are adolescents self-conscious about their changing appearance but there is a tremendous concern over not being different from one's peers and wanting to look like the cultural ideal.

Whether one matures early or late affects how one views oneself. Research has shown that males who mature early are more likely to be poised, popular with peers, and school leaders; while males who mature late are more likely to be insecure, aggressive, and dependent (Mussen & Jones, 1957; Peskin, 1973; Simmons & Blyth, 1987). Research also has shown that females who mature early are more likely to be introverted, shy, and less sociable (Peskin, 1973), although these characteristics often disappear as peers catch up (Faust, 1960; Simmons & Blyth, 1987). Apparently, the timing of puberty onset is more significant for males' self-concepts than it is for females' (Duke et al., 1982).

Most adolescents are dissatisfied with the image they see in the mirror (Siegel, 1982). Males want to be tall and broad-shouldered, whereas females want to be slim. These are the ideal body types for males and females in our culture, as portrayed in the media. The acceptance of the body for what it actually is rather than the way one thinks it should be affects the total self-concept. Research shows a strong correlation between how young people view their bodies and the way they judge themselves as people (Lerner & Spanier, 1980; Adams, 1991).

According to Erikson (1963; 1968), establishing a sense of identity is a major developmental task of adolescence. This stage is called *identity versus role confusion.* In this stage adolescents must reassess previous roles and concepts of self and derive a stable sense of who they are and where they are going. They have to connect the skills cultivated in childhood with the occupations available to them as adults, otherwise they risk a sense of role confusion. In trying to establish an identity, adolescents progress through the psychosocial stages again. In establishing an identity, the adolescent has to learn to take successes and failures as events to learn from instead of generalizing them to the whole personality. If you make the honor society, that does not mean you are a superior person but rather that you have good study skills. Thus, an identity is a concept of self that includes an individual's uniqueness and similarity to others, strengths and weaknesses, goals and beliefs, and how they came to be. Such an identity is possible by the end of adolescence because the individual has reached a level of maturity whereby the physical self, cognitive self, emotional self, social self, and moral self can be integrated.

According to Marcia (1980; 1991), the task of constructing an identity involves making certain commitments—choosing a career, an ethical code, a sexual orientation, and so on. To make a commitment, one must first experience a **crisis of choice**, a period of conscious decision making involving exploring and eliminating alternatives. According to Marcia, there are four statuses or ways of resolving the identity versus role-confusion crisis: *identity diffusion, identity foreclosure, identity moratorium,* and *identity achievement.*

**Identity diffusion** describes adolescents who have not experienced any crisis of choice (because they have not seriously examined opportunities available to them) nor have they made any commitments.

**Identity foreclosure** describes adolescents who have made a commitment toward a career, philosophy, or love object without having experienced a crisis of choice.

Until the mid 1970s many women experienced identity foreclosure because of society's expectations. It was assumed a woman would marry

nd have children. If she was employed, she would leave her job when she
ad children. Today women have many opportunities to explore identities
nd careers.

**Identity moratorium** describes adolescents in the middle of a crisis
f choice but their commitments are either absent or vaguely defined.

**Identity achievement** describes adolescents who have gone through
crisis of choice and who have made a commitment.

Identity formation may differ for females and males. Gilligan (1982)
ates that females more than males are socialized to prioritize relationships
nd responsibilities. Gilligan also says that for females development of
lentity and intimacy appear to be fused (one comes to know oneself
hrough relationships with others), whereas for males development of iden-
ty precedes intimacy.

This gender difference in identity formation is supported by
esearch. For example, among a group of 19-year-old college students,
omen were found to be higher than men in intimacy development; they
ere also higher in identity achievement (Schiedel & Marcia, 1985). Perhaps
heir experiences with relationships provide them not only with insight into
thers' perspectives but insight into themselves as well.

This candy striper has made a
determination that she wants
to pursue a career in medicine.
Being a hospital volunteer is a
way for her to learn about
people.

# SELF-ESTEEM

As children develop, their concept of self becomes increasingly com-
lex. They come to know how they look; they begin to define themselves by
heir skills and psychological traits; they begin to understand how they
neasure against others' standards; and they begin to evaluate themselves
ccordingly.

*Self-concept* refers to an individual's idea of his identity as distinct
rom others and emerges from the understanding of self as separate from
thers. **Self-esteem** refers to the value that an individual places on her iden-
ity and emerges from interactions with others. Self-esteem then is usually
escribed as high or low. One's level of self-esteem has been shown to influ-
nce such things as one's general satisfaction with life, one's relationships
vith others, and one's achievement.

Coopersmith studied hundreds of fifth- and sixth-grade white, mid-
lle-class, average males. He tested the level of their self-esteem via an
nventory, a sample of which is shown below (Coopersmith, 1967).

| | Like Me | Unlike Me |
|---|---|---|
| 'm pretty sure of myself. | _____ | _____ |
| often wish I were someone else. | _____ | _____ |
| never worry about anything. | _____ | _____ |
| here are lots of things about myself I'd change if I could. | _____ | _____ |
| can make up my mind without too much trouble. | _____ | _____ |
| 'm doing the best work that I can. | _____ | _____ |
| give in very easily. | _____ | _____ |
| My parents expect too much of me. | _____ | _____ |
| Kids usually follow my ideas. | _____ | _____ |

Coopersmith found the self-esteem of the children he tested to be
onstant, even after retesting them three years later. He also asked their

teachers to rate them on such behaviors as reactions to failure, self-confi-dence in new situations, sociability with peers, and need for encouragemen and reassurance. He then classified the children on the basis of their score on the self-esteem inventory and teachers' ratings.

The children were further assessed through clinical tests and obser vations on their behavior in various situations. In one situation, they wer tested to determine how readily they would yield to group influence in situation when their own judgment was actually superior. In another situa tion, the children were given tasks that were either difficult or easy to dete mine whether their interest in working on a task was sharpened or weak ened by success or failure. Finally, their classmates were asked to select th other children in the class whom they would like to have for friends, and record was kept of how often each child was chosen.

On the basis of this extensive study, Coopersmith concluded tha there are significant differences in the experiences and social interactions persons who differ in self-esteem.

> Persons high in their own estimation approach tasks and per-sons with the expectation that they will be well received and successful. They have confidence in their perceptions and judgments and believe that they can bring their efforts to a favorable resolution. Their favorable self-attitudes lead them to accept their own opinions and place credence and trust in their reactions and conclusions. This permits them to follow their own judgments when there is a difference of opinion and also permits them to consider novel ideas (Coopersmith, 1967).

> The picture of the individual with low self-esteem that emerges from these results is markedly different. These persons lack trust in themselves and are apprehensive about express-ing unpopular or unusual ideas. They do not wish to expose themselves, anger others or perform deeds that would attract attention. They are likely to live in the shadows of a social group, listening rather than participating, and preferring the solitude of withdrawal above the interchange of participation. Among the factors that contribute to the withdrawal of those low in self-esteem are their marked self-consciousness and preoccupation with inner problems (Coopersmith, 1967).

Coopersmith also investigated the child-rearing practices employed by his subjects' parents. He found that the boys with high self-esteem tend ed to have parents who were accepting, affectionate, and involved in thei activities. They also established consistent and reasonable limits that helped their sons know what was expected of them and gave them a sense of how to be successful in the world. While these parents were strict, they were no overly harsh in punishing their children. They used withdrawal of privi leges and explained the reasons for the consequences. The children wer allowed to participate in discussions, and their opinions were respected The parents were relatively self-assured; they had definite values that the communicated.

Baumrind (1967; 1971) found similar results in the relationship between parenting styles and competent children. The children who wer happy, self-reliant, and able to meet challenging situations directly had par ents who provided emotional support yet exercised a good deal of contro and demanded responsible independent behavior.

Parents who are actively involved in their children's activities and encourage them to succeed tend to have sons who have a strong sense of self-esteem.

Another study (Burkett, 1985) revealed a connection between parenting practices and the self-esteem of preschool children. Parents who were sensitive to their child's needs and who were consistent in discipline had children with high self-esteem. Particularly important was the parents' recognition of the child as a separate individual who warranted respect.

It appears that the quality of the relationship with one's parents continues to influence self-esteem after the child becomes an adolescent (Walker & Greene, 1986).

High self-esteem plays an important role in achievement. It has been found that students with high self-esteem are more likely to be successful in school and achieve more than children with low self-esteem (Purdey, 1970). This relation shows up as early as the primary grades and becomes stronger as a student gets older (Bednar, Wells & Peterson, 1989).

Achievement affects a students' perceptions of her own abilities and others' perceptions of those abilities as well (Harter & Connell, 1982).

The more positively children feel about their ability to succeed, the more likely they are to exert effort and feel a sense of accomplishment when they finish a task. Likewise, the more negatively children evaluate their ability to succeed, the more likely they are to avoid tasks in which there is an uncertainty of success, the less likely they are to exert effort, and the less likely they are to attribute any success or lack of it to themselves ("Oh, it was just luck."). Research supports the relation between perceived competence and subsequent performance on a task (Horn & Hasbrook, 1987).

People with low self-esteem tend to have a high fear of failure. This causes them to set easy goals or unrealistically difficult goals in tasks where goal setting is required. For example, in a ring-toss game where students could toss the rings at the goal from any distance they desired, those with low self-esteem stood either right next to the peg or too far away (Covington & Beery, 1976). Those who stood next to the peg avoided feelings of failure by ensuring success. Those who stood far away ensured failure, but the distance provided an excuse. Students with positive self-esteem were more likely to set goals of intermediate difficulty. In the ring-toss game, they were more likely to choose a distance they thought reasonable for success. If they were given a chance to try the game again, they adjusted the distance according to how they performed on the first try. Those with low self-esteem did not make use of this information.

Peers can influence a child's self-esteem by their acceptance or rejection. Children who are popular with their peers are generally physically attractive, come from a high social class, have certain names, are intelligent, friendly, and assertive (Hartup, 1983). Peer attitudes about "ideal" size, physique, and physical capabilities can influence children's self-esteem.

According to Rosenberg (1975), difference or similarity of social identity (race, religion, national origin, social class) to that of the majority of the people in one's neighborhood affects one's self-esteem. For example, Rosenberg found that Jewish children raised in Jewish neighborhoods were likely to have higher self-esteem than those raised in Catholic neighborhoods.

To summarize, Coopersmith (1967) believes self-esteem is composed of:

1. *competence*—one's success in meeting demands for achievement
2. *power*—one's ability to control and influence others
3. *virtue*—one's adherence to moral and ethical standards
4. *significance*—one's acceptance, attention, and affection from others

Successfully learning how to count gives children confidence to apply their new skills.

### F.Y.I.

Achievement of specific skills that were taught was found to improve self-esteem in adolescents (Bednar, Wells, & Peterson, 1989) because knowing how to accomplish a goal led to confidence in the ability to perform similar tasks.

African-American students in integrated schools were found to have lower self-esteem than those in nonintegrated schools. Lower-class children attending a school where the majority of children were from higher classes also had lower self-esteem than those attending a school where the majority of children were from lower-class environments. The same was true of upper-class children who were in the minority. Apparently, being different affects one's self-esteem.

While Coopersmith measured overall self-esteem, Harter (1983, 1985) measured the competence component. She developed a scale, called the Self-Perception Profile for Children, that measured general feelings of self-worth ("I am happy with myself") and five different areas of a child's perceived competence:

1. scholastic competence ("I am good at school work.")
2. athletic competence ("I do well at sports.")
3. social acceptance ("I have a lot of friends.")
4. physical appearance ("I like my looks.")
5. behavioral conduct ("I behave well.")

Harter postulates that achievement in any area affects how one feels about oneself in general; how one feels about oneself then influences the motivation to achieve.

The Self-Perception Profile for Children was designed to be used with third to sixth grade children. Recognizing the changes in self-perception as one gets older, Harter (1989) developed a scale for adolescents, which adds three categories to the ones used for children—job competence, romantic appeal., and close friendship.

Box 15.1 gives suggestions on how to enhance self-esteem.

## Box 15.1 ENHANCING SELF-ESTEEM

1. **Enable children to feel loved**—understand and attend to their needs; be affectionate and warm; accept their individuality; talk to them and listen to them.
2. **Enable children to be autonomous**—provide opportunities for them to do things for themselves; give them choices; encourage curiosity; encourage pride in achievement, provide challenges.
3. **Enable children to be successful**—be an appropriate model, set clear limits; praise accomplishments; explain consequences and how one can learn from mistakes.
4. **Enable children to interact with others**—provide opportunities for give and take; help them to understand others' perspectives; enable them to work out differences; help them deal with feelings.
5. **Enable children to be responsible**—provide opportunities for them to care for belongings, help with chores, help others; encourage their input; enable them to correct their mistakes.

## SELF-CONTROL: INTERNAL OR EXTERNAL LOCUS

**Self-control** refers to control of one's actions, emotions, and thoughts. The locus of self-control can be *internal* in that a person feels control over what happens to her or it can be *external* in that a person feels others control what happens to her. Rotter (1954) and Seligman (1975) studied *locus of control.* **Locus of control** refers to one's perception of responsibility for one's actions; it may be internal or external. These investigators found some consistent differences among individuals with respect to their sense of control over their lives. Some people feel they have the power to determine what happens to them and are responsible for their own success or failure. In other words, they feel outcomes are the result of their own actions. These individuals are said to have an *internal locus of control*—control of the self comes from inside. Other people feel that the things that happen to them are a result of luck or fate; they are helpless. These individuals are said to have an *external locus of control*—control of the self comes from outside (Harter, 1983). Children with high self-esteem assume more personal responsibility or are more internal in regard to their locus of control than children with low self-esteem. Perceived locus of control, the generalized belief about one's power and control in various situations, has been found to be a relatively stable characteristic, like self-esteem (Phares, 1976).

Rotter developed a locus-of-control scale (1971) that has been used to study the internal-external dimensions of personal responsibility. The Internal-External Scale is constructed so that each item can be scored as internal or external. Some sample items follow. In each pair of statements, participants indicate the more appropriate statement.

Preschool children, due to their cognitive development, generally have an external locus of control; for example they blame others for their situation.

### Measuring Locus of Control

I more strongly believe that:

1. a. Promotions are earned through hard work and persistence.

   b. Making a lot of money is largely a matter of getting the "right breaks."

2. a. There is usually a direct connection between how hard I study and the grades I get.

   b. Many times the grades teachers give seem haphazard to me.

3. a. The number of divorces in our society indicates that more people are not trying to make marriage work.

   b. Marriage is largely a gamble; it's no one's fault if it does not work.

4. a. When I am right, I can usually convince others that I am.

   b. It is silly to think that one can really change another person's basic attitudes.

5. a. In our society, earning power depends on ability.

   b. Getting promoted is a matter of being luckier than the next person.

Children's locus of control is often determined by administering the Intellectual Achievement Responsibility Questionnaire (Crandall, Katovsky & Crandall, 1965).

1+  If a teacher passes you to the next grade, would it probably be:

   a. because he or she likes you?

   b. because of the work you did?

1-  When you read a story and can't remember much of it, is it usually

   a. because the story was not well written?

   b. because you were not interested in the story?

Items marked with a 1+ are those dealing with success; those marked with 1- are those dealing with failure. The child receives a total 1+ score, the number of items in which success is attributed to an internal cause, and a total 1- score, the number of items in which failure was attributed to an internal cause. A child's overall score is the combination of these two scores; high scores indicate internal locus of control, while low scores indicate external locus of control.

Piaget's observations of infants led him to conclude that it is not until about the age of five or six months that children show awareness that their actions can bring about an effect. Behavior does not become intentional or goal-directed, however, until between about eight and 12 months. It is about the age of one, according to Piaget, that children begin to distinguish between events caused by their actions and those that are not (Flavell, Miller & Miller, 1985). When children begin to understand they have an impact on their environment, they begin to experiment with various autonomous behaviors.

Children gradually develop a sense of control when things that happen to them are contingent on their actions. Erikson's (1963) theory of personality development states that parental responsiveness to children's needs leads to attachment and a sense of trust (first year). When children are allowed to be autonomous, they gain a feeling of control; if not given opportunities to be autonomous, they feel self-doubt (age two to three). If children are allowed to initiate activities, they will feel a sense of control over their environment rather than guilt over wanting to control it (ages four to five). When children enter school, their experiences will impact their feelings of industry or inferiority (ages six to 12). These are crucial years for development of self-esteem.

Thus, locus of control develops through one's actions on the environment and one's interactions with others. The outcomes of these actions and interactions influence whether people attribute what happens to them to internal or external causes. For example, a correlation exists between socioeconomic status and locus of control, with higher statuses being more internal and lower statuses being more external (Young & Shorr, 1986). This is probably due to the accumulation of experiences in the lives of children born into low socioeconomic status families that bring about a feeling of being helpless to change their situation. Children see their parents work hard yet get laid off when the company has a deficit and end up on government welfare because at least it provides some steady income. These children become passive and lose the motivation to achieve. Seligman (1975) has presented evidence to show that when people perceive they have no control over their lives or they are pawns of external circumstances, they feel hopeless and give up. They have *learned helplessness*.

In a series of studies on learned helplessness, Dweck and colleagues (Dweck, 1975; Dweck & Reppucci, 1973) found that when children believe their failures are due to uncontrollable factors in themselves such as lack of ability (for example, "I failed the math test because I'm dumb in math"), their subsequent task performance deteriorates. However, if children believe their failure was due to lack of effort, they try harder on subsequent tasks and often show improved performance.

In several studies (Dweck & Bush, 1976; Dweck & Gillard, 1975; Dweck et al., 1978), Dweck found that females exhibited more learned helplessness than males and attributed failure to lack of ability, whereas males attributed failure to lack of effort even though, in actuality, their scores on chievement tests were similar. Dweck and colleagues looked to the teach-rs to see if there was differential feedback to females and males, relating to ailure. They found that when males submitted poor work, they were gen-rally reprimanded for sloppiness, not paying attention, or lack of effort. When females submitted poor work, they were generally told, "You didn't o it right even though you tried."

Dweck and colleagues then set up a classroom experiment. One roup of males and females was told when they did poorly on an anagram est, "You didn't do very well that time; you didn't get it right." Another roup of males and females was told that they did not do well and that they id not write the answers neatly enough. This feedback led both sexes in ne second group to believe that poor performance was due to lack of effort. When the task was administered again, the first group gave up more easily fter the initial failure, while the second group tried harder after the initial ailure. Thus, if adults treat children as if their mistakes can be remedied by neir own actions, the children are likely to reflect this opinion of them-elves and behave accordingly.

Table 15.1 is a summary of terms relating to the self.

## TERMS RELATING TO SELF

### TABLE 15.1

| Term | Definition | Influences | Measure |
|------|-----------|-----------|---------|
| Self-concept | perception of one's identity as distinct from others | maturation, cognitive development, culture | observation of mirror-image interviews |
| self-esteem | value one places on her identity | parenting, peer-interaction, achievement (history of success or failure), cultural ideal type | Piers-Harris Scale Self-Perception Profile |
| self-control | control of one's actions, emotions, thoughts | interactions with environment, interactions with others | Locus of Control Scale (internal or external) |

# BIOLOGICAL INFLUENCES ON DEVELOPMENT OF SELF

It has been demonstrated (Gallup & Suarez, 1986) that only humans nd certain species of apes are capable of recognizing their mirror images. All other species fail to recognize themselves, regardless of how long they re exposed to their images. This was determined by exposing chimpanzees nd orangutans to mirrors for a few days. At first, the apes treated their nirror images as if they were unfamiliar companions. But soon the apes egan to exhibit self-directed behavior. They made faces at the mirror, icked their teeth, blew bubbles, and used the mirror to groom parts of heir bodies they could not otherwise see. To confirm self-recognition, the apes were anesthetized and a mark was put on their faces. When they awakened and were shown their faces in the mirror, they put their finger where the mark was and tried to rub it off.

Biochemical and genetic studies (Yunis & Prakash, 1982) show that humans and the great apes are closely related. Evolution might be a biological explanation for self-recognition. If so, there must be an advantage to being aware of oneself. Gallup and Suarez (1986) believe that the ability to be aware of oneself is the cognitive precursor of the ability to understand others; by understanding one's experiences, one can infer the experiences of others. If one can infer and anticipate the experiences of others, one can respond to them appropriately—be empathetic, provide assistance, run away, fight, be deceptive, and so on. Such responses are advantageous for successful survival. Further evidence for a biological explanation of self development comes from the correlation of self-recognition in humans with the development of the brain, specifically increases in neural connections during the first two years of life.

Gallup and Suarez (1986) conclude that humans and certain species of apes possess a cognitive category in their brains that is essential for processing information about themselves and that self-concept emerges from this biological capacity rather than from experience. Others, especially those who subscribe to learning theories, disagree (Epstein & Koerner, 1986).

Wilson (1975), a sociobiologist, believes that the genes construct a brain organized so that it processes information a certain way. The genes dictate the pattern of neural structures. These structures impose the regularities in thinking and behavior that are reinforced by one's culture. Perhaps the development of the self originates in these structures and grows as a result of experience, or interaction with the environment.

## CONTEXTUAL INFLUENCES ON DEVELOPMENT OF SELF

The self-concept relates to how an individual perceives himself and his behavior. It is strongly influenced by the way others perceive him. Self esteem, or the evaluation of one's self-concept, relates to how one feels one has measured up to others' perceptions and expectations.

In general., a child who is accepted, approved of, and respected is one who will develop high self-esteem; a child who is rejected, criticized, and humiliated will develop low self-esteem.

### FAMILY

The family is the first context in which a child's self-concept is influenced. Briggs (1975) poignantly describes how infants gather general impressions about themselves from how they are treated before they understand words:

> Mother A focuses on her baby rather than the task to be done. She is relaxed when she holds him. She talks to him when she feeds him. She soothes him when he's tense. She responds to his smile with delight and she tickles him to get him to laugh. Her baby is getting early experiences that foster the sense he is valued.

> Mother B reads or talks on the phone while she feeds her baby. If he looks at her she is too engrossed to respond. She

These young ballerinas are likely to have high self-esteem due to the constant encouragement from family members, peers, and dance teachers.

rushes through his bath not taking time to talk or play or soothe him to accustom him to the water. She tenses up when he cries and jostles him and yells to get him to stop. This baby's early experiences give him a sense of rejection. (Briggs, 1975)

After children understand words, they label themselves as good or bad, coordinated or clumsy, and so on, according to the way others communicate with them. Statements such as "You're a bad boy," "When are you going to grow up?" result in low self-esteem. Statements such as "You're such a good eater," "You were so nice to share your toys" result in high self-esteem.

Research shows that the way parents relate to children influences development of self. For example, Marcia (1980; 1991) found parent-child relationships to be related to identity status among youth. Males in the status of *identity achievement* were most likely to have fathers who spent a lot of time interacting with them, praised their son's efforts, and exerted moderate control over their behavior. Males in the status of *identity foreclosure* were likely to come from families with dominant fathers who exerted considerable pressure to conform to family values. Males in the *identity moratorium* status appeared to have ambivalent relationships with their parents and were likely to view their parents as being disappointed with them. Males in the *identity diffusion* status were likely to perceive themselves as being rejected by their parents, particularly their fathers.

The picture for females is similar with identity-achievement females reporting close ties with their mothers, identity-foreclosure females coming from close families that encourage conformity, identity-moratorium females critical of their mothers yet still feeling affection for them, and identity-diffusion females reporting distance from their mothers.

Identity achievement for both genders was found to be related to self-esteem.

The way parents encourage or discourage their children has an impact of the child's development of self.

## SCHOOL

School is a context in which much self-development occurs. Children learn how to read, write, compute, cooperate, and compete. School achievement is related to high self-esteem (Wylie, 1979; Bednar, Wells & Peterson, 1989). Achievement affects a student's perceptions of his own abilities and others' perceptions of those abilities as well. For example, in a study of third through ninth graders, it was found that achievement in school influenced students' estimations of their competence. This estimation of their competence influenced their motivation to achieve (Harter & Connell, 1982). The relation between actual achievement and motivation to achieve works like this:

Two females have had about equal experiences in their exposure to science. One gets a good grade on the first science test; the other does poorly. The female who got the good grade is likely to think "I'm pretty good at science" and, therefore, will learn more about the subject, which will enable her to do well on the next test. If she does do well, her concept of herself as being good in science is confirmed. On the other hand, the female who did poorly in the test is likely to think "I can't do science " and, therefore, will not be optimally prepared for the next test. If she does not do well, her concept of herself as being bad in science is confirmed.

## PEERS

Belonging to a peer group is part of the process of developing an identity. As adolescents, children are identified by the group they are associated with. So group identity is a precursor to individual identity. This is because, as the child strives for independence from parents and in so doing rejects their support, she turns to peers to fill the void. The peer group is an important source of self-confirmation in that children learn by comparing their thoughts and feelings with those of others. They need reassurance that others share their perceptions, wishes, fears, and doubts and that others value them for who they are.

In trying to establish an identity, the child usually tries to be different in some way from the parents. This generally involves choice of clothes, hairstyle, language, music, and in some cases, values. It is easier to be different *with* others than to do it alone. Others provide support and serve as role models. To demonstrate the appeal of peer groups, a study of 766 students entering adolescence found that the youth spent more than twice as much time with peers as with parents during a weekend (Condry, Simon & Bronfenbrenner, 1968).

Peer groups, especially of children approaching adolescence, are clannish and sometimes cruel in their exclusion of those who are different from the group. Erikson (1963) explains this behavior as a defense against a sense of identity confusion. In entering the *identity versus role confusion* stage, preadolescents look to the peer group for their identity. The group's ways of dressing, behaving, attitudes, opinions, and approval and support help define what is good and what is bad thereby contributing to the development of self. Identifying with a group and excluding those who are not like the group members help children identify who they are by affirming who they are not. As children approach the end of adolescence, they begin to derive an identity from the accumulation of their experiences, abilities, and goals. They begin to look within themselves rather than to others for who they are.

Thus, while young children look to parents and other significant adults for their concept of self, children approaching adolescence (ages 11 to 13) look to peers. However, toward the end of adolescence (ages 16 to 18), children begin to look to themselves. This was documented by Berndt (1978) who found eleventh and twelfth graders to show signs of developing a decision-making style more independent of peer and parent influence than in previous years.

## CULTURE

Culture is the setting in which the self is expressed. It also provides the standards and values against which the self is judged. All cultures have means by which individuals are recognized and accepted as members. Some cultures have formal initiation ceremonies. These ceremonies usually coincide with the cultural conception of maturity and serve to complete the person's identity by teaching the person the expected adult role. At the completion of the ceremony, the individual is regarded by the members of the culture as having a separate identity; he is no longer a child whose identity is meshed with his family. Certain privileges and responsibilities come with that identity. The term for these ceremonies coined by anthropologist Van Gennep (1960) is **rites of passage**. They usually occur at puberty for both genders.

## F.Y.I.

The status of a new initiate into a primitive culture is usually proclaimed by visible signs such as body scars, pierced ears, and tatooing. The initiate is then allowed to participate in adult activities, including reproduction.

The ways initiation rites are conducted vary widely in different cultures (Muus, 1970). Generally, for females the initiation ceremony is likely to center on the onset of menstruation. The female is usually secluded from men and receives special instruction from an older woman in matters pertaining to sex, marriage, and childbearing. The conclusion of the period is marked by a feast or dance where the female is publicly adorned in some manner.

For males, the initiation ceremony involves separation from their families, circumcision, learning roles in the culture from older men, and public displays of endurance and courage. For example, Arunta boys of central Australia must go through a series of demanding tasks designed to test their manhood, to teach obedience, and to impart the secrets of the tribe.

In American society there is no consensus as to when an individual should be recognized as having attained an adult identity, a self. Instead of a single passage rite, there are several sequential passages, such as getting a driver's license (giving one the privilege and responsibility to drive), having a sweet 16 party (giving one the privilege and responsibility to date), graduating from high school (giving one the privilege and responsibility to make choices about one's future). In addition, specific subcultures or ethnic groups retain initiation ceremonies, especially around the theme of religious commitment. Status is recognized by ceremonies such as baptism, communion, bar or bat mitzvah, and confirmation.

Thus, the society or culture into which one is born influences the development of self in that it imparts certain privileges and responsibilities at certain ages thereby influencing one's supply of behaviors. It also imparts certain values and expectations. One's conformity to these values and expectations affects one's self-esteem. Havighurst (1972) coined the term *developmental task* to describe what society expects of individuals at certain points in their development; "the successful achievement of which leads to happiness and success with later tasks, while failure leads to unhappiness in the individual., disapproval by the society, and difficulty with later tasks."

Havighurst outlined eight major developmental tasks for the adolescent period, the accomplishment thereof leading to a self recognized by the adult community:

1. Accepting one's physique and using the body effectively
2. Achieving new and more mature relations with agemates of both sexes
3. Achieving a masculine or feminine social role
4. Achieving emotional independence from parents and other adults
5. Preparing for an economic career
6. Preparing for marriage and family life
7. Desiring and achieving socially responsible behavior
8. Acquiring a set of values and an ethical system as a guide to behavior (developing an ideology)

By achieving each task, one has established an individual identity by our cultural standards.

Arunta rites include separating the boy from women at about age 10 or 12, beating him and circumcising him. After recovery in the company of other initiates, there is a period of several months of celebration, which ends when the boy goes through tests of bravery—for example, having to kneel down on hot coals. The culmination of the rite of passage is receiving a symbolic object from the chief to designate manhood (Spencer & Gillen, 1966).

# INTERACTION OF BIOLOGICAL AND CONTEXTUAL INFLUENCES ON DEVELOPMENT OF SELF

According to a study by Sheldon (1940), body types can be classified into three types—*endomorphy*, *mesomorphy*, and *ectomorphy*, as shown in figure 15.6. **Endomorphy** refers to the body type of having primarily fat tissue; **mesomorphy** refers to the body type of having primarily muscle tissue; and **ectomorphy** refers to the body type of having primarily lean tissue. Most people are combinations of these types, but one type usually dominates, determined by a combination of physical measurements.

Sheldon suggested that human behavior is influenced by the body build and the genetic and physiological qualities that influence the physique. He studied 200 men over five years and clustered their personality traits into three groups:

- **Viscerotonia**—cluster of personality traits that includes love of food and comfort, being relaxed, and enjoying people.
- **Somatotonia**—cluster of personality traits characterized by a desire for power and dominance, a zest for physical activity and adventure, and relative indifference to other people.
- **Cerebrotonia**—cluster of personality traits that includes self-consciousness, inhibition, overreactiveness, and a preference for being alone.

**FIGURE 15.6**
**SHELDON'S CLASSIFICATION OF BODY-TYPE EXTREMES**

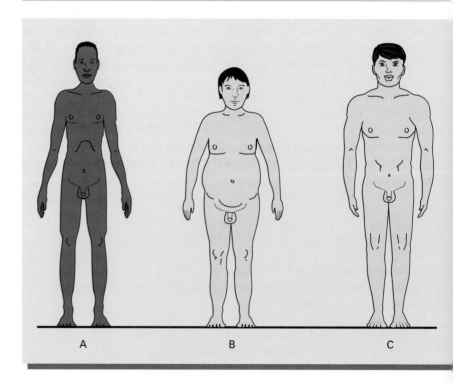

A   B   C

Sheldon found a relation between viscerotonia and endomorphy (fat subjects were lazy and jolly), somatotonia and mesomorphy (muscular subjects were assertive), cerebrotonia and ectomorphy (thin subjects were nervous and inhibited).

Biology plays a role in the perception of the self because certain physiques foster some behavior patterns over others. For example, a muscular body generally has more strength and energy than a fat one or a thin one. Strength and energy are needed to fight as well as in athletics. Thus, someone who is primarily a mesomorph might be advantaged in competitive sports. Participating in sports contributes to the development of strength and muscles, which contributes to enhanced performance and leads one to feel good about oneself. A fat body, on the other hand, is likely to carry excess weight, which makes it difficult to move quickly. Thus, the endomorph may appear to be relaxed or sluggish and may be disadvantaged in competitive sports so chooses to not engage in such activities because these activities make him feel bad about himself.

Another explanation of the role biology plays in the perception of the self is that significant people in various contexts (family, school, peer group, culture) have certain behavioral expectations for each body type and, therefore, reinforce certain exhibited characteristics. To illustrate, Staffieri (1967) studied the reactions of 90 males from six to ten years of age when presented with silhouettes that represented extreme endomorphy, mesomorphy, and ectomorphy. The males described the endomorph as someone who gets teased, lies, is stupid and dirty. The mesomorph was characterized as being strong, healthy, clean, and having many friends. The ectomorph was described as being quiet, afraid, worrisome, lonely, and sad. Such stereotypes are prevalent and are reinforced by media. They are already found in five-year-old children (Lerner & Korn, 1972). Thus, a thin person is assumed to be nervous and hyperactive, thus may become so in order to conform to the image of others.

In summary, the self is influenced by the interaction of biological and contextual factors. Biology is significant in determining what one does with the body. Context is significant in imparting expectations on one because of the body.

Evidence from various cultures indicates that satisfaction with one's body is influenced by self-imposed stereotypes (Mizuno et al., 1968). For example, in our culture males generally want to be taller and more muscular and females want to be thinner; the ideal physique is the mesomorph. One study (Tucker, 1983) showed a relation between self-esteem and how close one's actual physical self conformed to one's ideal physical self. The larger the discrepancy, the greater was the tendency to have low self-esteem.

## IS SELF-AWARENESS BIOLOGICALLY, CONTEXTUALLY, OR INTERACTIONALLY INFLUENCED?

Schneider-Rosen, K., & Cicchetti, D. (1991). Early self-knowledge and emotional development: Visual self-recognition and affective reactions to mirror self-images in maltreated toddlers. *Developmental Psychology, 27* (3), 471–478.

The development of self-awareness during infancy and early childhood has been examined through studies of visual self-recognition, which is a cognitive skill. For example, children of different ages have been observed looking into a mirror. Then, after an investigator unobtrusively puts a spot of rouge on the child's nose, the child's behavior when placed in front of the mirror is again observed.

Because the developing cognitive ability of distinguishing the self from others may be paralleled by unique emotional reactions, the investigation of children's affective responses to mirror self-images may be one way of indexing the feeling component of the self. Until this study, the emotional, or feeling, component of visual self-recognition had focused predominantly on analyzing children's affective reactions to their self-images after the application of rouge to their noses. The problem with such an analysis is that it is difficult to determine whether a child's emotional reaction is to herself or to the rouge. To ameliorate this problem, the investigators separated the cognitive aspect of self-recognition from the emotional. They first recorded a child's spontaneous emotional reaction to her image in the mirror for a minimum of 30 seconds. They did this by making detailed codings of the emotional expressions displayed as the child observed herself in the mirror. Four general categories were coded, including mouth position, eye direction, eye openness, and eyebrow position. Four major facial patterns were derived from the individual categories:

1. Positive affective expression (corners of mouth raised, lips relaxed and/or mouth opened, eyes directed up and/or straight ahead, and eyes opened)
2. Negative affective expression (corners of mouth lowered, eyes diverted from mirror and/or directed downward, eyes slightly squinted and eyebrows furrowed)
3. Neutral/attentive face (squared upper or lower lip or relaxed mouth, eyes ahead and/or up, eyes opened)
4. Coy expression (corners of mouth raised, lips relaxed and/or mouth opened, immediately followed by gaze aversion and then glances back to the mirror, sometimes repeated several times)

After a child's spontaneous emotional reaction to his mirror image was recorded, the child's capacity for visual self-recognition was assessed. An experimenter turned the child away from the mirror and secretly wiped some blue rouge on the child's nose. The experimenter then redirected the child back to the mirror, and the child's response to his image was observed. The cognitive capacity for visual self-recognition was operationally defined as touching one's reflection in the mirror. Any direct acknowledgement that the child recognized himself by stating his name while looking at his mirror image was also considered to be an index of visual self-recognition.

The sample for this study consisted of 250 maltreated and nonmaltreated children. The nonmaltreated children represented lower and middle socioeconomic statuses, whereas the maltreated children represented only the lower socioeconomic status. Children were assessed cross sectionally at 18, 24, and 30 months. Maltreated children were chosen for investigation to provide a more complete understanding of contextual variables that might mediate the development of self-awareness. Investigations have documented that maltreated children display delays or deviations in their emotional development, specifically as it relates to the self. For example, maltreated children have been described as having low self-esteem.

Thus, the specific purpose of this study was to examine the developing cognitive awareness of the self as distinct from others and the emotional responses to mirror self-images of maltreated and nonmaltreated lower and middle socioeconomic status children at 18, 24, and 30 months of age.

This study found there were developmental increases in the capacity to recognize mirror self-images, and this ability was not affected by socioeconomic status or the experience of maltreatment. Thus, it appears that biological maturation is responsible for the cognitive ability of visual self-recognition.

Regarding the emotional responses to the mirror self-image, the results indicated there is not a simple relation among age, maltreatment, socioeconomic status, and affective reactions. The data suggest there are multiple influences on the feeling component of the self. For those children who demonstrated the cognitive capacity for visual self-recognition, there were certain patterns of affective responses. Both the maltreated and lower socioeconomic status children were equally likely to show positive or negative/neutral affect in response to their mirror self-images, whereas the middle socioeconomic status children were significantly more likely to display positive affect. The experience of maltreatment *and* of growing up in a lower class appears to impact the child's emotional development.

Thus, cognitive development, specifically the development of visual self-awareness and ability to consider the self as distinct from others, may have an impact on subsequent emotional development. However, the experience of maltreatment and socioeconomic status impact emotional development as well. Research on attachment explains this interaction. Children securely attached to primary caregivers have been found to be more autonomous thereby developing a sense of self at a relatively earlier age, compared with insecurely attached children.

In conclusion, while children's self-awareness can be biologically influenced, certain contextual experiences affect how they feel about themselves, which can, in turn, impact the time at which biological programming is exhibited.

# DISTURBANCES IN DEVELOPMENT OF SELF

We have discussed self-concept, or identity. However, what happens when the process of developing a self becomes disturbed? Because much of self-concept is influenced by the *way we look*, we will first focus on eating disorders to exemplify disturbances in the development of self. Also, because part of our concept is influenced by the way we behave, especially with others, we will then focus on substance abuse to illustrate a second type of disturbance in the development of self. Finally, because much of our self-concept is influenced by how we feel about ourselves, we will look at depression and suicide to exemplify still another disturbance. All these disturbances have in common low self-esteem.

## OBESITY

**Obesity** is the most prevalent eating disorder. It is commonly defined as weight that is 20 percent above recommended weight for a person's height and age (Katchadourian, 1977). Because being fat in our society

Continually forcing this child to finish his meal may influence his eating habits as he gets older and may result in obesity.

is regarded negatively, the obese person's self-concept is affected. The person may depreciate herself, become passive, withdrawn, or may excessively try to please others (Bruch, 1974).

There are theories explaining the causes of obesity; some are biological., some are contextual., and some point to the interaction between a person's biological makeup and contextual events. Biologically, obese people are often found to have metabolisms that differ from others of average weight. They also have a larger numbers of fat cells, which make weight maintenance more difficult for them (Bruch, 1974). Contextually, obese people are frequently found to have been overfed as children (Schowalter 1983). Some may eat to fulfill unmet needs (Stankard, 1980). The interaction of biology and context is exhibited in the fact that due to continual overeating, many obese individuals have lost the ability to recognize the sense of hunger or fullness, biological regulators of food intake.

Regardless of cause, obese individuals have a disturbance in their sense of autonomy, independence, and control.

## ANOREXIA NERVOSA

**Anorexia nervosa**, a nervous loss of appetite characterized by severe undereating, malnutrition, and extreme weight loss, also signals a problem in the development of self. The cause may be partially biological. The signs of anorexia nervosa are intense fear of becoming obese, which does not diminish as the person loses weight, a disturbance of body image in that the person perceives herself as fat, even though she is emaciated, having experienced a weight loss of 25 percent of original body weight (Garbarino 1985).

Anorexia nervosa is more common in females than in males; most cases develop before age 25 (Halmi, 1985). Although anorexics vary in their psychological characteristics, what they have in common is a disturbance in their self-concept. Generally, this is manifested by feelings of inadequacy and inferiority. They do not feel in control of their lives. Thus, they direct their energy into masking these negative feelings about themselves and projecting an image of the ideal, or perfect, person. Their perception of a perfect body image is someone who is thin (Schwartz, Thompson & Johnson, 1982). Self-denial of food is a way for them to gain control of their lives. Many come from families where obedience is expected and autonomy and independence are discouraged (Liebman, Sargent & Silver, 1983). Some anorexic females may fear growing up, especially becoming a sexual being and a person responsible for herself (Bruch, 1974). By starving herself, the anorectic's menses and development of fat tissue stop. The anorexic's appearance, then, remains prepubertal.

## BULIMIA NERVOSA

**Bulimia nervosa** is an eating disorder primarily characterized by the ingestion of enormous amounts of food (binging) and followed by fasting, self-induced vomiting, and/or use of laxatives and diuretics (purging). The desire to binge may be due to a deficiency in the hormone that gives one a sense of fullness. Like anorectics, bulimics are preoccupied with weight gain. They fear they cannot stop eating and therefore purge themselves after a food binge to avoid getting fat. They have been described as having poor impulse control (Pyle, Mitchell & Eckert, 1981), and they feel guilt and shame over their behavior, which causes them to purge after binging. Their weight often fluctuates but remains at or slightly above the recommended range. Like anorexia nervosa, bulimia nervosa is more common in females than males (Halmi, Falk & Schwartz, 1981). The disorder occurs most often in the late teens to early twenties. Like anorectics, bulimics differ in specific psychological characteristics but what they have in common is a disturbance in self-concept, which involves the need to be perfect, an obsessive concern with food and body proportions, low self-esteem, social withdrawal., and excessive preoccupation with pleasing others (Boskind-White & White, 1983). The bulimic has not achieved an autonomous selfhood and is still struggling for self-control.

## SUBSTANCE ABUSE

Using drugs (including alcohol and tobacco) to satisfy unmet psychological needs signifies a disturbance in development of self. Psychological or physical dependency on drugs, alcohol, or tobacco is termed as **substance abuse**. Low self-esteem is a factor in substance abuse (Reardon & Griffing, 1983) as well as the relationship with parents. Abusers report a negative relationship with parents including excessive parental control without warmth, indifference, and lack of communication (Rice, 1990). The individual may initially use drugs because of curiosity or social pressure, especially in adolescence. The continued use of drugs, however, is to relieve anxiety and pressure and to escape from problems, particularly problems associated with developing an identity (making choices and commitments for the future). The substance abuser has not developed confidence in himself and turns to drugs to avoid becoming an independent, responsible, contributing individual.

## DEPRESSION

Seligman (1975) relates depression to *learned helplessness,* a feeling of having no control over what happens. **Depression** involves the development of unrealistically negative feelings, self-image, and expectations (Reynolds, 1976). Depressed individuals are extremely sad and withdraw from others. They tell themselves they are failures and begin to assume responsibility for everything bad that happens. Their behavior becomes increasingly self-destructive (Coleman, Butcher & Carson, 1980).

Depression can be due to a combination of causes, biological and contextual. Lack of support in dealing with an irretrievable loss, such as death or divorce, in childhood is commonly mentioned (Fuhrmann, 1986).

Depression, especially when prolonged, can lead to suicide (Cosand, Bourque & Kraus, 1982). Suicide is rare in childhood, but increases dramatically at age 15 (Fuhrmann, 1986). Suicidal adolescents feel alienated, alone, and unable to cope. Their emotional needs have not been met due to loss of a parent, parental detachment, or conflict (Caine, 1979), and they have not found a meaningful substitute attachment figure. They are in despair, hopeless, helpless, and out of contact with significant others. They have lost their sense of self and view death as the only thing left.

# CRITICAL THINKING & YOU

**ANALYSIS:** Being as objective as possible, describe yourself. Include physical self (appearance and physical ability), social self (relations with others), academic self, creative self, and emotional self.

**SYNTHESIS:** Using evidence from this chapter, describe five influences on your self-development.

**EVALUATION:** How would you rate your self-esteem? Why? Review this chapter and provide at least three reasons to support your self-evaluation

## SUMMARY

- Self-concept includes perception of the body as distinct; knowledge about abilities, wishes, beliefs, actions; personal ethical code; and feelings about oneself.
- The first task in developing a self-concept is the recognition that one is a separate being who initiates and controls his actions. The first sign of recognition of self has been demonstrated by infants' ability to recognize themselves in a mirror. This ability appears between 15 to 18 months and seems to develop with the concept of object permanence.
- Mahler believes the process of recognizing oneself as an individual., separate from one's mother, takes about three years.
- Erikson believes the sense of identity begins with a sense of trust. This occurs the first year. Building on a sense of trust is a sense of autonomy. This occurs between two and three years of age. Building on a sense of autonomy is a sense of initiative, this begins about age four.
- By preschool age, children understand they are separate beings with names, and they can perceive themselves in concrete terms.
- By schoolage, children begin to describe themselves in terms of personal qualities. Their self-con-

cept is influenced by whether they have a sense of industry. This occurs between ages 6 to 12. They also begin to consider how others perceive them.
- Adolescents have a more flexible and abstract sense of self. As they focus on their developing identities, they become self-conscious, which diminishes as they reach adulthood.
- Physical changes in puberty impact adolescent self image. Whether one matures early or late compared with friends affects how one views oneself.
- Establishing a sense of identity is a major developmental task of adolescence. According to Marcia this involves making certain commitments such as choosing a career and consolidating a personal ethical code. The four statuses, or ways of resolving the crisis of establishing an identity, are identity diffusion, identity foreclosure, identity moratorium, and identity achievement.
- A component of the self is self-esteem, which refers to the value an individual places on her identity and how one emerges from interactions with others. Influences on self-esteem include general satisfaction with life, relationship with others (especially parents), and achievements.
- Self-esteem is related to perception of control over life. Those who feel they have the power to determine what happens to them (an internal locus of control) tend to have high self-esteem. Those who

feel that what happens to them is a matter of luck or fate and they have little control over what happens to them (an external locus of control) tend to have low self-esteem. When people continually perceive of themselves as pawns of external circumstances, they feel hopeless and quit. They have learned helplessness.

A biological explanation of the development of self involves the organization of the brain. It is biologically advantageous to recognize oneself because the ability to be aware of oneself is the cognitive precursor of the ability to understand others. By understanding one's experiences, one can understand and respond appropriately to others' experiences.

- A contextual explanation of the development of self is that how one perceives oneself depends on how she is perceived by others. Contexts in influencing the development of self are the family, school, peers, and culture.

- Biology and context interact to explain the development of self in terms of body type. Genetic and physiological attributes of the physique influence what the individual can do and how others perceive the individual. Others' perceptions influence how the individual perceives himself. How one's physique conforms to the cultural ideal of body type (mesomorph in our culture) influences the self-esteem.

- Disturbances in self-development are exhibited in eating disorders such as obesity, anorexia nervosa, and bulimia and in substance abuse and depression.

## RELATED READINGS

Briggs, D.C. (1975). *Your child's self-esteem.* New York: Dolphin.

Coopersmith, S. (1967). *The antecedents of self-esteem.* San Francisco: Freeman.

Damon, W. & Hart, D. (1990). *Self understanding in childhood and adolescence.* New York: Cambridge University Press.

Erikson, E.H. (1968). *Identity: Youth and crisis.* New York: Norton.

James, M. & Jongeward, D. (1977). *Born to win.* Reading, MA: Addison-Wesley.

Kaplan, L.J. (1978). *Oneness and separateness: From infant to individual.* New York: Touchstone.

Ollendick, T.H. & Hersen, M. (Eds.). (1989). *Handbook of child psychopathology* (2nd. ed.). New York: Plenum.

Rosenberg, M. (1979). *Conceiving the self.* New York: Basic Books.

Seligman, M.E.P. (1975). *Helplessness.* San Francisco: W. H. Freeman.

Vandenberg, S.G., Singer, S.M. & Pauls, D.L. (1986). *The heritability of behavior disorders in adults and children.* New York: Plenum.

## ● ● ● ● ● ● ● ● ● ● ● ● ● ● ● ● ● ●  ACTIVITY  ● ● ● ● ● ● ● ● ● ● ● ● ● ● ● ● ● ●

To gain a better understanding of how the self develops, interview two preschoolers (one boy and one girl, aged four or five), two schoolagers (one boy and one girl, aged nine or ten), and two adolescents (one boy and one girl, aged 14 or 15).

1. Ask each one to describe himself.
2. Record what each one says.

3. Analyze the descriptions by age as to specifics (name, age, gender), personal qualities ("pretty," "smart," "good runner"), comparative qualities ("better than," "not as good as"), and abstract qualities ("truthful," "relaxed").
4. Analyze the descriptions by gender—differences and similarities among males and females.

# REFERENCES

Aamodt, A.M. (1975, August). *Social cultural dimensions of the concept of caring in the world of the Papago child.* Proceedings of the Transcultural Nursing Conference on Infants and Children. Snowbird, UT.

Abbeduto, L., Davis, B., & Furman, L. (1988). The development of speech act comprehension in mentally retarded individuals and nonretarded children. *Child Development, 59,* 1460–1472.

Abboud, T.K., Khoo, S.S., Miller, F., Doan, T., & Henriksen, E.H. (1982). Maternal fetal and neonatal responses after epidural anesthesia with bupivacaine, 2-chloroprocaine, or zedocaine. *Anesthesia and Analgesia, 61,* 638–643.

Abel, E.L. (1984). *Fetal alcohol syndrome and fetal alcohol effects.* New York: Plenum.

Abel, E.L. (1984). Smoking and pregnancy. *Journal of Psychoactive Drugs, 16*(327), 338.

Acredolo, L.P., & Hake, J.L. (1982). Infant perception. In B.B. Wolman (Ed.), *Handbook of developmental psychology.* Englewood Cliffs, NJ: Prentice-Hall.

Acredolo, L.P., Adams, A., & Goodwyn, S.W. (1984). The role of self-produced movement and visual tracking in infant spatial orientation. *Journal of Experimental Child Psychology, 38,* 312–327.

Adams, G.K. (1991). Physical attractiveness and adolescent development. In R.M. Lerner, A.C. Petersen, & J. Brooks-Gunn (Eds.), *Encyclopedia of adolescence.* (Vol. 2). New York: Garland.

Adler, A. (1927). *Practice and theory of individual psychology.* New York: Harcourt Brace Jovanovich.

Adler, J., & Carey, J. (1982). But is it a person? *Newsweek,* January 11, p. 44.

Ahr, P.R., & Youniss, J. (1970). Reasons for failure on the class inclusion problem. *Child Development, 41,* 131–143.

Aiken, S., & Bower, T.G.R. (1982). Intersensory substitutions in the blind. *Journal of Experimental Child Psychology, 33,* 309–323.

Ainsworth, M.D.S. (1973). The development of infant-mother attachment. In B.M. Caldwell & H.N. Ricciuti (Eds.), *Review of child development research.* (Vol. 3). Chicago: University of Chicago Press.

Ainsworth, M.D.S., Blehar, M., Waters, E., & Wall, S. (1978). *Patterns of attachment: A psychological study of the strange situation.* Hillsdale, NJ: Erlbaum.

Alexander, K.L., Cook, M., & McDill, E.L. (1977). *Curriculum tracking and educational stratifications: Some further evidence.* Baltimore, MD: Johns Hopkins University Center for Social Organization of Schools, Report No. 237.

Allen, M.C., & Capute, A.J. (1986). Assessment of early auditory and visual abilities of extremely premature infants. *Developmental Medicine and Child Neurology, 28,* 458–466.

American Academy of Pediatrics. (1989). *Focus on crack babies: A fact sheet.* Elk Grove Village, IL.

American Fertility Society. (1991). *Investigation of the infertile couple.* Birmingham, AL.

American Psychiatric Association. (1987). *Diagnostic and statistical manual of mental disorders* (3rd ed.). Washington, DC.

American Speech-Language Hearing Association (Committee on Language, Speech, and Hearing Services in the Schools) (1980). Definitions for communicative disorders and differences. *ASHA, 22,* 317–318.

Amoore, J.E. (1965). Psychophysics of odor. *Cold Springs Harbor Symposia in Quantitative Biology, 30,* 623–637.

Anders, T.F., & Chaldemian, R.J. (1974). The effect of circumcision of sleep-wake states in human neonates. *Psychosomatic Medicine, 36,* 174–179.

Anderson, D.R., Lorch, E.P., Field D.E., Collins, P.A., & Nathan, J.G. (1986). Television viewing at home: Age trends in visual attention and time with TV. *Child Development, 57,* 1024–1033.

Antell, S.E., Caron, A.J., & Myers, R.S. (1985). Perception of relational invariants by newborns. *Developmental Psychology, 21,* 942–948.

Apgar, V., & Beck, J. (1974). *Is my baby all right?* New York: Pocket Books.

Apgar, V. (1953). Proposal for a new method of evaluation of the newborn infant. *Anesthesia and Analgesia, 32,* 260.

Applebaum, M.I., & McCall, R.B. (1983). Design and analysis in developmental psychology. In P.H. Mussen (Ed.), *Handbook of child psychology* (4th ed.). (Vol. 1). New York: Wiley.

Apter, S.J., & Conoley, J.C. (1984). *Childhood behavior disorders and emotional disturbance.* Englewood Cliffs, NJ: Prentice-Hall.

Archer, J., & Lloyd, B. (1982). *Sex and gender.* Harmondsworth, Middlesex, England: Penguin Books.

Arjavalingam, V. (1989). *Summary of infant health statistics.* White Plains, NY: March of Dimes Birth Defects Foundation.

Aro, H., & Taipale, V. (1987). The impact of timing of puberty on psychosomatic symptoms among fourteen-to-sixteen-year old Finnish girls. *Child Development, 58,* 261–268.

Aronfreed, J. (1968). *Conduct and conscience: The socialization of internalized control over behavior*. New York: Academic Press.

Aronfreed, J., & Reber, A. (1965). Internalized behavioral suppression and the timing of social punishment. *Journal of Personality and Social Psychology, 1*, 3–16.

Asher, S.R. (1982). Some kids are nobody's best friend. *Today's Education, 71*, 23.

Asher, S.R., Gottman, J.M., & Oden, S.L. (1977). Children's friendship in school settings. In E.M. Hetherington & R.D. Parke (Eds.), *Contemporary readings in child psychology*. New York: McGraw-Hill.

Aslin, R.N. (1981). Experiential influences and sensitive periods in perceptual development: A unified model. In R.N. Aslin, J.R. Alberts, & M.R. Petersen (Eds.), *Development of perception: Psychobiological perspectives, Vol. 2 The visual system*. New York: Academic Press.

Aslin, R.N., Pisoni, D.B., & Jusczyk, P.W. (1983). Auditory development and speech perception in infancy. In P.H. Mussen (Ed.), *Handbook of child psychology* (4th ed.). (Vol. 2). New York: Wiley.

Atkinson, J., & Braddick, O. (1982). Sensory and perceptual capacities of the neonate. In P. Stratton (Ed.), *Psychobiology of the human newborn*. New York: Wiley.

Atkinson, R.C., & Shiffrin, R.M. (1971). The control of short-term memory. *Scientific American, 225*, 85–90.

Ault, R.L. (1983). *Children and cognitive development* (2nd ed.). New York: Oxford University Press.

Baillargeon, R. (1986). Representing the existence and the location of hidden objects: Object permanence in 6- and 8-month-old infants. *Cognition, 23*, 21–41.

Baillargeon, R., & DeVos, J. (1992). Object permanence in young infants: Further evidence. *Child Development, 62* 1227–1246.

Baldwin, D.A., & Markman, E.M. (1989). Establishing word-object relations: A first step. *Child Development, 60* 381–398.

Bandura, A. (1962). Social learning through imitation. In M.R. Jones (Ed.), *Nebraska symposium on motivation* Lincoln, NE: University of Nebraska Press.

Bandura, A. (1965). Influence of models reinforcement contingencies on the acquisition of imitative responses *Journal of Personality and Social Psychology, 1*, 589–595.

Bandura, A. (1969). Social learning theory of identificatory processes. In D.A. Goslin (Ed.), *Handbook of socialization theory and research*. Chicago: Rand McNally.

Bandura, A. (1974). Behavior theory and the models of man. *American Psychologist, 29*, 859–869.

Bandura, A. (1977). *Social learning theory*. Englewood Cliffs, NJ: Prentice-Hall.

Bandura, A. (1986). *Social foundations of thought and action: A social cognitive theory*. Englewood Cliffs NJ: Prentice-Hall.

Bandura, A. (1989). Social cognitive theory. In R. Vasta (Ed.), *Annals of child development, vol. 6: Six theories of child development*. Greenwich, CT: JAI Press.

Bandura, A., Ross, D., & Ross, S.A. (1961). Transmission of aggressive models. *Journal of Abnormal Social Psychology, 63*, 572–582.

Bandura, A., Ross, D., & Ross, S.A. (1963). Imitation of film-mediated models. *Journal of Abnormal and Social Psychology, 66*, 3–11.

Banks, M.S., & Bennett, P.J. (1988). Optical and photoreceptor immaturities limit the spatial and chromatic vision of human neonates. *Journal of the Optical Society of America, 5*, 2050–2070.

Banks, M.S., & Salapatek, P. (1978). Acuity and contrast sensitivity in 1-, 2-, and 3-month-old human infants *Investigative Opthalmology and Visual Science, 17*, 361–365.

Banks, M.S., & Salapatek, P. (1983). Infant visual perception. In P.H. Mussen (Ed.), *Handbook of Child Psychology* (4th ed.). (Vol. 2). New York: Wiley.

Barclay, L.K. (1985). *Infant development*. New York: Holt, Rinehart & Winston.

Bardouille-Crema, A., Black, K.N., & Feldhusen, J. (1986). Performance on Piagetian tasks of black children of differing socioeconomic levels. *Developmental Psychology, 22*, 841–844.

Barinaga, M. (1991). Is homosexuality biological? *Science, 253*, 956–957.

Barker, R.G., & Gump, P.V. (1964). *Big school, small school: High school size and student behavior*. Stanford, CA Stanford University Press.

Barnes, A., et al. (1980). Fertility and outcome of pregnancy in women exposed in utero to diethylstilbesterol. *New England Journal of Medicine, 302*, 609–613.

Barnes, D.M. (1989). "Fragile X" syndrome and its puzzling genetics. *Science, 243*, 171–172.

Barnett, J.T. (1969). Development of children's fears: *The relationship between three systems of fear measurement.* Unpublished Master's thesis. University of Wisconsin.

Barr, H.M., Streissguth, A.P., Darby, B.L., & Sampson, P.D. (1990). Prenatal exposure to alcohol, caffeine, tobacco, and aspirin: Effects on fine and gross motor performance in 4-year-old children. *Developmental Psychology, 26*(3), 339–348.

Barrera, M.E., & Maurer, D. (1981a). Recognition of mother's photographed face by the three-month-old infant. *Child Development, 52,* 714–716.

Barrera, M.E., & Maurer, D. (1981b). Discrimination of strangers by the three-month-old. *Child Development, 52,* 558–563.

Barron, F.(1958). The psychology of imagination. *Scientific American, 199*(3), 150–170.

Bartol, B. (1986). Cocaine babies: Hooked at birth. *Newsweek,* July 28, 56–57.

Basow, S.A. (1992). *Gender stereotypes and roles* (3rd ed.). Pacific Grove, CA: Brooks/Cole.

Bates, E., & MacWhinney, B. (1982). Functionalist approaches to grammar. In E. Wanner & L. Gleitman (Eds.), *Language acquisition: The state of the art.* Cambridge, MA: Cambridge University Press.

Bates, J.E. (1982). *Temperament as part of social relationships: Implications of perceived infant difficulties.* Paper presented at the International Conference on Infant Studies. Austin, Texas.

Baumrind, D. (1966). Effects of authoritative parental control on child behavior. *Child Development, 37,* 887–907.

Baumrind, D. (1967). Child care practices anteceding three patterns of preschool behavior. *Genetic Psychology Monographs, 75,* 43–88.

Baumrind, D. (1971). Current patterns of parental authority. *Developmental Psychology Monographs, 4*(1), Pt. 2.

Baumrind, D. (1968). Authoritarian vs. authoritative parental control. *Adolescence, 3,* 255–272.

Bayley, N. (1935). The development of motor abilities during the first three years. *Monographs for the Society for Research in Child Development.* No. 1.

Bayley, N. (1955). On the growth of intelligence. *American Psychologist, 10,* 805–818.

Bayley, N. (1956). Individual Patterns of development. *Child Development, 27,* 45–74.

Bayley, N. (1969). *Bayley scales of infant development.* New York: Psychological Corp.

Bayley, N. (1970). Development of mental abilities. In P.H. Mussen (Ed.), *Carmichael's manual of child psychology* (3rd ed.). (Vol. 1). New York: Wiley.

Beardslee, W.R., & Mack, J.E. (1986). Youth and children and the nuclear threat. *Newsletter of the Society for Research in Child Development,* (Winter), 1–2.

Beardsley, L.V., & Marecek-Zeman, M. (1987). Making connections: Facilitating literacy in young children. *Childhood Education, 63,* 159–166.

Bednar, R.L., Wells, M.G., & Peterson, S.R. (1989). *Self-esteem.* Washington, DC: American Psychological Association.

Beisel, W.R. (1977). Magnitude of the host nutritional responses to infection. *American Journal of Clinical Nutrition, 30,* 1236–1247.

Bell, S.M., & Ainsworth, M.D.S. (1972). Infant crying and maternal responsiveness. *Child Development, 43,* 1171–1190.

Belsky, J. (1988). The "effects" of infant day care reconsidered. *Early Childhood Research Quarterly, 3,* 235–272.

Belsky, J., & Rovine, M.J. (1988). Nonmaternal care in the first year of life and the security of infant-parent attachment. *Child Development, 59,* 157–167.

Belsky, J., Taylor, D.G., & Rovine, M. (1984). The Pennsylvania infant and family development project II: The development of reciprocal interaction in the mother-infant dyad. *Child Development, 55,* 706–717.

Bem, S.L. (1974). The measurement of psychological androgyny. *Journal of Consulting and Clinical Psychology, 42,* 155–162.

Bem, S.L. (1981a). Gender schema theory: A cognitive account of sex-typing. *Psychological Review, 88,* 354–364.

Bem, S.L. (1981b). *Bem sex-role inventory, professional manual.* Palo Alto, CA: Consulting Psychologists Press.

Bem, S.L. (1983). Gender schema theory and its implications for child development: Raising gender-aschematic children in a gender-schematic society. *Signs, 8*(4), (Summer), 598–616.

Bem, S.L. (1989). Genital knowledge and gender constancy in preschool children. *Child Development, 60,* 649–662.

Berbaum, M.L., & Moreland, R.L. (1985). Intellectual development with in transracial adoptive families: Retesting the confluence model. *Child Development, 56,* 207–216.

Bereiter, C., & Engelmann, S. (1966). *Teaching disadvantaged children in the preschool.* Englewood Cliffs, NJ: Prentice-Hall.

Berenda, R. (1950). *The influences of the groups on the judgment of children.* New York: Kings Crown Press.

Berg, C.A., & Sternberg, R.J. (1985). *Novelty as a component of intelligence throughout development.* Paper presented at the Meeting of the Society for Research in Child Development. Toronto, April.

Berko, J. (1958). The child's learning of English morphology. *Word, 14,* 150–177.

Berkowitz, M.W., & Gibbs J.C. (1983). Measuring the developmental features of moral discussion. *Merrill-Palmer Quarterly, 29*(4), 399–410.

Berndt, T.J. (1978, August). Developmental changes in conformity to peers and parents. *Paper presented at the annual meeting of the American Psychological Association.* Toronto, Canada.

Berndt, T.J. (1979). Developmental changes in conformity to peers and parents. *Developmental Psychology 15,* 608–616.

Berndt, T.J., & Perry, T.B. (1990). Distinctive features and effects of early adolescent friendships. In R. Montemayor (Ed.), *Advances in adolescent research.* Greenwich, CT: JAI Press.

Berns, R. (1993). *Child, family, community* (3rd ed.). San Diego: Harcourt Brace Jovanovich.

Berrueta-Clement, J.R., Schweinhart, L.J., Barnett, W.S., Epstein, A.S., & Weikart, D.P. (1984). *Changed lives: The effects of the Perry preschool program on youths through age 19.* Ypsilanti, MI: High Scope Press.

Bertenthal, B.I., Campos, J.J., & Barrett, K.C. (1984). Self-produced locomotion: An organization of emotional, cognitive, and social development in infancy. In R.N. Emde & R.J. Harman (Eds.), *Continuities and discontinuities in development.* New York: Plenum.

Bertenthal, B.I., & Fischer K.W. (1978). Development of self-recognition in the infant. *Developmental Psychology, 14,* 44–50.

Bianchi, S.M. (1990). America's children: Mixed prospects. *Population Bulletin, 45*(1). Washington, DC: Population Reference Bureau.

Biggs, J.B., & Collis, K.R. (1982). *Evaluating the quality of learning the SOLO taxonomy (structure of the observed learning outcome).* New York: Academic Press.

Bijou, S.W. (1989). Behavior analysis. In R. Vasta (Ed.), *Annals of child development, vol. 6: Six theories of child development.* Greenwich, CT: JAI Press.

Bijou, S.W., & Baer, D.M. (1961). *Child development: A systematic and empirical theory.* (Vol. 1). Englewood Cliffs, NJ: Prentice-Hall.

Bijou, S.W., & Baer D.M. (1965). *Child development.* (Vol. 2). New York: Appleton-Century- Crofts.

Birch, H.G., & Lefford, A. (1963). Intersensory development in children. *Monographs of the Society for Research in Child Development, 25*(5), Serial No. 89.

Birch, L.L. (1990). Development of food acceptance patterns. *Developmental Psychology, 26,* 515–519.

Bjorklund, D.F., & DeMarchena, M.R. (1984). Developmental shifts in the basis of organization memory: The role of associative versus categorical relatedness in children's free recall. *Child Development, 55,* 952–962.

Blakemoore, C., & Cooper, G.F. (1970). Development of the brain depends on the visual environment. *Nature, 228,* 477–478.

Blasi, A. (1980). Bridging moral cognition and moral action: A critical review of the literature. *Psychological Bulletin, 88,* 593–637.

Blehar, M.C., Lieberman, A.F., & Ainsworth, M.D. (1977). Early face-to-face interaction and its relation to later infant-mother attachment. *Child Development, 48,* 182–194.

Block, J.H. (1973). Conceptions of sex-role: Some cross-cultural and longitudinal perspectives. *American Psychologist, 28,* 512–526.

Bloom, B.S. (1964). *Stability and change in human characteristics.* New York: Wiley.

Bloom, B.S. (1973). Individual differences in achievement, In L.J. Rubin (Ed.), *Facts and feelings in the classroom.* New York: Viking.

Bloom, B.S. (1985). *Developing talent in young people.* New York: Ballantine Books.

Bloom, F.E., & Lazerson, A., & Hofstadter, L. (1988). *Brain, mind, and behavior* (2nd ed.). New York: W.H. Freeman.

Bloom, L. (1970). *Language development: Form and function in emerging grammars.* Cambridge, MA: MIT Press.

Blyth, D.A., Simmons, R.G., Bulcroft, R., Felt, D., VanCleave, E.F., & Bush, D.M. (1981). The effects of physical development on self-image and satisfaction with body-image for early adolescent males. In R.G. Simmons (Ed.), *Research in Community and Mental Health, 2,* 43–73. Greenwich, CT: JAI Press.

Blurton-Jones, N. (1972). Categories of child-child interaction. In N. Blurton-Jones (Ed.), *Ethological studies of child behavior*. Cambridge: Cambridge University Press.

Bobak, I.M., Jensen, M.D., & Zalar, M.K. (1989). *Maternity and gynecologic care*. St. Louis: C.V. Mosby.

Bohannon, J.N. III, & Warren-Leubecker, A. (1985). Theoretical approaches to language acquisition. In J. Berko Gleason (Ed.), *The development of language*. Westerville, OH: Merrill.

Bonjean, C.M., & McGee, R. (1965). Scholastic dishonesty among undergraduates in differing systems of social control. *Sociology of Education, 38*, 127–137.

Bornstein, M.H. (1976). Infants are trichromats. *Journal of Experimental Child Psychology, 21*, 421–445.

Bornstein, M.H. (1988). Perceptual development across the life cycle. In M.H. Bornstein & M.E. Lamb (Eds.), *Developmental psychology: An advanced textbook* (2nd ed.). Hillsdale, NJ: Erlbaum.

Bornstein, M.H., & Ruddy M.G. (1984). Infant attention and maternal stimulation. In H. Bouma & D.G. Bouwhuis (Eds.), *Attention and performance*. (Vol. 10). London: Erlbaum.

Bornstein, M.H., & Sigman M.D. (1986). Continuity in mental development from infancy. *Child Development, 57*, 251–274.

Boskind-White, M., & White, W.C. (1983). *Bulimarexia: The binge/purge cycle*. New York: W.W. Norton.

Bouchard, C. (1978). Genetics, growth and physical activity. In F. Landry & W.A.R. Orban (Eds.), *Physical activity and well-being*. Miami, FL: Symposia Specialists Inc., 29–45.

Bouchard, T.J. Jr., Lykken, D.T., McGue, M., Segal, N.L., & Tellegen, A. (1990). Sources of human psychological differences: The Minnesota study of twins reared apart. *Science, 250*, 223–250.

Bouchard, T.J., & McGue, M. (1981). Familial studies of intelligence: A review. *Science, 212*, 1056.

Bouchard, T.J. Jr., Lykken, D.T., McGue, M., Segal, N.L., & Tellegen, A. (1990). Sources of human psychological differences. Minnesota study of twins reared apart. *Science, 250*, 223–250.

Boukydis, C.F.Z., & Burgess R.L. (1982). Adult physiological response to infant cries: Effects of temperament of infant, parental status and gender. *Child Development, 53*, 1291–1298.

Bower, T.G.R. (1971). The object in the world of the infant. *Scientific American, 2225*, 30–38.

Bower, T.G.R. (1977). *The perceptual world of the child*. Cambridge, MA: Harvard University Press.

Bower, T.G.R. (1982). *Development in infancy* (2nd ed.). San Francisco: W.H. Freeman.

Bowerman, M. (1973). *Early syntactic development: A cross-linguistic study with special reference to Finnish*. Cambridge, England: Cambridge University Press.

Bowlby, J. (1958). The nature of the child's tie to his mother. *International Journal of Psychoanalysis, 39*, 35.

Bowlby, J. (1969). *Attachment and loss (Vol. 1): Attachment*. New York: Basic Books, 1969.

Bowlby, J. (1973). *Separation and loss*. New York: Basic Books.

Bowlby, J. (1979). *The making and breaking of affectional bonds*. London: Tavisock Publications.

Bowlby, J. (1980). *Attachment and loss (Vol. 3): Loss, sadness, and depression*. New York: Basic Books.

Bowlby, J. (1982). *Attachment and loss (Vol. 1): Attachment* (2nd ed.). London: Hogarth Press.

Bowlby, J. (1988). *A secure base: Parent-child attachment and healthy human development*. New York: Basic Books.

Bowman, H.E., & Ahrons, C.R. (1985). Impact of legal custody status on fathers' parenting post-divorce. *Journal of Marriage & the Family, 47*, 481–488.

Brackbill, Y. (1979). Obstetrical medication and infant behavior. In J.D. Osofsky (Ed.), *Handbook of infant development*. New York: Wiley.

Brackbill, Y., & Nichols P.L. (1982). A test of the confluence model of intellectual development. *Developmental Psychology, 18*, 192–198.

Brackbill, Y., McManus, K., & Woodward, L. (1985). *Medication in maternity: Infant exposure and maternal information*. Ann Arbor, MI: University of Michigan Press.

Bradley, R.H., & Caldwell, B.M. (1976). The relation of infants' home environment to mental test performance at fifty-four months: A follow-up study. *Child Development, 47*, 1172–1174.

Braine M.D.S. (1963). The ontogeny of English phrase structure: The first phase. *Language, 39*, 3–13.

Brainerd, C.J. (1978). The stage question in cognitive-developmental theory. *Behavioral and Brain Sciences, 2*, 173–213.

Brainerd, C.J. (1983). Varieties of strategy training in Piagetian concept learning. In M. Pressley & J.L. Levin (Eds.), *Cognitive strategy research: Educational applications*. New York: Springer-Verlag.

Brainerd, C.J., & Brainerd, S.H. (1972). Order of acquisition of number of liquid quantity conservation. *Child Development, 43*, 1401–1405.

Bradley, R.H., & Caldwell, B.M. (1976). The relation of infants' home environments to mental test performance at fifty-four months: A follow-up study. *Child Development, 47,* 1171–1174.

Bradley, R.H., & Caldwell, B. (1984). The relation of infants' home environments to achievement test performance in first grade: A follow-up study. *Child Development, 55,* 803–809.

Bradley, R.H., Caldwell, B.M., & Rock, S.L. (1990). Home environment classification system: A model for assessing the home environments of developing children. *Early Education and Development, 1,* 237–265.

Brandstadter-Palmer, G. (1982). Ontogenetic growth chart. In C.B. Kopp, & J.B. Krakow (Eds.), *The child. Development in a social context.* Reading, MA: Addison-Wesley.

Bransford, J.D., et al. (1981). Cognition and adaptation: The importance of learning to learn. In J. Harvey (Ed.), *Cognition, social behavior, and the environment.* Hillsdale, NJ: Erlbaum.

Brazelton, T.B. (1973). *Neonatal behavior assessment scale.* London: Spastics International Medical Publications.

Brazelton, T.B. (1985). *Working and caring.* Reading, MA: Addison-Wesley.

Brazelton, T.B., Koslowski, B., & Main, M. (1974). The origins of reciprocity. The early mother-infant interactions. In M. Lewis & J. Rosenblum (Eds.), *The origins of behavior.* New York: Wiley.

Brazelton, T.B., Nugent, K.J., & Lester, B.M. (1987). Neonatal behavioral assessment scale. In J.D. Osofsky (Ed.), *Handbook of infant development* (2nd ed.). New York: Wiley.

Breber, I., et al. (1962). *Homosexuality: A psychoanalytic study.* New York: Basic Books.

Breland, K., & Breland, M.(1972). The misbehavior of organisms. In M.E.P. Seligman & J.L. Hager (Eds.), *Biological boundaries of learning.* New York: Appleton-Century-Crofts.

Briggs, D.C. (1975). *Your child's self-esteem.* New York: Dolphin.

Brim, O.G. Jr. (1966). Socialization through the life cycle. In O.G. Brim & S. Wheeler (Eds.), *Socialization after childhood: Two essays.* New York: Wiley.

Brody, G.H., Stoneman, Z., & Burke, M. (1987). Child temperaments, maternal differential behavior, and sibling relationships. *Developmental Psychology, 23,* 354–362.

Bronfenbrenner, U. (1958). Socialization and social class through time and space. In E.E. Maccoby, T.M. Newcomb, & E.L. Hartley, (Eds.), *Readings in social psychology.* New York: Holt, Rinehart and Winston.

Bronfenbrenner, U. (1979). *The ecology of human development: Experiments by nature and design.* Cambridge, MA: Harvard University Press.

Bronfenbrenner, U. (1989). Ecological systems theory. In R. Vasta (Ed.), *Annals of child development.* (Vol. 6). Greenwich, CT: JAI Press.

Bronfenbrenner, U., Alvarez, W.F., & Henderson, C. R. (1984). Working and watching: Maternal employment status and parents' perceptions of their three-year old children. *Child Development, 55,* 1362–1378.

Bronfenbrenner, U., & Garbarino, J. (1976). The socialization of moral judgment and behavior in cross-cultural perspective. In T. Lickona (Ed.), *Moral development and behavior.* New York: Holt, Rinehart and Winston.

Bronson, G. (1977). Long exposure to waste anesthetic gas is peril to workers, U.S. safety unit says. *Wall Street Journal,* March 1, p. 10.

Bronson, G.W. (1972). Infants' reactions to unfamiliar persons and novel objects. *Monographs for the Society for Research in Child Development, 37*(3), Serial No. 148.

Brooks, J., & Lewis, M. (April, 1975). Person perception and verbal labeling: The development of social labels. *Paper presented at the Society for Research in Child Development Meeting.* Denver.

Brooks-Gunn, J., & Matthews, W.S. (1979). *He & she: How children develop their sex-role identity.* Englewood Cliffs, N J: Prentice-Hall.

Brooks-Gunn, J., & Petersen, A.C. (1983). *Girls at puberty: Biological and psychosocial perspectives.* New York: Plenum.

Brooks-Gunn, J., & Schempp, W. (1979). *He & she: How children develop their sex-role identity.* Englewood Cliffs, NJ: Prentice-Hall.

Brophy, J. (1986). Teacher influences on student achievement. *American Psychologist, 41,* 1069–1077.

Brophy, J.E., & Good, T.L. (1974). *Teacher-study relationships: Causes and consequences.* New York: Holt, Rinehart and Winston.

Brothers, J. (1982). Men and women—The differences. *Woman's Day, 45*(6), 58, 60, 138–140, 142.

Brown, R. (1958). *Words and things.* New York: Free Press.

Brown, R. (1983). *A first language: The early stage.* Cambridge, MA: Harvard University Press.

Brown, R., Cazden, C., Bellugi, U. (1969). The child's grammar from I to III. In J.P. Hill (Ed.), *Minnesota symposia on child psychology.* (Vol. 2). Minneapolis: University of Minnesota Press.

Brown, R.W. (1973). *A first language: The early stages.* Cambridge, MA: Harvard University Press.

Brozan, N. (1983). New look at fears of children. *New York Times,* (May 2, Pt. 1), p. 20.

Bruch, H. (1970). Juvenile obesity: Its course and outcome. In C. V. Rowlan (Ed.), *Anorexia and obesity.* Boston: Little Brown.

Bruch, H. (1974). Eating disturbances in adolescence. In G. Caplan (Ed.), *American handbook of psychiatry.* New York: Basic Books.

Bruner, J.S. (1957). On perceptual readiness. *Psychological Review, 64,* 123–152.

Bruner, J.S. (1972). The nature and uses of immaturity. *American Psychologist, 27,* 687–708.

Bruner, J.S. (1973). *Beyond the information given: Studies in the psychology of knowing.* New York: Norton.

Bruner, J.S. (1983). *Child's talk.* New York: Norton.

Bryant, B. (1982). Sibling relationships in middle childhood. In M. Lamb & B. Sutton-Smith (Eds.), *Sibling relationships: Their nature and significance across the lifespan.* Hillsdale, NJ: Erlbaum.

Bryden, M.P. (1982). *Laterality.* New York: Academic Press.

Bullock, M. (1985). Animism in childhood in thinking: A new look at an old question. *Developmental Psychology, 21,* 217–225.

Bureau of Labor Statistics (1990). *Handbook of labor statistics.* Washington, DC: U.S. Department of Labor.

Burkett, C.L. (1985, April). Child-rearing behaviors and the self-esteem of preschool aged children. *Paper presented at the meeting for the Society for Research in Child Development.* Toronto, Canada.

Burt, C. (1937). *The backward child.* New York: Appleton-Century-Crofts.

Burton, R.V. (1984). A paradox in theories and research in moral development. In W.M. Kurtines & J.J. Gewitz (Eds.), *Morality, moral behavior and moral development.* New York: Wiley.

Buss, A.H., & Plomin, R. (1975). *A temperament theory of personality development.* New York: Wiley–Interscience.

Buss, A.H., & Plomin, R. (1984). *Temperament: Early developing personality traits.* Hillsdale, NJ: Erlbaum.

Bushnell, E.W. (1981). The ontogeny of intermodal relations: Vision and touch in infancy. In R.D. Walk & H.L. Pick, Jr. (Eds.), *Intersensory perception and sensory integration.* New York: Plenum.

Butler, S.R., March, H.W., Sheppard, M.J., & Sheppard, J.L. (1985). Seven-year longitudinal study of the early prediction of reading achievement. *Journal of Educational Psychology, 77,* 349–361.

Buxton, C. (1973). *Adolescents in schools.* New Haven, CT: Yale University Press.

Byrnes, J.P. (1988). Formal operations: A systematic reformulation. *Developmental Review, 8,* 66–87.

Caine, D. (1979). Two contemporary tragedies: Adolescent suicide/adolescent alcoholism. *Journal of the National Association of Private Psychiatrists, 9,* 4–11.

Caldera, Y.M., Huston, A.C., & O'Brien, M. (1989). Social interactions and play patterns of parents and toddlers with feminine, masculine, and neutral toys. *Child Development, 60,* 70–76.

Caldwell, B.M. (1964). The effects of infant care. In M.L. Hoffman & L.W. Hoffman (Eds.), *Review of child development research.* (Vol. 1). New York: Russell Sage Foundation.

Caldwell, B.M. (1970). The effects of psychological deprivation on human development in infancy. *Merrill-Palmer Quarterly, 16,* 260–277.

Caldwell, B.M., & Crary, D. (1981). Why are kids so darned aggressive? *Parents Magazine, 52,* 2, 52–56.

Camara, K.A. (1986). Family adaptation to divorce. In M.W. Yogman, & T.B. Brazelton (Eds.), *In support of families.* Cambridge, MA: Harvard University Press.

Camara, K.A. (1985). *For the sake of the children: Interparental cooperation and conflict after divorce.* Paper presented at the American Orthopsychiatric Association Annual Conference. New York.

Campos, J.J., et al. (1978). The emergence of fear on the visual cliff. In M. Lewis & L.A. Rosenblum (Eds.), *The development of affect.* (Vol. 1). New York: Plenum.

Campos, J.J., Barrett, K.C., Lamb, M.E., Goldsmith, H.H., & Stenberg, C. (1983). Socioemotional development. In P.H. Mussen (Ed.), *Handbook of child psychology* (4th ed.). (Vol. 2). New York: Wiley.

Campos, J.J., Langer, A., & Krowitz, A. (1970). Cardiac responses on the visual cliff in prelocomotor human infants. *Science, 170,* 196–197.

Cann, A., & Newbern, S.R. (1984). Sex stereotype effects in childrens' picture recognition. *Child Development, 55,* 1085–1090.

Cantwell, D.P. (1975). *Epidemiology, clinical practice and classification of the hyperactive child.* New York: Spectrum.

Carey, W.B., & Earls, F. (1988). Temperament in early adolescence: Continuities and transitions. In M.D. Levine & E.R. McAnarney (Eds.), *Early adolescent transitions.* Lexington, MA: Lexington

Carlson E.A. (1984). *Human genetics.* Lexington, MA: D.C. Heath.

Carner, N.K. (1986). Reading readiness: Aspects overlooked in structured readiness programs and workbooks *Childhood Education, 62,* 256–259.

Case, R. (1974). Structures and strictures: Some functional limitations on the course of cognitive growth. *Cognitive Psychology, 6,* 544–574.

Case, R. (1980). The underlying mechanism of intellectual development. In J.R. Kirby & J.B. Biggs (Eds.), *Cognitive development and instruction.* New York: Academic Press.

Case, R., & Khanna, F. (1981). The missing links: Stages in children's progression from sensorimotor to logical thought. In K.W. Fisher (Ed.), *Cognitive Development (New Directions for Child Development,* (No. 12). San Francisco: Jossey-Bass.

Cate, R., & Sugawara, A.I. (1986). Sex role orientations and dimensions of self-esteem among middle adolescents. *Sex Roles, 15*(3/4), 145–159.

Caudill, W. (1971). Tiny dramas: Vocal communication between mother and infant in Japanese and American families. In W. Libra (Ed.), *Mental health research in Asia and the Pacific.* Vol II. Honolulu: East-West Center Press.

Caudill, W., & Schooler, C. (1973). Child behavior and child rearing in Japan and the United States: An interim report. *Journal of Nervous and Mental Disease, 157*(4), 323–339.

Caudill, W., & Weinstein, H. (1969). Maternal care and infant behavior in Japan and America. *Psychiatry, 32*(1), 12–43.

Chaney, C., & Frodyma D.A. (1982). A noncategorical program for preschool language development. *Teaching Exceptional Children, 14,* 152–155.

Charles, C.M. (1974). *Teacher's petit Piaget.* Belmont, CA: Fearon.

Cherry, L. (1975). The preschool teacher-child dyad: Sex differences in verbal interaction. *Child Development, 46,* 532–535.

Chess, S. (1971). Autism in children with congenital rubella. *Journal of Autism and Childhood Schizophrenia, 1,* 33–47.

Chess, S., & Thomas A. (1984). *Origins and evolution of behavior disorders: From infancy to early adult life.* New York: Brunner/Mazel.

Chess, S., & Thomas, A. (1987). *Know your child.* New York: Basic Books.

Chi, M.T.H.(1982). Knowledge development and memory performance. In M. Friedman, J.P. Das, & N. O'Connor (Eds.), *Intelligence and learning.* New York: Plenum.

Children's Defense Fund (1989). *A vision for America's future: An agenda for 1990s.* Washington, DC: Children's Defense Fund.

Children's Defense Fund (1990). *A report card, briefing book, and action primer.* Washington, DC.

Chomsky, C. (1969). *Acquisition of syntax in children from 5 to 10.* Cambridge, MA: MIT Press.

Chomsky, N. (1965). *Aspects of a theory of syntax.* Cambridge, MA: MIT Press.

Chomsky, N. (1968). *Language and mind.* San Diego, CA: Harcourt Brace Jovanovich.

Chomsky, N. (1980). *Rules and representations.* New York: Columbia University Press.

Chumlea, W.C. (1982). Physical growth in adolescence. In B.B. Wolman (Ed.), *Handbook of developmental psychology.* Englewood Cliffs, NJ: Prentice-Hall.

Claiborn, W. (1969). Expectancy effects in the classroom: A failure to replicate. *Journal of Educational Psychology, 60,* 377–383.

Clark, A.L. (Ed.). (1978). *Culture childbearing health professionals.* Philadelphia: F.A. Davis.

Clark E.V. (1973). What's in a word? On the child's acquisition of semantics in his first language. In T.E. Moore (Ed.), *Cognitive development and the acquisition of language.* New York: Academic Press.

Clark, E.V. (1976). From gesture to word: On the natural history of deixis in language acquisition. In J.S. Bruner & A. Gartner (Eds.), *Human growth and development.* Oxford: Clarenton Press.

Clark, E.V. (1977). First language acquisition. In J. Morton & J. C. Marshall (Eds.), *Psycholinguistic Series.* (Vol. I). London: Elek Science.

Clarke-Stewart, A. (1978). And daddy makes three: The father's impact on mother and young child. *Child Development, 49,* 466–478.

Clarke-Stewart, A., & Friedman, S. (1987). *Child development: Infancy through adolescence.* New York: Wiley.

Clarke-Stewart, K.A. (1973). Interactions between mothers and their young children: Characteristics and consequences. *Monographs of the Society for Research in Child Development, 38*(6 & 7), (Serial No. 153).

Clarke-Stewart, K.A., & Fein, G.G. (1983). Early childhood programs. In P.H. Mussen (Ed.), *Handbook of child psychology* (4th ed.). (Vol. 2). New York: Wiley.

Clausen, J.A. (1975). The social meaning of differential physical and sexual maturation. In S.E. Dragastin & G.H. Elder (Eds.), *Adolescence in the life cycle: Psychological change and the social context.* New York: Halsted.

Clifford, E. (1971). Body satisfaction in adolescence. *Perceptual and Motor Skills, 33,* 119–125.

Clifton, R., Morrongiello, B.A., Kulig, J., & Dowd, J. (1981). Developmental changes in auditory localization in infancy. In R. Aslin, J. Alberts, & M.R. Peterson (Eds.), *The development of perception: Psychological perspectives. Audition, somatic perception, and the chemical senses.* (Vol. 1). New York: Academic Press.

Coalition Concerned With Adolescent Pregnancy. (1988, October). *Adolescent sexual behavior and pregnancy fact sheet.* Santa Ana, CA.

Coates, B., Pusser, H.E., & Goodman, I. (1976). The influence of Sesame Street and Mister Rogers' Neighborhood on children's social behavior in the preschool. *Child Development, 47,* 138.

Cohen, L.B., Gelber, E., & Lazar, M. (1971). Infant habituation and generalization to differing degrees stimulus novelty. *Journal of Experimental Child Psychology, 11,* 379–389.

Cohen, L.B., DeLoache, J.S., & Strauss, M. S. (1979). Infant visual perception. In J.D. Osofsky (Ed.), *Handbook of infant development.* New York: Wiley.

Cohn, J.F., & Tronick, E.Z. (1983). Three-month-old infants' reaction to simulated maternal depression. *Child Development, 54,* 185–193.

Coie, J.D., & Koeppi, G.K. (1990). Adapting intervention to the problems of aggressive and disruptive students. In S.R. Asher & J.D. Coie (Eds.), *Peer rejection in childhood.* New York: Cambridge University Press.

Colby, A., & Kohlberg, L. (1987). *The measurement of moral judgement (Vol. 1). Theoretical foundations and research validation. Standard issue scoring manual (Vol. 2).* Cambridge, England: Cambridge University Press.

Colby, A., Kohlberg, L., Gibbs, J., & Lieberman, M. (1983). A longitudinal study of moral judgment. *Monographs of the Society for Research in Child Development, 48,* Whole No. 200.

Cole, M. (1978). How education affects the mind. *Human Nature, 1,* 50–59.

Cole, M., & Scribner, S. (1974). *Culture and thought: A psychological interpretation.* New York: Wiley.

Cole, M. & Scribner, S. (1977). Cross-cultural studies of memory and cognition. In R.V. Kail, Jr. & J.W. Hagen (Eds.), *Perspectives on the development of memory and cognition.* Hillsdale, NJ: Erlbaum.

Coleman, J.C., Butcher, J.N., & Carson, R.C. (1980). *Abnormal psychology and modern life* (6th ed.). Glenview, IL: Scott Foresman.

Coleman, J.S. (1961). *The adolescent society: The social life of the teenager and its impact on education.* New York: Free Press.

Coleman, M. (1976). *The autistic syndromes.* Amsterdam: North-Holland.

Coles, C.D., Smith, I.E., & Falek, A. (1987). Prenatal alcohol exposure and infant behaviors immediate effects and implications for later development. *Advances in Alcohol and Substance Abuse, 6,* 87–104.

Coletta, N.D. (1978). *Divorced mothers at two income levels: Stress, support and child-rearing practices.* Unpublished thesis, Cornell University, Ithaca, N Y.

Coley, J.D., & Gelman, S.A. (1989). The effects of object orientation and object type on children's interpretation of the word "Big." *Child Development, 60,* 372–380.

Collins, L.J., Ingoldsby, B.B., & Dellman, M.M. (1984). Sex-role stereotyping in children's literature: A change from the past. *Childhood Education, 60*(4), 278–285.

Collins, W.A., Berndt, T.J., & Hess, V.L. (1974). Observational learning of motives and consequences for television aggression: A developmental study. *Child Development, 45,* 799–802.

Comstock, G., & Paik, H. (1991). *Television and the American child.* San Diego, CA: Academic Press.

Condry, J. (1989). *The psychology of television.* Hillsdale, NJ: Erlbaum.

Condry, J.C., Simon M.L., & Bronfenbrenner, U. (1968). *Characteristics of peer- and adult-oriented children,* Unpublished manuscript. Ithaca, NY: Cornell University.

Conel, J.L. (1939-1963). *The postnatal development of the human cerebral cortex.* (7 Volumes). Cambridge, MA: Harvard University Press.

Constanzo, P.R., & Shaw, M.E. (1966). Conformity as a function of age level. *Child Development, 37,* 967–975.

Cook, V.J., & White, M.A. (1977). Reinforcement potency of children's reading materials. *Journal of Educational Psychology, 41,* 226–232.

Cooley, C.H. (1902). *Human nature and the social order.* New York: Scribners.

Coons, S., & Guilleminault, C. (1984). Development of consolidated sleep and wakeful periods in relation to the day/night cycle in infancy. *Developmental Medicine and Child Neurology, 26,* 169–176.

Cooper, H.M. (1979). Pygmalion grows up: A model for teacher expectation, communication and performance influence. *Review of Educational Research, 49,* 389–410.

Cooper, H., & Good, T. (1983). *Pygmalion grows up: Studies in the expectation communication process.* New York: Longman.

Coopersmith, S. (1967). *The antecedents of self-esteem.* San Francisco: Freeman.

Coren, S., Porac, C., & Duncan, P. (1981). Lateral preference behaviors in preschool children and young adults. *Child Development, 52,* 443–450.

Cosand, B.J., Bourque, L.B., & Kraus, J.F. (1982). Suicide among adolescents in Sacramento County, California, 1950-1979, *Adolescence, 17*(Winter), 917–930.

Covington, M.V., & Beery, R.G. (1976). *Self-worth and school learning.* New York: Holt, Rinehart and Winston.

Cowan, C.P., Cowan, P.A., Heming, G., Garrett, E., Coysh, W.S., Curtis-Boles, H., & Boles, A.J. III. (1985). Transitions to parenthood: His, hers, and theirs. *Journal of Family Issues, 6*(4), 451–481.

Cowan, W.M. (1979). The development of the brain. *Scientific American, 241,* 88–133.

Cowen, E.L., Pederson, A., Babijian, H., Izzo, L.D., & Trost, M.A. (1973). Long-term follow-up of early detected vulnerable children. *Journal of Consulting and Clinical Psychology, 41,* 438–446.

Cowart, B.J. (1981). Development of taste perception in humans: Sensitivity and preference throughout the life span. *Psychological Bulletin, 90,* 43–73.

Cozby, P.C., Worden, P.E., & Kee, D.W. (1989). *Research methods in human development.* Mountain View, CA: Mayfield.

Crandall, V.V., Katovsky, W., & Crandall, V.J. (1965). Children's beliefs in their own control of reinforcements in intellectual-academic achievement situations. *Child Development, 36,* 91–109.

Cratty, B.J. (1986). *Perceptual & motor development in infants & children.* Englewood Cliffs, NJ: Prentice-Hall.

Crawford, A.C. (1968). *Customs and culture of Vietnam.* Tokyo: Tuttle.

Cromer, R. (1979). The strengths of the weak form of the cognition hypothesis for language acquisition. In V. Lee. (Ed.), *Language Development.* New York: Wiley.

Curtiss, S.R. (1977). *Genie: A psycholinguistic study of a modern day "wild child."* New York: Academic Press.

Curtiss, S.R. (1980). The critical period and feral children. *Paper presented at the first annual conference: Language reading comprehension and products.* San Diego State University.

Cushner, I.M. (1981). Maternal behavior and perinatal risks: Alcohol, smoking, and drugs. *Annual Review of Public Health, 2,* 201–218.

Damon, W. (1977). *The social world of the child.* San Francisco: Jossey Bass.

Dannemiller, J.L., & Stephens, B.R. (1988). A critical test of infant pattern preference models. *Child Development, 59,* 210–216.

Dansky, J.L. (1980). Make believe: A mediator of the relationship between play and associative fluency. *Child Development, 51,* 576–579.

Darwin, C. (1877). A biographical sketch of an infant. *Mind, 2,* 285–294.

Dasen, P.R. (1972). Cross-cultural Piagetian research: A summary. *Journal of Cross-Cultural Psychology, 3,* 23–39.

Dasen, P.R. (Ed.). (1977). *Piagetian psychology: Cross-cultural contributions.* New York: Gardner Press.

Davis, S.M., & McCroskey, R.L. (1980). Auditory fusion in children. *Child Development, 51,* 75–80.

Day, R.H., & McKenzie, B.E. (1981). Infant perception of the invariant size of approaching and receding objects. *Developmental Psychology, 17,* 670–677.

De'carie, T.G. (1974). *The infant's reaction to strangers.* New York: International Universities Press.

De Casper, A.J., & Fifer, W.J. (1980). Of human bonding: newborns prefer their mothers' voices. *Science, 208,* 1174–1176.

Dembo, M.H. (1988). *Applying educational psychology in the classroom* (3rd ed.). New York: Longman.

DeMyer, M., Hingten, J., & Jackson, R. (1981). Infantile autism reviewed: Decade of research. *Schizophrenia Bulletin, 7,* 388–45.

Dennis, W. (1935). The effect of restricted practice upon the reaching, setting, and standing of two infants. *Journal of Genetic Psychology, 47,* 17–32.

Dennis, W. (1940). The effect of cradling practices upon the onset of walking in Hopi children. *Journal of Genetic Psychology, 56,* 77–86.

Dennis, W. (1960). Causes of retardation among institutionalized children: Iran. *Journal of Genetic Psychology, 96,* 47–59.

de Villiers, J.G., & de Villiers, P.A. (1973). A cross-sectional study of the acquisition of grammatical morphemes in child speech. *Journal of Psycholinguistics Research, 2,* 267–278.

Dodge, K.A. (1983). Behavioral antecedents of peer social status. *Child Development, 54,* 1386–1399.

Dodge, K.A. (1985). A social information processing model of social competence in children. In M. Perlmutter (Ed.), Cognitive perspectives on children's social and behavioral development, *Minnesota Symposium on Child Psychology.* (Vol. 18). Hillsdale, NJ: Erlbaum.

Dolgin, K.G., & Behrend, D.A. (1984). Children's knowledge about animates and inanimates. *Child Development, 55,* 1646–1650.

Dolgins, J., Myers, M., Flynn, P.A., & Moore, J. (1985). How do we help the learning disabled? In C. Borg (Ed.), *Educating exceptional children. (Annual eds.).* Guilford, CT: Dushkin

Dollard, J., Doob L.W., Miller, N.E., Mowrer, O.H., & Sears, R.R. (1939). *Frustration and aggression.* New Haven: Yale University Press.

Donahue, M., Pearl, R., & Bryan, T. (1982). Learning disabled children's syntactic proficiency during a noncommunicative task. *Journal of Speech and Hearing Disorders, 47,* 397–403.

Donahue, M., Pearl, R., & Bryan, T. (1983). Communicative competence in learning disabled children. In H. Bialer & K. Gadow (Eds.), *Advances in learning and behavioral disabilities.* (Vol. 2). Greenwich, CT: JAI Press.

Donaldson, M. (1979). *Children's minds.* New York: W.W. Norton.

Donovan, W.L., & Leavitt, L.A. (1989). Maternal self-efficacy and infant attachment; Integrating physiology, perceptions, and behavior. *Child Development, 60,* 460–472.

Dorr, A. (1980). When I was a child and thought as a child. In S.B. Withey & R.P. Abeles (Eds.), *Television and social behavior: Beyond violence and children.* Hillsdale, NJ: Erlbaum.

Dorr, A. (1986). *Television and children: A special medium for a special audience.* Beverly Hills, CA: Sage.

Dornbusch, S., Ritter, P., Liederman, P., Roberts, D., & Fraleigh, M. (1987). The relation of parenting style to adolescent school performance. *Child Development, 58,* 1244–1257.

Dorval, B., & Eckerman, C.O. (1984). Developmental trends in the quality of conversation achieved by small groups of acquainted peers. *Monographs of the Society for Research in Child Development, 49*(2), (Serial No. 206).

Drabman, R.S., & Thomas, M.H. (1976). Does watching violence on television cause apathy? *Pediatrics, 52,* 329–331.

Drake, C.T., & McDougall, D. (1977). Effects of the absence of a father and other male models on the development of boys' sex roles. *Developmental Psychology, 13,* 537–538.

Dryfoos, J.G. (1990). *Adolescents at risk.* New York: Oxford University Press.

Duke P.M., Carlsmith, J.M., Jennings, D., Martin, J.A., Dornbush, S.M., Gross, R.T., & Siegel-Gorelick, B. (1982). Educational correlates of early and late sexual maturation in adolescence. *Journal of Pediatrics, 100,* 633–637.

Duncan, P., Ritter, P.L., Dornbusch, S.M., Gross, R.T., & Carlsmith, J.M. (1985). The effects of pubertal timing on body image school behavior and deviance. *Journal of Youth and Adolescence, 14,* 227–235.

Dunkel-Schetter, C. Lobel, M., & Scrimshaw, S. (1990, August). *Stress during pregnancy and infant prematurity.* Paper presented at the annual convention of the American Psychological Association. Boston.

Dunn, J., & Plomin, R. (1990). *Separate lives: Why siblings are so different.* New York: Basic Books.

Dunn, J. (1985). *Sisters and brothers.* Cambridge, MA: Harvard University Press.

Dweck, C.S. (1975). The role of expectations and attributions in the alleviation of learned helplessness. *Journal of Personality and Social Psychology, 31,* 674–685.

Dweck, C.S., & Bush, E.S. (1976). Sex differences in learned helplessness, I: Differential debilitation with peer and adult evaluators. *Journal of Personality and Social Psychology, 12,* 147–156.

Dweck, C.S., Davidson, W., Nelson, S., & Enna, B. (1978). Sex differences in learned helplessness: II. The contingencies of evaluative feedback in the classroom, and III. An experimental analysis. *Developmental Psychology, 14,* 268–276.

Dweck, C.S., & Gillard, D. (1975). Expectancy statements as determinants of reactions to failure: Sex differences in persistence and expectancy change. *Journal of Personality and Social Psychology, 32,* 1077–1084.

Dweck, C.S., & Reppucci, N.D. (1973). Learned helplessness and responsibility in children. *Journal of Personality and Social Psychology, 25,* 109–116.

Dweck, C.S., Davidson, W., Nelson, S., & Enna, B. (1978). Sex differences in learned helplessness: II. The contingencies of evaluative feedback in the classroom, and III. An experimental analysis. *Developmental Psychology, 14,* 268–276.

Eakins, P.S. (Ed.). (1986). *The American way of birth*. Philadelphia: Temple University Press.

Egeland, B., & Farber, E.A. (1984). Infant-mother attachment. Factors related to its development and changes over time. *Child Development, 55*, 753–771.

Egeland, B., & Sroufe, C.A. (1981). Attachment and early maltreatment. *Child Development, 52*, 44–52.

Eichorn, D.H. (1970). Physiological development. In P.H. Mussen (Ed.), *Carmichael's manual of child psychology* (3rd ed.). Vol. 1. New York: Wiley.

Eichorn, D.H. (1979). Physical development: Current foci of research. In J.D. Osofsky (Ed.), *Handbook of infant development*. New York: Wiley.

Eid, E.E. (1970). Follow-up study of physical growth of children who had excessive weight in first six months of life. *British Medical Journal, 2*, 74–76.

Eimas, P.D. (1975). Auditory and phonetic coding of the cues for speech: Discrimination of the [r-l] distinction by young infants. *Perception and Psychophysics, 18*, 341–347.

Eimas, P.D. (1982). Speech perception: A view of the initial state and perceptual mechanism. In J. Mehler, M. Garrett, & E. Walker (Eds.), *Perspectives on mental representation*. Hillsdale, NJ: Erlbaum.

Eimas, P.D. (1985). The perception of speech in early infancy. *Scientific American, 252*, 46–52.

Eimas, P.D., Siqueland, E.R., Jusczyk, P., & Vigorito, J. (1971). Speech perception in infants. *Science, 171*, 303–306.

Eimas, P.D., & Tartter, V.C. (1979). *On the development of speech perception: Mechanism and analogies. Child behavior and development*. (Vol. 13). New York: Academic Press.

Eisenberg, N. (1986). *Altruistic emotion, cognition and behavior*. Hillsdale, NJ: Erlbaum.

Eisenberg, N., Shell, R., Pasternack, J., Lennon, R., Beller, R., & Mathy, R.M. (1987). Prosocial development in middle childhood: A longitudinal study. *Developmental Psychology, 23*(5), 712–718.

Einspieler, C., Widder, J., Holzer, A., & Kenner, T. (1988). The predictive value of behavioral risk factors for sudden infant death. *Early Human Development, 18*, 101–109.

Eitzen, D.S.(1975). Athletics in the status system of male adolescents: A replication of Coleman's the adolescent society. *Adolescence, 38*(10), 267–276.

Ekman, P. (1973). Cross-cultural studies of facial expression. In P. Ekman (Ed.), *Darwin and facial expression*. New York: Academic Press.

Ekman, P., & Friesen, W.V. (1972). Constants across cultures in the face and emotion. *Journal of Personality and Social Psychology, 17*, 124–129.

Ekman, P., & Friesen, W.V. (1978). *The facial action coding system (FACS)*. Palo Alto, CA: Consulting Psychologists Press.

Elardo, R., Bradley, R.H., & Caldwell, B.M. (1975). The relation of infant's home environment to mental test performance from 6 to 36 months: A longitudinal analysis. *Child Development, 46*, 71–76.

Elder, G.H. Jr. (1974). *Children of the great depression: Social change in life experience*. Chicago: University of Chicago Press.

Elder, G.H. Jr. (1979). Historical change in life patterns and personality. In P. Baltes & O. Brim (Eds.), *Life-span development and behavior*. (Vol. II). New York: Academic Press.

Elder, G.H. Jr., & Bowerman, C.E. (1963). Family structure and child-rearing patterns: The effect of family size and sex composition. *American Sociological Review, 30*, 81–96.

Elder, G.H. Jr., Van Nguyen, T.V., & Caspi, A. (1985). Linking family hardship to children's lives. *Child Development, 56*, 361–375.

Elkind, D. (1975). Perceptual development in children. *American Scientist, 63*, 533–541.

Elkind, D. (1978). *The child's reality: Three developmental themes*. Hillsdale, NJ: Erlbaum.

Elkind, D. (1981). *Children and adolescents: Interpretive essays on Jean Piaget* (3rd ed.). New York: Oxford University Press.

Elkind, D., & Bowen, R. (1979). Imaginary audience behavior in children and adolescents. *Developmental Psychology, 15*, 38–44.

Elliot, A.J. (1981). *Child language*. London: Cambridge University Press.

Emde, R., et al. (1971). Stress and neonatal sleep. *Psychosomatic Medicine, 33*, 491–497.

Emde, R.N. (1980). Levels of meaning for infant emotions: A biosocial view. In W.A. Collins (Ed.), Development of cognition, affect and social relations. *The Minnesota symposia on child psychology*. (Vol. 13). Hillsdale, NJ: Erlbaum.

Emde, R.N., & Harmon, R.J. (1972). Endogenous and exogenous smiling systems in early infancy. *Journal of the American Academy of Child Psychiatry, 11*, 77–100.

Emerick, L.L., & Haynes, W.O. (1986). *Diagnostic and evolution in speech pathology* (3rd ed.). Englewood Cliffs, NJ: Prentice-Hall.

Engen, T., Lipsitt, L.P., & Kaye, H. (1963). Olfactory responses and adaptation in the human neonate. *Journal of Comparative and Physiological Psychology, 56,* 73–77.

Engsner, G., & Woldemarian, T. (1974). Motor nerve conduction velocity in marasmus and kwashiorkan. *Neuropadiatrie, 5,* 34–48.

Enright, R.D., Shukla, D.G., & Lapsley, D.K. (1980). Adolescent egocentrism—Sociocentrism and self-consciousness. *Journal of Youth and Adolescence, 9*(2), 101–111.

Epstein, J.L. (1983). Longitudinal effects of family-school-person interactions on student outcomes. In J.L. Epstein (Ed.), *Research in sociology of education and socialization.* (Vol. 4). Greenwich, CT: JAI Press.

Epstein, L.H., & Wing R.R.(1987). Behavioral treatment of childhood obesity. *Psychological Bulletin, 101,* 331–342.

Epstein L.H., Wing, R.R., Koeske, R., & Valoski, A. (1987). Long-term effects of family-based treatment of childhood obesity. *Journal of Consulting and Clinical Psychology, 55,* 91–95.

Epstein, R., & Koerner, J. (1986). The self-concept and other daemons. In J. Suls & A.G. Greenwald (Eds.), *Psychological perspectives on the self.* (Vol. 3). Hillsdale, NJ: Erlbaum.

Erdman, M. (1986). *Perceptual constancy for auditory stimuli in infancy.* Unpublished Doctoral Dissertation. University of Toronto, Canada.

Erikson, E.H. (1963). *Childhood and society* (2nd ed.). New York: Norton.

Erikson, E.H. (1968). *Identity: Youth and crisis.* New York: Norton.

Erikson, E.H. (1980). *Identity and the life cycle.* New York: W.W. Norton.

Espenschade, A., & Eckert, H. (1974). Motor development. In W.R. Johnson & E.R. Buskirk (Eds.), *Science and medicine of exercise and sport.* New York: Harper & Row.

Eysenck, H.J. (Ed.). (1981). *A model for personality.* New York: Springer-Verlag.

Fabricus, W.V., & Wellman, H.M. (1983). Children's understanding of retrieval cue utilization. *Developmental Psychology, 19,* 14–21.

Fagan, J.F. (1984). Infant memory: History, current trends, and relations to cognitive psychology. In M. Moscovitch (Ed.), *Infant memory: Its relation to normal and pathological memory in humans and other animals.* New York: Plenum.

Fagan, J.F. (1985). *Early novelty preferences and later intelligence.* Paper presented at the Meeting of the Society for Research in Child Development. Toronto, April.

Fagot, B.I. (1973). Influences of teacher behavior in the preschool. *Developmental Psychology, 9,* 198–206.

Fagot, B.I. (1977). Consequences of moderate cross-gender behavior in preschool children. *Child Development, 48,* 902–907.

Fagot, B.I. (1981). Male and female teachers: Do they treat boys and girls differently? *Sex Roles, 7,* 263–272.

Fagot, B.I., Leinbach, M.D., & Hagan, R. (1986). Gender labeling and the adoption of sex-typed behaviors. *Developmental Psychology, 22*(4), 440–443.

Fagot, B.I., & Patterson, G.R. (1969). An in vivo analysis of reinforcing contingencies for sex-role behavior in the preschool child. *Developmental Psychology, 1,* 563–568.

Fanaroff, A.A., & Martin, R.J. (Eds.), (1987). *Neonatal-perinatal medicine: Disease of the fetus and infant* (4th ed.). St. Louis: C.V. Mosby.

Fantz, R.L. (1961). The origin of form perception. *Scientific American, 204,* 66–72.

Faust, M.S. (1960). Developmental maturity as a determinant in prestige of adolescent girls. *Child Development, 31,* 173–186.

Feingold, B.F. (1975). Hyperkinesis and learning disabilities linked to artificial food flavors and colors. *American Journal of Nursing, 75,* 797–803.

Feldman, D.H. (1982). A Developmental Framework for Research with Gifted Children. In D.H. Feldman (Ed.), *New directions for child development. Developmental approaches to giftedness and creativity.* (Vol. 17). San Francisco: Jossey-Bass.

Fentress, J.C., & McLeod, P.J. (1986). Motor patterns in development. In E.M. Blass (Ed.), *Handbook of behavioral neurobiology Vol. 8: Developmental psychobiology and developmental neurobiology.* New York: Plenum.

Fernald, A. (1985). Four-month-old infants prefer to listen to mothers. *Infant Behavior and Development, 8,* 181–195.

Fernald, A. (1987). Acoustic determinants of infant preference for motherese speech. *Infant Behavior and Development, 10,* 279–294.

Feshbach, S. (1970). Aggression. In P.H. Mussen (Ed.), *Carmichael's manual of child psychology*. New York: Wiley.

Field, T.M. (1977). Effects of early separation, interactive deficits, and experimental manipulation on mother infant interaction. *Child Development, 48*, 763–771.

Field, T.M. (1979). Interaction patterns of high-risk and normal infants. In T.M. Field, A. Sostek, S. Goldberg, & H.H. Shuman (Eds.), *Infants born at risk.* New York: Prentice-Hall.

Field, T.M. (1979). Visual and cardiac responses to animate and inanimate faces by young term and preterm infants. *Child Development, 50*, 188–194.

Field, T.M. (1980). Interactions of preterm and term infants with their lower-and-middle-class teenage and adult mothers. In T. M. Field, S. Goldberg, D. Stern, & A. Soskek (Eds.), *High-risk infants and children*. New York Academic Press.

Field, T.M., et al. (1985). Pregnancy problems, postpartum depression, and early mother-infant interactions *Developmental Psychology, 21*, 1152–1156.

Field, T.M. (1986). Intervention for premature infants. *Journal of Pediatrics, 109*, 183–191.

Field, T.M. (1990). *Infancy.* Cambridge, MA: Harvard University Press.

Fiorentine, M.R. (1973). Reflex testing methods for evaluating CNS development. Springfield, IL: Charles C Thomas.

Firush, R., & Mandler, J.M. (1985). Developmental changes in the understanding of temporal sequence. *Child Development, 56*, 1437–1446.

Fischer K.W., & Pipp, S.L. (1984). Process of cognitive development; optimal level and skill acquisition. In R.J. Sternberg (Ed.), *Mechanisms of cognitive development.* San Francisco: W.H. Freeman.

Fisher, K.W. (1980). A theory of cognitive development: The control and construction of hierarchies of skills. *Psychological Review,*

Fisher, K.W., & Canfield, R.L. (1986). The ambiguity of stage and structure in behavior: Person and environment in the development of psychological structures. In I. Levin (Ed.), *Stage and structure: Reopening the debate.* Norwood, NJ: Ablex.

Fisher, K.W., Hand, H.H., & Russell, S. (1983). The development of abstractions in adolescence and adulthood. In M.L. Commons, F.A. Richards, & C. Armon (Eds.), *Beyond formal operations.* New York: Praeger.

Fisher, K.W., & Lazerson, A. (1984). *Human development: From conception through adolescence.* New York: W.H. Freeman.

Flanagan, J.C. (1963). The definition and measurement of ingenuity. In W.C. Taylor & F. Barron (Eds.), *Scientific creativity: Its recognition and development.* New York: Wiley.

Flanery, R.C., & Balling, J.D. (1979). Developmental changes in hemispheric specialization for tactile spatial ability. *Developmental Psychology, 15*, 364–372.

Flavell, J.H. (1982). On cognitive development. *Child Development, 53*, 1–10.

Flavell, J.H. (1985). *Cognitive development* (2nd ed.). Englewood Cliffs, NJ: Prentice-Hall.

Flavell, J.H., Shipstead, S., & Croft, K. (1978). Young children's knowledge about visual perception: Hiding objects from others. *Child Development, 49*, 1208–1211.

Flavell, J.H., Beach, D.R., & Chinsky, J.M. (1966). Spontaneous verbal rehearsal in a memory task as a function of age. *Child Development, 37*, 283–299.

Flavell, J.H., Friedrichs, A.G., & Hoyt, J.D. (1970). Developmental changes in memorization processes. *Cognitive Development, 1*, 324–340.

Flavell, J.H., Miller, P.H., & Millec, S.A. (1983). Cognitive development (3rd ed.). Englewood Cliffs, NJ: Prentice-Hall.

Fontana, V.J. (1991). *Save the family, save the child.* New York: Dutton.

Foorman, B.R., & Siegel, A.W. (1985). *Acquisition of reading skills.* Hillsdale, NJ: Erlbaum.

Forman, G.E., & Kuschner, D.S. (1983). *The child's construction of knowledge: Piaget for teaching children.* Washington, DC: NAEYC.

Fraiberg, S.H. (1959). *The magic years.* New York: Charles Scribner's Sons.

Fraiberg, S. (1974). Blind infants and their mothers: An examination of the sign system. In M. Lewis & L.A. Rosenblum (Eds.), *The effect of the infant on its caregiver.* New York: Wiley.

Frankel, E. (1979). DNA: The ladder of life. New York: McGraw-Hill.

Frankenburg, W., Dodds, J., Fandal, A., Kazuk, E., & Cohrs, M. (1975). *Denver developmental screening test reference manual* (revised ed.). Denver, CO: LADOCA Project & Publishing Foundation.

Frankenburg, W.K., & Dodds, J.B. (1967). The Denver developmental screening test. *Journal of Pediatrics, 71*, 181–191.

Frankenburg, W.K. , Dodds, J.B., & Frandal, A. (1975). *The Denver developmental screening test.* Denver CO: LADO-CA Project & Publishing Foundation.

Frantz, R.L. (1966). Pattern discrimination and selective attention as determinants in infancy. In A.H. Kidd and J.L. Rivoire (Eds.), *Perceptual development in children.* New York: International University Press.

Freidrich, L.K., & Stein, A.H. (1975). Prosocial television and young children: The effects of verbal labeling and role playing on learning and behavior. *Child Development, 46,* 27–36.

Freud, S. (1900). The interpretation of dreams. In J. Strachey (Ed. & Trans.), *The standard edition of the complete psychological works of Sigmund Freud* (Vol. 5). London: Hogarth Press.

Freud, S. (1925). Some psychical consequences of the anatomical distinction between the sexes. In *Standard edition.* Condon: Hogarth Press, 1961.

Freud, S. (1927). *Beyond the pleasure principle.* New York: Bonj and Liveright.

Freud, S. (1935). *A general introduction to psychoanalysis.* New York: Liveright.

Fried, P.A., Watkinson, B., Dillon, R.F., & Dulberg, C.S. (1987). Neonatal neurological status in a low-risk population after prenatal exposure to cigarettes, marijuana, and alcohol. *Journal of Developmental and Behavioral Pediatrics, 8,* 318–326.

Friedman, W.J. (1991). The development of children's memory for the time of past events. *Child Development, 62,* 139–155.

Friedrich, C.K., & Stein, A.H. (1975). Pro-social television and young children. The effects of verbal labelling and role playing on learning and behavior. *Child Development, 46,* 27–38.

Friedrich-Cofer, L., & Huston A.C. (1986). Television violence and aggression: The debate continues. *Psychological Bulletin, 100,* 364–371.

Fuhrmann, B.S. (1986). *Adolescence, adolescents.* Boston: Little Brown.

Gagne, R. (1968). Contributions of learning to human development. *Psychological Review, 75,* 177–91.

Galinsky, E. (1981). *Between generations.* New York: Times Books.

Galler, J.R., Ramsey, F., Solimano, G., Kucharski, L.T., & Harrison, R. (1984). The influence of early malnutrition on subsequent behavioral development IV. Soft neurological signs. *Pediatric Research, 18,* 826–832.

Gallup, G.G. Jr., & Suarez, S.D. (1986). Self-awareness and the emergence of mind in humans and other primates. In J. Suls & A.G. Greenwald (Eds.), *Psychological perspectives on the self.* (Vol. 3). Hillsdale, NJ: Erlbaum.

Galton, F. (1936). Genius as inherited. From hereditary genius: An inquiry into its laws and consequences. London: Macmillan, 1869. Reprinted in A. Rothenberg & C.R. Hausman (Eds.), *The creativity question.* Durham, NC: Duke University Press.

Galton, L. (1980). *Your child in sports.* New York: Franklin Watts.

Garbarino, J. (1980). Some thoughts on school size and its effects on adolescent development. *Journal of Youth and Adolescence. 9*(1), 19–31.

Garbarino, J. (1985). *Adolescent development: An ecological perspective.* Columbus, OH: Merrill.

Garbarino, J. (1992). *Children and families in the social environment* (2nd ed.). New York: Aldine de Gruyter.

Garbarino, J. Guttman, E., & Seely, J.W. (1986). *The psychologically-battered child. Strategies for identification, assessment, and intervention.* San Francisco, CA: Jossey-Bass.

Garber, J., Cohen, E., Bacon, P., Egeland, B., & Sroufe, L.A. (1985). Depression in preschoolers: Reliability and validity of a behavioral observation measure. *Paper presented at the Society for Research in Child Development.* Toronto, Canada.

Gardner, H. (1983). *Frames of mind: The theory of multiple intelligences.* New York: Basic Books.

Gardner, K.E., & LaBrecque, S.V. (1986). Effects of maternal employment on sex-role orientation of adolescents. *Adolescence, 21*(84), 875–885.

Garvey, C. (1984). *Children's talk.* Cambridge, MA: Harvard University Press.

Garvey, C., & Hogan, R. (1988). Social speech and social interaction: Egocentrism revisited. In M.B. Franklin & S.S. Barten (Eds.), *Child language: A reader.* New York: Oxford University Press.

Garvey, C. (1990). *Play* (enlarged ed.). Cambridge, MA: Harvard University Press.

Gelfand, D.M., Jenson, W.R., Drew, C.J. (1988). *Understanding Child Behavior Disorders* (2nd ed.). New York: Holt, Rinehart and Winston.

Gattler, J.M. (1982). *Assessment of children's intelligence and special abilities* (2nd ed.). Boston: Allyn & Bacon.

Gellatly, A.R.H. (1987). Acquisition of a concept of logical necessity. *Human Development, 30,* 32–47.

Gelman, R. (1977). How young children reason about small numbers. In N.J. Castellan, D.P. Pisoni, & G.R. Potts (Eds.), *Cognitive theory.* Hillsdale, NJ: Erlbaum.

Gelman, R., & Baillargeon, R. (1983). A review of some Piagetian concepts. In P.H. Mussen (Ed.), *Handbook of child psychology* (4th ed.). (Vol. 3). New York: Wiley.

Gelman, R., & Shatz, M. (1977). Appropriate speech adjustments. The operation of conversational constraints on talk to two-year olds. In M. Lewis & L.A. Rosenbaum (Eds.), *Interaction conversation, and the development of language.* New York: Wiley.

Geschwind, N. (1979). Specialization of the human brain. *Scientific American, 241,* 180–201.

Geschwind, N., & Behan, P. (1982). Left-handedness: Association with immune disease, migraine, and developmental learning disorder. *Proceedings of the National Academy of Science, USA, 79,* 5097–5100.

Gesell, A. (1929). Maturation and infant behavior patterns. *Psychological Review, 36,* 307–319.

Gesell, A.L. (1925). *The mental growth of the pre-school child: A psychological outline of normal development from birth to the sixth year, including a system of developmental diagnosis.* New York: Macmillan.

Gesell, A., et al. (1940). *The first five years of life.* New York: Harper.

Gesell, A.L. (1946).The ontogenesis of infant behavior. In L. Carmichael (Ed.), *Manual of child psychology.* New York: Wiley.

Gesell, A. (1954). The ontogenesis of infant behavior. In L. Carmichael (Ed.), *Manual of child psychology.* New York: Wiley.

Getzels, J.W., & Jackson, P.W. (1962). *Creativity and intelligence: Explorations with gifted students.* New York: Wiley.

Gibson, E.J. (1969). *Principle of perceptual learning and development.* New York: Appleton-Century-Crofts.

Gibson, E.J. (1987) Introductory essay: What does infant perception tell us about theories of perception? *Journal of Experimental Psychology: Human Perception and Performance, 13*(4), 515–523.

Gibson, E.J., et al. (1963). An analysis of critical features of letters tested by a confusion matrix. *In Final Report on a Basic Research Program on Reading.* (Cooperative Research Project No. 639). Ithaca, New York: Cornell University & U. S. Office of Education.

Gibson, E.J., Shapiro, F., & Yonas, A. (1968). Confusion matrices for graphic patterns obtained with a latency measure. In *The Analyses of Reading Skill: A Program of Basic and Applied Research.* (Final Report Project No. 5-1213). Ithaca, New York: Cornell University Office of Education.

Gibson, E.J, Owsley, C.J., & Johnson, J. (1978). Perception of invariants by five-month-old infants: Differentiation of two types of motion. *Developmental Psychology, 14,* 407–415.

Gibson, E.J., & Walk, R.D. (1960). The "visual cliff." *Scientific American, 202,* 64–71.

Gibson, E.J., & Walker, A.S. (1984). Development of knowledge of visual-tactual affordances of substance. *Child Development, 55,* 453–460.

Gibson, J.J., & Gibson, E.J. (1955). Perceptual learning: Differentiation or enrichment? *Psychological Review, 62,* 32–41.

Gibson, J.J. (1979). *The ecological approach to visual perception.* Boston: Houghton-Mifflin.

Gillet, J.W., & Temple, C. (1982). *Understanding reading problems.* Boston: Little, Brown.

Gilligan, C. (1982). *In a different voice: Psychological theory and women's development.* Cambridge, MA: Harvard University. Press.

Ginsburg, A.P. (1978). *Visual information processing based on spatial filters constrained by biological data.* Doctoral dissertation. Cambridge University.

Glaser, R. (Ed.). (1982). *Advances in instructional psychology.* (Vol. 2). Hillsdale, NJ: Erlbaum.

Glass, G.V., Cohen, L.S., Smith, M.L., & Filby, N.N. (1982). *School class size: Research and policy.* Beverly Hills, CA: Sage.

Gleitman, H. (1991). *Psychology* (3rd ed.). New York: W.W. Norton.

Gleitman, L.R., & Wanner, E. (1982). Language acquisition. In E. Wanner & L.R. Gleitman. (Eds.), *Language acquisition.* Cambridge: Cambridge University Press.

Glick, J. (1975). Cognitive development in cross-cultural perspective. In F. Horowitz (Ed.), *Review of child development research.* (Vol. 4). Chicago: Chicago University Press.

Glover, J.A. (1980). *Becoming a more creative person.* Englewood Cliffs, NJ: Prentice-Hall.

Glover, J.A., & Bruning, R.H. (1987). *Educational psychology: Principles and applications* (2nd ed.). Boston: Little Brown.

Glover, J.A., & Gary, A.L. (1976). Procedures to increase some aspects of creativity. *Journal of Applied Behavior Analysis, 9,* 79–84.

Glover, J.A., Ronning, R.R., & Brunning, R.H. (1990). *Cognitive psychology for teachers.* New York: Macmillan.

Glover, J.A., & Sautter, F.J. (1977). Procedures for increasing four behaviorally defined components of creativity within formal written assignments among high school students. *School Applications of Learning Theory, 9* (11), 3–22.

Glucksmann, A. (1974). Sexual dimorphism in mammals. *Biological Review, 49,* 423–475.

Gold, D., & Andres, D. (1978). Developmental comparisons between ten-year old children with employed and non-employed mothers, *Child Development, 49,* 75–84.

Gold, D., Crombie, G., & Noble, S. (1987). Relations between teachers' judgments of girls and boys' compliance and intellectual competence. *Sex Roles, 16,* 351–358.

Goldberg, S. (1988). Premature birth: Consequences for the parent-infant relationship. In E.M. Hetherington & R.D. Parke (Eds.), *Contemporary readings in child psychology* (3rd ed.). New York: McGraw-Hill.

Goldberg, S., Brachfeld, S., & DiVitto, B. (1980). Feeding, fussing and play: Parent-infant interaction in the first year as a function of prematurity and prenatal medical problems. In F. M. Field, S. Goldberg, D. Stern, & A. Sostek (Eds.), *High-risk infants and children.* New York: Academic Press.

Goldberg, S., & DiVitto, B.A. (1983). *Born too soon: Preterm birth and early development.* San Francisco: W.H. Freeman.

Goldfield, B.A., & Reznick, J.S. (1990). Early lexical aquisition: Rate, content, and vocabulary spurt. *Journal of Child Language, 17,* 171–183.

Goldfield, E.C. (1989). Transition from rocking to crawling: Postural constraints on infant movement. *Developmental Psychology, 25*(6), 913–919.

Goldin-Meadow, S. (1979). Structure in a manual communication system developed without a conventional language model: Language without a helping hand. In H. Whitaker & H.A. Whitaker (Eds.), *Studies in neurolinguistics.* (Vol. 4). New York: Academic Press.

Goldin-Meadow, S., & Morford, M. (1985). Gesture in early language: Studies of deaf and hearing children. *Merrill Palmer Quarterly, 31,* 145–176.

Goldin-Meadow, S., & Mylander, C. (1983). Gestural communication in deaf children: Non effect of parental input on language development. *Science, 221,* 372–374.

Golding, W. (1954). *Lord of the flies.* New York: Putnam.

Goldman-Rakic, P.S. (1987). Development of cortical circuitry and cognitive function. *Child Development, 58,* 601–622.

Goldman-Rakic, P.S., Isseroff, A., Schwartz, M.L., & Bugbee N. M. (1983). The neurobiology of cognitive development. In P.H. Mussen (Ed.), *Handbook of child psychology* (4th ed.). (Vol. 2). New York: Wiley.

Goldsmith, H.H., & Campos, J.J. (1982). Genetic influence on individual differences in emotionality. *Infant Behavior and Development, 5,* 99.

Goldsmith, H.H., & Gottesman, J.J. (1981). Origins of variation in behavioral style: A longitudinal study of temperament in young twins. *Child Development, 54,* 356–360.

Goldsmith, H.H., et al. (1987). Round table: What is temperament? Four approaches. *Child Development, 58,* 505–529.

Goleman, D. (1980). 1,528 little geniuses and how they grew. *Psychology Today, 13,* 28–53.

Gollins, E.S. (1984). *Malformations of development.* New York: Academic Press.

Good, T., & Brophy, J.E. (1986). *Educational psychology* (3rd ed.). New York: Longman.

Good, T., & Brophy, J.E. (1984). *Looking in classrooms* (3rd ed.). New York: Harper & Row.

Goodenough, F.L. (1931). Anger in young children. *Institute of Child Welfare Monograph Series, No. 9.* Minneapolis: University of Minnesota Press.

Goodman, R.M. (1986). *Planning for a healthy baby: A guide to genetic and environmental risks.* New York: Oxford University Press.

Goodwin, D.W. (1979). Alcoholism and heredity: A review and hypothesis. *Archives of General Psychiatry, 36,* 57–61.

Goodwin, D.W. (1981). *Adoption studies of alcohol. Twin research 3: Epidemiological and clinical studies.* New York: A.R. Liss.

Gottesman, I.I. (1963). Heritability of personality: A demonstration. *Psychological Monographs, 77* (Whole No. 572).

Gottman, J.M., & Katz, L.F. (1989). Effects of marital discord on young children's peer interaction and health. *Developmental Psychology, 25*(3), 373–381.

Gould, D., & Horn, T. (1984). Participation motivation in young athletes. In J. Silva & R. Weinberg (Eds.), *Psychological foundations of sport.* Champaign, IL: Human Kinetics.

Goy, R.W. (1975). Early hormonal influences on the development of sexual and sex-related behaviors. In R.K. Anger & E.L. Denmark (Eds.), *Woman: Dependent or Independent Variable?* New York: Psychological Dimensions.

Gratch, G. (1975). Recent studies based on Piaget's view of object conception development. In L.B. Cohen & P. Salapatek (Eds.), *Infant perception: From sensation to cognition.* (Vol. 2). New York: Academic Press.

Green, J.A., Jones, L.E., & Gustafson G.E. (1987). Perception of cries by parents and nonparents: Relation to cry acoustics. *Developmental Psychology, 23,* 370–382.

Green, R. (1987). *The "sissy boy syndrome" and the development of homosexuality.* New Haven: Yale University Press.

Greenfield, P.M. (1982). The role of perceived variability in the transition to language. *Journal of Child Language, 9,* 1–12.

Greenfield, P.M., & Bruner, J.S. (1966). Culture and cognitive growth. *International Journal of Psychology, 1,* 89–107.

Greenfield, P.M., & Smith, J.A. (1976). *The structure of communication in early language development.* New York Academic Press.

Greenough, W.T., Black, J.E., & Wallace, C.S. (1987). Experience and brain development. *Child Development, 58,* 539–559.

Greenspan S., & Greenspan, N.T. (1985). *First feelings.* New York: Viking.

Gregg, Mc A. (1941). *Congenital cataract following German measles in the mother.* Transactions of the Ophthalmological Society of Austria, 3, 35–46.

Gregg, C.L., Huffner, M.E., & Korner, A.F. (1976). The relative efficacy of vestibular-proprioceptive stimulation and the upright position in enhancing visual pursuit in neonates. *Child Development, 47,* 309–314.

Griffiths, R. (1954). *The abilities of babies.* New York: McGraw- Hill.

Grueling, J.W., & DeBlassie, R.R. (1980). Adolescent suicide. *Adolescence, 59,* 589–601.

Gruen, C.E., & Vore, D.A. (1972). Development of conservation in normal and retarded children. *Developmental Psychology, 6,* 146–157.

Grusec, J.E., & Abramovitch, R. (1982). Imitation of peers and adults in a natural setting: A functional analysis *Child Development, 53,* 636–642.

Grusec, J.E., Kuczynski, L., Ruston, J.P., & Simutis, Z.M. (1979). Learning resistance to temptation through observation. *Developmental Psychology, 15,* 233–240.

Guilford, J.P. (1950). Creativity. *American Psychologist, 5,* 444–454.

Guilford, J.P. (1954). A factor analytic study across the domains of reasoning, creativity, and evaluation. I Hypothesis and description of tests. *Reports from the Psychology Laboratory.* Los Angeles: University of Southern California Press.

Guilford, J.P. (1959). Three faces of intellect. *American Psychologist, 14,* 469–479.

Guilford, J.P. (1982). Cognitive psychology's ambiguities: Some suggested remedies. *Psychological Review, 89,* 48–59.

Guilford, J.P. (1985). The structure-of-intellect model. In B.B. Wolman (Ed.), *Handbook of intelligence.* New York: Wiley.

Gunnar, M.R., Malone, S., Vance, G., & Fisch, R.O. (1985). Coping with aversive stimulation in the neonatal period: Quiet sleep and plasma cortisol levels during recovery from circumcision. *Child Development, 56,* 824–834.

Guttman, N., & Kalish, H.I. (1956). Discrimination ability and stimulus generalization. *Journal of Experimental Psychology, 51,* 79–88.

Haan, N., Aerts, E., & Cooper, B.A.B. (1985). *In moral grounds: The search for practical morality.* New York: University Press.

Hall, C.C. (1979). *A primer of Freudian psychology.* New York: New American Library.

Hall, E.T. (1959). *The silent language.* New York: Doubleday.

Hall, E.T. (1966). *The hidden dimension.* New York: Doubleday

Hallahan, D.P., & Kauffman, J.M. (1991). *Exceptional children: Introduction to special education* (5th ed.). Englewood Cliffs, NJ: Prentice-Hall.

Halliday, M. (1973). *Explorations in the functions of language.* London: Edward Arnold.

Halmi, K.A. (1985). The diagnosis and treatment of anorexia nervosa. In D. Shaffer, A.A. Erhardt, & L. Greenhill (Eds.), *The clinical guide to child psychiatry.* New York: Free Press.

Halmi, K.A., Falk, J.R., & Schwartz, E. (1981). Binge-eating and vomiting: A survey of a college population. *Psychological Medicine, 11,* 697–706.

Hammen, C., Burge, D., & Stansbury, K. (1990). Relationship of mother and child variables to child outcomes in a high-risk sample: A causal modeling analysis. *Developmental Psychology, 26*(1), 24–30.

Handyside, A.H., Lesko, J.G., Tarin, J.J., Winston, R.M.L., & Hughes, M.R. (1992). Birth of a normal girl after in vitro fertilization and preimplantation diagnostic testing for cystic fibrosis. *New England Journal of Medicine, 327*(13), 905–909.

Hanshaw, J.B., Dudgeon, J.A., & Marshall, W.C. (1985). *Viral diseases of the fetus and newborn* (2nd ed.). Philadelphia: Saunders.

Harding, C., & Golinkoff, R. (1979). The origins of intentional vocalizations in prelinguistic infants. *Child Development, 50,* 33–40.

Hargreaves, D.J. (1987). Psychological theories of sex-role stereotyping. In D.J. Hargreaves & A.M. Colley (Eds.), *The psychology of sex roles.* Cambridge: Hemisphere.

Haring, N.G., & McCormick, L. (Eds.). (1990). *Exceptional children and youth* (5th ed.). Columbus, OH: Charles E. Merrill.

Harlow, H.F., & Harlow, M.K. (1969). Effects of various mother-infant relationships on rhesus monkey behaviors. In B. M. Foss (Ed.), *Determinants of infant behavior.* (Vol. 4). London: Methuen.

Harlow, H.F., & Zimmerman, R.R. (1959). Affectional responses in the infant monkey. *Science, 130,* 421–432.

Harris, L.J. (1978). Sex differences in spatial ability: Possible environmental, genetic, and neurological factors. In M. Kinsbourne (Ed.), *Asymmetrical functions of the brain.* Cambridge, England: Cambridge University Press.

Harris, M.P. (1970). Reciprocity and generosity: Some determinants of sharing in children. *Child Development, 41,* 313–328.

Harris, P.L. (1989). *Children and emotion: The development of psychological understanding.* New York: Basil Blackwell.

Harter, S. (1985). *Manual for the self-perception profile for children.* Denver, CO: University of Denver.

Harter, S. (1983). Developmental perspectives on the self-system, In P.H. Mussen (Ed.), *Handbook of child psychology* (4th ed.). (Vol. 4). New York: Wiley.

Harter, S. (1989). *Manual for the self-perception profile for adolescents.* Denver, CO: University of Denver.

Harter, S., & Connell, J.P. (1982). A comparison of alternative models of the relationships between academic achievement, and children's perceptions of competence, control, and motivational orientation, In J. Nicholls (Ed.), *The Development of Achievement-Related Cognitions and Behaviors.* Greenwich, CT: JAI Press.

Hartshorne, H., & May, M.A. (1928). *Studies in deceit.* New York: Macmillan.

Hartup, W.W. (1974). Aggression in childhood: Developmental perspectives. *American Psychologist, 29,* 336–341.

Hartup, W.W. (1983). Peer relationships. In P.H. Mussen (Ed.), *Handbook of child psychology* (4th ed.). (Vol. 4). New York: Wiley.

Harvey, R. (1980). Learning ability/achievement discrepancy. In R. Woody (Ed.), *Encyclopedia of clinical assessment.* San Francisco: Jossey-Bass.

Havighurst, R.J. (1972). *Developmental tasks and education* (3rd ed.). New York: McKay.

Hawthorne, W., & Menzel, N. (1983). Youth treatment should be a programming priority. *Alcohol Health and Research World, 8,* 46–50.

Hay, D.F. (1984). Social conflict in early childhood. *Annals of Child Development, 1,* 1–44.

Hay, D.F., & Ross, H.S. (1982). The social nature of early conflict. *Child Development, 53,* 105–113.

Held, R., & Hein, A. (1963). Movement-produced stimulation in the development of visually-guided behavior. *Journal of Comparative and Physiological Psychology, 56,* 872–876.

Hellerich, R.L., & Johnson, T.G. (1981). *Test manual. Test for READY STEPS: A diagnostic approach to early identification of reading readiness needs.* Boston: Houghton-Mifflin.

Helms, J.E. (1992). Why is there no study of cultural equivalence in standardized cognitive ability testing? *American Psychologist, 47*(9), 1083–1101.

Hermann, K. (1959). *Reading disability: A medical study of word-blindness and related handicaps.* Springfield, IL: Charles C. Thomas.

Hermelin, B., & O'Connor, N. (1970). *Psychological experiments with autistic children.* New York: Pergamon.

Hershanson, M. (1964). Visual discrimination in the human newborn. *Journal of Comparative and Physiological Psychology, 58,* 270–276.

Hess, R.D., & McDevitt, T.M. (1984). Some cognitive consequences of maternal intervention techniques: A longitudinal study. *Child Development, 55,* 2017–2030.

Hetherington, E.M. (1966). Effects of paternal absence on sex-typed behaviors in Negro and White preadolescent males. *Journal of Personality and Social Psychology, 4,* 87–91.

Hetherington, E.M. (1972). Effects of father absence on personality development in adolescent daughters. *Developmental Psychology, 7,* 313–326.

Hetherington E.M. (1988). Parents, children and siblings six years after divorce. In R. Hinde & J. Stevenson-Hinde (Eds.), *Relationships within families.* Cambridge: Cambridge University Press.

Hetherington, E.M. (1989). Coping with family transitions: Winners, losers, and survivors. *Child Development, 60,* 1–14.

Hetherington, E.M. (1991). The role of individual differences and family relationships in children's coping with divorce and remarriage. In P.A. Cowan & M. Hetherington (Eds.), *Family transitions.* Hillsdale, NJ: Erlbaum.

Hetherington, E.M., & Baltes, P.B. (1988). Child psychology and life-span development. In E.M. Hetherington, R.M. Learner, & M. Perlmutter (Eds.), *Child development in life-span perspective.* Hillsdale, NJ: Erlbaum.

Hetherington, E.M., & Camara, K.A. (1984). Families in transition: The processes of dissolution and reconstitution. In R.D. Parke (Ed.), *Review of child development research.* (Vol. 7). Chicago: University of Chicago Press.

Hetherington, E.M., & Clingempeel, W.G. (1992). Coping with marital transitions. *Monographs of the Society for Research in Child Development, 57,* (Serial No. 227), 2 and 3.

Hetherington, E.M., Cox, M., & Cox, R. (1982). Effects of divorce on parents and children. In M. Lamb (Ed.), *Nontraditional families.* Hillsdale, NJ: Erlbaum.

Hetherington, E.M., & Feldman, S.E. (1964). College cheating as a function of subject and situational variables. *Journal of Educational Psychology, 55,* 212–218.

Hetherington, E.M., & Parke, R.D. (1986). *Child psychology: A contemporary viewpoint* (3rd ed.). New York: McGraw Hill.

Hetherington, E.M., Stanley-Hagan, M., & Anderson, E.R. (1989). Marital transitions: A child's perspective. *American Psychologist, 44*(2), 303–312.

Heward, W.L., & Orlansky, M.D. (1992). *Exceptional children* (4th ed.). Columbus, OH: Merrill.

Higgins, A.T., & Turnure, J.E. (1984). Distractibility and concentration of attention in children's development. *Child Development, 55,* 1799-1810.

Hiller, L., Hewitt, K.L., & Morrongielo, B.A. (1992). Infants' perception of illusions in sound localization: Reaching to sounds in the dark. *Journal of Experimental Child Psychology, 53,* 159–179.

Himmelfarb, S., Hock, E., & Wenar, C. (1985). Infant temperament and noncompliant behavior at four years: A longitudinal study. *Genetic, Social and General Psychology Monographs, 111,* 9–21.

Hinde, R.A. (1983). Ethology and child development. In P.H. Mussen (Ed.), *Handbook of child psychology* (4th ed.) (Vol. 1). New York: Wiley.

Hinde, R.A. (1989). Ethological and relationships approaches. In J.R. Vasta (Ed.), *Annals of child development.* (Vol. 6). Greenwich, CT: JAI Press.

Hoben, T.A. (1985). Theory of high mathematical aptitude. *Journal of Mathematical Psychology, 29,* 231–242.

Hobson, J.A., & Mc Carley, R.W. (1977). The brain as a dream state generator: An activation-synthesis hypothesis of the dream process. *American Journal of Psychiatry, 134,* 1335–1348.

Hock, E. (1978). Working and nonworking mothers with infants: Perceptions of their careers, their infants' needs, and satisfaction with mothering. *Developmental Psychology, 4,* 37–43.

Hoff-Ginsberg, E. (1986). Function and structure in maternal speech: Their relation to the child's development of syntax. *Developmental Psychology, 22,* 155–163.

Hoffman, L.W. (1974). Effects of maternal employment on the child: A review of the research. *Developmental Psychology, 10,* 204–228.

Hoffman, L.W. (1984). Work, family and the socialization of the child. In R.D. Parke (Ed.), *Review of child development research, Vol. 7: The family.* Chicago: University of Chicago Press.

Hoffman, L.W. (1989). Effects of maternal employment in the two-parent family. *American Psychologist, 44*(2), 283–292.

Hoffman, M.L. Moral development. (1970). In P.H. Mussen (Ed.), *Carmichael's manual of child psychology* (3rd ed.) (Vol. 2.) New York: Wiley.

Hoffman, M.L. (1977). Moral internalization: Current theory and research. In L. Berkowitz (Ed.), *Advances in experimental, social psychology.* (Vol. 10). New York: Academic Press.

Hoffman, M.L. (1982). Development of prosocial motivation: Empathy and guilt. In N. Eisenberg (Ed.), *Development of prosocial behavior.* New York: Academic Press.

Hoffman, M.L. (1984). Moral development. In M.H. Bornstein & M.E. Lamb (Eds.), *Developmental psychology.* Hillsdale, NJ: Erlbaum.

Hoffman, M.L. (1988). Moral development. In M.H. Bornstein & M.E. Lamb (Eds.), *Developmental psychology: An advanced textbook* (2nd ed.). Hillsdale, NJ: Erlbaum.

Hoffman, M.L., & Saltzstein, H.D. (1967). Parent discipline and the child's moral development. *Journal of Personality and Social Psychology, 5,* 45–47.

Hofman, J. (1984). Children's drawings portray their world...and themselves. *The Register,* February 29, pp. 1, 6.

Holden, C. (1987). The genetics of personality. *Science, 1*(237), 598–600.

Holleran, P.R., Pascale, I., & Fraley, J. (1988). Personality correlates of college-age bulimics. *Journal of Counseling and Development, 66,* 378–381.

Hollingsworth, C.E., Tanguay, P.E., Grossman, L., & Pabst, P. (1980). Long-term outcome of obsessive compulsive disorder in children. *Journal of the American Academy of Child Psychiatry, 19,* 134–144.

Holtzman, W.H. (1982). Cross-cultural comparisons of personality development in Mexico and the United States. In D.A. Wagner & H.W. Stevenson (Eds.), *Cultural Perspectives on Child Development.* San Francisco: W.H. Freeman.

Honig, A.S. (1980). The importance of fathering. *Dimensions,* October, 63, 33–38.

Horn, J.L., Loehlin, J., & Wellman, L. (1985). Preliminary report of the Texas adoption project. In H. Munsinger (Ed.), The adopted child's IQ: A critical review. *Psychological Bulletin, 82,* 623–659.

Horn, T.S., & Hasbrook, C.A. (1987). Psychological characteristics and the criteria children use for self-evaluation. *Journal of Sport Psychology, 9,* 208–221.

Horowitz, F.D., & Paden, L.Y. (1973). The effectiveness of environmental intervention programs. In B.M. Caldwell & H.N. Riccuiti (Eds.), *Review of Child Development Research.* (Vol. 3). Chicago: University of Chicago Press.

Horwitz, R.A. (1979). Psychological effects of the "open classroom." *Review of Educational Research, 49,* 1–12.

Hottinger, W. (1980). Early childhood. In C.B. Corbin (Ed.), *A textbook of motor development* (2nd ed.). Dubuque, Iowa: Wm. C. Brown.

Houston, J. (1985). *Motivation.* New York: Macmillan.

Hoyenger, K.B., & Hoyenger, K.T. (1979). *The question of sex differences.* Boston: Little Brown.

Hubel, D.H., & Weisel, T.N. (1959). Receptive fields of single neurons in the cat's visual cortex. *Journal of Physiology, 148,* 574–591.

Hudson, J.A. (1990). Constructive processing in children's event memory. *Developmental Psychology, 26*(2), 180–187.

Huesmann, L.R. Psychological processes promoting the relation between exposure to media violence and aggressive behavior by the viewer. *Journal of Social Issues, 42,* 125–139.

Hughes, J.G. (1980). *Synopsis of pediatrics* (5th ed.). St. Louis: C.V. Mosby.

Humphreys, A.P., & Smith, P. K. (1984). Rough-and-tumble in preschool and playground. In P.K. Smith (Ed.), *Play in animals and humans.* Oxford: Basil Blackwell.

Humphreys, L.G. (1939). The effect of random alternation of reinforcement on the acquisition and extinction of conditioned eyelid reactions. *Journal of Experimental Psychology, 25,* 141–158.

Hunt, J. McV. (1961). *Intelligence and experience.* New York: Ronald Press.

Huston, A.C. (1983). Sex-typing. In P.H. Mussen (Ed.), *Handbook of child psychology* (4th ed.). (Vol. 4). New York: Wiley.

Huston, A.C., Watkins, B.A., & Kunkel, D. (1989). Public policy and children's television. *American Psychologist, 44*(2), 424–433.

Huttenlocker, P.R. (1984). Synapse elimination and plasticity in developing human cerebral cortex. *American Journal of Mental Deficiency, 88,* 488–496.

Hynd, G.W., et al. (1991). Corpus callosum morphology in attention deficit-hyperactivity disorder. Morphometric analysis of MRI. *Journal of Learning Disabilities, 24,* 141–146.

Ilg, F.L., Ames, L.B., & Baker, S.M. (1981). *Child behavior* (revised ed.). New York: Harper & Row.

Imperato-McGinley, J., Peterson R.E., Gantier, T., & Sturla, E. (1979). Androgens and the evolution of male-gender identity among male pseudohermaphrodites. *New England Journal of Medicine, 300,* 1233–1237.

Inhelder, B., & Piaget, J. (1958). *The growth of logical thinking from childhood to adolescence.* New York: Basic Books.

Istomina, Z.M. (1975). The development of voluntary memory in preschool-age children. *Soviet Psychology, 13,* 5–64.

Ito, M. (1984). *The cerebellum and neural control.* New York: Raven.

Izard, C.E. (1971). *The face of emotions.* New York: Appleton.

Izard, C.E. (1979). *The maximally discriminative facial movement coding system (MAX).* Newark: Instructional Resources Center, University of Delaware.

Izard, C.E. (1982). Measuring emotions in human development. In C.E. Izard (Ed.), *Measuring emotions in infants and children.* New York: Cambridge University Press.

Izard, C.E., Porges, S.W., Simons, R.F., Hayes, O.M., Hyde, C., Parisi, M., & Cohen, B. (1991). Infant cardiac activity: Developmental changes and relations with attachment. *Developmental Psychology, 27*(3), 432–439.

Jacklin, C.N. (1989). Female and male: Issues of gender. *American Psychologist, 44*(2), 127–133.

Jacobson J.L., Boersma, D.C., Fields, R.B., Olson, K.L. (1983). Paralinguistic features of adult speech to infants and small children. *Child Development, 54,* 436–442.

Jencks, C., et al. (1972). *Inequality: A reassessment of the effect of family and schooling in America.* New York: Basic Books.

Jensen, A.R. (1969). How much can we boost IQ and scholastic achievement? *Harvard Educational Review, 39,* 1–123.

Jensen, A.R. (1980). *Bias in mental testing.* New York: Free Press.

Jerison, H.J. (1982). The evolution of biological intelligence. In R.J. Sternberg (Ed.), *The Handbook of human intelligence.* New York: Cambridge University Press.

Jersild, A.T. (1968). *Child psychology* (6th ed.). Englewood Cliffs, NJ: Prentice-Hall.

Jersild, A.T., & Holmes, F.B. (1935). Children's fears. *Child Development Monographs, No. 20.* New York: Teachers College, Columbia University.

Johnson, C.D., Driscoll, S.G., Hertig, A.T., Cole, P.T., & Nickerson, R.J. (1979). Vaginal adenosis in still-borns and neonates exposed to diethylstilbesterol and steroid estrogens and progestins. *Obstetrics and Gynecology, 53,* 671–679.

Johnson, D.W., & Johnson, R.T. (1974). Instructional goal structure: cooperative, competitive, or individualistic. *Review of Education Research, 44,* 213–240.

Johnson, D.W., & Johnson, R.T. (1991). *Learning together and alone: Cooperative, competitive, and individualistic learning* (3rd ed.). Englewood Cliffs, NJ: Prentice-Hall.

Johnson, E.S., & Meade, A.C. (1987). Developmental patterns of spatial ability: An early sex difference. *Child Development, 58*(3), 725–740.

Johnson, W., Emde, R.N., Pannabecker, B., Stenberg, C., & Davis, M. (1982). Maternal perception of infant emotion from birth through 18 months. *Infant Behavior and Development, 5*, 313–322.

Johnston, F.E. (1980). The causes of malnutrition. In L.S. Greene & F.E. Johnston (Eds.), *Social and biological predictors of nutritional status, physical growth and neurological development.* New York: Academic Press.

Johnston, J. & Ettema, J.S. (1982). *Positive images. Breaking stereotypes with children's television.* Newbury Park, CA: Sage.

Johnston, J.R., Kline, M., & Tschann, J.M. (1989). Ongoing post-divorce conflict: Effects on children of joint custody and frequent access. *Journal of Orthopsychiatry, 59*(4), 576–592.

Jones, K.L., Smith D.W., Ulleland, C.N., & Streissguth, A.P. (1973). Pattern of malformation in offspring of chronic alcoholic mothers. *Lancet, 1*, 1267–1271.

Jones, L. (1988). Survivors, other plumb tragedy of teen suicide. *Los Angeles Times*, March 12, Pt. II, p. 1, 6–7.

Jones, L. (1989). Procedures buy mothers time. *Los Angeles Times*, February 28, Prt II, 1, p. 4.

Jones, M.C. (1965). Psychological correlates of somatic development. *Child Development, 36*, 899–911.

Jones, M.C., & Mussen, P.H. (1958). Self-conceptions, motivations, and interpersonal attitudes of early- and late-maturing girls. *Child Development, 29*, 491–501.

Just, M.A., & Carpenter, P.A. (1984). Eye movements and reading comprehension. In D.E. Kieras & M.A. Just (Eds.), *New methods in reading comprehension research.* Hillsdale, NJ: Erlbaum.

Kagan, J. (1982). *Psychological research on the human infant: An evaluative summary.* New York: W.T. Grant Foundation.

Kagan, J. (1965). Reflection-impulsivity and reading ability in primary grade children. *Child Development, 36*, 609–626.

Kagan, J. (1984). *The nature of the child.* New York: Basic Books.

Kagan, J., et al. (1964). Information processing in the child: significances of analytic and reflective attitudes. *Psychological Monographs, 78*(1), (Whole No. 578).

Kagan, J., Kearsley, R.B., & Zelazo, P.R.(1978). *Infancy: Its place in human development.* Cambridge: Harvard University Press.

Kagan, J., & Moss, H.A. (1962). *Birth to maturity.* New York: Wiley.

Kagan, J., Pearson, L., & Welch, L. (1966). Conceptual impulsivity and inductive reasoning. *Child Development, 237*, 583–594.

Kail, R. (1990). *The development of memory in children* (3rd ed.). New York: W.H. Freeman.

Kalish, H.I. (1981). *From behavioral science to behavior modification.* New York: McGraw-Hill.

Kamii, C. (1982). Autonomy as the aim of education: Implications of Piaget's theory. In C. Kamii (Ed.), *Number in preschool and kindergarten.* Washington, DC: National Association for the Education of Young Children.

Kanner, L. (1965). Infantile autism and the schizophrenics. *Behavioral Science, 10*, 412–420.

Karmel, B.J., Kaye, H., & John, E.R. (1978). Developmental neurometrics: The use of quantitative analysis of brain electrical activity to probe mental functioning throughout the life span. In W.A. Collin (Ed.), *Minnesota symposia on child psychology.* (Vol. 2). Hillsdale, NJ: Erlbaum.

Karmiloff-Smith, A. (1979). Language development after five. In P. Fletcher & M. Garman (Eds.), *Language acquisition.* New York: Cambridge University Press.

Kasahni, J., Husain, A., Shekim, W., Hodges, K., Cytryn, L., & McKrew, D. (1981). Current perspectives on childhood depression. *American Journal of Psychiatry, 138*, 143–153.

Katchadourian, H.A. (1977). *The biology of adolescence.* San Francisco: Freeman.

Katcher, A. (1955). The discrimination of sex differences by young children. *The Journal of Genetic Psychology, 87*, 131–143.

Kaufman, J. & Cicchetti, D. (1986). *The effects of maltreatment on school-aged children. Assessments in a day camp setting.* Unpublished manuscript. University of Rochester.

Keeney, T.J., Cannizzo, S.R., & Flavell, J.H. (1967). Spontaneous and induced verbal rehearsal in a recall task. *Child Development, 38*, 953–966.

Keeton, W.T. (1973). *Elements of biological science* (2nd ed.). New York: W.W. Norton.

Keeton, W.T., & Mc Fadden, C.H. (1983). *Elements of biological science* (3rd ed.). New York: W.W. Norton.

Keller, A., Ford, L.H. Jr., & Meacham, J.A. (1978). Dimensions of self-concept in preschool children. *Developmental Psychology, 14*, 483–489.

Kellerman, J. (1981). *Helping the fearful child.* Chicago: Contemporary Books.

Kempe, R.S., & Kempe, C.H. (1978). *Child abuse.* Cambridge: Harvard University Press.

Kennell, J.H., & Klaus, M.H. (1984). Mother-infant bonding: Weighing the evidence. *Developmental Review, 4,* 275–282.

Kennter, G. (1969). Absolute differences and changes of the average stature among the Chileans. *Biological Abstracts, 50,* 3248.

Kenny, S.L. (1983). Developmental discontinuities in childhood and adolescence. *In levels and transitions in children's development.* (New Directions for Child Development, No. 21). San Francisco: Jossey-Bass.

Kershner, J.R., & Ledger, G. (1985). Effect of sex, intelligence, and style of thinking on creativity: A comparison of gifted and average IQ children. *Journal of Personality and Social Psychology, 48,* 1033–1040.

Kesner, R.P., & Baker, T.B. (1980). Neuroanatomical correlates of language and memory: A developmental perspective. In R.L. Ault (Ed.), *Developmental perspectives.* Santa Monica, CA: Goodyear.

Kinsbourne, M. (1989). Mechanisms and development of hemisphere specialization in children. In C.R. Reynolds & E. Fletcher-Janzen (Eds.), *Handbook of clinical child neuropsychology.* New York: Plenum.

Kite, W.R. (December, 1980). Presenting problems of adolescents in treatment: A survey of comprehensive-care adolescent programs. *Executive Summary.* St. Louis: Comprehensive Care Corp.

Klahr, D. (1989). Information processing approaches. In R. Vasta (Ed.), *Annals of child development.* (Vol. 6). Greenwich, CT: JAI Press.

Klaus, M.H., & Kennell, J.H. (1982). *Parent-infant bonding.* St. Louis, MO: C.V. Mosby.

Klaus, M.H., & Kennell, J.H. (1978). Parent-to-infant attachment. In J.H. Stevens, Jr. & M. Mathews (Eds.), *Mother/child father/child relationships.* Washington, DC: National Association for the Education of Young Children.

Klein, S.B. (1987). *Learning: Principles and applications.* New York: McGraw-Hill.

Klinnert, M., Campos, J., Sorce, J., Emde, R., & Svejda, M. (1983). Emotions as behavior regulators: Social referencing in infancy. In R. Plutchnik & Z.H. Kellerman (Eds.), *Emotions in early development.* New York: Academic Press.

Klinnert, M.D., Emde, R.N., Butterfield, P., & Campos, J.J.(1986). Social referencing: The infant's use of emotional signals from a friendly adult with mother present. *Developmental Psychology, 22*(4), 427–432.

Klissouras, V. (1976). Prediction of athletic performance: genetic considerations. *Canadian Journal of Applied Sport Sciences, 1,* 195–200.

Klopfer, P.H. (1971). Mother love: What turns it on? *American Scientist, 59,* 404–407.

Knobloch, H., & Pasamanick, B. (Eds.). (1974). *Gesell and Amatruda's developmental diagnosis.* Hagerstown, MD: Harper & Row.

Knudsen, E., & Knudsen, P. (1985). Vision guide to the adjustment of auditory localization in young barn owls. *Science, 230,* 545–548.

Kogan, N. (1983). Stylistic variation in childhood and adolescence: Creativity, metaphor, and cognitive style. In P.H. Mussen (Ed.), *Handbook of child psychology* (4th ed.). (Vol. 3). New York: Wiley.

Kohlberg, L. (1969). Stage and sequence: The cognitive-developmental approach to socialization. In D.A. Goslin (Ed.), *Handbook of socialization: Theory and research.* Chicago: Rand McNally.

Kohlberg, L. (1976). Moral stages and moralization: The cognitive developmental approach. In T. Lickona (Ed.), *Moral development and behavior.* New York: Holt, Rinehart and Winston.

Kohlberg, L.A. (1966). A cognitive-developmental analysis of children's sex-role concepts and attitudes. In E.E. Maccoby (Ed.), *The development of sex differences.* Stanford: Stanford University Press.

Kolata, G. (1984). Studying learning in the womb. *Science, 225,* 302–303.

Kolata, G.B. (1986). Obese children: A growing problem. *Science, 232,* 20–21.

Konner, M. (1982). *The tangled wing: Biological constraints on the human spirit.* New York: Holt, Rinehart and Winston.

Kopp, C.B. (1983). Risk factors in development. In P.H. Mussen (Ed.), *Handbook of child psychology* (4th ed.). (Vol. 2). New York: Wiley.

Koop, C.E. (1988). *Understanding AIDS.* (HHS-88-8404). Washington, DC: U.S. Government Printing Office.

Korner, A.F., & Grobstein, R. (1966). Visual alertness as related to soothing in neonate. *Child Development, 37,* 867–876.

Kotelchuck, M. (1976). The infant's relationship to the father: Experimental evidence. In M.E. Lamb (Ed.), *The role of the father in child development.* New York: Wiley.

Krashen, S. (1975). The critical period for language acquisition and its possible bases. In D. Aaronson & R.W. Reiber (Eds.), Developmental psycholinguistics and communication disorders. *Annals of the New York Academy of Sciences, 263*(2), 11–224.

Kreutzer, M.A., Leonard, C., & Flavell, J.H. (1975). An interview study of children's knowledge about memory. *Monographs of the Society for Research in Child Development, 40* (1 Serial No. 159).

Krogman, W.M. (1972). *Child growth.* Ann Arbor: University of Michigan Press.

Kuczaj, S.A. II. (1977). The acquisition of regular and irregular past tense forms. *Journal of Verbal Learning and Verbal Behavior, 16,* 589–600.

Kuczaj, S.A. II, & Brannick, N. (1979). Children's use of 'Wh' question modal auxilliary placement rule. *Journal of Experimental Child Psychology, 28,* 43–67.

Kuhn, D. (1989). Children and adults as intuitive scientists. *Psychological Review, 96,* 674–689.

Kupersmidt, J.B., & Coie, J.D. (1990). Preadolescent peer status, aggression, and school adjustment as predictors of externalizing problems in adolescence. *Child Development, 61,* 1350–1363.

Kurent, J.E., & Sever, J.L. (1977). Infectious diseases. In G. Wilson & F.C. Fraser (Eds.), *Handbook of teratology, Vol. 1. General principles and etiology.* New York: Plenum.

Kwakman, A.M., Zuker, F.A.J.M., Schippers, G.M., & DeWuffel, F.J. (1988). Drinking behavior, drinking attitudes, and attachment relationships of adolescents. *Journal of Youth and Adolescence, 17,* 247–253.

Labinowicz, E. (1980). *The Piaget primer: Thinking, learning, teaching.* Menlo Park, CA: Addison-Wesley.

Lachenmeyer, J.R., & Muni-Brander, P. (1988). Eating disorders in a nonclinical adolescent population: Implications for treatment. *Adolescence, 23,* 303–312.

Lamaze, F. (1970). *Painless childbirth.* Chicago: Henry Regnery.

Lamb, M.E. (1976). The role of the father: An overview. In M.E. Lamb (Ed.), *The role of the father in child development.* New York: Wiley.

Lamb, M.E. (1977). The development of mother-infant and father-infant attachment in the second year of life. *Developmental Psychology, 13*(6), 637–648.

Lamb, M.E., & Bornstein, M.H. (1987). *Development in infancy* (2nd ed.). New York: Random House.

Lamb, M.E., & Campos, J.J. (1982). *Development in infancy: An introduction.* New York: Random House.

Lamb, M.E., & Hwang, C.P. (1982). Maternal attachment and mother-neonate bonding: A critical review. In M.E. Lamb & A.L. Brown (Eds.), *Advances in developmental psychology.* (Vol. 2). Hillsdale, NJ: Erlbaum.

Landau, R. (1982). Infant crying and fussing. *Journal of Cross-Cultural Psychology, 13,* 427–443.

Langlois, J.H., & Downs, A.C. (1980). Mothers, fathers and peers as socialization agents of sex-typed play behaviors in young children. *Child Development, 51,* 1237–1247.

Langsdorf, P., Izard, C.E., Rayiss, M., & Hembree, C.A. (1983). Interest expression, visual fixation, and heart rate changes in 2- to 8-month-old infants. *Developmental Psychology, 19,* 375–386.

Lasko, J.K. (1954). Parent behavior toward first- and second-born children. *Genetic Psychology Monographs, 49,* 105–116.

Lazar, I., & Darlington, R. (1982). Lasting effects of early education: A report from the consortium for longitudinal studies. *Monographs of the Society for Research in Child Development, 47* (Whole No. 195).

Leboyer, F. (1975). *Birth without violence.* New York: Alfred Knopf.

Lecours, A.R. (1975). Myelogenetic correlates of the development of speech and language. In E.M. Lenneberg & E.H. Lenneberg, *Foundations of language development.* New York: Academic Press.

Lee, C.L., & Bates, J.E. (1985). Mother-child interaction at age two years and perceived difficult temperament. *Child Development, 56,* 1314–1325.

Lee, V. (Ed.). (1979). *Language development.* New York: Wiley.

Lefrancois, G.R. (1989). *Of children* (6th ed.). Belmont, CA: Wadsworth.

Leibert, R.M., & Sprafkin, J. (1988). *The early window* (3rd ed.). New York: Pergamon Press.

Leinbach, M.D., & Fagot, B.I. (1986). Acquisition of gender labels: A test for toddlers. *Sex Roles, 15*(11/12), 655–666.

Lempers, J.D., Clark-Lempers, D., & Simons, R.L. (1989). Economic hardship, parenting, and distress in adolescence. *Child Development, 60,* 25–39.

Lenneberg, E.H. (1967). *Biological foundations of language.* New York: Wiley.

Lenneberg, E.H. (1973). Biological aspects of language. In G.A. Miller (Ed.), *Communication language and meaning.* New York: Basic Books.

Leo, J. (1980). From mollusks to moppets. *Time, 116,* p. 55.

Leonard, L. (1986). The dynamic brain. In H.E. Fitzgerald & M.G. Walgren (Eds.), *Annual editions: Human development, 86/87,* Guilford, CT: Dushkin.

Leonard, L.B., Chapman, K., Rowan, L.E., & Weiss, A.C. Three hypotheses concerning children imitations of lexical items. *Developmental Psychology, 19,* 591–601.

Lerner, J., Mardell-Czudnowski, C., & Goldenberg, D. (1987). *Special education for early childhood years* (2nd ed.). Englewood Cliffs, NJ: Prentice-Hall.

Lerner, R.M. (1983). A "goodness-of-fit" model of person-context interaction. In D. Magnusson & V.L. Allen (Eds.), *Human development: An interactional perspective.* New York: Academic Press.

Lerner, R.M., & Korn, S.J. (1972). The development of body-build stereotypes in males. *Child Development, 43,* 908–920.

Lerner, R.M., & Spanier, C.B. (1980). *Adolescent development: A life-span perspective.* New York: McGraw-Hill.

Lever, J. (1976). Sex differences in the games children play. *Social Problems,* 478–487.

Lever, J. (1978). Sex differences in the complexity of children's play and games. *American Sociological Review, 43,* 471–483.

Levine, M.W., & Shefner, J.M. (1991). *Fundamentals of sensation and perception* (2nd ed.). Pacific Grove, CA: Brooks/Cole.

LeVine, R.A. (1986). Properties of culture: An ethnographic view. In R.A. Sweder & R.A. LeVine (Eds.), *Culture theory: Essays on mind, self and emotion.* Cambridge: Cambridge University Press.

Levy, J. (1980). Cerebral asymmetry and the psychology of man. In M.C. Wittrock (Ed.), *The brain and psychology.* New York: Academic Press.

Lewandowski, L.J., & Cruickshank, W.M. (1980). Psychological development of crippled children and youth. In W. M. Cruickshank (Ed.), *Psychology of exceptional children and youth* (4th ed.). Englewood Cliffs, NJ: Prentice-Hall.

Lewin, K., Lippitt, R., & White, R. (1939). Patterns of aggressive behavior in experimentally created social climate. *Journal of Social Psychology, 10,* 271–299.

Lewis, M., & Brooks-Gunn, J. (1979). *Social cognition and the acquisition of self.* New York: Plenum.

Lewis, T.L., Maurer, D., & Brent, H.P. (1985). The effects of visual deprivation during infancy on perceptual development. *British Journal of Ophthalmology, 70,* 214–220.

Liben, L.S., & Golbeck, S.L. (1980). Sex differences in performance on Piagetian spatial tasks: Differences in competence or performance. *Child Development, 51,* 594–597.

Lickona, T. (1983). *Raising good children.* New York: Bantam.

Lieban, J.N. (1977). *Playfulness: Its relationship to imagination and creativity.* New York: Academic Press.

Liebman, R., Sargent, J., & Silver, M. (1983). A family systems orientation to the treatment of anorexia nervosa. *Journal of the American Academy of Child Psychiatry, 22*(2), 128–133.

Lind, J. (1971). The infant cry. *Proceedings of the Royal Society of Medicine, 64,* 468.

Linney, J.A., & Seidman, E. (1989). The future of schooling. *American Psychologist, 44*(2), 336–340.

Lipsitt, L.P. (1974). Critical conditions in infancy: A psychological perspective. *American Psychologist, 34,* 973–980.

Lipsitt, L.P., Engen, T., & Kaye, H. (1963). Developmental changes in the olfactory thresholds of the neonate. *Child Development, 34,* 371–376.

Lipsitt, L.P., & Levy, N. (1959). Electrotactual threshold in the neonate. *Child Development, 30,* 547–554.

List, J.A., Collins, W.A., & Westby, S.D. (1983). Comprehension and inferences from traditional and nontraditional sex-role portrayals on television. *Child Development, 54,* 1579–1587.

Lockwood, A. (1978). The effects of value clarification and moral development curricula on school age subjects: A critical review of recent research. *Review of Educational Research, 48,* 325–364.

Livesley, W.J., & Bromley D.B. (1973). *Person perception in childhood and adolescence.* New York: Wiley.

Long, T.J., & Long, L. (1982). *Latchkey children: The child's view of self-care.* Washington, DC: Catholic University America (ERIC Document Reproduction Service, No. ED 211 229).

Longoni, A.M., & Orsini, L. (1988). Lateral preferences in preschool children: A research note. *Journal of Child Psychology & Psychiatry & Allied Disciplines, 29*(4), 533–539.

Lorenz, K. (1935/1970). *Studies in animal and human behavior.* R. Martin (Trans.). London: Methuen.

Lorenz, K. (1952). *King Solomon's ring.* London: Methuen.

Lorenz, K. (1966). *On aggression.* New York: Harcourt Brace.

Lozoff, B.(1988). Behavioral alterations in iron deficiency. *Advances in Pediatrics, 35,* 331–360.

Lozoff, B. (1989). Nutrition and behavior. *American Psychologist, 44*(2), 231–236.

Lubinski, D., Tellegen, A., Butcher, J.N. (1983). Masculinity, femininity and androgyny viewed and assessed as distinct concepts. *Journal of Personality and Social Psychology, 44,* 428–439.

Luria, A.R. (1976). *Cognitive development: Its cultural and social foundations.* Cambridge, MA: Harvard University Press

Lyon, J. (1985). *Playing god in the nursery.* New York: Norton.

Maccoby, E.E. (1980). *Social development: Psychological growth and the parent relationship.* New York: Harcourt Brace Jovanovich.

Maccoby, E.E., & Jacklin, C.N. (1974). *The psychology of sex differences.* Stanford, CA: Stanford University Press.

Maccoby, E.E., & Martin, J.A. (1983). Socialization in the context of the family: Parent-child interaction. In P.H. Mussen (Ed.), *Handbook of child psychology* (4th ed.). (Vol. 4.) New York: Wiley.

Maccoby, E.E., Snow, M.E., Jacklin, C.N. (1984). Children's disposition and mother-child interaction at 12 and 18 months: A short-term longitudinal study. *Developmental Psychology, 20,* 459–472.

MacDonald, K. (1986). Early experience, relative plasticity, and cognitive development. *Journal of Applied Developmental Psychology, 7,* 101–124.

MacDonald, K. & Parke, R.D. (1986). Parent-child physical play: The effects of sex and age of children and parents. *Sex Roles, 15*(7/8), 367–378.

MacFarlane, J.A. (1975). Olfaction in the development of social preference in the human neonate. In M.A. Hofer (Ed.), *Parent–infant interaction.* Amsterdam: Elsevier.

MacKinnon, D. (1962). The nature and nurture of creative talent. *American Psychologist, 17,* 484–495.

MacKinnon, D.W. (1975). IPAR's contribution to the conceptualization and study of creativity. In I.A. Taylor & J.W. Getzels (Eds.), *Perspectives in creativity.* Chicago: Aldine.

MacMillan, D.L. (1982). *Mental retardation in school and society.* (2nd ed.). Boston: Little Brown.

Madsen, C.H., & Madsen, C.K. (1970). *Teaching—Discipline.* Boston: Allyn & Bacon.

Madsen, M.C., & Shapira, H. (1970). Cooperative and competitive behavior of urban Afro-American, Anglo-American and Mexican-American and village children. *Developmental Psychology, 3*(1), 16–20.

Mahler, M.S. (1969). *On human symbiosis and the vicissitudes of individuation, Vol. 1: Infantile psychosis.* New York International Universities Press.

Mahler, M.S., Pine, F., & Bergman, A. (1975). *The psychological birth of the infant.* New York: Basic Books.

March of Dimes Birth Defects Foundation (1985). *The family health tree.* White Plains, NY.

March of Dimes Birth Defects Foundation (1987). *Report from International Conference on Prepregnancy Nutrition.* White Plains, NY.

March of Dimes Birth Defects Foundation (1989). *Pregnancy over 35.* White Plains, NY.

March of Dimes Birth Defects Foundation. (1991). *Be good to your baby before it is born.* White Plains, NY.

Marcia, J.E. (1980). Identity in adolescence. In J. Adelson (Ed.), *Handbook of adolescent psychology.* New York: Wiley.

Marcia, J.E. (1991). Identity and self-development. In R.M. Lerner, A.C. Petersen, & J. Brooks-Gunn (Eds.), *Encyclopedia of adolescence.* (Vol. 1). New York: Garland.

Marcus, L.C. (1983). Preventing and treating toxoplasmosis. *Drug Therapy, 13,* 129–144.

Marshall, H., & Weinstein, R. (1984, April). Classrooms where students perceive high and low amounts of differential teacher treatment. *Paper presented at the Annual Meeting of the American Educational Research Association.* New Orleans.

Matheny, A.J., and Dolan, A.B. (1975). Persons, situations and time: A genetic view of behavioral change in children. *Journal of Personality and Social Psychology, 32,* 1106–1110.

Malina, R.M. (1975). Anthropometric correlates of strength and motor performance. *Exercise and Sport Science Reviews, 3,* 249–274.

Malina, R.M. (1979). Secular changes in size and maturity, causes and effects. In A.F. Roche (Ed.), *Secular Trends in Human Growth and Development. Monographs for the Society for Research in Child Development, 44,* No. 3–4.

Malina, R.M. (1980). Biologically related correlates to motor development and performance during infancy and childhood. In C.B. Corbin (Ed.), *A textbook of motor development* (2nd ed.). Dubuque Iowa: Wm C. Brown.

Malina, R.M. (1980). Biosocial correlates of motor development during infancy and early childhood. In L.S. Greene & F.E. Johnston (Eds.), *Social and biological predictors of nutritional status, physical growth, and neurological development.* New York: Academic Press.

Malina, R.M., Harper, A.B., & Holman, J.D.(1970). Growth status and performance relative to parental size. *Research Quarterly, 41,* 503–509.

Mandler, J.M. (1983). Representation. In P.H. Mussen (Ed.), *Handbook of Child Psychology* (4th ed.). (Vol. 3). New York: Wiley.

Maratsos, M. (1983). Some current issues in the study of the acquisition of grammar. In P.H. Mussen (Ed.), *Handbook of child psychology*. (4th ed.). (Vol. 4). New York: Wiley.

Marcia, J.E. (1966). Development and validation of ego identity status. *Journal of Personality and Social Psychology, 3*, 551–558.

Marcia, J.E. (1991). Identity and self-development. In R.M. Lerner, A.C. Petyersen, & J. Brooks-Gunn (Eds.), *Encyclopedia of adolescence*. (Vol. 1). New York: Garland.

Marge, M. (1972). The general problems of language disabilities in children. In J.V. Irwin & M. Marge (Eds.), *Principles of childhood language disabilities*. Englewood Cliffs, NJ: Prentice-Hall.

Marland, M. (1983). School as sexist amplifier. In M. Marland (Ed.), *Sex differentiation and schooling*. London: Heinemanns.

Marler, P.R. (1970). A comparative approach to vocal learning: song development in white-crowned sparrows. *Journal of Comparative and Physiological Monographs 71* (No. 2, Part 2), 1–25.

Martens, R. (1978). *Joy and sadness in children's sports*. Champaign, IL: Human Kinetics.

Martin, C.L. (1989). Children's use of gender-related information in making social judgments. *Developmental Psychology, 25*, 80–88.

Martin, C.L., & Halverson, C.F. Jr. (1981). A schematic processing model of sex typing and stereotyping in children. *Child Development, 52*, 1119–1134.

Martin, C.L., & Halverson, C.F. Jr. (1983). The effect of sex-typing schemas on young childrens' memory. *Child Development, 54*(4), 563–574.

Martorell, R. (1980). Interrelationship between diet, infections disease, and nutritional status. In L.S. Greene & F.E. Johnston (Eds.), *Social and biological predictors of nutritional status, physical growth, and neurological development*. New York: Academic Press.

Matheny, A.P. Jr. (1983). A longitudinal twin study of stability of components from Bayley's Infant Behavior Record. *Child Development, 54*, 356–360.

Matheny, A.P. Jr., Dolan, A.B., & Wilson, R.S. (1976). Within pair similarity on Bayley's infant behavior record. *Journal of Genetic Psychology, 128*, 263–270.

Matheny, A.P. Jr., Wilson, R.S., Dolan, A. B., & Drantz, J.Z. (1981). Behavior contrasts in twinships: Stability and patterns of differences in childhood. *Child Development, 52*, 579–588.

Mathews, J.D. (1981). Genetics and alcohol: Implications for human disease. *Australian and New Zealand Journal of Medicine, 11*, 109–114.

Matthews, K. (1982). Psychological perspectives on the type A behavior pattern. *Psychological Bulletin, 91*, 293–323.

Maurer, D., & Maurer, C. (1988). *The world of the newborn*. New York: Basic Books.

Maurer, D., & Salapatek, P. (1976). Developmental changes in the scanning of faces by young infants. *Child Development, 47*, 523–527.

Maziade, M., Boudreault, M., Cote, R., & Thiverge, J. (1986). Influence of gentle birth delivery procedures and other perinatal circumstances on infant temperament: Developmental and social implications. *Journal of Pediatrics, 108*, 134–136.

McBride, W.G. (1961). Thalidomide and congenital abnormalities. *Lancet, 2*, 1358.

McCall, R.B. (1977). Childhood IQ's as predictors of adult educational and occupational success. *Science, 197*, 482–483.

McCall, R.B. (1984). Developmental changes in mental performance: The effect of birth of a sibling. *Child Development, 55*, 1317–1321.

McCall, R.B., Applebaum, M.I., & Hogarty, P.S. (1973). Developmental changes in mental performances. *Monographs of the Society for Research in Child Development, 38* (Serial No. 150).

McCarthy, D. (1954). Language development in children. In L. Carmichael (Ed.), *Manual of child psychology* (2nd ed.). New York: Wiley.

McCarthy, P. (1983). Fetal alcohol syndrome. *Nurse Practitioners: American Primary Health Care, 8*, 34.

McColl, R., Eichorn, D., & Hogarty, P. (1977). Transitions in early mental development. *Monographs of the Society for Research in Child Development, 43*, Serial No. 171, 3.

McCrary, J.L., & McCrary, S.P. (1982). *Human sexuality* (4th ed.). New York: D.Van Nostrand.

McCroskey, R.L., & Kidder H.C. (1980). Auditory fusion among learning disabled, reading disabled and normal children. *Journal of Learning Disabilities, 13*, 69–76.

McGraw, K.O. (1987). *Developmental psychology*. San Diego: Harcourt Brace Jovanovich.

McGraw, M.B.(1935). *Growth: A study of Johnny and Jimmy*. East Norwalk, CT: Appleton-Century-Crofts.

McGraw, M.B. (1940). Neural maturation as exemplified in achievement of bladder control. *Journal of Pediatrics*, 16, 580–589.

McGraw, M.B.(1945). *Neuromuscular maturation of the human infant.* New York: Hafner.

McGuiness, D. (1976). Sex differences in the organization of perception and cognition. In B. Lloyd & J. Archer (Eds.), *Exploring sex differences.* London: Academic Press.

McKean, K. (1987). Intelligence: New ways to measure the wisdom of man. In H.E. Fitzgerald & M.G. Walraven (Eds.), *Annual editions: Human development 87/88*, Guilford, CT: Dushkin.

Mc Neill, D. (1970). *The acquisition of language: The study of developmental psycholinguistics.* New York: Harper & Row.

Meacham, J.A. (1977). Soviet investigations of memory development. In R.V. Kail, Jr. & J.W. Hagen (Eds.), *Perspectives on the development of memory and cognition.* Hillsdale, NJ: Erlbaum.

Mead, G.H. (1934). *Mind, self, and society.* Chicago: University of Chicago Press.

Mead, M. (1935). *Sex and temperament in three primitive societies.* New York: Morrow.

Medrich, E.A., Rosen, J., Rubin, V., & Buckley, S. (1982). *The serious business of growing up.* Berkeley: University of California Press.

Meier, B. (1987). Companies wrestle threats to workers reproductive health. *Wall Street Journal*, February 5, p. 21.

Mehler, J., Bertoncini, J., Barriere, M., & Jassik-Gerschenfeld, D. (1978). Infant recognition of mother's voice. *Perception*, 7, 491–497.

Meltzoff, A. (1988). An imitation of televised models by infants. *Child Development*, 59, 1221–1229.

Meltzoff, A.N., & Borton, R.W. (1979). Intermodal matching by human neonates. *Nature*, 282, 403–404.

Mendelson, M.J. (1979). Acoustic-optical correspondences and auditory-visual coordination in infancy. *Canadian Journal of Psychology*, 33, 334–346.

Menyuk, P. (1983). Language development and reading. In T.M. Gallagher & C.A. Prutting (Eds.), *Pragmatic assessment and intervention issues in language.* San Diego: San Diego College-Hill Press.

Mercer, C.D. (1983). *Students with learning disabilities* (2nd ed.). Columbus, OH: Charles E. Merrill.

Mercer, J.R. (1972). IQ: The lethal label. *Psychology Today*, 6, 44–47.

Mercer, J.R., & Lewis, J.F. (1978). *System of multicultural pluralistic assessment.* New York: Psychological Corporation.

Merahn, S. (1987). Vision problems: Early detection in preschoolers. *Scholastic Pre-K Today*, 1, 33.

Meredith, D. (1986) Day-care: The nine-to-five dilemma. *Psychology Today*, 20, 36–39, 42.

Miller, N.E. (1985). Rx: biofeedback. *Psychology Today*, 16, 51–52.

Miller, L.B., & Dyer, J.L. (1975). Four preschool programs: Their dimensions and effects. *Monographs of the Society for Research in Child Development*, 40, (Serial No. 162), 5 and 6.

Miller, N., & Maruyama, G. (1976). Ordinal position and peer popularity. *Journal of Personality and Social Psychology*, 33, 123–131.

Milansky, A., Jick, H., Jick, S.S., MacLaughlin, D.S., Rothman, K.J., & Willet, W. (1989). Multivitamin/folic acid supplementation in early pregnancy reduces the prevalence of neural tube defects. *Journal of the American Medical Association*, 262, 2847–2852.

Millar, S. (1976). Spatial representation by blind and sighted children. *Journal of Experimental Child Psychology*, 21, 460–479.

Miller, L., & Dyer, J.(1975). Four preschool programs: Their dimensions and effects. *Monographs of the Society for Research in Child Development*, 40, (Serial No. 162), 5–6.

Miller, M.W. (1985). Study says birth defects more frequent in areas polluted by technology firms. *Wall Street Journal*, January 17, p. 6.

Miller, M.M. & Reeves, B.B. (1976). Children's occupational sex-role stereotypes: The linkage between television context and perception. *Journal of Broadcasting*, 20, 35–50.

Miller, P.M., Danaher, D.L., & Forbes, D. (1986). Sex-related strategies for coping with interpersonal conflict in children aged five and seven. *Developmental Psychology*, 22(4), 543–548.

Minton, C., Kagan, J., & Levine, J. (1971). Maternal control and obedience in the two-year-old. *Child Development*, 42, 1873–1894.

Minuchin, P.P., & Shapiro, E.K. (1983). The school as a context for social development. In P.H. Mussen (Ed.), *Handbook of child psychology* (4th ed.). (Vol. 4.) New York: Wiley.

Minuchin, P.P., Biber, B., Shapiro, E.K., & Zimiles, H. (1969). *The psychological impact of school experience.* New York: Basic Books.

Mischel, W. (1970). Sex-typing and socialization. In P.H. Mussen (Ed.), *Carmichael's manual of child psychology* (3rd ed.). (Vol. 2). New York: Wiley.

Mizuno, T., Hirata, H., Aoyama, S., Chan-Shi, J., & Ishikawa, N. (1968). An international comparative study on concepts of youths. *Research Journal of Physical Education (Japan), 12,* 141–146.

Moely, B.E. (1977). Organization factors in the development of memory. In R.V. Kail, Jr. & J.W. Hagen (Eds.), *Perspectives on the development of memory and cognition.* Hillsdale, NJ: Erlbaum.

Molfese, D.L. (1977). Infant cerebral asymmetry. In S.J. Segalowitz & F.A. Gruber (Eds.), *Language development and neurological theory.* Orlando, FL: Academic Press.

Montemayor, R., & Eisen, H. (1977). The development of self-conceptions from childhood to adolescence. *Developmental Psychology, 13,* 314–319.

Moore, K.L. (1983). *Before we are born* (2nd ed.). Philadelphia: W.B. Saunders.

Moorehouse, M. (1986). *The relationships among continuity in maternal employment, parent-child communicative activities, and the child's school competence.* Unpublished doctoral dissertation. Ithaca, New York: Cornell University.

Morrison, A., & McIntyre, D. (1971). *Schools and socialization.* Hammondsworth, Middlesex, England: Penguin Books.

Morrongiello, B.A., & Rocca, P.T. (1987). Infants' localization of sounds in the horizontal plane: Effects of auditory and visual cues. *Child Development, 58,* 918–927.

Morrongiello, B.A., Kulig, J.W., & Clifton, R.K. (1984). Developmental changes in auditory temporal perception. *Child Development, 55,* 461–471.

Morse, P.A., & Cowan, N. (1982). Infant auditory and speech perception. In T.M. Field, et al. (Eds.), *Review of human development.* New York: Wiley.

Moss, H.A. (1967). Sex, age and state as determinants of mother - infant interaction. *Merrill-Palmer Quarterly, 13,* 19–36.

Moss, H.A., & Robson, K.S. (1968). The role of protest behavior in the development of parent-infant attachment. *Symposium on Attachment Behavior in Humans and Animals,* American Psychological Association, September.

Munro, P. (Ed.). (1989). U.C.L.A. slang: A dictionary of slang words and expressions used at UCLA. *UCLA occasional papers in linguistics.* (No.8). Los Angeles: Department of Linguistics, UCLA.

Murray, A.D. (1985). Aversiveness is in the mind of the beholder. In B.M. Lester & C.F.Z. Boukydis (Eds.), *Infant crying.* New York: Plenum.

Mussen, P., & Eisenberg-Berg, N. (1977). *Roots of caring, sharing, and helping.* San Francisco: W.H. Freeman.

Mussen, P.H. (1989). Forward. In R. Vasta (Ed.), *Annals of child development.* (Vol 6). Greenwich, CT: JAI Press.

Mussen, P.H., & Jones, M.C. (1957). Self-conceptions, motivations, and interpersonal attitudes of late- and early-maturing boys. *Child Development, 28,* 243–256.

Muuss, R.E. (1970). Puberty rites in primitive and modern societies. *Adolescence, 5,* 109–128.

Muuss, R.E. (1986). Adolescent eating disorder: Bulimia. *Adolescence, 21*(82), 257–267.

Nathans, J. (1987). Molecular biology of visual pigments. *Annual Review of Physiology, 10,* 163–194.

National Center for Health Statistics (1987). Washington, DC: U.S. Department of Health and Human Services.

National Commission on Children (NCC) (1991). *Beyond rhetoric: A new American agenda for children and families.* Washington, DC: U.S. Government Printing Office.

National Institute of Child Health and Human Development (1984). *Facts about Down Syndrome.* Washington, DC: U.S. Government Printing Office.

National Institute of Child Health and Human Development (1985). *Facts about premature birth.* Washington, DC: U.S. Government Printing Office.

Neimark, E.D. (1982). Adolescent thought: Transition to formal operations. In B.B. Wolman (Ed.), *Handbook of developmental psychology.* Englewood Cliffs, NJ: Prentice-Hall.

Neisser, U., & Beller, H.K. (1965). Searching through word lists. *British Journal of Psychology, 56,* 349–358.

Neisser, U. (1963). Decision-time without reaction time. *American Journal of Psychology, 76,* 376–385.

Nelson, C.A. (1987). The recognition of facial expressions in the first two years of life: The mechanisms of development. *Child Development, 58,* 889–909.

Nelson, K. (1973). Structure and strategy in learning to talk. *Monographs of the Society for Research in Child Development, 38,* (1 & 2, Serial No. 149).

Nelson, K., & Gruendel, J.M. (1988). At morning it's lunchtime. A scriptal view of children's dialogue. In M.B. Franklin & S.S. Barten (Eds.), *Child language: A reader.* New York: Oxford University Press.

Nesselroade, J.R., & Baltes, P.B. (1974). Adolescent personality development and historical change: 1970–1972. *Monographs of the Society for Research in Child Development, 39* (Serial No. 154).

Newcomb, M.D., & Bentler, P.M. (1989). Substance use and abuse among children and teenagers. *American Psychologist, 44*(2), 242–248.

Nichols, P.L., & Anderson, V. E. (1973). Intellectual performance race and socioeconomic status. *Social Biology, 20*(4), 367–374.

Nielsen, A.C. (1990). *Nielsen report on television.* New York: A.C. Nielson Co.

Norcini, J., & Snyder, S. (1983). The effects of modeling and cognitive induction on the moral reasoning of adolescents. *Journal of Youth and Adolescence, 12*, 101–115.

Nowliss, G.H., & Kessen, W.M. (1976). Human newborns differentiate differing concentrations of sucrose and glucose. *Science, 191*, 865–866.

Oates, R.K. (1984). Similarities and differences between nonorganic failure to thrive and deprivation dwarfism. *Child Abuse and Neglect, 8*, 434–445.

Oates, R.K., Peacock, A., & Forrest, D. (1985). Long-term effects of nonorganic failure to thrive. *Pediatrics, 75*, 36–40.

O'Brien, M., & Huston, A.C. (1985). Activity level and sex stereotyped toy choice in toddler boys and girls. *Journal of Genetic Psychology, 146*, 527–534.

O'Conner, M.J., Cohen, F., & Parmelee, A.H. (1984). Infant auditory discrimination in preterm and full-term infants as a predictor of five-year intelligence. *Child Development, 20*, 159–165.

Oden, M.H. (1968). Fulfillment of promise: 40 year follow-up of the Terman gifted group. *Genetic Psychological Monographs, 77*, 3–93.

Oden, S., & Asher, S. (1977). Coaching children in social skills for friendship-making. *Child Development, 48*, 495–506.

Oller, D.K., & Eilers, R.E. (1988). The role of audition in infant babbling. *Child Development, 59*, 441–449.

Olweus, D. (1980). Familial and temperamental determinants of aggressive behavior in adolescent boys: A causal analysis. *Developmental Psychology, 16*, 644–666.

Olweus, D., Mattson, A, Schalling, D., & Low, H. (1980). Testosterone, aggression, physical and personality dimensions on adolescent males. *Psychosomatic Medicine, 42*, 253–299.

Orenberg, C.L. (1981). *DES: The complete story.* New York: St. Martin's Press.

Orlofsky, J.L. (1976). Intimacy status: Relationship to interpersonal perception. *Journal of Youth and Adolescence, 5*, 73–88.

Ornstein, P.A., Naus, M.J., & Stone, B.P. (1977). Rehearsal training and developmental differences in memory. *Developmental Psychology, 13*, 15–24.

Osherson, D., & Markman, E. (1975). Language and the ability to evaluate contradictions and tautologies. *Cognition, 3*, 213–226.

Osofsky, J.D., & Osofsky, H.S. (1984). Psychological and developmental perspectives on expectant and new parenthood. In R.D. Parke (Ed.), *Review of child development research. Vol. 7: The family.* Chicago: University of Chicago Press.

Overton, W.F., Ward, S.L., Noveck, I.A., Black, J., & O'Brien, D.P. (1987). Form and content in the development of deductive reasoning. *Developmental Psychology, 23*, 22–30.

Owen, M.T., Lewis, J.M., & Henderson, V.K. (1989). Marriage, adult adjustment, and early parenting. *Child Development, 60*, 1015–1024.

Packer, O., Hartmann, E.E., & Teller, D.Y. (1985). Infant color vision: The effect of test field size on Rayleigh discriminations. *Vision Research, 24*, 1247–1260.

Papousek, M., & Papousek, H. (1981). Musical elements in the infant's vocalization: Their significance for communication, cognition, and creativity. In P. Lipsitt (Ed.), *Advances in infancy research.* (Vol. 1). Norwood, NJ: Ablex.

Papousek, M., Papousek, H., & Bornstein, M.H. (1985). The naturalistic vocal environment of young infants. In T.M. Field & N. Fox (Eds.), *Social perception in infants.* Norword, NJ: Ablex.

Paris, S.G., & Lindaur, B.K. (1982). The development of cognitive skills during childhood. In B. Wolman (Ed.), *Handbook of developmental psychology.* Englewood Cliffs, NJ: Prentice-Hall.

Parizkova, J. (1973). Body composition and exercise during growth and development. In G.L. Rarick (Ed.), *Physical activity: Human growth and development.* New York: Academic Press.

Parizkova, J. (1984). *Growth, fitness and nutrition in pre-school children.* Prague, Czechslovakia: University of Prague Press.

Parke, R.D. (1974). Rules, roles and resistance to deviation: Recent advances in punishment, discipline and self-control. In A.D. Pick (Ed.), *Minnesota Symposium on Child Psychology.* (Vol. 8). Minneapolis: University of Minnesota Press.

arke, R.D. (1977). Punishment in children: Effects, side effects and alternative strategies. In H. Hom & P. Robinson (Eds.), *Psychological processes in early education.* New York: Academic Press.

arke, R.D. (1977). Some effects of punishment on children's behavior—revisited. In E.M. Hetherington & R.D. Parke (Eds.), *Readings in contemporary child psychology.* New York: McGraw-Hill.

arke, R.D. (1981). *Fathers.* Cambridge, MA: Harvard University Press.

arke, R.D. (1982). On prediction of child abuse: Theoretical considerations. In R. Starr (Ed.), *Prediction of abuse.* Philadelphia: Ballinger.

arke, R.D., & Sawin, D.B. (1976). The father's role in infancy: A re-evaluation. *The Family Coordinator, 25,* 365–371.

arke, R.D., & Slaby, R.G. (1983). The development of aggression. In P.H. Mussen (Ed.), *Handbook of child psychology* (4th ed.). (Vol. 4). New York: Wiley.

arker, J.G., & Asher, S.R. (1987). Peer relations and later adjustment: Are low-accepted children at risk? *Psychological Bulletin, 102,* 357–389.

arker-Cohen, N.Y., & Bell, R.Q. (1988). The relationship between temperament and social adjustment to peers. *Early Childhood Research Quarterly, 3,* 179–192.

arker, H.C. (1988). *The ADD hyperactivity workbook for parents, teachers, and kids.* FL: Impact Publications.

armelee, A.H., & Sigman, M.D. (1983). Perinatal brain development and behavior. In P.H. Mussen (Ed.), *Handbook of Child Psychology.* (4th ed.). (Vol. 2). New York: Wiley.

arten, M. (1932). Social play among preschool children. *Journal of Abnormal and Social Psychology, 27,* 243–269.

atterson, C.J. (1984). Aggression, altruism, and self-regulation. In M.H. Bornstein & M.E. Lamb (Eds.), *Developmental psychology.* Hillsdale, NJ: Erlbaum.

Patterson, G.R.(1982). *Coercive family processes.* Eugene, OR: Castilia Press.

Pavlov, I.P. (1927). *Conditioned reflexes.* (F.V. Anrep, Trans. & Ed.). New York: Dover.

Pavlov, I. (1927). *Conditional reflexes.* London: Oxford University Press.

Peare, C.O. (1959). *The Helen Keller story.* New York: Thomas Crowell.

Pearl, D. (Ed.). (1982). *Television and behavior: Ten years of scientific progress and implications for the eighties.* (Vol. l). U.S. Department of Health and Human Services. Washington, DC: U.S. Government Printing Office.

Pearl, D. (Ed.). (1982). *The impact of television on children.* Washington, DC: National Institute of Mental Health.

Pedersen, F.A., Rubenstein, J.L., & Yarrow, L.J. (1979). Infant development in father-absent families. *Journal of Genetic Psychology, 135,* 51–61.

Penning, M., & Barnes, G. (1982). Adolescent marijuana use: a review. *The International Journal of the Addictions, 17,* 749–791.

Pepler, D.J., & Ross, H.S. (1981).The effects of play on convergent and divergent problem solving. *Child Development, 52,* 1202–1210.

Peplau, L.A., et al. (1977). Sexual intimacy in dating relationships. *Journal of Social Issues, 33,* 86–109.

Peskin, H. (1973). Influences of the developmental schedule of puberty on learning and ego functioning. *Journal of Youth and Adolescence, 2,* 273–290.

Peters, D.L., Neisworth, J.T., & Yawkey, T.D. (1985). *Early childhood education: From theory to practice.* Monterey, CA: Brooks/Cole.

Petersen, A.C. (1988). Adolescent development. *Annual Review of Psychology, 39,* 503–607.

Phares, E.J. (1976). *Locus of control in personality.* Morristown, NJ: General Learning Press.

Phillips, J.L. (1975). *The origins of intellect: Piaget's theory.* San Francisco: W.H. Freeman.

Phillips, J.L. (1981). *Piaget's theory: A primer.* San Francisco: W.H. Freeman.

Piaget, J. Piaget's theory. (1970). In P.H. Mussen (Ed.), *Carmichael's manual of child psychology.* (Vol. 1). New York: Wiley.

Piaget, J. (1928). *Judgment and reasoning of the child.* New York: Harcourt Brace Jovanovich.

Piaget, J. (1950). *Introduction to genetic epistemology.* Paris: University Press.

Piaget, J. (1951). *Play, dreams, and imitation in childhood.* New York: W.W. Norton.

Piaget, J. (1952). *The child's conception of number.* New York: W.W. Norton.

Piaget, J. (1952). *The origins of intelligence in children.* New York: International Universities Press.

Piaget, J. (1954). *The construction of reality in the child.* New York: Basic Books.

Piaget, J. (1955). *The language and thought of the child.* (M. Gabain, Translator). New York: New American Library.

Piaget, J. (1960). *The child's conception of physical causality.* Totowa, NJ: Littlefield Adams.

Piaget, J. (1963). *The origins of intelligence in children.* New York: International Universities Press.

Piaget, J. (1964). Development and learning. In R.E. Ripple & V.N. Rockcastle (Eds.), *Piaget rediscovered: A report of the conference on cognitive studies and curriculum development.* New York: Cornell University.

Piaget, J. (1965). *The moral judgment of the child.* New York: Free Press.

Piaget, J. (1967). *Six psychological studies.* New York: Vintage Books.

Piaget, J. (1969). *The mechanism of perception.* New York: Basic Books.

Piaget, J. (1970). *Genetic epistemology.* New York: Columbia University Press.

Piaget, J. (1970). Piaget's theory. In P.H. Mussen (Ed.), *Carmichael's manual of child psychology* (3rd ed.). (Vol. 1). New York: Wiley.

Piaget, J. (1970). *Science and education and the psychology of the child.* New York: Orion.

Piaget, J. (1972). Intellectual evolution from adolescence to adulthood. *Human Development, 15,* 1–12.

Piaget, J. (1977). Problems in equilibration. In M. Apple & C. Goldberg (Eds.), *Topics in cognitive development, vol. 1. Equilibration theory, research, and application.* New York: Plenum.

Piaget, J. (1980). Language within cognition. In M. Piatelli-Palmarini (Eds.), *Language and learning: The debate between Jean Piaget and Noam Chomsky.* Cambridge, MA: Harvard University Press.

Piaget, J., & Inhelder, B. (1941). Le development des quantites chez l'enfant; Conservation et atomisme. Neuchatel: Delachaux et Niestle. Cited in E. Hall, M. Lamb, & M. Perlmutter (1986). *Child psychology today* (2nd ed.). New York: Random House.

Piaget, J., & Inhelder, B. (1969). *The psychology of the child.* New York: Basic Books.

Piaget, J., & Inhelder, B. (1976). The gaps in empiricism. In B. Inhelder & H. Chipman (Eds.), *Piaget and his school.* New York: Springer-Verlag.

Pick, H. (1974). Visual coding of nonvisual spatial information. In R. MacLeod & H. Pick (Eds.), *Perception: Essays in honor of James J. Gibson.* New York: Cornell University Press.

Pilling, D., & Pringel, M. (1978). *Controversial issues in child development.* New York: Schoken.

Pillow, B.H., & Flavell, J.H. (1986). Young children's knowledge about visual perception: Projective size and shape. *Child Development, 57,* 125–135.

Pirchio, M., et al. (1978). Infant contrast sensitivity evaluated by evoked potentials. *Brain Research, 141,* 179–184.

Plass, J.A., & Hill, K.T. (1986). Children's achievement strategies and test performance: The role of time pressure, evaluation, anxiety, and sex. *Developmental Psychology, 22,* 31–36.

Pleck, J.H. (1984). Husband's paid work and family roles: Current research issues. In H. Lapata & J.H. Pleck (Eds.), *Research in the interweave of social roles. Vol. 3: Families and jobs.* Greenwich, CT: JAI Press.

Plomin, R. (1990). *Nature and nurture: An introduction to human behavior genetics.* Pacific Grove, CA: Brooks/Cole.

Plomin, R., Defries J.C., & McClearn, G.E. (1990). *Behavior genetics: A primer* (2nd ed.). New York: Freeman.

Plomin, R., & Rowe, D.C. (1979). Genetic and environmental etiology of social behavior in infancy. *Developmental Psychology, 15,* 62–72.

Pope, B. (1953). Socio-economic contrasts in children's peer culture prestige values. *Genetic Psychology Monographs, 48,* 157–220.

Potter, W.J., & Ware, W. (1987). An analysis of the contexts of antisocial acts on prime time television. *Communication Research, 14(1),* 27–46.

Prechtl, H.F.R., & Beintema, D. (1965). *The neurological examination of the full-term newborn infant.* London: William Heineman Medical Books.

Prechtl, H.F.R. (1974). The behavioral states of the newborn infant. *Brain Research, 76,* 185–212.

Price-Williams, D., et al. (1969). Skill and conservation: A study of pottery-making children. *Developmental Psychology, 1,* 6, 769.

Purdey, W.W. (1970). *Self-concept and school achievement.* Englewood Cliffs, NJ: Prentice-Hall.

Pyle, R.L., Mitchell, J.E., & Eckert, E.D. (1981). Bulimia: A report of 34 cases. *Journal of Clinical Psychiatry, 42,* 60–64.

Rakic, P. (1985). Limits of neurogenesis in primates. *Science, 227,* 1054–1055.

Ramsay, D.S., & Weber, S.L.(1986). Infants: Hand preference in a task involving complementary roles for the two hands. *Child Development, 57,* 300–307.

Rauh, V.A., Achenbach, T.M., Nurcombe, B., Howell, C.T., & Teti D.M. (1988). Minimizing adverse effects of low birthweight: Four-year results of an early intervention program. *Child Development, 49,* 544–553.

Read, M. (1968). *Children of their fathers.* New York: Holt, Rinehart & Winston.

Reardon, B., & Griffing, P. (1983). Factors related to the self-concept of institutionalized white, male, adolescent drug abusers. *Adolescence, 18*(Spring), 29–41.

Reese, H.W. (1977). Imagery and associative memory. In R.V. Kail, Jr. & J.W. Hagen (Eds.), *Perspectives on the development of memory and cognition.* Hillsdale, NJ: Erlbaum.

Reich, P.A. (1986). *Language development.* Englewood Cliffs, NJ: Prentice-Hall.

Rest, J. (1983). Morality. In P.H. Mussen (Ed.), *Handbook of child psychology* (4th ed.). (Vol. 3). New York: Wiley.

Revill, S.I., & Dodge, J.A. (1978). Psychological determinants of infantile pyloric stenosis. *Archives of Diseases in Childhood, 53,* 66–68.

Reynolds, D.J. (1976). Adjustment and maladjustment. In J.F. Adams (Ed.), *Understanding adolescence.* (3rd ed.). Boston: Allyn & Bacon.

Rheingold, H.L., & Cook, K.V. (1975). The content of boys and girls' rooms as an index of parent behavior. *Child Development, 46,* 459–463.

Ribaupierre, A.D., Rieben, L., & Lautrey, J. (1991). Developmental change and individual differences: A longitudinal study using Piagetian tasks. *Genetic, Social, and General Psychology Monographs, 117*(3), 285–311.

Rice, F.P. (1990). *The adolescent: Development, relationships, and culture* (6th ed.). Boston: Allyn & Bacon.

Rice, L. (1984). Cognitive aspects of communicative development. In R.L. Schiefelbusch & J. Pickar (Eds.), *The acquisition of communicative competence.* University Park, PA: University Park Press.

Rice, M.L., Huston, A.C., Truglio, R., & Wright, J. (1990). Words from "Sesame Street:" Learning vocabulary while viewing. *Developmental Psychology, 26*(3), 421–428.

Rie, H.E., & Rie, E.D. (1980). *Handbook of minimal brain dysfunctions: A critical review.* New York: Wiley.

Roan, S. (1990). Ethics and the science of birth. *Los Angeles Times,* December 8, Section A, p. 1, 38–39.

Roche, A.F. (Ed.). (1979). Secular trends in human growth, maturation and development. *Monographs of the society for Research in Child Development, 44,* Nos. 3–4.

Rock, I. (1975). *An introduction to perception.* New York: Macmillan.

Rodgers, J.L. (1984). Confluence effects: Not here, not now! *Developmental Psychology, 20,* 321–331.

Roe, K.V., McClure, A., & Roe, A. (1982). Vocal interaction at 3 months and cognitive skills at 12 years. *Developmental Psychology, 18,* 15–16.

Roff, M., Sells, S.B., & Golden M.M. (1972). *Social adjustment and personality development in children.* Minneapolis: University of Minnesota Press.

Roffwarg, H.P., Muzio, J.W., & Dement, W.C. (1966). Ontogenetic development of the human sleep-dream cycle. *Science, 152,* 604–619.

Rogers, C.S., & Sawyers, J.K. (1988). *Play in the lives of children.* Washington, DC: National Association for the Education of Young Children.

Rogoff, B. (Ed.). (1990). U.S. children and their families: Current conditions and recent trends, 1989. *SRCD Newsletter,* Winter, 5.

Rogoff, B., & Morelli, G. (1989). Perspectives on children's development from cultural psychology. *American Psychologist, 44*(12), 343–348.

Roos, P. (1975). Parents and families of the mentally retarded. In J.M. Kauffman & J.S. Payne (Eds.), *Mental retardation: Introduction and personal perspectives.* Columbus, OH: Charles E. Merrill.

Rose, S.A. (1988). Shape recognition in infancy: Visual integration of sequential information. *Child Development, 59*(5), 1161–1176.

Rose, S.A., & Wallace, I.F. (1985). Visual recognition memory: A predictor of later cognitive functioning in preterms. *Child Development, 56,* 843–852.

Rosenberg, M. (1979). *Conceiving the self.* New York: Basic Books.

Rosenberg, M. (1975). The dissonant context and the adolescent self-concept. In S.E. Dragastin & G.H. Elder Jr. (Eds.), *Adolescence in the life cycle: Psychological change and social context.* New York: Wiley.

Rosenstein, D., & Oster, H. (1988). Differential facial responses to four basic tastes in newborns. *Child Development, 59,* 1555–1568.

Rosenthal, R. (1973). The pygmalion effect lives. *Psychology Today, 7,* 56–63.

Rosenthal, R., & Jacobson, L. (1968). *Pygmalion in the classroom.* New York: Holt, Rinehart and Winston.

Rosenzweig, M.R., Bennett, E.L., & Diamond, M.C. (1972). Brain changes in response to experience. *Scientific American, 226,* 22–29.

Rotter, J.B. (1954). *Social learning and clinical psychology.* Englewood Cliffs, NJ: Prentice-Hall.

Rotter, J.B. (1971). Who rules you? External control and internal control. *Psychology Today, 5,* 37–42.

Rovee-Collier, C.K., & Lipsitt, L.P. (1987). Learning adaptation, and memory in the newborn. In P. Stratton (Ed.), *Psychobiology of the human newborn.* New York: Wiley.

Rubin, K.H. (1973). Egocentrism in childhood: A unitary construct? *Child Development, 44,* 102–110.

Rubin, K.H., & Schneider, F.W. (1973). The relationship between moral judgment, egocentrism, and altruistic behavior. *Child Development, 44,* 661–665.

Rubin, J.Z., Provenzano, F.J., & Luria, A. (1974). The eye of the beholder: Parents' views on sex of newborns. *American Journal of Orthopsychiatry, 43,* 720–731.

Rubin, Z. (1980). *Children's friendships.* Cambridge, MA: Harvard University Press.

Ruble, D.N., Boggiano, A.K., Feldman, N.S., & Loebl, J.H. (1980). Developmental analysis of the role of social comparison in self-evaluation. *Developmental Psychology, 16,* 990–997.

Rushton, J.P., Fulker, D.W., Neale, M.C., Nias, D.K.B., & Eysenck, H.J. (1986). Altruism and aggression: The heritability of individual differences. *Journal of Personality and Social Psychology, 50,* 1192–1198.

Russell, M.J. (1976). Human olfactory communication. *Nature, 26,* 520–522.

Ruth, J., & Birren, J.E. (1985). Creativity in adulthood and old age: Relations to intelligence, sex, and mode of testing. *International Journal of Behavioral Development, 8,* 99–109.

Rutherford, E., & Mussen, P.H. (1968). Generosity in nursery school boys. *Child Development, 39,* 755–765.

Sachs, J. (1985). Prelinguistic development. In J.B. Gleason (Ed.), *The development of language.* Columbus, OH: Merrill.

Sadker, M., & Sadker, D. (1985). Sexism in the schoolroom of the '80s. *Psychology Today, 19,* 54–57.

Sadker, M., & Sadker, D. (1986). Sexism in the classroom: From grade school to graduate school. *Phi Delta Kappan, 67,* 512–515.

Sadker, M.P., & Sadker, D.M. (1991). *Teachers, schools, and society* (2nd ed.). New York: McGraw-Hill.

Saghir, M., & Robins, E. (1973). *Male and female homosexuality.* Baltimore: Williams & Wilkins.

Sahler, O.J., & Mc Anarney, E.R. (1981). *The child from three to eighteen.* St. Louis: C.V. Mosby.

Salapatek, P. (1975) Pattern perception in early infancy. In L.B. Cohen & P. Salapatek (Eds.), *Infant perception: From sensation to cognition.* (Vol. 1). Orlando, FL: Academic Press.

Salapatek, P., & Banks, M.S. (1978). Infant sensory assessment: Vision. In F.I. Minifie & L.L. Lloyd (Eds.), *Communication and cognitive abilities—early behavioral assessment.* Baltimore: University Park Press.

Salkind, N.J. (1985). *Theories of human development* (2nd ed.). New York: Wiley.

Salomon, J.B., Mata, L.J., & Gordon J.E. (1968). Malnutrition and the common communicable diseases of childhood in rural Guatemala. *American Journal of Health, 58,* 505–516.

Sameroff, A.J. (1983). Developmental systems: Contexts and evolution. In P.H. Mussen (Ed.), *Handbook of Child Psychology.* (Vol. 1). New York: Wiley.

Sameroff, A.J. (1987). The social context of development. In N. Eisenberg (Ed.), *Contemporary topics in developmental psychology.* New York: Wiley.

Sameroff, A.J., & Chandler, M.J. (1975). Reproductive risk and the continuum of caretaking casualty. In F.D. Horowitz (Ed.), *Review of child development research* (Vol. 4). Chicago: University of Chicago Press.

Samuels, M., & Samuels, N. (1986). *The well pregnancy book.* New York: Summit.

Sanger, D.E. (1987). Pregnancy transfers by AT & T. *New York Times,* January 14, p. 21.

Santrock, J.W. (1993). *Adolescence: An introduction.* Madison, WI: Brown & Benchmark.

Santrock, J.W. & Warshak, R.A. (1979). Father custody and social development in boys and girls. *Journal of Social Issues, 35,* 112–125.

Sarnat, H.B. (1978). Olfactory reflexes in the newborn infant. *The Journal of Pediatrics, 22*(4), 624–626.

Saunders, J.B. (1982). Alcoholism. New evidence for a genetics contribution. *British Medical Journal, 284,* 1137–1138.

Scanzoni, J., & Fox, G.L. (1980). Sex roles, family and society: The seventies and beyond. *Journal of Marriage and the Family, 42,* 743–756.

Scarr, S., & McCartney, K. (1983). How people make their own environments: A theory of genotype–environment effects. *Child Development, 54,* 424–435.

Scarr, S., & Weinberg, R.A. (1976). IQ test performance of black children adopted by white families. *American Psychologist, 31,* 726–739.

Scarr, S., Weinberg, R.A., & Levine, A. (1986). *Understanding development.* New York: Harcourt Brace Jovanovich.

Schardein, J.L. (1985). *Chemically induced birth defects*. New York: Dekker.

Schneider, W. (1985). Developmental trends in the metamemory- memory behavior relationship: An integrative review. In D.L. Forrest-Pressley, G.E. MacKinnon, & T.G. Waller (Eds.), *Metacognition, cognition, and human performance*. (Vol. 1). New York: Academic Press.

Schickendanz, J.A. (1986). *More than the ABCs: The early stages of reading and writing*. Washington, DC.: National Association for the Education of Young Children.

Schiedel, D.G., & Marcia, J.E. (1985). Ego identity, intimacy, sex-role orientation, and gender. *Developmental Psychology, 21*, 149–160.

Schieffelin, B.B., & Ochs, E. (1983). A cultural perspective on the transition from prelinguistic to linguistic communication. In R.M. Golinkoff (Ed.), *The transition from prelinguistic to linguistic communication*. Hillsdale, NJ: Erlbaum.

Schneider, B.A., Trehub, S.E., & Bull, D. (1979). The development of basic auditory processes in infants. *Canadian Journal of Psychology, 33*, 306–319.

Schneider, B.A., Trehub, S.E., & Bull, D. (1980). High-frequency sensitivity in infants. *Science, 207*, 1003–1004.

Schneider-Rosen, K., & Cicchetti, D. (1991). Early self-knowledge and emotional development: Visual self-recognition and affective reactions to mirror self-images in maltreated and nonmaltreated toddlers. *Developmental Psychology, 27*(3), 471–478.

Schowalter, J.E. (1983). Eating disorders: Introduction. *Journal of the American Academy of Child Psychiatry, 22*(2), 97–98.

Schorr, L.B., & Schorr, D. (1989). *Within our reach: Breaking the cycle of disadvantage*. New York: Doubleday.

Schwartz, D.M., Thompson, M.G., & Johnson, C.L. (1982). Anorexia nervosa and bulimia: The sociocultural context. *International Journal of Eating Disorders, 1*(3), 20–36.

Schwartz, J.C. (1972). Effects of peer familiarity on the behavior of preschoolers in a novel situation. *Journal of Personality and Social Psychology, 24*, 276–284.

Schwartz, R.G., & Leonard, L.B. (1984) Words, objects and actions in early lexical acquisition. *Journal of Speech and Hearing Research, 27*, 119–127.

Scrimshaw, N.S. (1969). Early malnutrition and central nervous system function. *Merrill-Palmer Quarterly, 15*, 375–388.

Seagoe, M.V. (1970). An instrument for the analysis of children's play as an index of degree of socialization. *Journal of School Psychology, 8*, 139–144.

Seaver, W.B. (1973). Effects of naturally induced teacher expectancies. *Journal of Personality and Social Psychology, 28*, 333–342.

Secord, P., & Peevers, B. (1974). The development and attribution of person concepts. In T. Mischel (Ed.), *Understanding other persons*. Oxford: Blackwell.

Segal, B. (1983). Drugs and growth: A review of the problem. *The International Journal of Addiction, 18*, 429–433.

Segal, N.L. (1985). Monozygotic and dizygotic twins: A comparative analysis of mental ability profiles. *Child Development, 56*, 1051–1058.

Seigler, R.S. (1991). *Children's thinking* (2nd ed.). Englewood Cliffs, NJ: Prentice-Hall.

Seligman, M.E.P. (1970). On the generality of the laws of learning. *Psychological Review, 77*, 406–419.

Seligman, M.E.P. (1975). *Helplessness*. San Francisco: W.H. Freeman.

Seligman, M.E.P., & Maier, S.F. (1967). Failure to escape traumatic shock. *Journal of Experimental Psychology, 74*, 1–9.

Selman, R.L., & Selman, A.P. (1979). Childrens' ideas about friendship: A new theory. *Psychology Today, 13*, 71–80, 114.

Selman, R.L. (1976). Social-cognitive understanding. In T. Lickona (Ed.), *Moral development and behavior*. New York: Holt, Rinehart and Winston.

Selman, R.L. (1980). *The growth of interpersonal understanding*. New York: Academic Press.

Selman, R.L., & Byrne, D.F. (1974). A structural-developmental analysis of levels of role taking in middle childhood. *Child Development, 45*, 803–806.

Sepkowski, C. (1985). Maternal obstetric medication and newborn behavior. In J.W. Scanlon (Ed.), *Prenatal anesthesia*. London: Blackwell.

Serbin, L.A. (1983). The hidden curriculum: Academic consequences of teacher expectations. In M. Marland (Ed.), *Sex differentiation and schooling*. London: Heinemanns.

Serbin, L.A., O'Leary, K.D., Kent, R.N., & Tonick, I.J. (1973). A comparison of teacher response to the preacademic and problem behavior of boys and girls. *Child Development, 44,* 796–804.

Serbin, L.A., & Sprafkin, C. (1986). The salience of gender and the process of sex-typing in three- to seven-year-old children. *Child Development, 57,* 1188–1199.

Sever, J.L. (1982). Infections during pregnancy: Highlights from the collaborative perinatal project. *Teratology, 25,* 227–237.

Shapira A., & Madsen, M.C. (1974). Between and within group cooperation among Kibbutz and non-Kibbutz children. *Developmental Psychology, 10,* 140–145.

Shapiro, J., & Doiron, R. (1987). Literacy environments: Bridging the gap between home and school. *Childhood Education, 63,* 263–269.

Shatz, M. (1983). Communication. In P.H. Mussen (Ed.), *Handbook of child psychology* (4th ed.). (Vol. 3). New York: Wiley.

Shatz, M., & Gelman, R. (1973). The development of communication skills. Modification in the speech of young children as a function of the listener. *Monographs of the Society for Research in Child Development, 38*(5), (Serial No. 152).

Shaw, C.A. (1985). The use of imagery by intelligent and creative school children. *Journal of General Psychology, 112,* 153–171.

Sheldon, W.H. (1940). *The varieties of human physique.* New York: Harper.

Shostak, M. (1981). *Nissa: The life and words of a !Kung woman.* Cambridge: Harvard University Press.

Siegel, L.S., et al. (1978). Evidence for the understanding of class inclusion in preschool children: Linquistic factors and training effects. *Child Development, 49,* 688–693.

Siegel, O. (1982). Personality development in adolescence. In B.B. Wolman (Ed.), *Handbook of developmental psychology.* Englewood Cliffs, NJ: Prentice-Hall.

Siegler, R. S. (1976). Three aspects of cognitive development. *Cognitive Psychology, 4,* 481–520.

Siegler, R.S. (1978). The origins of scientific reasoning. In R.S. Siegler (Ed.), *Children's thinking: What develops?* Hillsdale, NJ: Erlbaum.

Siegler, R.S. (1983). Information-processing approaches to development. In P.H. Mussen (Ed.), *Handbook of child psychology* (4th ed.). New York: Wiley.

Sigelman, C.K., Miller, T.E., & Whitworth, L.A. (1986). The early development of stigmatizing reactions to physical differences. *Journal of Applied Developmental Psychology, 7,* 17–32.

Siegler, R.S., & Liebert, R.M. (1972). Learning of liquid quantity relationships as a function of rules and feedback, number of training problems, and age of subject. *Proceedings of the 80th Annual Convention of the American Psychological Association, 7,* 117–118.

Signorielli, N. (1989). Television and conceptions about sex roles: Maintaining conventionality and the status quo. *Sex Roles, 21*(5/6), 341–360.

Simmons, R.G., & Blyth, D.A. (1987). *Moving into adolescence.* Hawthorne, NY: Aldine.

Simpson, C.C., & Beck, W.S. (1965). *Life: An introduction to biology.* New York: Harcourt, Brace and World.

Simpson, E.L. (1974). Moral development research: A case study of scientific cultural bias. *Human Development,* 81–106.

Sinclair-de Zwart, H. (1967). *Acquisition de language et development de la pensec.* Paris: Danod.

Singer, J.L., & Singer, D.G. (1980). *Television, imagination and aggression: A study of preschoolers' play.* Hillsdale, NJ: Erlbaum.

Singer, L.M., Brodzinsky D.M., Ramsey, D., Steir, M., & Waters, E. (1985). Mother-infant attachments in adoptive families. *Child Development, 56,* 1543–1551.

Siqueland, E.R. & DeLucia, C.A. (1969). Visual reinforcing of nonnutritive sucking in human infants. *Science, 165,* 1144–1146.

Skeels, H.M. (1966). Adult status of children with contrasting early life experiences. *Monographs of the Society for Research in Child Development, 31*(3) (Whole No. 105).

Skinner, B.F. (1938). *The behavior of organisms: An experimental analysis.* New York: Appleton-Century-Crofts.

Skinner, B.F. (1948). *Walden II.* New York: Macmillan.

Skinner, B.F. (1953). *Science and human behavior.* New York: Macmillan.

Skinner, B.F. (1957). *Verbal behavior.* New York: Appleton- Century-Crofts.

Skinner, B.F. (1958). *Teaching machines.* Science, 128, 969–977.

Skolnick, A. (1987). *The intimate environment: Exploring marriage and the family* (4th ed.). Boston: Little Brown.

Slobin, D.I. (1972). Children and language: They learn the same way all around the world. *Psychology Today, 5,* 71–74, 82.

Slobin, D.I. (1973). Cognitive prerequisite for the development of grammar. In C.A. Ferguson & D.I. Slobin (Eds.), *Studies of child language development.* New York: Holt, Rinehart and Winston.

Slobin, D.I. (1979). *Psycholinguistics.* Glenview, IL: Scott Foresman.

Slobin, D.I. (1983). *Cross linquistic evidence for basic child grammar.* Paper presented at the biennial meeting of the Society for Research in Child Development, Detroit.

Smart, M.S., & Smart, R.C. (1977). *Children: Development and relationships* (3rd ed.). New York: Macmillan.

Smirnov, A.A., & Zinchenko, P.I. (1969). Problems in the psychology of memory. In M. Cole & I. Malzman (Eds.), *A handbook of contemporary soviet psychology.* New York: Basic Books.

Smith, D.W. (1977). *Growth and its disorders.* Philadelphia: W.B. Saunders.

Smith, P., & Connolly, K. (1972). Patterns of play and social Interaction in preschool children. In N. Blurton-Jones (Ed.), *Ethological studies of child behavior.* Cambridge: Cambridge University Press.

Smith, P.K., & Connolly, K. (1981). *The behavioral ecology of the preschool.* Cambridge: Cambridge University Press.

Snow, C.E. (1986). Conversations with children. In P. Fletcher & M. Garman (Eds.), *Language acquisition* (2nd ed.). New York: Cambridge University Press.

Snowling, M. (1988). *Dyslexia.* New York: Basil Blackwell.

Sontag, L.W. (1944). War and the fetal maternal relationship. *Marriage and Family Living, 6,* 1–5.

Soroka, S., Corter, C., & Abramovitch, R. (1979). Infants tactual discrimination of novel and familiar stimuli. *Child Development, 50,* 1251–1253.

Sorrells-Jones, J. (1983). *A comparison of the effects of Leboyer delivery and modern "routine" childbirth in a randomized sample.* Unpublished doctoral dissertation, Chicago: University of Chicago.

Spearman, C. (1923). *The nature of "intelligence" and the principles of cognition.* London: Macmillan.

Spelke, E.S. (1979). Exploring audible and visible events in infancy. In A.D. Pick (Ed.), *Perception and its development: A tribute to Eleanor J. Gibson.* Hillsdale, NJ: Erlbaum.

Spelke, E.S. (1984). The development of intermodal perception. In L.B. Cohen & P. Salapatek (Eds.), *Handbook of infant perception.* New York: Academic Press.

Spence, J.T., & Helmreich, R.L. (1978). *Masculinity and femininity: Their psychological dimensions.* Austin: University of Texas Press.

Spence, J.T., Helmreich, R. L., & Stapp, J. (1974). The personal attributes questionnaire: A measure of sex-role stereotypes and masculinity-femininity. *JSAS Catalogue of Selected Documents in Psychology, 4,* 43.

Spence, J.T., Helmreich, R.L., & Stapp, J. (1975). Ratings of self and peers on sex-role attributes and their relation to self esteem and conceptions of masculinity and femininity. *Journal of Personality and Social Psychology, 32,* 29–39.

Spence, J.T., & Sawin, L.L. (1985). Images of masculinity and femininity: A reconceptualization. In V. O'Leary, R. Inger, & B. Wallston (Eds.), *Women, gender and social psychology.* Hillsdale, NJ: Erlbaum.

Spencer, B., & Gillen, F.J. (1966). *The Arunta: A study of a stone age people.* Atlantic Highlands, NJ: Humanities Press.

Sperling, C. (1960). The information available in brief visual presentation. *Psychological Monographs, 74*(11), (Whole No. 498).

Sperry, R. (1982). Some effects of disconnecting the cerebral hemispheres. *Science, 217,* 1223–1226.

Spitz, R.A. (1946). Hospitalism: An inquiry into the genesis of psychiatric conditioning in early childhood. In D. Fenschel, et al. (Eds.), *Psychoanalytic studies of the child.* (Vol. 1). New York: International Universities Press.

Spoher, K.T., & Lehmkuhle, S.W. (1982). *Visual information processing.* San Francisco: W.H. Freeman.

Spock, B.S. (1968). *Baby and child care.* New York: Pocket Books.

Spoth, R., & Rosenthal, D. (1980). Wanted: A developmentally oriented alcohol prevention program. *Personal and Guidance Journal, 59,* 212–216.

Sprafkin, J.M., Liebert, R.M., & Poulos, R.W. (1975). Effects of a prosocial example on children's helping. *Journal of Experimental Child Psychology, 20,* 119–126.

Springer, S.P., & Deutsch, G. (1985). *Left brain, right brain.* San Francisco: W.H. Freeman.

Staffieri, J.R. (1967). A study of social stereotype of body image in children. *Journal of Personality and Social Psychology, 7,* 101–104.

Stankard, A.J. (1980). Obesity. In H.I. Daplan, A.M. Freedman, & B. J. Sadock (Eds.), *Comprehensive textbook of psychiatry.* (Vol. 3). Baltimore, MD: Williams & Wilkins.

Stallings, J. (1975). Implementation and child effects of teaching practices in follow-through classrooms. *Monographs of the Society for Research in Child Development, 40,* (Serial No.163), 7–8.

Standley, K., Soule, B., & Copans, S.A. (1979). Dimensions of prenatal anxiety and their influence on pregnancy outcome. *American Journal of Obstetrics and Gynecology, 135,* 22–26.

Staub, E. (1971). The use of role playing and induction in children's learning of helping and sharing behavior. *Child Development, 42,* 805–816.

Stauffer, R.G. (1980). *The language experience approach to the teaching of reading.* New York: Harper & Row.

Stechler, G., & Halton, A. (1982). Prenatal influences on human development. In B.B. Wolman (Ed.), *Handbook of developmental psychology.* Englewood Cliffs, NJ: Prentice-Hall.

Stein, A.H. (1972). Mass media and young children's development. In I.J. Gordon (Ed.), *Early childhood education: 71st yearbook of NSSE.* Chicago: Chicago University Press.

Stein, Z., Susser, M., Saenger, G., & Marolla, F. (1975). *Famine and human development: The Dutch hunger winter of 1944–1945.* New York: Oxford University Press.

Steinberg, L. (1985). Early temperaments antecedents of adult type A behaviors. *Developmental Psychology, 21,* 1171–1180.

Steinberg, L., Elmen, J.D., & Mounts, N.S. (1989). Authoritative parenting, psychosocial maturity, and academic success among adolescents. *Child Development, 60,* 1424–1436.

Steiner, J.E. (1979). Human facial expressions in response to taste and smell stimulation. In H. Reese & L. Lipsit (Eds.), *Advances in child development and behavior.* (Vol. 13). New York: Academic Press.

Steinhausen, H.C. (1981). Chronically ill and handicapped children and adolescents: Personality studies in relation to disease. *Journal of Abnormal Child Psychology, 9*(2), 291–297.

Steinschneider, A. (1975). Implications of the sudden infant death syndrome for the study of sleep in infancy. In A.D. Pick (Ed.), *Minnesota symposia on child psychology.* (Vol. 9). Minneapolis, MN: University of Minnesota Press.

Steri, A., & Pecheux. M. (1986). Tactual habituation and discrimination of form in infancy: A comparison with vision. *Child Development, 57,* 100–104.

Stern, D. (1977). *The first relationship: Infant and mother.* Cambridge, MA: Harvard University Press.

Sternberg, R.J. (1977). *Intelligence, information processing, and analytical reasoning: The componential analysis of human abilities.* Hillsdale, NJ: Erlbaum.

Sternberg, R.J. (1979). Stalking the IQ quark. *Psychology Today, 13,* 42–54.

Sternberg, R.J. (1983). *Beyond IQ: A triarchic theory of intelligence.* Cambridge, England: Cambridge University Press.

Sternberg, R.J. (Ed.). (1985). *Human abilities: An information-processing approach.* New York: W.H. Freeman.

Sternberg, R.J. (1986). *Intelligence applied: Understanding and increasing your intellectual skills.* New York: Harcourt Brace Jovanovich.

Sternberg, R.J., & Berg, C.A. (1986). Quantitative integration: Definitions of intelligence—a comparison of the 1921 and 1986 Symposia. In R.J. Sternberg & D.K. Determan (Eds.), *What is intelligence? Contemporary viewpoints on its nature and definition.* Norwood, NJ: Ablex.

Sternberg, R.J., & Nigro, C. (1980). Developmental patterns in the solution of verbal analogies. *Child Development, 51,* 27–38.

Stevens, J.H., Jr. (1980). The consequences of early childbearing. *Young Children, 35*(2), 47–56.

Stevenson, H. (1983). How children learn—the quest for a theory. In P.H. Mussen (Ed.), *Handbook of Child Psychology.* (Vol 1). New York: Wiley.

Stillman, R.J. (1982). In utero exposure to diethylstilbestrol: Adverse effects on the reproductive tract and reproductive performance in male and female offspring. *American Journal of Obstetrics and Gynecology, 142,* 905–921.

Stoch, M.B., Smythe, P.M., Moodie, A.D., & Bradshaw, D. (1982). Psychosocial outcome and CT findings after gross undernourishment during infancy: A 20-year developmental study. *Developmental Medicine and Child Neurology, 24,* 419–436.

Stout, D.B. (1974). *San Blas Cuna acculturation: An introduction.* New York: Viking Fund Publications.

Streissguth, A.P., Barr, H.M., Sampson, P.D., Darby, B.L., & Martin, D.C. (1989). IQ at age 4 in relation to maternal alcohol use and smoking during pregnancy. *Developmental Psychology, 25*(1), 3–11.

Stucky, M.F., McGhee, P.E., & Bell, N.G. (1982). Parent-child interaction: The influence of maternal employment. *Developmental Psychology, 18,* 635–644.

Sudhalter, V., & Braine, M.D.S. (1985). How does comprehension of passives develop? A comparison of actional and experiential verbs. *Journal of Child Language, 12,* 455–470.

Sullivan, H.S. (1953). *The interpersonal theory of psychiatry.* New York: W.W. Norton.

Summey, P.S. (1986). Cesarian birth. In P.S. Eakins (Ed.), *The American way of birth.* Philadelphia: Temple University Press.

Super, C.M. (1981). Behavioral development in infancy. In R.H. Monroe, R.L. Monroe, & B.B. Whiting (Eds.), *Handbook of cross-cultural human development.* New York: Garland.

Surber, C.F., & Gzesh, S.M. (1984). Reversible operations in the balance scale task. *Journal of Experimental Child Psychology, 38,* 254–274.

Surgeon General's Advisory on Alcohol and Pregnancy. (1981). *FDA Drug Bulletin, 11*(2), 9–10.

Susman, E.J., Inoff-Germain, G., Nottelmann, E.D., Loriaux, D.L., Cutler, G.B. Jr., & Chrousos, G.P. (1987). Hormones, emotional dispositions, and aggressive attributes in young adolescents. *Child Development, 58,* 111–1134.

Sutton-Smith, B. (1971). Children at play. *Natural History, 80,* 54–59.

Swadish, M. (1971). *The origin and diversification of language.* Chicago, IL. Aldine-Atherton.

Tanner, J.M. (1978). *Fetus into man: Physical growth from conception to maturity.* Cambridge, MA: Harvard University Press.

Tanner, J.M. (1981). Growth and maturation during adolescence. *Nutrition Review, 39,* 43–55.

Tanner, J.M. (1990). *Fetus into man: Physical growth from conception to maturity* (2nd ed.). Cambridge, MA: Harvard University Press.

Tanner, J.M. (1990). *Foetus into man: Physical growth from conception to maturity* (revised ed.). Cambridge, MA: Harvard University Press.

Tavris, C., & Wade, C. (1984). *The longest war: Sex differences in perspective* (2nd ed.). San Diego: Harcourt Brace Jovanovich.

Tellegen, A., Lykken, D.T., Bouchard, T.J. Jr., Wilcox, K.J., Segal, N.L., & Rich, S. (1988). Personality similarity in twins reared together and apart. *Journal of Personality and Social Psychology, 54,* 1031–1039.

Teller, D.Y., Peeples, D.R., & Sekel, M. (1978). Discrimination of chromatic from white light by two-month-old infants. *Vision Research, 18,* 41–48.

Terman, L.M. (1925). *Genetic studies of genius.* Stanford, CA.: Stanford University Press.

Terman, L.M., & Merrill, M.A. (1937). *Measuring intelligence.* Boston: Houghton-Mifflin.

Thelen, E. (1987). The role of motor development in developmental psychology: A view of the past and an agenda for the future. In N. Eisenberg (Ed.), *Contemporary topics in developmental psychology.* New York: Wiley.

Thomas, A., & Chess, S. (1977). *Temperament and development.* New York: Bruner/Mazel.

Thomas, A., & Chess, S. (1980). *The dynamics of psychological development.* New York: Brunner/Mazel.

Thomas, A., Chess, S., & Birch, H.G. (1968). *Temperament and behavior disorders in children.* New York: New York University Press.

Thomas, A., Chess, S., Birch, H.G. (1970). The origin of personality. *Scientific American, 223,* 102–109.

Thomas, R.T. (1985). *Comparing theories of child development* (2nd ed.). Belmont, CA: Wadsworth.

Thompson, S.K. (1975). Gender labels and early sex-role development. *Child Development, 46,* 339–347.

Thompson, S.K., & Bentler, P.M. (1971). The priority of cues in sex discrimination by children and adults. *Developmental Psychology, 5,* 181–185.

Thorndike, E.L. (1898). Animal intelligence: An experimental study of the associative processes in animals. *Psychological Monographs, 2* (Whole No. 8).

Thornton, L. P., & DeBlassic, R.R. (1989). Treating bulimia. *Adolescence, 24*(95), 631–637.

Thurstone, L.L. (1938). *Primary mental abilities.* Chicago: University of Chicago Press.

Tieger, T. (1980). On the biological basis of sex differences in aggression. *Child Development, 51,* 943–963.

Timiras, P.S. (1982). The timing of hormone signals in the orchestration of brain development. In R.N. Emde & R. J. Harmon (Eds.), *The development of attachment and affiliative systems.* New York: Plenum.

Tinbergen, N. (1951). *The study of instinct.* Oxford: Oxford University Press.

Tobias, J.J. (1980). A glossary of affluent suburban juvenile language. *Adolescence, 15*(Spring), 227–230.

Tobias, P.V. (1975). Anthropometry among disadvantaged people: Studies in southern Africa. In E.S. Watts, F.E. Johnston, & G.W. Lasker (Eds.), *Biosocial interrelations in population adaptation: World anthropology series.* The Hague: Mouton.

Torgesen, J.K. (1988). Studies of children with learning disabilities who perform poorly on memory span tasks. *Journal of Learning Disabilities, 21*(10), 605–612.

Torrance, E.P. (1966a). *Torrance tests of creative thinking, verbal forms A and B.* Princeton, NJ: Personnel Press.

Torrance, E.P. (1966b). *Torrance tests of creative thinking: Norms technical manual.* Princeton, NJ : Personnel Press.

Torrance, E.P. (1974). *Torrance tests of creative thinking.* Lexington, MA: Ginn.

Tortora, G.J., & Anagnostakos, N.P. (1990). *Principles of anatomy and physiology* (6th ed.). New York: Harper & Row.

Trehub, S.E., Thorpe, L.A., & Morrongiello, B.A. (1987). Organizational processes in infants' perception of auditory patterns. *Child Development, 58,* 741–749.

Trevarthen, W. (1987). *Human birth: An evolutionary perspective.* New York: Aldine de Gruyter.

Triana, E., & Posnak, R. (1986). A distraction task as an assessment of object permanence. *Infant Behavior and Development, 9,* 151–165.

Trieberman, J. (1977). *Playfulness: Its relationship to creativity.* New York: Academic Press.

Tucker, L.A. (1983). Self-concept: A function of self-perceived somatotype. *Journal of Psychology, 14,* 123–133.

Tulkin, S.R., & Konner, M.J. (1973). Alternative conceptions of intellectual functioning. *Human Development, 16,* 33–52.

Turiel, E. (1983). *The development of social knowledge, morality and convention.* New York: Cambridge University Press.

Turnbull, A.P., Summers J.A., & Brotherson, M.J. (1984). *Working with disabled members: A family systems approach.* Lawrence, Kansas: Kansas University Affiliated Facility, University of Kansas.

Turnbull, C. (1972). *The mountain people.* New York: Simon & Schuster.

Tyack, D., & Ingram, D. (1977). Childrens' production and comprehension of questions. *Journal of Child Language, 4,* 211–224.

Ullman, C.A. (1957). Teachers, peers, and tests as predictors of adjustment. *Journal of Educational Psychology, 48,* 257–267.

U.S. Bureau of Census. (1991). *Statistical abstract of the United States* (111th Ed.). Washington, DC: U.S. Government Printing Office.

U.S. Department of Health, Education and Welfare. (1979). *Smoking and health: A report of the surgeon general.* Washington, DC: U.S. Government Printing Office.

U.S. Department of Health and Human Services (1983). *The health consequences of smoking for women: A report of the surgeon general.* Washington, DC: U.S. Government Printing Office.

U.S. Office of Education. (1977). Procedures for evaluating specific learning disabilities. *Federal Register, 42,* 65082–65085.

Uzgiris, I.C. (1964). Situational generality of conservation. *Child Development, 35,* 831–841.

Uzgiris, I.C., & Hunt, J. McV. (1975). *Assessment in infancy: Ordinal scales of psychological development.* Urbana, IL: University of Illinois Press.

Vandell, D.L., & Corasaniti, M.A. (1988). The relation between third graders after-school care and social academic and emotional functioning. *Child Development, 59*(4), 868–875.

Vander Zanden, J.W. (1989). *Human development* (4th ed.). New York: Alfred Knopf, 1989.

Vanderslice, V. (1984). Empowerment: A definition in process. *Human Ecology Forum, 14,* 2–3.

Van Gennep A. (1960). *Rites of passage.* (M.B. Vizedon & G. Caffee, Trans.). Chicago: University of Chicago Press (originally published in 1909).

Van Thorre, M.D., & Vogel, F.X. (Spring, 1985). The presence of bulimia in high school females. *Adolescence, 20,* 45–51.

Vaughn, V.C., McKay, J.R., & Behrman, R.E. (1984). *Nelson textbook of pediatrics* (12th ed.). Philadelphia: Saunders.

Vendovitskaya, T.V. (1971). Development of memory. In A.V. Zaporozhets & D.B. Elkonin (Eds.), *The psychology of preschool children.* Cambridge, MA: MIT Press.

Vellutino, F.R. (1987). Dyslexia. *Scientific American, 256,* 34–41.

Venezky, R.L. (1980). *Orthography, reading, and dyslexia.* Baltimore: University Park Press.

Ventura, J. (1987). The stresses of parenthood re-examined. *Family Relations,* January, 26–29.

Von Bargen, D.M. (1983). Infant heart rate: A review of research and methodology. *Merrill-Palmer Quarterly, 29,* 115–150.

Von Hofsten, C. (1989). Motor development as the development of systems: Comments on the special section. *Developmental Psychology, 25*(6), 950–953.

Vurpillot, E. (1976). *The visual world of the child.* New York: International Universities Press.

Vygotsky, L.S. (1978). The prehistory of written language. *In Mind in Society.* Cambridge, MA: Harvard University Press.

Vygotsky, L.S. (1962). *Thought and language.* Cambridge, MA: MIT Press.

Vygotsky, L.S. (1978). *Mind in society: The development of higher psychological processes.* Cambridge, MA: Harvard University Press.

Wadsworth, B.J. (1978). *Piaget for the classroom teacher.* New York: Longman.

Wadsworth, B.J. (1984). *Piaget's theory of cognitive and affective development* (3rd ed.). New York: Longman.

Wagner, M.E., & Schubert, H.J.P. (1985). Family size effects: A review. *Journal of Genetic Psychology, 146,* 65–78.

Walk, R.D. (1981). *Perceptual development.* Monterey, CA: Brooks/Cole.

Walker, J.E., & Shea, T.M. (1980). *Behavior modification: A practical approach for educators* (2nd ed.). St. Louis, MO: Mosby.

Walker, L.J. (1983). Sources of cognitive conflict for stage transition in moral development. *Developmental Psychology, 19,* 103–110.

Walker, L.J., & Taylor, J.H. (1991). Family interactions and the development of moral reasoning. *Child Development, 62,* 265–283.

Walker, L.S., & Greene, J.W. (1986). The social context of adolescent self-esteem. *Journal of Youth and Adolescence, 15,* 315–322.

Wallace, G., & McLoughlin, J.A. (1979). *Learning disabilities: Concepts and characteristics* (2nd ed.). Columbus, OH: Charles E. Merrill.

Wallach, M.A., & Kogan, N. (1965). *Modes of thinking in young children: A study of the creativity-intelligence distinction.* New York: Holt.

Wallerstein, J.S., & Kelly, J.B. (1980). *Surviving the breakup: How children and parents cope with divorce.* New York: Basic Books.

Wallerstein, J.S., Corbin, S.B., & Lewis, J.M. (1988). Children of divorce: A ten-year study. In E.M. Hetherington & J. Arasteh (Eds.), *Impact of divorce, single parenting and stepparenting on children.* Hillsdale, NJ: Erlbaum.

Wallis, C., Booth, C., Ludtke, M., & Taylor, E. (1985). Children having children. *Time, 126*(23), 76, 79–84, 87–90.

Walters, R.H., & Parke, R.D. (1964). Influence of response consequences to a social model on resistance to deviation. *Journal of Experimental Child Psychology, 1,* 260–280.

Watson, J.B., & Raynor, R. (1920). Conditional emotional reactions. *Journal of Experimental Psychology, 3,* 1–14.

Watson, J.B. (1925). *Behaviorism.* New York: Norton.

Watson, J.D., & Crick, F.H.C. (1953). Molecular structure of nucleic acids. *Nature, 17,* 737–738.

Webb, H. (1967). Professionalization of attitudes toward play among adolescents. In G.S. Kenyon (Ed.), *Aspects of contemporary sport sociology.* Chicago: The Athletic Institute.

Weikart, D.P., Rogers, L., Adcock, C., & McClelland, D. (1971). *The cognitively oriented curriculum.* Urbana, IL: ERIC-NAEYC.

Weil, W.B. (1975). Infantile obesity. In J.M. Winick (Ed.), *Childhood Obesity.* New York: Wiley.

Weiss, M.R. (1989). Youth sports. Is winning everything? *Childhood Education, 65*(4), (Summer)195–196.

Weiss, G., & Hechtman, L.T. (1986). *Hyperactive children grown up: Empirical findings and theoretical considerations.* New York: Guilford Press.

Wellman, H.M., Ritter, K., & Flavell, H. H. (1975). Deliberate memory behavior in the delayed reactions of very young children. *Developmental Psychology, 11,* 780–787.

Wells, G. (1981). *Learning through interaction: The study of language development.* Cambridge: Cambridge University Press.

Werker, J.F., Gilbert, J.H.V., Humphrey, K., & Tees, R.C. (1981). Developmental aspects of cross—language speech perception. *Child Development, 52,* 349–355.

Werner, J.S., & Lipsitt, L.P. (1981). The infancy of human sensory systems. In E.S. Gollin (Eds.), *Developmental plasticity: Behavioral and biological aspects of variations in development.* New York: Academic Press.

Wertheimer, M. (1961). Psychomotor coordination of auditory and visual space at birth. *Science, 134,* 1692.

West, S.E. (1984). Children and divorce. *Human Ecology Forum, 13,* 21–23.

Westoff, L.A. (1976). Kid's with kids. *Annual editions: Readings in early childhood education, 77/78.* Guilford, CT: Dushkin.

White, B.L. (1971). *Fundamental early environmental influences on the development of competence.* Paper presented at the Third Western Symposium on Learning: Cognitive Learning, Western Washington State College, Bellingham, Washington, October 21-22.

White, B.L. (1971). *Human infants: Experience and psychological development.* Englewood Cliffs, NJ: Prentice-Hall.

White, B.L. (1975). *The first three years of life.* Englewood Cliffs, NJ: Prentice-Hall.

White, B.L., & Watts, J.C. (1973). *Experience and environment: Major influences on the development of the young child.* (Vol. 1). Englewood Cliffs, NJ: Prentice-Hall.

Whitehurst, G.J. (1982). Language development. In B.B. Wolman (Ed.), *Handbook of developmental psychology.* Englewood Cliffs, NJ: Prentice-Hall.

Whitehurst, G.J., & Valdez-Menchaca, M.C. (1988). What is the role of reinforcement in early language acquisition? *Child Development, 59,* 430–440.

Whiting, B.B., & Edwards, C.P. (1988). *Children of different worlds: The formation of social behavior.* Cambridge, MA: Harvard University Press.

Whiting, B.B., & Whiting, J.W.M. (1973). Altruistic and egoistic behavior in six cultures. In L. Nader & T.W. Maretski (Eds.), *Cultural illness and health: Essays in human adaptation.* Washington, DC: American Anthropological Association.

Whiting, B.B., & Whiting, J.W.M. (1975). *Children of six cultures.* Cambridge, MA: Harvard University Press.

Whiting, J.W.M., & Child, I.L. (1953). *Child training and personality: A cross-cultural study.* New Haven, CT: Yale University Press.

Whorf, B.L. (1952). Language mind and reality. *Etc: A Review of General Semantics, 9,* 167–188.

Witkin, H.A. (1959). The perception of the upright. *Scientific American, 200,* 50–56.

Witkin, H.A. (1967). A cognitive style approach to cross-cultural research. *International Journal of Psychology, 2,* 233–250.

Wideman, M.V., & Singer J.F. (1984). The role of psychological mechanisms in preparation for childbirth. *American Psychologist, 34,* 1357–1371.

Wiig, E.H. (1984). Language disabilities in adolescents: A question of cognitive strategies. *Topics in Language Disorders, 4*(2), 41–58.

Wiig, E.H., & Semel E.M. (1980). *Language assessment and intervention for the learning disabled.* Columbus, OH: Merrill.

Williams, C.D. (1959). Elimination of tantrum behavior by extinction procedures. *Journal of Personality and Social Psychology, 59,* 269.

Willis, J. (1981). Genetic counseling. Learning what to expect. Reprinted from *FDA Consumer,* September, 1980. U.S. Government Printing Office.

Wilson, D.M., & Rosenfeld, R.G. (1987). Treatment of short stature and delayed adolescence. In C.P. Mahoney (Ed.), *Pediatric Clinics of North America, 34,* 865–879.

Wilson, E.O. (1975). *Sociobiology: The new synthesis.* Cambridge, MA: Harvard University Press.

Winick, M. (1976). *Malnutrition and brain development.* New York: Oxford University Press.

Winsom, S. (1985). *Brain and psyche: The biology of the unconscious.* New York: Doubleday.

Wise, K.L., Wise, L.A., & Zimmermann, R.R. (1974). Piagetian object permanence in the infant Rhesus monkey. *Developmental Psychology, 10,* 429–437.

Witelson S.F. (1987). Neurobiological aspects of language in children. *Child Development, 58,* 653–688.

Witkin, H.A., & Moore, C.A. (1974, April). Cognitive style and the teaching-learning process. *Paper presented at the Annual Meeting of the American Educational Research Association.* Chicago.

Witkin, H.A., Moore, C.A., Goodenough, D.R., & Cox, R.W. (1977). Field dependent and field independent cognitive styles and their educational implications. *Review of Educational Research, 47,* 1–64.

Wohlwill, J.F. (1980). Cognitive development in childhood. In O.C. Brim, Jr. & J. Kagan (Eds.), *Constancy and change in human development.* Cambridge, MA: Harvard University Press.

Wolff, P.H. (1966). The causes, controls, and organization of behavior in the neonate. *Psychological Issues, 5*(1) Monograph No. 17, 7–11.

Wolff, P.H. (1969). The natural history of crying and other vocalizations in early infancy. In B.M. Foss (Ed.), *Determinants of infant behavior.* (Vol. 4). New York: Wiley.

Woolley, J.D., & Wellman, H.M. (1990). Young childrens' understanding of realities, nonrealities, and appearances. *Child Development, 61,* 946–961.

Wylie, R.C. (1979). *The self-concept theory and research on selected topics.* (Vol. 2). Lincoln: University of Nebraska Press.

Young, J.C.(1985). What is creativity? *Journal of Creative Behavior, 19,* 77–87.

Young, T.W., & Shorr, D.N. (1986). Factors affecting locus of control in school children. *Genetic, Social, and General Psychology Monographs, 112*(4), 405–417.

Youniss, J.E. (1980). *Parents and peers in social development.* Chicago: University of Chicago Press.

Youniss, J., & Volpe, J.A. (1978). A relational analysis of childrens' friendship. In W. Damon (Ed.), *New Directions for Child Development.* Vol I. San Francisco: Jossey-Bass.

Yunis, J.J., & Prakash, O. (1982). The origin of man: A chromosomal pictorial legacy. *Science, 215,* 1525–1530.

Zahn-Waxler, C., Kochanska, G., Krupnick, J., & McKnew, D. (1990). Patterns of guilt in children of depressed and well mothers. *Developmental Psychology, 26*(1), 51–59.

Zahn-Waxler, C., Radke-Yarrow, M., & King, R.A. (1979). Child-rearing and children's pro-social initiation toward victims of distress. *Child Development, 50,* 319–330.

Zaichkowzky, L.D., Zaichkowsky, L.B., & Martinek, T.J. (1980). *Growth and development: The child and physical activity.* St. Louis: C.V. Mosby.

Zajonc, R.B. (1983). Validating the confluence model. *Psychological Bulletin, 93,* 457–480.

Zajonc, R.B. (1976). Family configuration and intelligence. *Science, 192,* 227–236.

Zajonc, R.B., Markus, H., & Markus, G.B. (1979). The birth order puzzle. *Journal of Personality and Social Psychology, 37,* 1325–1341.

Zajonc, R.B., & Markus G.B. (1975). Birth and intellectual development. *Psychological Review, 82,* 74–88.

Zaslow, M.J. (1987). *Sex differences in response to maternal employment.* Unpublished manuscript, prepared for the Committee on Child Development Research and Public Policy, National Research Council, Washington, D C.

Zelnicker, T., Jeffrey, W.E., Ault, R.L., & Parsons, J. (1972). Analysis and modification of search strategies of impulsive and reflective children on the matching familiar figures test. *Child Development, 43,* 321–335.

Zelson, C., Lee, S.J., & Casalino, M. (1973). Neonatal narcotic addiction: Comparative effects of maternal intake of geroin and methadone. *New England Journal of Medicine, 289,* 1216–1220.

Zeskind, P.S., & Ramey, C.T. (1981). Preventing intellectual and interactional sequelae of fetal malnutrition: A longitudinal transactional and synergistic approach to development. *Child Development, 52,* 213–218.

Zuckerman, B., et al. (1989). Birth outcomes for infants of drug-abusing mothers. *New York State Journal of Medicine, 89,* 256–261.

# GLOSSARY

**accommodation**–process by which something is adjusted to become part of the whole or to allow the whole to work

**achievement tests**–measure what one has already learned

**active genotype–environment correlation**–refers to environments one seeks as a result of genotypic predisposition

**adaptation**–change in structure, function, or form that produces better adjustment of an organism to its environment; any genetically controlled characteristic that helps an organism to survive and reproduce in its environment

**alleles**–alternative forms of a gene coded for particular traits

**alpha-fetoprotein (AFP) testing**–several prenatal diagnostic techniques (blood analysis, amniocentesis, ultrasound) to detect neural tube defects

**amniocentesis**–prenatal diagnostic technique in which a hollow needle is inserted in the uterine wall and amniotic fluid is withdrawn

**amniotic sac**–membrane filled with amniotic fluid surrounding the embryo

**androgenital syndrome**–type of pseudohermaphroditism in which a genetic female has masculine sex organs because of prenatal exposure to androgens

**anorexia nervosa**–nervous loss of appetite characterized by severe undereating, malnutrition, and extreme weight loss

**anoxia**–lack of oxygen that is a leading cause of brain damage in newborns

**antisocial behavior**–behavior that includes disregard for rights of others, including being mean and hurtful

**anxiety**–psychological state characterized by tension and general apprehension

**Apgar scale**–standard measure of the condition of a newborn that assesses circulation and reflexes

**apnea**–spontaneous interruptions in breathing

**aptitude tests**–measure potential for learning

**archival research**–use of existing information to answer research questions (public records, anthropological reports, written records, computer-based data)

**assimilation**–process by which something is incorporated to become part of the whole

**associative play**–type of play in which children interact socially, with little or no organization

**assumptive realities**–theories about reality that are assumed to be true without examining or evaluating contradictory data

**auditory canal**–part of the ear that conducts sound waves

**authoritarian parenting**–parenting style in which parents attempt to direct and control a child's behavior according to absolute standards

**authoritative parenting**–parenting style in which parents consider a child's needs as well their own in making decisions about the child's behavior

**autism**–severe disorder appearing in early childhood and affecting how an individual relates to things and people in the environment; individual is self-bound

**autonomous morality**–term to describe children who understand that rules are arbitrary agreements that can be questioned and even changed with consensus

**autosocial stage**–first stage in development of heterosexuality in which pleasure and satisfaction originate from self

**autosomes**–refers to the first 22 pairs of chromosomes; they are similar compared with the 23rd pair (sex chromosomes), which are different

**autosomal dominant inheritance**–refers to dominant genes on the first 22 pairs of chromosomes that cause abnormalities if defective

**autosomal recessive inheritance**–refers to recessive genes on the first 22 pairs of chromosomes that can cause abnormalities if two defective alleles are inherited

**babbling**–reduplication of syllables composed of sequences of consonants and vowels

**behaviorism**–school of psychology that focuses on observable behavior only and investigates relations between stimuli and responses

**bilineal**–system of descent in which both parents are responsible for a child

**bulimia nervosa**–eating disorder characterized by ingestion of enormous amounts of food (binging) and followed by fasting, self-induced vomiting, and/or use of laxatives and diuretics (purging)

**case study**–thorough description of a person or a setting, such as a school or community

**centration**–Piagetian term to describe thinking about only one aspect of a problem while neglecting other aspects

**cephalocaudal development**–principle that human development proceeds from head to foot

**cerebrotonia**–cluster of personality traits that includes desire to be alone, inhibition, self-consciousness, and overreactivity

**cesarean section**–surgical incision in abdominal wall to deliver an infant

**chorionic villi sampling (CVS)**–prenatal diagnostic technique in which a sample of the chorionic villi is removed for analysis

**chromosome**–rodlike structure in the cell nucleus that stores and transmits genetic information

**chunking**–cognitive strategy of organizing into groups what one wants to remember

**circumcision**–surgical removal of the foreskin of the penis

**classical conditioning**–process whereby reflex (innate) action or involuntary response comes to be associated with a stimulus that does not ordinarily elicit it; also called simple learning

**classification**–ability to arrange things by categories based on some similarity or relation

**clinical interview**–flexible and open-ended questioning technique that probes for a subject's perspective

**cochlea**–internal part of the ear that contains the auditory nerve endings

**co-dominance**–pattern of inheritance whereby both alleles in a heterozygous condition are expressed phenotypically

**cone cells**–light-sensitive receptor cells that give rise to color vision

**cognitive behavior modification**–therapy that tries to change some habitual ways of thinking so a person's behavior will consequently change

**cognitive conceit**–opinion that one is wiser or more knowledgeable than others

**cognitive development**–growth and change in knowledge or thought

**cognitive-developmental theory**–view that an individual is an active participant in the developmental process; the individual interacts with the environment and thinks about it in ways that complement his maturity and previous experience

**cohort effect**–effect of cultural or historical change on subjects born at the same time or era

**concrete operations**–Piagetian term for the stage in which logical operations develop and are used on real things

**conditioned response (CR)**–learned reaction to a conditioned stimulus

**conditioned stimulus (CS)**–something that is paired with an unconditioned stimulus that after several pairings elicits a response

**conduct disorders**–childhood disorders marked by persistent acts of aggressive or antisocial behavior

**conscience**–conception of actions and behavior that are morally wrong or bad and that should be punished

**conservation**–Piagetian term that comes from the principle that energy is never conserved but only changes form; it is the understanding that if nothing is added or taken away from an object, the object remains the same although its appearance can change

**contingency contract**–agreement between parent or teacher or psychologist and child specifying what the child must do to earn rewards

**continuous reinforcement**–reinforcing a response each time it occurs

**conventional level of morality**–Kohlberg's description of individuals whose moral reasoning is based on the perspectives of others or the law

**convergent thinking**–mental process that singles out the one response to a problem

**cooperative play**–type of play in which children interact, share toys, or take turns; it involves some purpose and division of roles and is organized

**coordination of secondary reactions**–Piagetian term for ability to coordinate previously unrelated acts to produce interesting outcomes

**cornea**–clear covering on the front of the eye that helps focus light rays

**correlation**–degree to which one variable is related to another

**control group**–those subjects in an experiment who do not receive the experimental treatment (independent variable) but for whom all other conditions are held comparable with those of the experimental group

**correlation coefficient**–statistic calculating the direction and strength of a correlation

**correlational design**–research method that examines relations between certain variables

**creativity**–unique mental process whereby a novel (new) end product is developed and valued

**crisis of choice**–period of conscious decision making that involves exploring and eliminating alternatives

**critical period**–time in development that an organ system, body part, or behavior is developing most rapidly and, therefore, is susceptible to being disturbed by harmful environmental influences

**cross-cultural research**–studies that compare development in different cultures throughout the world

**cross-sectional study**–study of a group of subjects of different ages to obtain information about changes in one or several aspects of development at certain times

**culture**–knowledge, habits, beliefs, morals, law, customs, and traditions of a group of people; shared organization of ideas, including intellectual, moral, and aesthetic standards prevalent in a community

**deduction**–reasoning from the general to the particular or from a premise to a conclusion

**defense mechanisms**–processes by which the ego keeps unacceptable impulses and thoughts in the unconscious thereby preventing them from becoming conscious

**deferred imitation**–ability to produce an action after having previously observed it

**deoxyribonucleic acid (DNA)**–biochemical substance that makes up chromosomes, segments of which are genes containing the hereditary blueprint for individual characteristics

**dependent variable**–observed condition in an experiment that is affected by an independent variable

**depression**–state of pervasive dejection and hopelessness, accompanied by apathy and a feeling of personal worthlessness; involves development of unrealistically negative feelings, self-image, and expectations

**deprivation dwarfism**–condition appearing in childhood (between 2 to 15 years) involving a retardation in physical growth

**development**–quantitative or qualitative progressive changes over time

**developmental milestone**–significant or important event in the life of a person

**developmental psychology**–science that studies how individuals change over time and factors that influence or produce the changes

**developmental tasks**–what society expects of individuals at certain points in their development

**differential emotions theory**–primary emotions are innate, each having a distinctive neurological system

**differentiation**–principle of human development stating that infants' abilities become increasingly distinct and specific over time

**differentiation emotions theory**–emotions develop from the general to the specific becoming more differentiated as individuals mature

**differentiation theory**–view that explains perception as being a process of discrimination of significant features of stimuli from the vast array of potential sensory information already in the environment

**disequilibrium**–Piagetian term for the state of imbalance due to cognitive conflict resulting from difficulty integrating new information into existing schemes

**dishabituation**–renewed tendency to respond to a new stimulus when habituation has initially occurred with another stimulus; increase in response after being exposed to a stimulus slightly different from one to which an individual habituated

**divergent thinking**–mental process represented by the quantity and quality of different and novel responses that one makes

**dizygotic twins**–siblings resulting from two ova fertilized by two different sperm; commonly termed fraternal twins

**dominant**–powerful gene that is expressed

**Down syndrome**–condition in which a child has inherited an extra 21st chromosome; also called trisomy 21.

**eclectic**–view that incorporates aspects of several theories

**ecology**–science of the relations between organisms and their environments

**ecological theory**–view that development is influenced by the settings one is in at a particular time and by their relations

**ectomorphy**–body type of having primarily lean tissue

**ego**–Freudian part of the personality that represents conscious awareness of reality

**egocentrism**–Piagetian term for the inability to consider another's view or perspective

**ego-ideal**–conception of what is morally good that should be rewarded

**embryonic period**–second phase of prenatal development that lasts until eight weeks after conception

**emotion**–physiological change in arousal level (such as an increase in heart rate) expressed subjectively by various responses (such as a smile)

**encoding**–process of putting information into a form by which it can be stored

**endogenous**–something elicited by an internal or physical stimulus.

**endomorphy**–body type of having primarily fat tissue

**enrichment theory**–view that explains perception as being an increase in understanding of a stimulus each time an individual experiences it

**equilibrium**–Piagetian term for the state of balance achieved through active reactions to cognitive conflict that results in the integration of new information

**erogenous zones**–Freud's reference to areas of the body that are the focus of pleasure

**ethology**–study of the behavior of different species in their natural habitats

**evocative genotype–environment correlation**–refers to the influence of different genotypes on evoking different reactions from the environment

**evoked potentials**–specific responses in the brain that can be detected after stimulation by an electroencephalograph (EEG)

**exogenous**–something elicited by an external or social stimulus

**exosystem**–settings in which children are not active participants but that affect them in one of their microsystems

**expansions**–elaborations of a child's speech by adults

**experimental design**–research method that examines the effect of manipulating one variable on another

**experimental group**–those subjects receiving a treatment (independent variable) in an experiment

**extinction**–disappearance of a response by eliminating the association between conditional and unconditional stimuli or by removing the reinforcement

**failure to thrive**–condition appearing in infancy involving growth retardation with no organic or nutritional signs to account for it

**fetal alcohol syndrome (FAS)**–specific cluster of abnormalities such as microcephaly and malformations of the heart, limbs, joints, and face as well as behavioral abnormalities that appear in the offspring of women who abuse alcohol

**fetal period**–third phase of prenatal development that includes the third month until birth

**fetoscopy**–prenatal diagnostic technique in which a small tube with a light source is inserted into the uterus to visually inspect the fetus and/or take fetal samples of blood

**field dependence**–cognitive style in which one relies on contextual cues to solve a problem

**field independence**–cognitive style in which one analyzes a problem without being constrained by the context in which it is presented

**fixated**–Freud's term to describe being "stuck" at a particular stage of development because of excessive indulgence of needs at that time

**fixed interval reinforcement schedule**–responses are reinforced at certain intervals

**fixed ratio reinforcement schedule**–reinforcement follows a fixed number of responses

**formal operations**–Piagetian term for the stage in which logical operations can be performed on abstract and real things

**Fragile-X syndrome**–compressed or broken X chromosome associated with mental retardation

**games**–play in which children engage in activities for pleasure with rules and often compete with one another to win

**gender constancy**–concept that one's gender remains the same despite superficial changes in appearance or behavior

**gender identity**–perception of being male or female

**gender stability**–concept that one's gender always remains the same (that it cannot change)

**gender role**–constellation of qualities an individual understands to characterize males and females in a culture

**gene**–segment on a chromosome that carries the hereditary instructions from one generation to the next

**generational chauvinism**–devotion to one's own generation and contempt (dislike) of other generations

**genotype**–total genetic endowment

**germinal period**–first phase of prenatal development that includes time from conception to implantation

**gestation**–period when an infant is carried in the womb

**gonads**–ovaries that produce eggs or testes that produce sperm

**grammar**–part of language that includes the form and structures of words (morphology) and customary arrangement in phrases and sentences (syntax)

**gustation**–sensation of taste

**gustatory perception**–ability to detect various tastes

**habituation**–decrease in response after being repeatedly exposed to a stimulus

**Head Start**–an early childhood federally funded educational program designed for disadvantaged children from age three to five that enables them to enter elementary school prepared to learn

**heredity**–all the genetic characteristics transmitted from parents to a child at conception

**hermaphrodite**–having both male and female organs; term comes from the Greek legend of the son of Hermes and Aphrodite who becomes joined in one body with a nymph while bathing

**heteronomous morality**–Piaget's term to describe children who view rules as absolute and unquestionable

**heterosexuality**–sexual attraction to the opposite biological sex

**heterosocial stage**–third stage in the development of heterosexuality involving pleasure and friendship from both sexes

**heterozygous**–having two different alleles for a particular trait, one allele is dominant and the other recessive

**holophrase**–use of a single word to convey a whole thought

**homosexuality**–sexual attraction to those of the same biological sex

**homosocial stage**–second stage in the development of heterosexuality involving pleasure and satisfaction from being with others of the same sex for companionship (not sexual purposes)

**homozygous**–having two identical alleles for a particular trait

**hypothalamus**–structure in the brain that controls the endocrine system informing the glands when and how much hormone to secrete

**hypothesis**–specific prediction that can be tested

**id**–Freudian part of the personality representing the unconscious drives and needs

**ideal principle**–striving for perfection rather than reality or pleasure

**identification**–process by which one takes on the characteristics of another person

**identity achievement**–one status in Marcia's process of achieving an identity characterized by one who has gone through a crisis of choice and who has made a commitment

**identity diffusion**–one status in Marcia's process of achieving an identity characterized by one who has not experienced a crisis of choice nor has made a commitment

**identity foreclosure**–one status in Marcia's process of achieving an identity characterized by one who has made a commitment without having experienced a crisis of choice

**identity moratorium**–one status in Marcia's process of achieving an identity characterized by one who is in the middle of a crisis of choice but whose commitments are absent or vaguely defined

**idiot savants**–individuals who have very low intelligence quotients (IQs) yet possess extraordinary talent in some area

**imagery**–cognitive strategy of forming a pictorial representation of what one is trying to remember

**imaginary audience**–belief that one is "on stage" and others are as concerned about an adolescent's thoughts and actions as is she

**imminent justice**–belief that if one does something wrong, one will inevitably be punished

**impulsive**–cognitive style characterized by a tendency to respond to cognitive tasks in a rushed and inaccurate manner

**independent variable**–condition in an experiment that is manipulated so its effects are observed

**induction**–reasoning from particular facts to a general conclusion

**information processing**–how information is processed, remembered or forgotten, and used

**inner speech**–Vygotsky's term for private speech critical to the organization of thoughts

**instrumental learning**–another term for operant conditioning; the organism is instrumental in operating the process

**integration**–principle of human development (complementary to differentiation) stating that simple, differentiated skills come to be combined and coordinated into more complex skills

**interactive synchrony**–coordination between individuals whereby each responds to subtle verbal and nonverbal cues of the other

**interview**–research technique in which people are questioned about various aspects of their lives

**isolette**–special crib in which temperature can be regulated

**jaundice**–yellowish appearance to the skin due to the liver's overproduction and accumulation of bilirubin in the tissues

**Klinefelter syndrome**–condition that affects males in which an extra chromosome is inherited (XYY)

**labor**–process of giving birth

**Lamaze method**–preparation method for childbirth that provides exercises to build stamina and training to relax

**language acquisition device (LAD)**–universal grammatical structure believed by some linguists to be the foundation for all human languages, enabling humans to combine words so they are understood

**lateralization**–process by which cerebral hemispheres specialize their functions

**law of effect**–consequences of a response determine whether the response will be strengthened or weakened; rewarded responses are strengthened, and nonrewarded responses are weakened

**learned helplessness**–perception of not having control over outcomes, which then leads to loss of motivation to try to perform effectively thereby exhibiting helpless behavior that has been learned

**learning**–permanent change in behavior that occurs over time and results from experience

**Leboyer method**–childbirth method that ensures ease of transition for the infant from womb to world

**lens**–tissue on the eye that bends light to focus it on the retina

**linguistics**–study of language

**locus of control**–perception (either internal or external) of responsibility for one's actions

**longitudinal study**–study of developmental processes by taking repeated measures of the same group of children at various stages of development

**long-term memory**–memory system that keeps information for a long time and that has a large storage capacity

**low-birth weight infants**–infants who are born weighing less than 5½ pounds

**macrosystem**–developing person's society and subculture with particular reference to belief systems, lifestyles and options, and patterns of social interchange

**mapping**–process of representing the relative position of objects

**marasmus**–disease resulting in emaciation that is caused by a diet insufficient in all essential nutrients

**matrilineal**–system of descent in which the family of the mother is primarily responsible for a child

**maturation**–unfolding of genetically determined traits, structures, and functions

**mean length utterance (MLU)**–measurement of the average number of morphemes in an utterance that is used as an index of a child's language development

**meiosis**–process by which chromosomes in the ovum or sperm (sex cells) duplicate and separate so the cell divides into four cells, each having half the number of chromosomes as the original cell

**menarche**–first menses

**mesomorphy**–body type of having primarily muscular tissue

**mesosystem**–linkages and relationships between two or more of a developing person's microsystems

**metamemory**–denoting knowledge of a person's memory processes including strengths, weaknesses, and strategies

**microsystem**–activities and relationships with others experienced by a developing person in a particular context

**mitosis**–process by which chromosomes in a single cell duplicate and the cell divides into two identical cells each having the same number of chromosomes as the original cell

**monozygotic twins**–siblings resulting from one ova fertilized by one sperm that has undergone separation during early cell division; commonly called identical twins

**morality**–concept of right and wrong in relationships with others

**morpheme**–smallest unit of a language that by itself has a recognizable meaning

**morphology**–study of form and structure of words

**motherese**–special form of language spoken to infants that includes simple sentences with exaggerated intonation, high pitch, and slow and clear pronunciation; also called child-directed speech

**motion parallax**–cue to depth perception originating from the fact that visual images of distant objects are displaced less than visual images of near objects when objects move or when the observer moves

**myelinization**–process by which myelin, a white fatty tissue, forms around neurons thus facilitating transmission of impulses or messages

**naturalistic observation**–study that involves observing and recording behavior as it occurs in a subject's natural environment

**negative reinforcement**–termination of an unpleasant condition following a desired response

**neonatal behavioral assessment scale (NBAS)**–measure of a newborn's behavior and adaptive responses to the environment that assesses social responses and reflexes

**neurometrics**–measurement of nerve responses

**neuron**–nerve cell that receives and transmits impulses

**nonexperimental design**–research method used to study behaviors that occur naturally

**norms**–scores, which are standards based on measurement, of a large sample of similar people used for comparison purposes; scientifically established averages or standards of performance; typical patterns that describe the way in which important attributes and skills develop and approximate ages at which they appear

**obesity**–weight of over 20 percent the average weight for one's age, gender, and height

**object permanence**–understanding that an object still exists when it is partially or completely removed from immediate perception

**observational learning**–another term for social learning or vicarious conditioning; learning by watching others

**obsessive compulsiveness**–disorder in which persistent and irrational thoughts and uncontrollable repetitive acts occur as a defense against anxiety

**Oedipus complex**–psychoanalytic term referring to a boy's desire to possess his mother; term comes from Greek mythology wherein Oepidus unwittingly kills his father and marries his mother

**olfaction**–sense of smell

**olfactory perception**–ability to detect various odors

**open class words**–one type of word appearing in children's two-word combination whose position is not fixed; the number of open words is greater than the number of pivot words

**operant**–response that produces an effect

**operant conditioning**–a voluntary response to an environmental stimulus is reinforced and as a result reoccurs; the organism is instrumental in operating the process; also termed instrumental learning operation–reversible mental manipulation on an object or experience

operational definition–defining a variable in terms of concrete operational techniques a researcher uses in measuring or manipulating it

organization–system of parts working together as a whole

ossification–process by which bones harden as a result of deposition of calcium and other minerals

overextension–use of a single word to mean many different things

overregularization–in language development, the application of a rule to all cases, including ones that are exceptions

parallel play–play in which two or more children simultaneously use similar toys or play next to each other but the children do not interact

parenting–implementing a series of decisions about socialization of a child

partial or intermittent reinforcement–reinforcing a response according to the number of times they occur or the interval between them

passive genotype–environment correlations–a child's genes and environment are influenced by the parents' genes and therefore correlate with the child's genes

patrilineal–system of descent in which the family of the father is primarily responsible for a child

perception–process by which the brain interprets messages the body receives through its senses

perceptual constancy–ability to recognize sizes or shapes regardless of their distances or position

permissive parenting–parenting style in which the parent accepts a child's impulses and avoids exercising control over the child's behavior

personal fable–belief that one is unique or special and not subject to the system or rules by which society is governed nor liable for the consequences of not following the rules

personality–sum of physical, mental, and emotional traits and behaviors that characterize an individual

phenotype–visible expression of certain genes

phobia–intense and exaggerated fear that interferes with one's functioning

phonemes–basic units of sound in language

phonology–study of speech sounds

pivot class words–one type of word appearing in children's two-word combinations whose position is fixed; the number of pivot words is smaller than the number of open words

placenta–organ through which an infant is attached to the mother

plasticity–flexibility in structure and function

play–pleasurable activity engaged in for its own sake

pleasure principle–avoidance of pain and seeking pleasure or gratification of needs

positive reinforcement–pleasing things such as food, physical contact, or praise that follow desired behavior and increase the likelihood the behavior will reoccur

postconventional level of morality–Kohlberg's description of individuals whose moral reasoning is based on contracts or universal principles of ethics and justice

practice play–play in which children repeat a behavior while learning new skills or improving coordination

pragmatics–study of rules governing how language is used in different social contexts

precedence effect–perception that sounds separated by a few microseconds are heard as a single sound, although the sounds come from different directions

preconventional level of morality–Kohlberg's description of individuals whose moral reasoning is based on the consequences of the act

preimplantation diagnosis–technique used in cases of assisted reproduction whereby embryos are tested for disease in vitro before implantation

prenatal–period of development from conception to birth

preoperational–Piagetian term for the stage before development of logical operations; prelogic; distinguished by development of symbolic functions

preparedness–predisposition of a species to learn certain response-reinforcement relations more easily than others

preterm infants–infants born before 37 weeks of gestation

primary circular reaction–Piagetian term for a response centered on an infant's body that is discovered accidentally and repeated because it is pleasurable

proprioception–sense that informs humans about the orientation of the body in space and position of arms, legs, and other body parts when they move

prosocial behavior–helping, sharing, or cooperating with others; behavior that includes respecting other's personal and property rights and being kind and helpful

proximodistal development–principle that human development proceeds from the center of the body to its extremities

psychoanalysis–process of analyzing unconscious aspects of the mind

psychoanalytic–approach that analyzes unconscious forces that motivate behavior

**psychometrics**–branch of psychology concerned with measuring mental abilities

**psychosexual theory**–Freud's view that sexual instinct influences behavior

**psychosocial theory**–Erikson's view that social interactions influence psychological development

**psychosomatic ailments**–physical disorders in which psychological factors play a major causative role

**puberty**–biological processes involved in attaining sexual maturation

**punishment**–application of an aversive stimulus after a response to decrease its frequency

**pupil**–opening in the iris of the eye that allows light to enter

**rapid eye movement (REM) sleep**–state of irregular sleep in which the eyes move rapidly beneath the eyelids and brain wave activity is typical of wakefulness

**reaction range**–limits within which effects of genes can vary depending on changes in environments

**reality principle**–postponing the gratification of a need until an appropriate object that will satisfy the need has been found

**recall**–ability to produce information from memory

**recasting**–restructuring a child's speech by adults

**recessive**–weak gene that is hidden

**recognition**–ability to identify information one has been previously experienced

**referential operations**–way in which children name or call attention to things during the two-word combination stage of language development

**reflective**–cognitive style characterized by a tendency to respond to cognitive tasks in a slow, deliberate, and accurate manner

**rehearsal**–cognitive strategy of continually repeating something in order to remember it

**reinforcer**–stimulus event that increases the probability that the operant response that immediately preceded it will occur again

**reliability**–degree to which a research design is consistent or stable in producing repeatable results

**response cost**–punishment procedure that results in loss of previously earned rewards

**retina**–back surface of the eye that contains visual receptors

**rites of passage**–public ceremonies that recognize an individual's passage from one stage or process to another

**rod cells**–light sensitive receptor cells that give rise to colorless vision

**scheme**– organized pattern of behavior that can be generalized to various situations

**secondary circular reactions**–Piagetian term for ability to coordinate previously unrelated acts to produce interesting outcomes

**selective attention**–awareness of only part of the available environmental stimuli

**self-concept**–one's perception of his identity as distinct from others that emerges from the understanding of one's self as being separate from others

**self-esteem**–value a person places on her identity that emerges from her interaction with others

**self-fulfilling prophecy**–process by which initial beliefs, predictions, or impressions elicit behavior that confirms the belief, prediction, or impression

**semantics**–study of word meanings and their combinations

**sensorimotor**–Piagetian term for the stage in which sensing and motor activities predominate

**sensation**–physiological process by which senses receive stimuli from the environment

**sequential processing**–capacity to solve problems in a stepwise fashion

**sequential study**–examination of aspects of developmental change by studying several samples of same-aged children in sequence over a certain period

**seriation**–ability to arrange objects in order of number, size, weight, volume, and so forth

**sex-linked inheritance**–genes carried on the chromosome; males need to inherit only one defective gene to be affected, whereas females need to inherit two defective genes

**sex-role stereotype**–standardized mental picture of behavior expected of males and females held in common by group members that represents an oversimplified attitude or perception

**sex-role typing**–taking on societal or cultural characteristics (masculine or feminine) of one's gender

**sexuality**–acceptance of one's sexual role as male or female

**shaping**–reinforcing successive approximations of a desired response

**short-term memory**–memory system that keeps information for a short time (one minute or less) and that has a small storage capacity

**simple learning**–another term for classical conditioning

**simultaneous processing**–involves the ability to elicit meaning from various stimuli at the same time

**skeletal age**–measure of the extent to which bones in the human skeleton have hardened

**social cognition**–another term for observational learning or vicarious conditioning; learning by watching others and by cognitively processing the experience

**socialization**–process by which individuals acquire knowledge, skills, and dispositions that enable them to participate as more or less effective members of groups and society

**social learning or cognition**–behavior change in the form of imitation that results from observing another person performing actions and experiencing the consequences

**social referencing**–looking for cues from others about how to behave in an unfamiliar situation

**social speech**–speech used for communication

**sociocentrism**–ability to understand and relate to views and perspectives of others

**sociometric measures**–measures of patterns of attraction and rejection among group members

**solitary play**–play in which a child plays with toys by himself, independent of others

**somatotonia**–cluster of personality traits that includes desire for physical activity, adventure, and dominance

**sound waves**–successive pressure variations in the air that vary in amplitude, wavelength, and frequency

**stage**–period of development that differs markedly in quality from other periods; development of stages is discontinuous

**standardized**–when something has been tested with a large sample and the result is a measure of performance

**standardized test**–one in which an individual's results are compared with those of a large group of similar individuals

**stimulus discrimination**–process by which an individual distinguishes among stimuli that are different from the one to which she was conditioned to respond

**stimulus generalization**–process by which an individual responds to stimuli similar to the original one for which he was conditioned

**substance abuse**–excessive and harmful use of alcohol and drugs or the psychological or physical dependency on drugs, alcohol, or tobacco

**sudden infant death syndrome (SIDS)**–sudden and unexplained death of an apparently healthy infant who stops breathing during sleep

**superego**–Freudian part of the personality representing morals and ideals of society

**surfactant**–substance coating the air sacs of the lungs that aids in transporting oxygen into and carbon dioxide out of the lungs

**survey**–instrument that uses questioning techniques to get subjects to report on specific aspects of themselves

**symbolic play**–play in which children transform physical objects, actions, or events into substitute ones

**symbolic representation**–ability to use one object or item (word, picture, action) to stand for another

**synapse**–connective space between two neurons

**syntax**–study of the rules that govern how words are organized into phrases and sentences

**systems**–sets or arrangements of items linked to each other in order to function as a whole; the functioning of the whole is different from the sum of its parts

**telegraphic speech**–sentences that contain nouns and verbs and convey meaning without grammatically functional words such as articles and prepositions

**temperament**–characteristic way (including mood, activity level, and intensity of reaction) that one responds emotionally to objects and people; individual differences in physiological responsiveness to various experiences

**teratogen**–environmental agent that causes damage during the prenatal period

**tertiary circular reactions**–Piagetian term for exploratory behavior and trial-and-error experimentation

**theory**–set of statements that relate different facts or events, explain past events, and predict future outcomes

**time-out**–removing a child from an apparently reinforcing setting to one that is not reinforcing for a specified period

**transduction**–reasoning from the particular to particular so events that occur together are assumed to have a casual relation

**Turner syndrome**–condition that affects females in which one less chromosome than normal is inherited (XO)

**tympanic membrane**–another name for eardrum

**ultrasound**–prenatal diagnostic technique in which sound waves are used to scan the womb

**umbilical cord**–organ that attaches infant to placenta; contains vessels that carry nutrients, oxygen, and other substances from mother to child and wastes from child to mother

**unconditioned response (UCR)**–reaction, usually reflexive, elicited by an unconditional stimulus

**unconditioned stimulus (UCS)**–anything that elicits a response in the absence of learning

**underextension**–restriction of the meaning of a single word

**unoccupied play**–activity in which a child is not engaged in what is commonly defined as play but may stand in one place and observe or randomly wander around looking at others play

**validity**–degree to which a research design measures or predicts what it was intended to measure or predict

**variable**–general class or category of objects, events, situations, responses, or characteristics of a person

**variable interval reinforcement schedule**–responses are reinforced at different intervals between them although the average time per reinforcement is constant

**variable ratio reinforcement schedule**–reinforcement varies for the number of responses made although the average number of responses per reinforcement is constant

**vicarious operant conditioning**–association between a response and its consequences or between a conditioned stimulus and a conditional response by watching others; also termed observational or social cognition

**viscerotonia**–cluster of personality traits that includes desire for food, comfort, and people

**visual acuity**–sharpness or clearness of vision

**zone of proximal development**–distance between actual developmental level determined by independent problem solving and level of potential development determined through problem solving under adult guidance or in collaboration with more capable peers

**zygote**–single cell resulting from an ovum fertilized by a sperm

# CREDITS

## Chapter 1

p.8 (top) Photograph courtesy of the Irish Tourist Board.

p.8 (bottom) From Bentzen, *Seeing Young Children: A Guide to Observing and Recording Behavior*, 2nd edition, copyright 1993 by Delmar Publishers Inc.

p.10 (top) Photograph courtesy of Marilyn Nolt.

p.13 From Essa, *Introduction to Early Childhood Education*, copyright 1992 by Delmar Publishers, Inc.

p.14 From Essa, *Introduction to Early Childhood Education*, copyright 1992 by Delmar Publishers Inc.

p.16 From Essa, *Introduction to Early Childhood Education*, copyright 1992 by Delmar Publishers Inc.

p.18 Photograph courtesy of Marilyn Nolt.

Figure 1.1 Adapted from "The control of short-term memory," by R. C. Atkinson and R.M. Shiffrin. Copyright © 1971 by Scientific American, Inc. All rights reserved.

Table 1.4 "Ecological Systems and Influences on Development" Garbarino, J. (1992). *Children and Families in the Social Environment* (2nd ed), NY: Aldine de Gruyter. Reprinted by permission of the author.

Box 1.1 Reprinted with permission of the National Easter Seal Society.

Table 1.5 Georgia Brandstadter-Palmer from Kopp/Krakow, *The Child*, © 1982 by Addison-Wesley Publishing Company, Inc. Reprinted with permission of the publisher.

## Chapter 2

Figure 2.3 From *Human Development* by Fischer and Lazerson. Copyright © 1984 by Kurt Fischer and Arlyne Lazerson. Reprinted by permission of W.H. Freeman.

## Chapter 3

p.61 Photograph courtesy of Bethlehem Central High School. Photo by Jolene Roe.

Figure 3.1b From Anderson and Shapiro, *Basic Maternal/Newborn Nursing*, 5th edition, copyright 1989 by Delmar Publishers Inc.

p.64 (illustrations) From Anderson and Shapiro, *Basic Maternal/Newborn Nursing*, 5th edition, copyright 1989 by Delmar Publishers Inc.

Figure 3.3 From Burke, *Human Anatomy and Physiology in Health and Disease*, 3rd edition, copyright 1992 by Delmar Publishers Inc.

Figure 3.4 Frankel, E. (1979). *DNA: Ladder of Life*. Copyright © 1979 by McGraw-Hill, Inc. Reprinted with permission of McGraw-Hill, Inc.

Figure 3.5 From Burke, *Human Anatomy and Physiology in Health and Disease*, 3rd edition, copyright 1992 by Delmar Publishers Inc.

Figure 3.8 (a,b,c) Reprinted with permission of the March of Dimes Birth Defects Foundation.

p.80 (illustration) From Anderson and Shapiro, *Basic Maternal/Newborn Nursing*, 5th edition, copyright 1989 by Delmar Publishers Inc.

p.80 (ultrasounds) From Anderson and Shapiro, *Basic Maternal/Newborn Nursing*, 5th edition, copyright 1989 by Delmar Publishers Inc.

Figure 3.10 From Burke, *Human Anatomy and Physiology in Health and Disease,* 3rd edition, copyright 1992 by Delmar Publishers Inc.

Figure 3.11 Moore, K.L. (1989). *Before We Are Born* (3rd ed). Philadelphia, PA: W.B. Saunders.

Box 3.2 (graph) Adapted from Gottesman, I.I. (1963). "Genetic aspects of intelligent behavior." In N. Ellis (ed.) *Handbook of Mental Deficiency: Psychological Theory and Research*. New York: McGraw-Hill.

## Chapter 4

p.101 Photograph courtesy of Marilyn Nolt.

Figure 4.1 Adapted from *Child Development: A Topical Approach* (1985) by Clarke-Stewart, A.K. and Friedman S Copyright © 1985 by John Wiley & Sons, Inc. Reprinted by permission of John Wiley & Sons, Inc.

p.104 From Anderson and Shapiro, *Basic Maternal/Newborn Nursing*, 5th edition, copyright 1989 by Delmar Publishers Inc.

p.105 From Anderson and Shapiro, *Basic Maternal/Newborn Nursing*, 5th edition, copyright 1989 by Delmar Publishers Inc.

Table 4.1 Apgar, V. (1953). "A proposal for a new method of evaluation of the newborn infant." *Anesthesia and Analgesia*, 32, 260.

p.107 Photograph by Marjorie Pyle, Copyright © LIFECIRCLE.

p.108 Photograph courtesy of the Hewlett-Packard Company.

p.111 (top) Photograph courtesy of Marilyn Nolt.

p.111 (bottom) From Anderson and Shapiro, *Basic Maternal/Newborn Nursing*, 5th edition, copyright 1989 by Delmar Publishers Inc.

Table 4.2 Adapted from Allen and Marotz, *Developmental Profiles: Prebirth to Age Eight*, 2nd edition, copyright 1994 by Delmar Publishers Inc.

p.117 Photographs courtesy of Robert E. Mikrut.

p.118 Photograph courtesy of Marilyn Nolt.

p.120 (bottom) Photograph courtesy of the LaLeche League International.

Figure 4.2 From *Studies in Animal and Human Adulthood,* by K. Lorenz. Copyright © 1971 by Harvard University Press. Reprinted by permission.

# Chapter 5

Figure 5.1 Hall, E. et al. (1986). *Child Psychology Today* 2nd edition. Copyright © 1986 by McGraw-Hill, Inc. Reprinted with permission of McGraw-Hill, Inc.

Figure 5.2 (a,b) From Allen and Marotz, *Developmental Profiles: Prebirth to Age Eight*, 2nd edition, copyright 1994 by Delmar Publishers Inc.

Figure 5.3 From *Brain, Mind and Behavior*, by Bloom and Lazerson. Copyright © 1988 by W.H. Freeman and Company. Reprinted with permission.

p.138 (x-ray) From Burke, *Human Anatomy and Physiology in Health and Disease*, 3rd edition, copyright 1992 by Delmar Publishers Inc.

Figure 5.4 From Burke, *Human Anatomy and Physiology in Health and Disease*, 3rd edition, copyright 1992 by Delmar Publishers Inc.

Figure 5.6 From Burke, *Human Anatomy and Physiology in Health and Disease*, 3rd edition, copyright 1992 by Delmar Publishers Inc.

Figure 5.7 Reprinted with the permission of Macmillan Publishing Company from *Children: Development and Relationships* 3rd ed. by Mollie S. Smart and Russell C. Smart. Copyright © 1977 by Macmillan Publishing Company.

Figure 5.8 From Burke, *Human Anatomy and Physiology in Health and Disease*, 3rd edition, copyright 1992 by Delmar Publishers Inc.

Figure 5.9 Reprinted by permission of the publishers from *Fetus Into Man: Physical Growth From Conception to Maturity* by J.M. Tanner, Cambridge, Mass.: Harvard University Press, Copyright © 1978, 1989 by J.M. Tanner.

p.149 Photograph courtesy of the New York State Library for the Blind and Visually Handicapped.

p.150 (chart) Courtesy of Pathways Awareness Foundation. Endorsed by the Illinois Chapter of the American Academy of Pediatrics.

Figure 5.10 From Burke, *Human Anatomy and Physiology in Health and Disease*, 3rd edition, copyright 1992 by Delmar Publishers Inc.

p.156 Photograph courtesy of the United Nations.

p.159 Photograph courtesy of Vannucci Foto Services.

Figure 5.11 Graph courtesy of Denver Developmental Materials, Inc.

# Chapter 6

Figure 6.1 Reprinted with the permission of Macmillan Publishing Company from *An Introduction to Perception* by Irwin Rock and Carl B. Zuckerman. Copyright © 1975 by Macmillan Publishing Company.

p.171 Photograph courtesy of the Geisel Estate.

Figure 6.2 From "Pattern discrimination and selective attention as determinants in infancy," by R.L. Fantz. In A.H. Kidd and J.L. Rivoire (eds.) *Perceptual Development in Children*. New York: International University Press.

p.172 Photograph courtesy of Marilyn Nolt.

Table 6.1 From *Brain, Mind and Behavior* by Bloom and Lazerson. Copyright © 1988 by W.H. Freeman and Company. Reprinted by permission.

Figure 6.4 Adapted from "The Origin of Form Perception" by R.L. Fantz. Copyright © 1961 by Scientific American, Inc. All rights reserved.

Figures 6.7 & 6.8 Elkind, D. (1978). *The child's reality. Three developmental themes*. Hillsdale, N.J.: Lawrence Erlbaum. Reprinted with permission.

Figure 6.9 Vurpillot, E. (1976). *The Visual World of the Child*. Madison CT: International University Press.

Figure 6.11 From Schirrmacher, *Art and Creative Development for Young Children*, copyright 1988 by Delmar Publishers Inc.

Figure 6.12 From "The Origin of Form Perception" by R.L. Fantz. Copyright © 1961 by Scientific American, Inc. All rights reserved.

Figure 6.13 Dannemillar & Stephens (1988). "A critical test of infant pattern preference models." *Child Development*, 59, 210-216. Copyright © 1988 by The Society for Research in Child Development, Inc.

Figure 6.14 From Burke, *Human Anatomy and Physiology in Health and Disease*, 3rd edition, copyright 1992 by Delmar Publishers Inc.

p.191 (bottom) Photograph courtesy of Marilyn Nolt.

Figure 6.17 From Burke, *Human Anatomy and Physiology in Health and Disease*, 3rd edition, copyright 1992 by Delmar Publishers Inc.

Figure 6.18 From Morrison, *World of Child Development*, copyright 1990 by Delmar Publishers Inc.

Figure 6.19 Held, R. & Hein, A. (1963). "Movement-produced stimulation in the development of visually-guided behavior." *Journal of Comparative and Physiological Psychology*, 56, 872-76. Copyright © 1963 by Richard Held. Reprinted with permission.

## Chapter 7

p.212 (bottom) From Essa, *Introduction to Early Childhood Education*, copyright 1992 by Delmar Publishers Inc.

Table 7.1 Madsen, C.H., and Madsen, C.K. (1970). *Teaching—Discipline*. Boston: Allyn & Bacon.

Figure 7.2 Photograph courtesy of Albert Bandura.

## Chapter 8

p.239 Photograph courtesy of Marilyn Nolt.

Figure 8.5 From *Human Development: From Conception Through Adolescence* by Kurt Fischer and Arlyne Lazerson. Copyright © 1984 by Fischer and Lazerson.

Table 8.1 Adapted from *Teacher's Petit Piaget* by C.M. Charles. 1974 © Fearon Teacher Aids. P.O. Box 280, Carthage, L 62321.

Figure 8.7 Santrock, J.W., and Yussen, S.R. (1987). *Child Development: An Introduction.* Dubuque, Iowa: Wm. C. Brown

## Chapter 9

Figure 9.4 Siegler, R.S. (1978). "The origins of scientific reasoning." In R.S. Siegler (ed.), *Children's thinking: What Develops?* Hillsdale, N.J.: Lawrence Erlbaum Associates, Inc. Reprinted with permission.

Table 9.1 Siegler, R.S. (1978). "The origins of scientific reasoning." In R.S. Siegler (ed.), *Children's thinking: What Develops?* Hillsdale, N.J.: Lawrence Erlbaum Associates, Inc. Reprinted with permission.

Figure 9.5 From *Handbook of Intelligence.* B.B. Wolman (ed.). Copyright © 1985 by John Wiley & Sons, Inc. Reprinted by permission of John Wiley & Sons, Inc.

Table 9.2 Sattler, J.M. (1982). *Assessment of Children's Intelligence and Special Abilities.* Boston: Allyn & Bacon.

Figure 9.7 Conel, J.L. "The postnatal development of the human cerebral cortex." Copyright © 1939, 1959 by Harvard University Press. Reprinted by permission.

Figure 9.8 Kagan, J. "Reflection-impulsivity and reading ability in primary grade children." *Child Development*, 36, 609-626. Copyright © 1965 by The Society For Research in Child Development, Inc.

Figure 9.9 Reprinted by permission of Educational Testing Service, the copyright owner.

p.296 Photograph courtesy of the Irish Tourist Board.

Table 9.3 Lefrancois, G.R. (1992). *Of Children* (7th ed.). Belmont, CA: Wadsworth. Reprinted by permission of Wadsworth Publishing Co.

Figure 9.10 Lefrancois, G.R. (1992). *Of Children* (7th ed.). Belmont, CA: Wadsworth. Reprinted by permission of Wadsworth Publishing Co.

p.300 Photograph courtesy of Marilyn Nolt.

## Chapter 10

Table 10.1 Adapted from Bayley, N. (1969). *Bayley Scales of Infant Development.* New York: Psychological Corp.; Lennenberg, E.H. (1967). *Biological Foundations of Language.* New York: Wiley, and McCarthy, D. (1954). "Language development in children," in L. Carmichael (ed.) Manual of child psychology (2nd ed.). New York: Wiley.

Table 10.2 Reprinted by permission of the publishers from *A First Language: The Early Stages* by Roger Brown, Cambridge, Mass.: Harvard University Press, Copyright © 1973 by the President and Fellows of Harvard College.

p.319-329 (quote) Nelson, K., and Gruendel, J.M. (1988) "At mornings it's lunchtime. A scriptal view of children's dialogue." In M.B. Franklin and S.S. Barten (eds.), *Child Language: A Reader.* New York: Oxford University Press.

Table 10.3 Abbeduto, L. et al. (1988). "The development of speech act comprehension in mentally retarded individuals & non-retarded children." *Child Development* 59, 1460-1472. Copyright © 1988 by The Society for Research in Child Development, Inc.

p.323 Photograph courtesy of Marilyn Nolt.

Table 10.4 Reprinted with the permission of Merrill, an imprint of Macmillan Publishing Company from *Exceptional Children and Youth*, Fifth Edition by Norris G. Haring and Linda McCormick. Copyright © 1990 by Merrill Publishing Company.

# Chapter 11

Figure 11.1 Izard, C.E. (1979). "The maximally discriminative facial movement coding system (MAX)." Newark University Media Services, University of Delaware. Reprinted with permission.

Table 11.1 Campos, J.J. et al. (1983). Socioemotional Development. In P.H. Mussen (ed.) *Handbook of Child Psychology. Vol.2.* Copyright © 1983 by John Wiley & Sons, Inc. Reprinted by permission of John Wiley & Sons, Inc.

Table 11.2 Sroufe, L.A. (1979). Socioemotional Development. In J.D. Osofsky (ed.) *Handbook of Infant Development.* Copyright © 1979 by John Wiley & Sons, Inc. Reprinted by permission of John Wiley & Sons, Inc.

Figure 11.2 Reprinted by permission of the publisher. From Jersild, A. & Holmes, F.B., *Children's Fears*, Child Development Monographs, no. 20, 1935. (New York: Teachers College Press, © 1935 by Teachers College, Columbia University. All rights reserved.), "An Experimental Study of the Fears of Young Children," p.237.

Figure 11.3 Barnett, J.T. (1969). Development of children's fears: The relationship between three systems of fear measurement. Unpublished master's thesis. University of Wisconsin. Reprinted with permission.

p.[354] Photograph courtesy of Marilyn Nolt.

# Chapter 12

Table 12.2 Erickson, E.H. (1980). *Identity and the Life Cycle.* New York: W.W. Norton.

p.[372] Photograph courtesy of Vannucci Foto Services.

Table 12.4 Adapted from "The origin of personality" by Thomas S. Chess & H.G. Birch, 1970, *Scientific American, 223*, 102-109. Copyright © 1970 by Scientific American, Inc. All rights reserved.

p.[386] (bottom) Photograph courtesy of Marilyn Nolt.

Table 12.5 Maccoby, E.E., and Martin, J.A. (1983). "Socialization in the context of the family: Parent-child interaction." In P.H. Mussen (ed.), *Handbook of Child Psychology* (4th ed.). New York: Wiley

p.[393] Photograph courtesy of Marilyn Nolt.

p.[396] Photograph courtesy of Marilyn Nolt.

Figure 12.2 Constanzo, P.R. & Shaw, M.E. (1966). Conformity as a function of age level. *Child Development, 37,* 967-975. Copyright © 1966 by The Society for Research in Child Development, Inc.

Figure 12.3 Berndt, T.J. (1979). "Developmental changes in conformity to peers and parents." *Developmental Psychology, 15,* 608-616. Copyright (1979) by the American Psychological Association. Reprinted by permission.

p.[399] Photograph courtesy of Marilyn Nolt.

p.[402] Photograph courtesy of Family Communications, Inc. Photo by Walt Seng.

## Chapter 13

Figure 13.2 From Sloane, *Biology of Women*, 3rd edition, copyright 1993 by Delmar Publishers Inc.

Figure 13.4 Hetherington, E. & Parke, R. *Child Psychology: A Contemporary Viewpoint* 3rd edition. Copyright © 1986 by McGraw-Hill, Inc. Reproduced with permission of McGraw-Hill, Inc.

Figure 13.5 Permission to reprint by John Money, Professor of Medical Psychology and Pediatrics, Emeritus, Johns Hopkins Univ., School of Medicine.

Table 13.1 From *The Intimate Environment: Exploring Marriage and the Family* 4th edition by Arlene S. Skolnick. Copyright © 1987 by Arlene S. Skolnick. Reprinted by permission of HarperCollins Publishers.

Box 13.1 Bem, S.L. (1974). The measurement of psychological androgyny. *Journal of Consulting and Clinical Psychology, 42,* 155–162.

p.[434] Photograph courtesy of Marilyn Nolt.

## Chapter 14

p.[449] Photograph courtesy of Police Department, Town of Colonie, NY.

Table 14.1 Kohlberg, L. (1978). "Moral Stages & Moralization." In T. Lickona (Ed.) *Moral Development and Behavior.* Reprinted with permission.

Box 14.1 From *Raising Good Children* by Thomas Lickona, Ph.D. Copyright © 1983 by Thomas Lickona. Used by permission of Bantam Books, division of Bantam Doubleday Dell Publishing Group, Inc.

p.[459] Used with permission of Girl Scouts of the U.S.A.

p.[465] Photograph courtesy of Family Communications, Inc.

Figure 14.1 Reprinted from Eisenberg, N. (1986). *Altruistic Emotion, Cognition & Behavior,* with permission of Lawrence Erlbaum Associates, Inc.

## Chapter 15

Figures 15.1-15.5 Reprinted with the permssion of Merrill, an imprint of Macmillan Publishing Company from *Early Childhood Development: Prenatal through Age Eight* by Sandra Anselmo. Copyright © 1987 by Merrill Publishing Company.

p.[483] Photograph courtesy of Marilyn Nolt.

p.[484] Photograph courtesy of Marilyn Nolt.

p.[486] (quote) From *The Antecedents of Self Esteem* by S. Coopersmith. Copyright © 1967 by W.H. Freeman and Co. Reprinted by permission.

p.[492] Photograph courtesy of *The Gazette Newspapers.*

# INDEX

Conditioning, 9, 210-11
Conduct disorders, 358
Cone cells, 177
Conformity, 397-98
Conscience, 367
Conservation, 243-44, 254-55
Contextual orientation, 44
Contingency contract program, 218
Conventional rules, 452
Convergent thinking, 296, 300
Cooing, 310
Cooperative play, 394
Coordination of secondary reactions, 246
Cornea, 176
Corpus callosum, 141, 204
Correlation, 50
Correlational design, 45, 48-50
Correlation coefficient, 50
Creativity, 296-301
  biological and contextual influences on, 300
  biological influences on, 299
  contextual influences on, 299-300
  measurement of, 297-99
Crisis of choice, 484
Critical period, 85-86, 224, 325-26
Cross-cultural research, 53
Crossing over, 70
Cross-sectional study, 54-55
Crying, 125-26, 310
Cultural theories, 10-11
Culture
  definition of, 286
  and gender-role development, 431
  influence on learning, 227-29
  and moral development, 466
  and self-concept, 494-95
  and social and personality development, 399-400
Curvilinear relation, 49
Cytomegalovirus (CMV), 89

**D**

Day care
  and attachment, 349-50
Decentering, 180
Decibels, 186
Defense mechanisms, 367, 368 (table)
Deferred imitation, 248
Denver Developmental Screening Test, 158, 160
Deoxyribonucleic acid (DNA), 67
Dependent variable, 50
Depression, 358-59, 501
Deprivation dwarfism, 157
Depth perception, 197-201
Development
  cognitive. *See* Cognitive development
  definition of, 4-5
  emotional. *See* Emotional development
  gender-role. *See* Gender-role development
  language. *See* Language development
  milestones of, 23-30 (table)
  moral. *See* Moral development
  perceptual. *See* Perceptual development
  physical and motor. *See* Physical and motor development prenatal.
    *See* Prenatal development of self. *See* Self-concept
  social and personality. *See* Social and personality development
  theories of, 5-6
    biological, 7-8
    cognitive, 16-18
    cultural, 10-12

ecological, 19-21
information processing, 18-19
learning, 8-10
psychoanalytic, 13-16
systems, 19
Developmental change, 53-56
Developmental milestones, 7, 23-30 (table)
Developmental tasks, 477, 495
Diethylstilbesterol (DES), 90-91
Differential emotions theory, 341
Differentiation, 133-34
Differentiation emotions theory, 341
Differentiation theory of perception, 170
Difficult infant, 376
Disequilibrium, 17, 241
Dishabituation, 209, 271
Divergent thinking, 296, 300
Divorce
  and social and personality development, 383-84
Dizygotic twins, 65
Dominant, 74
Down's syndrome (trisomy 21), 71-72
Dreams, 250
Dyslexia, 203

**E**
Eardrum, 185
Easy infant, 376
Ecological systems theory, 19-21, 403-5
Ecology, 403
Ectoderm, 83
Ectomorph body type, 162, 496-97
Educational programs, 391-92
Effacement, 102
Ego, 13, 366
Egocentric speech, 318-20
Egocentrism, 250-51, 257, 260
Ego-ideal, 367
Embryonic period, 82-83
Emotional abuse and neglect, 359-60
Emotional development, 340-60
  abuse and neglect, 359-60
  biological and contextual influences on, 343-44
  biological influences on, 340-41
  contextual influences on, 341-43
  emotional ties, 344, 346-50
  milestones of, 345-46 (table)
  out of control emotions, 357-59
  specific emotions, 350-56, 351 (table)
Emotional health, 157
Emotional stress, 88-89
Emotions
  definition of, 338
  significance of, 339-40
Empathy, 446-47
Encoding, 269
Endocrine system, 143-49, 154 (table)
Endoderm, 83
Endogenous smile, 341
Endomorph body type, 162, 496-97
Enrichment theory of perception, 170
Environmental hazards, 92-94
Epiphyseal closure, 159
Episiotomy, 116
Equilibration, 244, 301
Equilibrium, 17, 241
Erogenous zones, 367
Eros, 461
Erythroblastosis fetalis, 94, 96
Estrogen, 147

Ethics, 56-58
Ethology, 7-8
Evoked potentials, 174
Exercise, 157-58
Exogenous smile, 341
Exosystem, 404
Experimental design, 45, 50-51
Experimental group, 51
Extinction, 213-14

F
Face perception, 182-84
Failure to thrive, 157
Family
  and gender-role development, 422-25
  and intelligence, 289-90
  and learning, 226
  and moral development, 462-63, 466-67
  and self-concept, 492-95
  and social and personality development, 377, 382-89
Fantasy, 250
Fathers, 121-22
  and attachment, 349
  and gender-role development, 422-23
Fear, 353-54
Feature detectors, 196
Fels Longitudinal Study, 54
Females
  biological distinction from males, 411-15
  characteristics of, 432 (table)
  cognitive distinction from males, 415-16
  social/emotional distinction from males, 415
Fetal alcohol syndrome (FAS), 91
Fetal period, 83-84
Fetoscopy, 81
Field dependence, 295-96
Field experiment, 51
Field independence, 281, 295-96
Fontanels, 137
Formal operational stage, 17, 242, 258-61
Form perception, 179-80
Fragile-X syndrome, 73
Fraternal twins, 375
Friendship, 395-96

G
Games, 395
Gender, 152, 154, 411. *See also* Gender-role development
Gender constancy, 421
Gender identity, 420
Gender-role development, 410-39
  androgyny, 434-35
  biological and contextual influences on, 428-34
  biological influences on, 416-18
  contextual influences on, 422-28
  development of sexuality, 435-38
  sex-role typing theories, 418-22
Gender schema theory, 421-22
Gender stability, 420
Generational chauvinism, 260
Genes, 62, 74
Genetic abnormalities, 76-78
Genetic counseling and diagnostic procedures, 78-81
Genetic inheritance, 74-76
Genital stage, 369
Genotype, 74
Genotype-environment interaction, 96-97
Germinal period, 81-82
Gestation period, 108

Gonads, 143, 147, 411
Grammar, 308-9, 313-17
Growth disorders, 157
Guilt, 446-47
Gustation, 188
Gustatory perception, 189-91

H
Habituation, 173-74, 209, 271
Head Start, 227
Hearing, 184-86
Heredity, 62. *See also* Heredity and prenatal development
  and intelligence, 289
  and social and personality development, 375
Heredity and prenatal development
  biological and contextual influences on, 94-97
  biological influences on, 62-84, 151-52
  contextual influences on, 84-94
Hermaphrodite, 429
Herpes, 89
Heteronomous morality, 448
Heterosexuality, 435-36
Heterosocial stage, 436
Heterozygous, 74
High amplitude sucking procedure, 173
Historical theory, 12
Holophrase, 311
Homebirth, 117
HOME (Home Observation for the Measurement of the Environment), 290
Homosexuality, 436-37
Homosocial stage, 436
Homozygous, 74
Hormones, 143-49, 152, 154 (table), 428-29
Hospital birth, 116
Human growth hormone (HGH), 144-46
Hyperbilirubinemia, 109
Hypothalamus, 143
Hypothesis, 44

I
Id, 13, 366
Ideal principle, 367
Identical twins, 375
Identification, 368
Identity, 410
Identity achievement, 485, 493
Identity diffusion, 484, 493
Identity foreclosure, 484, 493
Identity moratorium, 485, 493
Idiomorphs, 310
Imagery, 273
Imaginary audience, 260
Imaginary companions, 250
Imitation, 220-21
Imminent justice, 448
Implantation, 82
Impulsive thinking, 294-95
Incus, 185
Independent variable, 50
Individual differences, 134, 137
Infants. *See also* Newborn
  emotional development of, 352-56
  self-concept of, 477-79
  and sensorimotor stage, 245-47
  temperament differences in, 376
Information processing, 18-19, 270-71
  theories of, 281-82
Instinct, 13, 223

# NAME INDEX